D1519437

Entrancing Muse

A DOCUMENTED BIOGRAPHY OF FRANCIS POULENC

Francis Poulenc
(The Fred and Rose Plaut Archives, Irving S. Gilmore Music
Library, Yale University)

Entrancing Muse

A DOCUMENTED BIOGRAPHY OF

Francis Poulenc

Carl B. Schmidt

LIVES IN MUSIC No. 3

PENDRAGON PRESS
HILLSDALE, NY

Other titles in the series LIVES IN MUSIC:

No. 1 *Hugues Cuenod: With a Nimble Voice*
Conversations with François Hudry

No. 2 *Nicolae Bretan: His Life—His Music*
by Hartmut Gagelmann

No. 4 *Pied Piper: The Many Lives of Noah Greenberg*
by James Gollin

TO BETSEY,

in lasting gratitude for a lifetime of happiness

*"Sans doute notre passé se pare-t-il toujours de couleurs
enchanteresses . . ."*

(Probably our past always takes on magic colors.)

(Poulenc to Stéphane Audel)

Library of Congress Cataloging-in-Publication Data

Schmidt, Carl B.
  Entrancing muse: a documented biography of Francis Poulenc/ Carl B. Schmidt.
      p. cm. -- (Lives in music; no. 3)
  Includes bibliographical references (p. 515), discography (p. 503), and index.
  ISBN 1-57647-026-1
    1. Poulenc, Francis, 1899-1963 2. Composers--France--Biography. I. Title
  II. Lives in music series; no. 3

  ML410.P767 S35 2001
  780'.92--dc21
  [B]   00-068824

Contents

Preface

Entrancing Muse: A Documented Biography of Francis Poulenc is the sequel to *The Music of Francis Poulenc: A Catalogue* (Clarendon Press, 1995). In 1990, when I could no longer resist the temptation to write a Poulenc biography, I realized that considerable research was required to avoid a mere rehash of Henri Hell's eloquent but aging biography. In spite of over one hundred graduate theses and dissertations on Poulenc, no satisfactory catalogue of his music existed, his own personal writings and interviews had never been thoroughly scrutinized in print, and few periodicals had been systematically culled for their references to Poulenc. Moreover, his voluminous correspondence was available only in the modest 1967 sampling edited by Hélène de Wendel. The biography was postponed so that a detailed catalogue of Poulenc's music could be compiled and the many problems of compositional history clarified. In particular, I made significant efforts to locate and study the numerous unpublished letters and to find Poulenc's scattered musical manuscripts. The catalogue became a source book describing manuscripts and printed editions, excerpting reviews and letters in which each work was discussed, providing compositional histories, and even revealing a small group of previously unknown Poulenc works.

As the catalogue progressed, a much expanded and annotated version of Poulenc's letters appeared in 1991 in Sidney Buckland's excellent English translation, a monograph on Poulenc by Wilfred Mellers was published in 1993, and a new edition of Poulenc's own *Journal de mes mélodies*, edited by Renaud Machart, in 1993. Some months after the catalogue went to press, Myriam Chimènes' superb annotated volume of letters by and to Poulenc containing in excess of one thousand items appeared in 1994. Scholarly interest in key aspects of Poulenc's life and works has increased dramatically dueto the increasing interest in his music as well as the celebration of the composer's centennial in 1999.

Although Poulenc himself remarked "My music is my portrait," we know that he yearned to see his life and music described in print as early as 1942.[1] He first approached his friend André Schaeffner about such a project in the early 1940s, but Schaeffner, who preferred to write about Debussy and ethnomusicology, penned only a brief article entitled "Francis Poulenc: Musicien français" for the January 1946 issue of *Contrepoints*.[2] Claude Rostand thought about the possibility, but produced instead *Entretiens avec Claude Rostand* in 1954.[3] Several years later, impressed by Henri Hell's review of his recent works, Poulenc proposed he write his biography.[4] When Hell's interest in the project temporarily flagged, the American critic Allen Hughes considered writing a biography.[5] Hell finally produced a book in 1958 borrowing a title used earlier by Schaeffner, and Hughes moved on to other projects. Six years later Jean Roy, who also knew Poulenc personally, wrote a useful study entitled *Francis Poulenc: L'Homme et son œuvre*. Hell's book, revised in 1978 to include Poulenc's final years, remained the standard source for Poulenc's biography until Keith Daniel's doctoral dissertation *Francis Poulenc: His Artistic Development and Musical Style* was turned into a monograph in 1982. While Hell had the advantage of knowing Poulenc and benefited from his direct assistance in producing the book, Daniel provided a more thorough and better documented study concentrating on Poulenc's music, which also presented new information about his life. In the 1990s Renaud Machart wrote a concise biography of Poulenc containing excellent illustrations. Finally, Benjamin Ivry, an American arts correspondent who has lived in Paris, has contributed a 1996 biography in which Poulenc's sexuality is interpreted, and Sidney Buckland and Myriam Chimènes have edited *Francis Poulenc: Music, Art and Literature* (1999), a volume full of new information and significant reinterpretations.

The present volume charts a brand new course in Poulenc scholar-

---

[1] André Schaeffner's 21 Oct. 1942 letter to Poulenc in Poulenc 1994, p. 24.
[2] At the beginning of this piece (p. 50), Schaeffner wrote, "If I were to write about French music between the two wars, at the risk of shocking the soothsayers, I would consecrate two chapters to Francis Poulenc, certainly one of the first and perhaps the last."
[3] Poulenc's letter of "mercredi" [May 1945] to Bernac in Poulenc 1994, 45-11.
[4] "Les dernières œuvres de Francis Poulenc," *Fontaine: Revue mensuelle de la poésie et des lettres française* 11 (1947), 499-501.
[5] Private conversation with Allen Hughes on 13 July 1999. Hughes wrote frequently about Poulenc in *The New York Times*, the *Saturday Review, Musical America*, and elsewhere. He wrote a very fine "portrait" of Poulenc for *Show* magazine (see Hughes 1963), which has escaped Poulenc scholars. At no time did he consider translating Hell's biography as suggested in Poulenc 1994, p. 898, note 4. For a partial list of Hughes' writings on Poulenc see Keck, pp. 190-3.

ship by relying on thousands of primary sources, many of which have not been consulted by any previous Poulenc biographer. It is a detailed scrutiny of his day-to-day activities and his relationships with numerous friends and acquaintances. This study not only seeks to examine Poulenc's life as a composer, but to place proper emphasis on his extensive career as a pianist, accompanist, and recording artist. Previous biographers have paid little attention to Poulenc the performer, ignoring the fact that like Mahler in a previous generation or Bernstein in a more recent one, Poulenc devoted considerable time and energy to public performance. From the early days with the soprano Suzanne Peignot, to the quarter-century he spent touring the world with the baritone Pierre Bernac; from the frequent appearances as soloist in his own *Aubade, Concert champêtre, Le Bal masqué*, Concerto in D minor, or Concerto for Piano and Orchestra, to his many radio broadcasts and colloquia, Poulenc was a steady contributor to the European musical scene.

Beginning with his first North American tour in 1948-1949 Poulenc made his presence known to another huge and receptive musical population. Other tours to America followed, and one was planned when his death intervened. The fact that some of his pianistic legacy from the 1920s until his death in 1963 was recorded permits us to do more than contemplate Poulenc through the eyes and ears of earlier critics. Moreover, the possibility to interview some of Poulenc's chief collaborators and friends, has helped us view the man in decidedly more human terms. Poulenc's own words, contemporary memoirs and accounts, journal and newspaper articles, the testimony of his friends and family, and his own recordings form the foundation on which this documented biography is constructed.

Above all, Poulenc was inspired by his constant collaboration with fellow artists and their œuvre. Some, such as the renowned impresario Serge Diaghilev, made a career of bringing creative artists together. His commission for the ballet *Les Biches* catapulted the young Poulenc into the international limelight that was to shine on him virtually undiminished for his entire career. Poulenc also had a strong personal attachment to fellow musicians such as Erik Satie, Georges Auric and Darius Milhaud of *Les Six*, Henri Sauguet, Serge Prokofiev, and Igor Stravinsky. His devotion to visual artists like the venerable Zurbarán and Mantegna as well as to Raoul Dufy, Pablo Picasso, Henri Matisse, Georges Braque, Pierre Bonnard, Paul Klee, and others from his own time was equally strong. Moreover, Poulenc showed a remarkable affinity for the prose and poetry of Guillaume Apollinaire, Jean Cocteau, Max Jacob, Paul Eluard, and Georges Bernanos to name but a few of those with whom the bond was the strongest. Poulenc was one of the century's most gifted writers for the voice.

Poulenc's own words remind us that his biography must consider his music even though my documented biography makes no attempt to analyze Poulenc's numerous compositions beyond casual description. Like its predecessor *The Music of Francis Poulenc (1899-1963): A Catalogue*, the present documented biography is a source book for future investigations.

Baltimore, Maryland   C.B.S.
2001

Acknowledgments

This documented biography is built on the factual foundation laid in my 1995 book *The Music of Francis Poulenc (1899-1963): A Catalogue.* The numerous individuals and institutions acknowledged in that work, must, by extension, be reacknowledged here. Given the length of the list, I beg their indulgence if I do not repeat their names. They have my unfailing thanks now as then. Without their loving attention to detail, their constant encouragement, and their willingness to devote untold hours of personal time to aiding my research, this book would be much the poorer. Their extraordinary efforts on my behalf eloquently testify to the love and affection they share for the life and music of Francis Poulenc. I have encountered this boundless love in every corner of my research.

The entire Poulenc project would never have come about without the opportunities my father Harold Schmidt gave me as a Stanford University student to sing the Mass in G, various motets, Stabat Mater, Gloria, and to conduct *Litanies à la Vierge noire.* Through the generosity of Winifred and Raymond Chrisman I was able to study in France with Nadia Boulanger through whom I met Pierre Bernac and heard my first Poulenc *mélodies.* Finally, my classmate Roland John Wiley, then writing an undergraduate honors thesis on Poulenc, "commissioned" me to go to Salabert and bring home an armload of Poulenc scores. These events lighted the fire.

There are, nevertheless, a number of other people who richly deserve individual acknowledgment for their generous assistance with the present volume. I continue to be indebted to Rosine Seringe, Poulenc's niece and goddaughter, and Les Amis de Francis Poulenc for their personal support, numerous kindnesses, and financial assistance which permitted me to make the first of several trips to France for work on this documented biography.

With two people in particular, I share a great love for Poulenc's music. Rosine Lambiotte-Donhauser, who knew Poulenc personally, has been a source of constant inspiration. Her incredible generosity in reading the full manuscript has saved me from missteps and I have constantly benefited from her considerable knowledge of French arts and letters. Unpublished photographs from her collection further enrich this biography. Catherine Massip, Director of the Département de la Musique, Bibliothèque Nationale, has not only helped make my visits to the BN enormously productive, but her magnificent and continuing effort to collect Poulenc sources there has met with extraordinary success. One can only hope that future donors will consider the Bibliothèque Nationale for gifts of materials related to Poulenc and *Les Six*.

Several people who have consistently aided my research are fellow Poulenc scholars. Without their pioneering books of Poulenc letters, no documentary biography could seriously be undertaken. To Sidney Buckland goes my continued gratitude and thanks for friendship, hospitality, and a wealth of direct assistance with the present volume. Her generosity and encouragement are deeply appreciated. To Myriam Chimènes goes my profound respect for the brilliance of her copiously annotated book of Poulenc correspondence and for her generosity in sharing personal knowledge. To Madeleine Milhaud goes my continued gratitude for years of kindnesses. She and her husband Darius collaborated on performances of Milhaud works such as *Trois Psaumes de David* and the grand opera *David* with Harold Schmidt and it is through this association that I first met them in 1954. It has been a great honor.

I am pleased to thank Oliver Davies of the Royal College of Music, London (Department of Portraits and Performance History) for aid in tracking down numerous programs performed by Poulenc and Bernac. His help has gone far beyond what any researcher could expect, and his assistant Margaret Murray most generously continues to send new information as she uncovers it. The interlibrary loan department of Cook Library at Towson University (Sharon P. Mollock, Head) has been of constant assistance with this book as has Ned Quist and his staff at the Arthur Friedheim Library, Peabody Institute of the Johns Hopkins University.

I am further pleased to have met and benefited from the great generosity of Ornella Volta, director of the Archives de la Fondation Erik Satie in Paris. Jay McKeon Fisher, Senior Curator of Prints, Drawings and Photographs at the Baltimore Museum of Art, has aided my study of Matisse's working methods as a model. Once again, Alice Davison Humez has most graciously provided me with unpublished materials related to the Harvard Glee Club 1921 European tour.

Numerous libraries and their staffs have also continued to support my research. Among them I thank in particular The Library of Congress Music Division (particularly Wayne Shirley), The Boston Public Library, the John Herrick Jackson Music Library at Yale University (especially Kendall Crilly), and Harvard University Libraries (especially John Howard, former Richard French Librarian of the Eda Kuhn Loeb Music Library). I also thank the staffs of Durand (especially Jean-Manuel Mobillon de Scarano) and Salabert in Paris, and Chester in London for publishing Poulenc scores I have either found or which I have newly edited. In addition, I am grateful to Barbara Owen, librarian of The Organ Library of the Boston Chapter, American Guild of Organists at Boston University, for her help with correspondence between E. Power Biggs and Poulenc. Marcella A. Gulledge deserves particular praise for her technical expertise exhibited in the map listing places of importance to this biography.

I thank Denise Duval for the enormous pleasure of a visit that helped her association with Poulenc come alive in a most extraordinary fashion. I shall never forget our hours together. Since my catalogue was published, several people who so generously assisted my research in France have now passed away: Suzanne Peignot and Doda Conrad, I thank you once again for making aspects of Poulenc's life vivid in my imagination.

After this biography was completed, serendipity, a constant presence during a decade of Poulenc research, once again intervened. My decision to print a letter to Virgil Thomson from Allen Hughes led to our meeting. Hughes had known Poulenc from the middle 1950s and, as I have mentioned, contemplated writing a Poulenc biography himself. Once again Poulenc is responsible for initiating friendships.

In addition to those named above, the following individuals have been of assistance in the preparation of this book, and I thank them all: Harriett Woodworth Koch, Roger Poirier, Carol Jacobs (archivist of the Cleveland Orchestra), JoAnne Barry (archivist of the Philadelphia Orchestra), Patricia Harper (contributing editor of the new Chester edition of Poulenc's Sonata for Flute and Piano), and Frédéric Cellier.

Finally, I express my deepest gratitude to Claire Brook and Robert Kessler of Pendragon Press for the extraordinary effort they have made to publish this book in the wake of the Poulenc centenary. Working with an editor like Claire Brook, who not only knew Poulenc, but who is intimately familiar with the entire milieu in which this biography takes place, has been an extraordinary pleasure. Quelle bonne chance!

A decade ago, when I decided to write a biography, I did not immediately realize that a catalogue would have to be written first. Nor did I realize the extent of Poulenc's epistolary prowess. The inexorable chain of events set in motion by a meeting with Poulenc in August 1961 has now run full circle. Francis, your music changes lives.

*   *   *   *   *

My immediate family — Betsey, Brandon, Stephen, and Lindsay — has my lasting gratitude for "living" this book with me for a decade. Each has been of enormous support and has contributed to whatever success this biography can claim. Dear Percy knows best the travails of writing this book. His companionship and purr have been constant and reassuring. Poulenc's Mickey would have understood!

List of Illustrations

[3] To the extent of its authority, permission to publish has been granted by Spelling Entertainment Group, Inc., which owns The Bulletin Company.

Library Sigla

(Standard RISM sigla have been used where possible.)

F   France
Pa	Paris: Bibliothèque de l'Arsenal
Pbodin	Paris: Private Library of Thierry Bodin (Les Autographes)
Pgm	Paris: Bibliothèque Musical Gustav Mahler
Pn	Paris: Bibliothèque Nationale, Département de la Musique
Po	Paris: Bibliothèque de l'Opéra
Psalabert	Paris: Editions Salabert, 22, rue Cauchat
Rmtfp	Rocamadour: Musée trésor Francis Poulenc

GB   England
Lchester	London: J. & W. Chester Ltd., 8/9 Frith Street (materials stored at Bury St Edmunds)
Lcm	London: Royal College of Music
Rbbc	Reading: BBC Written Archives Centre at Caversham

I   Italy
Vgc	Venice: Fondazione Giorgio Cini

CH   Conféderation Helvétique (Switzerland)
Bsacher	Basel: Paul Sacher Foundation

US   United States of America

AUS	Austin, TX: University of Texas at Austin, Harry Ransom Humanities Research Center (Carlton Lake Collection)
Bchristie	Boston, MA: Private Library of James David Christie
Bp	Boston, MA: Boston Public Library
But	Boston, MA: The Organ Library of the Boston Chapter, American Guild of Organists at Boston University, School of Theology
Cn	Chicago, IL: The Newbury Library
NH	New Haven, CN: John Herrick Jackson Music Library, Yale University
NHb	New Haven, CN: Beinecke Rare Book and Manuscript Library, Yale University (now contains Koch collection materials reported in Schmidt 1995 as in US-NYpm)
NYlambiotte -donhauser	New York, NY: Private Library of Rosine Lambiotte-Donhauser
NYp	New York, NY: New York Public Library (Lincoln Center)
NYpa	New York, NY: New York Philharmonic Archive
NYpm	New York, NY: The Pierpont Morgan Library
NYpriv. coll,	New York, NY
TCshapiro	Tucson, AZ: Private Library of Robert Shapiro

Abbreviations

Bar.	baritone
bsn.	bassoon
c.a.	cor anglais
cl.	clarinet
cond.	conductor
d.b.	double bass
fl.	flute
FP	[Francis Poulenc] work numbers from Schmidt 1995
hp.	harp
hps.	harpsichord
hn.	horn
Mez.	mezzo-soprano
ob.	oboe
pn.	piano
S.	soprano
str.	strings
T.	tenor
timp.	timpani
trb.	trombone
tr.	trumpet
vla.	viola
vc.	violoncello
vn.	violin

Key places in France of importance to Poulenc's biography. Départment in square brackets; Cities in capital letters shown on map. Numbers give approximate locations.

1 Amboise [Indre-et-Loire], 24Km NE of TOURS

2 Anost [Saône et Loire], 23Km NW of Autun

3 Autun [Saône et Loire], 23 m SE of Anost; 85Km SW of DIJON

4 Bagnols-en-Forêt [Var] , Afew Km W of CANNES

5 Beaulieu-sur-Dordogne [Corrèze], 44Km SE of BRIVE-LA-GAILLARDE

6 Fontainebleau [Seine et Marne], 36.5Km SE of PARIS

7 Kerbastic ("Kekker," Near Guidel & Guidel Plages) [Morbihan]   A few Km NW of L'ORIENT

8. Larche [Corrèze], 11Km W of BRIVE-LA-GAILLARDE

9 Nazelles [Indre-et-Loire] A few Km E of Noizay

10 Nogent-sur-Marne [Val de Marne], Suburb 8Km W of PARIS

11 Noizay (Le Grand Coteau) [Indre-et-Loire], Ca. 24Km NE of TOURS

12 Offranville [Seine-Maritime], A few Km S of DIEPPE

13 Rocamadour [Lot] 54Km SE of BRIVE- LA-GAILLARDE

14 Tourrettes-sur-Loup [Alpes-Maritimes] 30Km NW of NICE

15 Le Tremblay (Neubourg par Evreux [Eure]), Ca. 28Km NW of EVREUX

16 Uzerche [Corrèze] 34Km N of BRIVE-LA-GAILLARDE

Cities:PARIS, DIJON, LYON, CANNES

Map of France indicating places of special interest to Poulenc

I

Background and Beginnings: 1899-1912

The penultimate year of the nineteenth century dawned auspiciously in Paris, even though France was still in the throes of "The Dreyfus Affair," which divided even important artists such as Camille Pissaro and Alfred Sisley from Auguste Renoir and Paul Cézanne.[1] At approximately three o'clock in the afternoon on New Year's Eve the first flakes of an unanticipated snow storm began to fall. "Tiens! il neige," [Look! it's snowing] *Le Petit Journal* in its New Year's Day issue reported one Parisian as having remarked. Suddenly the streets filled with the curious, greeting each other animatedly. As the snow intensified, becoming a squall, café awnings whipped in the wind, umbrellas turned inside out, and sheet metal chimneys were set swaying. "It seemed to all," *Le Petit Journal* added, "as if the snow in its white shroud would obscure all the sad memories of the year passed."[2] Eight days later, under more moderate weather conditions, Francis Poulenc was born.[3] The intervening week had contained few noteworthy events except for the death of Édouard Hervé, respected director of *Le Soleil* and revered member of the Académie

---

[1] Weber, p. 122.
[2] *Le Petit Journal* (1 Jan. 1899), 1.
[3] Poulenc's birth year was shared with his close colleagues Pierre Bernac (12 Jan.) and Georges Auric (15 Feb.), as well as with Alexander Tcherepnin (20 Jan.), Randall Thompson (21 Apr.), Duke Ellington (29 Apr.), Carlos Chavez (13 June), Helen Traubel (20 June), Eugene Ormandy (18 Nov.), and Sir John Barbirolli (2 Dec.), among other musicians, plus Federico Garcia Lorca, Vladimir Nabokov, Noël Coward, and Maurice Carême among writers. It also marked the deaths of Ernest Chausson (44) and Johann Strauss (74).

1

Plate 1: Poulenc's birthplace at 2, rue Saussaies (Paris, 1991)

française. News of Hervé's obsequies, which occupied the front page of *Le Figaro* the day of Poulenc's birth, was even carried across the channel by the *London Times*.[4]

FAMILY BACKGROUND AND BIRTH (1899-1906)

Poulenc was born in Paris on Saturday, 7 January 1899, in a large building at 2, place des Saussaies (Plate 1).[5] Located in the heart of the city, the building, which is still standing today, is situated within easy walking distance of the Place de la Madeleine and the Élysée Palace.[6] Though the day's news was of little significance, several musical events seemed harbingers of his life to come. *Le Figaro* published its brief monthly musical selections including Louis Diémer's *Minuetto* (especially written for *Le Figaro*), lauded for its elegant and charming melodic line, and an excerpt from Alexandre Brody's *Resignation*, described as "a sort of funeral march."[7] During that same evening Parisians ushered in the new year with a splendid ball at the Opéra which featured the following *entrées*:

10:00 pm	"The bells of Saint-Hubert"
11:00	"Musical novelties" played by the orchestra in the "avant-foyer" under the direction of M. Mélé
11:30	"First performance of waltzes, polkas, sung mazurkas" (200 performers), under the direction of L. Ganne
12:00 am	"Fairy dance of the diamonds and precious stones"
12:30	"Battle of the flowers and game of fishing for presents"[8]
1:00	"Triumphal entry of the Twelfth Night Cake and distribution of the traditional cake"[9]
2:00	"Huge farandole dance and general apotheosis"[10]

Poulenc's family was one of more than comfortable means and artistic inclination. On the paternal side, it originated in Aveyron,

[4] André Maurel, "Les obsèques de M. Édouard Hervé," *Le Figaro* (6 Jan. 1899), 2 and A. Claveau,"Édouard Hervé," *Le Figaro* (6 Jan. 1899), 1 ff.
[5] Poulenc's parents lived on the rue Faubourg St-Honoré. Poulenc 1935a, p. 522.
[6] Pierre Bernac, who viewed photographs of the apartment, noted that it "was large, comfortable, and lavishly furnished with upholstered suites, draped curtains and potted palms, according to the taste of the times." Bernac 1977a, p. 21.
[7] Music in *Le Figaro* (7 Jan. 1899), 5-6. Diémer (1843-1919) was a noted French pianist and composer; Brody was a professor at the Conservatoire de Genève.
[8] A game in which one uses a fishing pole to snag a present (as at a "foire").
[9] This cake contained a charm which entitled the winner to pick a queen.
[10] A. Mercklein, "Spectacles & Concerts," *Le Figaro* (3 Jan. 1899), 4.

in the south-central part of France, while on the maternal side, as Poulenc would note, the Royer family had been "pure" Parisians for generations.[11]   Poulenc always considered himself Parisian at heart, and the artistic climate of that great city stimulated him enormously.[12] His father Émile, along with uncles Gaston and Camille (all sons of Étienne Poulenc), owned a business established in the last quarter of the nineteenth century devoted to manufacturing high quality industrial chemicals.[13]   Camille possessed the degree "Docteur ès sciences" and was a regular contributor to the chemical literature of his day.[14] In the fashion of the time, his mother Jenny, who "came from a line of cabinet-makers, bronze workers and upholsterers," never sought employment.[15] Income from the Poulenc business allowed Émile and Jenny to engage in their passion for the arts. This same income later provided Francis with the independence to compose and perform as he chose without the necessity of maintaining a full-time job.[16] It also afforded the family the luxury of summer vacations and the ability to employ a nurse to care for

[11] Poulenc told Rostand: "In marrying my father, who was Aveyronnais, my mother made an exception to a sort of family rule [i.e., to marry only Parisians]." Poulenc 1954, p. 12.

[12] In later chapters it will be seen that the preponderance of his compositional activity was centered in the Touraine, where he bought an estate in 1927. He also worked in a variety of venues in Southern France and at his sister's estate Le Tremblay (Eure). When inspiration flagged, a pilgrimage to Rocamadour — with its fifteenth-century chapel containing an image of the black virgin on the altar — was often the perfect cure to restore Poulenc's creativity.

[13] For details of the firm's history and activity see Cayez. After Étienne's death the firm took the name *Veuve Poulenc et Fils* with the modest capital of 450,000 francs (1878). When Étienne's widow Pauline retired, the firm was renamed *Etablissements Poulenc Frères* (1881). In 1883 Gaston established a store on rue de Cluny which was moved in 1893 to 122, boulevard St-Germain. In 1887, just twelve years before Francis's birth, his father Émile directed a factory at 92, rue Vieille-du-Temple which manufactured photographic equipment. (Cayez, p. 18.) Today, Rhône-Poulenc is a powerful international conglomerate listed on the New York Stock Exchange.

[14] His thesis was entitled *Thèse présentée à la Faculté des sciences de Paris pour obtenir le grade de docteur ès sciences physiques, par M. C. Poulenc [. . .] 1ʳᵉ thèse. . . .* (Paris: Gauthier-Villars et fils, 1893). In 1891 he published an article in *Annales de chimie et de physique*, 6ᵉ series, vol. XXIV, p. 548; in 1894 he published another in the 7ᵉ series, vol. 2; and in 1908 a book entitled *Les Produits chimiques purs en photographie*. From 1896-1911, 1913-1914 he published a yearly volume entitled *Les Nouveautés chimiques,* and there are still other scientific books credited to him.

[15] Statements in Poulenc 1954, p. 13, and Poulenc 1963a, pp. 31-2 (Poulenc 1978, p. 29). Schneider, p. 213 notes that Poulenc found the rue Turenne (where Schneider lived) "divine" because his mother was born there and was married in the church of St-Denys-du-St-Sacrement.

[16] Two world wars, however, contributed to financially difficult moments for Poulenc during which his independence was severely threatened.

the young boy. Years later, Poulenc recalled the lasting affect that walks with his nurse had on him.

> When I say the word *tree*, I think immediately of the celebrated magnolia on the Champs-Elysées, today dead and gone, and, if it is a question of a palace, I inevitably think of the installation at the President's palace of M. Fallières, a sight which intoxicated both my nurse and myself, I assure you. It seems to me impossible for a human being and most especially an artist not to be branded by his memories of childhood. That is why, even if I am in the most beautiful city in the world, in Rome or in Grenada, I must return for the blooming of the Parisian lilacs. Otherwise it seems to me like a lost spring.[17]

According to Poulenc's published recollections (which occasionally vary in details), his family was quite musical. ". . . If my father rarely missed a rehearsal at the Colonne concerts, or a first night at the Opéra or the Opéra-Comique, he did not play an instrument."[18] Émile's taste included "Beethoven and Berlioz, then César Franck and—finally—Massenet. *L'Enfance du Christ* [Berlioz] and *Marie-Magdaleine* [Massenet] brought tears to his eyes."[19] His mother was an accomplished amateur pianist who had studied with Mme Riss-Arbeau, incorrectly noted in the Poulenc literature as having been one of Franz Liszt's last students.[20] "My mother," Poulenc recalled, "had a charming touch and perfect musical understanding allied to great virtuosity. She idolized Mozart, Schubert and Chopin."[21] Her tastes extended to Domenico Scarlatti and Robert Schumann on the one hand, and to several of the more popular pieces by Edward Grieg (*Berceuse*) and Anton Rubinstein (*Romance*) on the other.[22] It was she who instilled in Poulenc a love for music in general and for the piano in particular.[23] It was she who, beginning in 1904, provided her young son with his training on the instrument which later accounted

[17] Poulenc 1935a, p. 521. For a photograph of Poulenc and his nurse see Poulenc 1979, p. 1. Rosine Seringe has kindly informed me that M. Jean Liger has recently identified her as Marie-Françoise Lauxière (née Pastour), 1860-1931.
[18] Poulenc 1963a, p. 32 (Poulenc 1978, p. 29) and Poulenc 1954, pp. 20-1.
[19] Poulenc 1954, p. 21. In an earlier interview (Guth 1952, p. 4) Poulenc had stated: "As for my father: Berlioz, César Franck, Massenet... And then Beethoven!... Oh! yes... Beethoven, Beethoven!..."
[20] Alan Walker, the noted Liszt authority, found no trace of Mme Riss-Arbeau having been Liszt's student. (E-mail of 27 Jan. 1996 solicited with the kind assistance of Fred Schock.)
[21] Poulenc 1963a, p. 32 (Poulenc 1978, p. 30).
[22] Poulenc 1954, pp. 13-14. In an earlier interview (Guth 1952, p. 4) Poulenc had stated: "For my mother, Chopin came before everyone. And then Mozart, Schubert, Scarlatti..."
[23] Poulenc 1935a, p. 521.

for a portion of his livelihood.[24] Poulenc paid her the ultimate com-
pliment in the dedication to his opera *Dialogues des Carmélites* which
begins "To the memory of my mother, who revealed music to me."[25]
One of the most charming photographs of Poulenc's early childhood, probably taken when he was three, shows him playing in front
of a miniature toy piano.[26] White lacquered and decorated with rep-
resentations of cherries, this piano remained in Poulenc's toy cupboard until he was eight. At nine, however, he developed a disdain
for it and it was given away. He boasted to Stéphane Audel that at
two he sight-read everything he thought was music, mostly old store
catalogues and railway timetables![27]

As Poulenc's childhood progressed, his education became a family issue. His father, an industrialist at heart, could not brook the
idea that a son might prefer the Conservatoire over finishing sec-
ondary school. His mother, who loved music and recognized her
son's passionate interest for both the arts and the piano, coveted an
education for him at the Conservatoire, one of Europe's premier
musical institutions. The father's position prevailed and Poulenc
stayed at the lycée Condorcet through graduation.[28]

Jenny Royer was not the only Royer who provided an artistic
stimulus to the young boy. Marcel Royer, or "Uncle Papoum" as
Poulenc dubbed him, was thirty-seven years Poulenc's senior. He
lived in an apartment opposite the Luxembourg Gardens at 5, rue
de Médicis, where Poulenc himself took up residence beginning in
1936. Royer, Poulenc's godfather and according to Audel "the doyen
of subscription-ticket holders at the Odéon theater," was an amateur artist who frequently visited his sister Jenny.[29] The young boy
enjoyed hearing his uncle discuss the theater, movies, and concerts
with her while he was thought to be playing with his toy trains under a table.[30]

Moreover, it was at the Royer's family estate in nearby Nogent-
sur-Marne, a small village some eight kilometers west of Paris edg-
ing on the Bois de Boulogne, where Poulenc spent countless sum-

[24] Poulenc 1954, p. 28. See also Roland-Manuel, p. 98 where Poulenc states he
began his piano lessons at age four.
[25] See the published score.
[26] Poulenc 1935a, p. 523. Poulenc told Roland-Manuel he was given the toy piano
at the age of two. Roland-Manuel, p. 98.
[27] Audel, an actor, did a series of radio interviews with Poulenc. Poulenc 1963a,
p. 32 (Poulenc 1978, p. 33).
[28] The French *lycée* is a private preparatory school where tuition must be paid.
Sachs 1933, p. 103.
[29] Poulenc claimed Royer painted under the influence of Toulouse-Lautrec and
that his apartment was filled with valuable porcelain vases juxtaposed with
cheap Japanese curios. Poulenc 1963a, p. 33 (Poulenc 1978, p. 30).
[30] Poulenc 1963a, p. 33 (Poulenc 1978, p. 30).

mer months during the first twenty-five years of his life.[31] (French places of interest to this biography may be found on a map on page xx.) In addition to the spacious white house at 4, rue de la Muette, the grounds also included a tennis court.[32] Nogent was the locus of Poulenc's musical imagination, and its atmosphere left an indelible impression on him. At the turn of the century, Nogent could easily be reached by electric tramways (Chemins de Fer Nogentais: Plates 2 and 3). The incomparable Baedecker guide notes that the trams started "from the station of the *Métropolitain Railway*, at the Porte de Vincennes. The Champigny tramway connected Vincennes with Nogent-sur-Marne and Le Plant-Champigny."[33] For Henri Sauguet's first visit to Nogent Poulenc sent the following directions:

> Take the Métro to the Vincennes station. There, take the Champigny or the Bry sur Marne tramway which depart from the same gate. Get off at Nogent rue de Beauté. Follow the rue de Beauté which de-scends and the first street on the right is rue de la Muette. You see that it is quite simple.[34]

Poulenc later confided to Claude Rostand the importance Nogent held for him.

> *La Madeleine* is the city of my birth, and *le Marais* my village. And then . . . a little farther away, continuing to the east of Paris, there is also my "country:" dear Nogent-sur-Marne where I spent my entire childhood. What you sometimes call my "bad boy" side developed quite naturally in Nogent.[35]

> . . . it was paradise for me, with its open-air dance-halls, its purveyors of French-fries, and its *bals musettes*. . . . It is there that I learned the tunes of Christiné and Scotto which became my folklore. The bad-

[31] Concerning Nogent-sur-Marne see Poulenc 1954, pp. 17-18 and Poulenc 1963a, pp. 33-4 (Poulenc 1978, p. 31).

[32] For a photograph of the three-story house see Poulenc, 1979, p. 12. Houdin 1964a, p. 70 describes the house as follows: ". . . on one side it abutted the rue de Beauté providing access from a gated entryway. Enclosed by high walls, planted with hundred-year-old trees, everything there bespoke of quiet and peace. . . . It was a very large house, quite tall, the two corners of which jutted out dominating the slope of the valley. Its gracious well-lighted porch supported by semicircular columns, opened onto a large stone staircase." For another brief description see Schneider, p. 213. According to Houdon 1964a, p. 75, the house was left to Ernest-Louis Royer in 1926, who bequeathed it to the S.N.C.F. in 1945, at which time it was made into a nursery for children.

[33] Baedecker: Paris, appendix, p. 35.

[34] Unpublished [1923] letter to Sauguet in F-Pn (Sauguet, no. 6).

[35] Poulenc 1954, p. 17. Poulenc's friend Marcel Schneider wrote that Poulenc signed their correspondence "Francis Marquis du Marais." (Schneider, p. 218.)

Plate 2: Turn-of-the-century view of Nogent-sur-Marne.

Plate 3: Turn-of-the-century view of "Ile de Beauté" in Nogent-sur-Marne

boy side of my music, you see, is not artificial, as one sometimes be-lieves, because it is associated with my fondest childhood memories.[36]

Poulenc's nostalgia for Nogent, never very remote in his conscious-ness, welled up in a later letter to his friend Marthe Bosredon:

> I am writing from my home town, where I am spending a day of pilgrimage. Nothing is as melancholy as this type of introspection into the past; however, I can never resist it. But where are the banks of the Marne of long ago, today devoid of open-air dance-halls and accordion bands, without Bébert in his cap, and Nini in her pink silk blouse![37]

It was in Nogent that Poulenc met several neighbors of his grand-parents who were later influential in his childhood and teenage years. One was the pianist Simone Tilliard with whom Poulenc discussed music and who participated in a number of early concerts which included Poulenc's compositions.[38] Another was Jacques Soulé, Poulenc's boyhood companion, who lived with his parents at 9, rue du Moulin from June to September.[39] At Soulé's house in 1916, Poulenc met a third person, Edouard Souberbielle, who became important in his life and with whom he maintained a brief but ex-tremely valuable correspondence in 1918-19.[40] Tilliard, Soulé, and Souberbielle will receive greater attention in subsequent chapters.

When Poulenc was fifty-one he revealed to his friend Paul Eluard one more bit of information about his youthful habits Eluard had just moved into a new house at 52, rue de Gravelle in Charenton-le-Pont, nine kilometers outside of Paris. Poulenc told him, "I must congratulate you for choosing the plateau of Gravelle—which I tra-versed by bicycle throughout my childhood."[41]

AN INTRODUCTION TO MUSIC IN THE ÎLE DE FRANCE (1907-10)

In 1907, when Poulenc was eight years old, his mother passed her piano protégé on to Mlle Melon, coach of César Franck's niece Cécile

---

[36] Poulenc 1954, pp. 17-18. Henri-Marius Christiné and Vincent Scotto were composers of popular music admired by Poulenc. Poulenc devoted two radio broadcasts to them in 1948. See the transcriptions in Poulenc 1999, pp. 49-58.

[37] Poulenc 1994, 43-8 (Poulenc 1991, no. 163) (dated "mercredi 5 heures"[août 1943]).

[38] Poulenc dedicated his Sonata for Piano Four Hands (FP 8) to her in June 1918; also "L'Espionne," the first song in *Calligrammes* (FP 140) in May 1948. Schmidt 1995, pp. 21 and 383.

[39] Soulé's recollections in Poulenc 1979, pp. 13-28.

[40] Souberbielle, composer and organist tied to Ricardo Viñes, was the dedicatee of the Sonata for Two Clarinets. Chimènes' commentary in Poulenc 1994, p. 1051.

[41] "Dimanche" [June 1950] letter to Eluard. Poulenc 1994, 59-19 (Poulenc 1991, no. 208).

Boutet de Montvel. Poulenc remembered her as possessing excellent technical principles.[42] Under her supervision he practiced one hour every afternoon after lycée; whenever he had spare time during the day he sight-read as well.[43] In a later interview Poulenc recalled: "When I was eight, this fantasy [Mozart's Fantasy in C minor, K. 475?] represented for me the grandeur, the nobility of the piano."[44] That same year was also memorable for providing Poulenc his first known contact with contemporary music when he heard Claude Debussy's *Danse sacrée et danse profane* (1904: for harp and string orchestra).[45]

> I was literally enthralled: "How beautiful it is! It is a little off key," I wrote, and upon returning home I tried to reproduce on the piano these ninth chords, so new, which had intoxicated me. Next, I would not stop pestering them to let me play some Debussy, alas too difficult for my inadequate pianistic abilities. Moreover, at the age of ten I purchased some [Debussy] surreptitiously, by "buying" my complicitious silence from our cook, who was receiving her lover, a delivery man from *La Belle Jardinière*, evenings on which my parents were out. . . . that's how I obtained *Jardins sous la pluie* and *La Soirée dans Grenade*.[46]

The impression Debussy's music made on the young Poulenc cannot be overstated. "In spite of an anti-Debussyist crisis in self defense at the time I knew Satie in 1917, Debussy has always remained the musician whom I prefer after Mozart. I cannot do without his music. It is my oxygen."[47]

The same cannot be said for the music of Gabriel Fauré. Around his seventh or eighth year Poulenc heard Fauré accompany some of his songs during a student recital at the home of Mme Ronceret. He had attended because his sister Jeanne (twelve years his senior) was Ronceret's student.[48] In a 1952 letter to the writer Gabriel Faure he remembered:

> Alas, dear sir, I would like to explain equitably my position vis-à-vis Fauré so that you can accept it with indulgence. Brought up in a profoundly musical family, from my earliest age I understood music well. I have some exhilarating memories: at the age of eight an audi-

[42] Poulenc 1954, p. 28.
[43] Poulenc 1954, p. 28.
[44] Roland-Manuel, p. 102.
[45] Poulenc 1954, pp. 24-5.
[46] Poulenc 1954, p. 24. Poulenc also told a similar story to Roland-Manuel: "An *Arabasque* by Debussy played for me when I was six elicited this cry: 'Oh! how beautiful it is; it is a little off key.' . . ." Roland-Manuel, p. 98.
[47] Poulenc 1954, p. 24. When Christian Bérard painted Poulenc's portrait, it was Mozart whose likeness he placed in a picture on the wall behind Poulenc.
[48] 11 June [1952] letter in Poulenc 1994, 52-15.

tion for *Pour la musique* [sic] at the home of Madame Griset, dedicatee of the work.[49] Alas, I have two nightmares: Fauré and the Capet Quartet. When my sister who studied with Raunay and Croiza sang Schumann, Schubert, Debussy, perfectly accompanied by my mother, I went to the piano and I closed my eyes with happiness. When Fauré's turn came I said, "Not Fauré!"[50]

In his later years Poulenc developed a respect for Fauré, but before thirty he hated his music. Paul Guth (1952) quoted him as saying: "People often confuse my total lack of taste for Fauré with a lack of respect. It is the opposite. The older I get, the more I admire him and the less I like him."[51]

Finally, the young Poulenc was an insatiable reader of sophisticated literature with a great interest in the famous actors and actresses of his day. By eight he was already familiar with Réjane, Sarah Bernhardt, and Eve Lavallière, as well as Lucien Guitry.[52] For his entire life Poulenc was an avid playgoer who cherished associations with many of France's most gifted performers and playwrights including Maurice Chevalier, Yvonne Printemps, Jean Cocteau, Raymond Radiguet, and Jean Anouilh.

Poulenc's next several years are the subject of few documented anecdotes other than the sometimes contradictory statements made in interviews with Stéphane Audel and Claude Rostand. He told Audel that "As far back as I can go in memory my sole preoccupation was music,"[53] and "that Edmond Clément, a fine tenor and friend of his Uncle Royer, came to his house regularly."[54] Poulenc heard him sing des Grieux in *Manon* at the Opéra-Comique when he was ten. For five years Poulenc dreamed of becoming a singer until his voice changed and developed what he himself called "a composer's squawk."[55] At ten he could recite Stéphane Mallarmé's poem *Apparition* by heart, and harbored the desire to become a great tragedian.[56]

In the last of a series of radio broadcasts entitled "A Bâtons

---

[49] Chabrier's song *A la Musique*.
[50] Poulenc 1994, 52-15. Faure (1877-1962), not to be confused with Fauré, was a writer and inspector of historic monuments.
[51] Guth 1952, p. 4. In a 29 Sept. 1962 letter to Michel Garcin in Poulenc 1994, 62-15 Poulenc remarked: "God knows that I detest Fauré (it is a frightful allergy). . . ."
[52] Poulenc 1954, p. 132. Poulenc notes that these authors were as well known to him as were Général Dourakine or Sophie Ficini to other children. Poulenc had told Guth 1952, p. 4 that "From the age of eight I saw Réjane, Sarah Bernhardt, [and] Jane Granier perform."
[53] Poulenc 1963a, p. 36 (Poulenc 1978, p. 33). "I was raised on the knees of Edmond Clément, the tenor," he told Guth 1952, p. 4.
[54] Poulenc 1963a, p. 36 (Poulenc 1978, p. 33).
[55] Poulenc 1963a, pp. 36-7 (Poulenc 1978, p. 33).
[56] Poulenc 1954, p. 69.

rompus," Poulenc discussed and played music by Louis Ganne, the prolific composer of more than two-hundred works, a number of which were written for the popular opera balls at which he conducted the orchestra.[57] In the course of this broadcast Poulenc reminisced about events in the spring of 1909. We learn that he was taken for walks by his nurse in the Bois de Boulogne to avoid the Champs-Élysées where diseases such as measles were prevalent; that he sometimes went by Métro to the Chinese pavilion or by other conveyance to Le Pré-Catelan restaurant (where he first heard Ganne's *Valse des brunes*); and that he was already reading copies of *Théâtre illustré* which his father kept in his study.[58]

The winter of 1909-10 was unusually wet in Paris, and not long after Poulenc's eleventh birthday the Seine River overflowed its banks inundating the city. Bridges were submerged, the Métro disabled, and water stood approximately five meters deep at the Quai d'Orsay station. To make matters worse, sewers backed up and looters preyed on the unwary.[59] Joining thousands of Parisians, Poulenc's family fled taking up residence in neighboring Fontainebleau, "a quiet place with broad, clean streets and just under 15,000 inhabitants."[60] Having brought along few belongings, Poulenc, starved for music to read, bought a score of Franz Schubert's *Winterreise* at a shop across the street from where the family had settled.

> I went from magic moment to magic moment. By a strange coincidence, child of the city that I was, I discovered all at once the beauty of the country, the winter, and its sublime musical transmutation. I played and replayed without stopping "La Corneille" [Die Krähe], "Le Tilleul" [Der Lindenbaum], "Le Joueur de Vielle" [Der Leiermann] and above all this astonishing "Soleil d'Hiver" [Die Nebensonnen], which remains for me the most beautiful art song in the world.[61]

Poulenc enjoyed turning his piano around to face the window so that he could play "Die Nebensonnen" [The Phantom Suns] while viewing the sun, which he said looked like a red cheese from Holland. Later in his career, Poulenc occasionally performed Schubert lieder with Bernac, but the two left no commercial recordings of Schubert's numerous art songs.[62]

---

[57] For a transcription see Poulenc 1999, pp. 73-81.
[58] About this radio series see Chapter X. See also Buckland/Chimènes: e, p. 368 and Poulenc 1999.
[59] Gosling, p. 161 and Cronin.
[60] Baedecker: Paris, p. 411.
[61] Poulenc 1947c, pp. 507-8.
[62] Marya Freund epitomized Poulenc's ideal of Schubert interpretation as his inscription in a copy of *Cocardes* given to her indicates: "à Madame Freund unique interprète de Schubert avec toute mon admiration Fr. Poulenc [rule] 1921." Also Schmidt 1995, p. 47.

The impressionable young Poulenc had two other "musical encounters" during 1910, both of great significance. In his eleventh year he first became aware of Erik Satie's music, though he apparently did not formally study any at his piano lessons until six years later (in 1916).[63] He also heard music by Igor Stravinsky for the first time at a Colonne concert during which Gabriel Pierné conducted *Feux d'artifice* and the "Berceuse" from *L'Oiseau de feu*. Pierné's conducting of the "Berceuse" (he had earlier conducted the premiere of the complete ballet), as well as the "sound" of the music itself, impressed Poulenc deeply. He would encounter Stravinsky's music again in 1913 at the Théâtre des Champs-Élysées, where he witnessed a performance of *Le Sacre du Printemps* by Serge Diaghilev's Ballets Russes, and in 1914 at the Casino de Paris, where Pierre Monteux conducted a concert performance of *Le Sacre* memorable for its sensational success.[64]

Sometime around his tenth year Poulenc also learned how to play bridge.[65] Knowlege of this sophisticated cardgame was useful to him later. He played regularly with the composer/pianist Serge Prokofiev when he was in Paris.

A GROWING PASSION FOR MUSIC: POULENC'S EARLY TEENS (1911-12)

Before Poulenc began his extensive correspondence in 1915, virtually all testimony concerning his life up to the time of World War I was given many years after the fact. An exception is a *Journal de vacances* he kept as a boy of twelve during a summer vacation at the Hôtel Sacaron in Luchon (15 August-2 September 1911) and at thirteen during a spring vacation in Biarritz (late April 1912).[66] Taken in the aggregate, the exuberant entries show his growing passion for music as well as for art and architecture. Those concerning the Luchon vacation, some of which are quaintly illustrated with drawings of opera singers and stage sets, record his youthful impressions for relatives (notably his Uncle Royer) who had remained behind in Nogent. In addition to discussing activities at the thermal baths and commenting on the various one-day excursions the family took to nearby lakes, waterfalls, and other natural attractions of the

---

[63] Poulenc 1963a, p. 81 (Poulenc 1978, p. 63). Georges Auric also shared a youthful interest in Satie. See his "Erik Satie: musicien humoriste," *Revue française de musique* 12 (10 Dec. 1913), 138-42, written when Auric was only fourteen.

[64] Poulenc 1963a, pp. 187-9 (Poulenc 1978, pp. 135-6) and Guth, p. 4. Poulenc was also greatly impressed by Vaslav Nijinsky's choreography for *Le Sacre*. For Stravinsky's personal recollection of the Casino de Paris performance see Stravinsky 1962, p. 164 and Stravinsky 1984, pp. 59-60.

[65] Recalled in his "vendredi" [29 Sept. 1922] letter to Milhaud. Poulenc 1994, 22-31.

[66] Excerpts in Poulenc 1979 (see also Poulenc 1999). Luchon, a popular vacation spot in the Pyrénées some 841Km from Paris, rests at an altitude of 630 meters at the end of the Luchon Valley nestled under Mt. Superbagnères, which rises to

Pyrénées, Poulenc made remarkably perspicacious observations about the music he had heard including Giacomo Puccini's *Tosca* and Georges Bizet's *Carmen*.

> 15 Aug.: We are going to revel in the thermal baths. Oh! how funny it is! the ladies make noises like poorly oiled motors. The men spitting and snorting. Then the Mass, where Mr. Jean Laure sang very well, was filled with elegances. We returned home for lunch before going to the open air theater where Campagnola sang the role of Cavaradossi in *Tosca*. I cried gently, I assure you because everything was very well performed. Campagnola, in the Italian manner, was marvelous. Besides, he has a splendid voice. Bergès, she, has a very pretty voice and excellent diction. She was especially good in the last two acts because her voice is a little piercing in its upper register; in the first act, she had a horrible costume, orange and transparent. The costume of C[avaradossi] was not very appropriate, it was [rather] the costume of Werther.[67] That of J[ean] L[aure] was very sinister especially in the first act where he wore a coat. I liked the first act very much because to my great surprise the role of the Sacristan is very funny. Then we departed the open air theater at six o'clock. [The *Journal* includes three drawings which accompany this entry: one of Scarpia, one of the décor of the first act, and one of Tosca after the murder.][68]

> 28 Aug.: In the afternoon we went to *Carmen* because Mr. Laure had given us two very good seats. I had a very good time; besides it was very well sung and truly it is a masterpiece which will never become pompous like many others. The art of music is developed in it and also it seems that the artist puts his heart into certain passages where you are taken by some kind of passion. Indeed! this is not modern, no dissonances, but who cares. It seems that this is a story that happened to him, and that he puts sad and gay thoughts into his harmonies. It is an art!!! The motif which occurs often in the score is a gem. Here is *Toréador* [Poulenc transcribes the melody of the Toréador and includes three pictures of characters from the opera.][69]

In a 19 August entry, Poulenc noted having seen two noteworthy churches, the first of which he likened to one in Edouard Lalo's and Edouard Blau's opera *Le Roy d'Ys*.[70]

2,260 meters. Numerous thermal baths there had been famous since Roman times. The Poulenc family had reached Luchon by train, a trip which then took approximately seventeen and a half hours. Baedecker: Paris, p. 165.

[67]Poulenc probably refers to Jules Massenet's opera *Werther*, which he must have seen earlier in Paris.

[68]Poulenc 1979, pp. 3-5 and Poulenc 1999, pp. 25-6 (lacks the drawings).

[69]Poulenc 1979, p. 9: "8 aôut" and Poulenc 1999, p. 30.

[70]Lalo's work, premiered at the Paris Opéra in 1888, is set in Ys, "a legendary Breton city submerged by the sea many centuries ago." Macdonald 1992, p. 6.

Poulenc's diary of the 1912 trip to Biarritz discusses architecture more than music. Among the musical anecdotes, however, several are of interest. After a lengthy automobile ride during which he recited Molière, Racine, and Corneille, the family arrived in Mauléon at the villa of friends surnamed Gorre.

> To my great surprise there was a very good harmonium there. I had never played one, but I burned with desire to do so. When I played it it was very amusing and it permitted me to compose my orchestra because there was a flute, fife, etc. Mme Gorre, who played it, gave me some Bach to read, but composing pleased me more.[71]

At twelve, according to the well-known French singer and radio commentator Hélène Jourdan-Morhange, the young boy also discovered Modeste Moussorgsky through a set of piano pieces entitled *Les Enfantines (Souvenirs d'enfance)*.[72] Later, Poulenc acknowledged his debt to Moussorgsky in songs such as *La Grenouillère* and the dedication to his opera *Dialogues des Carmélites*. Poulenc also met the famous mezzo-soprano and teacher Claire Croiza at whose house he played piano accompaniments during his sister Jeanne's voice lessons. He preferred Debussy's *Ariettes oubliées* to Fauré's *La Bonne Chanson*.[73]

At fifty-one Poulenc was still haunted by a dream he had had in 1927, which recalled an event from 1912. It confirms that some of Poulenc's musical tastes were shaped in his very early years.

> Please pardon me if I now have the desire to retranscribe a bizarre dream I had in 1927. [. . .] The event took place in Monte Carlo during 1912 at the Hôtel de Paris where I was eating lunch with my parents. An old white-bearded gentleman wearing a fez was seated at the next table. "It's Saint-Saëns," whispered my father, "and the large lady accompanying him is Félia Litvinne."[74] At the end of the meal, the black waiter in charge of the Turkish coffee, approached the singer and whispered into her ear. She stood up immediately and sang *La Marseillaise*. The maestro applauded as if to bring the house down, and to my amazement, his hands were two hands of fatma, in gold filigree. As stupid as that may appear, the fez and the hands of fatma have hampered me across the years from any impartial judgment of Saint-Saëns' music.[75]

[71]Poulenc 1979, p. 11 and Poulenc 1999, p. 33.
[72]Jourdan-Morhange, p. 130.
[73]Poulenc 1935a, pp. 521-2. Later Poulenc accompanied Croiza in recitals, and in 1929 he made several Columbia records with her including repertoire by Duparc ("L'Invitation au voyage"), Debussy (*Ariettes oubliées*), and Fauré ("Claire de lune"). See Appendix 3.
[74]Félia Litvinne (1861-1936) was a dramatic soprano who had studied with Pauline Viardot and Victor Maurel.
[75]Poulenc 1950c, p. 66 and Poulenc 1999, pp. 223-4.

II

Crosscurrents and Encounters: 1913-1916

CROSSCURRENTS

In the years 1913-16, Poulenc's fourteenth through seventeenth, the number of documentable events which shaped his artistic and personal life expanded exponentially. The fact that Europe's political situation deteriorated rapidly in these years, culminating with Germany's declaration of war on Russia (1 Aug. 1914) and on France two days later, seems not to have affected Poulenc's life in Paris.[1] The closing on 2 August 1914 of all of France's theaters, movie houses, and music-halls, however, must have seriously intruded upon one of his chief pleasures.[2] He himself noted that after the initial shock of the war, which saw important artists such as Henri Matisse, Georges Braque, Guillaume Apollinaire, Fernand Léger, Maurice de Vlaminck, and André Derain quickly join French military regiments, in 1916 the avant-garde once again raised its head, lowered since the advent of hostilities.[3] The revival was led by Apollinaire, who had returned to Paris after being seriously wounded at the front,

---

[1] Hausser, pp. 535-8 summarizes these events as reported in the press.
[2] Details about the effect of World War I on the daily life of French civilians appears in Perreux. Especially pp. 273-92 and 293-309. Perreux points out that the first Parisian theaters to reopen were the Théâtre des Capucines on 15 Nov. 1914 (followed in quick succession by neighboring theaters), then two state theaters, the Opéra-Comique on 6 Dec. 1914 and the Comédie-Française eight days later. Two other state theaters opened later: the Odéon in Mar. 1915 and the Opéra did not receive permission to present full-length works until the beginning of Nov. 1916.
[3] See Silver, passim.

16

and by various painters who had been recalled to the Paris region to camouflage buildings.[4]

> Everything began to fuse together in the extraordinary crucible of Paris. Of course, there was the "Nouvelle Revue française" group, the "Cocteau" group, but all the writers, when they went in the direction of the Luxembourg [Gardens] had the habit of stopping in a bookstore which has now, alas, disappeared: that of Adrienne Monnier at 7, rue de l'Odéon.[5]

This was a period of new and important musical, literary, and artistic experiences for Poulenc, who saw Guillaume Apollinaire for the first time in late 1916.[6] It was a time when his musical horizon was expanded and challenged by diverse musical currents that seemed diametrically opposed. Foremost among the currents were: his introduction to the Second Viennese School; his chance discovery of Chabrier's piano music; his fascination with the café-concerts, theaters, and music-halls of the Quartier de la République in Paris; and his meeting with four people who were enormously important to his life: the great Catalan pianist Ricardo Viñes (whose student he would become), Georges Auric, Darius Milhaud, and Raymonde Linossier.

Shortly after his encounter with Stravinsky's *Le Sacre du Printemps*, Poulenc bought Arnold Schönberg's *Six Little Piano Pieces*, Op. 19 (1911). Poulenc wrote that the pieces "stupefied me by their conciseness and their chromaticism."[7] He also knew *Pierrot lunaire* in 1914 from the published score, though he would not hear the music performed until Marya Freund and Milhaud presented it at a Concert Jean Wiéner.[8] In late January and February 1922 Poulenc joined Milhaud and Freund for a trip which included a stop in Vienna. It was during this trip, which will be discussed later, that he met Schönberg, Alban Berg, and Anton Webern, among others, for the first time. Though Poulenc found little reason to assimilate their styles into his own, he nevertheless maintained a lifelong interest in their music.

---

[4] Poulenc 1963a, p. 130 (Poulenc 1978, pp. 97-8).

[5] Poulenc 1963a, pp. 130-1 (Poulenc 1978, p. 98).

[6] Poulenc had read Apollinaire earlier, however. In 1950 he told Roland Gelatt (in an interview facilitated by Doda Conrad): "I find myself able to compose music only to poetry with which I feel total contact — a contact transcending mere admiration. This quality I felt for the first time when I encountered the poems of Guillaume Apollinaire. That was in 1912, when I was thirteen." Gelatt, p. 58.

[7] Poulenc 1954, p. 199, where he gives his age as fourteen (1913). In Audel's preface to Poulenc 1963a, p. 21, the dates read "fifteen" and "1914" respectively. Poulenc 1978, p. 22 errs in ascribing Op. 19 to Webern.

[8] Poulenc 1963a, p. 21 (Poulenc 1978, p. 22). The first Freund/Milhaud performance of Part One was at the Salle des Agriculteurs on 15 Dec. 1921. The first

One of the few anecdotes he told about himself concerns a visit from a friend of his mother known as "la raseuse" [the bore]. Poulenc notes how she found him playing Edward Grieg's Piano Concerto only to see that his music rack contained pieces by Schönberg as well as Stravinsky's *Le Sacre du Printemps* and *Rossignol*. Horrified, she is quoted as having remarked "My dear, it is truly time to get him to work seriously."[9]

Whatever stylistic affinity Poulenc lacked for music of the Second Viennese School was made up for by his affection for that of his compatriot Emmanuel Chabrier (1841-94). One day, while visiting a small shop near the Madeleine, Poulenc placed "deux sous" in a machine to hear Chabrier's *Idylle* played by the French pianist Edouard Risler.[10] He was captivated by what he heard. "Poulenc told me recently," Jourdain-Morhange recounted shortly before 1955, "with a passion which was completely juvenile, that he had played the record more than ten times. His passion for Chabrier, which marked many of his works, dates from this radiant day."[11] Years later Poulenc purchased scores and letters of Chabrier at auction, devoted time to him in illustrated lectures, and ultimately wrote his biography.[12] He also paid the following homage in one of his published conversations:

> Ah! Chabrier, I love him as one loves his father! An indulgent father, always happy, pockets full of tasty morsels. Chabrier's music is a treasure that cannot be exhausted; "I could not do without it". It consoles me on my most somber days, because you know, faithful friend, I am a melancholic man . . . who likes to laugh, as do all sad men.[13]

For Poulenc, the "crucible of Paris" not only contained a variety

---

complete performance in France occurred in the Salle Gaveau on 12 Jan. 1922 with subsequent performances on 10 Mar. at the Salle Gaveau and 14 Dec. at the Théâtre des Champs-Élysées.
[9] Poulenc 1954, pp. 16-17.
[10] Arthur Rubinstein called Risler "a wonderful interpreter of Beethoven sonatas." Rubinstein 1973, p. 41.
[11] Jourdan-Morhange, p. 130. *Idylle* is the 6th of *Dix pièces pittoresques* (1881). Daniel, p. 4 cogently summarizes Chabrier's impact on French music and Poulenc's musical debt to Chabrier in particular, reminding us of Poulenc's own statement in Poulenc 1961a, p. 46, that "I gave much thought to *l'Etoile* while composing *Les Mamelles de Tirésias*."
[12] Poulenc 1994, p. 383, note 8 concerning Poulenc's purchase of two Chabrier scores from the Hôtel Drouot sale of Vincent d'Indy's library (20-1 Jan. 1933); for Poulenc's biography of Chabrier see Poulenc 1961a. He also dressed as Chabrier for the 14 Feb. 1956 "Bal des artistes." Faucigny-Lucinge 1987, p. 83 prints a photograph of Poulenc in costume.
[13] Poulenc 1963a, pp. 67-8 (Poulenc 1978, pp. 53-4).

of art musics, but a world of popular music as well, which paralleled that found in the cabarets and dance halls of Nogent mentioned earlier.[14] He developed this interest independently but shared it later with Cocteau, Milhaud, and Auric, among others. Moreover, the influence of popular music is often found in Poulenc's later compositions. One of the most telling accounts of his experiences came in conversations with Claude Rostand. Poulenc teased Rostand that he might sing his early chanson entitled *Toréador:*

> Imagine that at sixteen I was fascinated by a friend one year older than me. The boxing champion of his lycée, he was the lover of a boot seamstress from the Quartier de la République, which seemed to me just as chic as being a mannequin on the rue de la Paix. This young woman, quite attractive besides, had a sister, who sold feathers and was just as pretty as she. All four of us frequented the cafés concerts and the theaters of the quarter. With what enthusiasm I remember the enormous Jeanne Bloch in *Prostitution, Vierge flétrie,* on which I dreamed of composing an opera. [. . .] In any case, what we preferred above all was [Maurice] Chevalier, the Chevalier of the Petit Casino and of the Carillon. [. . .] Chevalier, God be praised, is still around to enchant us. Chevalier sang, among others, a chanson which intoxicated me. The title was *Si fatigué.* [. . .] This chanson influenced me in some of the prosody in *Les Mamelles de Tirésias.*[15]

ENCOUNTERS: FOUR INFLUENTIAL PEOPLE

Between 1914 and 1916 Poulenc met three individuals who significantly shaped his life and saw an earlier friendship take on new significance. These are his first encounters with Ricardo Viñes, Georges Auric, and Darius Milhaud, and the maturing of his childhood friendship with Raymonde Linossier. Through them Poulenc met numerous other artists, writers, and musicians who shaped his artistry. Through them the world of opportunity opened ever wider for a young man whose ambition and eagerness seemingly knew few bounds.

•Ricardo Viñes (1875-1943)

In 1914 Poulenc was introduced to Ricardo Viñes.[16] "At sixteen [*recte* fifteen], my parents had taken me to Viñes' house understand-

---

[14] Perloff, pp. 86-111. See also the extensive discussions in Whiting, passim.
[15] Poulenc 1954, p. 136. In the recording of a 16 May 1958 concert with Denise Duval at the "Mai Musical de Bordeaux," Poulenc had fun with the audience by explaining the subject of this *mélodie.* See CLIO 001 listed in Appendix 3. Poulenc does sing with Duval on another selection!
[16] Poulenc, whose precise memory of dates is often contradictory, writes: "Thus, in 1916, during my first year of study with Viñès, I had only one desire, that of knowing Satie." Poulenc 1963a, p. 82 (Poulenc 1978, p. 63).

ing that my pianistic gifts, fairly good for a lycée student, were in-sufficient for a boy dedicated to music."[17] The introduction was ar-ranged through Geneviève Sienkiewicz, a passionate lover of mu-sic, an excellent pianist, and a friend of Poulenc's mother.[18] At the age of fifteen, by his own admission, he "got by reasonably well [at the piano], no more," so a change of teacher to Viñes was suggested.[19] Catalan by birth, Viñes had come to France in 1887 to study at the Paris Conservatoire with Charles de Bériot (piano), Albert Lavignac (harmony), and Benjamin Godard (composition).[20] He had a stellar record as the premier interpreter of contemporary French piano music (Debussy, Ravel, Mompou, Satie, etc.) and numbered among his other students the respected Marcelle Meyer. M.D. Calvocoressi, who frequently wrote about Parisian musical events and who knew Viñes personally, described his friend in the following words:

> Viñes, alert and cheerful, ever on the track of new music and new ideas, as keen on literature and painting as on his own art, was, when-ever he turned up, the life and soul of our meetings. We loved his childlike ingenuity as much as we admired his playing and appreci-ated the colossal amount and rare quality of his disinterested work as a pioneer. He played in public the piano music of Debussy and Ravel years before any other pianist dreamt of touching it. Indeed, for a long time, all the first performances of these two composers' piano works were given by him, as well as countless first performances of music by other composers, French, Russian, and Spanish.[21]

Poulenc never missed an opportunity to praise Viñes.

> I admired him madly, because, at this time, in 1914, he was the only virtuoso who played Debussy and Ravel. That meeting with Viñes was paramount in my life: I owe him everything. [. . .] In reality it is to Viñes that I owe my fledgling efforts in music [i.e., composition] and everything I know about the piano.[22]

To Claude Rostand he added:

> He was a delightful man, a bizarre hidalgo with large mustaches, who wore a brown "sombrero" in the purest Barcelonaise style, and who wore fine buttoned boots which he used to kick my shins when I didn't change the pedals properly. The art of pedaling, this essen-tial ingredient in modern music; no one could teach it better than

[17] Poulenc 1935a, p. 522.
[18] Sienkiewicz's activity as a pianist and accompanist is discussed in Poulenc 1994, p. 1051 and Buckland/Chimènes:b, pp. 212-14.
[19] Poulenc 1963a, p. 42 (Poulenc 1978, p. 36).
[20] About Viñes' performing career see Brody 1977 and Brody 1987, pp. 169-89.
[21] Calvocoressi, p. 63.
[22] Poulenc 1963a, pp. 42-3 (Poulenc 1978, p. 37).

Viñes since he managed to play clearly in a wash of pedaling, which seems paradoxical. And what science he demonstrated in staccato![23]

At this time Viñes lived on rue Sergent-Hoff, a few steps from Avenue Niel in a building inhabited predominantly by women of questionable morals who enjoyed noisy evenings.[24] During his first lesson, Poulenc played Schumann's *Faschingschwank aus Wien [Carnaval of Vienna]* and Debussy's *Minstrels*.[25]

> Initially it was agreed that I would take a half-hour lesson each week, but this lesson soon lasted for an hour, then two and, imperceptibly, I spent my life with this hidalgo who had the face of a benevolent inquisitor.[26]

Poulenc was also introduced to Serge Prokofiev's piano music during 1916. In an article on Prokofiev's piano music published in 1953, Poulenc related that Léon Bakst, returning to France from America in 1916, had brought Viñes copies of Prokofiev's *Quatre pièces* (op. 4), the *Sarcasmes* (op. 17) and the Sonata no. 2 for piano (op. 14).[27] Poulenc particularly delighted in watching his teacher sight-read these pieces. Viñes also encouraged Poulenc to study the music of Chabrier in detail. Several years later he wrote his first piano work under Viñes' influence, and lessons became a place where poetry was read and discussed. Viñes championed various early Poulenc piano works, particularly *Trois mouvements perpétuels, Trois pastorales,* and *Suite pour piano* all three of which he premiered.

•Georges Auric (1899-1983)

Next to Raymonde Linossier, Poulenc developed the closest kinship with Georges Auric, referring to him as his "true brother in spirit" (Plate 4).[28] For fifteen years, Linossier, Poulenc, and Auric enjoyed each other's company. Poulenc and Auric, born just sixteen days apart in 1899, were friends for nearly fifty years. During this time they were anointed fellow members of "Les Six," frequently attended concerts involving music of the other, played the piano together in concert, sought the other's advice in compositional matters, and shared numerous friends. Each man dedicated works to the other, and Ned Rorem wrote that according to Henri [José] Hell, "Poulenc and Auric were intimate (platonic) friends, [and] that

[23] Poulenc 1954, pp. 29-30 and Poulenc 1963a, p. 43 (Poulenc 1978, p. 37).
[24] Poulenc's description in Poulenc 1935a, p. 522.
[25] Poulenc 1954, p. 4.
[26] Poulenc 1935a, p. 522.
[27] Poulenc 1953b.
[28] Poulenc 1954, p. 38. In a 17 Apr. [19]47 letter to Collaer Poulenc wrote: "You know that Auric is for me a spiritual brother who cannot be surpassed. His intelligence, lucid to the point of cruelty, has always been indispensable for me. [. . .]" Collaer 1996, 47-2.

Plate 4: Caricature of Georges Auric by Jean Cocteau

the former never showed his music to anyone before getting the latter's approval."[29] Moreover, Poulenc occasionally asked Auric to proofread his music prior to publication.[30] Later, Auric was responsible for introducing Poulenc to Satie. Poulenc also became quite friendly with Nora Vilter, the artist Auric married in 1930, the year of Linossier's tragic demise. Auric, whose praise Poulenc never found easy to win, fondly remembered his friend when writing his own memoirs. "Poulenc, born the same year as I, my elder by several weeks, was my best friend, my best companion and, in the area of music, the person closest to me."[31]

Auric came to Paris from the south of France where he had studied at the Montpellier Conservatoire. As a youth of fourteen (1913), he was a student of the French composer and pedagogue Georges Caussade at the Paris Conservatoire. In 1914, with the assistance of Léon Vallas (a musicologist and friend of Vincent d'Indy), Auric had several songs publicly performed by Mme Paule de Lestang accompanied by the composer Alfredo Casella, and *Trois interludes* (texts by René Chalupt) appeared on an important Société Nationale de Musique program.[32] Between 1914 and 1916 he worked with d'Indy at the Schola Cantorum where he widened his circle of Parisian acquaintances to include Milhaud, Honegger, and Satie.[33] Poulenc, who attended neither the Conservatoire nor the Schola Cantorum, was introduced to Auric privately by Viñes in 1916. He quickly recognized Auric's precociousness. "At fifteen he [Auric] discussed sociology with Léon Bloy and theology with [Jacques] Maritain; at seventeen Apollinaire read him *Les Mamelles de Tirésias* asking for his advice."[34] Poulenc remembered that Auric's piano was surmounted by "a mountain of accumulated music which testified to a perfect eclecticism, ranging from 16th-century polyphony to the operettas of Messager, while including *Pierrot lunaire* of Schönberg and the *Allegro barbaro* of Bartók."[35]

[29] Rorem 1994, p. 406.

[30] Proof sheets for the solo piano reduction of *Concert champêtre*, copiously corrected by Auric, are described in Schmidt 1995, FP 51, p. 162.

[31] Auric 1979, p. 183.

[32] Auric discussed the events of his fourteenth year in Auric 1979, pp. 17-20.

[33] Milhaud wrote: "It was at this period that I got to know Georges Auric, whom I met sometimes in the corridors of the Conservatoire. He made me marvel at the extent of his culture and his extraordinarily penetrating intelligence and uninhibited ease of composition." Milhaud 1953, p. 51. [Milhaud errs in stating that he met Auric in 1909-10.] Auric met Satie as the result of having published an article on Satie in the Dec. issue of *Revue française de musique*. Satie, who read the article, wrote to Auric suggesting they meet. Auric 1979, pp. 21-33.

[34] Poulenc 1954, p. 38.

[35] Poulenc 1954, pp. 38-9. Auric lived at 36 bis, rue Lamarck in Montmartre behind Sacré-Cœur. Poulenc 1994, 20-13.

•Darius Milhaud (1892-1974)

In 1915 Poulenc met Darius Milhaud at the house of a friend (in Nogent?) where they played tennis together.[36] Shortly thereafter they met again following a concert at the Salle des Agriculteurs in Paris, during which several Milhaud works were performed, including a quartet in which Milhaud played viola. Too tired for a lengthy talk with the young Poulenc, who sought an autograph, Milhaud enclosed one in a letter from L'Enclos (the estate on the outskirts of Aix-en-Provence which belonged to his grandparents), probably dating from June 1915.[37]

A native of Aix-en-Provence, Milhaud came from a wealthy Jewish family with close ties to the cultural life of the area. Though a purveyor and distributor of almonds by trade, Milhaud's father "was the pillar of the Musical Society of Aix, and accompanied all its vocalists."[38] Reminiscing about his mother, Milhaud remarked: "[she] had a powerful contralto voice, and up to the time I was born had studied in Paris under [Gilbert-Louis] Duprez, who taught her to interpret operatic arias. Thus music was already a familiar friend in our house."[39] The year Poulenc was born, Milhaud began to study the violin and over the next decade he made such progress that he was able to play quartets as well as a varied repertory of solo literature. In 1908 Milhaud completed his Classics baccalaureate and soon set off for Paris with his friend, the writer Armand Lunel. Milhaud successfully passed the entrance examinations for the Conservatoire, where he studied violin and harmony. After several years without placing in the annual violin juries, Milhaud, who had been composing for some time, turned increasingly in that direction. While at the Conservatoire, he studied with pedagogues such as Xavier-Henry Leroux, Paul Dukas, André Gédalge, and Charles-Marie Widor. He also befriended numerous musicians and artists including Francis Jammes, Jean Wiéner, and Arthur Honegger.

Although Poulenc and Milhaud first met in 1915, Milhaud notes that the two did not become friends until several years later. Milhaud had left Paris for Brazil in the company of Paul Claudel, the French ambassador to Brazil, in early 1917, arriving in Rio de Janeiro on 1 February 1917 after an eighteen-day crossing. He remained there until his return to Paris in November 1918.[40] Milhaud recalled the

---

[36] Milhaud 1953, p. 95 (Milhaud 1987a, p. 81) and Poulenc 1954, p. 44.
[37] Milhaud's letter to Poulenc in Poulenc 1994, 15-1 (Poulenc 1991, no. 1). Chimènes' commentary discusses the repertoire played at the concert and reprints both Milhaud's and Poulenc's recollections of the events.
[38] Milhaud 1953, p. 14 (Milhaud 1987a, p. 17).
[39] Milhaud 1953, p. 14 (Milhaud 1987a, p. 17).
[40] For details of the voyage to Brazil see Milhaud 1953, pp. 69-93 (Milhaud 1987a, pp. 63-75).

real beginning of his friendship with Poulenc, which must date from sometime after May 1919:

> Louis Durey and Poulenc had been added to the musicians I had known before the war. I met Poulenc at René Chalupt's while he [Poulenc] was still in the army. He played us his *Mouvements perpétuels* and sang the *Bestiaire*, which he had just completed. I thought that day of a saying of d'Indy concerning the development of music: "French music will become what the next musician of genius wants it to be." After all the vapors of impressionism, would not this simple, clear art renewing the tradition of Mozart and Scarlatti represent the next phase in the development of our music? At all events, I remember feeling that day that Poulenc would achieve greatness and would attain to a place in music's history. [. . .] The fresh charm of Poulenc's music was the most endearing feature of that period.[41]

Poulenc and Milhaud remained close friends until the former's death and at least as early as 1924 Poulenc became friendly with Madeleine Milhaud, whom Milhaud married on 4 May 1925.

•Raymonde Linossier (1897-1930)

Poulenc's most intimate childhood friend, and "with Auric the true intellectual ferment of my adolescence," was Raymonde Linossier.[42] Born into a financially comfortable Vichy family and the daughter of Georges Linossier, a well-known physician, Linossier was the youngest of three talented sisters.[43] Poulenc maintained a friendship with both other sisters, Suzanne Latarjet (née Linossier, 1886-1962) and Alice Ardoin (née Linossier, 1893-1964), throughout his life. Linossier, a woman of remarkable intelligence and culture, earned the academic degrees and obtained the positions that Poulenc never coveted. Her influence on his literary shaping was seminal, and her importance to his musical creativity was equally important. On 7 February 1918 she published a curious brief work entitled *Bibi-la-Bibiste* (translated by Sylvia Beach as *One's Self the One's Selfist*) and dedicated it to Poulenc, who was then eighteen.[44] She

---

[41] Milhaud 1953, p. 95 (Milhaud 1987a, pp. 81-2). Poulenc had only finished his *Bestiaire* (FP 15a) in May of 1919 and was not assigned to Paris until July 1919. In a 1970 conversation with Henry Breitrose, Milhaud said: "Poulenc and I met only after the war. He was still in the army. I met him at the house of a poet, René Chalupt, and he played me his music, which immediately I liked very much." Milhaud 1970, p. 56.

[42] Poulenc 1954, p. 39. A wealth of new information concerning Linossier appears in Buckland/Chimènes: j.

[43] Poulenc 1994, pp. 1034-5.

[44] Linossier 1918 (original publication) and Linossier 1991 (modern edition with notes). It was also published in *The Little Review* (Sept.- Dec. 1920). See Monnier 1976, p. 459 concerning Beach's translation and Buckland/Chimènes: j, pp. 138-9 for a new translation.

studied law at the University of Paris and was admitted to the bar in 1920 after which she had a brief career as secretary to the lawyer Charles Chanvin.[45] Concurrent with her legal work she took courses in Orientalism which led to an association with the photographic department of the Musée Guimet (the national museum devoted to Asiatic arts) in 1923 and to a regular position at the museum in 1925. A member of the Société Asiatique, her untimely death on 30 January 1930 prevented her from inevitably assuming the conservatorship of this august museum.[46]

According to Sylvia Beach, proprietress of the famous Parisian bookstore Shakespeare and Company:

> She had grown up with him [Poulenc], and their tastes and their ways of seeing things were identical. She divided her time between her poets in the Rue de l'Odéon and her musical friends in the group known as "The Six."[47]

Although virtually nothing is known of their youthful relationship beyond that they were occasional childhood playmates, Poulenc probably met Raymonde through her friendship with his sister, Jeanne.[48] Her influence on his intellectual development from 1916 forward, however, was demonstrably profound. It was she who, in that year, introduced Poulenc to Adrienne Monnier's famous bookstore, later to be called Maison des Amis des Livres, which opened in November 1915 at 7, rue de l'Odéon.[49]

> If you opened the door of Monnier's bookstore between the hours of four and seven in the afternoon, most of the time you would find

---

[45] Monnier 1976, pp. 101-02. Linossier's status was probationary at this point.
[46] Concerning Poulenc's feelings about her passing see Poulenc 1994, pp. 28 and 1034.
[47] Beach as quoted in Monnier 1976, p. 459. Beach wrote of Linossier: "Her chin and her mouth were very developed, her lips likewise — large and strong, they resembled a wide-open flower. Dominating that intense and almost savage lower part of her face, her eyes showed all the sweetness, all the discretion, that one expects of beautiful feminine souls; they were of the purest and lightest blue that can be seen, like clear sapphires. Beautiful eyes that grief and care could never veil, but in which thought and joy passed like the smoke of incense. The voice of Raymonde Linossier was no less remarkable than her face — how shall I describe it? It was quivering, subdued, tender. It clung to words lightly like the feet of a bird; it made them flutter with innumerable little wings; it had silken starts and hoverings that at one and the same time were distracted and attentive." Quoted in Monnier 1976, pp. 98-9.
[48] Poulenc 1994, p. 48. In a [summer 1910] letter to her son Francis, written from Vichy, Jenny Poulenc said that she was about to present Raymonde with a picture Poulenc had drawn. Poulenc 1994, 10-1.
[49] Poulenc 1956a, p. 72.

Léon-Paul Fargue there, who was the guiding light, Valéry Larbaud and James Joyce. They were the faithful ones, the regulars; and then the most varied types of writers often crossed the threshold: Valéry as often as Max Jacob, Paul Claudel as often as Apollinaire. [. . .] Now, one afternoon in 1916, three young men, whose names I hardly knew, crossed the threshold of the shop: they were André Breton, Paul Éluard and [Louis] Aragon. [. . .] Adrienne Monnier introduced us, but I felt of little consequence in front of these fellows who had already published writings in avant-garde publications. [. . .] None among them, moreover, was interested in music, and, naturally, they paid no attention to me in spite of Adrienne Monnier's indulgent words: "He's such a gifted boy!"[50]

Linossier was "the Youngest *Potasson* in the world," whose literary connections were to provide the young Poulenc with important entrée. A close friend of the poet Léon-Paul Fargue, she was reputed to own a copy of everything he had written, including most of his manuscripts.[51] It was Fargue who coined the term *Potasson*, moniker for a group Monnier noted "knew an extraordinary power and influence from 1918 to 1923."[52] *Potassons* were, she said:

[A] variety of the human species that is distinguished by its kindness and its sense of life. For the *potassons* pleasure is a positive; they are immediately in the know, they have goodheartedness and pluck. When the *potassons* meet everything goes well, everything can be put to rights, they enjoy themselves without effort, the world is clear, they cross it from one end to the other, from the beginning to the end, from the huge animals of the beginning—they have seen them, they were there—until the end of ends when everything begins again, always with good appetite and good humor.[53]

In a brief memoir written following Monnier's death in 1955, Poulenc recalled:

When I become melancholic, which often happens to me, I have only to remember her smile, and to relive in my thoughts the time long ago when I saw Adrienne Monnier almost daily. [. . .] She [Raymonde Linossier] knew that Adrienne was, as we said then, "made for me".

---

[50] Poulenc 1963a, pp. 131-2 (Poulenc 1978, pp. 98-9). In Poulenc 1954, p. 93 Poulenc dates the meeting as 1917.
[51] Monnier 1976, p. 459.
[52] Quoted by Monnier 1976, p. 38.
[53] Quoted by Monnier 1976, p. 38. *Potassons* included Monnier, Linossier, Valery Larbaud, Fargue, Léon Pivet (artist), Jean-Gabriel Daragnès (painter, engraver, and illustrator), Thérèse Bertrand-Fontaine (physician), Beach (bookseller), and Satie (composer), among others. According to Orledge 1990, p. 221, "As 'Potasson' was the name of Fargue's fat cat, Satie's final *Ludion*, the *Chanson du chat*, was adopted as the *Marche des Potassons* by his admirers."

In effect, we suddenly became a pair of friends. I loved her gourmande nun-like face, and she amused herself to see me, nose in the air, "sniffing" her store. [. . .] What rare and marvelous memories I owe to this friendship. It is at the Rue Odéon that I had the privilege of meeting Apollinaire many times. It is there that I knew Fargue, that I heard Valéry read *Le Cimetière marin*, Gide *Le Retour de l'Enfant Prodigue*, Claudel *L'Ours et la Lune*. It is there that Satie unveiled to us one evening his *Socrate*.[54]

Until her death, Poulenc presented Linossier with each of his published works and a selection of manuscripts, many if not all of which have touching inscriptions. At least some use a cryptic code which had meaning only to themselves.[55] In the score for *Cocardes*, Poulenc wrote: "To Raymonde who loves as do I French fries, mechanical pianos, chromos, shell-covered jewelry boxes, and Paris. Her friend Francis. Summer 1921."[56] It was she who accompanied Poulenc and Auric to Monte Carlo for the respective 1924 premieres by Diaghilev's Ballets Russes of *Les Biches* and *Les Fâcheux*. It was also she who, in an extraordinarily perceptive and compassionate letter to the absent Poulenc, detailed Satie's death and funeral in early July 1925. With an eye toward practicality and a heart full of gentility, Linossier had "a very beautiful wreath of flowers (salmon pink roses and hydrangeas of the same color)" sent to the church in Arcueil.[57] Upon her own death after a brief illness on 30 January 1930, Poulenc paid her the ultimate tribute by placing the original orchestral manuscript of *Les Biches* between her hands in the coffin in which she is buried in Valence, France.[58] This deeply personal gesture eloquently captures his affection for Raymonde better than anything he ever penned. Later he recalled her often in words filled with nostalgia and melancholy, but it was through music a decade later that he expressed his most profound feelings. To her memory he dedicated his ballet *Les Animaux modèles*, based on fables by La Fontaine, composed and orchestrated from August 1940 to June 1942.[59] Shortly before composing this ballet he returned to *Les Biches*,

[54] Poulenc 1956a, p. 72. The performance of Part One of *Socrate* by Suzanne Balguerie and Satie took place at Monnier's bookstore on 21 Mar. 1919. Orledge 1990, p. 317.
[55] Chimènes discusses codes in Poulenc 1994, p. 257. For other inscriptions see Schmidt 1995, passim. According to Soulé in Poulenc 1979, p. 17, Poulenc referred to Linossier as "La naïade."
[56] Poulenc 1994, p. 1035 and Schmidt 1995, p. 46.
[57] Poulenc 1994, 25-9 (Volta 1989, pp. 206-09 and Poulenc 1991, no. 90).
[58] Schmidt 1995, p. 101. Linossier died of an intestinal occlusion (Poulenc 1993, p. 85).
[59] Schmidt 1995, p. 312. Earlier, Poulenc had dedicated his Sonata for Horn, Trumpet, and Trombone (1922), *Epitaphe* (1930), and *Ce doux petit visage* (1939) to her. Later, he added "Voyage" from *Calligrammes* (1948).

reorchestrating it between May 1939 and January 1940.[60] His final gesture was to dedicate his *Entretiens avec Claude Rostand* (1954) "A Georges AURIC en souvenir de Raymonde Linossier."

UNDATED EVENTS OF CHILDHOOD

The descriptions of Poulenc's earlier years often do not provide a clear chronology of when the events took place. One of the most provocative anecdotal accounts, written by Poulenc's childhood friend Soulé, randomly chronicled experiences shared over the "more than ten years" they saw each other frequently before 1918.[61] Soulé knew Poulenc in Nogent during the traditional summer vacation months, but also encountered him in Paris during the winter at Poulenc's family home (Faubourg St Honoré) and at his own (rue Debelleyme). Soulé's memoir vividly portrays Poulenc's youth, juxtaposing accounts of tennis matches with grandiose performance projects, and indications of his musical preferences with accounts of early compositional efforts.

A recurrent theme is Poulenc's propensity for talk about music, literature, and poetry with, among others, the pianist Simone Tilliard and Soulé's sister-in-law Andréa Soulé. One anecdote, to which Soulé listened as a silent spectator, followed a discussion of how the prominent pianists of the era interpreted Chopin, Beethoven, and others.

> Finally, Francis asked my sister-in-law, "In your opinion, Madame, who is the pianist who plays Debussy the best?" Her response, after reflection, was the following: "I believe that it is Debussy himself." "Oh! Madame, how happy I am!," exclaimed Poulenc, "That is precisely what I thought."[62]

Music was not the only subject that Soulé and Poulenc discussed. Poulenc's Uncle Royer, allied with numerous artists, was surely at least partially responsible for Poulenc's life-long interest in art. Once in the family gardens at Nogent, Soulé remembered Poulenc saying to him, "You see that large man who is talking to Papoum, it is Hermann Paul." Soulé also noted that Poulenc:

> . . . often showed him designs or engravings by friends of his uncle and notably expressed a great admiration for Steinlen.[63] I am unaware if his tastes in painting were those favored by M. Royer. I only know that one day he astonished us once again by saying that, among painters, he placed Manet and Monet above all.[64]

[60] Schmidt 1995, p. 101.
[61] Soulé, p. 13.
[62] Soulé, p. 16.
[63] This may refer to Théophile Steinlen (1859-1923), whom Whiting, p. 533 refers to as "the old Chat Noir artist."
[64] Soulé, pp. 25-6.

Soulé also reminisced about Poulenc's pianistic ability.

> Often, after a snack, we went up to his room where there was a nar-
> row piano in front of which he could not wait to install himself. I was
> astonished then to see his large hands with round fingers run across
> the piano with agility; and while listening to him play with the velvet
> touch which already characterized his playing, I asked myself if this
> was the same Francis whom I had just seen spoil so many tennis
> shots.[65]

Occasionally Poulenc used music for his boyish flights of imagination.

> On a certain day he played for me a frenetic air of his own composi-
> tion, ended with one of his quick tempered traits which was familiar
> to him and that he accompanied with a particular facial expression.
> When I asked him what this air purported to represent, "Wait" he
> said, "you are going to see." He disappeared in his bathroom only to
> come out clothed only in a towel tied around his waist and he began
> to perform a savage dance while singing the air that he had just played.
> Then he left to put his clothes on and we talked about other things.[66]

During 1916 Poulenc also made the acquaintance of Edouard
Souberbielle, a young man of identical age born in Tarbes.
Souberbielle's mother was Soulé's first piano teacher and during
the war years Souberbielle and Soulé became friends in Paris. After
hearing Edouard's brilliant performance of a Chopin piece, Soulé
reports that his mother exclaimed "We must introduce you to
Poulenc."[67] Apparently Francis accepted the invitation and came to
the Soulé's to hear Souberbielle play. They immediately became
friends. When Soulé departed for the military and lost track of
Souberbielle, Poulenc maintained his friendship with the latter, en-
trusting to him the most private details about his compositions in
progress via a series of letters.

In more serious moments, Poulenc also entertained Soulé with
music by Stravinsky, Debussy (*La Terrasse des audiences du Clair de
Lune* and *En Blanc et Noir*), Satie (*Tendrement*), and his own *Rapsodie
nègre* while he was composing it.[68] Following Poulenc's 1918 military induction, and particularly after Soulé married, his relationship with Poulenc became more distant and the two saw each other
infrequently over the next 45 years.

[65] Soulé, p. 14.
[66] Soulé, p. 14.
[67] Soulé, p. 21.
[68] Soulé, pp. 20-1. *Tendrement*, originally an instrumental waltz in B-flat and later
a waltz song in A-flat, was probably played in the solo piano version. Orledge
1990, pp. 286-7.

Finally, the years 1914-16 were bounded on either end by Poulenc's first adventures into the world of musical composition. In 1914, under the influence of Stravinsky's *Le Rossignol*, Poulenc wrote *Processional pour la crémation d'un mandarin* (FP 1) for piano.[69]

> I recall that the day after the first performance of Stravinsky's *Rossignol*, still under the spell of the March funèbre of the Chinese Emperor, I wrote a piano piece entitled *Processional pour la crémation d'un mandarin*.[70]

Then, in 1916, while studying piano with Viñes, he "composed several preludes of incredible complexity [. . .] written on three or four staves à la Debussy."[71] Neither piece is known to have survived, and Poulenc said that only Auric knew the latter. Perhaps the *Trois pastorales*, composed in late 1917, share some similarity with their cousins.

These years also held an event of decidedly more tragic consequences. On 7 June 1915, Poulenc's mother died. Since she had given her son a strong musical beginning, the loss must have had a serious impact on Poulenc (then sixteen) and his sister Jeanne (then in her late twenties). Sadly, there is no direct mention of her death in any of Poulenc's known writings at this time. During the second half of 1915, Poulenc made his first significant foray into the world of letter writing, inquiring of such famous composers as Debussy, Saint-Saëns, Satie, Vincent d'Indy, Guy Ropartz, Dukas, and Stravinsky what they thought of César Franck's role in musical evolution.[72] Brief responses, including a marvelously enigmatic one by Satie, exist from all but Ropartz and Dukas. These letters set in motion Poulenc's inexorable epistolary passion, which was nearly matched by his dislike of the telephone as a means of "artistic" communication.[73]

Poulenc's interest in music stands in stark opposition to his dislike of life at the lycée Condorcet. Although Poulenc's published writings generally ignore this subject, his lifelong friend and lycée

---

[69] Stravinsky's *Rossignol*, later reworked as a ballet for Diaghilev, was premiered at the Paris Opéra on 26 May 1914.
[70] Roland-Manuel, p. 99.
[71] Schmidt 1995, FP 2.
[72] Poulenc 1994, 15-2 (Debussy to Poulenc), 15-3 (Saint-Saëns to Poulenc), 15-4 (Satie to Poulenc) [English translation in Volta 1989, pp. 91-2], 15-5 (Poulenc to Stravinsky) [English translation in Stravinsky 1985, p. 198], 15-6 (Roussel to Poulenc). The Debussy, Saint-Saëns, Roussel, and Satie responses were first published in *La Revue musicale* (1921).
[73] Ironically, this notion was expressed in an interview with Denise Duval for whom Poulenc set Cocteau's *La Voix humaine*, a telephone monologue with an unseen lover.

Condorcet classmate Jean Nohain, author of more than two dozen books, reminisced about classroom life with Poulenc in *La Main chaude*. Nohain remembered that he used to position his own work so that Poulenc could see it clearly.

> Dreaming only of music and at that only of "his" music, he totally messed up subjects such as the Oubanghi, isosceles triangles, or the quantitative and qualitative study of red cells about which our professor M. Huot spoke to us. . . . Francis Poulenc was not a dunce hopeless and tiresome like some poor boys that we have all encountered. He was the "disinterested" student whom our scholarly preoccupations left utterly impassive and flabbergasted.[74]

Nohain goes on to relate several amusing stories of Poulenc being questioned by his instructors:

> ——Monsieur Poulenc. Yes. You! What's the Aube?
> ——The Aube... It's a tributary of the Seine?
> ——Well yes, very good, monsieur Poulenc. The Aube is a tributary of the Seine. Right bank or left bank?
> ——That depends on which side you're on.[75]

It is no wonder that when Poulenc received his *baccalauréat* in 1917 he did so without distinction. His friendship with Nohain would endure beyond school days and in 1934 Poulenc set some of Nohain's childish rhymes to music in *Quatre chansons pour enfants*.

Marking as it did the midpoint of World War I, 1916 also witnessed Poulenc's first flight into the provocative realm of multimedia entertainments. Soulé recounted one such event, probably dating from 1916:

> . . . he came to see me one morning and after having spoken of Gaspard de la Nuit by Aloysius Bertrand and having shown me the score written by Ravel based on three of these poems, he talked to me about a project that he had conceived. He wished to organize with me and the five young girls with whom we played tennis a matinée of dancing in costume. He took charge of everything — costumes, program of dances, choice of music. The home of M. and Mme Tilliard in Fontenay-sous-Bois was chosen as the place for this garden party. As for me, afraid of showing myself to be a very poor dancer, I observed to Francis that during the war dance was forbidden and that my mother might be opposed to my participation in the projected spectacle. Francis, wishing to see his project to fruition while taking my

---

[74] Nohain 1980, p. 101.
[75] Nohain 1980, pp. 101-02.

suggestion into account, decided to give up the dances and to replace them with "tableaux vivants."[76]

In the long run, this entertainment was a harbinger of Poulenc's strong interest in the theater which included writing music for films, plays, ballets, and operas. This interest culminated in his consuming passion to set Georges Bernanos' *Dialogues des Carmélites* to music in the 1950s. In the short run, it predated Poulenc's involvement with the Séance Music-Hall "happenings" masterminded by Cocteau in the late teens and early 1920s. Innocent though it was, this modest entertainment marked in spirit if not in fact the end of Poulenc's adolescence and the beginning of his entrée into the more public world of performance and composition. His coming of age, so to speak, was characterized by a growing fascination with the multifarious activities of his teacher Viñes and a new interest in Satie as mentor and composer of *Parade*. It was further marked by the realization that he had not received the comprehensive musical training expected of France's finest musical talent. Having attended neither the Conservatoire nor the Schola Cantorum, and though family wealth had provided him with many advantages, he lacked many musical skills requisite to the composer's craft. The time to face these problems and to launch his career as a composer had come: 1917 would be decisive.

---

[76] Poulenc 1979, p. 15.

III

Under the Influence of Satie and Apollinaire: 1917

Though the phrase which captioned a published cartoon "Be patient . . . time is working for us" might have been an appropriate slogan for the war in 1916, 1917 saw patience lost on several important fronts.[1] In February Germany declared unlimited submarine warfare, in March the Russian Revolution broke out, and in April the United States entered World War I. Moreover, early in the year Paris saw lengthy lines for coal when the water level on the Seine was so low that coal barges could no longer navigate. An early February snowfall only exacerbated an already difficult situation. Nevertheless, the first half of the year did not provide the challenge to Parisians that it would a year hence when the city was bombarded by air and long-range cannons. Ever resourceful French artists rose to the occasion on 10 January 1917, holding a gala at the Opéra "To benefit the Front." Edmond Rostand recited *Le Vol de la Marseillaise*, while [Gabrielle Réju, called] Réjane, [Jeanne-Julia Regnault, called] Bartet, Marguerite Carré, Signoret, Polin and others interpreted *La Victoire en chantant* (written by Funck-Clemens Brentano). The ballet *Les Abeilles* also enjoyed a run of ten performances.[2]

[1] Hausser, p. 585: this cartoon depicts a uniformed general pointing to an hour glass bearing the inscription "Victoire," behind which appears the ghost of Father Time.

[2] Hausser, p. 621. Ballet based on Stravinsky's *Scherzo Fantastique* with choreography by Leo Staats and scenario from Maeterlinck's *La Vie des abeilles*. According to White, p. 179 neither Stravinsky nor Maeterlinck authorized use of their work. See also Taruskin, I, pp. 316-18.

For Poulenc 1917 was a watershed year during which he exhibited impatience at his lack of formal musical training; developed ties to a number of Paris' most important artists, writers, and musicians; faced family tragedy again with the death of his father; expressed pride at the first significant public performance of one of his compositions; and witnessed the premiere performances of *Parade (Ballet réaliste)* by Erik Satie, Jean Cocteau, and Pablo Picasso (given by Diaghilev's Ballets Russes on 18 May) and *Les Mamelles de Tirésias* by Apollinaire (given on 24 June 1917). In Poulenc's words:

> The 1914 war so little resembled our present wars that at only eighty kilometers from the German lines Paris was in a lather about the famous Picasso-Matisse exhibition, the first performance of *Parade,* or the premiere of Apollinaire's *Les Mamelles de Tirésias.*[3]

The war itself did not touch him directly until his mobilization in January 1918, and then only peripherally. In 1917, however, he encountered Satie and Apollinaire, two men whose influence proved decisive. With Satie influence included admiration for the individuality of his music and friendship that lasted until a variety of events including a thoughtless prank with Auric estranged them shortly before Satie's death. With Apollinaire, who died not long after their first meeting, influence came from his poetry and prose, which Poulenc often set to music over the years.

SATIE AND *PARADE*

Among the encounters of 1917, none had more significance for the impressionable eighteen-year-old Poulenc than the premiere of *Parade*. Cocteau later called *Parade* "The greatest battle of the war," referring in part to the intellectual ferment of the Montparnasse district inhabited by so many artists, but more directly to the intrigue and in-fighting between collaborators, Diaghilev and Misia Edwards.[4] For Poulenc it qualified as "The greatest triumph of the war."[5] Although he had met Satie in 1916, knew some of "le bon maître d'Arcueil's" piano works, and had at least limited experience with the Ballets Russes (particularly Stravinsky ballets), the

---

[3] Poulenc 1963a, p. 94 (Poulenc 1978, p. 73).

[4] Gold, pp. 183-96. Earlier Cocteau had worked for Diaghilev designing a playbill for the 1911 season and collaborating with Frédéric de Madrazo to provide the scenario for Reynaldo Hahn's *Le Dieu bleu* (1912). Garafola, p. 388. Cocteau was a member of the Paris homosexual set led by Diaghilev, which included Hahn, Daudet, and Marcel Proust. Buckle, p. 146. Misia, born Marie Sophie Olga Zenaïde Godebska, was successively married to Thadée Natanson (founder of *La Revue blanche*), Alfred Edwards (wealthy entrepreneur whose businesses ran from theaters to mines), and José-Maria Sert (Spanish painter). She had a strong financial and artistic hand in Diaghilev's Ballets Russes, was quite musical, and had her portrait painted by many of France's most illustrious artists.

[5] Steegmuller 1970, p. 160.

entire concept of *Parade* fascinated him. *Parade*, in Cocteau's oft-quoted words, "brought together Erik Satie's first orchestral score, Pablo Picasso's first stage décor, Massine's first Cubist choreography, and a poet's first attempt to express himself without words."[6] Cocteau, whom Satie referred to as "the *idea* man," and who always considered *Parade* as his personal brainchild, told anyone who would listen that the collaborators were hand-picked by himself.[7] Critics with less to gain than Cocteau, however, have pointed out that he was a clever manipulator of ideas already conceived by others.

> Cocteau's true genius [Lynn Garafola writes] lay not in the originality of his ideas, but in the ability to appropriate the ideas of the avant-garde for essentially conservative ends. Purged of radicalism, his sanitized art became the stuff of élite entertainment.[8]

She also establishes that some of Cocteau's early notes for the "Little American Girl" in *Parade*, given to Satie in 1916, make clear but unacknowledged reference to Apollinaire's writings.[9]

The genesis and performance history of *Parade* have been thoroughly documented elsewhere.[10] Relevant here is that Satie, without Cocteau's prodding, already had a history of collaborating with artists. "It was from painters that he [Satie] derived most influence in his quest for modernity."[11] Before *Parade* was performed Satie provided special music for exhibitions featuring works by Matisse, Picasso, Modigliani, Kisling, and others. Satie, André Derain's close friend and collaborator, wrote music inspired by other painters such as Botticelli and Watteau.[12] Later Poulenc followed Satie's lead, or, as Cocteau put it in his tract *Le Coq et l'Arlequin*, "Satie leaves a clear road open upon which everyone is free to leave his own imprint."[13]

Precisely what impact did *Parade* have on Poulenc? It established, with a single blow, an alternative to Stravinsky and Debussy in Poulenc's thinking and provided him with a valuable mentor beyond Viñes.[14] In the 11 May 1917 issue of the newspaper *Excelsior*,

[6] Gold, p. 183.
[7] Satie's letter in Steegmuller 1970, p. 147.
[8] Garafola, p. 100.
[9] Garafola, p. 100.
[10] Rothschild and Volta 1992.
[11] Orledge 1990, p. 222.
[12] Orledge 1990, p. 223 points out that Satie's unfinished violin and piano work entitled *L'Embarquement pour Cythère* and *La Naissance de Vénus* were inspired by Botticelli and Watteau paintings respectively. Poulenc later wrote his own *L'Embarquement*, which he called "an evocation of the banks of the Marne dear to my childhood."
[13] Translated by Steegmuller 1970, p. 206.
[14] Stravinsky remained a major influence in Poulenc's musical life. For example, Poulenc wrote Stravinsky in Feb. 1917 requesting a copy of a trio saying that "My

which was reprinted in the ballet program for *Parade*, Apollinaire wrote a now-famous introduction extolling Satie's music, calling it "astonishingly expressive" and "so clean-cut and so simple that it mirrors the marvelously lucid spirit of France itself."

> In short, [Apollinaire wrote] *Parade* will upset the ideas of quite a number of spectators. They will be surprised, to be sure, but in the pleasantest way, and fascinated; and they will learn how graceful modern movement can be — something they had never suspected. A magnificent music-hall Chinaman will give free rein to the flights of their imagination, and the American girl, by turning the crank of an imaginary automobile, will express the magic of their everyday life, while the acrobat in blue and white tights celebrates its silent rites with exquisite and amazing agility.[15]

It would be fairer to say that *Parade* challenged Poulenc rather than upset him. Poulenc acknowledged his debt to both ballet and composer whenever afforded the opportunity.

> • • I was conquered! Though I idolized Debussy, with the shortsightedness of my youth I permitted myself to renounce him a bit since I longed for this new spirit that Satie and Picasso were bringing us.[16]

> • • *Parade* succeeded in tying us together, and its music remains for me one of the dearest treasures in all of music.[17]

> • • *Parade* is, in effect, a landmark in the history of art. The collaboration, I nearly said conspiracy, between Cocteau, Satie, and Picasso, inaugurated the cycle of Diaghilev's great modern ballets.[18]

> • • Satie's influence on my music was profound and immediate.[19]

> • • Erik Satie considerably influenced me, as much spiritually as musically.[20]

> • • All I knew about Satie's music, and I knew everything, seemed to me to signal a new direction in French music.[21]

---

good friends Satie and Viñes have encouraged me to hope that you might give me the honor of a favorable reply. . . ." On 5 Mar. 1917 Poulenc corrected his previous letter noting that "I meant to request the Three Pieces for String Quartet: those three pieces, performed for the first time at the Salle des Agriculteurs by Yvonne Astruc, Darius Milhaud, et al." See the letters quoted from Stravinsky 1985, pp. 198-9.
[15] Translated in Steegmuller 1970, pp. 513-14.
[16] Poulenc 1963a, pp. 47-8 (Poulenc 1978, p. 39).
[17] Poulenc 1954, p. 46.
[18] Poulenc 1963a, p. 88 (Poulenc 1978, p. 68).
[19] Poulenc 1954, p. 47.
[20] Poulenc 1935a, p. 522.
[21] Poulenc 1963a, p. 83 (Poulenc 1978, p. 64). Poulenc also acknowledged *Socrate*

Satie's impressions of Poulenc before and after *Parade* are equally interesting. Thirty-three years Poulenc's senior, Satie was fifty and Poulenc seventeen when the two first met; Satie was not impressed. Jourdan-Morhange, who knew them both, wrote: "In spite of the warm recommendation of Ricardo Vinès, Erik Satie (the doyen of the group), at first saw him only as a middle-class son, a greenhorn, who would remain an amateur."[22] But Satie's opinion changed.

> In short, Satie, after having had nothing to do with him on several occasions (he walked out of the room when Poulenc was played), quickly recognized that the young Francis was not only talented, but one of the most "nouveaux jeunes" of the group.

Poulenc's lavish praise of *Parade* was undoubtedly in part responsible for Satie's change in attitude.

On 15 July, a month after the *Parade* premiere, Poulenc's father Émile died. Having heard the news from Vinès, Satie wrote Poulenc a brief letter of condolence.[23] Then just eighteen, Poulenc moved to the home of his sister Jeanne (whom Sauguet later referred to as a member of "the great Parisian bourgeoisie")[24] and her husband André Manceaux, a distinguished Parisian notary.[25] The couple lived comfortably in the 8th arrondissement at 76, rue de Monceau, a street which connects the Faubourg St Honoré and the rue du Rocher. Poulenc stayed there through the spring of 1919. When his sister moved to 83, rue de Monceau that summer, Poulenc took an apartment at the end of the courtyard above what had been the stables.[26]

We do not know the precise nature of the elder Poulenc's estate but it can be surmised that he left his Parisian property and financial interest in the family business to his children Francis and Jeanne. In the next two decades Francis did not have to earn a living outside of composition or playing the piano and he invested at least some of his capital in a comfortable home in the Touraine which he completely renovated. His inheritance plus earnings as a composer and performer permitted him a comfortable life-style.

---

as on an equal footing with *Parade*, but did not believe it was the greater piece. Poulenc 1963a, p. 89 (Poulenc 1978, p. 69).
[22] Jourdan-Morhange, p. 127 (and subsequent quotation).
[23] Poulenc 1994, 17-1 (Poulenc 1991, no. 2).
[24] Sauguet, p. 140.
[25] Jeanne Manceaux (1887-1974) married André in 1913. The couple had three children: Brigitte Manceaux (1914-63), Rosine Manceaux (b. 1918), and Denis Manceaux (1921-79). Jeanne was an amateur musician who studied singing with Jeanne Raunay and Claire Croiza.
[26] Poulenc 1991, no. 2, note 2. Sauguet, p. 140 briefly described the dwelling: "At that time Francis Poulenc was living with his older sister. [. . .] [She lived] in an opulent-looking ground floor apartment located at the corner of the rues Monceau and Miromesnil. In the courtyard above what had been the stables when

Before the year was out, Satie took Poulenc under his wing adding him to the group of Auric, Durey, and Honegger called "Les Nouveaux Jeunes." Poulenc was aware of the debacle which followed Satie's having written an insulting postcard to the music critic Jean Poueigh. Poueigh, with whom Satie had had an acrimonious exchange in 1911-12, described *Parade* as "an outrage to French taste," and Satie's rejoinder resulted in a lawsuit which Satie lost.[27] That Cocteau rose ardently to Satie's defense would also have been known to Poulenc. The interest Cocteau had shown in Satie's group of young composers peaked in his tract *Le Coq et l'Arlequin* written in 1918. Dedicated to Auric, *Le Coq et l'Arlequin* "deifies Satie as the leading musical spirit behind the post-war *esprit nouveau* (with its vital elements of surprise, simplicity, popular artistic roots and essential Frenchness)."[28] Poulenc's relationship with Satie became strained in November 1918. On 1 November Satie wrote to Durey indicating his resignation from the "Nouveaux Jeunes" group.[29] Poulenc attempted a reconciliation to take place during an evening presented by the "Art et Liberté" society, but Satie, referring to Poulenc's "comico-idiotic maneuvers," disgustedly rejected his plan.[30]

IN SEARCH OF A COMPOSITION TEACHER

During 1917, hungry to study composition seriously, Poulenc followed Viñes' advice.

> Viñes sent me to Paul Dukas who gave me a very pleasant reception and looked over my first compositions with indulgence; but Dukas, who gave few lessons during the war, thought it better that I present myself to Paul Vidal, composer of *La Korrigane*, a Breton ballet that was formerly well-known.[31]

The visit to Vidal, then principal conductor at the Opéra-Comique, took place on Wednesday, 26 September. Poulenc described their meeting to Viñes in a letter of the same date brimming with disappointment. Things started to go badly when Vidal asked if Poulenc had brought some music:

---

people traveled in two-wheeled vehicles, Poulenc occupied a bachelor flat furnished with his exquisite and original taste. That evening, for the dinner to which Milhaud and I had been invited (Auric was among the guests and I believe [also] Jean Cocteau), Jeanne Manceau[x] received us in the circular dining room (the room was at the angle of the two streets), furnished in Louis XVI style, with Corots on the walls."
[27] Satie 1980, pp. 29 and 176. Poueigh's review appeared in *Carnets de la Semaine* (27 May 1917).
[28] Orledge 1990, p. xxxiv.
[29] Volta 1989, p. 96.
[30] Satie's Thursday [Nov. 1918] letter to Bertin in Volta 1989, p. 97.
[31] Poulenc 1963a, p. 48 (Poulenc 1978, p. 40).

I handed him the manuscript of my *Rapsodie nègre*. He read it attentively, furrowed his brow and, upon seeing the dedication to Erik
Satie, rolled his eyes furiously, got up and yelled these very words:
"Your work stinks, it is ridiculous, it is merely a load of balls. You are
trying to make a fool of me with these parallel fifths everywhere.
And what in hell is this 'Honoloulou?' Ah! I see that you are running
with Stravinsky, Satie, and company. Well then, good day!" and he
all but threw me out.[32]

Poulenc also spoke of this lamentable event to Auric, who in turn
mentioned it to Satie. On Saturday, 29 September, Satie, amused but
not surprised by Vidal's reaction, wrote Poulenc that he should like
to see him and not to be discouraged.[33]

In the 26 September 1917 letter to Viñes, Poulenc also asked for a
recommendation to Ravel or André Gédalge. Poulenc thought they
might be able to set him on the right track; failing that, he suggested
enrolling in the Schola Cantorum. There is no evidence that he met
either man as the result of intercession by Viñes after 26 September,
but Viñes did write a recommendation.[34] Moreover, that he should
have even suggested Ravel is curious. Poulenc remembered a
strained meeting with Ravel in March 1917 at which he wanted to
play Ravel's *Sonatine* and the "Forlane," "Menuet," and "Rigaudon"
from *Le Tombeau de Couperin*. Ravel stopped him after only about
three minutes and turned the conversation to composition, asking
to see some piano compositions Poulenc had brought. He criticized
them severely, but not unkindly before moving to more general
matters. Ravel also gratuitously criticized Schumann saying that
Mendelssohn's *Songs Without Words* were a thousand times better
than *Carnaval*. He added that Debussy's late works were not "good"
Debussy, that Chabrier's orchestration did not fit his music, and
praised Mendelssohn's and Saint-Saëns' compositions in general.[35]
Poulenc, quite put off, stayed clear of Ravel (except for a 1920 meeting at Misia's apartment)[36] until a 1925 encounter with *L'Enfant et les
Sortilèges* at Monte Carlo caused him to reconsider his viewpoint.[37]
If Poulenc's memory was accurate, a second overture to Ravel would

[32] Poulenc 1994, 17-4 (Volta 1989, pp. 92-3 and Poulenc 1991, no. 4).
[33] Poulenc 1994, 17-5 (Poulenc 1991, no. 5).
[34] 14 Oct. 1917 letter to Viñes in Poulenc 1994, 17-6 (Poulenc 1991, no. 6).
[35] Details of their meeting and subsequent relationship are provided in Poulenc
1963a, pp. 173-86 (Poulenc 1978, pp. 125-34; excerpts reprinted in Nichols 1988,
pp. 116-18).
[36] Poulenc was there to hear *La Valse* played for Diaghilev by Ravel and Marcelle
Meyer. Poulenc 1963a, pp. 178-9 (Poulenc 1978, pp. 128-9).
[37] In 1941 Poulenc published a most complimentary article entitled "Le Cœur de
Maurice Ravel," in which he reminisced about Ravel's compositions and their
interpreters. Poulenc 1941b.

have been highly unlikely. Poulenc did not study with a bona fide composition teacher until 1921 when, on Darius Milhaud's advice, he began five off and on years under Charles Koechlin's tutelage.

A GROWING CIRCLE OF FRIENDS: JANE BATHORI, ARTHUR HONEGGER, CHARLES KOECHLIN, GERMAINE TAILLEFERRE, LOUIS DUREY, MAX JACOB

"Le bon Viñès, toujours le bon Viñès" [The good Viñes, always the good Viñes], in Poulenc's words, was also responsible for introducing him to Jane Bathori during the spring of 1917. A French mezzo-soprano, sometime producer of musical events, author, and radio commentator, Bathori was more than twenty years Poulenc's senior. She had an outstanding reputation as the first performer of works by Debussy, Ravel, Fauré, Roussel, Satie, and Milhaud.[38] At her home on the Boulevard Péreire, young musicians including Poulenc gathered on Sundays to make music and meet other artists. It was there that Poulenc first heard Debussy's Sonata for Harp, Flute, and Viola read from the manuscript and participated in a sight-reading conducted by André Caplet of Ravel's *Trois chansons* (featuring Koechlin and Honegger among others).[39] This was certainly Poulenc's first encounter with Honegger and most probably with Koechlin as well. Poulenc admits to having made several solfège errors while singing only to have Honegger chide him. He also remembered their meeting as his second with a future member of *Les Six*, but his memory was imperfect. He had actually met both Milhaud and Auric by this time.[40] Germaine Tailleferre and Louis Durey completed his acquaintanceship with future members of *Les Six*.[41]

Poulenc also met Max Jacob, then in his early forties. Jacob was the next poet, after Cocteau, to write poems specifically for Poulenc to set. Poet and artist, a Jew who converted to Catholicism after experiencing a vision, Jacob had come to Paris penniless around 1901.[42] As a resident of Montmartre, "the hard and terrible Montmartre of the young Utrillo, of Modigliani, of the unknown Picasso, of Reverdy, of Juan Gris," he had met Picasso at an Ambroise Vollard show in 1901, and they had become friends.[43] The two even

---

[38] Poulenc 1954, p. 41.
[39] Poulenc 1963a, p. 144 (Poulenc 1978, pp. 106-07). Caplet was recently returned from the Front.
[40] Poulenc 1954, p. 40. Poulenc forgot that even though Milhaud was in Brazil in 1917, the two had met earlier at a concert.
[41] Poulenc 1954, p. 42.
[42] Fernande Olivier (quoted in Richardson 1991, p. 206), who became Picasso's mistress, referred to Jacob as "a singer, a singing-teacher, a pianist, a comedian if called upon to be, and the life-and-soul of all our parties."
[43] Sachs 1933, p. 209 and Richardson 1991, pp. 203-07 (which includes Jacob's description of Picasso).

shared living-quarters when Picasso spoke little French. Poulenc held him in extremely high regard, and Max Jacob was one of the few individuals discussed at length in *Moi et mes amis.*

> I admired without reservation that astonishing work by Max Jacob: *Le Cornet à dés*, which I hold as one of the three masterpieces among French prose-poems. The two others are Baudelaire's *Le Spleen de Paris* and Rimbaud's *Une saison en enfer.* That strange miscellany is at the source of an entire poetic style in French, one that has given rise to surrealism and, to a lesser degree, Mr. [Jacques] Prévert. Apollinaire's reputation, so well deserved, has often eclipsed that of Max Jacob; they influenced each other in turn, like Picasso and Braque, between the years 1911 and 1913.[44]

According to Poulenc, he met Max Jacob through fifteen-year-old Raymond Radiguet, with whom he took a cab one morning and drove to Montmartre where Jacob lived in the rue Gabrielle near the Sacré-Cœur.[45] What Poulenc found was a conversationalist, in fact a gossip, of the first order.[46] By the time Jacob wrote the poems set by Poulenc in *Quatre poèmes de Max Jacob* (1920-21), the poet was living at a monastery in Saint-Benoît-sur-Loire, near Orléans. In 1931 Poulenc returned to Jacob's poetry completing *Cinq poèmes de Max Jacob,* and a year later he used his text for the cantata *Le Bal masqué. Parisiana: Deux mélodies sur des poèmes de Max Jacob* (1954) completed his Jacob settings. Jacob died in the Drancy concentration camp on 24 February 1944.

EMERGENCE AS A COMPOSER: *RAPSODIE NÈGRE*

Parade was not Poulenc's only interest during 1917. While studying with Viñes, he continued to try his hand at composing. During the spring he wrote *Rapsodie nègre* (FP 3), five movements for seven instruments and voice. Though three of five are for instrumental ensemble alone, the middle number entitled "Honoloulou" and the last number require a baritone to intone repeated descending four-note patterns B-A-G-sharp-F-sharp "Lent et monotone." According

---

[44] Poulenc 1963a, pp. 94-5 (Poulenc 1978, p. 73).

[45] Poulenc 1963a, pp. 95-6 (Poulenc 1978, p. 74).

[46] Sachs 1933, p. 210, states: "Max Jacob is short of stature; his face is kindly and grave, but his eye is full of mischief. His upper lip is thin, his lower laughing and sensual. He looks at times like a Roman emperor, at others like a prophet of Israel, at still others like one of La Fontaine's fauns. Everything in him is multiple and opposite; he is the most torrential person it has ever been given me to know. His soul, far from being static, gives rise in him to abundant floods; like those rivers swollen with rain which sweep along living and inanimate things, mineral rocks, and the lush vegetation they have uprooted, the length of their triumphant course, his soul is rich with everything which is life. Max Jacob is as difficult to define or harness as life itself."

to Poulenc, the text is from a collection of poems entitled *Les Poésies de Makoko Kangourou* which he found in a bookstall along the banks of the Seine.[47] Ornella Volta, well-known for her work on Satie and his times, suggested that Makoko Kangourou is a pseudonym for the Parisian poet Marcel Ormoy, who was part of Roland-Manuel's entourage.[48] The three strophes, each of which contains four lines, are mostly pure gibberish.

Honoloulou, poti lama!   Wata Kovsi mo ta ma sou
Honoloulou, Honoloulou,   Etcha pango, Etche panga
Kati moko, mosi bolou,   tota nou nou, nou nou ranga
Ratakou sira, polama!   lo lo lulu ma ta ma sou.
                    Pata ta bo banana lou
                    mandes Golas Glebes ikrous
                    Banana lou ito kous kous
                    pota la ma Honoloulou.[49]

The cult of *art nègre*, visible in Paris before Poulenc wrote his *Rapsodie*, became firmly established toward the end of World War I.[50] Glenn Watkins, writing about this movement, points out that the cakewalk, ragtime, jazz, and negro dancers inspired numerous "artists" including Cocteau, Picasso, Debussy, Stravinsky, Milhaud and, of course, the young Poulenc.[51]

[47] This book was edited by Marcel Prouille and Charles Moulié, frontispiece by Guy Tollac (Paris: Dorbon Aîné, 1910). Information kindly supplied by Sidney Buckland.
[48] Volta 1990, p. 9. Ormoy played the part of Polycarpe in the private first performance of Satie's *Le Piège de Méduse* performed in late 1913 or early 1914. Orledge 1990, pp. 297-8. Ormoy's name is actually cited in the program for the premiere performance on 11 Dec. 1917. (Facsimile in Laurent, p. 246.) Roland-Manuel also set two Ormoy poems in *Sept poèmes de Perse*. It is not clear when Poulenc first met Roland-Manuel, a composer and writer about music, but in March 1923 he gave Roland-Manuel a signed photographic copy of his sketched portrait by Roger de La Fresnaye and over the years presented him with signed copies of assorted published scores. See *Archives Roland-Manuel*, nos. 78-89.
[49] "The textual model was to be found in the Dada poetry of Tristan Tzara, who had introduced the mock-African textual element in his 1916 play *La Première Aventure céleste de M. Antipyrine*." Watkins, p. 104.
[50] Poulenc later said that *Rapsodie* was "a reflection of the taste for negro art which had flourished since 1912 under the impetus of Apollinaire" and "It was the time of wooden negro statues, of Picasso's negro period. It was thus natural that a young musician would submit to the ambiance of the day." Poulenc 1963a, p. 50 (Poulenc 1978, p. 41) and Poulenc 1935a, p. 523.
[51] Watkins, pp. 100-11 speaks of the interaction of the arts saying: "Sponsorship of such a fusion appeared in numerous quarters. By the time of the Société Lyre et Palette's first *séance* of music and painting, organized by Blaise Cendrars and

The *Rapsodie nègre* was premiered on 11 December 1917 during one of Jane Bathori's afternoon concerts produced by the actor Pierre Bertin at the Théâtre du Vieux-Colombier. Again Viñes had interceded on Poulenc's behalf, and Poulenc thanked him saying "For me it's a dream."[52] Jane Bathori had taken over management of the Vieux-Colombier while Jacques Copeau (its regular director) was performing in the United States. In a 1953 interview with Stéphane Audel recorded for Radio-Lausanne, Bathori recalled how she learned of Poulenc's *Rapsodie:*

> Francis Poulenc arrived one day at the Vieux-Colombier, presented by his teacher Ricardo Viñes. He was then very young and he suddenly showed me a work [. . .] which was the *Rapsodie nègre.* We presented it immediately and its success was such that we had to repeat it many times.[53]

Sharing the spotlight with Poulenc's *Rapsodie* were first performances of Louis Durey's *Scènes de cirque,* Auric's *Huit poèmes de Jean Cocteau,* and R. de Fontenoy's *mélodie* "A Clara d'Ellébeuse."[54] The *Rapsodie* caused a scandal. Poulenc recalled:

> At the last minute the singer threw in the towel, saying it was too stupid and that he didn't want to be taken for a fool. Quite unexpectedly, masked by a big music stand, I had to sing that interlude myself. Since I was already in uniform, you can imagine the unusual effect produced by a soldier bawling out songs in pseudo-Malagasy![55]

The piece was frequently reprised over the next several years, at the Salle Huyghens on 15 December 1917, at the Beaumonts' on 30 August 1918 (it was an event featuring jazz), at the Vieux-Colombier on 15 January (at a "Causerie de M. René Chalupt") and 3 November 1918, and at the Salle des Agriculteurs on 9 March 1919 and 24 January 1920.[56] The 15 January performance at the Vieux-Colombier helped solidify Poulenc's reputation as a composer inextricably linked to Satie, Cocteau, and "Les Nouveaux Jeunes."[57]

Before the year was out Poulenc turned his hand to four new pieces: *Poèmes sénégalais* (FP 6), *Zèbre* (FP 4), *Trois pastorales* (FP 5),

---

Moïse Kisling from November 19 to December 5, 1916, the appeal of *art nègre* to high society was under way. At the vernissage which took place at the Salle Huyghens on the afternoon of 19 November, music of Satie was played alongside works by Picasso, Matisse, and examples of *sculptures nègres.* [. . .]"
[52] [14 Oct. 1917] letter in Poulenc 1994, 17-6 (Poulenc 1991, no. 6).
[53] Copeau, pp. 813-14.
[54] Laurent, p. 246.
[55] Poulenc 1963a, pp. 50-1 (Poulenc 1978, p. 41) and Poulenc 1935a, p. 523.
[56] Schmidt 1995, pp. 14-15 and Buckland/Chimènes: f, pp. 9-10 and b, p. 219.
[57] Daniel, p. 15. For a facsimile of the 15 Jan. 1918 program see Laurent, p. 247.

and *Fanfare à quatre pianos* mentioned as his Op. 4 and dated winter 1917 in an early [October 1918] letter to Souberbielle.[58] The earliest of these pieces, *Poèmes sénégalais*, was composed in August 1917, though it was not performed until 19 March 1918 at a Jane Bathori Théâtre du Vieux-Colombier concert.[59] Scored for voice and string quartet, Poulenc's work shared the stage with Ravel's Trio, Désiré-Émile Inghelbrecht's Quintet for String Quartet and Harp, two songs by Fernand Lamy, and the premiere of Honegger's Violin Sonata in C-sharp minor. No trace of these songs has been found, and the origin of the texts is unknown. We know little more about *Zèbre* than what Poulenc told Viñes while the latter was vacationing in Paramé:

> I have done no practicing at all on the piano because the hotel piano is atrocious. As to composing, I am for the same reason at the same point that I was before my departure, that is to say I have a scherzo for two pianos on my desk. It is called *Zèbre* and is inspired by a Cocteau poem. I believe that it will please you very much because its rhythm is very amusing.[60]

Zèbre was probably never completed, and only the briefest fragment of a sketch remains today bound among the leaves of the holograph manuscript of *Rapsodie nègre*.[61]

The *Trois pastorales*, on the other hand, long thought to exist only in their 1928 version as *Trois pièces* (FP 48), survive in a manuscript Poulenc gave to Alfredo Casella "avec l'assurance de ma profonde admiration."[62] The second piece, marked "Très lent," is dated "Automne 1917," and "Décembre 1917" appears at the end of the manuscript. Poulenc dedicated the work to Viñes, who premiered

---

[58] Poulenc 1994, 18-11: "op. 4 *Fanfare* à 4 pianos — hiver 1917 à rester en carton, mais peut être jouée."

[59] The first reference to the *Poèmes* appears in Poulenc's letter to Souberbielle written at the beginning of Oct. 1917, where it is listed as Op. 2. Poulenc 1994, 18-11. In a 21 June [1919] letter to Souberbielle Poulenc refers to "4 *Chants sénégalais*." Poulenc 1994, 19-15. Poulenc still possessed a manuscript of them at this point. Facsimile of the program in Laurent, p. 248.

[60] [25 Aug. 1917] letter in Poulenc 1994, 17-3. Poulenc discusses having read a collection of twelve lectures given in Lyon between Mar. and June of 1915 by "Normaliens et Sorbonnards" (members of the École normale de musique and the Sorbonne). He is particularly attracted to lectures on how Wagner and Bizet judged Nietzsche by Paul Huvelin and on Rameau by Edmond Goblot. He excoriates a third lecture by Maurice Boucher on the School of César Franck. These lectures appeared in *Pour la musique française*, 12 causeries avec une préface de Claude Debussy (Paris/Zurich: Éditions Georges Crès & Cie, 1917).

[61] F-Pn (MS Mus. 17676).

[62] The inscription to Casella is quoted from the manuscript in I-Vgc (MS MUS 115). This manuscript was copied by Monsieur Roy, who resided at 20, rue Cambon.

it at the Théâtre du Vieux-Colombier between 12 and 20 May 1918. Subsequent performances took place in Madrid at the Hôtel Ritz on 5 November and in Rome at the Teatro Quirino on 23 January 1919.[63] Viñes' numerous concerts and tours are poorly documented, but in 1921 the piece was still in his repertoire when he played it in Italy.[64]

As Poulenc's first extant piano piece (the earlier *Processional pour la crémation d'un mandarin* [1914] and *Préludes* [1916] were almost certainly destroyed), this work warrants a brief discussion. A comparison of the manuscript and the 1928 printed version shows that Poulenc used only part of two *pastorales* as the first and second numbers of the 1928 set, abandoning the rhapsodic second piece altogether and replacing it with a "Toccata." When he revised the work in 1953, the second and third numbers were reversed so that the flashy "Toccata," made famous by Vladimir Horowitz, would conclude the work. The relationships are clarified on the facing page.

Undeterred by Paul Vidal's harsh criticism of his *Rapsodie nègre*, Poulenc did not hesitate to thumb his nose at the establishment again. The opening *Pastorale,* in simple A-B-A' form, begins with a chord containing only the superimposed fifths A-E-B followed by a section containing eight bars of parallel fifths and another containing six bars in parallel fourths.[65] The B section, written on four staves *à la Debussy,* maintains the interest in parallel fourths (this time two sets superimposed over a pedal point of another fourth). The final A' section is a near verbatim echo of A. We can already see Poulenc's predisposition to one- or two-bar units used to construct phrases. The second *Pastorale* is predominantly based on the descending figure E-flat-D-C-sharp-B-sharp-E-flat-B-flat, which is sometimes embellished or presented in parallel intervals outlining a major seventh. Again the form A-B-A' appears with the B section a series of repetitions of the motif accompanied by the interval of a minor second played *tremolando.* Poulenc's writing for his own large hands can be seen in chords for the left hand consistently spanning a tenth. The final *Pastorale* combines the rapid reiteration of chords based on fifths in the left hand with a melodic figure occurring twice each bar in thirty-second notes. Occasionally the left hand takes up a short melodic figure, treated like an *ostinato,* and the right hand accompa-

---

[63] Poulenc 1994, 18-1, 18-2, 18-3, and 18-21 plus Chimènes' notes.
[64] The modern "premiere" after its rediscovery, was played by Sandrine Erdeley-Sayo in the course of a lecture by this author printed as Schmidt 1996.
[65] Poulenc's predilection for parallel fifths early in his career is reminiscent of the fake "Conservatory Catechism" published in the 15 Feb. issue of *Revue musicale SIM* and falsely attributed to Satie. Items four and five state: "(4) With greatest care shalt thou violate The ancient rudimentary rules (5) Parallel fifths shalt thou create And octaves in like style." Translation in Satie 1980, p. 81. See Orledge 1990, p. xxxi concerning the false attribution to Satie and his demand that the editor, Jules Ecorcheville, print a retraction.

THREE INCARNATIONS OF *TROIS PASTORALES*		
1917 Trois Pastorales	**1928 Trois pièces pour piano**	**1953 Rev. Trois pièces**
1. Très vite (Gai et très rhythmé)	1. Pastorale (Calme et nystérieuse) Uses opening of 1917/2	1. Pastorale (Identical to 1928 version)
2. Très lent (Très triste - rhythmé dans la douceur)	2. Toccata (Très animé) Uses opening of 1917/1 followed new material	2. Hymne (Modéré) (Identical to 1928 version)
3. Vite	3. Hymne (Modéré) Newly composed	3. Toccata (Très animé) Uses opening of 1917/1 followed by new material

nies in parallel major-seventh chords. The movement concludes with an ascending five-octave scale in parallel diminished fifths leading to a pentatonic chord which resolves to a stratospheric A natural followed by the lowest A on the keyboard.

Poulenc spoke of this piece several times in discussions with Stéphane Audel and Claude Rostand, remarking to the latter:

> Next I dedicated three pastorales to Viñes (1918 [*recte* 1917]). These three pastorales remained unedited for a long time, but in 1928, Casella having written "What has become of your pastorales. I liked them very much," I had the idea of taking them up again. Published under the title *Trois pièces pour piano*, the first is nearly identical to the original version; of the second, keeping only the first four bars and the conclusion, I wrote a *Toccata* which is very well known today thanks to Horowitz; finally, I replaced the last with a Hymne very close [in style] to the *Concert champêtre*.[66]

Nothing further is known of the last piece, the *Fanfare à quatre pianos*, except that Poulenc completed it and still possessed a copy in early October 1918.[67] Here there can be no question of influence from Stravinsky's *Les Noces*. The composer had only unveiled *Noces* in April 1917 when he played it for Diaghilev at Ouchy, and it was not yet scored for the four pianos found in the final version.[68]

---

[66] Poulenc 1954, pp. 30-1 and Poulenc 1963a, p. 48 (Poulenc 1978, p. 38). Poulenc's 1954 recollection of the relationship between the 1917 version (misdated 1918) and the 1928 revision is not borne out by the extant sources. The relationships in Table 1 are correct.
[67] "Jeudi" [early Oct. 1918] letter to Souberbielle in Poulenc 1994, 18-11.
[68] Craft 1992, p. 341.

APOLLINAIRE AND *LES MAMELLES DE TIRÉSIAS*

Among the many poets whom Poulenc came to know, none was more influential than Apollinaire. Only Paul Eluard (1895-1952) later emerged as a significant rival. The friend of numerous artists intent on radically changing the arts in pre-war Paris, Apollinaire, "the poet of the Avant-Garde,"[69] found himself the object of notoriety when he was wrongly accused of complicity in the theft of the *Mona Lisa* from the Louvre in 1911.[70] In particular, Apollinaire was friendly with Picasso (from ca. 1905) and Jacob, and had a tempestuous love affair with Marie Laurencin, who provided the décor for Poulenc's beloved *Les Biches* in 1924. Looking back at Apollinaire's career in 1954, Poulenc said, "Apollinaire is my first poet."[71] By 1954 he had composed thirty-four songs to Apollinaire poetry and made an opera of his *Les Mamelles de Tirésias*. Later he set several other poems.[72] Although Apollinaire died when Poulenc was only eighteen, he wrote that "From 1912 I was fascinated by everything I read of his."[73] He spoke particularly of Apollinaire's voice:

> Most important: I heard the sound of his voice. I think there is here something essential for a musician who does not want to betray a poet. Apollinaire's timbre, like his entire œuvre, was at the same time melancholic and joyful. There was, in his speech, sometimes, a point of irony, but never *le ton pince-sans-rire* of a Jules Renard. That is why one must sing my Apollinaire songs without insisting on the comical sound of certain words.[74]

Poulenc probably first met Apollinaire at Valentine Hugo's home and saw him on several other occasions including the premiere of Apollinaire's play *Les Mamelles de Tirésias*, which Poulenc attended on 24 June 1917 at the Théâtre René Maubel, rue l'Orient, in Montmartre.[75] Originally subtitled *"Drame surnaturaliste"* before

[69] Shattuck, chapter 9.
[70] Steegmuller 1963, pp. 182-219.
[71] Poulenc 1954, p. 65.
[72] Bernac 1977a, pp. 50-90 (Bernac 1978, pp. 57-90). The songs include *Le Bestiare* (1919: originally twelve songs of which only six were published [FP 15a] plus two recently discovered unpublished songs [15b]), *Trois poèmes de Louise Lalanne* (1931 [FP 57: actually Marie Laurencin wrote the poetry for nos. 1 & 3 and Apollinaire no. 2]), *Quatre poèmes de Guillaume Apollinaire* (1931 [FP 58]), *Deux poèmes de Guillaume Apollinaire* (1938 [FP 94]), *La Grenouillère* (1938 [FP 96]), *Banalités* (1940: five songs [FP 107]), *Montparnasse* and *Hyde Park* (1945 [FP 127]), "Le Pont" and "Un poème" (1946 [FP 131]), *Calligrammes* (1948: seven songs [FP 140]), *Rosemonde* (1954 [FP 158]), *Deux mélodies* (1956 [FP 162]).
[73] Poulenc 1947c, p. 508.
[74] Poulenc 1947c, p. 509.
[75] Poulenc 1994, pp. 60-1 and Poulenc 1993, p. 14. Steegmuller 1963, p. 168 wrote: "In her *Carnet des Nuits* Marie Laurencin mentions a resemblance [between how

Apollinaire decided on *"Drame surréaliste," Les Mamelles* was directed by Pierre Albert-Birot and featured incidental music composed by Germaine Albert-Birot performed on a piano.[76] Cubist sets and costumes were executed by Serge Férat.[77] It was probably in the special program for this production that Poulenc first encountered Cocteau's poem *Zèbre*, which was printed on the first page and inspired his piano piece of the same name.[78] The work created something of a sensation, and Apollinaire said it "was played in an atmosphere most suitable to a work which I think resembles nothing known, but which if we must have comparisons, could be said to have affinities with Plautus and Beaumarchais, as well as Goethe."[79] Poulenc remembered that a veritable Who's Who of artists including Matisse, Picasso, Braque, Derain, Modigliani, Dufy, Léger, Cocteau, Eluard, Aragon, Breton, Satie, Auric, Diaghilev, and Massine were present at the premiere, that Jacob sang in the chorus, and that Marcel Herrand mounted the spectacle.[80] "To tell the truth," Poulenc said, "although immensely amused by all this, I would never have thought that this farce would one day occupy a significant place among my works."[81] He refers to the fact that as early as 1935 he had again been attracted to Apollinaire's play, had turned it into a libretto, and set it to music between May and October of 1944.[82]

At the close of 1917, Poulenc, who had viewed Cocteau from a distance through *Parade* and from a slightly closer vantage point when he chose *Zèbre* as inspiration for a two-piano scherzo, was poised to work directly with him. Collaborations with Cocteau provided Poulenc desperately needed diversion during his military service, which began on 17 January 1918 and ended precisely three years later. Moreover, Cocteau's involvement with other artists provided Poulenc with entrée into an ever-widening and diversified circle of friends and acquaintances.

Poulenc set Apollinaire and how the poet recited his own poetry]: Apollinaire had a way of reciting his poems in a low, chanting voice which is almost like the music of Poulenc. And yet Poulenc never knew Apollinaire, unless I am mistaken [she was]." See also Poulenc 1954, pp. 65 and 144.

[76] Silver, p. 166, indicates that *Les Mamelles* was "presented under the auspices of Birot's *Sic*."

[77] See Adéma's bibliographical essay on Apollinaire's play. For a fragment of Albert-Birot's music and a brief discussion of what Poulenc might have remembered of it when he set the work in the 1940s, see Bellas 1965, pp. 45-8. A photograph of three costumes appears in Richardson 1996, p. 425.

[78] Adéma, p. 56, describes the entire contents of the program and lists the cast.

[79] Quoted in Steegmuller 1963, p. 316.

[80] Poulenc speaks of Jacob's contribution in Poulenc 1963a, p. 94 (Poulenc 1978, p. 73).

[81] Poulenc 1954, p. 145.

[82] Bellas 1965, p. 41 suggests 1935.

IV

Military Service: 1918-1920

Mobilization on 17 January 1918, just ten days after his nineteenth birthday, could not have come at a worse time. With the war in its final phase, he faced the reality of serving France for three years just when his fledgling compositional career was taking flight. Unlike Apollinaire, Cocteau, Misia, and Count Etienne de Beaumont, for whom service to France held a certain glamour, Poulenc showed no appetite for military rigor let alone the horrors of the front.[1] Apollinaire, a foreigner under no obligation to serve in the French army, succeeded in enlisting in the artillery in December 1914.[2] He received a severe head wound on 17 March 1916, which bothered him continuously, but his death the evening of 9 November 1918 (just two days before the Armistice), resulted from Spanish influenza.

Early in the war Misia, a most influential Parisian patroness of the arts and Diaghilev confidante, "obtained . . . authorization to form a convoy of ambulances to administer First Aid."[3] After putting together fourteen trucks and a variety of linens and medicines, she found it nearly impossible to obtain volunteers to drive the vehicles to the front. In her own words, "Finally I formed my team with [José-Maria] Sert, Jean Cocteau, Paul Iribe, François le Gris, Vautier, Vignal, Madame Rumilly, a professional nurse, and our dear coachmaker Saoutchik!"[4] Only slightly later Beaumont, also eager to serve in spite of his exemption, founded an ambulance corps under the auspices of the French Red Cross.[5] Poulenc wrote to Viñes

---

[1] For discussion of these four individuals see Chapter III.
[2] Steegmuller 1963, pp. 281-332.
[3] Sert, p. 141.
[4] Sert, p. 142.
[5] Steegmuller 1970, p. 140 and Poulenc 1994, 18-7 (Poulenc 1991, no. 10). About Beaumont see note 7.

on 3 Sept. 1918 that his greatest desire was to be able to drive for Beaumont. Toward the end of 1915, Cocteau (whose military career began in March 1915 when "he had been called to join an artillery regiment, only to be plucked out, two weeks later, and made a clerk of the Quartermaster Corps"[6] from which he was released on 13 November 1915) interrupted his personal work to join Beaumont's "Convoi Automobiles No. 2."[7] Beaumont, Cocteau, and Misia survived the war. Cocteau managed to juggle "duty" at the front with various artistic projects, and Beaumont lavished personal financial resources on numerous concerts and costume balls. Such was the luxury of voluntary service as opposed to military conscription.

For Poulenc, a decade Cocteau's junior, the constraints of military service chafed mightily.[8] Throughout his service, he tried desperately to improve his growing public visibility as a composer, to widen his circle of friends and acquaintances, to participate in or attend Parisian entertainments, and to resist a strong urge to overstay furloughs and be absent without leave![9] He succeeded remarkably at all but the last; on several occasions he was briefly incarcerated for ignoring terms of furloughs. Poulenc's letters speak enthusiastically of compositional activity, literary interests, and concerts attended in Paris once he was stationed near enough to get there.

[6] Steegmuller 1970, p. 139. In 1914, classified as unfit for duty in the French army, Cocteau joined a Red Cross ambulance corps organized by Misia, who subsequently introduced him to the aviator Roland Garros with whom he went on reconnaissance flights over enemy lines.
[7] Beaumont's service and his relationship to Cocteau are discussed in Steegmuller 1970, pp. 138-60. Steegmuller points out that Beaumont was "A model, for Cocteau, of aquiline, aristocratic appearance (especially later in Cocteau's life, when silvery or bluish hair was appropriate); of manners, of taste and flair and frivolity; of *bien-pensant* but very French Catholicism; of obsession with perpetual youth; of homosexuality at once overt and discreet, much of it sublimated in benevolent artistic activity with attractive artists." See also Steegmuller 1984, pp. 20-2, and Harding 1972, p. 75.
[8] Maurice Sachs, who chronicled the twenties, aptly described military conscription. "In France we have an institution made obligatory by the government for all young Frenchmen — military service. Everyone is compelled to give a year to it (in my time it was a year and a half); no one escapes through physical disability. This sojourn in the army is intolerable because of conditions in the military administration; the young soldiers dream only of leaves of absence, hospital, liberation; they anxiously count the days separating them from civil life. They come to hate anything that wears a uniform, they actually suffer." Sachs 1933, pp. 3-4. Harding 1972, pp. 195-217 provides a perceptive portrait of Sachs.
[9] Poulenc's [2 Sept. 1918] letter to Souberbielle and [3 Sept. 1918] letter to Viñes note that he was imprisoned for a week for having slept in Paris without permission. Poulenc wrote the latter, "Let's say to be more precise that I am truly beginning to feel the stupid and strict discipline of the army." Poulenc 1994, 18-6 and 18-7 (Poulenc 1991, no. 10).

However, they seldom mention his "military" activity except for loneliness caused by squalid conditions before his final assignments in Pont-sur-Seine and Paris. At best Poulenc was a reluctant soldier.

During these years Poulenc was assigned duties in diverse locations, all no farther than 163 kilometers (ca. 100 miles) from Paris. Except for a brief stint with a mobile anti-aircraft division in the Vosges during late September 1918, he was not directly subject to the horrifying rigors of the Front itself.[10]

POULENC'S MILITARY SERVICE		
Date	Assignment	Proximity to Paris
17 Jan.-July 1918	Called up and sent to Vincennes (Val de Marne) and assigned to duty as a "chauffeur non instruit"	6.5KM
23 Aug.-Sept. 1918	Assigned to 63ᵉ Régiment d'Artillerie at Arnouville-lès-Gonesse (Val d'Oise)	Paris region
Late Sept.-Dec. 1918	Assigned to the 66ᵉ Régiment d'Artillerie at Saint-Martin-sur-le-Pré near Châlons-sur-Marne (G. Champagne)	163KM
End of Dec. 1918	Assigned to the 60ᵉ Régiment d'Artillerie at Villenauxe and Villeneuve-La-Grande (Aube)	66KM and 106KM
Mid-Jan. 1919	Centre de D. C. A. Pont-sur-Seine (Aube)	20KM
July 1919	Secretary at the war office (Paris)	Paris
17 Jan. 1921	Demobilized[11]	

[10] A [3 Sept. 1918] letter to Viñes indicates that Poulenc's unit left Tremblay on 24 Aug. for Arnouville-lès-Gonesse to undergo three weeks of training before being sent to the Front. Poulenc 1994, 18-7 (Poulenc 1991, no. 10). Poulenc was still in Paris on 18 Sept. when he thanked Irène Lagut for having sent him "a ravishing drawing" and told her that he looked forward to the liberation. Unpublished "Paris le 18 septembre [1918]" letter in US-AUS.

[11] Compiled from Poulenc 1994, pp. 59-117 (especially the note on p. 59). Hell 1978, pp. 35-6, errs stating that Poulenc served in Paris until his demobilization in Oct. 1921. In fact he traveled to Italy early in 1921 and by mid-summer was in Nogent-sur-Marne.

Common threads during his service years include Poulenc's genuine dislike for being stationed away from Paris and his growing circle of friends and acquaintances. That he found life divorced from Paris' artistic ferment stifling is amply documented. His depression was particularly acute in late 1918 when he vented his frustration to Beaumont, Monnier, Souberbielle, and Viñes.

> I am writing you from a little town in the country [Villenauxe], frightfully depressing. I am worn down and alone to face my sad thoughts. This time all work seems impossible to me.[12]

> And this evening, at your house Mademoiselle, one will be playing the piano, one will be reading some Fargue, one will be with friends, in the warmth of sympathetic surroundings. How badly this makes me feel to think of all these joys while I am here shivering in a hovel which lacks doors. This time it's the last straw. Never have I been so unhappy. I am in a hole where there isn't even a piano.[13]

> If you only knew how bored I am here, far from my friends and everything. Fortunately I have the prospect of soon leaving this frightful place, otherwise one would beat one's head against the wall.[14]

> Truly the countryside is something frightful for young persons, especially in circumstances such as those in which I find myself.[15]

The new year found Poulenc in better humor. "... I am so happy," he told Souberbielle, "I leave in two or three days for Pont-sur-Seine. You see there a step to my definitive return to Paris."[16] By mid-January Poulenc had moved to his new station where he remained until July 1919. From July 1919 to mid-January 1921, he had a desk job in Paris and seldom wrote about military service.

Milhaud referred to his own return to Paris from Brazil in late 1918 saying "Fortunately I was soon caught up in the artistic movement that developed around me and tore me away from these memories. The nightmare of the war as it faded gave birth to a new era."[17] For Poulenc the return to Paris and the end of the war provided the same catharsis.

Poulenc's compositional output during his mobilization shows astonishing fertility even if military life left little time to devote to

---

[12] [Late Dec. 1918] letter in Poulenc 1994, 18-19.
[13] 19 Dec. 1918 letter in Poulenc 1994, 18-20. Poulenc ended this letter with music for a "Petite complainte" ("Ah que la vie est insipide; Ah que la vie est morne et triste a a a; Crois-moi mon cher Aristide a a.") to be sung by his friends. He wrote: "This chanson repeats itself indefinitely, it is background music."
[14] [31 Dec. 1918] letter to Souberbielle in Poulenc 1994, 18-22.
[15] 31 Dec. [1918] letter to Viñes in Poulenc 1994, 18-21.
[16] 11 Jan. [1919] letter to Souberbielle in Poulenc 1994, 19-1.
[17] Milhaud 1953, p. 94.

his art.[18] At least nineteen works were contemplated or completed by January 1921, twelve in the months away from Paris, the rest after his return. Seven of these were published, and the others were either lost, destroyed, or may never have progressed beyond the assignment of working titles. Compositions include six sonatas (two completed; four lost or destroyed), four groups of songs, piano pieces, incidental music for a play, two sections of a collaborative ballet, a pair of aborted chamber works (one a trio for clarinet, violoncello, and piano; the other a string quartet), and miscellaneous compositions including three studies for pianola, possibly suggested by Stravinsky.[19] At this point two of Poulenc's greatest affinities are already visible: writing for winds or voice.

Three pieces — *Trois mouvements perpétuels* (1918: FP 14), "Valse" for piano from *Album des Six* (1919: FP 17), and *Le Bestiaire, ou Le Cortège d'Orphée* (1919: FP 15a) — were among Poulenc's most popular. A fourth work, *Suite pour piano* (FP 19), apparently begun by November 1919, but not finished until March 1920, also enjoyed considerable popularity. Poulenc himself had a particular affection for two other pieces. "I love this work [*Cocardes*] as I love the Sonata for Two Clarinets," he told Edouard Souberbielle.[20] He proudly sent Stravinsky the newly published Sonata on 26 September 1919,[21] and on 21 January 1920, in a report to Paul Collaer about music composed by members of *Les Six*, Poulenc listed among his own works the same Sonata "which I love most particularly."[22] Most of these works were heard in Parisian performance spaces including the Théâtre du Vieux-Colombier, Salle Huyghens, Salle des Agriculteurs, Galerie L'Effort moderne (an art gallery), Salle du Vieux Conservatoire, Théâtre Michel, and Salle de la Ville l'Evêque. The first three were the most important for Poulenc.

[18] Unpublished [early 1918] postcard to Cocteau (?) from Vincennes in US-AUS.
[19] Concerning Stravinsky's interest in the pianola, manifest in his 1917 *Etude* for pianola and numerous transcriptions, see Lawson, pp. 284-301(which catalogues Stravinsky's known output for this instrument); Craft 1992, p. 287 and Satie 1980, p. 96, which quotes Satie's view on the pianola published in *Les Feuilles libres* (1922). Stravinsky boasted to Ansermet that his *Etude* for pianola was "*the first in the world!*" (Stravinsky 1982, p. 139 [6 June 1919 letter].)
[20] Poulenc 1994, 19-15.
[21] Poulenc 1994, 19-19 (Poulenc 1991, no. 21) and 19-21 (Poulenc 1991, no. 22) for Stravinsky's acknowledgment sent 1 Oct. 1919. Stravinsky fondly remembered an evening spent with Poulenc at the Hugo's Rue Royale apartment at which (according to Hugo) Poulenc, Auric, Picasso, Diaghilev, and Massine heard Stravinsky play his *Piano Rag Music*. Hugo 1976, p. 31.
[22] Poulenc 1994, 20-1. Poulenc's letter, written in response to a querry from Collaer, marks the beginning of an important friendship. Collaer, centered near Brussels, was a remarkable champion of new French music, and under his auspices Poulenc received numerous performances in Belgium. Collaer also arranged for Poulenc to appear as a performer.

From 1917 to 1920 the Montparnasse studio of the painter Émile Lejeune, called the Salle Huyghens (6, rue Huyghens), was the venue for a series of concerts featuring music by "Les Nouveaux Jeunes" presented in conjunction with art (by such notables as Picasso, Juan Gris, Georges Braque, and Amadeo Modigliani) and poetry (Blaise Cendrars, Cocteau, etc.).[23] The multimedia events, soon called "Lyre et Palette,"[24] were sponsored by the writer Cendrars, the actor Pierre Bertin (married to the pianist Marcelle Meyer), and the cellist turned conductor Félix Delgrange.[25] Cocteau and Milhaud, who frequented these concerts, left the following memoirs:

> I detest sentimentalizing over meager souvenirs, but the Salle Huyghens was not without its charm. We listened to music and po- etry standing — not as a matter of respect, but owing to a lack of chairs. The stove used to burn well in the spring, but in winter it refused to draw. Beautiful ladies in furs could be seen next to the "djibbahs" of Montmartre and Montparnasse. These miracles did not last long, but while poets and painters were learning to hate each other, our musicians came together, supported by one another, and formed under the title "Nouveaux Jeunes."[26]

> Delgrange abandoned the cello to devote himself wholly to the cause of the new art; he organized concerts in a little hall in Montparnasse, the Salle Huyghens; the backless benches were uncomfortable, and the atmosphere was unbreathable because of the fumes of the stove, but all that was elegant in Parisian society, as well as the artists and devotees of the new music, rubbed shoulders there. Jane Bathori and Ricardo Viñes, the faithful pioneers, the (female) Capelle Quartet,[27] the pianists Juliette Meerovitch and Marcelle Meyer, and the actor Pierre Bertin, who also sang, lent us their devoted help and disinter- ested services.[28]

Four early Poulenc works were premiered in this small space: the Sonata for Two Clarinets, the Sonata for Piano Four Hands, the So- nata for Violin and Piano [I], and *Trois mouvements perpétuels.*

---

[23] Arvid Fougstedt's color drawing of a Lyre et Palette "exposition," is repro- duced in Machart, p. 17. A drawing of the 19 Nov. 1916 opening exhibition is in Klüver, p. 81. See also Whiting, p. 491.
[24] The Société Lyre et Palette existed as early as 18 Apr. 1916, when Roland- Manuel gave a talk about Satie. Orledge 1995, p. 174 and Klüver, p. 80.
[25] Harding 1972, pp. 58-9.
[26] Jean Cocteau, "The Six," *Fanfare*, p. 3 (quoted by Daniel, p. 14). See also the description from Cocteau's *Carte blanche* quoted in Halbreich, p. 43.
[27] The Capelle Quartet included Ferdinande Capelle, Alice Piantini, Marguerite Lutz, and Marika Bernard. Their picture appeared in the Mar. 1922 issue of *Le Monde musical*, p. 109.
[28] Milhaud 1953, p. 96 (Milhaud 1987a, p. 82).

The Théâtre du Vieux-Colombier (21, rue du Vieux-Colombier), which Cocteau described to Stravinsky as "the theater of the young, of the contemporary movement,"[29] normally housed legitimate theater under Jacques Copeau's direction.[30] Copeau had opened it in late 1913 with a "call" in the form of a challenge to re-energize French theatrical arts:

Théâtre du Vieux Colombier

Call

•**to youth,** to react against all the pusillanimity of commercial theaters and to defend the freest, most sincere manifestations of a new dramatic art;

•**to the literate public,** to maintain the cult of classic, French, and foreign masterpieces, which will form the foundation of the repertoire;

•**to all,** to sustain a company which will succeed owing to the low cost of its spectacles, their variety, the quality of their interpretation, and of their production.[31]

Later, when Copeau took his troupe to America financed by the American banker Otto Kahn, he asked Jane Bathori to accompany him. When she declined, he implored her to maintain the flame he had kept so well lighted in Paris and left the theater in her charge.[32] Copeau's printed announcement, dated "Paris, septembre 1917" reads in part:

Several writers, several artists, all sympathetic to our effort, join with Jane Bathori to keep burning on our hearth during this fourth winter of the war, a flame that the frightful storm will not force to waiver. These artists lead the same fight we do for an art that is sincere, free, without affectation, showiness, or histrionics.[33]

Bathori directed the theater for several years producing and occasionally performing in music as venerable as Adam de la Halle's *Le Jeu de Robin et Marion* (staring Bathori and Bertin) and as modern as

[29] Stravinsky 1982, p. 77 (letter postmarked 14 Feb. 1914).
[30] Copeau had purchased the Athénée Saint-Germain theater in 1913 and renamed it for the street on which it was located. According to Cuneo-Laurent, p. 87, "Bathori and Engel were engaged by Copeau to train the artists for any singing necessary for the productions, and to provide incidental music for various works." For excellent essays on this theater, as well as photographs of its facade in 1920 (p. 13) and interior in 1913 before Copeau renamed the theater (p. 17), see Christout.
[31] Color facsimile in Christout, p. 49.
[32] Copeau, p. 813.
[33] Facsimile in Cuneo-Laurent, pp. 88-9.

premieres by "Les Nouveaux Jeunes." Initially her success led Roger Martin du Gard to write Copeau that: "Bathori's Colombier attracts all of Paris. Limousines fill the streets and go all the way to my door on the [rue] Cherche-Midi."[34] Poulenc's *Rapsodie nègre* was premiered at the 11 December 1917 concert.[35] In late March 1918, the threat of aerial bombardment forced Bathori to close the theater.[36] When re-opened for its second season in December 1918, she terminated her working relationship with Bertin because the literary portion of the program had not gone especially well. Hoping to present a twenty-one week season, she turned her attention to some larger musical productions that required staging and orchestra.[37]

A third theater of importance to Poulenc and other musicians in the late teens and early twenties was the Salle des Agriculteurs (8, rue d'Athènes). There Vladimir Golschmann, the young violinist turned conductor, inaugurated a series of concerts which often favored music by young French composers.[38] Later, Golschmann specifically championed works by Poulenc, Milhaud, Honegger, and other French composers, and conducted some of the Concerts Wiéner in the early 1920s.

During this time Poulenc made important additions to his circle of friends. He courted artists, writers, musicians, publishers, and wealthy patrons and patronesses of the arts, and during these three years he established two working relationships of paramount importance. The first was with Cocteau, who solicited Poulenc's contribution to several planned entertainments. One was a "Séance Music-Hall" in 1918, which was planned but never given, and the other was a Spectacle-Concert on 21 February 1920. Their friendship continued until 1963, the year both men died. The second important working relationship was as a member of the group anointed *Les Six* by the Parisian critic Henri Collet on 16 January 1920. This provided Poulenc with status by association, improving his visibility immediately after the war. In truth, Cocteau served as something of a philosophical and artistic spokesperson for *Les Six*, often participating in their joint concerts and appearing in their group photographs. His provocative tract *Le Coq et l'Arlequin*, dated 1918 but published in January 1919, is filled with maxims describing the music and aesthetics of Satie and "Les Nouveaux Jeunes."[39] As a

[34] Copeau, vol. 1, 266.

[35] Harding 1972, pp. 60-2.

[36] See Cuneo-Laurent, pp. 98-100 for Bathori's poignant letters (originals in F-Pa), and Hausser, p. 660 for the dates Paris was bombarded.

[37] Concerning the debacle involving a late 1917 talk by Apollinaire see Cuneo-Laurent, p. 95.

[38] Milhaud 1953, p. 96 (Milhaud 1987a, p. 92).

[39] Volta 1990, p. 7.

result of Cocteau's interest in Auric and Poulenc, both composers were able to put down roots in the fertile soil of Montparnasse, the cradle of much significant Parisian artistic activity.

FIRST COLLABORATION WITH COCTEAU: WORKS FOR THE 1918 "SÉANCE MUSIC-HALL"

Until mobilization, Poulenc's most significant contacts with Cocteau were through *Parade,* a few personal encounters, and his use of a Cocteau verse for the lost composition entitled *Zèbre.* Poulenc was keenly aware, however, that Cocteau was at the center of many of Paris' most exciting collaborative events and was well connected to its artists of all trades. During the late summer of 1918, Cocteau asked Poulenc to join other members of "Les Nouveaux Jeunes" in a projected "Séance Music-Hall" performance devised in collaboration with the actor Pierre Bertin.[40] This was Poulenc's first collaboration with all the future members of *Les Six* plus Satie. It is ironic that a project which never came to fruition and for which almost no music remains could stimulate and frustrate Poulenc for so long. In many respects this project acted as a surrogate for the friends he left behind and for the Parisian artistic events he could not personally attend.

Precisely when Cocteau and Bertin first conceived this "Séance" is unknown, but Poulenc knew about it by the beginning of September when he wrote glowingly to Souberbielle:

> Jean Cocteau, at the instigation of Bathori, has accepted to direct the Vieux-Colombier Theater for fifteen days, transformed during this period into a music-hall. There will be a "séance" four times a week. True acrobats, jugglers, wrestlers, boxers, will be conjured up on the stage and will move to the sound of music by Messieurs Satie, Auric, Durey, and Poulenc. Here entirely in secret are our projects. For décor, nothing at all. Everything will take place in front of a large black velvet curtain lighted by two projectors. During the entr'actes, there will be background music by all of us.[41]

A draft program outlines Cocteau's conception, which involved the future *Les Six* and Satie[42] (see facing page).

---

[40] Volta 1990, p. 30, no. 62 cites a 13 Sept. 1918 letter from Cocteau to Louise Lara in which Cocteau, at Bathori's request, "dreams of organizing a séance music-hall or, more precisely, a café-concert for the young musicians who 'very much want to give him the honor of considering him as their spokesperson'."
[41] [2 Sept. 1918] letter in Poulenc 1994, 18-6. Poulenc also wrote Viñes on Tuesday [3 Sept. 1918] sending news and reminding him that he had already played him a fragment of *Le Jongleur* when they last met. Poulenc 1994, 18-7 (Poulenc 1991, no. 10).
[42] Volta 1990, p. 7 suggests the date Sept. 1918.

Programme

Nouveaux jeunes's marche ————————— auric

1ère Partie

2 Cycliste (avec prelude) ————————— Honnegger
5 Gymnastes (avec prelude) ————————— Taillefere
3 Siffleur (pour siffet imitant oiseau siffle) - Durey
6 Bertin dans son repertoire

          Les 3 couleurs — Honnegger
          un Romance = Poulenc
          ~ chansonette

Entracte
musique d'ameublement

2.e Partie

ouverture   Pot Pourri — Taillefere

8 Virtuose
     Mlle meerwild.
     1er Prix du conservatoire
     Molange   gai luron (polka) Caprice brillant Satie
1 Jongleurs [43]   avec Prélude ————————— Poulenc
4 Danse modernes ————————————— auric
7 chanteur a voix —————————————— Satie
                                       auric
                                       Durey

À bientôt (Retraite) — Satie

---

[43] The name of this piece varies frequently both in Poulenc's writings and in the Poulenc literature: *Le Jongleur, Jongleur, Jongleurs.* Except in quotations, we have adopted *Le Jongleur.*

Poulenc's progress on compositions intended for Cocteau's Séance Music-Hall is revealed in more than thirty letters written between 2 September 1918 and 15 October 1920. Most valuable are exchanges with Cocteau and Souberbielle which give specific details about Poulenc's compositions. This project must have relieved Poulenc of the stifling boredom of military life, and he vigorously attacked his assignment. Cocteau clarified that each composer would work without knowledge of what the others were doing "in order to preserve the atmosphere of surprise."[44] Poulenc was responsible for three separate parts: "Une chanson espagnole" (called "Une Romance" and "Une chansonette" in Cocteau's program), "Musique d'ameublement pour l'Entracte," and "*Jongleurs* (avec Prélude)."[45] Music for the first, *Toréador* (FP 11), still exists today; music for *Le Jongleur* (FP 9 [Prélude] & 10) was either destroyed or has not yet been found; and Poulenc's contribution to the *Musique d'ameublement* was most probably never written.[46] He already had *Le Jongleur* on his drawing board by September because Cocteau noted "I am adopting your *Jongleurs*, and the *Prélude percussion* pleases me very much. So, then, I am counting you in: *Jongleurs* [will be] on our program."[47] Letters to Souberbielle on 2 September and the beginning of October exude optimism. The former deserves quotation even if Poulenc thought a work could not be recounted by letter!

Chapter 1

Analysis of the *Prélude*

List of the instruments:

> 2 Trompettes chinoises à son unique (Yan)
>
> Timbales
>
> Grosse caisse (which never plays loudly)
>
> Cymbales
>
> Tam-tam (very sober use of this instrument, two strokes alone
>   separated)

[44] Cocteau's 13 Sept. 1918 letter in Poulenc 1994, 18-9 (Poulenc 1991, no. 11). A letter to Durey of the same date is mentioned by Volta 1990, p. 30, no. 64.

[45] Poulenc 1994, 18-9 (Poulenc 1991, no. 11). Cocteau included the text for the "chanson espagnole" entitled *Le Toréador*. The text includes twelve strophes and a refrain in the form R, 1-4, R, 5-8, R, 9-12, R. Cocteau remarked, "One should be able to sing the song seriously at the Bobino for example." The Bobino was a famous music-hall located at 20, rue de la Gaîté in Montparnasse.

[46] Milhaud 1953, p. 122 wrote that Poulenc and Auric disapproved of the concept of *musique d'ameublement* when he and Satie experimented with it at a concert given at the Galerie Barbazanges on 8 Mar. 1920. See also Orledge 1990, p. 320.

[47] Cocteau's 2 Sept. 1918 letter in Poulenc 1994, 18-5 (Poulenc 1991, no. 9).

Tambour basque

Castagnettes

Tambour militaire

Triangle

Xylophone

Glockenspiel

At the beginning the two trumpets howl lugubriously, the kettledrums make a gentle roll, the cymbals a trill. Violent accord of all the instruments, but I realize suddenly that you will understand poorly, I will do better. I will immediately send my manuscript to the copyist, and shortly you will receive the orchestral score which you can study at leisure. I move on to *Jongleurs.*

Chapter 2

A long silence between the *Prélude* and the beginning of the piece. Then the orchestra begins quietly. The tonality of the piece is as soft and sad as the *Prélude* was streaming and frenetic (you will see the combinations of rhythm). *Jongleurs*, I say, starts softly. And it is the *Basse continue* which begins. This bass will remain nearly the same for the entire piece. But that is not monotonous for that, you will see. Soon the first theme advances majestically and with a sad poignancy, in a rather long curve, it is only interrupted to make way for the second theme, this one nonchalant, rubato, and sensitive to the utmost finishes with some kind of desperate melodic fragments. After, *basse continue* alone with variations, then a third theme rather embellished and fast, bass again with a great descent into the lower register. Then, a combination of themes, trying to outmatch each other, combined, the first theme returns sumptuous and triumphant, then everything loses its luster, the bass goes out as it has come with a really poignant sadness, an oboe holds the main note of the piece (a "g") for many bars, a vestige of the former spectacle as one sometimes sees when a fête is over, a lantern forgotten by accident which recalls the sadly joyful time. Here is how I have conceived *Jongleurs*, my friend. You will judge better what it's about soon when you receive the transcription for two pianos. I do not doubt that you will be moved then by what you are calling now fantasy. The orchestration will be very clear like Mozart, while that of the other, the *Prélude* is ultra complex.[48]

[48] Poulenc 1994, 18-11. He also wrote to Valentine Gross on 1 Oct. [1918] saying: "Although very busy, I still find time to put a few notes onto paper. My *Jongleurs* grows by several bars each day; my *Prélude pour instruments à percussion* is finished. This last work, which will precede the music-hall number, will please you I believe, since it is something very novel and which will not leave one indifferent, that is the main point." Poulenc 1994, 18-10.

By mid-October Cocteau pressed Poulenc to compose background music and urged that *Toréador* not sound too much like Chabrier.[49] Although Poulenc said nothing about progress, he nevertheless assured Valentine Gross that he was working:

> Having nothing to do in the way of duty permits me to accomplish a great deal of work. A few days ago I finished the orchestral score of my *Prélude pour instruments à percussion* which will precede the *Jongleurs* number for the Colombier music-hall performance. At the moment I am completing the two-piano transcription of *Jongleurs* itself and am rather pleased with the whole.[50]

Seeking approbation for his work and assistance with having his scores copied, Poulenc wrote Souberbielle on five occasions between 30 October and 20 November. In the first letter he chastised "Vilain Edouard" for not having written. He had finished composing *Le Jongleur*, the two-piano score was with his copyist, and he had finally written the Sonata for Two Clarinets (dedicated to Souberbielle) and completed the piano transcription.[51] Poulenc enclosed the orchestral score for the *Prélude* with a 2 November letter asking that Souberbielle transport it to Monsieur Roy, the copyist.[52] Poulenc's next letter (undated, but early November), addressed "My dear, you are a beast," exhibited still less patience.[53] He demanded to know if the *Prélude* had been received and said that the copyist was to deliver the two-piano transcription of *Le Jongleur* and the Sonata for Two Clarinets as soon as they were finished. Souberbielle was twice asked for his opinion about the music, but none was forthcoming until mid-November.

In the interim Poulenc wrote Cocteau that he had just finished a Sonata for Violin and Piano using ragtime, and that the completion of *Toréador* and the orchestration of *Le Jongleur* were next on his desk.[54] Finally, in a 20 November letter, Poulenc acknowledged receipt of

[49] Poulenc 1994, 18-12 (Poulenc 1991, no. 12). Perloff traces the popular origins of this song, which Poulenc later called "une fausse chanson de caf'conç." Perloff, pp. 153-61 and Poulenc 1954, p. 135.
[50] Poulenc 1994, 18-13 (Poulenc 1991, no. 13).
[51] Poulenc 1994, 18-14. The orchestral score of *Le Jongleur*, however, was not completed until 1919. See Poulenc 1994, 18-19. A fragment of a 5 Nov. 1918 letter from Cocteau to Poulenc reports: "I have your *Jongleurs* (alone) but very, very good. We were able to take it with Bertin at Gaumont Palace in the entr'acte of a showing of *Twenty Thousand Leagues Under the Sea*. I wish that our whole group would work as quickly as you." Poulenc 1994, p. 62, note 3.
[52] Poulenc 1994, 18-15.
[53] Poulenc 1994, 18-16. Poulenc's complaints and questions were echoed in his 13 [Nov.] letter. Poulenc 1994, 18-17.
[54] Fragment in Poulenc 1994, p. 77, note 2. This piece was dedicated to Jourdan-Morhange, who gave the first performance. Poulenc had not completed the piano part and so only the first two movements could be played. In an early

news from Souberbielle diplomatically assigning blame to logistical problems with the mail.[55] By year's end he was in very low spirits as correspondence with Beaumont[56] and Souberbielle attests.[57] To Beaumont he expressed hope to be reassigned to Paris as a driver ("au Service automobile") and to complete the orchestral score of *Le Jongleur* by the end of March 1919. To Souberbielle, speaking with more candor, he confessed: "I have no taste for work. In effect I have my visual field obstructed by the orchestra of *Jongleurs;* work which cannot be done here."[58] With the advent of a new year and pending assignment to Pont-sur-Seine, his moroseness disappeared quickly. Poulenc wrote Cocteau: "I will be living then in Pont-sur-Seine. I will have there: a room, piano, etc. . . .etc. . . . In a week you will have *Toréador,* handsome and pungent like a Spanish forest."[59] On 11 January he wrote to Souberbielle with similar news noting that upon his arrival he would work on the orchestral score of *Le Jongleur* and send the second of his *Trois mouvements perpétuels.*[60]

Once in Pont-sur-Seine Poulenc diligently orchestrated *Le Jongleur.*[61] The work proceeded swiftly, because letters to Souberbielle on [21 January] and Cocteau the next day confirm that the task was completed. "You know that my *Jongleur* is absolutely ready, orchestral score, parts, etc.," he told Cocteau.[62] Poulenc's sense of urgency is again revealed on 9 February when he discussed a scheme for Cocteau to concoct a letter signed with an English name to facilitate Poulenc's request for leave.[63] He told Cocteau that versions of *Toréador* for piano and voice as well as voice and instruments were at the copyist.[64]

Nov. 1918 letter to Souberbielle in Poulenc 1994, 18-16, Poulenc said "This work is very curious." In a radio broadcast in the *A Bâtons rompus* series, Poulenc spoke with interest of Satie's use of ragtime in *Parade.* See Chapter X concerning these broadcasts.

[55] Poulenc 1994, 18-18. This letter clarifies that the sonatas for violin and for two clarinets had not been returned by the copyist, and Souberbielle was instructed to go to Roy's at 20, rue Cambon, fetch them, and transport them to Durey, who would arrange for their performance. Chimènes' note in Poulenc 1994, p. 77.

[56] [Late Dec. 1918] letter in Poulenc 1994, 18-19.

[57] [31 Dec. 1918] letter in Poulenc 1994, 18-22.

[58] Poulenc 1994, 18-22. Poulenc also alludes to a *Sonate pour cimbalum et quatuor à bois,* about which nothing else is known.

[59] Unpublished [9 Jan. 1919?] letter in US-AUS. Poulenc also included several lines of music for *Toréador.*

[60] Poulenc 1994, 19-1.

[61] Poulenc 1994, 19-2 (Poulenc 1991, no. 15).

[62] Unpublished letter in US-AUS.

[63] Poulenc 1994, 19-4 (Poulenc 1991, no. 16).

[64] This is the only mention of an orchestral version, of which no copy has been located.

The morning of 14 March Poulenc spoke to Cocteau about a possible performance of *Le Jongleur* and wrote Valentine Gross from Pont-
sur-Seine reviewing his conception of the work, which had not
changed since he first discussed it with Souberbielle in September
of 1918:

> You know precisely what my idea is for this spectacle. For décor I
> want only a large black velvet curtain. For lights, no footlights or
> very faint footlights but very strong projectors. And there it is, I lack
> costumes. You have asked me why I do not ask Picasso. It is because
> I do not want anything that will make one think of *Parade*. For the
> same reason I have not wanted to ask a Picasso disciple. I then thought
> of you because I am sure you would make a striking costume for me.
> Though you are very busy, do not refuse me that, for you it is such a
> trifle and for me it is so much. Besides, I believe that *Jongleur* can be
> a beautiful thing with an enormous prélude of noises and then the
> calm and classic spectacle up until a certain point.[65]

When no "Séance Music-Hall" performance materialized,
Cocteau's involvement with *Le Jongleur* ended and Poulenc turned
elsewhere for assistance in presenting it.[66] *Le Jongleur* is mentioned
in a [3 June 1919] letter to Milhaud which states that Poulenc thought
it would be performed with Milhaud's *Les Choéphores* on 15 June.[67]
He expressed concern that both works dealt heavily with percussion and that the concert might be too long. For whatever reason, *Le
Jongleur* was not performed. Instead it was premiered, probably in
its piano reduction, at a "Grand Gala d'avant-garde" organized by
Pierre Bertin at the Galerie Barbazanges (109, Faubourg St -Honoré)
in conjunction with an exhibition of theatrical works by Natalia
Goncharova and Mikhail Larionov on 24 June 1919.[68] It was inter-
preted by Caryathis (née Elise Toulemon, later Mme Elise
Jouhandeau), the well-known but eccentric character dancer.
Caryathis had been Gabrielle "Coco" Chanel's dance instructor in
1911 when the latter maintained a rue Lamarck studio high up in
Montmartre.[69] Virtually nothing is known of this performance, but

[65] Poulenc 1994, 19-6.
[66] *Toréador* was apparently never performed and Poulenc finally let Deiss publish
it in 1933. Cocteau contributed a lithograph for the cover signed "Jean." (Reproduced in Machart, p. 22.)
[67] Poulenc 1994, 19-12. "Exhortation" from *Les Choéphores* was performed 19 June
with Cocteau, Honegger, Auric, Poulenc, and Lucien Daudet augmenting the
hired percussion. See Madeleine Milhaud's account in Nichols 1996, pp. 17-18.
[68] Poulenc 1994, p. 92. Larionov and Goncharova had left Pivotins (Russia) on 5
May 1919 to return to Paris, and the exhibition based on one they had mounted
the year before at the Galerie Sauvage celebrated their arrival. Parton, p. 178.
Concerning the Galerie see Klüver, pp. 62-4.
[69] Charles-Roux, p. 118.

there must have been some story involved because on Monday [5 April 1920] Poulenc wrote Milhaud:

> The story of Caryathis is true but ... take off a zero and put in its place a thousand francs. It's already enough. This for a version of 2 hands; another for 4 hands and another for small orchestra. I am not usually reticent, but as I don't like *Jongleurs*, I don't attach any importance to it and remain silent about it.[70]

During the summer of 1920 Poulenc wrote, "I have finished my orchestra for *Jongleurs* which this time will be heard, I assure you."[71] He also mentioned to Durey on 7 October that he had worked with Caryathis the evening before on Satie's theater piece *La Belle Excentrique* scheduled to receive its private premiere on 8 January 1921 *chez* Pierre Bertin.[72] He tried to entice his new Belgian friend Paul Collaer to come to Paris for the performance.

> Now, if you come to Paris, come in January, because at this time will take place the first performance of a dance spectacle by Mme Caryathis with the first hearing of a large twenty-minute piece by Satie *La Belle Excentrique*, which is the work of a genius; then a ten-minute number by Auric; one by me, *Jongleurs*; and various other spectacles by Ravel etc.[73]

Le Jongleur was finally put to rest when it was performed on 21 June 1921 at the Théâtre du Colisée, Vladimir Golschmann conducting. A letter from Satie to Poulenc notes that he could not attend a rehearsal scheduled for a Sunday morning at 9. Satie asked Poulenc to stand in if Auric was unable to oversee the rehearsal of *La Belle Excentrique*.[74] Once again Caryathis danced, dressed in a costume designed by Goncharova. J. -L. Croze's *Comœdia* review focusing on Caryathis stated that "Poulenc's *Le Jongleur*, interpretation of a music-hall number, obtained a great success due to her acrobatic ingenuity."[75]

---

[70] Poulenc 1994, 20-3. The precise nature of the negotiations is not known beyond this reference.

[71] Poulenc 1994, 20-8. Poulenc also lunched with Satie on 9 Sept., perhaps to discuss his latest works. Satie's 9 Sept. 1920 letter to Cocteau in Volta 1993, p. 117.

[72] Poulenc 1994, 20-10 and Satie's "vendredi" [7 Jan. 1921] letter to Cocteau announcing the same event in Volta 1993, p. 118. Bertin lived at 120, boulevard du Montparnasse (Orledge 1990, p. 321).

[73] 15 Oct. [1920] letter to Collaer in Poulenc 1994, 20-12 and Collaer 1996, 20-7.

[74] Poulenc 1994, 21-9 where the [10 June] letter is misdated [10 July 1921].

[75] Review of the "Répétition générale" entitled "Les Danses de Mlle Caryathis originales et curieuses, ont passioné le public au Théâtre du Colisée" (16 June 1921), 1. The program also included Auric's *Paris Sport*, a dance by Granados, Ravel's *Rapsodie Espagnole* and two "morceaux de concert" by Milhaud (*Symphonie pastorale*) and Honegger.

Unlike *Le Jongleur*, the *Prélude percussion* was never performed. Its use of ten percussion instruments and two "Trompettes chinoises à son unique" places it among the very first works intended for percussion orchestra. Although the *Prélude* postdates Milhaud's use of percussion and spoken voices in the third and fourth movements of *Les Choéphores* ("Omen" and "Incantation" written in 1915-16), Poulenc probably did not know this music, which had neither been published nor performed by the time his *Prélude* was completed in October of 1918.[76] More important, it predates Edgard Varèse's famous *Ionisation* (1929-31) by nearly a decade and a half.[77] Unfortunately, the fate of the score and parts both for the *Prélude percussion* and *Le Jongleur* is unknown.

OTHER WORKS

Poulenc also wrote other works early in his military service. These pieces include the Sonata for Two Clarinets (FP 7) and the Sonata for Piano Four Hands (FP 8), completed in March and June 1918 respectively while he was stationed at Vincennes;[78] the *Trois mouvements perpétuels*, completed in December 1918 at Saint-Martin-sur-le-Pré, and *Le Bestiaire*, composed between February and May 1919 at Pont-sur-Seine.[79] Poulenc rarely mentions them except in a "Petit catalogue de mes œuvres" included in several letters.[80]

The Sonata for Two Clarinets inaugurates a series of sonatas for winds that Poulenc particularly prized. Poulenc was strongly influenced by Stravinsky's wind writing in works such as *Pribaoutki* and by Satie:

> But whereas Stravinsky tended to exploit contrasts of mood ironically, Poulenc followed Satie in making us laugh not in a satiric or parodistic spirit, but simply at the incongruities inherent in the everyday world. In the 1918 *Sonate* the two clarinet-pipers chortle like mountebanks at a Petrouchka-style fair in the quick movements, while in the slow movement they lament in peasant monotone.[81]

Poulenc wrote to Jean-Aubry:

---

[76] Milhaud was in Brazil during this period.

[77] Born in Paris in 1883, Varèse had introduced Debussy to Schönberg's atonal works and was acquainted with Apollinaire and Satie.

[78] In an early Oct. 1918 letter to Souberbielle Poulenc lists the Sonata for Piano Four Hands as having been written in May 1918. Poulenc 1994, 18-11. The printed score gives June. Both Sonatas are listed by Poulenc as having been written in "Boulognes [sic]-sur-Seine."

[79] But see Bellas 1964.

[80] See those to Souberbielle of early Oct. 1918 (Poulenc 1994, 18-11), Sauguet of 14 Oct. 1920 (Poulenc 1994, 20-11), and Archibald T. Davison of July 1921 (facsimile in Schmidt 1995, xxi-xxiv). Ansermet also received a catalogue.

[81] Mellers, p. 12.

I am writing little for the moment and I prefer to think rather than to realize. I also listen very little to music; besides, few things this winter have presented a real interest save three first performances of works of the first order. I am speaking here of *Pribaoutki* and of *Berceuses du chat* by Stravinsky and above all of *Socrate* by Satie, a work which I love equally with the Passions and Cantatas of Bach.[82]

Poulenc frequently commented that writing for solo winds was much more satisfying than composing for solo strings, and his actions confirm this assertion. He abandoned four violin sonatas before permitting one to be published, never completed several other chamber works for strings, and threw a string quartet down a Parisian sewer![83]

Trois mouvements perpétuels was dedicated to his friend Valentine Gross [subsequently Valentine Hugo]. Later he disparaged some of his own piano music, but played this piece often and also recorded it.[84] He was a fine pianist, and his statement on a manuscript of the work that "the pianist must forget he is a virtuoso" presents a certain irony.[85] Not only did Poulenc play it often, but Viñes premiered it. Poulenc's use of ostinati in each movement of *Trois mouvements* shows him to be an excellent student of Satie and Stravinsky. Along with the "Valse" from *Album des Six,* these short movements remain among Poulenc's most popular compositions. Poulenc himself arranged the work both for chamber orchestra and nine solo instruments, and it has also been arranged for violin and piano by Jascha Heifetz, for symphonic winds by Bram Wiggins, for wind instruments and percussion by Quinto Maganini, and for winds by Samuel Baron. Still other arrangements exist for bayan, flute and guitar, two guitars, and two pianos.

The last works written in 1919 and early 1920 while Poulenc was in military service include *Le Bestiaire* (his first for voice) and *Suite pour piano.* Poulenc was already aware of Apollinaire's writings when he received a copy of *Le Bestiaire* in a new edition with woodcuts by Raoul Dufy, among books sent by Adrienne Monnier in January 1919.[86] Over the next months he set twelve of Apollinaire's poems

---

[82] 10 June 1919 letter in Poulenc 1994, 19-13. Poulenc says he had also heard Ravel's *Le Tombeau de Couperin* (which he disliked, although he enjoyed the Trio), and "Alborada dal gracioso" (which was fantastic from the point of view of orchestration).

[83] See, for example, his (late Mar. 1919) letter to Souberbielle in Poulenc 1994, 19-7 announcing the destruction of one violin sonata (FP 12): "I am immensely happy. This work was truly too abominable."

[84] Schneider, p. 216 (concerning a string quartet) and p. 222 (concerning his piano music).

[85] Schmidt 1995, p. 31.

[86] Apollinaire's thirty poems were originally published in 1911.

for voice and instruments including a string quartet, flute, clarinet, and bassoon.[87] But at the same time, Louis Durey also set the entire *Bestiaire,* a fact Poulenc was surprised to learn when the two met in Paris during one of his leaves. Heeding Auric's and Linossier's advice,[88] he published only six: "Le Dromadaire," "La Chèvre du Thibet," "La Sauterelle," "Le Dauphin," "L'Écrivesse," and "La Carpe," dedicating them to Durey. When first performed on 8 June 1919 in Léonce Rosenberg's gallery "L'Effort moderne" (rue de la Baume) during a *matinée poétique* devoted to Apollinaire's memory, all twelve songs were sung by Jeanne Borel accompanied by Poulenc.[89] Manuscripts of two more songs, "Le Serpent" and "La Colombe," (FP 15b) sold in 1992 at the Richelieu-Drouot (Paris), found their way to the Bibliothèque Nationale. Poulenc also reset and published "La Puce" in 1960 in a book honoring Dufy.[90] The missing songs not yet found include "La Tortue," "La Mouche," and "Le Bœuf."[91] Poulenc used two other poems from *Le Bestiaire,* "La Souris" and "Nuage," in *Deux mélodies* (1956: FP 162) dedicated to his friends Marya Freund and Rose Dercourt-Plaut.

The first private performance of *Le Bestiaire* was given by Suzanne Rivière and Poulenc at the home of Mme Vignon (avenue Latour-Maubourg) most likely in May 1919.[92] Rivière may have been introduced to Poulenc and other members of "Les Nouveaux Jeunes" by her cousin Emmanuel Faÿ. On 31 July 1920 Rivière married Charles Peignot, heir to a prosperous Parisian family of typographers.[93] Soon the couple was entertaining "Le Tout-Paris" each Sunday in their 5, quai Voltaire apartment. Poulenc later counted Suzanne as the most important early interpreter of his "feminine" songs, and the two were life-long friends.

---

[87] Perloff, pp. 168-70 describes various folk elements in "Le Dauphin."

[88] Poulenc 1989, pp. 20-1. Poulenc 1993, p. 14 credits Linossier's involvement.

[89] At this event, Cocteau met the young poet Raymond Radiguet, who was one of the readers. Concerning the performance see the letters in Schmidt 1995, p. 41 and Poulenc 1994, 19-10 (to Rosenberg), 19-11 (to Viñes), and 19-13 (to Georges Jean-Aubry). In a 15 July 1919 diary entry entitled "In the den of cubism," the art dealer René Gimpel described the gallery as follows: "A quiet little house harbors the revelation. An unobtrusive plate on the door: L'EFFORT MODERNE. I rang the bell and was let into a low-pitched entrance way, tiled very simply in black and white. I was shown upstairs to a large, long room forming a gallery. Here he has displayed cubes of canvases, canvases in cubes, marble cubes, cubic marble, cubes in color, cubic colorings, incomprehensible cubes and the incomprehensible divided cubically." Gimpel, p. 107, described Rosenberg as "tall, blond, and elegant like a pink shrimp."

[90] For "La Puce," which Poulenc dates "Noizay - 9 Novembre [19]60," see Oury, p. 106.

[91] Poulenc 1994, pp. 90-1.

[92] Schmidt 1995, p. 41. Peignot recalled that Poulenc asked her to sing this cycle.

[93] Concerning Peignot see Pistone.

The *Suite pour piano* (FP 20), probably begun in late 1919, consists of three contrasting movements (Presto, Andante, Vif) dedicated to Viñes.[94] It was finished in Paris during March and performed by Viñes on 10 April 1920 at a Société Nationale de Musique concert in the Salle du Vieux Conservatoire along with diverse works by Sangra, Rimsky-Korsakov, Alimenko, Falla, Tommassini, and Debussy.[95] The comment when the work was revised and printed in 1926 was:

> This work [. . .] is a remarkable example of certain phases in the evolution of modern piano music. Its very name and subtitles, in their total avoidance of any extra-musical suggestion, are significant of the present-day reaction, especially among French composers, against romanticism, impressionism, expressionism, in fact of any "ism" that tends to lead music away from its own ends. [. . .] Neatly and crisply handled, these three movements have an irresistible fascination.[96]

Poulenc contemplated or sketched a number of other compositions and the diversity of their instrumentations reflects the influence of Stravinsky, Satie, and Viñes and shows a certain interest in novelty. Works include the Sonata for Violin and Piano [I] (Op. 7) mentioned in a 23 October letter to Valentine Gross and performed on 21 December in the painter Émile Lejeune's studio at 6, rue Huyghens by Marcelle Meyer and Hélène Jourdan-Morhange;[97] Sonata for Piano, Violin, and Violoncello (FP 13) mentioned in a 23 October letter to Valentine Gross;[98] *Sonate pour cimbalum et quatuor à bois* alluded to in a [31 December 1918] letter to Souberbielle;[99] *Quadrille à quatre mains* (FP 18) mentioned in an 8 November 1919 letter to Georges Jean-Aubry; three songs including *Côte d'Azur, Paul et Virginie,* and *Victoire* on poems by Raymond Radiguet mentioned in a [5 April 1920] letter to Milhaud;[100] and a suite of *Pièces en trio pour*

---

[94] An unpublished letter to Viñes (postmarked 8 Nov. 1919) in US-NH suggests he is composing a suite for piano.

[95] Poulenc's "vendredi" 9 Apr. 1920 letter to Collaer in Collaer 1996, 20-4.

[96] The *Chesterian* 8/17 (Sept.-Oct. 1926), 31 and Schmidt 1995, p. 57 (where one review is quoted in part).

[97] Letters to Gross (23 Oct. [1918]) and Cocteau (14 Nov. [1918]) in Schmidt 1995, FP 12. See also his 20 Nov. [1918] letter to Souberbielle in Poulenc 1994, 18-18 and p. 77 concerning the first performance. Jourdan-Morhange, p. 74 states that Poulenc had only finished two movements by the time of the performance.

[98] Poulenc 1994, 18-13.

[99] Poulenc 1994, 18-22.

[100] Poulenc 1994, 20-3. In 1946 Poulenc composed music for *Paul et Virginie* (FP 132), but no music for the others is known. That Poulenc actually wrote music in 1920 and, in thinking about Radiguet in 1946 tried to reconstruct the song from memory, is indicated in his [Aug. 1946] letter to Bernac. (Schmidt 1995, FP 132 and Poulenc 1994, 46-10.) English translation of *Côte d'Azur* in Crosland, p. 39. See also the unpublished letter from Poulenc to Jean Hugo in US-AUS (date based on Poulenc's remark that he would become a civilian in just eight days).

piano, violoncelle et trompette mentioned in a 14 October 1920 letter to Henri Sauguet.[101] Only the Sonata for Violin and Piano [I] was complete enough to perform. Not a note of these works has come to light, and it is likely that Poulenc destroyed whatever music he wrote.

When Chester issued its inaugural advertisement for Poulenc's first four publications (*Trois mouvements perpétuels*, Sonata for Piano Four Hands, Sonata for Two Clarinets, and *Rapsodie nègre* [the last still in press]) in the October 1919 issue of the *Chesterian* it did so using words obtained from the composer.

> The *Rapsodie Nègre* was written in the Spring of 1917, under the influence of Stravinsky. It is emphatically not meant as a work of the "picturesque" order, but as an essay of free melody, and of reaction against what the composer calls "Impressionist snow." At this moment the influence of Erik Satie begins to render his style more definite. This new outlook leads him to write, a year later (Spring 1918), the two sonatas, one for piano duet, the other for two clarinets. These two works show a still greater tendency to get away from mere harmony, not by the obvious device of orthodox counterpoint, but by what the composer styles as "polytony." In December, 1918, the *Mouvements perpétuels* follow — a new step towards simplicity. The first three months of the present year are occupied by the setting of quatrains from Guilleaume [sic] Apollinaire's *Le Bestiaire ou le Cortège d'Orphée*, with accompaniment of string quartet, flute, clarinet and bassoon. To this succeed the *Cocardes*, a set of songs, which are in a manner the summing up of the methods developed in the previous works. The music of Francis Poulenc may be likened in some ways to the art of Picasso; there is no perspective, as it were, and no elaborate detail. But it must not be surmised from this that he is a "cubist" or "futurist" composer; he is too refined an artist and too great an individual to be dismissed with one of these vaguely comprehensive labels.[102]

ENTR'ACTE: COCTEAU'S *LE COQ ET L'ARLEQUIN;* COLLET'S ANOINTING OF *LES SIX;* AND *LE COQ* AND *LE COQ PARISIEN*

In addition to impresarial interests exhibited in ventures such as the aborted "Séance Music-Hall" performance, Cocteau began to pay much greater attention to music in his published writings. Already comfortable using musical imagery, he exploited knowledge gained through collaboration with Satie on *Parade* and the association with members of "Les Nouveaux Jeunes." His principal literary piece directly related to music is the brief tract *Le Coq et*

---

[101] Poulenc 1994, 20-11.
[102] The *Chesterian* 1/2 (Oct. 1919), 58-9.

l'Arlequin.[103] The composer Ned Rorem has remarked that Cocteau "did not write *about* music, but *around* it, and was careful to subtitle *Le Coq et l'Arlequin* as *Notes autour de la musique.*"[104] *Le Coq et l'Arlequin* was the inaugural offering of the small publishing firm Éditions de la Sirène founded in 1916 by Paul Lafitte and reconstituted by Cendrars and Cocteau.[105] *Le Coq*, a collection of aphorisms and epigrams *à la Nietzsche* or La Rochefoucauld,[106] presents a fervent plea for a "purely French music" in which "The music-hall, the circus, American Negro bands — all this is as fertilizing to an artist as life itself."[107] Numerous writers have attempted to define the intent of this tract, some by calling it the aesthetic doctrine of "Les Nouveaux Jeunes,"[108] others by calling it the flag bearer for an anti-impressionistic stance.[109] Although Poulenc was not in Paris on a regular basis when Cocteau wrote *Le Coq et l'Arlequin*, he was definitely aware of it. Early in 1919, he told Cocteau he awaited a copy of the collection impatiently.[110]

Various members of "Les Nouveaux Jeunes" reflected on Cocteau and his importance to the group. Poulenc wrote:

> He was, if you will, our poetic chronicler far more than our theoretician. [. . .] In fact, *Le Coq et l'Arlequin* is not so much a manifesto of the group, but rather a defense of Satie's aesthetic as opposed to that of the pre-War masters: Debussy, Ravel, and Stravinsky. Cocteau, who had just mounted *Parade* with Satie and Picasso, wished that our aesthetic was his own.[111]

Responding to Stéphane Audel's question about the role Cocteau played in *Les Six*, Poulenc noted:

[103] Concerning the possible play on words involving "Coq" and "Cocteau" see Steegmuller 1970, p. 206.
[104] Rorem 1984, p. 155.
[105] Concerning this press and its publications see Fouché. Cocteau's work was illustrated by Picasso, who contributed two emblems of a cock and a harlequin plus a portrait of Cocteau. Auric, Durey, Honegger, Milhaud, Poulenc, Debussy, Ferroud, Martinu, Rosenthal, Satie, Schmitt, Tansman, Wiéner, among others, were published by this firm.
[106] Hurard-Viltard 1988, p. 36.
[107] Translated in Steegmuller 1970, p. 207.
[108] Harding 1972, p. 65.
[109] Perloff, pp. 7-11.
[110] Unpublished [probably 22 Jan.] letter to Cocteau in US-AUS. When Poulenc attended a Casella-Malipiero-Castelnuovo concert he met Viñes, recently returned from Rome. Moreover, the letter reveals the extent to which Poulenc pushed his own works. He had, he tells Cocteau, asked Bathori about getting pieces by Auric, Durey, Tailleferre and himself performed on a Wednesday concert at the Vieux-Colombier, but had been told to discuss the matter with Walter Straram.
[111] Poulenc 1954, pp. 45-6.

Jean Cocteau, who is attracted by novelty of all sorts, wasn't our theoretician, but our friend and brilliant spokesperson. As a matter of fact, his little musical summary, *Le Coq et l'Arlequin*, is a disguised defense of Satie's aesthetic against Stravinsky's. It is impossible to regard it as a manifesto of *Les Six* because the violent and romantic art of Arthur Honegger is alone enough to contradict it.[112]

Poulenc called Cocteau "a manager of genius, a faithful and marvelous friend," and Honegger (1951) remarked:

> Without being genuinely a musician, Cocteau served as a guide to many young folk. He stood for the general sense of a reaction against the pre-war aesthetic. Each one of us translated that in a different manner.[113]

By the end of 1919, "Les Nouveaux Jeunes" had become a group of artistic consequence: Milhaud had returned from Brazil; Poulenc had been transferred to Paris; and Cocteau, though unsuccessful in getting his works published by *La Nouvelle Revue française*, had succeeded in garnering an increasing share of the spotlight. Although Satie had formally resigned from "Les Nouveaux Jeunes" to pursue a more independent course, his name was still very much attached to the group. In a 16 January 1920 *Comœdia* article, the critic-composer-musicologist Henri Collet compared Rimsky-Korsakov's *Ma Vie musicale* with Cocteau's *Le Coq et l'Arlequin* and the Russian Five with "Les Nouveaux Jeunes."[114] Entitled "Un livre de Rimsky et un livre de Cocteau — les cinq Russes, les six Français et Erik Satie," this article extolled the virtue of Cocteau's pronouncements and affirmed Satie's importance. Collet's second article, printed 23 January, focused on music by six young composers rather than on Cocteau's aesthetic issues.[115] Entitled "Les six Français: Darius Milhaud, Louis Durey, Georges Auric, Arthur Honegger, Francis Poulenc et Germaine Tailleferre," this article forever changed the collective name of these composers from Satie's "Les Nouveaux Jeunes" to "Les Six Français," later simply "Les Six." Poulenc expressed personal enthusiasm for the content telling Collet, "I wish for only one thing; that we will not disappoint you."[116] The group plus Cocteau collectively expressed its gratitude by letter that same month.[117]

The fact is, however, that these composers had appeared together on concert programs well before Collet's pronouncement, and even

---

[112] Poulenc 1963a, p. 52 (Poulenc 1978, pp. 42-3).
[113] Honegger 1966, p. 104.
[114] Reprinted in Roy 1994, pp. 192-8.
[115] Reprinted in Roy 1994, pp. 198-203.
[116] [Ca. 28 Jan. 1920] letter to Collet in Poulenc 1994, 20-2.
[117] Letter to Collet in Volta 1990, pp. 11 and 31.

during Milhaud's absence, Honegger had kept Milhaud's name alive. As a regular reviewer of Parisian concerts, Collet would have known this. Moreover, Poulenc knew Collet was interested in several of his compositions and arranged complimentary copies from Chester. He also listed works by Auric, Durey, and Tailleferre, in case Collet was not yet familiar with them.[118] The publisher Eugène Demets had conceived a volume including music by "notre groupe" plus Satie as early as the summer of 1919.[119] A letter from Milhaud to Honegger lists the composers' names and prospective titles of the pieces.[120] Ultimately published in 1920 as *L'Album des Six*, this thin volume contains six piano pieces: Auric's "Prélude," Durey's "Romance sans paroles," Honegger's "Sarabande," Milhaud's "Mazurka," Poulenc's "Valse," (FP 17), and Tailleferre's "Pastorale." Collet mentioned this unpublished collection in his 16 January article. A guest at Milhaud's apartment for a concert given by these musicians on 8 January 1920, Collet was probably shown a proof copy of *L'Album des Six*.[121] Sometime after Milhaud's return from Brazil—eyewitnesses vary in placing the date between late 1919 and early 1920—his apartment became the place for Saturday evening gatherings by a small group of friends.[122]

> For two years [Milhaud wrote] we met regularly at my place every Saturday evening. Paul Morand would make the cocktails, and then we would go to a little restaurant at the top of the rue Blanche [IXᵉ]. [. . .] After dinner, lured by the steam-driven merry-go-rounds, the mysterious booths, the Daughter of Mars, the shooting-galleries, the games of chance, the menageries, the din of the mechanical organs [. . .] we would visit the Fair of Montmartre, or occasionally the Cirque Médrano to see the Fratellinis in their sketches. [. . .] We finished the evening at my house.[123]

[118] 24 Oct. 1919 letter to Collet in Poulenc 1994, 19-22. By late 1918 Poulenc was already showing great interest in his fellow composers. In an unpublished (typed) letter of 18 Nov. 1918 from Paris to an unnamed person in London Poulenc lists the publishers associated with Milhaud (Durand), Auric (Demets), and himself (Chester) while pleading the need to find a publisher for Durey's first string quartet, which he thought to be "une chose très bien." The quartet, dedicated to Auric, was not published by La Sirène until 1927. Letter in private collection of the author and see Robert, p. (228), op. 10.

[119] Poulenc 1994, p. 98, note 9 (fragment of Durey 's 4 Aug. 1919 letter to Milhaud).

[120] Poulenc 1994, p. 98, note 9 (fragment of Milhaud's 13 Aug. 1919 letter to Honegger). See also Poulenc's 30 Aug. 1919 letter to Cocteau in Poulenc 1994, 19-17 (Poulenc 1991, no. 20).

[121] Poulenc 1994, p. 104.

[122] Perloff, p. 91 summarizes the dates given by Auric and various biographers of *Les Six*, and proffers 1919 as the probable commencement of the "Saturday Soirées."

[123] Milhaud 1953, pp. 98-9 (Milhaud 1987a, p. 84). Hugo 1983, p. 154 also writes of

Poulenc's interest in such gatherings is revealed in a spring 1920 letter to Milhaud in Aix-en-Provence describing an evening divided between Lucien Daudet's home on the rue Bellchasse and that of Valentine and Jean Hugo:

> My dear friend we missed you Saturday. Never has that been as successful. Cocktails 7 o'clock at Lucien's place, then we dined at Gauclair's on the rue Richelieu followed by drinks at the Hugos. Lucien [Daudet], [Count Etienne de] Beaumont, Jean [Cocteau], Radi[guet], Emmanuel [Faÿ], [Marcel] Herrand, [Andrée] Vaurabourg, Simone [Tilliard], [Caspar-Emile Honegger called] Zigo, [Louis] Gautier-Vignal, Durey, [Paul] Morand, Irène [Lagut], Auric, etc. The evening at Valentine's was insane! They put me in a costume and with Jean [Cocteau] at the piano I did a Jean Borlin number. A dance almost in the altogether was above all quite a success. You were sorely missed I can assure you.[124]

Still a third witness to these Saturday evenings was the composer-conductor-pianist Jean Wiéner, another 1911 Milhaud classmate at the Paris Conservatoire. Wiéner was responsible for acting on Milhaud's suggestion that "we find a bistro" so that the group could meet some place other than at his apartment. Wiéner found a wine store on the rue Duphot, near the Madeleine, owned by Louis Moysès which, with the assistance of Milhaud and Cocteau, was turned into a bar called the Gaya, later renamed *Le Bœuf sur le toit*.[125] In his autobiography, Wiéner recounts the events of "a certain evening at the Gaya, in 1920:

> At one table, André Gide, Marc Allégret, and a lady. To their side, Diaghilev, Kochno, Picasso, and Misia Sert. A little farther away, Mlle Mistinguett, Volterra, and Maurice Chevalier. Against the wall, Satie, René Clair, his wife, and Bathori. Then I noticed Picabia debating with Paul Poiret and Tzara . . . Cocteau and Radiguet are saying hello to every table. They embrace Anna de Noailles whom Lucien Daudet, just having entered, rejoins. He is with Marcel Herrand. Yvonne George, all the way at the back, laughs heartily with Auric and the Princess Murat. Léon-Paul Fargue is all alone, standing, in front of the door: Jacques Porel signals him to come to his table. Fernand

---

these Saturday evenings saying that he had known of them through letters from Cocteau until he and Valentine Hugo were able to attend them in Oct. 1920.
[124] "Lundi" [5 Apr. 1920] letter in Poulenc 1994, 20-3. Poulenc 1994, p. 106 contains part of a 4 Apr. 1920 letter from Durey to Milhaud in which he says he accompanied Poulenc in a number entitled "Visions de beauté." Durey reports that Poulenc danced completely in the buff and that Valentine Hugo was afraid her maid would be scandalized by the incident! Cocteau, who called Poulenc's act "difficult to describe," did so in a "Lundi de Pâques" letter to Milhaud in Cocteau 1992, no. 22.
[125] Wiéner 1978, pp. 43-4 and Perloff, p. 92.

Léger gets up and comes to ask us to play *Saint-Louis Blues*[126] . . . Moysès tries to elbow a passage to the middle of this throng. In passing behind me, he says that Arthur Rubinstein will come this evening after his concert. We can already be sure that he will ask me to relinquish my place and that he will play mazurkas by Chopin for the beautiful ladies accompanying him. . .While waiting, Cocteau has come to sit down in front of his drums and,[127] with his sleeves rolled up, he strikes the cymbal a small blow with his stick, from time to time, and right on cue to accompany us in *Old Fashion[ed] Love* which Poulenc listens to religiously, leaning on the piano . . . I did not see Ravel enter, but he is there with Hélène Jourdan-Morhange: they must have passed by the courtyard, too many friends standing blocking the door. They are seeking Misia's table. . . .[128]

If *L'Album des Six* represents the musical maiden voyage of *Les Six*, four issues of the broadsheet *Le Coq* or *Le Coq parisien*, represent the group's first and only literary effort.[129] Though short-lived, this audacious series of broadsheets contained fragments of music, poems, maxims, articles, announcements of events and works in progress, and other items all printed in different type sizes which were arranged in a multitude of directions.[130] Principal contributors include Cocteau and the brilliant young writer Radiguet,[131] Morand and Daudet, plus Jacob and Cendrars. As Cocteau favorites, Poulenc and Auric represented the musicians. Cocteau had already contrib-

[126] Wiéner recorded Handy's piece for Columbia records. Wiéner 1978, p. 213.

[127] We know little about Cocteau's involvement with music as a performer aside from this reference and one of 1921 indicating Cocteau beat the drum at the Gaya (see Chapter V). Ned Rorem, who has given the most complete account of "Cocteau and Music," is silent on this particular point. See Rorem 1984.

[128] *Old Fashioned Love*, a jazz tune from the Broadway musical *Runnin' Wild*, was composed in 1923 by James P. Johnson (pianist and composer 1894-1955). See Bruyninckx, vol. 6, p. 2382 and Perloff, p. 93. Wiéner 1978, pp. 44-5 says he found this quotation written in a small notebook he had kept at the time. It is probable the event took place in 1921, not 1920. Francis Picabia's *L'Oeil cacodylate* (a 1921 ink, gouache, and collage on canvas piece created at Picabia's apartment and later hung for some time in the bar) is a remarkable reminder of the many artists who frequented the establishment. The canvas consists almost entirely of graffiti and signatures written by Milhaud, Poulenc, Cocteau, and others. Reproduced in Volta 1990, p. 12 and Camfield, color plate XI.

[129] Facsimile of the May and June 1920; July-Aug.-Sept., and Nov. 1920 issues in *L'Approdo musicale* 19-20 (1965).

[130] Steegmuller 1970, p. 247 writes: "Le Coq imitated Picabia's *391* in its folded format, fragmented text and variegated typography, and surpassed it in wit and high spirits; it was merrily anti-Dada, although in adopting Dada's methods of slogan and, occasionally, scurrility, it became itself anti-Dada Dada; it was put together chiefly by Cocteau himself and the now seventeen-year-old Raymond Radiguet, with contributions by all the members of the clan."

[131] Radiguet, age seventeen, edited the June issue of *Le Coq* while Cocteau was in England. Crosland, p. 35.

uted to other literary magazines such as *Schéhérazade*, as early as 1908, and with Paul Iribe to *Le Mot*. He founded *Le Coq* partly because he was under siege from other literary magazines.[132] *Le Coq* was brazen in its pronouncements, unflinching in its desire to surprise, and unafraid to parry and thrust with the Parisian establishment.[133] The first of Poulenc's published literary contributions, "Accent populaire," appeared in the November 1920 issue.[134]

Any discussion of *Les Six* embraces intertwined musical, literary, and philosophical issues. Paul Rosenfeld, one of the earliest critics to make distinctions between members of *Les Six*, penetrated the style of each. His September 1921 remarks provide an appropriate end to this brief discussion.

> Individualities do protrude from the pile. The shapes of men are as apparent in the Group as underneath the hide of the elephant on the stage. There is, in the foreground, Germaine Tailleferre, the woman of the house, "die Muse des Montparnasse." She and Arthur Honegger stand out from the group for the reason that they fit into it a little less than the remaining three [Durey having already resigned], Darius Milhaud, Francis Poulenc, and Georges Auric. There is the distinctest family resemblance between the trio. But the resemblance is far less pronounced in the features of Tailleferre and Honegger; almost as indistinct as it was in Durey's case. Tailleferre has nothing of great novelty to say. There is a certain charm and cleverness in what she writes that is feminine. She may in time prove herself a sort of Marie Laurencin of composition. But, at the present moment, the personage she resembles most is Chaminade; a vitriolic Chaminade, it is true, who prefers drinking *amer Picon* straight, musically speaking, to sipping *eau de cologne* off loaves of sugar . . . But her talent is very frail; and her inclusion in the group must be attributed chiefly to a fine enthusiasm for the sex on the part of the five male members. [. . .] The attraction of Poulenc, Auric, and Milhaud lies in the quality of openness they have. They have some contact with the flood of life, and respond to it with a certain directness which even in its exaggeration remains vivid. They, too, are more conventional than they would know; but if they err, it is on the more pardonable side of insolence, indifference, slanginess. One recognizes in their muse the unsentimentality of some of those amazing junior leaguers which the accelerated modern world is casting up. [. . .] Of the three, Poulenc is as yet the least developed. Auric is just as young in years as he; they were both of them born in 1899, later than the rest of the band; but Poulenc rests more juvenile. His music makes one represent him to oneself as a child playing gleefully with toys; chuck-

---

[132] Crosland, pp. 34-5. See also *Les Nouvelles littéraires* (10 Oct. 1925), 7.
[133] Concerning Parisian literary magazines see Steegmuller 1970, pp. 219-33.
[134] Poulenc 1920.

ling and grinning and holding up objects to show them to the elders, and throwing them exuberantly about the nursery. He is gentle, amiable, and devoid of the cruel mockery which makes its appearance in Milhaud at times, and in Auric often. He comes out of "Petrushka"; but he has added Gallic salt and coolth to the playfulness of Strawinsky. He writes sophisticatedly childish tunes for the piano; rhythms repeated over and over again as the improvisations of children sometimes are; "perpetual movements," but subtly varied, subtly prevented from becoming monotonous. There is no one so simple or so complex, so young or so old, who would not smile with pleasure at hearing Poulenc's little gamineries. High spirits, wit, and animal grace break out of the merry brass in the "Ouverture" composed by him for Cocteau's "Spectacle-Concert." The best of his work is still contained in the setting of the *Bestiaire* of Guillaume Apollinaire for soprano, string quartet, flute, clarinet, and bassoon. We will not pretend that the work manifests a rich or a profound musical gift. The music is thin; and witty more than moving, although a genuine poetry sounds from the last song, "Les Carpes." But it is exquisitely appropriate to the mood of Apollinaire's polished little epigrams; and lightly and surely executed. It is said that the newer of Poulenc's works exhibit a satisfactory development.[135]

THE FIRST DADA PROGRAM IN PARIS

In mid-January Poulenc had some of his music included in a "Matinée of *Littérature*," which took place on the 23rd. This first Dada program in Paris was planned by Louis Aragon, André Breton, and Philippe Soupault, coeditors of *Littérature*. The program was conceived

> . . . as moving from a base in the poetry of such established men as Apollinaire, Jacob Reverdy and [Blaise] Cendrars to recitations of poems by themselves, Tzara, Picabia and others. Separating those blocks of readings were interludes devoted to the music of Satie, Milhaud, Auric, Poulenc and [Henri] Cliquet[-Pleyel], and a presentation of the paintings of [Juan] Gris, [Fernand] Léger, [Georgio] de Chirico, [Jacques] Lipchitz, [Georges] Ribemont-Dessaignes and Picabia.[136]

The event caused a scandal when André Breton presented some controversial paintings by Picabia including one entitled *Riz au nez [Laugh in Your Face]*. Not even the introduction of Tristan Tzara, who arrived in Paris on the 17th, could quell the disturbance and in the end many of those present left leaving a nearly empty house.

---

[135] Rosenfeld, pp. 150-3. See the lengthy discussions in Hurard-Viltard 1988 and Roy 1994.
[136] Camfield, p. 135.

Though Poulenc did not ally himself closely with the Dadists, the "Matinée" provided further exposure for the young composer.

SECOND COLLABORATION WITH COCTEAU: THE 1920 "SPECTACLE-CONCERT" AT THE THÉÂTRE DE COMÉDIE DES CHAMPS-ÉLYSÉES

His first attempt to produce a "Séance-Music Hall" having come to naught, Cocteau conceived a second event sometime later during 1919.[137] Called a Spectacle-Concert, it was the first of two Séances financed by Etienne de Beaumont.[138] Auric later wrote that the Séance "was supremely organized by our poet" Cocteau.[139] When presented, beginning with the *répétition générale* on 21 February 1920, the concert included an *Ouverture* by Poulenc, *Adieu, New-York* a fox-trot by Auric,[140] *Cocardes* by Poulenc, and Satie's *Trois petites pièces montées* on its first half followed by Milhaud's *Le Boeuf sur le toit*, the featured piece on the second. Cocteau's attention may have been drawn to *Le Boeuf sur le toit* by an article which appeared in the April 1919 issue of *Littérature* under the pseudonym "Jacaremirim," actually Milhaud himself.[141] Cocteau used the famous Fratellini clowns (Paul, François, and Albert) from the Cirque Médrano for various roles and Guy-Pierre Fauconnet to create the décor, masks, and costumes. When Fauconnet died five days before the premiere, his masks were retained but Raoul Dufy took over.[142]

On the first half, only Poulenc's *Ouverture*, an orchestration of the finale of his Sonata for Piano Four Hands, was not new for the occasion.[143] *Cocardes* (FP 16), however, was conceived for this event, and the texts by Cocteau (then in his Dada period) were tailored to evoke a certain atmosphere. Perloff, discussing popular elements in the music for this concert, writes:

> Each of Cocteau's texts in *Cocardes* presents a kaleidoscopic succession of popular images: "caramel mous", "bonbons", "trapèze",

---

[137] Harding 1972, pp. 75-85; Steegmuller 1970, pp. 238-45; Perloff, pp. 171-86; and Whiting, pp. 498-9.

[138] Milhaud 1953, p. 102 (Milhaud 1987a, p. 87) notes that Cocteau went to Beaumont after he had decided to turn *Le Boeuf sur le toit* into a ballet with a scenario entirely different from Milhaud's conception. The second Spectacle-Concert was a Festival Erik Satie.

[139] Auric 1979, p. 158.

[140] Auric said that this piece was written by someone who had never set foot in New York. Auric 1979, p. 159. It was danced by Tommy Footit and Jackly.

[141] Steegmuller 1970, p. 239. The word means "little crocodile."

[142] Fauconnet was asphyxiated by fumes from his stove. Shead, p. 52 and Cocteau 1992, p. 22.

[143] Concerning Satie's piece see Orledge 1990, p. 319; concerning Auric's see Auric 1979, p. 159. Peignot recalled that she gave the first performance of *Cocardes* at a Princesse de Polignac *soirée*. Peignot 1964, but there is no other substantiation of this claim.

"girafe", "air de Mayol", "cinéma". The impression that words are selected randomly stems from Cocteau's tendency to take the final syllable of one line and use it to begin the next. [. . .] The utter lack of subtlety in Cocteau's manipulation of the text contributes to the hilarity and imparts an irreverence reminiscent both of Satie's comical annotations in his piano pieces of the 1910s and the Dadaist word games.[144]

Cocteau's second poem clearly illustrates these points:

Técla: notre âge d'or. Pipe, Carnot Joffre.	Tecla: our golden age. Pipe, Carnot Joffre.
J'offre à toute personne ayant des névralgies . . .	I offer to everybody who has neuralgia . . .
Girafe. Noce. Un bonjour de Gustave.	Giraffe. Wedding. A good day from Gustave.
Ave Maria de Gounod, Rosière,	Ave Maria by Gounod, Queen of the village
Air de Mayol, Touring-Club, Phonographe.	Air by Mayol, Touring-Club, Phonograph.
Affiche, crime en couleurs. Piano méchanique,	Poster, crime in coulours. Mechanical piano,
Nick Carter; c'est du joli!	Nick Carter; that's a nice thing!
Liberté, Egalité, Fraternité.	Liberty, Equality, Fraternity.[145]

The poems are "remarkable for their lack of cohesion and direction; Cocteau seems to have conceived them aleatorically, with words and images that can be placed in any order, any pattern."[146]

Later, Poulenc wrote:

Cocardes [. . .] were written under the orchestral influence of Stravinsky, though that is less visible here than elsewhere, and under the aesthetic influence, "*tricolore*," of Roger de la Fresnaye. This cycle, also, must be sung without irony. The principal point is to believe in the words which fly like a bird from one branch to another. Médrano of 1920, Paris before 1914 (Bonnot's gang!), Marseilles of 1918 are evoked here. One must try to discern them, like scenes you view in a penholder. I would include *Cocardes* among my "Nogent" works with the smell of frites, the accordion, Piver perfume. In a word, everything that I loved at that age and that I still love. Why not?[147]

---

[144] Perloff, pp. 178-9.
[145] Text and Winifred Radford's translation from Bernac 1977a, p. 182, where all three poems are printed.
[146] Daniel, p. 17.
[147] Complete French texts in Poulenc 1993, p. 15; see also Poulenc 1989, pp. 20-3.

Closer to the time, Poulenc communicated certain details to Paul Collaer in Brussels:

> There is something very special about these songs, namely that the words and the music were written at the same time which led to a perfect understanding. We didn't go our separate ways. I wanted a work devoid of artifice and *earthy*, which makes a statement and rings out. I believe I have succeeded in this. It is above all very Parisian.[148]

Raymond Radiguet, a precocious young writer from Cocteau's circle, wrote after hearing the cycle sung at the Spectacle-Concert:

> Too often it is to the detriment of the words that the music is heard. That of Poulenc does not smother, but underlines these poems which, in some thirty lines, summarize what might be called the patriotism of Paris, the love of a Parisian for his city. A tri-colored flag awakens in us the idea of our country far better than speaking the word "country." Similarly Cocteau's lines do not name Paris. They do better — they evoke it. At café concerts, refreshments can be taken without leaving the seats. Poulenc's music seems to me a musical refreshment.[149]

The first reference to Poulenc's musical setting appears in a 21 June [1919] letter to Souberbielle. After having put aside *Le Bestiaire*, *Poèmes sénégalais*, *Trois pastorales*, and the Sonata for Violin and Piano [I], Poulenc wrote:

> The result, I have composed a *mélodie* (the first of three *Cocardes*) *absolutely* good; I love this work as I love the Sonata for Two Clarinets, you will probably be astonished because it scarcely resembles what I have done up to now; it is rather complex, longer than the *mélodies* of Debussy and absolutely new as vocal writing. The singer will sing what in our time is something rare. There is even a certain bel canto side which would not perhaps have displeased Gounod.[150]

Two months later the piano version of all three songs was complete and Alfredo Casella suggested he offer them to Chester for publication.[151] When Poulenc orchestrated *Cocardes* for small orchestra (violin, cornet, trombone, bass drum, triangle, and cymbals) is unknown, but he announced its instrumentation to Collaer in a 21 January 1920 letter, and the work was first performed in this version.[152] Auric, taken by Poulenc's choice of instruments, wrote, "The

---

[148] Poulenc 1994, 20-1.
[149] Quoted from Bernac 1977a, p. 183 (Bernac 1978, pp. 166-7).
[150] Poulenc 1994, 19-15. The printed score indicates that the pieces were composed between Apr. and June 1919, but this seems to be incorrect.
[151] 30 Aug. 1919 letter to Cocteau in Poulenc 1994, 19-17. The pieces were actually published by Éditions de la Sirène in mid-1920.
[152] Poulenc 1994, 20-1.

small orchestra of *Cocardes* by Francis Poulenc delighted me as much as a page of Rameau."[153]

Not only did Poulenc develop a close working relationship with Cocteau during his years of military service, but he also gained entry into Diaghilev's world. In 1920 (Poulenc mistakenly says 1921) he was invited to Misia's apartment to hear Ravel play *La Valse* for Diaghilev. Marcelle Meyer (who assisted at a second piano), Léonide Massine, Stravinsky, several Diaghilev secretaries, and Misia's husband José-Maria Sert also attended. Diaghilev dismissed it as "a portrait of a ballet." Poulenc recalls being humbled that day. "Ravel proceeded to give me a lesson in modesty which has remained with me my entire life: he picked up his music very quietly and, without worrying about what we thought of it, calmly left the room."[154]

According to Ballets Suédois historian Bengt Häger, Poulenc also contributed music to *Sculpture nègre* choreographed and danced by Jean Börlin in his first solo recital at the Comédie des Champs-Élysées on 25 March 1920.[155] Pierre Scize, who witnessed the production, wrote, "Dressed in a costume [by Paul Colin] imitating a wooden African statuette (later echoed in *La Création du monde*), he danced this piece in a deliberately ponderous fashion."[156] Poulenc's score is quite probably his earlier *Rapsodie nègre*.[157] Börlin danced *Sculpture nègre* on at least two other occasions: 30 November and 24 December 1929 at the Théâtre des Champs-Élysées with the Orchestre Straram conducted by Vladimir Golschmann and Eugène Bigot respectively.[158]

As the spring Parisian performing arts season neared its end, Diaghilev presented the second of his three new 1920 offerings, Stravinsky's *Pulcinella*, which opened at the Opéra on 15 May.[159] Picasso designed the sets, costumes, and drop curtain. Jean Hugo, who witnessed the premiere with Picasso from Misia Sert's box, has left a splendid account of the party that followed. Given by Persian Prince Firouz, the party took place in a suburb called Robinson at an establishment run by René de Amouretti. Hugo remembers that the guests included Diaghilev, Picasso and his wife, Léonide Massine, Misia and José-Maria Sert, Princess Eugène Murat, Hoytie Wiborg,

---

[153] *Le Coq* (May 1920) and Volta 1990, pp. 12-13.
[154] Poulenc 1963a, p. 179 (Poulenc 1978, p. 129 and Nichols 1988, p. 118).
[155] Häger, pp. 67-71.
[156] Quoted in Häger, p. 68 (includes several illustrations).
[157] Watkins, p. 108.
[158] *Le Guide du concert et des théâtres lyriques* 16 (22 Nov. 1929), 230 and 20 (Dec. 1929), 353.
[159] The other productions were Stravinsky's *Le Chant du rossignol*, with sets, costumes, and curtain by Henri Matisse and choreography by Massine (which opened on 2 Feb.) and *Le Astuzie femminili*, with sets, costumes, and curtain by José-Maria Sert. The music for this ballet, originally by Domenico Cimarosa, was

Lucien Daudet, Jean Cocteau, Georges Auric, Poulenc and Raymond Radiguet.[160] Champagne flowed and Stravinsky became so drunk that he ascended to one of the bedrooms, gathered bedding, and threw it from a balcony into the assembled guests. A pillow fight ensued and the party did not end until three in the morning. Poulenc was to attend other Stravinsky premieres before the twenties passed, but not one produced such frivolity!

MILITARY YEARS AT A CLOSE

In the summer before Poulenc's discharge, while *Le Boeuf sur le toit* was being premiered in London as *The Nothing-Doing-Bar*, Poulenc visited Albert Roussel and his wife at "Vastérival," their home in Varengeville-sur-Mer, just to the southwest of Dieppe.[161] From there he wrote letters to Cocteau (undated, but probably 7 July),[162] Milhaud (8 and 26 July),[163] and Radiguet (undated, but early in his stay).[164] Poulenc, who valued Roussel's advice and counsel, told Cocteau, "Roussel is truly charming and so clairvoyant, what a difference from Maurice R[avel]."[165] To Milhaud he added: "Who of his generation could offer works of such equal quality as *Evocations*, *Le Festin*, *Padmâvati*, the *Symphonie*, and the *Sinfonietta*. I converted him to *Socrate*."[166] The letter to Radiguet suggests that he was waiting for Radiguet to send him some poetry, "I have the intention of making a suite of five or six *mélodies* in the style 'Ile d'amour'."

He also spent a few days in Offranville, some kilometers southwest of Dieppe, with Jacques-Emile Blanche, the noted painter, writer, and art critic. Precisely how he met Blanche is unknown, but Blanche was friendly with Cocteau and Stravinsky, having painted them in 1913 and 1915 respectively. Blanche, whom Poulenc later frequently visited during the 1930s, painted three portraits of Poulenc in his military uniform. The first verson dates from 18 July 1918 and belonged to Mme Paul Liénard; a second version painted the next day and dedicated to Milhaud is in a private collection, and a third version is known only from a 1920 photograph in Blanche's studio.[167]

---

orchestrated and provided with recitatives by Ottorino Respighi. It debuted on 27 May, also at the Opéra.

[160] Hugo 1976, p. 67. See also Gold, p. 233.

[161] Poulenc stayed at the Hôtel de la Terrasse.

[162] Unpublished letter to Cocteau in US-AUS. Poulenc had arrived that morning.

[163] 8 July letter in Poulenc 1994, 20-5, and p. 103, note 3.

[164] Unpublished letter in US-AUS.

[165] In early 1929, Poulenc wrote "Pièce brève sur le nom d'Albert Roussel" (FP 50), one of the eight pieces in a collective *Hommage à Albert Roussel* for his sixtieth birthday.

[166] Poulenc 1994, p. 103, note 3.

[167] François Bergot, "Mes modèles" in Blanche, p. 186. The portraits of Cocteau and Stravinsky are also reproduced and discussed.

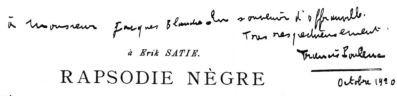

à *Erik SATIE.*

RAPSODIE NÈGRE

Poème de
Makoko Kangourou

Musique de
Francis POULENC.

I. Prélude

Plate 5: *Opening page of* **Rapsodie nègre** *inscribed to Jacques-Emile Blanche (former collecton of Dame Joan Sutherland and Richard Bonynge)*

(Concerning portraits of Poulenc see Appendix 4.) Two years later Blanche completed his famous painting of five members of *Les Six*, Marcelle Meyer, and Jean Wiéner (who replaced Durey).[168] In October Poulenc presented Blanche with an inscribed printed copy of *Rapsodie nègre* in gratitude for their time together in Offranville (Plate 5).[169]

As Poulenc's military years ended, four other works were on his drawing board, all of which were performed after his discharge from active duty: three pieces for piano entitled *Napoli* (1919-summer 1920: FP 40), six *Impromptus* (September 1920-May 1921: FP 21), incidental music for Cocteau's and Radiguet's *Le Gendarme incompris* (October-November 1920: FP 20),[170] and *Quatre poèmes de Max Jacob* (July 1920-September 1921: FP 22) which he was already discussing with Jacob and Milhaud during the summer of 1920.[171]

---

[168] Discussed in the next chapter.
[169] Formerly owned by Dame Joan Sutherland and Richard Bonynge, now in the author's collection.
[170] Cocteau 1971.
[171] First mentioned in an 8 July [1920] letter to Milhaud: "I am working not too

"It is paradoxical, but true [. . .] that my piano music is the least representative genre in my output."[172] Poulenc's observation surely applies to *Napoli* and the six *Impromptus*. The earliest history of *Napoli* is obscure, and the information contradictory.[173] In a letter to Sauguet, Poulenc dates the work "summer 1920."[174] In one to Collaer just over two years later, however, he suggests "1919-1920."[175] The holograph manuscript gives "1922-24" next to which Poulenc has written, "I promise to finish this suite before 1930."[176] Poulenc actually wrote a three-movement suite ("Barcarole," "Nocturne," "Caprice italien"), completing the final movement by early October 1920. [177] This version was never published, and the final movement was revised before publication in 1926.

The six *Impromptus*, as they were listed in the 1922 publication, dedicated to Marcelle Meyer, mark the beginning of a period in which Poulenc was obviously searching for his compositional identity.[178] He could no longer rely exclusively on instinct, but required the tutelage of a composition teacher to make up for Viñes' waning influence and his lack of formal training at an institution such as the Conservatoire. All four works under discussion were either later suppressed by Poulenc or considerably revised. Moreover, all show struggles with greater complexity of texture, flirtation with increasing dissonance juxtaposed with more familiar popular elements,

---

badly, I am preparing some songs full of surprises for voice, trumpet, flute, clarinet, oboe, and bassoon in a pastoral genre." Poulenc 1994, 20-5. It is probable that this letter was sent after 20-7 (Jacob to Poulenc in which Jacob enclosed the poems) and 20-8 (Poulenc to Milhaud in which Poulenc copied the fourth poem "Dans le buisson de mimosa") which Chimènes dates "summer 1920."

[172] Quoted in Jourdan-Morhange, p. 133.

[173] *Napoli* must have changed considerably in length. Poulenc first estimated its duration at five minutes ("vendredi" [7 July 1922] letter to Collaer in Poulenc 1994, 22-14 and Collaer 1996, 22-14). The published version takes longer to perform. Paul Crossley's performance for CBS Records (M3K 4491) takes 11'16" and Gabriel Tacchino's for EMI (CMS 7 62551 2) takes 9'30".

[174] 14 Oct. 1920 letter in Poulenc 1994, 20-11.

[175] Collaer 1996, 22-19 (fragment in Poulenc 1994, p. 112, note 4).

[176] Transcription in Schmidt 1995, FP 40.

[177] 7 Oct. 1920 letter to Durey in Poulenc 1994, 20-10 and fragment of his 26 July [1920] letter to Milhaud in note 4. La Sirène did not publish the work and in a [6 Dec. 1921] letter to Cœuroy Poulenc suggested that it would be published by Demets. (Poulenc 1994, 21-26.) Poulenc also submitted one movement to Robert Brussel, who had asked for something he could print in *Le Figaro*, but this too came to naught. ("Samedi" [15 Apr. 1922] letter to Milhaud in Poulenc 1994, 22-5.) Poulenc's [July 1922] letter to Milhaud in Poulenc 1994, 22-1 informs us that Demets reneged.

[178] Poulenc certainly met Meyer much earlier at Viñes' studio. Meyer appears prominently in Blanche's famous ca. 1921 portrait of *Les Six* (color reproduction in Volta 1990, p. 9).

experimentation with changing meters, and a general lack of formal counterpoint. In *Impromptu* no. 1, for example, C major is the frame of reference, but certainly not the innocent C of "Valse" from *Album des Six*. Rather, Poulenc places augmented seconds and augmented unisons on strong beats, and in the last five bars including the final chord simultaneously sounds both the minor and major third (E and E-flat) above the tonic. No. 3 is reminiscent of Milhaud's 1920 shimmy *Caramel mou*, which Poulenc heard frequently. The jazzy opening, with its jaunty dotted-rhythm melody over a six-note (one measure) ostinato, owes a debt to Milhaud, whose work is in turn indebted to Auric's equally popular fox-trot *Adieu, New-York!*[179] This impromptu also deals with changing meters, but Poulenc did not approach the problem of shifting numbers of eighth notes as seen later in *Promenades* or *Les Biches*. None was particularly successful, even after revision in 1924.[180]

Le Gendarme incompris was apparently initially conceived by Radiguet, who "had persuaded Cocteau to take part in writing a short play in which Mallarmé and admirers of Mallarmé would be attacked, amusingly, of course."[181] Cocteau and Radiguet wrote this play during the latter's summer 1920 visit to Le Picquey. Because Cocteau had contracted a bad cold, "Radiguet was made to stay on the balcony outside Cocteau's room so that *he* would not catch the cold. Cocteau wrote to his mother that he 'dictated' to his young friend from ten in the morning until three in the afternoon."[182]

> The plot tells of a country policeman who, while on his beat through lands owned by the marquise de Montonson, observes a priest behaving in an equivocal manner. A charge is brought, the case is heard, and it turns out that the "priest" was none other than the marquise. Dressed in a black robe and wearing a hat, the ancient noblewoman had been contorting her body into peculiar stances in order to get at some inaccessible flowers she wanted to pick. The marquise invites the judge to dinner, and the policeman, whose zeal for promotion had inspired the charge, is laughed out of court. The big joke of the proceedings is that the report which the policeman reads in broad, comic tones is none other than Mallarmé's prose-poem "l'Ecclésiastique", where the priest, his blood stirred by the approach of spring, gambols among the shrubs of the bois de Boulogne in a highly unecclesiastical manner.[183]

[179] Perloff, pp. 173-7.
[180] In a "samedi" [25 Mar. 1922] letter to Collaer Poulenc said the *Impromptus* would be published in a week. Collaer 1996, 22-5.
[181] Crosland, pp. 69-70.
[182] Crosland, p. 70.
[183] Harding 1972, p. 96.

When Poulenc wrote to Paul Collaer in late 1920, he was under the impression that *Le Gendarme incompris* would be produced in Paris in late January.[184] Instead, it concluded a program given at the Théâtre Michel (rue des Mathurins) on 24-26 May 1921 during a "Spectacle de Théâtre bouffe" presented by Pierre Bertin.[185] The remainder of the program included *La Femme fatale* ("Drame lyrique en un acte" by Jacob, now lost), *La Piège de Méduse* ("Comédie lyrique en un acte" in 9 scenes with music [seven dances] for clarinet, trumpet, trombone, percussion, violin, violoncello, and contrabass by Satie),[186] *Caramel mou* ("Shimmy pour jazz-band" [clarinet, saxophone, trumpet, trombone, and piano] on words by Cocteau set by Milhaud, and danced by the American Negro Gratton);[187] and *Les Pélicans* ("Pièce en deux actes" by Radiguet with incidental music by Auric).[188]

Poulenc's music for *Le Gendarme incompris,* including an overture, two songs, two duets, and a finale with a little dance,[189] was championed by Milhaud. "*Le Gendarme incompris* is a marvelous thing for the instruments, of so clear a sensibility, and one feels it full of music throughout. The charm and the abundance of melodies make it something that is exceedingly successful."[190] Later, he recalled, "Poulenc had composed music so witty and pungent that I have always felt sorry he would not allow it to be played again."[191] In fact, Poulenc's arrangement as an "Ouverture, Madrigal, Final," was performed in London as an entr'acte by the Ballets Russes on 11 July during the 26 May-30 July run of performances, and again by Milhaud for a Salle des Agriculteurs concert arranged by Jean Wiéner on 15 December 1921.[192] Ansermet also performed it on 22 February

---

[184] Collaer 1965, p. 49 (French), Poulenc 1991, pp. 316-7 (English), Poulenc 1994, 20-13 (dated 5 Dec. 1920), Collaer 1996, 20-8), and Schmidt, FP 20.
[185] French text in Cocteau 1946, vol. 6, 11-50 and Cocteau 1971, pp. 39-69 (which also includes Cocteau's article on the performance published in *Comœdia* (28 May 1921).
[186] Orledge 1990, pp. 297-8.
[187] Collaer 1988, p. 296. For Milhaud's recollection see Milhaud 1953, p. 120 (Milhaud 1987a, pp. 101-02).
[188] Translation in Benedikt, pp. 117-29.
[189] "Samedi" [5] Dec. [1920] letter to Collaer in Poulenc 1991, pp. 326-7; Poulenc 1994, 20-13; Collaer 1996, 20-8; and Schmidt, FP 20. Poulenc misdates this letter 6 Dec.
[190] Milhaud's [24 May 1921] letter to Collaer in Collaer 1996, 21-22 (Collaer 1956, pp. 53-4).
[191] Milhaud 1953, p. 120 (Milhaud 1987a, p. 101).
[192] Ansermet wrote Poulenc on 20 July [1921] from London telling him that he had been especially pleased with *Le Gendarme,* but that at the first performance the audience had whistled loudly. Poulenc 1994, 21-13. Poulenc immediately transmitted this news to Milhaud (fragment of his letter quoted in Poulenc 1994,

1923 in Geneva.[193] After that it was suppressed, only to be reconstructed by Roger Nichols for the Exeter Festival in 1987 and edited by Daniel Swift based on a piano score Poulenc gave to Raymonde Linossier and a full score in a private French collection. Poulenc had hoped to have the work published by Éditions de la Sirène, Chester, or some unnamed American firm, but it never was.[194]

Quatre poèmes de Max Jacob, the third and final work begun in the months before return to civilian life, is alluded to in a summer 1920 letter from Jacob to Poulenc.[195] With it Jacob sent poems Poulenc had requested earlier. Although no titles are given, Poulenc transcribed the text of "Dans le buisson de mimosa" (no. 3) to Milhaud a short time later, noting that he had written music for it.[196] The cycle was mentioned publicly in the November 1920 issue of *Le Coq parisien*, which prematurely announced a Salle Gaveau performance at a Golschmann concert.[197] Since Poulenc composed the bulk of the music in August and September 1921, we will discuss it in the next chapter. This cycle continues the stylistic exploration described in discussions of the *Impromptus* and *Le Gendarme incompris*.

Poulenc's three-year conscription, begun in depressing surroundings often some distance from his beloved Paris, ended with a desk job which allowed him ample time for composing, attending concerts, and performing. By 1921 he was an established composer whose music was well-known to the Parisian avant-garde, and who could claim a wide circle of friends including artists, musicians, writers, critics, and noteworthy performers. This is symbolized by two more high-profile appearances: (1) participation in the 10 December 1920 opening of an *Exposition Picabia* at the Galerie Povolozky as part of Cocteau's "infernal jazz band"[198] and (2) 31 December 1920 participation in *Les Bal des artistes* "Grande fête de bienfaisance" organized by *Comœdia* and held at the Olympia theater.[199] *Bal* patrons were urged to come masked, and *de rigueur* costumes had to include

p. 130, note 1) and Collaer (Poulenc's "jeudi" [28 July 1921] letter in Poulenc 1994, 21-16 and Collaer 1996, 21-27). He then wrote Ansermet in late July that he was transcribing the Waltz for orchestra without voice and asking him to intercede with Kling to get the work published. Poulenc 1994, 21-14.

[193] Precisely what Ansermet performed, however, is clouded by Poulenc's 5 Aug. 1921 letter to Collaer in which he says he had just finished the suite that same day. Collaer 1996, 21-28.

[194] Details about revivals and manuscripts in Schmidt 1995, FP 20.

[195] Poulenc 1994, 20-7 (Poulenc 1991, no. 35: misdated 1921).

[196] Poulenc 1994, 20-8.

[197] Full entry in Schmidt 1995, FP 22.

[198] Camfield, pp. 157-8. Apparently they played Auric's *Adieu, New-York* and Milhaud's "Tango" from *Le Bœuf sur le toit* "on piano, drums, cymbals, castanets, reed pipes, Klaxon horn and glasses."

[199] Brief history of this theater in Feschotte, pp. 109-11.

the colors red and white. Guests were entertained by two orchestras, one "Le Jazz-Band de l'Olympia" and the other "Le Jazz-Band
Parisien" consisting of Auric, Cocteau, Poulenc, Milhaud, and
Honegger.[200] In a 1935 lecture/recital, Poulenc confessed his dislike
for jazz as an art form. To a lady who asked if he liked jazz, he
responded:

> Certainly not! I do not like it and I especially don't want to hear about
> its influence on contemporary music. Born in New York [. . .] this
> substitute amuses me when I listen to it on records while bathing, but
> it is frankly odious to me in the concert hall. [. . .] Can anyone cite a
> single work of quality that it has inspired![201]

As the military years closed his works had not only been published in Paris by Éditions de la Sirène and Demets, but also in London by J. & W. Chester. Poulenc, who had a long and close association with this London firm, later thanked Stravinsky and Diaghilev
for the introduction which made it possible.[202] Chester, then directed
by Otto Marius Kling, did much to promote Poulenc's European
reputation.[203] Through its house journal the *Chesterian,* they often
advertised and feted Poulenc and the association with Chester later
flourished under Robert Douglas Gibson, who continued to publish
and promote his music.

The Twenties had now dawned and Poulenc faced a compositional
crisis already manifested in works of later 1920. He addressed the
crisis by taking Milhaud's advice to study with Charles Koechlin,
by making trips to Austria-Hungary-Yugoslavia (1921) and Italy

---

[200] Listing in *Comœdia* (27 Dec. 1920), 1. Extensive articles were also printed in the
22-26, and 28-31 Dec. issues. Entertainers included Mistinguett, Harry Pilcer,
Germaine Sallandri of the Opéra-Comique, and the Sherry Girls. Hundreds of
items from perfumes to works of art were donated for charity. A 2 Jan. 1921
article called the receipts "magnificent" and the event "a grand success."
[201] Poulenc 1935a, p. 524. Few Poulenc works show any jazz influence in spite of
the fact he played jazz occasionally in the early 1920s. Exceptions are "Rag-
Mazurka" from *Les Biches* and the third *Impromptu* from the revised 1924 set.
[202] Poulenc 1935a, p. 524. Poulenc sent the following letter to Chester, which was
printed in English in the *Chesterian* (June 1947), 3: "Dear Friend, I was very
delighted to hear that THE CHESTERIAN was to be revived under your direction. I
feel quite sure that this will be beneficial to the cause of French music, of which
you have been for so long the faithful and efficient friend. And I need hardly
remind you of my attachment to the House of Chester — I shall never forget that
it was they who published my first works on the recommendation of Stravinsky.
Wishing you every success and with warmest greetings to our friend Gibson.
FRANCIS POULENC."
[203] Poulenc received a great boost from Ansermet, who favorably reviewed the
Chester edition of his Sonata for Piano Four Hands in *La Revue romande* (1 Oct.
1919; reprinted in Machart, pp. 30-1.)

(1922) to experience new lands and new music, and by association with Diaghilev, who offered him commissions. In the early 1920s Poulenc also realized that though Paris could provide the ferment for his musical ideas, with its busy concerts and performance opportunities, it was unsuitable for their distillation into works of art. For that he sought the relative tranquillity of Touraine locations such as Amboise and later "Le Grand Coteau," the Noizay estate he purchased. By the end of the 1920s, the pattern of Poulenc's life was established and he settled down to write some of the enduring works of his compositional career.

V

Expanding Horizons: 1921-1926

The years 1921 through 1926 are framed by *Les Mariés de la Tour Eiffel* (FP 23), the zany collaborative work for the Ballets Suédois, and the Trio (for Oboe, Bassoon, and Piano: FP 43). Poulenc's world expanded greatly during these years, and although Paris remained the center of his musical orbit, he began to compose in the Touraine region, residing in Nazelles (five kilometers to the east of Noizay) or Amboise. His fondness for the region led to his purchase of a sixteenth-century Noizay estate named "Le Grand Coteau" in 1927. He also began traveling outside France, expanded his already extensive musical repertoire, and his circle of friends and acquaintances grew to include Béla Bartók, Serge Prokofiev, Arnold Schönberg, Anton Webern, Alban Berg, Egon Wellesz, Marya Freund, Alfredo Casella, Gian Francesco Malipiero, Vittorio Rieti, Mario Labroca, Henri Sauguet, and Wanda Landowska.[1]

Studying composition formally for the first time, Poulenc wrote his maiden choral piece *Chanson à boire* and the ballet *Les Biches*. The former was an American commission for the Harvard Glee Club and the latter a Diaghilev commission for the Ballets Russes. *Les Biches* and the Trio both show compositional maturity and rank among Poulenc's best works. Finally, 1926 marked the beginning of an extraordinary performance collaboration with Pierre Bernac, the baritone who premiered Poulenc's *Chansons gaillardes* accompanied by the composer. Nearly a decade later they gave their initial full recital together, becoming, along with Peter Pears and Benjamin Britten, one of this century's premier piano/vocal duos.

As Poulenc's world expanded, Paris in the 1920s became a magnet for Americans seeking new stimuli and experiences.[2] During

---

[1] Poulenc had actually met several of these individuals earlier.
[2] Partially based on material in Carpenter, Morton, and Rosenstiel.

the teens a small number of Americans, including Gertrude Stein, Alice B. Toklas, and Sylvia Beach (proprietress of the Shakespeare and Company bookstore), became fixtures of Parisian cultural life. They joined Princess Edmond de Polignac (née Winnaretta Singer), whose sewing machine fortune financed one of Paris' most successful artistic salons, and Sylvia Barney, the noted lesbian artist who came to Paris after the turn of the century. In the next decade the trickle became a flood with Shakespeare and Company the locus where many immigrant writers congregated. Among them were Sherwood Anderson (then in his late forties), Ernest Hemingway (recovered from wounds received in Europe during World War I), and Robert McAlmon (who befriended James Joyce during the writing of *Ulysses*). Ever mindful of the debt owed to the United States for its entry as an ally into World War I on 6 April 1917, France welcomed Americans to a stimulating environment.

Writers were not the only Americans attracted to Paris. As the war raged, an organization called American Friends of Musicians in France was formed, through which a considerable amount of money was donated to maintain cultural activities.[3] Central figures to this effort such as Walter Damrosch later played a significant role in the founding of the Conservatoire Américain at Fontainebleau in 1921. Once established, this institution and one of its teachers, the exceedingly talented Nadia Boulanger, attracted countless Americans to Paris including Aaron Copland, Herbert Elwell, Virgil Thomson, and Walter Piston. George Gershwin was another early arrival. Though Poulenc's path seldom crossed those of the American writers, he became friendly with Nadia Boulanger, Aaron Copland, and Virgil Thomson and, like Boulanger, thought highly of America.

During the 1920s several writers with whom Poulenc later became associated established or enhanced their reputations. Poulenc had already met Eluard, Fargue, Aragon, and Breton at Monnier's bookstore. In the 1930s he frequently turned to Eluard for texts, and in the 1940s Eluard's *Liberté* supplied the requisite patriotic message for Poulenc's cantata *Figure humaine*. André Gide, author of *La Symphonie Pastorale* (1919), continued to solidify his reputation in the 1920s by publishing *Les Faux-Monnayeurs* in 1926; Poulenc corresponded with him in the 1930s. He also came to know Paul Valéry's writings during the early 1920s. Valéry and Gide were important figures who helped shape French literary thought through the influential journal *La Nouvelle Revue française* (NRF). Poulenc later set to music one of Valéry's poems written in 1920.

Three further contributors to French literature of the 1920s, whose words he used, were Colette, Jean Giraudoux, and George Bernanos.

---

[3] Concerning American musicians in Paris see Brody 1987, pp. 225-47.

Colette's works *Chéri* (1920) and *Fin de Chéri* (1929) framed the decade. Later she became his friend and critic, and he set one of her poems to music in 1938. Giraudoux mostly produced stories in the 1920s, but was writing plays in the 1930s when Poulenc became associated with him. Later Poulenc was mesmerized by the final work of Bernanos, another Catholic writer whose masterpiece *Dialogues des Carmélites* he set as an opera. It is no doubt Bernanos' "compassion for human suffering" that appealed to him most.[4] Poulenc always preferred poetry to prose, however, and formed his closest bonds with poets. He also knew François Mauriac, one of several important Catholic writers of the 1920s from the time when Jacques-Emile Blanche painted his portrait.[5] The two saw each other frequently during World War II.

After returning to civilian life, politics in the aftermath of World War I seem to have affected Poulenc little, and his letters seldom refer to political events. For example, when the German government asked for a three- to four-year moratorium on war reparations to the French Government , the French answered in January 1923 by sending 40,000 French troops into the Ruhr. Eventually, buoyed by world public opinion, the Germans refused to cooperate and the debacle cost the French dearly. The money needed to sustain the expeditionary force adversely affected the franc, and the French were labeled as isolationists. Through it all, Poulenc kept his sights on becoming a more disciplined composer and solidifying his position among his peers. He worried only when his inheritance was jeopardized by the effect of political events on the economy.

TRANSITION BACK TO CIVILIAN LIFE

Eight days before release from military service Poulenc was finishing work on *Le Gendarme incompris*, the piano *Impromptus*, and the *Quatre poèmes de Max Jacob*.[6] Once released in January 1921, he left for southern France and spent time with the gifted artist Roger de La Fresnaye (1885-1925) to whom he was introduced by the Hugos.[7] La Fresnaye, then staying at the Villa Félicie in Grasse, made several pencil drawings of Poulenc on 1 and 7 February 1921 and complained to Jean Hugo a few days later that he could not complete work because Poulenc had left.[8] During his stay Poulenc also had lunch

---

[4] Tint, p. 43.
[5] Poulenc 1994, p. 1037.
[6] Unpublished [9 Jan. 1921] letter to Hugo in US-AUS.
[7] Meeting date unknown. Poulenc was already inquiring after La Fresnaye in a 23 Oct. [1918] letter to Valentine Gross. Poulenc 1994, 18-13.
[8] A late [27?] Jan. postcard to Valentine says he had already visited La Fresnaye once and would return "lundi" [31?] for two more days. Poulenc left for Paris on 3 Feb. Unpublished card in US-AUS. Two La Fresnaye drawings are repro-

with the writer Lucien Daudet at Cap d'Ail and said he might attend a Paul Poiret fête at the casino.

Poulenc soon ventured farther afield. In early March he wrote Valentine Hugo: "Today I depart for Rome. [I am] very moved to leave FRANCE for the first time in my life."[9] He was then thinking about "my first *large work* an *opéra-ballet bouffe* (in the style of *Don Giovanni*) for Diaghilev."[10] This is his earliest mention of what became *Les Biches*.[11] Poulenc and Milhaud remained in Rome until the end of March playing a concert of music by Satie and *Les Six* on the 21st.[12] At least several concerts were arranged by the composer Gian Francesco Malipiero, who would become Poulenc's devoted friend.[13] Poulenc ate breakfast with the artist André Derain, who was about to return to Paris, and a week later he wrote Viñes that his last concert tour had made a great impression.[14]

COLLABORATION ON *LES MARIÉS DE LA TOUR EIFFEL*

Before leaving for Rome Poulenc composed at least one of his assigned sections for Cocteau's ballet *Les Mariés de la Tour Eiffel* (FP 23).[15] Originally entitled *La Noce* or *La Noce massacrée*, this work was commissioned by Rolf de Maré, who had brought his Ballets Suédois to Paris during the winter of 1920-21.[16] The Ballets Suédois boldly advertised itself as "the only one which 'dared'," "the only one representative of contemporary life," and "the only one truly against

duced in Seligman, p. 247, no. 489 (inscribed "Grasse le 1er Février 21 | R de la Fresnaye") and no. 490 (inscribed "Grasse - Portraits | Photographe d'art"). One which appears to be identical to no. 490, is reproduced in Kochno 1970, p. 200, but this copy contains the added inscription in Poulenc's hand "à Boris [Kochno] | son fidèle | Poulenc | 1926." In 1921, La Fresnaye also drew portraits of Poulenc's friends including the Hugos, Radiguet, Cocteau, Chalupt, Marie Laurencin, Lagut, and Auric. In a 7 May [1921] letter to Collaer Poulenc added "Ci-joint mon portrait par La Fresnaye." Poulenc 1994, 21-8 (Collaer 1996, 21-16).
[9] [5 Mar. 1921] postcard in Poulenc 1994, p. 120, note 1. Poulenc's precise departure date is unknown. Auric wrote Collaer on "vendredi" [11 Mar. 1921] that Milhaud and Poulenc had left on "mardi" [9 Mar.]. Collaer 1996, 21-9.
[10] "Dimanche" [6 Mar. 1921 letter, incorrectly dated 9 Mar.] in Poulenc 1994, 21-3 (Collaer 1996, 21-8).
[11] *Les Demoiselles*, intended as a collaboration with Germaine Bongard, is discussed later. Poulenc 1994, 21-3 (Collaer 1996, 21-8).
[12] Poulenc 1994, p. 147, note 1. Poulenc played the first piano part of *Le Boeuf sur le toit* "passably."
[13] Malipiero's moving tribute after Poulenc's death is in JournalMF 1963.
[14] Unpublished postcard to Valentine in US-AUS and [Rome, 28 Mar. 1921] postcard in Poulenc 1994, p. 120, note 1 (Poulenc 1991, p. 326) respectively.
[15] In a "dimanche" [6 Mar. 1921] letter to Collaer, Poulenc wrote: "I am working. I finished my 'Dance for the Trouville Bathing Girl' for the *Wedding*." Poulenc 1994, 21-3 (Collaer 1996, 21-8). See also Cocteau 1965.
[16] See Häger's superbly illustrated volume and Maré.

academicism."[17]   When Diaghilev declined to produce Milhaud's and Claudel's unperformed *L'Homme et son Désir*, Maré accepted the challenge.   Maré also asked Cocteau to write a *pièce-ballet* or play-ballet for his inaugural season. *La Noce massacrée* was read for Maré and members of his troupe on 23 February 1921 at the Hugo's home in the Palais-Royale. This reading was probably not attended by Poulenc.[18] Auric was supposed to write all the music, but with time short music became the collective work of Auric, Honegger, Milhaud, Poulenc, and Tailleferre.[19] Durey opted out for reasons of health, and formally resigned from *Les Six*.[20]

Steegmuller sees the plot of *Les Mariés* as "an updating in more ways than one of Emile Zola's famous wedding party in *L'Assommoir* and its hilarious visits to the Louvre and the Vendôme column."[21] Watkins notes that "in *Les Mariés* a popular French tradition of ancient stock was appropriated in the service of caricaturing bourgeois rites, big game hunters, sideshow entertainers, and flatulent generals."[22] Milhaud left the following description:

> The plot was quite simple: a young newly married couple, accompanied by their parents and an old friend, a general, have come to have their wedding banquet on the first-floor terrace of the Eiffel Tower. They partake of a banquet during which the general mimes a speech. A wedding-group photograph is taken, but every time the fateful words: "Watch the birdie!" are uttered, some unexpected apparition interrupts the proceedings. First of all it is the "Bathing Beauty from Trouville," then "Telegrams" — for the Eiffel Tower has been the handmaiden of the post office ever since its aerial was installed— and finally a lion appears that devours the general. This is only the beginning of the misfortunes that befall this unlucky wedding party, for it ends by being "massacred" as in games at the fair by the "Child of the Future."[23]

[17] Advertisement announcing the opening of the Ballets Suédois at the Théâtre des Champs-Élysées on 20 Nov. 1920 (color reproduction in Häger, p. 27).
[18] Based on Steegmuller 1970, p. 265: "The script was apparently approved with enthusiasm: after the reading the clan attended the Swedish Ballet, sitting in the box of the choreographer, Jean Borlin, and then went on to the Gaya, where Cocteau beat the bass drum."
[19] Tailleferre said Cocteau wrote during spring 1921 asking her to compose the "Quadrille." Tailleferre, p. 47. In an 11 Apr. 1921 letter Cocteau begged Poulenc to tell Auric to write his "two other ritournelles." Poulenc 1994, 21-6.
[20] 25 Mar. 1921 letter to Poulenc in Poulenc 1994, 21-4. Durey was to have composed the "Valse des dépêches" (Waltz of the Telegrams), but asked Tailleferre to replace him. Tailleferre, p. 29 says she completed this number in three days and that Milhaud orchestrated it.
[21] Steegmuller 1970, p. 265.
[22] Watkins, p. 300.
[23] Milhaud 1953, p. 111 (Milhaud 1987a, pp. 94-5) and Häger, pp. 141-6. English translation of the play and of Cocteau's 1922 preface in Benedikt, pp. 93-115.

Les Mariés includes ten musical numbers requiring just over twenty minutes to perform. Only three (*) are actually dances.

1	Ouverture "Le 14 juillet"	Auric
2	Marche nuptiale	Milhaud
3	Discours du général (Polka pour deux cornets à pistons)*	Poulenc
4	La Baigneuse de Trouville (Carte postale en couleurs)	Poulenc
5	Fugue du massacre	Milhaud
6	Valse des dépêches*	Tailleferre
7	Marche funèbre sur la mort du Général	Honegger
8	Quadrille: Pantalon, Été, Poile, Pastourelle Final*	Tailleferre
9	Trois ritournelles	Auric
10	Sortie de la Noce	Milhaud

The production was fraught with problems. Cocteau had initially planned to have Auric's girlfriend, the artist Irène Lagut, design the set and costumes under his supervision. Finding her sketches unsatisfactory, Cocteau had Jean Hugo take over.[24] In the end, Lagut designed the backdrop and Hugo, with the aid of his fiancée, Valentine Gross, designed the costumes and elaborate masks.[25] Angered by Cocteau's decision to drop Lagut, Auric threatened to withdraw but was mollified.[26] Cocteau charged Poulenc with gathering the music and delivering it to Jacques Hébertot, director of the Théâtre des Champs-Élysées, where the work was performed.[27] A distinguished audience was invited for the 18 June gala *avant-première*.

Rolf de Maré assembled a curiously mixed audience: Paul Claudel, the Duchess de Rohan, the Princess Murat, Rouché, director of the Opéra, Georges Casella, Alfred Cortot, Maurice Ravel, Roger Cousin, André Warnod, Robert de Rothschild and his wife, and Rachilde, to mention only a handful of the important people present. The Cubists sat *en masse*, the entire group of the Six was there, and the Dadaists,

Trouville is a well-known coastal resort in Normandy.
[24] Hugo 1975, p. 19 and Hugo 1976, p. 107 say Cocteau's displeasure with Lagut came from her suggestion that electric lights be used for the eyes of the lion.
[25] Iconography in Häger and Maré. A photograph of the "Valse des dépêches" is in Laloy's review in *Comœdia* (20 June 1921), 1. On 22 June Maré hosted the performers and collaborators for lunch on the Eiffel Tower, and several photographs were taken. Roy 1994, pp. 32-3 and Poulenc 1994, photograph no. 11.
[26] Häger, p. 30.
[27] Cocteau's 6 Apr. 1921 letter to Poulenc in Poulenc 1994, 21-5.

sensing competition (Cocteau's supernaturalism anticipated Surrealism) came armed with whistles.[28]

The Dadaists caused a significant disturbance.

The Dadaists were in a particularly belligerent mood because of a frustration they had just suffered in the same building. For the past few weeks a "Salon Dada" had been in progress in the Studio des Champs-Elysées (a small hall on the theatre's top floor). Temporarily rechristened the Galerie Montaigne, it had been filled by Dada artists with an assortment of readymades, sculpture and paintings, including works by Arp, Max Ernst and Man Ray—an exhibition important in the annals of Dada. The night of the seventeenth, the theatre itself was rented to Marinetti and other Italian Futurists for a *"concert bruitiste."* This was invaded by Tzara and other Dadaists, who began a demonstration, whereupon the management, which had already been annoyed by rowdy Dada demonstrations in the gallery upstairs, retaliated by locking the Dadaists out of their own exhibition, where a Dada matinée had been scheduled for the afternoon of the eighteenth. The Dadaists were doubly frustrated: by the lockout, and by the certain prospect of making themselves ridiculous if, after all their self-proclaimed anarchism, they were to appeal to the law. That evening a number of them, infiltrating the smart invited audience of the Swedish Ballet, kept standing up and sitting down at various points in the theatre, shouting "Vive Dada!" with the result that the critics were unable to hear enough of the words or music to be able to write proper reviews.[29]

On opening night, 19 June, *Les Mariés* created a scandal. Aaron Copland, newly arrived in Paris to study with Nadia Boulanger, saw a billboard advertisement and attended the performance.

The audience was shocked by the modernity of the music and the fanciful nature of the production; they whistled and hooted each time the curtain descended. I recall seeing Milhaud take a bow from the stage to mixed applause and hisses. It was the perfect way to spend one of my first nights in Paris—to get right into the action, where controversial music and dance were happening.[30]

Maré kept the ballet in his repertory, giving thirty performances over four seasons. Reaction from the press was predictably mixed, though there were favorable accounts.[31] As the ballet historian Cyril Beaumont remarked, *Les Mariés* "completes the trilogy of experi-

---

[28] Häger, p. 32. Durey, of course, was absent.
[29] Steegmuller 1970, p. 273. Volta 1993, pp. 59-65 discusses the relationships between Cocteau and the Dadaists.
[30] Copland 1984, p. 44.
[31] Several quoted in Häger, p. 32.

ment by Cocteau, of which the two previous works were *Parade*, written for Diaghilev, and *Le Bœuf sur le toit*."[32]

The hastily composed music draws considerably on popular styles. Since the action takes place on Bastille Day, Auric's *Ouverture* sets the tone, skillfully blending military marches with fanfares grotesquely punctuated by tuba and timpani within a polytonal context. Milhaud's march continues both the fanfares and the polytonal idiom, deftly characterizing the members of the bridal party as they make their entry. Poulenc's numbers, the only contiguous ones by the same composer, follow. The first, a discourse for the general, is intended to be mimed. Through the use of two cornets, appropriate snare drum flourishes to caricature pomp, and clever trombone glissandos (all in the context of a polka), Poulenc creates a scene straight out of a silent film of the epoch.[33] In the "Baigneuse de Trouville" his music "started as a slow galop [sic] and veered into a slow waltz of the type Satie favored in his days as a Montmartre café pianist."[34] Désiré-Emile Inghelbrecht, who conducted the first performance, told Poulenc that his orchestration was not as effective as it could have been. Poulenc wrote Paul Collaer:

I am far from having found "my orchestration" and Inghelbrecht was correct: *La Baigneuse* does not come off. It is neither "brash" enough for the theater nor "subtle" enough for good music. *Le Discours* is not bad, that I grant you.[35]

Poulenc may have found it daunting to write in the shadows of Milhaud and Honegger, both of whom had already composed many orchestral works. Or perhaps, as he noted in the same letter à propos *Le Gendarme incompris*, he was simply more accustomed to writing for small ensemble, "which I do know something about."

Milhaud's "Fugue du massacre" does not survive among the original manuscripts and had to be recomposed for a revival.[36] James Harding described the remaining musical numbers:

Germaine Tailleferre deputized for Durey with a fairground *Valse des dépêches* in steam-organ style. Her *Quadrille*, which contained the hal-

[32] Quoted in Häger, p. 151. In *La Danse* (1921), Cocteau explained his intentions in writing *Les Mariés*. See Häger, pp. 147-8.
[33] Concerning "caricatures of pomp" see Perloff, pp. 188-9.
[34] Harding 1972, p. 103.
[35] [12 July 1921] letter in Poulenc 1994, 21-11 (Collaer 1996, 21-26). In a [29 July 1923] letter to Collaer Poulenc gave a much less flattering account: "As for the music, aside from Auric's overture, it is still crap. . . ." Poulenc 1994, 23-19 (Collaer 1996, 23-30).
[36] Collaer 1988, p. 321. Milhaud recomposed the missing number in Geneva during 1971.

lowed movements of "Pantalon," "Été," "Poule," "Pastourelle" and "Finale," unwound with all the exuberance of a Garde Républicaine brass band. The General's demise was celebrated by Honegger's *Marche funèbre*. Its lugubrious mockery of formal pomp was all the more effective in that he incorporated, *adagio* and in a minor key, the theme from Milhaud's *Marche nuptiale*. At the double forte he also introduced in counterpoint the waltz song from Gounod's *Faust*, a joke that Saint-Saëns had played with Berlioz' *Danse des sylphes* in *Carnaval des animaux*. An unwary critic praised Honegger for having written "real music at last". As well as his *Marche nuptiale*, Milhaud wrote the crisp *Fugue du massacre de la noce*.[37]

For Poulenc, Auric, and Milhaud, the most important result of the collaboration was that Diaghilev attended the premiere and was impressed with their contributions.[38] He had heard their music earlier at such venues as the Salle Huyghens, but not in the context of a ballet. Each composer later received at least one Ballets Russes commission: Poulenc wrote *Les Biches* , Milhaud *Le Train bleu*, and Auric *Les Fâcheux*, *Les Matelots*, and *La Pastorale*. The collaboration was also a financial success. Poulenc wrote Cocteau that he had gone to the Society of Authors and had collected his share which was 432 francs.[39]

While Poulenc was in Rome, Raymond Radiguet suggested that he might like to set some of his lengthy poems written in southern France. After all, he noted, in 1910 Debussy had used three fragments from *Le Promenoir des deux amants*, a long poem by Tristan L'Hermite.[40] Nothing immediate came of Radiguet's suggestion, but Poulenc set his short *Paul et Virginie* in 1946. Cocteau, Radiguet, and Poulenc were all together again for the matinee performances of *Le Gendarme incompris* which concluded the "Spectacle de Théâtre bouffe" presented by Pierre Bertin at the Théâtre Michel from 24-26 May 1921.[41] In the midst of preparations for it Poulenc attended the first Paris performance of Prokofiev's new Piano Concerto no. 3, premiered in Chicago the previous December.[42]

As spring turned to summer, Poulenc had new projects in mind.

---

[37] Harding 1972, p. 104.
[38] Poulenc probably saw Diaghilev during performances of *Parade* in 1917. On 28 Apr. 1919, he wrote Diaghilev (having obtained his address from Picasso) to thank him for helping to get his *Rapsodie nègre* published by Chester. They had earlier conversed at Misia's home. Poulenc 1994, 19-8 (Poulenc 1991, no. 17). See acknowledgment of Diaghilev's earlier assistance in Poulenc 1935a, p. 524.
[39] [July 1921] letter in Poulenc 1994, 21-15.
[40] Radiguet's [Apr. 1921] letter sent to Paris in Poulenc 1994, 21-7 (Poulenc 1991, no. 26).
[41] Playbill facsimile in Volta 1997, p. 133.
[42] 17 Jan. [1923] letter to Prokofiev in Poulenc 1994, 23-5.

He read avidly, including scores by Gioacchino Rossini and Giuseppe Verdi (especially *Rigoletto*), in preparation for Diaghilev's commission. By July, at his family home in Nogent-sur-Marne, Poulenc had sketched a string quartet and *Promenades,* a set of piano pieces for Arthur Rubinstein, and completed the *Quatre poèmes de Max Jacob.*[43]

He also lamented the typical mid-summer phenomenon that virtually all his friends had vacated the city. His lament, however, was temporarily muted by the arrival in Paris of "the Harvard University Glee Club," as they were announced on period posters. The Glee Club, conducted by the renowned Archibald Thompson "Doc" Davison, had embarked 11 June for France on the steamer La Touraine and reached land at Le Havre late on the 20th.[44] By the end of the next day the men had arrived in Paris by train and were ensconced in a student residence at 100, rue de Vaugirard. Their visit engendered considerable advance publicity, and they were officially welcomed at the Hôtel de Ville by M. Le Corbeiller (President of the Municipal Council), Ambassador Wallace (American Ambassador to France), and other dignitaries. What really piqued public attention was a luncheon at the Cercle Interallié, Marshal Foch presiding, attended by Charles-Marie Widor, André Messager, Henri Rabaud, Albert Wolff, Reynaldo Hahn, and three members of *Les Six* (Milhaud, Auric, and Poulenc). Satie and Ravel had also been invited, but are not known to have attended.[45] After lunch the Glee Club sang a short but excellent program for the assembled guests. Then, on the 24th, Wolff hosted the men for an evening performance of Debussy's *Pelléas et Mélisande* at the Opéra-Comique.

The next day they went to the Ballets Suédois as Milhaud's guests to see *L'Homme et son Désir* and *Les Mariés de la Tour Eiffel.* At intermission Auric, Poulenc, and Milhaud came to Davison's box to congratulate him on the Cercle Interallié performance. A triumphant concert at Fontainebleau in the Galerie Henri II (part of the opening festivities for the Conservatoire Américain), during which Saint-Saëns' *Saltarelle* was sung to the composer's delight, was followed by five more in Paris on 28, 30 June and 1 July (Salle Gaveau), 3 July (Church of St Eustache), and 4 July (Trocadéro).[46] Glowing reviews were a welcome sendoff as the Glee Club left Paris for performances in Dijon, Nancy, Verdun, Strasbourg, Mulhouse, Coblenz, Venice,

---

[43] [July 1921] letter to Durey in Saint-Tropez in Poulenc 1994, 21-10.
[44] Details from Glee Club, passim.
[45] Halbreich, p. 80 quotes 22 June and 3 July 1921 letters from Honegger to his mother indicating who was supposed to attend the lunch and how things went. Honegger indicates that his invitation to represent French music had come from Marshal Foch himself.
[46] Information from Glee Club, Milhaud 1953, pp. 134-5 (Milhaud 1987a, p. 114), and Rosenstiel, p. 154.

Pesaro, Ravenna, Milan, and Geneva. According to information contained in Davison's personal diary of the Glee Club tour, he heard works by Poulenc, Milhaud, and others on Saturday, 2 July:

> ... After lunch [I] went to a reception given us by French students at the Sorbonne. The Minister of Beaux[-]Arts made an address and there was a concert of modern music by different members of the Six. Some piano music and songs by Poulenc which he played and accompanied; a string quartet by Milhaud. Other music also. We sang.[47]

Poulenc's encounter with Davison led to a male chorus commission fulfilled by *Chanson à boire* (FP 31: Plate 6 on p. 117) in September 1922, and Milhaud wrote a Psalm (Op. 72) for the Glee Club. It is ironic that Poulenc's first choral work should have been commissioned by a visiting American chorus.

During the July heat Poulenc also suffered from "an attack of Stravinsky-itis." Not only had he read and digested Ansermet's lengthy article on Stravinsky in the July issue of *La Revue musicale*, but he had spent two days immersed in *Renard*. "The counterpoint is unbelievable," he said, "The secret is that his contrapuntal writing is a superimposition of very appropriate 'themes' rather than the Wagnerian hairsplitting exhibited by Honegger."[48] Poulenc felt entirely inadequate. In early August he talked with Ansermet, himself a Stravinsky champion, when the conductor passed through Paris following a London Ballets Russes engagement.[49] Also during July Poulenc's Uncle Royer visited Paul Collaer in Brussels, taking with him Poulenc's gift of the original orchestral manuscript of *Cocardes*. The two must have discussed Honegger's new oratorio *Le Roi David*, for upon his return Royer told Poulenc that Collaer called it a masterpiece. Not one quick to criticize fellow members of *Les Six*, Poulenc thought the oratorio thirty years out of date and unworthy of such praise.[50] At summer's end, Poulenc read the 1919 orchestration of Stravinsky's suite from *L'Oiseau de feu*, finding it striking, and further vented steam at Collaer concerning *Le Roi David*.[51]

---

[47] 2 July 1921, p. 26 entry in the unpublished diary kept by Davison documenting the tour. Private collection of Alice Davison Humez.
[48] [12 July 1921] letter to Collaer in Poulenc 1994, 21-11 and Collaer 1996, 21-26 (Poulenc 1991, no. 28). Craft says Stravinsky inscribed Poulenc's piano score of *Renard*: ". . . in all friendship. Igor Stravinsky, Paris, May 18, day of the premiere of *Renard* at the Opéra."
[49] In Poulenc's [3 Aug. 1921] letter to Milhaud in Poulenc 1994, p. 130, note 2.
[50] "Jeudi" [28 July 1921] letter in Poulenc 1994, 21-16 (Collaer 1996, 21-27).
[51] Fragment of Poulenc's [Aug. 1921] letter to Milhaud in Poulenc 1994, p. 134, note 3. The two took up this subject again in 1924 when Poulenc was afraid *Les Biches* would be eclipsed by *Le Roi David*. "Mardi" [8 Apr. 1924] letter to Collaer

STUDY WITH CHARLES KOECHLIN[52]

When Paris came back to life in the fall of 1921, Poulenc immediately took action concerning his inadequate formal musical training. Initially he had been prevented from entering the Conservatoire by a father who coveted a more traditional lycée education for his son. "He can do what he likes afterwards," Poulenc quoted his father as having said.[53] Clearly his father, a respected scientist and businessman,was concerned that his son receive a more traditonal education. Next Poulenc had been thwarted by conscription into the military. Now twenty-two and associated with influential members of the Parisian avant-garde, he could boast entry into the salons of wealthy Parisians, and enjoyed a budding career as pianist and composer. It would have been all too easy for this darling of Parisian society to let early successes go straight to his head. Fortunately, better judgment prevailed, judgment significantly shaped by Milhaud who encouraged him to approach Charles Koechlin for composition lessons. Poulenc contacted Koechlin from Vaux-le-Pénil near Melun. Anticipating returning to the city around 20 September, he confessed that until now he had obeyed instinct rather than intelligence.[54] A day later Milhaud wrote Koechlin:

> Poulenc is delighted to be going to study with you. I hope that you will be very demanding. It is only with you that he will be able to learn his trade. He is a charming boy marvelously talented and wealthy (his father sold many chemical products in order that he might pursue music).[55]

By mid-October, Poulenc wrote to Georges Jean-Aubry in London: "I return to Paris tomorrow. There I am going to work hard both alone and with Koechlin."[56] Later he added, "I am going to study with Koechlin for the entire winter (orchestration, fugue, etc.) because I am soon to throw myself into my 'important works'."[57] In 1935 Poulenc remarked that he found Koechlin a teacher who was both marvelously comprehensive and indulgent.[58] Still later discussions with Stéphane Audel elicited the following recollection:

---

in Poulenc 1994, 24-9 (Collaer 1996, 24-27) and Milhaud's "dimanche" [13 Apr. 1924] and [5 May 1924] letters in Collaer 1996, 24-28 and 24-30 respectively.

[52] Robert Orledge has published important new information based on his study of Poulenc's 58 lessons with Koechlin in Buckland/Chimènes: f.

[53] Poulenc 1963a, p. 40 (Poulenc 1978, p. 35).

[54] [Sept. 1921] letter to Koechlin in Poulenc 1994, 21-19 (Poulenc 1991, no. 31).

[55] Fragment of Milhaud's 21 Sept. [1921] letter in Poulenc 1994, p. 136, note 2.

[56] Unpublished postcard in US-NH.

[57] Fragment of Milhaud's "dimanche soir" [23 Oct. 1921] letter to Jean-Aubry in Poulenc 1994, p. 136, note 2. In a "samedi" [25 Mar. 1922] letter to Collaer Poulenc said he was studying "contrepoint, choral, orchestre, etc." Collaer 1996, 22-5

[58] Poulenc 1935a, p. 523.

After the death of André Gédalge [1926], Charles Koechlin was by far the best counterpoint teacher in France. His knowledge was prodigious, but his finest attribute was the ability to adapt to the pupil. Having sensed, as a result, that like most Latins I was more of a harmonist than a contrapuntist, he had me harmonize Bach chorale melodies in four parts, along with the customary contrapuntal exercises. This work, which fascinated me, had a decisive influence. It is thanks to this that I acquired my feeling for choral music.[59]

Robert Orledge has established that Poulenc took 38 lessons between November 1921 and July 1922 for which Koechlin was paid "20 francs/hour."[60] Lessons took place on "8, 11, 15, 18, 22, 25 November; 2, 6, 9, 23, 27 December (plus a visit on 13, but no lesson); 3, 6, 17 January 1922." During this span lessons were on Mondays and Thursdays. Then they were switched to Tuesdays and Fridays as follows: "on 3, 7, 10, 14, 17, 21, 24, 31 March; 4, 7, 11, 21, 25, 28 April; 2, 9, 12, 23, 30 May; 6, 13, 23 June; 18, 25 July."

Poulenc remained Koechlin's student until 1925 taking lessons only sporadically due to the busy schedules of both master and pupil. Moreover, in spite of Poulenc's protestations that he needed formal training, his compositional habits were enough ingrained that teaching him was a challenge. In mid-summer 1922, as noted above, he briefly resumed working with Koechlin studying Nikolai Rimsky-Korsakov's *Traité d'instrumentation* and Henri Reber's *Traité d'harmonie*.[61] Then, following a trip to Salzburg, he wrote to Koechlin:

You must wonder at my silence, since there has been no news from me in more than a month. Don't be angry with me because the only reason is that I have been traveling. I was very pleased with my stay in Salzburg. The French have had an immense success there. [. . .] I cannot impress upon you enough the extent to which I have benefited from my study with you during the winter, from the point of view of counterpoint as well as harmony. I am anxious now to begin three- and four-part harmony and fugue. I have so much to accomplish, however, that I shall not return to Paris until around the 15th or 20th of December. So it is at about that time that I shall contact you. Be it understood that I will write to you often about my work. My Sonata for Clarinet and Bassoon is finished. I am pleased with it. The counterpoint is sometimes quite amusing.[62]

---

[59] Poulenc 1963a, p. 41 (Poulenc 1978 , pp. 35-6).
[60] Information and quotations of dates and payments from Buckland/Chimènes: f, pp. 13-14. Orledge prints examples of Poulenc's exercises and Koechlin's corrections noting that dissonant chorale harmonizations were not discouraged and that a Bach theme was first introduced in Mar. 1922.
[61] [July 1922] letter in Poulenc 1994, 22-19.
[62] Early Sept. letter from Nazelles in Poulenc 1994, 22-26 (Poulenc 1991, no. 51).

Orledge further establishes that Poulenc resumed his studies between January and March 1923 taking lessons "on 23, 26 and 30 January; 2, 6, 9, 20, 23, and 27 February; and on 2, 6, 9, and 16 March."[63] In May 1923 Koechlin wrote that he would be residing in Méry-sur-Oise, but would be unavailable from 15 June to about 5 July. His 20 francs per hour private lesson fee would rise to 30 francs except for students who could come to Méry.[64] Poulenc was ashamed to have withheld news from Koechlin for so long and he had hardly worked on technique the previous winter. He promised to be more diligent and accepted Koechlin's new rate.[65] Subsequently he explained that feverish work on *Les Biches* had limited his correspondence, and promised Koechlin a visit in October to show off his new orchestral work.[66] In late October, called to Monte Carlo by Diaghilev, Poulenc apologized again.[67]

While orchestrating *Les Biches* and composing recitatives for Charles Gounod's *La Colombe,* Poulenc sought his teacher's advice on orchestral details.[68] Koechlin finally saw the completed *Les Biches* in August 1924 when Poulenc sent him an inscribed printed piano score.[69] Evidently he took no lessons during the first half of 1924.

> Please excuse my unspeakable silence. I am completely ashamed and beg your unqualified pardon. What I say to you now is that I am firmly counting on working with you twice a week for one hour after 15 January [1925] the date on which I shall return to Paris. Until then I will not be leaving the Touraine, where I am finishing various things.[70]

Flush from the international success of *Les Biches,* however, Poulenc did not immediately recommence lessons, though he always valued Koechlin's counsel. His final seven lessons with Koechlin did not take place until March 1925.[71]

---

[63] Buckland/Chimènes: f, pp. 24-5.
[64] 1 May [1923] letter in Poulenc 1994, 23-13.
[65] "Jeudi" [24 May 1923] letter in Poulenc 1994, 23-14.
[66] 3 Sept. [1923] letter from Nazelles in Poulenc 1994, 23-26 (Poulenc 1991, no. 60). Poulenc also noted, "Once again the chorales have served me."
[67] "Samedi" [27 Oct. 1923] letter in Poulenc 1994, 23-38.
[68] Fragment in Poulenc 1994, p. 207, note 1. In this [Sept.?] letter, Poulenc indicates that he had sought guidance in Charles-Marie Widor's *Technique de l'orchestre moderne* (Paris: Henry Lemoine et Cie, 1904). Orledge discusses details of Koechlin's suggestions in Buckland/Chimènes: f, pp. 25-7.
[69] Archives Li-Koechlin. Poulenc 1994, p. 131, note 1. It is unknown if Koechlin attended the Parisian premiere of *Les Biches* at the Théâtre des Champs-Élysées on 26 May 1924.
[70] Undated [autumn] letter from the Hôtel du Lion d'Or in Amboise in Poulenc 1994, 24-24.
[71] These will be discussed below.

COMPOSITIONS OF SUMMER AND FALL 1921

During the summer of 1921, before his composition lessons began, Poulenc was busy completing three works: the brief and inconsequential *Esquisse d'une fanfare* (FP 25) (overture for act V of Cocteau's *Roméo et Juliette*),[72] the more problematical *Promenades* (FP 24), and *Quatre poèmes de Max Jacob* (FP 22). In the previous chapter, where the *Quatre poèmes* were introduced, mention was made that Poulenc was going through a period of "stylistic exploration." Wilfred Mellers writes of the *Promenades*.

> ... [they] flirt with the polyharmonies and luxuriant textures of Ravel, as well as with Stravinskian polytonality and polymetre. Temporarily, Poulenc's true self is obscured, though he never really wavered in his loyalty to his spiritual father, Satie.[73]

These pieces, written for the virtuoso pianist Arthur Rubinstein, are slightly reminiscent of Satie's *Sports et Divertissements*, a set of twenty-one brief works composed in 1914.[74] Poulenc gives us a glimpse of his struggles.

> As for *Promenades*, this is how I have resolved the problem of short pieces. Here is the plan: Prelude. 10 Promenades. Finale. I see the ten promenades as ten variations on ten different themes (one for each promenade). The special technique used for each piece will create in the end a sort of *trompe-l'oreille* given that there will be one in thirds, another in repeated octaves, etc. In this manner I shall achieve a semblance of unity.[75]

The critic Jean Marnold heard Rubinstein play the Parisian premiere on 7 May 1923:

> *Promenades* is an extremely remarkable work which marks a turn in the composer's evolution. [. . .] The native qualities of this musician,

[72] This work has been published only in Poulenc's piano transcription. Its dissonant harmonic language (full of minor seconds) is similar to that of other music written that summer. Poulenc acknowledged receipt of *Roméo* in a postcard to Cocteau [summer 1921] saying he would see what the work had to say to him. Unpublished postcard in US-AUS. Poulenc next wrote Cocteau [summer 1921] indicating he was thinking about *Roméo*, but was not sure he would do it. Unpublished postcard in US-AUS. Poulenc then wrote Collaer [12 July 1921], "The Fanfare is good (I am sure of it) . . . but there are better things." Poulenc 1994, 21-11 (Poulenc 1991, no. 28) and Collaer 1996, 21-26. When Cocteau's play was published in 1926, no mention of Poulenc can be found. The publication indicates "Musique de scène d'après les airs populaires anglais arrangés et instrumentés par Roger Desormière."
[73] Mellers, p. 12.
[74] Concerning Satie's collection see Whiting, pp. 399-408.
[75] [12 July 1921] letter to Collaer in Poulenc 1994, 21-11 (Poulenc 1991, no. 28 and Collaer 1996, 21-26).

his impulsive verve and his melodic freshness combine themselves with a more substantial polyphony of an unexpected richness and variety.[76]

"The public liked the *Promenades,* to my astonishment," [Rubinstein recalled], "but disapproved of the Milhaud and [Karol] Szymanowski pieces. . . . I was proud to have a major piece by Poulenc dedicated to me."[77] Poulenc later acknowledged that these pieces were not "the best of Poulenc." But Alfred Cortot, in a survey of French piano music, thought Poulenc's judgment too harsh: "On the contrary, I confess not being clearly able to perceive for what reasons Poulenc quite recently strove to retire the *Promenades* of 1921 from circulation."[78]

The *Quatre poèmes* also presented Poulenc with problems. "I am finishing the *Max Jacob,*" he told Paul Collaer, "this time I think I've got it right."[79] They had kept Poulenc busy since summer 1920. Jacob's brief poems, later published in *Le Laboratoire central* (no. 3) and *Les Pénitents en maillot rose* (nos. 1, 2, and 4), are full of juxtaposed references to Turkish wanderers, balalaïkas, fox-trots, harlequin, Narcissus, Persia, men at a monastery, wine, and Christ. The first completed song was no. 3 "Dans le buisson de mimosa."[80] In February 1921 Poulenc told Milhaud that the cycle was dedicated to him and that:

> I am enchanted with them. The last one kicks up a din. The second contains a fugue "en simili" for trumpet and oboe, which is not lacking in the unexpected, and naturally there are huge faults in it.[81]

According to the manuscript, they were finished in August-September 1921 at Nogent.[82]

Barely eight minutes long, they exhibit Poulenc's interest at this time in shifting or conflicting meters, ostinati, acerbic dissonance, and considerable virtuosity due to excessively fast tempi in nos. 2 and 4.[83] Like *Promenades,* these pieces represent something of a dead end for the composer. Although they were performed in Paris on 7 January 1922 at the Salle des Agriculteurs by the Société moderne d'instruments à vent[84] and in Brussels on 17 January 1923 at the Salle

---

[76] *Mercure de France* (1 July 1923). Text in Schmidt 1995, FP 24, pp. 78-9.
[77] Rubinstein 1980, pp. 246 and 105 respectively.
[78] Cortot, p. 41.
[79] Poulenc 1994, 21-11 (Poulenc 1991, no. 28) and Collaer 1996, 21-2. See also his letter to Durey in Poulenc 1994, 21-10.
[80] Poulenc 1994, 20-8.
[81] Poulenc 1994, 21-2.
[82] Schmidt 1995, FP 22, pp. 66-7.
[83] Timing in a [7 July 1922] letter to Collaer in Poulenc 1994, 22-14.
[84] 22 Dec. 1921 letter from Jacob in Poulenc 1994, 21-28 (Poulenc 1991, no. 36).

du Conservatoire,[85] Poulenc lost interest in them telling the conductor Ernest Ansermet: "As for the *Poèmes de Max Jacob*, don't make any mention of them in your 'Poulenc.' I burned them."[86] Poulenc must have forgotten that Milhaud possessed an autograph manuscript.[87] On the basis of Milhaud's copy we can consider a work about which critics held conflicting views. In *La Revue musicale*, the sympathetic Roland-Manuel wrote:

> These poems represent Poulenc at his best and mark clear progress in the style of the young composer, whose tasty gifts do not need to be heralded here. What gives these burlesques the prize is that they are written with precise care and with a never-ending charming cleverness.[88]

The anonymous reviewer for *L'Action française*, however, was less receptive:

> This work must belong, at least in the broad sense, to this misconfigured province that one still calls dadaisme. M. Milhaud, who is very much a joker, conducted in a very fraternal fashion. [. . .] I interpret these brief works as humorous, as a form of derision or as a parody representing a cruel hoax on all forms known to musical pathos. Derision has merit when it is witty. It is healthy. Who knows! Those devils will perhaps arrive to give back to music a little of this sharpness, of this precise clarity that it has with the French of times past and that it had lost in the endless balancing act of Wagnerian music, and of "continuous melody." But if their comical schemes tend to that end, and maybe despite them, they are still only a rough basis.[89]

Poulenc contemplated four other works during the summer of 1921: *Trois études de pianola* (FP 26), *Première suite d'orchestre* (FP 27), *Trio pour piano, clarinette et violoncelle* (FP 29), and a String Quartet [I] (FP 28). The pianola etudes are mentioned in a letter to Collaer, and it is cited, along with the suite, in a July 1921 work list Poulenc sent to Archibald Davison at Harvard University. No evidence suggests either was ever written.[90] On the other hand, the String Quartet and Trio were actually begun.

---

[85] The 17 Jan. concert was given by Collaer in the series Concerts Pro Arte. Poulenc 1994, p. 186, note 12.
[86] [Oct. 1923] letter in Poulenc 1994, 23-34.
[87] Salabert edition with a preface in French and English by this author (1997).
[88] Feb. 1922 issue quoted in Schmidt 1995, FP 22 and the Salabert edition preface.
[89] 10 Jan. 1922 issue quoted in Schmidt 1995, FP 22, pp. 67-8 and preface to the Salabert edition.
[90] [6 Mar. 1921] letter to Collaer in Poulenc 1994, 21-3 and Collaer 1996, 21-8. Letter to Davison reproduced in Schmidt 1995, pp. xxi-xxiv.

My quartet is going poorly. I tore up the sketch [of movement] 1. I began again no. 1 which now rather pleases me. The finale will be a rondo. That's all I can tell you about it.[91]

A year later he considered resuming the work for a concert of first performances promised to Jean Wiéner, but writing for strings was more daunting than writing for winds, and he gave up.[92]

Poulenc completed a sketch of the *Trio pour piano, clarinette et violoncelle* in August,[93] and told Georges Jean-Aubry in October that the work was coming along.[94] This piece has not been located but it could be related to his Trio for Oboe, Bassoon, and Piano.

REMAINDER OF 1921

The remainder of the year was predominantly spent corresponding with friends, arranging concerts, and composing. Poulenc also established contact with Béla Bartók in Budapest, sending him copies of his Sonata for Piano Four Hands and Sonata for Two Clarinets, and asked how to obtain a score of Bartók's *The Wooden Prince*.[95]

Working with Prunières, editor of *La Revue musicale,* Poulenc arranged to have the great soprano Marya Freund sing his *Le Bestiaire* at the Théâtre du Vieux-Colombier in a 19 November concert.[96] Freund, associated with Gustav Mahler's music, had also sung in the premiere of Schönberg's monumental *Die Gurrelieder* (1913). Poulenc also heard *Suite du Gendarme incompris* performed at a Jean Wiéner concert during which Freund sang Part One of Schönberg's *Pierrot lunaire* with Milhaud conducting.[97] He heard her sing *Pierrot* again during a trip to Vienna made with Milhaud.

In November and December Poulenc became the Parisian correspondent for Leigh Henry's short-lived periodical *Fanfare.* His two articles, hitherto unrecorded in Poulenc studies, shed valuable light on his already extensive knowledge of musical repertoire, his concert attendance habits, and his championing of new music. A November contribution reviews three new works for string quartet: Stravinsky's *Concertino* dedicated to the Flonzelay Quartet,

---

[91] Fragment of Poulenc's [Sept. 1921] letter to Milhaud in Poulenc 1994, p. 126, note 2.

[92] "Vendredi" [7 July 1922] letter to Milhaud in Poulenc 1994, 22-13.

[93] Fragment of Poulenc's [Aug. 1921] letter to Souberbielle in Poulenc 1994, p. 197, note 3.

[94] Partial transcription in Poulenc 1994, p. 197, note 3.

[95] Ascertained from Bartók's Nov. 1921 response in Poulenc 1994, 21-24.

[96] Poulenc 1994, 21-21 (14 Oct. [1921] letter to Freund) and 21-22 (14 Oct. [1921] letter to Prunières).

[97] Roussel attended this 15 Dec. concert at the Salle des Agriculteurs and enjoyed Poulenc's work. "Vendredi" [16 Dec. 1921] letter to Poulenc in Poulenc 1994, 21-27.

Malipiero's *Rispetti e Strambotti* (which had won the Coolidge prize the previous year), and Bartók's String Quartet no. 2.[98] Speaking of the Bartók quartet, Poulenc suggests that he would be delighted to see Diaghilev stage Bartók's *The Woodcut [recte Wooden]Prince* and *The Miraculous Mandarin*. Diaghilev never did, but what a fascinating thought! In December he focused on works presented in a Colonne concert. First he highlights "the very special position occupied by Albert Roussel in French music," commenting on the premiere of *Pour une fête de Printemps*.[99] Then he turns to Rimsky-Korsakov's *Antar*, which he found "insipid and crude." His review concludes with the prophetic words: "For me Russia has two certain geniuses, Moussorgsky and Stravinsky. One must also set many hopes on Prokofief." Poulenc's command of music literature is already impressive and, like his more prolific fellow critic Auric, he is unabashed about speaking candidly. The year ended with a small disappointment when Poulenc learned that Jacob would not leave the monastery of St-Benoît-sur-Loire to attend the *Quatre poèmes de Max Jacob* premiere.[100]

TO VIENNA AND BEYOND WITH FREUND AND MILHAUD: EARLY 1922

Late in 1921 Milhaud decided to make a concert tour to central Europe, in his words "to renew our contacts with the Austrian musicians from whom we had been separated by the war."[101] He asked Poulenc to go along.[102] Members of *Les Six* had reestablished contact with Schönberg in the first issue of *Le Coq* (May 1920) stating "Arnold Schönberg, *Les Six* salute you." Schönberg's music reappeared in Paris on 22 April 1921 when André Caplet conducted *Five Orchestral Pieces* at a Pasdeloup concert attended by Florent Schmitt, Ravel, Poulenc, Roland-Manuel, Henry Prunières, and Maurice Delage.[103]

Arrangements for the tour were set in motion via a 19 December 1921 letter to Robert Brussel, Chef du Service d'Etudes d'Action

[98] Poulenc 1921b.
[99] Poulenc 1921c. Poulenc apparently destroyed a diary he had been keeping in 1937 because it was too critical of Roussel. See Lucie Kayas' commentary in Poulenc 1999, p. 14.
[100] Jacob's 22 Dec. [1921] letter in Poulenc 1994, 21-28 (Poulenc 1991, no. 36).
[101] Milhaud 1953, p. 138 (Milhaud 1987a, p. 117). An unpublished letter from Brussel to Dunan in early Jan. notes "Mm. Darius Milhaud et Francis Poulenc ont formé le projet d'accomplir une tournée en Autriche, Hongrie, Pologne, Roumanie, dans le but de révéler au public dans ces pays les expressions les plus récentes de la musique moderne en France." This and subsequent unpublished letters about this tour in F-Pn (Fonds Montpensier: Poulenc).
[102] Poulenc 1963a, p. 22 (Poulenc 1978, p. 22).
[103] Freund's letter to Schönberg in Stuckenschmidt, p. 278. A near riot broke out at the concert and Schmitt, defending the piece "like a lion," was struck and left the concert with a swollen face.

Artistique à l'Etranger, Direction des Beaux-Arts, requesting his assistance. On 31 December, acting for the composers, Louis Bouchet forwarded letters to Yves Auger (Professor of Literature at the University of Kluj, Romania), Marcel Dunan (Vienna), and Mathéus Glinski (Warsaw). Brussel also explained his efforts to the composers.[104] Milhaud and Poulenc were joined on the trip by Marya Freund.[105]

The trio embarked in late January or early in February.[106] On 7 February all three performed in a Vienna Musikverein concert: Milhaud played Poulenc's *Trois mouvements perpétuels* and Poulenc accompanied Freund in *Le Bestiaire*.[107] While there, Poulenc wrote Picasso that Viennese painting, poetry, and music were unimpressive. Speaking more precisely about Viennese art, he noted, "I am disgusted by all these horrors."[108] He much preferred his beloved Louvre. They also visited Alma Mahler-Werfel's home, in whose red music salon they met Schönberg, Berg, Webern, Egon Wellesz, and Hugo von Hofmannsthal. She conceived the idea of performing *Pierrot lunaire* in two versions: one in French by Freund and Milhaud, the other in German by Erika Wagner and Schönberg.[109] Milhaud left the following account:

> Erika Wagner, who sang Schönberg's works in Germany, happened to be in Vienna at the same time as we, and Frau Mahler thought that it might be a good idea to organize a double performance of *Pierrot Lunaire* in the German and French versions. Schönberg agreed, and we used the same instrumentalists. [. . .] It was a most exciting experience; Schönberg's conducting brought out the dramatic qualities of his work, making it harsher, wilder, more intense; my reading, on the other hand, emphasized the music's sensuous qualities, all the sweetness, subtlety, and translucency of it. Erika Wagner spoke the German words in a strident tone, with less respect for the notes as written than Marya Freund, who if anything erred on the side of observing them too closely.

[104] Unpublished 7 Jan. 1922 letter in F-Pn.

[105] Freund, born in Poland, had become a naturalized French citizen.

[106] A Poulenc 22 Jan. 1922 letter (probably written to Kling), for which only a summary has been available, " . . apologizes for being unable to go to Le Havre with him, because he is embarking on a trip to Vienna, Warsaw and Budapest, for a festival of music by Bartók, Milhaud, and himself, promising to visit him in London later in the year, asking him to speed up the publication of his six *Impromptus* for piano, and mentioning the poet Max Jacob." Description in the 29 Nov. 1985 Sotheby auction catalogue, no. 182.

[107] Poulenc 1994, 22-2. Accompanied by Edouard Steuermann, Freund also performed Poulenc songs (from *Le Bestiaire* ?) in Vienna at an *ordentlicher Vereinsabend* on 11 Oct. 1923. Hilmar, p. 90.

[108] Letter from Vienna in Poulenc 1994, 22-2.

[109] Playbill in Wiéner 1978, p. 50.

Milhaud also described a visit to Schönberg's home in Mödling for a meal:

> After the performance [. . .] Schönberg and I discussed our respective points of view, so different, yet equally justified. [. . .] We spent a wonderful afternoon together [at Mödling]. At his request, I played my Second Suite. Francis played his *Promenades* for the piano, which he had just completed. Schönberg talked to us at length of his works, especially of the operas *Glückliche Hand* and *Erwartung*, whose scores I had just bought. He gave me a copy of his Five Orchestral Pieces, the score he had himself used for conducting the first performance, with all his penciled annotations. A princely gift![110]

Poulenc and Hans Stuckenschmidt, the German music critic and musicologist, both report an anecdote. This provides us the unusual opportunity to test Poulenc's powers of recollection at different times.

> The atmosphere of his study was that of a laboratory. The walls were adorned with expressionist paintings and the simplest events felt suddenly bewitched. So it was, just as we sat down at the table when the sorcerer Arnold Schönberg was going to serve the soup, that a soccer ball, projected with force from his son's room, became an edible melon in the tureen.[111]

> When she brought in the steaming bowl of soup a football flew through the open window from the garden into the middle of it; her son Georg was playing with it and was even more alarmed by this accident than the laughing guests. Poulenc, who took a couple of good photos during this visit, told me this story.[112]

That day Poulenc and Milhaud also played the four-hand arrangement of *Le Boeuf sur le toit* for Schönberg and Edward Steuermann played Bartók's *Allegro barbaro*.[113] Finally, the Italian composer Vittorio Rieti, in conversations with Franco Carlo Ricci in 1985, recollected that he had first met Poulenc at the Schönberg's that February day.[114] Rieti had first heard Poulenc's music in Rome "around 1920" during one of Riccardo Viñes' recitals. He remembered that Poulenc was favorably impressed by his 1923 *Concerto per quintetto*

---

110 Milhaud 1953, pp. 139-40 (Milhaud 1987a, p. 118).
111 Poulenc 1945, p. 5.
112 Stuckenschmidt, p. 279. Poulenc also recounted this story to Audel in Poulenc 1963a, pp. 22-3 (Poulenc 1978, p. 23.) The photographs, printed in Stuckenschmidt, p. 280, show Mathilde and Arnold against a wall outside their dwelling, and Arnold and Francis in the same location.
113 Stuckenschmidt, p. 279. A 1922 photograph of Milhaud and Poulenc playing four hands is reproduced in Milhaud 1953, between pp. 148/9. See also Poulenc 1945, p. iv.
114 Ricci, p. 232. I am grateful to Claire Brook for pointing me to this source.

di fiati e orchestra, and that their friendship grew over the years, particularly as the result of Diaghilev ballet commissions.[115]

Little is known about the subsequent trip to Warsaw and Kalisz (a town in central Poland situated on the Prosna River) organized by Freund. When Poulenc later presented Freund with a copy of his *Poèmes de Ronsard,* he fondly remembered their travels together: "To dear Marya Freund in remembrance of Warsaw, of Vienna, of Salzburg. In testimony of deep and admiring affection. Francis Poulenc 1925."[116]

The trip ended poorly for Poulenc who developed a throat abscess that was operated on the afternoon of 13 February. Milhaud wrote Freund from Vienna that he had seen him through the crisis.[117] Wellesz brought Poulenc a jar of jam to speed his recovery.[118]

FIRST MEETINGS WITH HENRI SAUGUET AND BÉLA BARTÓK

Before leaving for Vienna in January 1922, Poulenc finally met Henri Sauguet, with whom he had corresponded since October 1920. From Bordeaux, where he lived, Sauguet had requested information about his music with the goal of including some in an "Erik Satie et la Jeune Musique Française" concert. When the concert took place at the Salle Delmouly on 12 December 1920, Sauguet performed the finale from Poulenc's Sonata for Piano Four Hands (with Louis Émié) and the "Valse" from *Album des Six,* along with works by Satie (*Parade*), Honegger, Tailleferre, Jean Marcel-Lizotte, Émié, Durey, and himself.[119] Sauguet, who became one of Poulenc's lifelong friends, moved to Paris at Milhaud's urging, arriving at the Orsay station on Sunday, 15 January 1922.[120]

A day later, Milhaud, Auric, Cocteau, and Poulenc took him to the Boeuf sur le toit bar on the rue Boissy-d'Anglas where he met several artists and writers.[121] Within days, Sauguet and Milhaud were invited to lunch at Poulenc's apartment before a Pasdeloup concert at the Théâtre des Champs-Élysées and an evening Ballets

---

[115] First performances of this and other works from the 1920s were conducted by Alfredo Casella, another important Poulenc acquaintance.

[116] Schmidt 1995, FP 38, p. 117.

[117] Unpublished letter in US-NYpriv. coll.

[118] Milhaud 1953, pp. 138-9 (Milhaud 1987a, p. 117). Milhaud and Poulenc brought back two Schönberg scores for Honegger. See Halbreich, p. 87.

[119] Schmidt 1995, FP 8, p. 23; program facsimile in Sauguet, pp. 288-9; affiche in Roy 1994, p. 22.

[120] Sauguet, p. 132. Milhaud had offered Sauguet room in his apartment at 5, rue Galliard.

[121] Sauguet, p. 144 lists Picasso, Paul Morand, Satie, Radiguet, Derain, Picabia, Borlin, Rolf de Maré, Fargue, Salmon, etc. One year later, Kessler described the bar as ". . . a sort of artists' tavern on the most modern lines, in the Rue Boissy d'Anglas. English furniture, Picassos on the walls." Kessler, p. 209.

Suédois performance of *L'Homme et son Désir* and *Les Mariés de la Tour Eiffel*.[122] Sauguet remembered that the telephone incessantly interrupted conversation, but had no recollection of the Pasdeloup concert except that he was seated between Ravel and Milhaud. The two ballets, however, greatly impressed him. He also recalled another visit to Poulenc's apartment on 10 March 1922 before the second complete French performance of *Pierrot lunaire* at the Salle Gaveau.[123] Sauguet noticed that many people greeted Poulenc and Auric at the concert. Over the years, they saw each other often, exchanged numerous letters, and Sauguet became Koechlin's pupil.

In March Poulenc participated in what was probably his only performance of music by Schönberg. He and Milhaud joined Mathilde Veillé-Lavallée and Jean Wiéner for a 30 March performance of "Feuillage du Cœur" from Schönberg's *Herzgewächse* at the Salle Gaveau (45, rue la Boétie). Poulenc played the celeste, Milhaud conducted, Veillé-Lavallée sang, and Wiéner performed the harmonium part.[124]

Shortly thereafter, Poulenc finally met Béla Bartók, whose music he had admired since childhood. Bartók was on a European tour that also included London, and while in Paris he made an effort to meet members of *Les Six*. Earlier Bartók had written, "I hold a very keen interest in the efforts of the 'Groupe des Six,' from which I expect a transformation of French music."[125] Public and private concerts plus a symposium devoted to Bartók's music were held in April, and Poulenc may have attended them all.[126] Poulenc described "the very beautiful session" chez Mme Dubost saying that the violinist Jelly d'Arányi, who had played Bartók's First Violin Sonata, had even asked him to write a sonata or concerto, but that he would

---

[122] Sauguet, pp. 134-5.

[123] Sauguet, pp. 140-1. Sauguet says Auric was present and possibly Cocteau. Sauguet also met Satie and Stravinsky at this concert.

[124] Program in US-NYp Job 91-30 (V/6), Schönberg-Freund materials. See also Milhaud 1953, p. 130 (Milhaud 1987a, pp. 109-10) and Milhaud 1987b, p. 133 (where Milhaud explains that he had bought scores of *Erwartung, Die glückliche Hand, Pelléas und Mélisande, Die Guerrelieder, Verklärte Nacht*, and *Herzgewächse* directly from Universal Edition).

[125] Bartók's 12 Apr. 1921 letter to Milhaud in Volta 1990, p. 19. According to Milhaud, Bartók's String Quartet no. 1 had been played at a concert in Mar. 1921 sponsored by *Les Six* at the Galerie Montaigne. Milhaud 1987b, p. 61.

[126] The concerts included one at the Théâtre du Vieux-Colombier sponsored by *La Revue musicale* on 8 Apr. and two chez Mme Dubost on 9 and 14 Apr. The 4 Apr. symposium at the Sorbonne, organized by the Cercle musical universitaire, was entitled "Le mouvement musical contemporain en Europe." Prunières was assisted by Bartók, Milhaud, Freund, d'Arányi, and Meyer. Stravinsky, Poulenc, Honegger, Roussel, Caplet, and Ravel were present. Poulenc 1994, p. 149, note 2.

never write even a note.[127] He presented Bartók with a signed copy of *Bestiaire*, asked him to forward copies of his *Improvisations* and *Quatre chansons*, and promised to send his *Impromptus*.[128]

Poulenc also invited Bartók to lunch with Satie and Auric.

> I remember a strange lunch, on 8 April 1922, where Bartók and Satie met at my house for the first and last time. Several of their works, that they signed for me that day, singularly confirm the date. Like two birds who do not sing the same tune, Bartók and Satie observed each other with suspicion and maintained an overwhelming silence that Auric and I tried in vain to break. For me it is an extraordinary and symbolic memory.[129]

Satie and Bartók "looked at each other as a Martian would look at an inhabitant of the moon," Poulenc said.[130]

While Bartók was in Paris, Poulenc maintained a busy schedule attending an 11 April 1922 performance of Fauré's *Pénélope, Pavane,* and *Masques et Bergamasques* at the Opéra,[131] the first performance of Stravinsky's *Mavra* given privately at the Hôtel Continental on 29 May and publicly at the Opéra on 3 June.[132] He played a four-hand version of Milhaud's *Protée*, Op. 17 with Wiéner on 13 and 22 April for the Russian conductor Serge Koussevitzky.[133] Poulenc found *Mavra* "une œuvre *très importante*," and rallied to its defense when it was attacked by critics such as Émile Vuillermoz.[134] "A propos de *Mavra*" was the first of several articles Poulenc devoted to

---

[127] "Jeudi saint" [13 Apr. 1922] letter to Milhaud in Poulenc 1994, 22-3. Jeanne and René Dubost maintained an important Parisian salon at their apartment on the avenue d'Iéna. Mme Dubost commissioned the private ballet *L'Eventail de Jeanne* (FP 47) performed at her home on 16 June 1927.
[128] 14 Apr. 1922 letter to Bartók in Poulenc 1994, 22-4. Chimènes located the score Poulenc sent Bartók, which bears an inscription dated July 1922 (note 3).
[129] Poulenc 1954, p. 47.
[130] Poulenc 1963a, p. 24 (Poulenc 1978, p. 24).
[131] "Jeudi saint" [13 Apr. 1922] letter to Milhaud in Poulenc 1994, 22-3.
[132] "Vendredi" [June 1922] letters to Durey (Poulenc 1994, 22-8) and "samedi" [June 1922] to Milhaud (Poulenc 1994, 22-9). Poulenc said that while he and Auric found *Mavra* marvelous, "the whole Société musicale indépendante crowd (Ravel, Delage, Schmitt, etc.) disliked it." After the premiere, Poulenc, Auric, Stravinsky, and Ansermet went to hear some sublime jazz. In a "dimanche" [9 July 1922] letter to Stravinsky, Poulenc said that he and Auric often spoke of the fine times they spent with Stravinsky during the spring. Poulenc 1994, 22-15.
[133] "Jeudi saint" [13 Apr. 1922] and "samedi" [15 Apr. 1922] letters to Milhaud in Poulenc 1994, 22-3 and 22-5. The piece is actually the *Deuxième suite symphonique*, Op. 57 reduced for piano. Koussevitzky conducted it on his 5 May 1922 concert.
[134] Vuillermoz (1878-1960), a constant thorn in Poulenc's side, was a prolific critic for numerous Parisian and foreign periodicals and journals who seldom complimented Poulenc or any member of *Les Six*. Concerning Poulenc's article see

Stravinsky.[135] Early in June Collaer, his wife Elsa, and sister Jeanne visited Paris dining with Satie on the 5th, lunching with Poulenc the 6th, and attending an evening Ballets Russes performance.[136]

Later in June Poulenc pressed the famous Russian artist Léon Bakst for tickets to Debussy's ballet *Le Martyre de Saint Sébastien*, starring Ida Rubinstein, that Bakst had designed for the Paris Opéra.[137] In an end-of-season report to Milhaud, Poulenc also spoke of attending a marvelous gala.[138] Before it, he dined at the petit Durand (avenue Victor Hugo) with Audrey Parr; afterwards they attended a party, probably at the *hôtel* of the Princess Edmond de Polignac, who maintained one of Paris' most flourishing salons. Among the attendees were Maurice Barrès, Mme de Noailles, Picasso, and Stravinsky. Poulenc also spoke of having seen Prokofiev's new ballet *Chout*, commending Nijinska for her role as the Bouffon, and of having seen Freund frequently. "You missed an amusing spring season," he concluded.[139]

SALZBURG, THE TOURAINE, AND NEW WORKS: SUMMER AND FALL 1922

Poulenc's thoughts turned to compositions just completed, works on his drawing board, and what should be played at the August Salzburg International Music Festival. He had worked on a *Caprice espagnol* (FP 34) for oboe and piano which he intended to dedicate to Falla and have Jean Wiéner play in Salzburg.[140] *Caprice* was sufficiently complete to rehearse in early June, but by the 22nd he with-

---

Poulenc 1994, 22-13, where he mentions the article to Milhaud [7 July 1922] and 22-21 (Poulenc 1991, no. 45), where he sends a copy to Stravinsky [31 July 1922]. Stravinsky, in turn, sent a copy to Ansermet on 5 Aug. with a request to return it. Stravinsky 1982, p. 158. For Satie's derogatory remarks about Vuillermoz see his 1 Mar. 1923 letter to Collaer in Collaer 1996, 23-11.

[135] Poulenc 1922. Poulenc sent his article to Marcel Raval, founder of *Les Feuilles libres*. Unpublished "vendredi" [May? 1922] letter to Raval in US-AUS and Poulenc 1931 (about the *Symphonie de psaumes*) and Poulenc 1941a (about Stravinsky in general).

[136] "Mercredi 24" [May 1922] letter in Collaer 1996, 22-10 and p. 157, note 1.

[137] Poulenc 1994, 22-10. Milhaud wanted Poulenc to buy a program for him, but Poulenc thought it "ugly" and refused. "Vendredi" [7 July 1922] letter from Nogent in Poulenc 1994, 22-14.

[138] A gala staring Tamara Karsavina, *première danseuse* of the Ballets Russes, took place at the Théâtre Mogador on 27 June. Karsavina danced in *Les Femmes de bonne humeur*, *Les Sylphides*, *Le Spectre de la rose*, and *Schéhérazade*. This performance, however, took place five days after Poulenc's letter, and we have been unable to identify the specific event to which Poulenc refers.

[139] "Jeudi 22" [June 1922] letter in Poulenc 1994, 22-11.

[140] In a 29 Jan. 1923 letter to Falla Poulenc said he had abandoned this unworthy work. Poulenc 1994, 23-6 (Poulenc 1991, no. 53).

drew it from consideration.[141]   Instead, the newly published
Impromptus were played, and Poulenc promised Wiéner the Parisian premieres of new chamber works including Sonata for Clarinet
and Bassoon (FP 32), Sonata for Horn, Trumpet, and Trombone (FP
33), *Napoli* (FP 40), and possibly a string quartet.[142] Concurrently,
Poulenc planned a *Chanson à boire* for the Harvard Glee Club, worked
on his Diaghilev ballet, and made fleeting noises about a piece called
Marches militaire for piano and orchestra.[143]

During early July, in league with Stravinsky, Poulenc met with
the distinguished Swiss-American pianist and conductor Rudolph
Ganz (then conductor of the St. Louis Symphony Orchestra) and
Richard Hammond to arrange publication of their recent compositions. Hammond was a board member of the Franco-American
Music Society which was then connected with the New York Composers' Music Corporation.[144] Stravinsky proposed a series of long-
term contractual possibilities at the same time Poulenc hoped to have
Hammond publish *Napoli, Quatre poèmes de Max Jacob,* both new
sonatas, and *Chanson à boire.*[145] The exercise proved fruitless.[146]

Poulenc traveled to Salzburg for the 7 and 10 August International Music Festival staying at a villa rented by Véra Janacopoulos,
who was studying with Lili Lehmann.[147] He kept a detailed record
of various works heard while attending five of the seven concerts,
ranking each composer on a +20 to -20 scale. Scoring highest were
Webern (+19), Bartók and Milhaud (+18); scoring lowest were three
unknowns, Wilhelm Grosz (-20 "abominable"), Hugo Kauder (-19),
Fidelio Finke (-18), followed by Busoni and Felix Petyrek (both -
15).[148] Poulenc rated his own work a modest +13. The festival, attended by over 300 critics and many composers, was stimulating.

---

[141] "Vendredi" [June 1922] letter to Durey in Poulenc 1994, 22-8.

[142] Milhaud's "vendredi" [7 July 1922] letter in Poulenc 1994, 22-13. *Promenades*
was explicitly excluded from the list, and any chamber work not performed by
Wiéner would be promised elsewhere.

[143] Discussed in Chapter VI.

[144] Stravinsky 1982, p. 155 and Poulenc 1994, p. 161, note 7.

[145] Fragment of Poulenc's 3 July [1922] letter to Milhaud in Poulenc 1994, p. 161,
note 7. The account of meeting Hammond is in Poulenc's "dimanche" [9 July
1922] letter to Stravinsky in Poulenc 1994, 22-15.

[146] Poulenc told Milhaud that Hammond and Ganz would take the four works,
but they took none. [July 1922] letter in Poulenc 1994, 22-19.

[147] Poulenc was still in Paris on 31 July (letter to Stravinsky in Poulenc 1994, 22-
21). Richard Strauss headed the organizing committee, which included Egon
Wellesz, Heinrich Damisch, Paul Stefan, Heinrich Kralik, Joseph Reitler, and
Rudolf Réti. [July 1922] letter in Poulenc 1994, 22-19.

[148] 16 Aug. [1922] letter to Milhaud and Poulenc 1994, p. 171, note 9. Poulenc had
earlier written a postcard to Valentine Hugo complimenting Salzburg as a city,
the people he had met, and saying that the trip was a "gros succès." Unpublished 9 Aug. 1922 card in US-AUS.

Years later, in homage to the English music critic Edwin Evans, Poulenc recalled their poignant initial meeting.

> I had the eminent honor of giving the world premiere performance of Manuel de Falla's *Chansons espagnoles* with the singer Marya Freund at the International Music Festival. The very evening of the concert I was desperate in the lobby of my hotel because my bag was lost and I was going to have to play in my travel clothes, while, as you can well imagine, from ten o'clock in the morning my German colleagues displayed pretentious frock coats. Suddenly, behind me I heard an ironic and affectionate voice saying: "Unfortunately, young man, I can not lend you my jacket because we do not have the same [sized] stomach." It was Edwin Evans who, taking my arm, with a big laugh invited me to have lunch with him after the concert. Thus our friendship was sealed.[149]

Poulenc gave the *Chansons espagnoles* a +16 rating.

Returning to France, he spent a week visiting his sister and her family at Houlgate before going to Nazelles, nestled on the north side of the Loire River just above Amboise.[150] Until 1922 Poulenc summered at the family home in Nogent. After that he stayed in "La Lézardière," which belonged to Virginie Liénard, familiarly known as "Tante Liénard."[151] This remarkable woman, who had seen Richard Wagner conduct *Lohengrin* in Brussels and Franz Liszt play in Italy, went out of her way to hear Stravinsky's music.[152] Poulenc adored her company and often visited her Cannes apartment. Before purchasing his Noizay estate in the spring of 1927, he often stayed at the neighboring Hôtel du Lion d'Or in Amboise.

As Poulenc passed the remainder of 1922 in Nazelles he had a revelation. "I believe I am entering my great period of which *Les Biches* will be number one," he confided to Jean Wiéner, "But I must not sacrifice, quite to the contrary, the smaller works, which show a parallel evolution."[153] Except for interruptions by friends, Poulenc tried to complete works promised to Davison and Wiéner and to advance the ballet.[154] *Chanson à boire*, the beginning of which Poulenc

---

149 Poulenc 1946f. Poulenc 1994, pp. 171-2, note 10.
150 He was at his sister's Houlgate estate by 16 Aug. (16 Aug. [1922] letter to Milhaud in Poulenc 1994, 22-22).
151 Poulenc's first-known letter bearing this return address was to Wiéner. Poulenc 1994, 22-24. Liénard, whose husband Paul had been killed in the War of 1870, was a great music lover. Machart, p. 49 (photograph).
152 Poulenc 1994, 22-24. Poulenc dedicated his piano pieces *Les Soirées de Nazelles* (FP 84: sketched in 1930, completed in 1936) to her memory.
153 "Lundi" [Sept. 1922] letter in Poulenc 1994, 22-27 (partial transcription in Poulenc 1991, pp. 334-5).
154 Jacob visited Poulenc for lunch on 9 Sept. and they talked at length about Picasso. [10 Sept. 1922] postcard to Picasso in Poulenc 1994, 22-29.

Plate 6: Opening page of Poulenc's first choral work, Chanson à boire, inscribed to Archibald Davison, conductor of the Harvard Glee Club.

told Milhaud sounded like "drunken Orlando de Lassus," was written in September, predominantly during a five-day period when he had reached an impasse on *Les Biches*.[155] It is interesting that one of the twentieth-century's most accomplished French choral composers dedicated his first effort in the genre to Davison and an American Glee Club.[156] Largely through Davison's efforts, choral music in America moved from the realm of light entertainment to the serious concert stage. It is ironic, however, that unwittingly Poulenc set an eighteenth-century drinking song text at a time prohibition in America made performance of such material virtually impossible.[157] Milhaud, however, did not miss the French connection of this piece.

> He wrote a chorus for the Harvard Glee Club in the style of an eighteenth-century drinking song. But it is an eighteenth century full of joy and happiness, seen through the eyes of a young Frenchman of 1923 [sic] who loves Paris, Montmartre, and good wine.[158]

During September and October Poulenc completed two of his favorite sonatas: the Sonata for Clarinet and Bassoon[159](dedicated to Audrey Parr) and the Sonata for Horn, Trumpet, and Trombone (dedicated to Raymonde Linossier).[160] With them he stepped away from the Russian influence exhibited in Sonata for Two Clarinets. Studies with Koechlin had made his wind writing much more assured and idiomatic. In September 1922, before he had heard the new sonatas and the drinking song, Durey had written:

> The composer whose evolution I have traced has undergone the most variegated influences, but whether he happens to think of Chopin, Haydn, Chabrier, Scarlatti, Stravinsky, Mozart or Satie, it is always Francis Poulenc who expresses himself, clearly and without danger of being mistaken. It may thus be judged how this young personal-

---

155 "Vendredi" [29 Sept. 1922] letter to Milhaud in Poulenc 1994, 22-31.

156 In 1950 Poulenc heard a male choir from The Hague rehearse his *Chanson*. He had never before heard it sung and remarked that he would not change a single note despite his penchant to revise. Poulenc 1954, p. 97.

157 For the origins of this text see Schmidt 1995, FP 31. Poulenc successfully threw everyone off its trail when he listed it as deriving from the seventeenth century. Poulenc asked Jean Hugo to do the English translation which he sent in a letter (postmarked 20 July 1922). Unpublished letter in US-AUS.

158 Milhaud 1987b, p. 201.

159 Manuscript dated "Touraine - Eté 1922" and "September 1922."

160 Manuscript dated both "Houlgate-Touraine (P.G.Q.) Août-Octobre 1922" and "Septembre-Octobre 1922"). In an [early Sept. 1922] letter to Koechlin, Poulenc says that the Sonata for Clarinet and Bassoon was finished, that he was particularly pleased with its counterpoint, and that the other sonata was still in progress. Poulenc 1994, 22-26.

ity has already asserted itself and how it keeps in good countenance next to the most notable of its predecessors.[161]

Stravinsky was most impressed when he saw the sonatas.

> While in Paris I saw Satie and Poulenc many times. The latter has composed two sonatas. One for horn, trumpet, and trombone and the other for clarinet and bassoon. Both are very well written and seem to me very significant in the sense that he visibly rids himself of the "modern prejudices" of which you have spoken to me. I very much loved the music of these two sonatas, very fresh music where the originality of Poulenc manifests itself as it does in none of his other works. Moreover, this music is very, very French. . . .[162]

When the sonatas were premiered on 4 January 1923 before a packed Théâtre des Champs-Élysées at a Jean Wiéner Concert, the audience included important people like Philippe Gaubert, Gabriel Pierné, Satie, Désiré-Emile Inghelbrecht, Robert Casadesus, the sculptor Fernand Ochsé, and the critics G. Azaïs (*L'Action française*), Roland-Manuel (*La Revue musicale*), Paul Souday (*Paris-midi*), and Émile Vuillermoz (*Excelsior*).[163] Count Harry Kessler also attended:

> In the evening with Wilma to a Satie and Poulenc concert in van de Velde's theatre. In the entrance I ran into Misia Edwards (now married to Sert), Sert and Diaghilev. Our first encounter since the war.[164]

The concert included Satie's *La Belle Excentrique* plus *Trois mouvements perpétuels* played by Poulenc. Suzanne Balguerie's performance of Satie's *Socrate* was the principal attraction.[165]

BRUSSELS AND LANDOWSKA: THE FIRST PART OF 1923

In January Poulenc traveled to Brussels, a city he frequented throughout his life.[166] As a guest of Paul and Elsa Collaer, he performed *Le Bestiaire* with Véra Janacopoulos at a Ysaye Concert.[167] The featured event was a 17 January mostly Poulenc Pro Arte concert including *Le Bestiaire* (sung by Évelyne Brélia to his accompaniment), *Quatre*

---

[161] Durey, p. 4.
[162] Excerpt of Stravinsky's 17 Nov. 1922 letter in Auric 1979, p. 57 (partially transcribed in Volta 1990, p. 19). Poulenc sent published copies to Stravinsky with a "samedi" [9 Feb. 1924] letter. Poulenc 1994, 24-6 (Poulenc 1991, no. 79) and 24-7 (Poulenc 1991, no. 80) for Stravinsky's 11 Feb. 1924 acknowledgment.
[163] [Jan. 1923] letter to Milhaud in Poulenc 1994, 23-3.
[164] Kessler, pp. 207-08. Kessler (1868-1937), whose diaries are particularly rich, was primarily an art patron and book publisher, though he wore numerous other hats. Trilingual in French, German, and English, he befriended many significant artists and writers.
[165] Concerning an important score of *Socrate* belonging to Freund see fn. 324.
[166] [20 Nov. 1922] and 4 Dec. [1922] letters to Collaer in Collaer 1996, 22-27 and 22-33 respectively. Collaer was told he planned to arrive on 9 or 10 Jan.
[167] Janacopoulos was the dedicatee of "Ballet" from Poulenc's *Poèmes de Ronsard*.

poèmes de Max Jacob (Maurice Weynandt, tenor), the premiere of *Prom-enades* (played by Collaer), the Sonata for Clarinet and Bassoon, *Napoli, Trois mouvements perpétuels,* and *Cocardes.*[168] The concert also included Stravinsky's *L'Histoire du soldat* suite and music by Honegger and Auric. Afterwards Poulenc enjoyed speaking with Edouard-Léon-Théodore Mesens and some young Belgian compos-ers at a small café.[169] He also heard Prokofiev's *Scythian Suite* and wrote complimentary letters to both Stravinsky and Prokofiev about their works.[170]

By 28 January he was back in Paris for a concert version of Falla's *El Amor Brujo.*[171] Two days later he wrote to Milhaud in America with news that the Section française de la Société Internationale de Musique Contemporaine had been founded with Gabriel Fauré as honorary president and Paul Dukas as active president.[172] Though the society's goal to promote foreign music in France and French music abroad was lofty, Poulenc found the society rife with intrigue. Vuillermoz wanted no part of Milhaud or Satie on the executive com-mittee; Stravinsky, elected to the executive committee, was against the society; and Prunières thought that French music was now saved. Poulenc gave this "new Société Musicale Indépendante" two years before it would be defunct!

The early months of 1923 were propitious because Ernest Ansermet included several Poulenc works in a *Nouvelles Auditions* concert at the Geneva Conservatory on 22 February.[173] Poulenc's Sonata for Clarinet and Bassoon and Suite from *Le Gendarme incompris* were played along with Stravinsky's *L'Histoire du soldat,* which was heard twice. Poulenc also advised Ansermet that Paul Budry had proposed a book of articles about contemporary composers. He suggested that Auric (not Roland-Manuel) write about Satie, Paul Landormy about Milhaud, Vuillermoz about Honegger, and Roland-Manuel about Auric. He implored that Cocteau not be asked to write (because he was incapable of dealing with musical examples), said

[168] Poulenc 1994, p. 186, note 12 and Collaer 1996, 22-33. Poulenc thanked Collaer in a 19 Jan. [1923] letter (Collaer 1996, 23-5), and Auric told Collaer ("lundi" [12 Feb. 1923] letter in Collaer 1996, 23-7) that Poulenc had been moved by the Belgian performances. Andrée Vaurabourg noted that Poulenc thought the concert had gone very well, particularly Collaer's performance of *Promenades,* but that his Sonata for Clarinet and Bassoon had been unrecognizable. 18 Feb. 1923 letter to Collaer in Collaer 1996, 23-10.
[169] Collaer's "mercredi matin" [16 Jan. 1923] letter to Mesens in Collaer 1996, 23-3. About Mesens, a composer, pianist, poet, etc., see p. 459.
[170] Letters of 17 Jan. [1923] in Poulenc 1994, 23-4 and 23-5 respectively. He told Prokofiev that he loved his music dearly.
[171] 29 Jan. 1923 letter in Poulenc 1994, 23-6.
[172] [30] Jan. [1923] letter in Poulenc 1994, 23-7 and note 5.
[173] "Mardi" [27 Mar. 1923] letter to Ansermet in Poulenc 1994, 23-8 and note 1.

Ansermet himself was the only sensible choice to cover Poulenc, and admonished Ansermet for excluding Falla. The book, scheduled for October, was never published.

In late March or early April Poulenc developed hepatitis. Expecting to be sent to Vichy for a cure, he declined Count Etienne de Beaumont's request to compose music for a 30 May *Bal Louis XIV*. He did, however, promise a Sonata for Organ for Beaumont's wife, a promise never honored.[174] Poulenc's illness was particularly unfortunate because it prevented him from playing fourth piano in the 13 June premiere of Stravinsky's *Les Noces* at the Théâtre de la Gaîté-Lyrique, though he attended the performance.[175] Juggling brief trips to Paris from Vichy before going to Nogent in July, he also applauded Roussel's *Padmâvatî* at the Paris Opéra.[176] During his illness he contemplated composing a Sonata for Flute and English Horn and began a Sonata for Flute, Clarinet, and English Horn.[177] No music remains for either if, in fact, Poulenc refers to two different pieces.

In the late spring Poulenc met the renowned harpsichordist Wanda Landowska. Born in Warsaw in 1879, Landowska had immigrated to Paris in 1900 to explore 17th- and 18th-century keyboard music. By 1903 she was performing on the harpsichord, and became its most famous exponent. The occasion of their meeting was a performance in which she played Falla's *El Retablo de Maese Pedro* at a private *soirée* in the Princesse de Polignac's home.[178] Viñes, involved as a

[174] 4 Apr. [1923] letter to Beaumont in Poulenc 1994, 23-10. Although Poulenc's initial reason for not accepting may have been his illness, an [Aug. 1923] letter to Beaumont makes clear that Diaghilev had forbidden it. Poulenc 1994, 23-23. Jealous, Diaghilev threatened Auric with banishment if he wrote for Beaumont. Only Milhaud, claiming a prior commitment, wrote for Beaumont and still remained in the impresario's good graces. Concerning Satie's contribution for Beaumont's ball see Orledge 1990, pp. 226-30; concerning famous people who attended see Hugo 1983, 224-5; for a photograph of Valentine Hugo in costume and of Jean Hugo's designs see Faucigny-Lucinge 1987, pp. 18-19. Poulenc had earlier attended a *Bal des Jeux* dressed (along with Auric and Milhaud) as a football player. See Gold, p. 239.

[175] Poulenc 1963a, p. 191 (Poulenc 1978, p. 137). The piano parts were taken by Auric, Meyer, Hélène Léon, and Edouard Flament (replacing Poulenc). Poulenc played more than forty performances during his career. Poulenc 1963a, p. 191 (Poulenc 1978, p. 137). Chimènes located the piano score Stravinsky gave Poulenc on 5 May (dedication reproduced in Poulenc 1994, p. 197, note 1).

[176] "Mardi le 12" [June 1923] letter to Collaer in Poulenc 1994, 23-15 and Collaer 1996, 23-22. Poulenc told Koechlin ("jeudi" [24 May 1923] letter) that he would return to Paris on 28 May and stay for a week (through 4 June). Poulenc 1994, 23-14.

[177] Letters to Collaer of "mardi le 12" [June 1923] in Poulenc 1994, 23-15 and Collaer 1996, 23-22, and Fleury of 16 Apr. [1923] in Poulenc 1994, p. 197, note 4.

[178] Sauguet was invited to attend this 25 June 1922 performance by Milhaud and met Princess Edmond de Polignac for the first time. After, Falla decided not to

puppeteer, had invited Poulenc to rehearsals, and probably provided the introduction. Poulenc considered her in the most favorable light when he wrote:

> My meeting with Landowska is, in effect, a major event in my career. I have for Wanda Landowska as much artistic respect as human affection. I am proud of her friendship, and I will never be able to say enough about what I owe her. It is she who gave me the key to the harpsichord works of Bach. It is she who taught me what I know about our French harpsichordists. What is incredible about Landowska is that she makes the music of the past real and alive.[179]

Landowska requested harpsichord concerti from both Falla and Poulenc. Falla wrote his between 1923-26, but Poulenc, not immediately inspired, did not compose his *Concert champêtre* until April 1927-August 1928.[180]

The 1923 spring season ended on 5 July with a housewarming at Milhaud's Boulevard de Clichy residence. Jean Hugo reports that Cocteau, Satie, Radiguet, Cendrars, Constantin Brancusi, Stravinsky, Diaghilev, Misia, José-Maria Sert, Cypa and Ida Godebski, Jacques and Anne-Marie Porel, Marie Laurencin, Poulenc, Honegger, Paul Morand, Auric, Pierre Bertin, Marcelle Meyer, Léopold Survage, and a bird trainer (!) were all present.[181]

OTHER WORKS ON POULENC'S DESK DURING 1923

Poulenc's "desk" was seldom devoid of music, whether barely sketched or still part of his imagination. He could manage some works with considerable speed (though none of *Les Six* could match Milhaud in that regard), but more often they required significant gestation before becoming definitive. Although *Les Biches* and the recitatives for *La Colombe* preoccupied Poulenc during 1923 and early 1924, he also worked on a *Quatuor à cordes et clarinette* (FP 37) which

---

attend a supper given by the Princess because she had not invited the musicians and singers. Instead, Landowska, Falla, Milhaud, Viñes, Auric, Poulenc, and a few others accompanied the rest of the cast to a *brasserie*. Sauguet, p. 199.

[179] Poulenc 1954, pp. 74-5.

[180] Poulenc's interest in the harpsichord also manifested itself in other works composed during 1935: *La Belle au bois dormant* (music for an animated film produced by Alexandre Alexeieff for Vins Nicolas), *Margot* (music for Édouard Bourdet's play), and *Suite française d'après Claude Gervaise* (extracted from *Margot*). Landowska and Poulenc remained friends until her death in 1959, and Poulenc visited her in Lakeville, Connecticut after she moved to the United States. For a charming photograph of Landowska and Poulenc inscribed by Poulenc "Chez Wanda à Lakeville, pour mon cher Rollo [Myers] très affectueusement," see Harding 1972, pp. 122/23.

[181] Steegmuller 1970, p. 309.

sprang from a Pro Arte Quartet request for a string quartet.[182] Though partially sketched, it was set aside in favor of *Les Biches* and eventually abandoned. He also completed the first two movements and sketched the last movement of a piano piece entitled *Napoli* (FP 40).[183]

WORKING FOR DIAGHILEV: *LES BICHES* AND RECITATIVES FOR GOUNOD'S *LA COLOMBE*

Poulenc first announced his intention to write a large-scale work for Diaghilev in early March 1921.[184] Its origin, however, was older still:

> From 1918, Diaghilev, always on the lookout for young musicians, attended our seances at the rue Huyghens. It is thanks to him that my first works were published in London. The day when, accompanied by Stravinsky, he came to ask me to write a ballet for his company, I could not believe my eyes. I was wildly intimidated, as much because I was seeing Stravinsky for the first time. Like all the musicians of my generation, I was feeding on Stravinsky, and I confess that I owe to Stravinsky my most important musical emotions since 1916. I cried at *Les Noces*, celebrated at *Mavra*. Full of indulgence, Stravinsky convinced me to tempt fate and, after eighteen months of trial and error, in agreement with Marie Laurencin, I set out to write *Les Biches*.[185]

In this account Poulenc conflates a series of events not recalling that it was Diaghilev's attendance at the May 1921 performance of Radiguet and Cocteau's play *Le Gendarme incompris* at the Théâtre Michel which prompted the commission.[186] Numerous letters shed light on his compositional progress for this important ballet.

Once Poulenc shared with friends his decision to write for Diaghilev, Cocteau quickly tried to become his artistic collaborator, writing Poulenc: "The ballet for Serge will be childishly simple. We will compose it together after my return [to Paris from Carqueiranne]."[187] The ballet historian and critic Lynn Garafola, citing a letter from Cocteau to Diaghilev dated a year and a half later, concludes that Cocteau instigated the scenario and suggested the actual collaborators to Diaghilev.[188] Not only did Cocteau speak in

---

[182] Letters in Poulenc 1994: [Aug. 1923] to Prokofiev, 23-25; [Sept. 1923] to Sauguet, 23-27; and [Sept. 1923] to Stravinsky, 23-32.

[183] [Oct. 1923] letter to Ansermet in Poulenc 1994, 23-34. Poulenc said Meyer had the manuscript and that she had performed the first two movements on 17 Mar. 1924 at the Salle des Agriculteurs in the first Auric-Poulenc concert. Poulenc finished the last movement in Sept. 1925.

[184] "Dimanche" [6 Mar. 1921, incorrectly dated 9 Mar.] letter to Collaer in Poulenc 1994, 21-3 (Collaer 1996, 21-8).

[185] Poulenc 1935a, p. 524.

[186] Kochno 1970, p. 200.

[187] 11 Apr. 1921 card to Poulenc in Poulenc 1994, 21-6.

[188] Cocteau wrote "If it vexes you to write, give your commissions to Poulenc or

terms of Poulenc and Laurencin, but he asked Diaghilev, "Are you pleased with Biches?" Erik Aschengreen, basing his opinion on interviews with Auric and Kochno, denies Cocteau's contribution, but he was unaware of Cocteau's letter.[189]

Diaghilev's November letter to Poulenc explains that "Germaine Bongard [sister of the couturier Paul Poiret] had written [the scenario for] a ballet with singing for which Poulenc would compose the music, Laurencin the costumes, and Nijinska would star. . . ."[190] The ballet was initially entitled *Les Demoiselles*.[191] By July Poulenc was discussing it with Laurencin and informing Milhaud that he was working on the music.[192] He told Stravinsky:

> After consulting with Diaghilev and Marie Laurencin, I have a clear conception of my ballet which will have no subject, simply dances and songs. I am thrilled by this decision and plan to begin work on it right away.[193]

In the end *Les Biches* had no plot, which put to rest any direct influence by Cocteau. Rather, "*Biches* explored a host of taboo themes - narcissism, voyeurism, female sexual power, castration, sapphism - with a directness hitherto unparalleled on the ballet stage."[194]

In late July Poulenc again wrote Stravinsky:

> I have been spending long hours in the Bibliothèque Nationale seeking song texts for my ballet. I have found some excellent ones and will commence work on them in earnest as soon as I get back from Salzburg in the second half of August.[195]

Texts occur in three numbers ("Chanson dansée," "Jeu," and "Petite chanson dansée"): the first for a playful dance song questioning "What is love?," the second for a game about how to marry off four

---

Marie Laurencin - but Poulenc is stricter about terms." Cocteau's 24 Oct. 1922 letter in F-Po quoted in Garafola, p. 107.

[189] See also Garafola, p. 432. Ries, pp. 86 and 218, on the other hand, argues convincingly that Cocteau's sketches for both *Les Fâcheux* and *Les Biches* were quite close to the final forms of the ballets.

[190] Poulenc 1994, 21-23 (Poulenc 1991, no. 33) and Poiret 1931, p. 210.

[191] Poulenc used this name when he told Milhaud he was again thinking about it in mid-June 1922. "Jeudi 22" [June 1922] letter in Poulenc 1994, 22-11.

[192] Laurencin's [July 1922] letter to Poulenc in Poulenc 1994, 22-17(Poulenc 1991, no. 41) and Poulenc's [July 1922] letter in Poulenc 1994, 22-19.

[193] [9 July 1922] letter in Poulenc 1994, 22-15 (Stravinsky 1985, pp. 199-201). In July Poulenc abandoned the idea of working with Bongard and turned to Laurencin.

[194] Garafola, pp. 129-30. Concerning Lydia Sokolova's reservations about having to dance the female pas de deux in the "Petite chanson dansée" with Luba Tchernicheva's arm around her neck and bosom, see Sokolova, pp. 216-17.

[195] [31 July 1922] letter in Poulenc 1994, 22-21 (Poulenc 1991, no. 45).

daughters, and the third for a coy proposal of flowers and love leading to marriage.

Before leaving Nazelles for Salzburg, Poulenc wrote Robert Lyon
in Paris that thanks to his loan of a marvelous piano the ballet was
coming along well.[196] When Poulenc returned to France he found
some slightly obscene eighteenth-century texts for the sung numbers.[197] Composition continued over the next eleven months though
the orchestration was not completed until mid-fall 1923.

> I've finished the introduction, which takes about two minutes and
> fifteen seconds, also the presto (I); the song for the three men will be
> number II. I have put it there because as No. VII it would not have
> provided enough contrast, being in the same spirit as the final num-
> ber (VIII). So now the slow song of the three women will be number
> VII. I have finally found my number III (solo for the star), but how
> difficult it was. I hope now that I've avoided the 1830 waltz, the 1870
> waltz, the Italian adagio, the Casella "false-note waltz," and the sad
> waltz (*Parade*). Actually, it is a very supple dance in 2/4 time, very
> danceable and andantino; it begins in C flat, then slips into the most
> unexpected modulations. I am sure it is what is required. I am at the
> beginning of the *Jeu* now (IV). For the first few bars the singers count
> *ams, tram, dram, pic et pic et colédram*, etc. Then the dancers divide into
> groups and the game begins. A kind of hunting game, very Louis
> XIV. The *Rag-Mazurka* (V) is terrifying. Tell Nijinska that she can
> think in terms of frenetic movements in triple metre. Still to be done
> is No. VI (a *pas de deux*), for which I have, alas, not the slightest idea;
> also the song No. VII, and the *Rondeau final*, for which I do have a few
> ideas. . . . What do you think of all this?[198]

Diaghilev was also informed that by popular consensus the ballet would be called *Les Biches*. Asked later who found the title,
Poulenc unabashedly remarked:

> Me, one July evening when I was returning from the Bastille in an
> open carriage with Valentine Hugo. I was looking for an animal title,
> such as *Les Sylphides*, and suddenly I cried out: "Why not *Les Biches?*",
> playing on the animal-like side of certain of Marie Laurencin's women,
> and on the *double entendre* of the word *biche* in the French language.
> *Biches*, for that reason, is untranslatable in English. That is why in
> London the ballet is called *House Party*.[199]

---

[196] Unpublished card postmarked 4 Aug. 1922 in US-AUS.
[197] "Mercredi" [Aug. 1922] letter in Poulenc 1994, 22-25.
[198] 24 Sept. 1922 letter to Diaghilev in Poulenc 1994, 22-30 (Kochno 1970, pp. 200-
05 and Poulenc 1991, no. 48). Poulenc also told Collaer in Nov. that the ballet
was going well. [20 Nov. 1922] letter in Collaer 1996, 22-27.
[199] Poulenc 1954, pp. 54-5. The change must have dated from July 1922.

In late January 1923 Poulenc studied Gounod operas at the Bibliothèque de l'Opéra. This is his first oblique indication that he was one of those Diaghilev, at Stravinsky's instigation, had commissioned to compose recitatives to three Gounod operas for the 1924 Monte Carlo season.[200] Satie was to write for *Le Médecin malgré lui*, Poulenc for *La Colombe* (FP 35), and Auric for *Philémon et Baucis*.[201] *La Colombe* is not mentioned by Poulenc again until late July when it had been relegated to a closet as the source of trouble and diversion. He also complained that Juan Gris had been retained to design *La Colombe* though he would have preferred a different artist.[202]

In February 1923 Poulenc left for the country to finish *Les Biches*, but by late May he was still having difficulty with several numbers.[203] He had begun the "Rag-Mazurka" four times, had touched up a number of spots, and was nearly finished.[204] He would orchestrate at Nogent in late June.[205] Music for the "Chanson dansée," however, eluded him until the end of July. "I am joyous because I have finally found the "Chanson dansée," a sort of game," he told Milhaud, "which comes in the middle of the ballet. It is at once bursting with energy, coy, and charming."[206] Poulenc also complimented one of Laurencin's costumes:

> . . . she has created an adorable costume for the principal female dancer. It is a short dress, very full, very *décolletée* of grayish tulle, faced with pieces of pink moiré, [and] a round flat hat with feathers of the same color.

He was finally able to play all but the last few pages for Diaghilev later in August and was pleased by the reception.[207] Concerned about

200 Milhaud 1953, p. 155 (Milhaud 1987a, p. 129).
201 [30] Jan. [1923] letter to Milhaud in Poulenc 1994, 23-7. In summer 1923, Milhaud was commissioned to compose sung recitatives for Chabrier's *Une éducation manquée*. Poulenc 1994, p. 201, note 7.
202 "Dimanche" [29 July 1923] letter to Milhaud in Poulenc 1994, 23-18.
203 18 Feb. [1923] letter to Collaer in Collaer 1996, 23-8.
204 "Jeudi" [24 May 1923] letter to Koechlin in Poulenc 1994, 23-14.
205 "Mardi le 12" [June 1923] letter to Collaer in Poulenc 1994, 23-15 (Collaer 1996, 23-22).
206 "Dimanche" [29 July 1923] letter in Poulenc 1994, 23-18. Costumes and scenery for *Les Biches* are reproduced in numerous sources. See in particular Kochno 1924; Kochno 1970, pp. 202-03; Beaumont 1956, pp. 810/11 (*The Times*, London photograph of the *Adagietto* showing Nemtchinova and Anatole Wilzak; Costumes, Dec. 19 Cat. pp. 76-8 (description of costumes for two of the Three Men [Nicolas Zverew and Léon Woizikowsky], two of the Girls in Pink, one of the Girls in Grey, with a photograph of Zverew and Woizikowsky taken in 1924); and Pozharskaya, pp. 214-17. The art dealer René Gimpel, p. 243, in a 26 Sept. 1923 diary entry, noted that he had visited Laurencin's house that day and that she was working on scenery and costumes for *Les Biches*.
207 On 13 Aug. 1923 Satie wrote Poulenc that Diaghilev was in Venice, returning

the second commission, however, he implored Diaghilev to send *La Colombe* quickly so that he could complete his assignment.[208] Poulenc finished the recitatives later in September.[209] "I completed and sent to Serge my recitatives for *La Colombe*," he wrote Stravinsky. "I did the job meticulously, attempting to avoid a pastiche or a harmony lesson *à la Reber*. I hope this will not seem too bad to you."[210] He then resumed *Les Biches*, seeking assistance from Koechlin and Sauguet.[211]

Poulenc played the ballet again for Diaghilev and Auric in early October, both of whom were pleased.[212] Milhaud, however, was less complimentary. In a rare disparaging statement about his friend, he confided to Collaer: "Poupoule plays his score everywhere and one likes it a little less each time one hears it."[213] "Poupoule" is a nickname for Poulenc which quite probably came from *Viens poupoule*, a

---

to Paris around the 20th. Poulenc 1994, 23-21. Poulenc told Sauguet he was coming to Paris on a Monday to talk with Diaghilev, bringing with him the ballet minus its last few pages. (Fragment of a postcard in Poulenc 1994, p. 205, note 1). Poulenc must have met Diaghilev on either 20 or 27 Aug., probably the former.
[208] [Aug. 1923] letter to Diaghilev in Poulenc 1994, 23-22 (Poulenc 1991, 59). In a 3 Sept. [1923] letter to Koechlin, Poulenc complained that he had to write eight recitatives, some of which were very long. He also boasted that he knew the stage works of Gounod quite well. Poulenc 1994, 23-26 (Poulenc 1991, no. 60). In a 21 July 1923 letter to Milhaud, Satie mentioned Diaghilev's desire to have Milhaud complete Chabrier's opera *Une éducation manquée*. As a postscript, he wrote that Poulenc had already done wonders for *La Colombe*. This and other pertinent letters in Milhaud 1953, p. 154 ff. (Milhaud 1987a, p. 129 ff.). In a 3 Aug. 1923 letter, Satie wrote Poulenc that his Gounod was not going well, but that he understood Poulenc's was "striking. " Poulenc 1994, 23-20.
[209] [Sept. 1923] letter to Sauguet in Poulenc 1994, 23-27.
[210] [Sept. 1923] letter in Poulenc 1994, 23-30 (Stravinsky 1985, p. 203 and Poulenc 1991, no. 62). Satie's 8 Oct. 1923 letter to Collaer indicates he knew Poulenc's music for *La Colombe* and liked it very much. Collaer 1996, 23-33. Henri Reber, Saint-Saens' immediate predecessor as professor of composition at the Paris Conservatoire, wrote a well-known *Traité d'harmonie* in 1862.
[211] Concerning Sauguet's guidance see Poulenc 1994, 23-27. He thanked Sauguet telling him he had followed his advice for four bars of no. 5 ("Jeu").
[212] [5 Oct. 1923] letter to Stravinsky in Poulenc 1994, 23-35 (Stravinsky 1985, p. 204 and Poulenc 1991, no. 66). Kochno writes: "When Diaghilev was back in Paris, he got together frequently with Poulenc, who would play him bits from the ballet he was composing. They met at the Hôtel Meurice, in the apartment of Misia Sert, to whom Poulenc dedicated the score of *Les Biches*. Poulenc was a brilliant pianist, but his attitude baffled Diaghilev. When Diaghilev asked him to repeat a piece he had just played, Poulenc used to improvise, saying that this final version would be 'on the same order.' Sometimes Poulenc would break off playing and ask Diaghilev, anxiously, 'Doesn't that sound like *Mavra?*' When this was repeated to Stravinsky, he laughed and said, 'In some cases, it's better to imitate good music than to write one's own'." Kochno 1970, p. 205.
[213] Milhaud's [Paris, 8 Oct. 1923] letter to Collaer in Collaer 1996, 23-35.

popular song sung first by Félix Mayol in 1902 and later by Maurice Chevalier.[214] By late October Poulenc was frequently being summoned to Paris for consultation, and Diaghilev pressed him to come to Monte Carlo to observe the choreography.[215] Arriving there on 4 November,[216] he settled in the Hôtel des Princes which had an ocean view and was only three minutes from the Villa Bellevue, where work on the ballet was progressing.[217] Poulenc rented a piano, completed his orchestration, attended rehearsals, and wrote friends about his impressions. He found the choreography "ravishing" and thought that "Nijinska this time truly understands my music."[218] "The choreography of *Biches* is a masterpiece," he told Sauguet. "It is ravishing from start to finish and precisely what I wanted."[219] At first Diaghilev was concerned that Nijinska's choreography might resemble too much what she used for Stravinsky's *Les Noces* in 1923. A letter from Diaghilev to Kochno, however, clarifies that it did not.

> Here everything is going along much better than I had expected. Poulenc is enthusiastic about Bronya's [Nijinska's] choreography, and they get along excellently together. The choreography has delighted and astonished me. But then, this good woman, intemperate and antisocial as she is, does belong to the Nijinsky family. Here and there her choreography is perhaps a bit too ordinary, a bit too *feminine*, but, *on the whole*, it is very good. The dance for the three men has come out extremely well, and they perform it with bravura— weightily, like three cannon. It doesn't at all resemble *Noces*, any more than Tchaikovsky's *Eugene Onegin* resembles his *Queen of Spades*. All the girls in the corps de ballet are mad about Poulenc. They go about humming his music, and say that he's an accomplished flirt. This is the picture. Tomorrow is a holiday, and all Monte Carlo is hung with splendid flags.[220]

At about the same time Poulenc wrote Kochno:

I'm eager to show you my orchestra and Nijinska's choreography,

---

[214] Poulenc occasionally signed his letters "Poupoule" and among his friends, Milhaud used this appellation more frequently than most others.

[215] "Samedi" [27 Oct. 1923] letter to Koechlin in Poulenc 1994, 23-38.

[216] Date established by Juan Gris who had left for the south on 9 Oct. and set up shop at Beausoleil, in the Villa Tosca, 3, rue du Marché. Kahnweiler 1947, p. 28.

[217] [Nov. 1923] postcard to Milhaud in Poulenc 1994, 23-39. Poulenc arrived two days before Diaghilev. Buckle, p. 416. Auric 1979, p. 183 incorrectly remembered that they went south together in early Dec.

[218] [Nov. 1923] postcards to Milhaud in Poulenc 1994, 23-39.

[219] [Nov. 1923] letter in Poulenc 1994, 23-40 (Poulenc 1991, no. 70).

[220] Translated by Foulke in Kochno 1970, p. 206. Buckle, pp. 418 and 575, suggests this letter was written 17 Nov. on the eve of Ste Dévote, the local saint celebrated on 18 Nov.

which is *truly splendid*. The pas de deux is so beautiful that all the dancers insist on watching it. I am enchanted.[221]

Diaghilev's Monte Carlo season of "Ballets-Classiques" began on 25 November with *Les Sylphides, Cléopâtre*, and the Polovtsian dances from Borodin's *Prince Igor*; it ended on 31 December.[222] The impresario was in Monte Carlo for the opening, but returned to Paris to oversee work for his French Festival, to begin on New Year's Day 1924. One Friday evening, most likely 30 November, Poulenc wrote:

Excellency:

You cannot imagine what you have missed for the last two days. When Nemtchinova's dance is finished—and what a *miracle*—they start the game. I must say that as *madness* it surpasses anything one could imagine. Nijinska is really *a genius*. Listen to this: having decided that the sofa is a "star," just as she herself is, she is making it dance throughout the game!!! Grigoriev asked the Casino for the loan of a magnificent sofa, and they fell to work (in an entirely proper fashion, naturally). I shan't try to describe to you what happens. In a "presto" movement, the women take sitting positions, leap into the air, fall onto the tufted cushions, roll over on their backs (although the two men are straddling the sofa back), and then they drag the poor sofa, which must be ultra solid, in all directions. When, in the middle section, the music calms down, the Star and Vilzak bounce on stage. Thereupon the Girls turn the sofa (its back is now to the audience) into an observatory, their heads popping up over the back and then dropping out of sight; when the game resumes—now listen to this— the two men quickly turn the sofa around and there are the two women lying down in a position that, thinking of Barbette, I can only describe as head to tail. You see, this is not at all bad. As to the last detail, I think it's the same sort of thing as the horse on Marie's curtain, and that it's myopia rather than sadism on Nijinska's part. Be that as it may, our two ladies complement each other very well indeed. [Koscov always seems to have a hot backside. This morning I helped him to do his pirouettes.] This is all the news I have for you. It's good news, you must admit. At rehearsals, I laugh until I cry. It seems to me, furthermore, that from the public's point of view, all this will be irresistible. Come back soon. A thousand greetings to dear Boris, whom I miss, and to you, "Milord."

Poulenc [223]

---

[221] Translated by Foulke in Kochno 1970, p. 206. Nijinska's choreography for *Les Biches* was revived by several companies including the Royal Ballet and the Oakland Ballet. Both are documented on film. Still photographs of the former are in Shead, pp. 128-32.

[222] Steegmuller 1970, p. 313.

[223] Translated by Foulke in Kochno 1970, p. 206 (French in Poulenc 1994, 23-47).

Late in November Cocteau told Valentine Hugo that the Gounod family had accepted Satie's recitatives for *Le Médecin malgré lui* and Poulenc's *La Colombe,* but had rejected Auric's for *Philémon et Baucis.*[224] By early December, Poulenc had not finished orchestrating *La Colombe* and told Milhaud that three days of work remained.[225] Euphoria at watching his dual commissions for Diaghilev come to life was shattered by a telegram which said: "Radiguet died during the night. Poor Jean [Cocteau] in a frightful state. Darius."[226] Raymond Radiguet, not twenty-one and a brilliantly talented writer, died in a Le Piquey nursing home; he was interred at Le Père Lachaise cemetery following a Requiem Mass in the chapel of Notre-Dame de la Cité Paroissiale of Saint-Honoré d'Eylau.[227] Gabrielle "Coco" Chanel and Misia paid the expenses.[228] Poulenc wrote the writer and philosophy professor Armand Lunel that he and Auric were so upset neither had been capable of any creative activity. He also sent condolences to Radiguet's father Maurice.[229]

Cocteau, so devastated by Radiguet's death that he could not attend the funeral, now viewed his own participation in Diaghilev's Monte Carlo 1924 season as impossible.[230] Having written the scenario for Milhaud's *Le Train bleu,* Cocteau's presence in Monte Carlo was expected, but several letters clarified the extent of his inability to face life without Radiguet. Abbé Mugnier and Valentine Hugo were told that his sole reason for living was not to hurt his mother.[231] Following a visit from Diaghilev about a week after Radiguet's death, Cocteau abruptly changed his mind. He wrote Diaghilev in Monte Carlo that he could only live in an atmosphere of birth, not death, and that he also needed the company of Auric, Poulenc, and Gris. Cocteau asked Diaghilev to have Poulenc and Auric arrange for his arrival on the 30th and to have Kochno post the details.[232]

[224] Cocteau's 23 Nov. 1923 letter in Steegmuller 1970, p. 313.

[225] Fragment of Poulenc's 11 Dec. 1923 letter in Poulenc 1994, p. 217, note 2.

[226] 12 Dec. 1923 telegram from Milhaud in Poulenc 1994, 23-42 (Poulenc 1991, no. 70). Valentine Hugo, who was in Montpellier having just undergone an operation, also received a telegram from Milhaud. Her grief is recounted in Steegmuller 1970, p. 317.

[227] Funeral announcement sent to Poulenc in Poulenc 1991, no. 71.

[228] Crosland, p. 140.

[229] 15 Dec. [1923] letter from R. Radiguet in Poulenc 1994, 23-44 (Poulenc 1991, no. 73) and Poulenc's "vendredi" [14 Dec. 1923] letter to Lunel in Poulenc 1994, 23-43. On this same date, perhaps as an effort to cheer him up, Poulenc received a photograph from Nijinska inscribed "A Monsieur Poulenc avec mes Meilleurs sentiments et admiration pour son musique de 'Biches' a mémoire de notre travaille 14 déc. 1923." Diaghilev, p. 121, no. 354 (from Poulenc's collection).

[230] For Nina Hamnett's description of the funeral see Hamnett 1932, pp. 299-301.

[231] Fragments of Mugnier's undated letter and Hugo's "lundi" [18 Dec. 1923] letter in Steegmuller 1970, pp. 316-17.

[232] Cocteau's 20 Dec. 1923 letter to Diaghilev in Aschengreen, p. 117.

Poulenc learned in December that Laurencin would not attend *Les Biches,* preferring to be represented by Cocteau.[233] Perhaps Laurencin's reticence was due to the fact that Kochno and Vera Soudeikine (the future Mme Igor Stravinsky) had had difficulty translating her vague designs into actual costumes. In Buckle's inimitable words, "Her suggestions for costumes . . . were about as helpful to the dressmaker as poems by Verlaine."[234] Laurencin repeatedly required both Soudeikine and the scene painter Prince Alexandre Schervashidze to redo their work and then, indecisive, told them to return it to its previous state.[235] Schervashidze was so upset with Laurencin's backcloth he complained, "It has no connection with the design, either in color, or in drawing, or in composition, giving the impression that the curtain has been painted by an amateur. . . ."[236] When Soudeikine finally brought the costumes to Monte Carlo in late December, she warned Diaghilev that they differed somewhat from his approved designs. Based on eyewitness testimony, Buckle recounted Diaghilev's reception.

> Nemtchinova appeared before Diaghilev's eyes in a long blue velvet frock-coat [for the adagietto], like that of a head porter in an hotel. 'Give me the scissors, Grigoriev!' Diaghilev exclaimed. He cut away the collar, to make a wide V-neck. He cut away the velvet, till it barely covered the buttocks. Nemtchinova had never shown so much leg before (what ballerina had?) and she protested. "I feel naked!" "Then go and buy yourself some white gloves!" said Diaghilev. The celebrated white gloves became almost a part of the choreography.[237]

The French Festival included eight works: four new ballets and four opera revivals, three by Gounod and one by Chabrier. New works were performed along with standards such as *Schéhérazade, L'Après-midi d'un faune,* and *Daphnis et Chloë.* (See p. 132)

The dizzying January production schedule—eighteen performances in only thirteen dark days, many of which were used for rehearsals—greatly strained the company. After financial difficulties in 1923, the new year dawned auspiciously, and aspirations of making Monte Carlo a mecca for opera and ballet seemed assured. The opera company manager, however, considered Diaghilev a rival.[238]

---

[233] Laurencin's [Dec. 1923] letter in Poulenc 1994, 23-46 (Poulenc 1991, no. 74).
[234] Buckle, p. 416.
[235] Buckle, p. 419.
[236] Brief excerpt translated from his 10 Dec. [1923] letter in Sotheby 1991, p. 209, no. 373, item 51.
[237] Buckle, p. 420.
[238] Buckle, p. 424. Massine brought a rival troupe to Monte Carlo giving Diaghilev further reason to want his productions to shine. Milhaud 1953, p. 157 (Milhaud 1987a, p. 131).

REPERTOIRE FOR DIAGHILEV'S FRENCH FESTIVAL

Date	Work	Composers/ Additions	Sets/ Costumes	Choreographer
1 Jan.	*La Columbe*	Gounod/Poulenc	Gris	[None]
3 Jan.	*Les Tentations de la Bergère*	Montéclair/ Casadesus	Gris	Nijinska
5 Jan.	*Le Médecin malgré lui*	Gounod/Satie	A. Benois	[None]
6 Jan.	*Les Biches*	Poulenc	Laurencin	Nijinska
8 Jan.	*Ballet de l'Astuce feminine*	Cimarosa	J.-M. Sert	Massine
10 Jan.	*Philémon et Baucis**	Gounod	A. Benois	[None]
17 Jan.	*Une éducation manquée*	Chabrier/Milhaud	Gris**	[None]
19 Jan.	*Les Fâcheux*	Auric	Braque	Nijinska

*Poulenc reported that the premiere, scheduled for earlier in the month, had to be postponed owing to the illness of a singer. Poulenc's [8 Jan. 1924] letter to Collaer in Poulenc 1994, 24-2 and Collaer 1996, 24-2. (Poulenc 1991, no. 75).

**Picasso had been asked to do the set and costumes. He did not. On 20 Dec. Gris said: "I have had to leave my painting aside just now, as I have suddenly been called on to do a setting and costumes for Diaghilev. They are for *L'Education manquée* by Chabrier, which Picasso was to have done but at the last moment has not. They took four days."

He convinced the management of the *Société des Bains de mer* to frown on the plethora of lesser-known operas, and Diaghilev stopped them after the 28 January performance of *Une éducation manquée*. When the troupe moved to the Théâtre des Champs-Élysées in Paris for a "Grande Saison d'art de la VIIIᵉ Olympiade," only *Une éducation manquée* was performed.[239] Poulenc's *Les Biches* (FP 36), the hit of Diaghilev's 17th season, may have been given as many as six times in Monte Carlo, and it opened the Paris season on 26 May. Subsequently it was danced on four of the thirteen remaining Paris dates (6, 11, 22, 25 June), more than any other new work.[240]

Immediately after the Monte Carlo premiere Poulenc labeled *Les Biches* a triumph. "It is the very essence of dance [. . .]," he said, "Can you imagine, there were no less than 72 rehearsals—about 250 hours of work. That is how one assures results. The sets, curtain, [and] costumes are a total success."[241] Poulenc was particularly proud of the eight curtain calls and Auric's hard-won approval. Only

239 Performances (on 13, 20, and 29 June) listed in Diaghilev, p. 163.
240 Diaghilev premiered the work at the London Coliseum Theatre on 25 May 1925 (Macdonald, pp. 303-07). It remained in their repertory through 1928. Dates for premieres across Europe are cited in Schmidt 1995, FP 36.
241 "Mardi soir" [8 Jan. 1924] letter to Collaer in Poulenc 1994 , 24-2 (Poulenc 1991, no. 75).

Edouard Flament's conducting displeased him.[242] He would have preferred Ernest Ansermet, a much finer musician. Word of the success quickly reached Marie Laurencin, who wrote the unforgettable words "It seems that *Biches* moves the Rich of Monte Carlo."[243] Complimentary letters also arrived. Satie sent bravos from Paris on 11 January, and Stravinsky on 3 February.[244] Milhaud, in an about face, told Paul Collaer: "I was filled with wonder by *Les Biches*, I dream of it. It is a masterpiece. The music is adorable. . . ."[245] The dancer Lydia Sokolova (née Hilda Munnings) wrote a particularly flattering description of Véra Nemtchinova.[246] Numerous critics reviewed *Les Biches* during its 1924 Monte Carlo and Paris runs. Maurice Martin du Gard, the influential editor of *Les Nouvelles littéraires* (for which Auric was a music critic), saw the Monte Carlo production and wrote a glowing front page article with a photograph of Auric, Cocteau, and Poulenc. "Quel charmant spectacle," he exclaimed, before making complimentary remarks about the music.[247] Only Émile Vuillermoz and Adolphe Boschot were unimpressed.

While documentation about *Les Biches* is plentiful, that for *La Colombe* is scarce. Poulenc mentioned it infrequently and left no known account of its performance or reception. For him it paled by comparison. One problem not of Poulenc's making is described in letters from Gris to the art dealer Daniel-Henry Kahnweiler.

[242] In a "vendredi" [May 1924] letter to Durey Poulenc wrote: "This time I will have a good conductor since Messager will conduct." Poulenc 1994, 24-10.

[243] Laurencin's [Jan. 1924] letter to Poulenc in Poulenc 1994, 24-3 (Poulenc 1991, p. 76). She also asked Poulenc to have Diaghilev return her designs and pay for her work. For a letter from Poulenc urging Kochno to arrange for Laurencin to be paid see Sotheby 1991, p. 221.

[244] Letters in Poulenc 1994, 24-4 (Poulenc 1991, no. 77) and 24-5 (Poulenc 1991, no. 78) respectively. Satie warned Poulenc not to become too close to the critic Louis Laloy, who had prepared an article for the souvenir program. Laloy also favorably reviewed *Les Biches* for the 11 Jan. 1924 issue of *Comœdia* (see Buckle, p. 422).

[245] Milhaud's "mardi" [22 Jan. 1924] letter in Collaer 1996, 24-3. Years later he wrote, "From the first note to the last, this ballet is truly enchanting!" (Milhaud 1987b, p. 120.)

[246] Sokolova, p. 216. When Nemtchinova finally left Diaghilev's troupe, Poulenc wrote Picasso: "I weep for my departed Biche. Serge began to find her too 'old'!! I hope that there are those with such beautiful gifts among the young." (Poulenc 1994, p. 224, note 1.)

[247] Auric (*Les Nouvelles littéraires*, 31 May), Adolphe Boschot (*L'Echo de Paris*, 28 May), Cocteau (*La Nouvelle Revue française*, no. 126, Mar. and *La Revue de Paris*, 15 June), Cœuroy (*La Nouvelle Revue française*, 1 Aug.), Fernand Gregh (*Les Nouvelles littéraires*, 14 June), Laloy (*Le Figaro*, 10 Jan., *Comœdia*, 11 Jan., and *Le Courrier musical* 26, no. 3, 1 Feb.), Henry Malherbe (*Le Temps*, 11 June), Jean Marnold (*La Revue de Paris*, 14 Oct.), Martin du Gard (*Les Nouvelles littéraires*, 12 Jan.), Schloezer (*La Revue musicale* 5, no. 4, Feb. and *La Nouvelle Revue française*, July), and Vuillermoz (*Excelsior*, 22 June).

[9 Dec. 1923] I have had a lot of trouble with *Colombe*, as on the day we put it up in the theatre—last Tuesday—I saw that the colours were nothing like those of the design. The painters have got to re-paint all the scenery. I hope I don't get a similar shock with the Montéclair.

[6 Jan. 1924] I have received a number of compliments on *La Colombe*, although the piece is too long and tedious. The costumes look well with the scenery, although they have been badly made. Barrientos' dress is very nicely done, but it is nothing like my design and does not look right. The Montéclair ballet has been a great success. The costumes for it are also badly made but they go well with the setting. I had to take a curtain call, and Nijinska says that she has never seen such a complete harmony. But Oh! how frantic I was during the last days. Except for Nijinska, who takes her work seriously, and Diaghilev who knows his job, nobody uses his brains or forsees anything. No-one has any common sense. I cannot wait to get away from this infuriating *milieu*.[248]

Polunin also commented on the scene construction:

Owing to the peculiarities of construction of the scene and the strong lighting, light penetrated the canvas from behind, completely changing the fundamental tones. For example, the walls, painted with a practically pure white, appeared to be of a brownish-ochre, the black tones seemed reddish and so on, resulting in a vague cacophony.[249]

The French canvas was too coarse, however, and ultimately an entirely new method had to be created to solve the problem. "We glazed the whole scene with a thin wash of aniline, which should neutralise the brownish tint without affecting the values."[250] The results pleased Diaghilev and all was well.

Altogether, Poulenc's recitatives for *La Colombe* contain only about 165 measures of music.[251] Despite his reticence about this commission, the music shows a refined understanding of Gounod's harmonic language, is decidedly tuneful, and sustains interest. Poulenc uses much more linear chromaticism in the progressions than Gounod did in his original music. He also shows a particularly fine sense of line. But Poulenc, not a musical grammarian, occasionally runs afoul of preferred chord spellings.

---

[248] Kahnweiler 1947, pp. 28-9 (Kahnweiler 1946, p. 63) and Buckle, p. 423.
[249] Polunin, p. 70 and Buckle, pp. 424-5. According to Maur, p. 278 (where the set is reproduced) no costume designed by Gris has been located and the model for the set (painted paper and cardboard), formerly in the Collection Maurice Raynal, can no longer be found. Laloy in *Comœdia* (11 Jan. 1924).
[250] Polunin, p. 70.
[251] Poulenc scored the recitatives for fl., 2 ob., 2 cl., 2 bsn., 4 hn., 2 tr., 2 trb.

La Colombe and particularly *Les Biches* for the Ballets Russes placed Poulenc in the international spotlight.[252] Notoriety gained from his earlier participation with the Ballets Suédois was provincial by comparison. Milhaud, reflecting on the relative merits of the two companies, summarized the difference: "Despite the laudable efforts by the Ballet Suédois and all the esteem in which they were held, the Ballets Russes achieved a greater technical perfection."[253] Diaghilev's palette of talent outdistanced the competition. Poulenc, the darling of many of his colleagues, received increasing attention in the international press. The success of *Les Biches* throughout Europe between 1925-28 kept him in the limelight. Max Jacob gave it a poetic slant:

> I have learned of your great success in Monte Carlo because entire newspapers are filled with your name. More than of Deputies, Francis, they speak of you from the banks of the Ganges to the Phlegethon.[254]

There was, however, a significant problem involving Satie who had already questioned Poulenc's and Auric's moral attitude and who took offense at his treatment in Monte Carlo.[255] Poulenc received bravos for *Les Biches*, but was warned not to get too close to Louis Laloy, with whom Satie had been at odds for years.[256] Satie believed that Laloy had purposefully omitted his name from the festival program and was also offended that Auric and Poulenc, like Cocteau, basked in the glow of direct success.[257] The wound fes-

---

[252] Three other examples of Poulenc's growing international fame include Rubinstein's performances of *Promenades* in Havana, Cuba in Aug. 1923 (*Chesterian* 5, no. 35 (Dec. 1923), 103); an "Association for Contemporary Music" concert devoted to piano works and songs by Ravel, Honegger, Poulenc, Milhaud, Satie, and Mompou given in Moscow (Victor Belaiev in his "Letter from Moscow" in the *Chesterian* 6, no. 43 (Dec. 1924), 93); and the performance of *Le Bestiaire* suggested by Poulenc's [19 Jan. 1925] letter to Hoérée stating that his favorite set of parts was currently in Budapest, Hungary. Poulenc 1994, 25-2 contains valuable information about performing these songs.

[253] Milhaud 1953, p. 153 (Milhaud 1987a, p. 129). Ricciotto Canudo, who founded an avant-garde magazine called *Montjoie!*, wrote an interesting comparison in *Comœdia* (27 Feb. 1922). See also Aschengreen, p. 103.

[254] Jacob's 12 May [1924] letter to Poulenc in Poulenc 1994, 24-12 (Poulenc 1991, no. 81). One final bright spot in early 1924 was Marcelle Meyer's 17 Mar. premiere of the "Barcarole" and "Nocturne" from *Napoli*.

[255] For Sauguet's account of the entire affair see Sauguet, pp. 205-06 and the 6 February 1924 letter to Koechlin in Volta 1989, p. 98.

[256] Satie's 11 Jan. 1924 letter to Poulenc in Poulenc 1994, 24-4 (Poulenc 1991, no. 77). Laloy was an influential critic and musicologist who had been Debussy's friend, but who had written uncomplimentary reviews of Satie and *Les Six*. His dislike of Cocteau's criticism of Debussy in *Le Coq et l'Arlequin* had also soured him on the poet. Steegmuller 1970, p. 321.

[257] Orledge 1995, p. xxxvii adds that the break with Poulenc, Auric, and Cocteau was also owing to opium smoking and homosexuality.

tered quickly, and Satie became so distraught that he left Monte Carlo after "covering his friends with incredible abuse . . . standing up during the entire journey home in the corridor of his sleeping car."[258] Subsequently, he wrote a brief article for the 15 February 1924 issue of *Paris-Journal* in which he referred to *Les Biches* and *Les Fâcheux* as "Lots of syrupy things . . . buckets of musical lemonade." He excoriated Laloy calling him "more ghastly than ever," and cast aspersions upon Cocteau who "Continues his mysterious and shady relationship with the said Laloy . . . Hm!"[259] The rift widened when Auric took a pot-shot in print at Satie's *Mercure* (performed 15 June 1924) and Satie retaliated.[260] The last straw involved a childish prank perpetrated by Auric and Poulenc.

> During this period Auric and Poulenc played poker every week in the company of Arthur Honegger and of the singer Claire Croiza. One morning Poulenc entered "Au nain bleu" (rue Saint-Honoré) in order to buy poker chips. His glance was suddenly attracted to a child's rattle decorated with a bearded head which unmistakably resembled Satie. [Later,] Auric proceeded to buy it and, with Poulenc's complete approval, sent it to the "bon maître d'Arcueil."[261]

For the rest of his life, Satie refused to talk with or to accept visits from Poulenc and Auric. Even Milhaud complained that although he and Sauguet loved Satie's *Relâche*, and attended every performance they could, Auric and Poulenc had a poor opinion of it.[262] Of *Les Six*, only Milhaud remained in his good graces. Poulenc, who later spoke reverently of Satie, infinitely regretted the incident, and never missed an opportunity to praise Satie.[263]

---

[258] Steegmuller 1970, p. 322.

[259] Satie and Steegmuller 1970, pp. 322-3. Orledge points out that the first cracks in the relationship between Auric and Satie date from the late summer of 1919. By 1922-23 Satie was quite concerned about Auric's familiarity with the homosexual group including Cocteau and Radiguet. Orledge 1990, p. 248. Poulenc noted Satie's intentions to publish uncomplimentary articles in a "samedi" [9 Feb. 1924] letter to Stravinsky. Poulenc 1994, 24-6 (Stravinsky 1985, p. 206 and Poulenc 1991, no. 79). He also mentioned the matter to Durey in a "vendredi" [May 1924] letter in Poulenc 1994, 24-10: "You know the celebrated quarrel between Satie - Cocteau - Auric - Poulenc, priceless!!" Poulenc commented about the situation in a [7 Oct. 1924] letter to Monnier. Excerpt in Poulenc 1994, p. 234, note 14. Jacob told Poulenc that he had been the object of Satie's wrath years earlier and that Satie's fit of temper would pass. Jacob's 12 May [1924] letter to Poulenc in Poulenc 1994, 24-12 (Poulenc 1991, no. 81).

[260] Hell 1978, pp. 74-5. For Auric's review see *Les Nouvelles littéraires* (21 June 1924), 7.

[261] Hell 1978, p. 75 (Hell 1959, p. 30).

[262] Milhaud's [Paris, 1 Dec. 1924] letter to Collaer in Collaer 1996, 24-47.

[263] For example, in Apr. 1952 Poulenc wrote an article on Satie's piano music. Poulenc 1952.

While the Satie debacle unfolded, Poulenc sought to have *Les Biches* published but was resolved to wait for a good offer.[264] "Still no publisher," he wrote Paul Collaer in mid-February, "I am greedy and I have reason to be: 10,000 francs or nothing."[265] A fortnight later he told Collaer that Heugel would publish the ballet.[266] Poulenc confirmed the arrangement, telling Durey:

> I have signed with Heugel for the edition. As soon as it appears I will send you the piano score and this autumn the miniature orchestral score. This venerable house, wildly rich, now desires to publish a modern catalogue. I have thus decided to give them my ballet. They pay better than any other French publisher.[267]

The piano score, with Laurencin's cover sketch, was published in July 1924, and Poulenc dispatched inscribed copies to Linossier, the Peignots, Jacques Heugel, Koechlin, Roussel, Dukas, and Falla.[268] The orchestral score, however, was not copyrighted until 1943, and the first printing occurred 13 April 1948.[269] One reason for the delay is that Poulenc tinkered with the orchestration during autumn 1924, to simplify certain passages.[270] Another is its association with Linossier mentioned in Chapter II.

The success of Poulenc's and Auric's ballets was celebrated on 26 June 1924 at a banquet organized by the English critic Maurice Brillant just before *Les Biches* was published. Over the next decades Poulenc presented Brillant with signed copies of his scores, and Brillant occasionally reviewed Poulenc's works.[271] *Les Biches* also had exceedingly strong emotional ties for Cocteau. Still suffering from Radiguet's death and from a new opium addiction (thanks to

---

[264] Mardi soir" [8 Jan. 1924] letter to Collaer " in Poulenc 1994, 24-2 and Collaer 1996, 24-2 (Poulenc 1991, no. 75).

[265] "Jeudi" [21 Feb. 1924] letter in Poulenc 1994, 24-8 and Collaer 1996, 24-9.

[266] "Mardi" [8 Apr. 1924] letter to Collaer in Poulenc 1994, 24-9 and Collaer 1996, 24-27.

[267] "Vendredi" [May 1924] letter to Durey in Poulenc 1994, 24-10.

[268] Locations of piano-vocal scores presented to Linossier, the Peignots, and Heugel are given in Schmidt 1995, FP 36, p. 107. Concerning the others see the letters to Poulenc from Koechlin, Roussel, Dukas, and Falla in Poulenc 1994, 24-14, 24-15, 24-16, and 24-18 respectively. Four *Morceaux détachés* for piano solo were published on 19 July 1924. Schmidt 1995, FP 36, pp. 105-06.

[269] Schmidt 1995, FP 36, p. 103. World War II probably accounts for why the score was not published between 1943 and 1948.

[270] [Sept. 1924] letter to Milhaud and [autumn 1924] letter to Schaeffner in Poulenc 1924, 24-19 and 24-23 respectively.

[271] Jean Hugo's notice in Cocteau 1989a, p. 333. About Brillant see Roger Martin du Gard, "Maurice Brillant," *Les Nouvelles littéraires* (21 June 1924), 1. Concerning Brillant's party, which fêted Honegger, Auric, Poulenc, and Milhaud, see the notice in *Les Nouvelles littéraires* (28 June 1924), p. 4.

Laloy who supplied him with the drug), Cocteau wrote Poulenc that *Les Biches*, as played to him by Auric, helped him to live.[272]

In mid-summer 1924 Poulenc left Paris for a vacation in Vichy, a place his family had frequented during his childhood. There, "thirsty for air," he played golf, spent time with Charles Peignot, went dancing, and enjoyed the excellent jazz.[273] He then returned briefly to Nogent before departing for the Touraine where he hoped to compose until January 1925. Numerous compositions were contemplated, resurrected, and/or completed over the next several years. Before considering them, let us discuss one piece that vexed Poulenc for many years, the so-called *Marches militaires* for piano and orchestra. The *Marches* do not fit into any particular year, but they occupied Poulenc's thinking more at this time than at any other.

UNREMITTING STRUGGLE WITH *MARCHES MILITAIRES* (1918-1932)

An accomplished pianist, Poulenc used the instrument in various early chamber and solo pieces. The idea of writing for piano and orchestra, however, did not occur to him until late 1918. "I am thinking on another account of something new, a sonata for piano and orchestra, but don't speak about it to anyone because it is too much in limbo," he told Valentine Hugo.[274] The paucity of evidence between 1918 and 1922 suggests that Poulenc did not compose any such music. Sometime in spring 1922, however, Poulenc confided to Milhaud that he was writing a *"Marche militaire"* (FP 30).[275] Then, in early July 1922, he told Collaer about a *Symphonie pour piano et orchestre.*[276] Although we may never be certain, a connection between the Sonata for Piano and Orchestra and what was later called *Symphonie pour piano et orchestre, Marche militaire*, or *Marches militaires*, is probable. Over the next eight years, Poulenc spoke often about *Marches militaires*, to Milhaud, Stravinsky, Koechlin, Cœuroy, Schaeffner, Cocteau, and Marie-Laure de Noailles. Reports of progress were published in *Modern Music*, the *Chesterian*, *Le Monde musical*, *La Revue musicale*, and *Les Nouvelles littéraires.*[277] Perfor-

272 Cocteau's Aug. 1924 letter to Poulenc in Poulenc 1994, 24-17 (Poulenc 1991, no. 82).
273 [Early Aug. 1924] letter to Milhaud in Poulenc 1994, 24-13.
274 1 Oct. [1918] letter in Poulenc 1994, 18-10. To Edouard Souberbielle he confided, "I am thinking about a sonata for piano and orchestra." Poulenc's "jeudi" [early Oct. 1918] letter in Poulenc 1994, 18-11.
275 Milhaud's [June 1922] letter to Poulenc from Aix-en-Provence in Poulenc 1994, 22-12 (Poulenc 1991, no. 46). Milhaud's reference is in the singular.
276 "Vendredi" [7 July 1922] letter to Collaer in Poulenc 1994, 22-14 and Collaer 1996, 22-14.
277 Concerning progress and anticipated performances see Schmidt 1995, FP 30 and Poulenc 1994, passim. Concerning *Le Monde musical* see Poulenc 1994, p. 237, note 3.

mances were planned for Brussels (1925), Boston (1926), and Paris (1930-32).

Poulenc shared his concept of *Marches* with Stravinsky: ". . . this last work is very complex to do, at least from the point of view of construction. I think I may try some sort of 'Harlequin' of short marches sounding together, each of them giving the sense of developing the other."[278] It was probably at this time that Sauguet, a frequent visitor to Poulenc's rue de Monceau apartment, heard Poulenc play "a sort of symphony comprised of military marches . . . which he had not finished."[279] Work was interrupted by *Les Biches*, however, and only in early February 1924 were they again on his mind.[280] By May he saw the work more clearly: "I am now working on a large piece for piano and orchestra entitled *Marches militaires* in three parts. The largo in the middle is very far along."[281] After Poulenc's Vichy vacation, composition continued from September through November.[282] A piano sonata in the style of Saint-Saëns was destroyed after four pages: "The *Marches militaires* by comparison are advancing slowly but surely. It will be for next winter in Brussels."[283]

Between November 1924 and August 1925 Poulenc does not mention *Marches*. In September Cocteau wrote of his impatience to hear the *Marches,* and Poulenc told Valentine Hugo he was continuing them mainly for her.[284] No 1926 performance occurred and they are only mentioned in a letter from Vittorio Rieti and Poulenc's telegram to Serge Koussevitzky. Rieti, who had moved to Paris in 1925, was friendly with Milhaud at whose house he had apparently heard Poulenc play part of *Marches*.[285] Poulenc also dispatched a telegram to Koussevitzky in Boston telling him not to count on the unfinished "Concerto." The *Marches* go unmentioned for several years.

André Laphin, who interviewed Poulenc for *L'Intransigeant*, noted that the pianist Henri Gil-Marchex had told him: "Poulenc is composing some military marches in the genre of those by Schubert."

---

[278] [Sept. 1923] letter to Stravinsky. Poulenc 1994, 23-32 (Stravinsky 1985, p. 204).
[279] Sauguet, p. 197 says Poulenc frequently visited his room on the rue d'Orsel.
[280] "Samedi" [9 Feb. 1924] letter to Stravinsky in Poulenc 1994, 24-6 (Stravinsky 1985, p. 206 and Poulenc 1991, no. 79).
[281] "Vendredi" [May 1924] letter to Durey in Poulenc 1994, 24-10.
[282] Letters to Milhaud [Sept. 1924], Valentine of "vendredi" [10 Oct. 1924], Schaeffner [autumn 1924], Koechlin [autumn 1924], Schaeffner of "dimanche soir" [Nov. 1924], and Collaer [22 Nov. 1924] in Poulenc 1994, 24-19, 24-22, 24-23, 24-24 (Poulenc 1991, no. 85), 24-28, and 24-30 (Collaer 1996, 24-43) respectively.
[283] [22 Nov. 1924] letter to Collaer in Poulenc 1994, 24-30 and Collaer 1996, 24-43.
[284] Cocteau's [Sept. 1925, which must have arrived after he wrote Hugo] letter to Poulenc and Poulenc's [25 Sept. 1925] letter to Hugo in Poulenc 1994, 25-13 (Poulenc 1991, no. 93) and 25-17 (Poulenc 1991, no. 95) respectively.
[285] Rieti's 17 Feb. 1926 letter to Poulenc from Rome in Poulenc 1994, 26-2. He inquired about what followed a particularly chromatic theme copied in his letter.

This remark was repeated in a special Schubert issue of *La Revue musicale* with assorted other Poulenc quotes about Schubert.[286]

In 1929 André Schaeffner received four bars from *Marches* featuring a worked-out version of the theme about which Rieti had inquired earlier.[287] Poulenc also told Croiza, "I am working in very good form on a grand concerto for piano and orchestra, *Marches militaires.*"[288] Still composing in May 1930, he wrote Alice Ardoin from Grenada of his intention to dedicate *Marches* to Linossier's memory.[289] Poulenc alerted Marie-Laure de Noailles that she would hear *Marches* the winter of 1930-31,[290] and public notice of Pierre Monteux's proposed performance with the Orchestre Symphonique de Paris appeared in the *Monthly Musical Record.*[291] No performances took place, and *Marches militaires* is last heard of in 1932. In *Les Nouvelles littéraires* (4 June), André George wrote that he was still waiting for the work. In October, Poulenc wrote Schaeffner that work continued, and Monteux that he still owed him the concerto.[292]

"Ouf!," as Poulenc would say, *quelle histoire!* We may never know what became of this music, which was quite advanced by 1932. It probably had nothing to do with *Aubade* and *Concert champêtre*, both of which were written while work on the *Marches* ostensibly progressed. Nor is it likely that any connection exists with the Concerto in D minor composed in 1932. Poulenc never mentions the fate of this score which occupied so much time, and the few bars of music noted above link it to no known work.

CULMINATION OF A COMPOSITIONAL CYCLE: FALL 1924-SPRING 1926

Aside from work on the *Marches militaires*, the major portion of

---

286 *L'Intransigeant* (21 Feb. 1929) and "Les Revues de la Presse: Schubert chez Pou-lenc ," *La Revue musicale* (1 Dec. 1928), 91-2.

287 Music and letter dated 11 Nov. [1929] in Poulenc 1994, 29-20. Partial facsimile in Reibel, p. 34. He also told Schaeffner, artistic secretary of the Orchestre Symphonique de Paris, that a passage for trombone would astound him and that the piano part was more virtuosic than that in *Aubade*. Chimènes says Schaeffner used Poulenc's letter as the basis for program notes which included the statement: "les *Marches militaires*, concerto pour piano et orchestra, encore inédit et dont l'O.S.P compte donner la première audition cette saison même." Poulenc 1994, p. 317, note 4 and the fragment of a letter from Ansermet to Jean Gehret of 15 July 1929. Poulenc 1994, p. 328, note 5.

288 [Nov. 1929] letter to Croiza in Poulenc 1994, 29-21.

289 [May 1930] postcard in Poulenc 1994, 30-8 and letters to Ardoin of "jeudi" [9 Oct. 1930] in Poulenc 1994, 30-13 (promising a spring performance), and Suzanne Latarjet of 9 Oct. 1930 in Poulenc 1994, 30-14.

290 "Mercredi" [1 Oct. 1920] letter in Poulenc 1994, 30-11.

291 1 Oct. 1930 and Schmidt 1995, FP 30, p. 87.

292 Excerpts from Poulenc's 1 Oct. 1932 letter to Schaeffner and Milhaud's 31 Oct. 1932 letter to Poulenc in Poulenc 1994, p. 329, note 3.

Poulenc's compositional time between fall 1924 and spring 1926 was consumed by the *Impromptus,* a set of *Etudes pour Pleyela,* the Trio (for Oboe, Bassoon, and Piano), and the *Poèmes de Ronsard* (FP 38). A piano transcription of Mozart's *Ein musikalischer Spass (Dorfmusikanten-Sextett von Mozart)* (FP 41), a Sonata for Violin and Piano [II] (FP 39), the final movement of *Napoli* (FP 40), and the *Chansons gaillardes* (FP 42) were also on his desk.

One of the first works left unfinished was the *Etudes pour Pleyela* first called *Etudes de pianola,*[293] on which Poulenc worked in November 1921, but abandoned.[294] He also revised his 1922 piano *Impromptus.* The 1924 version, dated September in the publisher's copy, suppresses nos. 2 (Lent) and 6 (Brusque) entirely, turns old no. 3 into no. 2, and adds a new no. 3 (Très modéré).[295] There are also extensive revisions, most of which Poulenc wrote on *collettes* (pasted over pieces of paper) affixed to the first printed edition.[296]

The genesis of the very popular Trio is unclear. The first references to what may be this piece date from early 1923.[297] Always promoting his works, Poulenc informed Paul Collaer that he had sketched a Trio, which he would be glad to play for him next winter (1924). Almost a year later Poulenc repeated the scenario.[298] In May 1924 Armand Lunel was told: "I am beginning a trio for piano, oboe, and bassoon. The combination of instruments having excited me greatly, I hope to do good work."[299] Despite interruptions, such as work on *Marches militaires,* Poulenc's Trio had progressed sufficiently by September to inform Milhaud: ". . . [it] is much more important than my other chamber music. [It has a] length nearly that of a Haydn or Mozart trio, but is not at all in that style."[300] Autumn letters sug-

---

[293] "Dimanche" [6 Mar. 1921] letter to Collaer in Poulenc 1994, 21-3 and Collaer 1996, 21-8.

[294] Letters to Collaer of "dimanche" [6 Mar. 1921] and Milhaud [early Aug. 1924] in Poulenc 1994, 21-3 and Collaer 1996, 21-8, and 24-13 respectively. See also the fragment of his "vendredi" [4 Nov. 1921] letter in Poulenc 1994, p. 233, note 3. In 1924, without his permission, Kling permitted Odéola to issue a piano roll of the first movement of Sonata for Piano Four Hands (replete with mistakes!).

[295] Comparative table in Schmidt 1995, FP 21, p. 61.

[296] Schmidt 1995, FP 21, p. 62 and Poulenc's [Sept. 1924] letter to Milhaud from Nazelles in Poulenc 1994, 24-19.

[297] Letters to Collaer of 18 Feb. [1923] in Collaer 1996, 23-8 and "mardi le 12" [June 1923] in Poulenc 1994 23-15 and Collaer 1996, 23-22.

[298] "Mardi" [8 Apr. 1924] letter in Poulenc 1994, 24-9 and Collaer 1996, 24-27. The Trio remained unmentioned between letters to Collaer, but it was announced publicly in the *Chesterian* 5, no. 9 (May 1924), 222, suggesting that the pieces are the same.

[299] [10 May 1924] letter to Lunel in Poulenc 1994, 24-11. Poulenc probably met Lunel through Milhaud. See Chapter VIII for discussion of a proposed collaboration with Lunel.

[300] [Sept. 1924] letter to Milhaud in Poulenc 1994, 24-19.

gest it was nearly completed or actually finished.[301] That the Trio underwent significant revision can be assumed because Poulenc said the Andante was 6 minutes long.[302] His later recording of the final version is significantly shorter, only 4 minutes and 25 seconds.[303]

Work on the Trio was interrupted to set the *Poèmes de Ronsard*.[304] André Schaeffner had written for a 1924 issue of *La Revue musicale* devoted to Ronsard and had also contributed to a volume of Pierre de Ronsard poems obtained by Poulenc.[305] Poulenc chose five texts from this edition.[306] By November Poulenc was still composing the last movement of the Trio, "an Italian allegro that I hope is brilliant and joyous,"[307] and telling Paul Collaer to put the Trio on his 16 February 1925 Brussels Pro Arte program. Finally, he worked on the third movement of *Napoli*, two movements of which had been composed years earlier, and by mid-November the movement was half written.[308] A December letter suggests that Collaer himself should play the piano part plus the revised version of the *Impromptus*.[309]

Poulenc devoted more time to the Ronsard settings than to the Trio, however, because in mid-January 1925 the Trio remained incomplete but the *Poèmes* were finished.[310] No Poulenc music ap-

---

[301] Letters to Schaeffner [autumn 1924], Koechlin [autumn 1924, but after 20 Oct.], and Sauguet [Oct. 1924] in Poulenc 1994, 24-23, 24-24 (Poulenc 1991, no. 85), and 24-25 respectively. For Poulenc's [Oct. 1924] letter to Stravinsky see Stravinsky 1985, p. 207 (which says the Trio is finished).

[302] [Oct. 1924] letter to Sauguet in Poulenc 1994, 24-25.

[303] July 1959 recording with Pierre Pierlot (ob.) and Maurice Allard (bsn.).

[304] Poulenc announces the interruption in an [Oct. 1924] letter to Schaeffner in Poulenc 1994, 24-27. In another undated letter, he invited Schaeffner to dine at 83, rue de Monceau on Wednesday, 15 [Oct. 1924] before he settled in Amboise for ten weeks. Unpublished letter in F-Pgm (Fonds Schaeffner, no. 195).

[305] *Poésies choisies de Pierre de Ronsard*, ed. Roger Sorg and Bertrand Guégan (Paris: Payot, 1924).

[306] Poulenc listed the poems as I. "Le Tombeau," II. "Le Soir qu'Amour vous fit en la salle descendre," III. "Attributs," IV. "A son page," and V. "Je n'ai plus que les os." Ultimately the order was changed and the second poem was replaced by "Ballet." Each song was dedicated to a different singer: "Attributs" to Peignot, "Le Tombeau" to Freund, "Ballet" to Janacopoulos, "Je n'ai plus que les os" to Croiza, and "A son page" to Bathori. See Schmidt 1995, FP 38.

[307] "Dimanche soir" [Nov. 1924] letter to Schaeffner in Poulenc 1994, 24-28. The last movement of the final version is entitled "Rondo."

[308] [22 Nov. 1924] letter to Collaer in Poulenc 1994, 24-30 and Collaer 1996, 24-43. It must have been finished by Sept. 1925, because Cocteau told Poulenc that he longed to hear it after learning about it from Daudet. Cocteau's [Sept. 1925] letter to Poulenc in Poulenc 1994, 25-13. Poulenc sent a proof copy to Collaer together with a "lundi" [11 Jan. 1926] letter, see Poulenc 1994, 26-1 and Collaer 1996, 26-1.

[309] [12 Dec. 1924] letter to Collaer in Poulenc 1994, 24-32 and Collaer 1996, 24-45.

[310] The printed edition of the *Poèmes* dates nos. 1-3 "Amboise Décembre" and

Plate 7: Suzanne Peignot holding a manuscript of **Poèmes de Ronsard** *which Poulenc had given her (Paris 1991 by the author)*

peared on Collaer's 16 February concert, and the *Poèmes* and Trio were rescheduled for a 16 March Poulenc/Schönberg concert.[311] The Trio was dropped again, though the revised *Impromptus* (played by Poulenc) and the *Poèmes de Ronsard* (sung by Suzanne Peignot) received Belgian premieres.[312] Six days earlier Peignot and Poulenc had given the world premiere of the *Poèmes* at the Salle des Agriculteurs in Paris (Plate 7).[313]

In March Poulenc also took the last seven of his 58 composition lessons with Koechlin. Orledge indicates that these lessons took place "on 6, 9, 11, 13, 19, 25 and 27."[314] It is not known precisely what they did during these lessons, but Koechlin may have offered advice about Poulenc's latest compositions. If Poulenc's expectations were realized, the spring would include a performance of *Poèmes de Ronsard* by Claire Croiza at Mme de Polignac's *hôtel particulier* and a trip to Monte Carlo for the revival of *Les Biches* with a side trip to visit Tante Liénard in Cannes.[315] He planned to attend the premiere of Vladimir Dukelsky's *Zéphire et Flore* (Monte Carlo,

---

nos. 4-5 "Amboise Janvier 1925." Poulenc's 17 Jan. [1925] letter to Collaer in Poulenc 1994, 25-1 and Collaer 1996, 25-1. Poulenc's letter contains a brief discussion of possible singers for the *Poèmes*. He suggested Freund or Croiza, but definitely not Evelyne Brélia. Poulenc compared his new songs to those of Fauré and Debussy in length, and thought they were something quite new in spirit.

[311] "Mardi" [20 Jan. 1925] letter to Collaer in Poulenc 1994, 25-3 and Collaer 1996, 25-4 .

[312] "Mardi" [3 Mar. 1925] letter to Collaer in Poulenc 1994, 25-4 and Collaer 1996, 25-4 (which is here dated 'samedi"[24 Jan. 1925]). Two letters from Milhaud to Collaer ([7 and 8 Mar. 1925] in Collaer 1996, 25-11 and 25-13) clarify that Freund had declined to sing the *Poèmes* because they were too difficult. She had recommended the tenor Maurice Weynandt, but Poulenc chose Peignot instead. Poulenc was extremely upset by the episode. (Poulenc 1994, pp. 250-1, notes 1-3.) Poulenc and Peignot departed for Brussels on 16 Mar., returning the next afternoon.

[313] George's review in *Les Nouvelles littéraires* (21 Mar. 1925), 7 (Schmidt 1995, FP 38, pp. 117-18). Years later Poulenc told Latarjet ". . . Peignot sings them as I myself would sing them if Heaven had made me a soprano." (Poulenc 1994, 34-10). Poulenc's "dimanche" [15 Mar. 1925] letter to Auric in Poulenc 1994, 25-5, says the performance went very well and that Schaeffner, George, Brillant, and Cœuroy were enchanted. Picasso drew a guitar for the published cover. ([Spring 1925] letter to Picasso in Poulenc 1994, 25-6.) When the work was published, he sent Picasso a copy. [19 July 1925] letter to Picasso in Poulenc 1994, 25-11.

[314] Buckland/Chimènes: f, p. 28. Following these lessons Poulenc had much less contact with Koechlin for most of the rest of the decade. Orledge indicates that Poulenc lent his teacher 2000 francs on 15 Jan. 1926 and that on 13 Jan. he attended the premiere of Koechlin's Sonata for Clarinet no. 2, expressing his pleasure in an unpublished letter (see pp. 29-30).

[315] "Dimanche" [15 Mar. 1925] letter to Auric in Poulenc 1994, 25-5.

28 April)[316] and the 4 May marriage of Madeleine to Darius Milhaud at the synagogue in Aix,[317] and to spend two weeks with Russel Greeley, the wealthy American, and his companion Count François de Gouy d'Arcy, at their "Clavary" estate near Grasse.[318]

Poulenc's Cannes visit is documented in an arresting reminiscence of the artist Nina Hamnett which provides rare commentary on the composer's earlier years.[319] The following extended excerpt describes Poulenc's vitality in 1925.

F[rançois de Gouy d'Arcy] heard from Francis Poulenc to say that he was coming to Cannes to stay with his Tante Léna [Liénard], who was eighty, and F. wrote and asked him to stay with us for a few weeks. I knew him quite well and was delighted, as he was most amusing and intelligent, as all *Les Six* were. We went to Cannes to fetch him from his Aunt's house. [. . .] Poulenc composed all the morning; I painted the pear-tree and F. came and gave first Poulenc, and then myself, advice on our respective arts. It was delightful to paint in the sun and hear pleasant music at the same time, and I was perfectly happy. I taught Poulenc some of my songs, which he invented accompaniments to, and I sang them sometimes to the French people who visited us. Poulenc was terrified of birds and one morning, at about five o'clock, I heard a knock on my door, and there was Poulenc, who said, "Venez ici, j'ai peur." And under the water-pipes of his room was a fluttering sparrow, which he could not bear to pick up. I put my hand underneath and took it out and threw it out of the window. [. . .] We went to Grasse one day and found Nicole Groult, the dressmaker, and Madame Jasmy van Dongen. They arranged a luncheon-party at the hotel, which we went to. There were only French people present and we had a wonderful time. Poulenc and I found some gambling machines in the bar of the hotel and proceeded to lose francs until we were dragged away by F. and R[ussel Greeley].

[316] For Poulenc's impressions of Diaghilev's season see his [19 July 1925] letter to Picasso in Poulenc 1994, 25-11. He was particularly caustic about Braque's costumes for *Zéphire et Flore*, which he said "killed the choreography."
[317] Unpublished [Apr. 1925] postcard to Hugo in US-AUS. Milhaud married his cousin, ten years his junior, who had been his childhood friend in Aix. Concerning their honeymoon see Harding 1972, pp. 179-80 and Collaer 1996, 25-15 and 25-18. She had a distinguished career as an actress and has devoted her life to her husband. She wrote libretti for various of his stage works, performed in some, and has been the unfailing friend of researchers who have visited her at her Boulevard de Clichy apartment.
[318] Concerning Greeley's relationship to the Cocteau, Radiguet, Auric group (through whom Poulenc probably met the pair) see Steegmuller 1970, pp. 310-11. Sachs 1933, p. 165 called François "a charming man whose home is of unforgettable beauty and whose intelligence is the subtlest possible." Clavary is described in Hugo 1983, p. 267.
[319] Hamnett 1932, pp. 311-16.

Grasse is a dreadful place and smells of bad scent. I asked Poulenc
to sit for me, which he did, for an hour every day. I thought that he
should wear a button-hole, and we all walked round the estate to
choose a flower of a suitable colour. The ground was covered with
wild anemones of all colours and I chose a pinkish purple one, which
looked well on a grey-green suit. The portrait was a very good likeness but a drawing I did I liked better. The drawing was reproduced
in the *Burlington Magazine* some years ago, with one of Auric also.
Picabia [. . .] came to lunch with us and brought with him Marthe
Chenal, the famous opera-singer. [. . .] Poulenc tried to induce her to
sing, but she would not, but asked us all to a box at the Casino at
Cannes, where she was playing "Carmen." Poulenc sang his latest
songs which were composed for the words of some old and rather
naughty French poems of the sixteenth and seventeenth century,
which delighted Chenal, and I was finally induced to sing my sailor
songs which Poulenc played for me.[320] Poulenc's Tante Léna was
invited to the Opera also and asked us if we would like to come and
dress at her flat at Cannes. She was the sweetest old lady I have ever
met, very active and talkative, and was so kind and nice to me, treat-
ing me as if I was a young thing of twenty. [. . .] I had enormous pearl
earrings, a large pearl ring, and a very good imitation gold chain
bracelet, all of which had been given to me by R., F., and Poulenc one
day, when they left me alone at the Café de Paris, and went out and
showered false jewelry upon me, with which I was delighted; and
they really looked magnificent with my fine dress. [. . .] Chenal hired
a motor-boat sometimes and took her friends to the smaller of the
two islands opposite Cannes, called St. Marguerite. She invited us
all to lunch with her one day. F. was not feeling well and so Poulenc
and I went off in the car together. We had to meet at a small café and
had to explain that F. could not come. One motor went back and
Poulenc and I got into Chenal's Hispano-Suiza, which was very large
and grand. There were Picabia and Gaby and two other people. [. . .]
When we got to Cannes we went to the Casino. One can play boule
without a special ticket, but for the roulette and more serious gambling rooms one has to have one. [. . .] Poulenc played boule, I did
not play anything, but continued to watch the roulette. Our motor
came to fetch us, and Poulenc and I drove back to the Château.

Hamnett goes on to discuss a lunch they had with Stravinsky at a
restaurant called the Pavillon Henry IV noting that Cocteau, over
from Monte Carlo, joined them afterwards.

Poulenc was in Vichy during early July when Erik Satie died.[321]

---

[320] The songs in question are his *Chansons gaillardes*.
[321] Telegram in Poulenc 1994, 25-8 (Poulenc 1991, no. 89). Satie died on 1 July and
a list of those present at his funeral was published under the heading "Les
obsèques d'Erik Satie à l'église d'Arcueil" in *Comœdia* (7 July 1925), 1. Poulenc's

He telegramed Raymonde Linossier immediately asking that she consult Cocteau about flowers, but in the end she simply sent a bouquet of salmon pink roses and hydrangeas in his name.[322] She attended the funeral and wrote Poulenc about the ceremony and trip to Arcueil for burial.[323] Though estranged from Satie since the Monte Carlo debacle, Poulenc felt a deep sense of loss at the passing of one whose influence had been so pervasive.[324] Later, Milhaud and Cocteau attempted to locate the libretto and music Satie had left for his projected opera *Paul et Virginie*.[325] When the libretto was found but not the music, it was given to Poulenc who was asked to set it, but he never did.[326]

Poulenc spent much of the rest of the summer in the Touraine, where he heard from Milhaud and Cocteau with news of Jane Bathori, Stravinsky, Picasso, and others.[327] He sent a printed copy of his *Poèmes de Ronsard* to Stravinsky.[328] Then, in September, he wrote:

> I have worked a great deal this summer but with few results. I will not hide from you the fact that I am in a certain state of anxiety at this time. I am tired of all the fashionable "alla Scarlatti," "alla Haydn." I find that musicians have poorly understood the lesson of the *Octet* and the *Concerto*. I want to take better advantage of that lesson. The

name is erroneously listed among those attending. Orledge 1995, pp. 216-17 for the article by "M.F." in English translation.

[322] Deduced from Linossier's 6 July letter.

[323] 6 July letter in Poulenc 1994, 25-9 (Poulenc 1991, no. 90) and Chimènes' notes based on Milhaud's written accounts and Madeleine Milhaud's memories. Recollections of Satie's "Final Illness and Death" in Orledge 1995, pp. 205-20.

[324] Touching evidence of the affection Poulenc and Milhaud held for Satie appears in a score of *Socrate* given to Freund by Satie and inscribed "A Madame Marya Freund | A vous, chère Grande | Artiste, cet ouvrage que vous | chantez si divinement. | Merci de tout coeur. | Erik Satie | [rule]". To this Milhaud added "Commemoration de la mort de Satie | Arcueil 30 juin 1929 De tout [drawing of a heart] Milhaud" and Poulenc added "Pour fêter, encore une fois, notre | admirable "bon maître" | Francis Poulenc | [rule] | 25 Février 54 | [rule]." All three signed the title page. Copy in a private collection.

[325] Libretto by Cocteau and Radiguet. Letters to Poulenc from Cocteau of 14 July [1925] and Milhaud of [Sept. 1925] in Poulenc 1994, 25-10 (Poulenc 1991, no. 92) and 25-14 (Poulenc 1991, no. 91).

[326] Sauguet's 28 Mar. 1931 letter to Poulenc and Poulenc's 31 Mar. 1931 response in Poulenc 1994, 31-7 and 31-8 respectively. In Mar. 1931 Poulenc bequeathed the livret to Sauguet.

[327] Letters from Milhaud [early Aug. 1925] and Cocteau [Sept. 1925] in Poulenc 1994, 25-12 and 25-13 respectively.

[328] [Autumn 1925] letter from Nazelles in Stravinsky 1985, pp. 208-09. The copy is inscribed "à vous mon cher Stravinsky à qui je dois mes plus grandes joies musicales, en réclamant votre indulgence et en témoignage de profonde affection. Francis Poulenc [rule] 1925."

taste of perfection and of science is what I owe to your latest works, but it is difficult for those who do not possess your giant's muscles. I am writing a sonata for piano and violin, which shows you that I am taking the bull by the horns. This sonata in four movements includes a largo, an allegro, a romance, and a gigue. The first three movements move along diversely, the final one is in limbo. I hope nonetheless to work more quickly now.[329]

He busied himself correcting proofs, orchestrating *Trois mouvements perpétuels*, and transcribing Mozart's *Ein musikalischer Spass* for piano. He also received a flattering letter from the great French pedagogue Nadia Boulanger, to which he responded that he would be delighted to meet and discuss his music.[330] Their friendship grew, nurtured by a mutual admiration of Stravinsky, and during the thirties Poulenc relied on her for advice, correcting proofs, and conducting his music.

The Trio apparently lay dormant until fall 1925, when Poulenc resumed it while working on *Marches militaires*.[331] He had to put it down because of an accident in the Amboise station. When the train lurched unexpectedly, Poulenc accidentally put his right hand through a window severing two tendons in his thumb. He was rushed to Paris, operated on, and after ten days in a clinic, fifteen changes of bandage, and two months of recuperation was fortunate to be able to play the piano again. "You realize," he told Collaer, "that this little drama has not aided my work and that the Trio is unfinished."[332] By year's end his hand was mending and he planned to be in the Midi about 20 January and visit Stravinsky in Nice.[333] Count Harry Kessler wrote in his diary:

> Lunched with Misia Edwards-Sert, Poulenc, Jean and Valentine Victor-Hugo, Pierre Bertin of the Comédie[-]Française, and the pianist Marcelle Meyer. We ate in the hotel-room downstairs and then sat in Misia's small silver brocade cage on the sixth floor. Poulenc, whom I met for the first time, is a big, broad-shouldered farmer's son, rather taciturn and difficult of approach but likable.[334]

[329] [Sept. 1925] letter to Stravinsky in Poulenc 1994, 25-15 (Stravinsky 1984, p. 207).

[330] [25 Sept. 1925] letter in Poulenc 1994, 25-16.

[331] [25 Sept. 1925] letter to Valentine Hugo and [autumn 1935] letter to Cœuroy in Poulenc 1994, 25-17 (Poulenc 1991, no. 95) and 25-18 respectively.

[332] "Lundi" [11 Jan. 1926] letter in Poulenc 1994, 26-1 and Collaer 1996, 26-1.

[333] Letter from Moncontour, Vouvray (Indre-et-Loire) [30 Dec. 1925] in Stravinsky 1985, p. 209. Poulenc, writing Stravinsky from 16, boulevard Carnot in Cannes in Jan. or early Feb., had the flu, was running a fever, and had to postpone his visit for a few days. "Mercredi" [late Jan. or early Feb. 1926] letter in Stravinsky 1985, p. 209.

[334] Kessler, p. 273, 2 Jan. 1926: Paris entry.

The printed Trio indicates that it was composed in Cannes between February and April 1926, but the evidence suggests he worked
past the April date.[335] A letter from Cannes to Stravinsky written
just before Poulenc's return to Paris for a 2 May concert, thanks him
for advice leading to modification of the first movement tempo and
other unspecified changes.[336] Work continued up to the premiere.

Another piece revisited during late 1925 and early 1926 was his
Chansons gaillardes, first mentioned in August 1922.[337] He must have
completed it at Greeley's estate, because the manuscript is dated
"NAZELLES | CLAVARY 1925-1926."[338] How these songs progressed is
unknown, but they were ready for engraving by January 1926.
Poulenc was satisfied with them, but considered the texts "too im-
proper" for a Pro Arte concert.[339]

Spring culminated with the 2 May Salle des Agriculteurs "Auric-
Poulenc" concert to which critics came in force. Poulenc and Pierre
Bernac performed the *Chansons gaillardes*, Marcelle Meyer premiered
Napoli, and oboist Roger Lamorlette, bassoonist Gustave Dhérin, and
Poulenc played the Trio.[340] In his "Paris Letter" for the *Chesterian*,
René Chalupt wrestled with the direction of the two composers:

> Crowds flocked to an Auric-Poulenc recital, where these two com-
> posers gave some specimens of their most recent manner, which turns
> back more and more decidedly toward simple, direct, consonant, and
> "anti-modern" music. The public followed them with joy, but one
> grows soon tired of too easy pleasures and it may be presumed that

[335] Schmidt 1995, FP 43, p. 129. The manuscript indicates Mar.-Apr.
[336] Stravinsky 1985, p. 210. On 8 [Apr.] 1926, Poulenc cabled Stravinsky that he
would come to his house around 6:15 pm on Monday (probably the 12th).
Stravinsky 1985, p. 210. Poulenc was still in Cannes on 19 Apr. (letter to Jacob in
Poulenc 1994, 26-4).
[337] [Aug. 1922] letter to Wiéner and [Oct. 1922] letter to Milhaud in Poulenc 1994,
22-24 and 22-24, note 5 respectively.
[338] Schmidt 1995, FP 42, p. 127. Poulenc was in Nazelles during autumn 1925.
[339] Poulenc wrote "Textes anonymes du XVIIe Siècle" on the printed edition, but
told Milhaud they were from the 18th century ([Oct. 1922] letter in Poulenc 1994,
p. 174, note 5). Chimènes indicated that Poulenc had erred, but the texts are from
an 18th-century anthology (Schmidt 1995, FP 42, pp. 125-6) still in the Poulenc
estate. When premiered in Paris, George remarked on their bawdy quality
(Schmidt 1995, FP 40, p. 123). Once published, Poulenc sent Collaer a copy inscribed: "It seems to me that it is uniquely 'Poulenc' and no one would have been
able to succeed in this genre of half-erotic, half-elegiac song. I am in a hurry to
have your opinion. In any case I believe that this collection is *important.*"
Poulenc's 22 Nov. [1926] letter in Poulenc 1994, 26-9 and Collaer 1996, 26-13. In
Poulenc 1993, p. 16 (Poulenc 1989, pp. 22-3) the composer wrote: "I am very fond
of this collection where I tried to show that obscenity can adapt itself to music."
[340] The Poulenc/Bernac collaboration will be discussed in Chapter VII.

the present reaction in which they have taken the lead will in its turn, and probably before long, provoke a counter-reaction.[341]

REMAINDER OF 1926

Before beginning a stint as pianist with the Ballets Russes in London, Poulenc attended an important "Festival d'œuvres posthumes d'Erik Satie" on 17 May at the Théâtre des Champs-Élysées. Organized by Count Etienne de Beaumont, this concert featured *Geneviève de Brabant* (orchestrated by Roger Désormière) and included among its performers Marcelle Meyer, Désormière, Viñes, Roger Bourdin, Jane Bathori, and others. Poulenc reviewed the concert for *Le Ménestrel*.[342] Poulenc then played two final concerts: on 19 May he accompanied Mme De Lormoy in *Poèmes de Ronsard* at the Salle des Agriculteurs and on 26 May he accompanied Max Moutia in *Cocardes* at the Sorbonne (Amphithéatre Descartes).[343] Count Harry Kessler also encountered him at a private Pro Arte Quartet concert chez Mme Dubost.[344] Diaghilev was alerted that Poulenc, Croiza, and Auric planned to give a prestigious concert at Baroness d'Erlanger's London home on Tuesday, 5 July. Poulenc programmed his new Trio, invited Diaghilev, and asked his assistance in distributing 300 or 400 advertising flyers in Ballets Russes programs.[345] It was also suggested that he and Auric play Chabrier waltzes in front of the curtain during the interval of the ballet.[346]

Poulenc embarked for London on 2 June accompanied by Sauguet. Once there Poulenc was occupied by rehearsals for Stravinsky's *Les Noces* on 14 June at His Majesty's Theatre, Haymarket.[347] Diaghilev also presented Poulenc's *Les Biches* about which Poulenc commented: "Excellent orchestra. I *finally* 'heard' *Les Biches*."[348] Poulenc's artist friend Nina Hamnett, who was in London at the time, wrote:

> The Russian Ballet was having a season in London and Poulenc and Auric had come over to see their own ballets being played. I could go as often as I liked with Poulenc. We stood at the back of the circle if

341 *Chesterian* 8, no. 57 (Sept.-Oct. 1926), 25. George's review in Schmidt 1995, FP 40, p. 123.

342 Poulenc 1926.

343*Le Guide du concert et des théâtres lyriques* 12 (14 and 21 May 1926), 915-16 and (28 May and 4 June 1926), 926.

344 Kessler, p. 298. Auric and Milhaud were also present.

345 [Late May 1926] letter to Diaghilev. Poulenc 1994, 26-5 (Poulenc 1991, no. 97).

346 It is unknown if Diaghilev accepted Poulenc's offer for a nominal £12 fee.

347 The production, conducted by Eugene Goossens, featured pianists Vladimir Dukelsky, Rieti, Auric, and Poulenc. Performances were on 14, 16, 18, 22-24, and 26 June.

348 [July 1926] postcard to Valentine Hugo in Poulenc 1994, 26-6. *Les Biches* was given on 29 June and 2, 8, 10, and 14 July.

there was not a seat. During the intervals, we stood on the staircase leading down to the stalls, where Diaghilev, Stravinsky and the musical critics talked. Poulenc adored riding on 'buses. Auric liked 'buses too, but it was as difficult to induce him to move from place to place in London as it had been in France.[349]

Poulenc returned to France on 7 July, after participating in an exceptionally well-paid performance of his Trio for an American patroness named Wiborg [*recte* Wibord?] on the 5th.[350]

He spent the summer months in Nazelles where he entertained Elsie and Vittorio Rieti in mid-August. Afterwards he worked assiduously on a Sonata for Violin and Piano [II] which he hoped to accompany in Copenhagen on 23 October.[351] In the style of the Vivaldi-Leclair-Loeillet eighteenth-century violin school, it contained a largo, allegro, romance, and gigue. He hoped to return to London the following season to play the same work with the Polish violinist Paul Kochanski. Poulenc was still at work on the sonata in mid-November while waiting impatiently for proofs of the Trio from Hansen in Copenhagen. He had completed the largo and the romance, but was struggling with the presto [earlier called allegro]. The gigue was in limbo.[352] He discussed possible works for a Pro Arte concert on 13 December, but nothing came of this idea. The year closed with a most mundane matter resolved. Poulenc thought he had used a theme from Alfredo Casella's *Italia* (rhapsody for large orchestra, op. 11) in *Napoli* only to have Casella tell him that the theme was actually a slightly altered Neapolitan popular song. Casella then confessed to having "swiped" a theme from Poulenc for his ballet *La Jarre* performed by the Ballets Suédois on 19 November 1924.[353] In the spirit of Bach's time, Casella suggested that each forgive such petty intellectual larcenies!

---

[349] Hamnett 1955, p. 12. An unpublished letter [probably late Aug. 1926, see Poulenc 1994, 26-7] from "La Lézardière-Nazelles-Indre et Loire" to "Amour de Nina" [Hamnett], speaks of photographs which Poulenc had promised to send her, thanks her for having sent him some "gigues," and hopes that her elegant lady friends will invite him to London next spring. (Did the gigues have anything to do with the Sonata for Violin and Piano [II] mentioned above?) Poulenc also asks her to try to arrange payment for an article on Stravinsky's latest works from the director of *Apollo*. (Letter in a private collection.)

[350] [Summer 1926] letter to Milhaud in Poulenc 1994, 26-7.

[351] Poulenc and Auric went to Copenhagen for a joint concert of chamber music, but the Violin Sonata was not performed. Concerning this trip see Knudaage Rhsager, "Auric et Poulenc à Copenhague," *La Revue musicale* 8 (1 Dec. 1926), 171.

[352] [17 Nov. 1926] letter to Collaer in Poulenc 1994, 26-8.

[353] Casella's [late 1926] letter to Poulenc in Poulenc 1994, 26-10. See also Häger, pp. 237-48.

Plate 8: Caricature (1922) of Poulenc playing the piano by Jean Cocteau

VI

The Close of the Twenties: 1927-1930

As the twenties closed, much of the excitement that had propelled Poulenc to quick and lasting fame had dissipated. *Les Six* had long since ceased to be a cohesive group, if it ever was one, and in the future would only be resurrected every decade or so at an "Anniversary Concert." Milhaud and Auric, though, remained Poulenc's closest artistic advisors and friends. Cocteau, responsible for some of Poulenc's earliest public exposure, continued to wage a relentless battle against his opium addiction, while gaining sufficient stature to garner the artistic collaboration with Stravinsky he had coveted for a decade.[1] Never again would he have to badger a composer to set his poetry or prose to music, or coerce anyone to write his film scores.[2] He too remained Poulenc's lifelong friend, though future collaboration came decades later.

Paris no longer held quite the same allure for American writers although generations of American musicians flocked there to work with Nadia Boulanger. Nor was the city still the forum for endless confrontations in theaters and art galleries between the followers of André Breton and those of Tristan Tzara. Dadaism, which had produced works of anti-art that purposefully defied reason, gave way

---

[1] The two collaborated on *Oedipus Rex*. Robert Craft (Stravinsky 1982, p. 94) indicates that Stravinsky heard Cocteau read his play *Orphée* in later 1923 and wrote Cocteau inviting his collaboration.

[2] Stravinsky's folder containing his Cocteau correspondence concerning *Oedipus Rex* is inscribed, "Annoying and useless correspondence with J. Cocteau* concerning the first performance of *Oedipus,* in which many people wanted to have their say, and which greatly frayed my nerves. [*And many others.]" Stravinsky 1982, p. 94.

to Surrealism, which emphasized positive expression. Poulenc had been an observer at some of the confrontations, but not a direct participant. In comparison to the Surrealists, whose history was riddled with personal disputes, expulsions, and defections, *Les Six* was a familial group. Only Durey had chosen to remove himself. "What distinguished the Surrealists from many other intellectual revolutionaries of the twenties was that they carried their reforming zeal into the political field," states the British historian Herbert Tint. Members of *Les Six,* by comparison, harbored no desire to ally themselves with any other group—artistic, political, or social.[3] Although Poulenc exhibited little interest in Breton's Surrealist Manifesto and its attempt at doctrinal control, he later acknowledged the surrealist Paul Eluard as the most significant poet of his *mélodies.*[4]

The end of the decade was extremely important for Poulenc from the personal standpoint: it witnessed a weakening relationship with Raymonde Linossier, thoughts of marriage, and a deepening crisis concerning his own sexual identity. It was also a time during which friendships with several influential and wealthy Parisian patrons, including the Viscount and Viscountess de Noailles and Marie-Blanche and Jean de Polignac, solidified.

A PERMANENT PLACE TO WORK, "LE GRAND COTEAU:" 1927

Evidence of Poulenc's activities for 1927 is sparse compared to that for earlier years in the 1920s. Nevertheless, the highlight of the year was his purchase of a large house with ample property in Noizay (near Amboise) called "Le Grand Coteau" (Plate 9).[5] A frequent guest of his beloved eighty-two year old Tante Liénard in neighboring Nazelles, Poulenc finally bought property in the region that was so fertile for his compositional imagination. Le Grand Coteau, a name he found poetic and Schubertian, was initially built in the sixteenth century and enlarged in the eighteenth. The property is surrounded by acres of vineyards in a part of France famous for its production of white wines. Maurice Sachs, who knew virtually *Le Tout-Paris* in the 1920s, described Poulenc and clarified the importance of this house:

> Poulenc had a curious speech, a little heavy, a little nasal. Broad-shouldered, tall, his body well wrapped in a handsome fur coat, he always looked marvelously comfortable. His life was divided between Amboise and the capital; I have met him alternately on the streets of Paris and Tours. Everybody teased him constantly for be-

[3] Tint, p. 39.
[4] Poulenc first set Eluard's poetry in *Cinq poèmes de Paul Eluard* composed in 1935.
[5] For photographs of Le Grand Coteau see Gouverné, nos. 12 (front gate), 13-16 (music room), 21 (Poulenc's bedroom); Machart, p. 165 (Sophie Peignot's color photograph of the terrace designed by André Manceaux).

ing so meticulous with his pennies; he had, however, a well-to-do air. He seemed strong and soft at the same time, but his keen mind interested itself in everything. His contribution to contemporary music is considerable, although his career is still young; in the solitude of his home in Amboise he is creating beauty which Paris is preparing to hear.[6]

Poulenc purchased the property from Mme Rolland de Réneville, who lived at 11, rue Émile Zola in Tours. Apparently her brother-in-law assisted Poulenc in Paris, probably on 28 June, in negotiating the purchase agreement.[7] In August and September Poulenc happily wrote Milhaud, Picasso, and Valentine Hugo sending photographs of his purchase as they became available. Though the property required considerable renovation, Poulenc optimistically expected to receive guests by October.[8] To complicate matters, in late July and early August, amidst weeks of dust and dirt, Poulenc's family emptied and rented the Nogent-sur-Marne property.[9] Poulenc sent what was his to Noizay. By November, however, he still resided at the Hôtel Lion d'Or which was, he said, "lugubrious" notwithstanding the fairy-tale appearance of his estate when an early winter storm covered it with snow. Renovation continued for several years. Details shared with his sister Jeanne Manceaux, whose husband André had designed a new terrace, clarify the situation:

My home is coming along but I became crimson with anger last week. The carpenter claimed that it was ready, the locksmith the same, and the mason as well, but each blamed the other for the delay. I assembled all three of them, and they explained each other as well as they could, and most importantly did the job in double quick time. I hope thus that André will see the masonry finished. Tell him that if the carpenter is stupid, he was in spite of everything the only one ready, and that his windows are very successful. The plasterer worked since 4 November. The first floor is finished. These three white-walled rooms are very pretty. I assure you that the more I go to this lovely house the more enamored I am with it, whether in the snow or in cloudy weather, it is never sad and especially never damp. One would nearly be able to sleep in every room without heat and this despite the fact it has not been inhabited for eighteen months. I am in a hurry to live there.[10]

---

[6] Sachs 1933, pp. 29-30. See also the excellent description in Hughes 1963, p. 30.
[7] Unpublished letters to Mme Réneville: [5 May 1927] and [18 June 1927] in US-TCshapiro; and postmarked 23 June 1927 transcribed in Albrecht. I am grateful to Robert Shapiro and Carol Padgham Albrecht for access to these letters.
[8] Unpublished 13 Sept. 1927 letter to Hugo in US-AUS.
[9] "Mardi" [9 Aug. 1927] letter to Milhaud in Poulenc 1994, 27-6.
[10] "Lundi" [Nov. 1927] letter in Poulenc 1994, 27-10.

Plate 9: Drawing of Noizay (ca 1960) by Marie-Thérèse Mabille.(Private collection of Rosine Lambiotte-Donhauser and used with her kind permission and that of Rosine Seringe.)

Poulenc established some semblance of a staff at Le Grand Coteau because he also told Jeanne that his housekeeper cooked well and that for the first time he had had "un panier de légumes [a basket of vegetables] du 'Grand Coteau' that was very good."[11] He was unable to move in permanently, and letters to friends still bear Tante Liénard's "La Lézardière, Nazelles" address.[12]

Though a landowner, Poulenc rejected the appellation "Tourangeau,"[13] notwithstanding that he inscribed a copy of *Napoli* "à Madame Rol[l]and [de Réneville] avec ma bien vive sympathie Francis Poulenc [rule] Tourangeau de cœur 27 Février 1927 [rule]."[14] Later he clarified his reasons:

> I am not a Tourangeau, no matter what one says. The critics bury me in country adjectives with the bouquet of fine wine. Though I own a pleasant home in Noizay, the only place where I am able to work, I have no roots in this area.[15]

> I beg of you, never let anyone refer to me as *le musicien tourangeau*, for I have *always* worked here as if I were in prison, dreaming of those fairy-tale countries: Monte Carlo, Nogent, the Boulevard de la Chapelle [Paris], etc.[16]

[11] In Nov. 1928 Poulenc hired André Rocheron to oversee his vineyards and gardens as well as the property in general. Chimènes says he was also "chef de la musique à Noizay." His wife Suzanne, who helped care for Poulenc's house and lived on the grounds with their daughter Micheline, committed suicide shortly after Poulenc's death, unable to deal with the loss. Poulenc 1994, pp. 1045-6.

[12] In an [early Oct. 1928] letter to Maurice Lecanu, Poulenc said his house was coming along. In another "mercredi" [3 Dec. 1928] letter to Sauguet, he said he was trying to move, but apparently could not. Poulenc 1994, 28-10 and 28-13 respectively. Poulenc's first-known letter bearing the return address Le Grand Coteau, was written to Koechlin on "mardi" [Mar. 1929], Poulenc 1994, 29-3 (Poulenc 1991, no. 103). Poulenc also speaks of the great renovation expenses.

[13] "Tourangeau" indicates a person from the Touraine region.

[14] Schmidt 1995, FP 40, p. 122.

[15] Poulenc 1935a, p. 526. One of these critics was the distinguished writer, Colette. Reviewing Poulenc's ballet *Les Animaux modèles*, she wrote: "On the edge of a calcareous hill, surrounded by his vineyards, Poulenc lives in a large, airy house, where he makes and drinks his own wine. Across his sequined instrumentation, listen to the sound, see the gold gleam and the bubble come out of a rich soil. Look at Poulenc: are these the physical characteristics of a teetotaler? He has a strong and sensitive nose, eyes that quickly change expression. He is self-confident and cautious, at ease with his friends, and a country poet." "A propos d'un ballet" in *Comœdia* (22 Aug. 1942). Poulenc rejected her comments about his ballets in Poulenc 1942b.

[16] 27 July [1944] letter to Marie-Blanche in Poulenc 1994, 44-9 (Poulenc 1991, no. 167): Poulenc 1993, p. 49, recalling times past spent with Radiguet on the banks of the Marne, wrote: "My music is often *nogentaise*: it is *never tourangelle*, because, although I write at Noizay, it is the spirit of elsewhere, and when I write elsewhere, the spirit never turns toward the banks of the Loire. It is without a

Renovation dragged on and by 1929 structural work was nearly finished, but in early September the kitchen was still not ready so again he stayed with his Tante Liénard.[17] From 1930 until his death in 1963, Poulenc spent many summers at Noizay, often staying through the fall. Guests were frequent and he kept a small but devoted staff to maintain the property and manage his household.

OF MARRIAGE AND SEXUAL ORIENTATION

In mid-1927, as word spread that Poulenc had bought a substantial estate with his inheritance,[18] the artist Jacques-Emile Blanche initiated rumors from London that Poulenc intended to marry.[19] Aix-en-Provence was buzzing with news that "The ring is already on the finger."[20] Poulenc was going to marry a young lady from London! Shortly after receiving photographs of Noizay, Milhaud teased Poulenc about seeing him married with many children and a dog.[21] Poulenc emphatically denied everything.[22]

> My dear friend Jacques-Emile, here is the house that I have just bought in the Touraine, but for the time being I have absolutely no interest in getting married. You are very kind nevertheless to have thought of me. No matter how charming your delicious "Miss" is, I believe I prefer one from France. Perhaps my lack of matrimonial internationalism will seem to you bourgeois. I am not making a general rule. I speak for myself.[23]

Blanche found Poulenc's lack of interest unfortunate, adding that his wife had heard from a young lady wishing to see more of Poulenc, and that he knew French artists who would jump at such an offer from an adorable young lady.[24]

---

doubt because this ravishing countryside is for me perfectly neutral that I work there so well."
[17] 2 Sept. [1929] letter to Marie-Laure in Poulenc 1994, 29-17.
[18] Concerning what little is known about his inheritance see Chapter II.
[19] 6 Oct. 1927 letter in Poulenc 1994, 27-8. Poulenc told Mme Rolland de Réneville: ". . . I must leave for concerts in London on 4 July. . . ." Could his presence have led to further speculation? Unpublished "samedi soir" [envelope dated 19 June 1927] letter in US-TCshapiro.
[20] Fragment of Milhaud's [July 1927] letter in Poulenc 1994, p. 279, note 2.
[21] Fragment of Milhaud's second [July 1927] letter in Poulenc 1994, p. 279, note 2.
[22] "Mardi" [9 Aug. 1927] letter in Poulenc 1994, 27-6. Chimènes determined that the young lady in question was one of Saxton William Armstrong Noble's two daughters. As he was part of Diaghilev's circle in London, Poulenc may have met her during June or early July of 1927. Sauguet, p. 250 remembered that he, Poulenc, and Auric were entertained by "les Seston-Noble [sic]" that year. Noble, Director of the Royal Academy in London, owned Kent House which became the object of an interior decorating confrontation between Jacques-Emile Blanche and the Serts. See Gold, p. 218.
[23] [Sept. 1927] letter to Blanche in Poulenc 1994, 27-8.
[24] 6 Oct. 1927 letter to Blanche in Poulenc 1994, 27-9.

This episode was but one of several that deepened Poulenc's need to assess his own sexuality, and in the next eighteen months he experienced a personal crisis of significant proportions. Not only did his relationship with Raymonde Linossier change before her sudden death on 30 January 1930, but by early 1929 (if not before) Poulenc believed he had fallen in love with the artist Richard Chanlaire while working on *Concert champêtre* and *Aubade*.[25] Direct evidence concerning the beginning of the crisis is scarce, but letters to Raymonde's sister Alice Ardoin and Chanlaire assist in clarifying the situation.

At thirty, Poulenc enjoyed or was rapidly developing significant relationships with various women. Throughout his life he had a very special affection for Geneviève Sienkiewicz, at whose Parisian salon he met numerous musicians. Already in the teens, Valentine Gross nurtured his artistic activities and helped expand his circle of friends. During the 1920s, Virginie Liénard became his surrogate mother who provided him with a home away from home in Nazelles and whose love of music made her an excellent companion. He found favor with Marie Laurencin during their work on *Les Biches*, and there were also singers such as Marya Freund, Suzanne Peignot, and Claire Croiza with whom he performed and for whom he wrote *mélodies*. In the 1920s, Poulenc received the first of many invitations from Marie-Blanche de Polignac to visit the estate she and her husband Jean maintained in Brittany and at which numerous summer guests were received. Marie-Laure and Charles de Noailles also entertained Poulenc both in Paris and Hyères.[26] They found him a delightful guest who was willing to compose for them upon request. Poulenc was, of course, also associated with Germaine Tailleferre, a fellow member of *Les Six*, and became Nadia Boulanger's good friend.

Linossier, the only woman with whom he developed a special bond, had been his friend from childhood. Nothing suggests their relationship was other than platonic, but the two developed a deep love for each other's company, and Poulenc considered her his closest artistic confidant.[27] She is among the few women who received a specially signed copy of virtually every piece he published, and she was also the recipient of dedications and manuscript scores given as gifts. Their friendship peaked in the early 1920s, but by mid-de-

---

[25] Chanlaire maintained a Paris shop and a gallery in Tourrettes-sur-Loup, a town in the mountains above Nice. Poulenc had made his acquaintance in the mid-1920s in the Touraine where Chanlaire frequently stayed at the Château du Perreux. Poulenc 1994, p. 1016.

[26] Poulenc's relationship with his patrons is discussed in great detail in Buckland/Chimènes: b.

[27] Poulenc never tutoyed Linossier in letters nor she him, yet they developed a secret written code for thoughts they did not want intercepted. See Chapter II.

cade she reproached him for mishandling his relationship with Satie, and thereafter they slowly drifted apart.

Deeply troubled, Poulenc wrote Alice Ardoin in July 1928 seeking assistance with a rapprochement.[28] "Did you think that I have bought a large house for myself alone?," he queried. He had been afraid to say anything about this to Raymonde. "The longer I live," he said, "the more I feel that she is the only person with whom I would like to live." Poulenc knew that his plea might already be too late, that he was losing Raymonde to her increasing passion for oriental studies at the Musée Guimet, and that two years earlier she would have accepted his offer to become Madame Poulenc. He even envisioned where Raymonde would put her books and personal belongings at Le Grand Coteau. He asked Alice to share the letter with no one but her husband (especially not the Latarjets), and said that he had told only his Tante Liénard, who fervently desired a reconciliation. "Be a good ambassador," he pleaded, as he asked her to make the marriage proposal he could not bring himself to tender.

We do not know how often Poulenc and Linossier saw each other during 1929, but she made her first visit to Le Grand Coteau late in the fall. When she left, Poulenc gave her a fragmentary sketch of a *Valse* (FP 53) inscribed "Pour Raymonde sa partie en pleurant parce qu'elle part et en souvenir de son *premier* séjour à Noizay. Tendrement Francis 3 Novembre 1929."[29] She died on 30 January 1930 leaving Poulenc "frightfully unhappy, dreadfully unhappy."[30]

Raymonde must have noticed Poulenc's increasing attachment to the homosexual group of artists with whom he had worked for years. Though close friends such as Milhaud, Picasso, and Stravinsky showed no interest whatsoever in other than heterosexual relationships, such was not the case for numerous other friends. In particular, the Cocteau-Radiguet group, Diaghilev and his circle, Count François de Gouy d'Arcy and Russel Greeley to mention a few, were all part of a male-oriented culture; Linossier knew about this group and acknowledged that Satie had become suspicious years earlier. References to homosexual activity, virtually absent from Poulenc's earlier correspondence, begin to appear in early May 1929. He not only privately avowed his "love" for Chanlaire in letters accompa-

[28] "Samedi" [21 July 1928] letter in Poulenc 1994, 28-4. This important letter has been translated in Buckland/Chimènes: j, pp. 97-8.
[29] "For Raymonde her part weeping because she is leaving in memory of her *first* stay at Noizay. . . ." Poulenc, who reacquired the manuscript when Linossier died, gave it to Boulanger from whose estate it passed to the Bibliothèque Nationale. He also spoke warmly of a Dec. Linossier visit in a "dimanche" [29 Dec. 1929] letter to Marie-Laure in Poulenc 1994, 29-23.
[30] "Vendredi midi" [31 Jan. 1930] *pneumatique* to Ardoin in Poulenc 1994, 30-1.

nying gifts of drafts for *Concert champêtre* (FP 49) and *Aubade* (FP 51),[31] but expressed it more "publicly" to Valentine Hugo.

> How happy I was to be able to confide to you my great secret, my grave secret. This *amazing,* but so anguishing love of which I spoke to you being now the *sole* raison d'être of my life, you understand how hard, due to this anomaly, it is to hide it.[32]

Even Poulenc's choice of subject for *Aubade,* dealing with the goddess Diana's eternal chastity, may be read as a commentary on his conception of love. One year later, in 1930, Poulenc's dear friend Auric married the painter Nora Vilter. Throughout his life Poulenc maintained friendships with many women, but from the late twenties his intimate relationships, whether long term or casual, were virtually all with men.

The vexing question of how much Linossier knew of the reasons for Poulenc's angst may be answered in his own remark to Ardoin after Raymonde's death:

> There are moments when I feel abominably low. Raymonde was so good and indulgent to me in all these past months, excusing my worst follies and endlessly trying to pull me from this inextricable quagmire in which I have sunk... I am trying to work in her memory, but physically very drained I am not doing good work.[33]

A brilliant and compassionate woman, Linossier no doubt understood Poulenc's plight all too well, and Poulenc felt guilt at what he apparently viewed as his own betrayal.

COMPOSITIONS OF 1927: THE SHORTER WORKS

Preoccupation with new responsibilities at Noizay did not limit his compositional activities. Though hardly a stellar year, he worked on various short pieces as well as the *Concert champêtre* for Landowska. During February he composed a brief *Vocalise* for high voice and piano (FP 44), often referred to as an *Air sans parole,* destined for inclusion in one of the numerous volumes of vocalizes collected by Amédée Hettich.[34] Poulenc dedicated the 1929 printed edition to the memory of Evelyne Brélia, Paul Collaer's singer friend, who had been murdered in July 1928.[35] He also performed *Poèmes*

[31] 10 May 1929 and "lundi" [*recte* "mardi"] 18 June 1929 letters in Poulenc 1994, 29-8 and 19-11 respectively. See also Schmidt 1995, pp. 151-2 and 161.
[32] "Mardi" [21 May 1929] letter. Apparently Poulenc also told Landowska. "Samedi" [May 1929] letter in Poulenc 1994, 29-10.
[33] "Jeudi" [summer 1930] letter in Poulenc 1994, 30-9.
[34] Though infrequently performed, this piece captured the fancy of later Russian arrangers who published it in versions for trumpet or violin and piano during the 1970s.
[35] Poulenc 1994, p. 247, note 2.

de Ronsard with Brélia in Nancy during late March.[36] In February Poulenc gave a concert with Collaer in Brussels on the 21st. They performed Debussy's four-hand piano works *En blanc et noir* and *Lindaraja* on a concert that included Poulenc's Trio and pieces by the Brussels composer and organist Paul de Maleingrau, by Vittorio Rieti, and by Stravinsky.[37]

In April, Poulenc composed a brief "Pastourelle" for a one-act ballet entitled *L'Eventail de Jeanne* [Jeanne's Fan] (FP 45) written by ten composers for Mme Jeanne Dubost. "A charming, elegant, whimsical woman who liked to surround herself with artists and writers," Dubost was a frequent patroness of visiting musicians such as Bartók and Horowitz.[38] She gathered artists and left-wing politicians in the salon of her apartment on the Avenue d'Iéna for Wednesday entertainments as diverse as wailing Russian singers and a red Indian chief uttering war-cries while strutting up and down the room.

> As a token of our appreciation for all she had done for us [Milhaud wrote], Auric, Delannoy, Ferroud, Ibert, Roland-Manuel, Poulenc, Ravel, Roussel, Florent Schmitt, and I decided to give her a surprise. Each of us wrote a little dance, and we had them all performed in her drawing-room by students from the Opéra. My *Polka* was danced by the petite Tamara Toumanova, then just eight. Marie Laurencin, one of Jeanne's personal friends, did the décor as well as the organdy costumes and plumed headdresses.[39]

On 16 June 1927, Roger Désormière conducted the rather large orchestra that accompanied the dancers, who numbered twenty-six girls and two boys. Enchanted by what he had seen, Jacques Rouché, director of the Paris Opéra, arranged the first public performance of the ballet there two years later on 4 March 1929. Although the ballet had a short life, a piano transcription of Poulenc's "Pastourelle" had sold more than 31,000 copies by 1992![40]

During the spring Poulenc also set the first of four poems by Jean Moréas which became *Airs chantés* (FP 46). "I do not like this poet," Poulenc sputtered, "but as a game, in order to tease my editor and friend François Hepp, who adored him, I decided to set four of his sonnets to music promising myself all the sacrileges possible."[41]

---

[36] [2 Apr. 1927] letter to Collaer in Collaer 1996, 27-6.

[37] "Mardi matin" [15 Feb. 1927] letter to Collaer in Collaer 1996, 27-3 and "mercredi soir" [16 Feb. 1927] letter in Poulenc 1994, 27-2 and Collaer 1996, 27-4.

[38] Madeleine Milhaud in Nichols 1996, p. 81.

[39] Milhaud 1953, pp. 208-09 (Milhaud 1987a, p. 170).

[40] Schmidt 1995, FP 45, p. 137. Horowitz helped popularize the piece through his piano recording (V.S.M. DB 2247), made on 11 Nov. 1932. Bloch, p. 144 and Plaskin, pp. 537-8. The "Toccata" from *Trois pièces* was released on the same album.

[41] Poulenc 1954, pp. 67-8.

Elsewhere Poulenc was harsher. "I detest Moréas and I chose these poems precisely because I found them suitable for mutilation."[42] According to the autograph manuscripts no. 4 was composed in May 1927, no. 1 in August, and nos. 2 and 3 not until May 1928.[43] Jane Bathori and Poulenc premiered nos. 1 and 4 on 3 March 1928 at the Théâtre du Vieux-Colombier and the complete cycle was presented on 10 June 1928 in an Auric-Poulenc Salle Pleyel concert by Suzanne Peignot and Poulenc. Poulenc also performed his Trio at the Salle Pleyel on 6 March, and he and Madeleine Grey gave a 6 May recital at the Ancien Conservatoire featuring Ravel's *Chansons Madécasses* and his own *Rapsodie nègre*.[44] Slowly but surely Poulenc's repertoire as an accompanist was expanding to include vocal works by composers other than himself.

Poulenc departed Paris for London immediately following a 14 June performance of *L'Eventail de Jeanne*, traveling by ferry between Calais and Dover in Henri Sauguet's and Georges Auric's company. Sauguet's new ballet *La Chatte* received its London premiere that evening at the Prince's Theatre and there were reprises of Auric's *Les Fâcheux* and Poulenc's *Les Biches*.[45] Sauguet and Poulenc stayed at a small hotel "For gentlemen only" on Down Street near the Foreign Office, and Poulenc delighted in showing Sauguet the London sights. During their stay Auric and Poulenc performed one or more of Chabrier's *Valses romantiques* at the interval of a 4 July Ballets Russes performance.[46] A day later, they played two-piano works by Debussy and Chabrier, and took turns accompanying Claire Croiza in *mélodies* by Debussy, Poulenc, Auric, and Chabrier. Every day they were invited to meet important people such as Baron Erlanger, Lady Emerald Cunard, Lady Colefax, Mrs. Mathews, the Saxton-Nobles, Miss Wibord, and others.[47] Throughout his life, Poulenc was as at home with the exalted as he was with folk of lower origin.

---

[42] Poulenc 1993, p. 16. In brief comments about each song, Poulenc was extremely caustic, denigrating the songs in general and no. 3 in particular. In Buckland/Chimènes: h, p. 144 Poulenc lists all of Moréas' books as works he would dislike possessing.

[43] In a 9 Sept. 1927 letter to Sauguet Poulenc wrote that he had composed three new *Airs variés*: no. 1 was at the publisher, and he expected to write two others. Fragment in Poulenc 1994, p. 277, note 2. In an unpublished 13 Sept. 1927 letter in US-AUS he told Valentine that he was beginning a cycle of *Airs variés*.

[44] Grey, a French soprano, was associated with modern French music. She recorded with Poulenc and sang various premieres including Fauré's *Mirages*.

[45] *Biches* was apparently presented on 20 and 30 June, and 13 July.

[46] Sauguet, p. 250. Poulenc had suggested this idea to Diaghilev a year earlier in an [end of May 1926] letter in Poulenc 1994, 26-5.

[47] Sauguet, p. 250. Poulenc and Auric also accompanied Croiza in a similar concert on 5 July 1927 for which Cocteau designed the program. See Volta 1990, no. 188.

In November 1927 Poulenc reported having just written three of five or six projected *Novelettes* for piano that he planned to introduce at an Auric-Poulenc concert.[48] He felt they would please pianists and judiciously gave Horowitz the original manuscript of the first, dedicated to his Tante Liénard.[49] Only two *Novelettes* exist, however, one in C major ("Nazelles Octobre 1927") and another in B-flat minor ("Amboise 1928:" both FP 47).[50] On 8 November Poulenc also performed nos. 1, 4-5, and 7-8 of his *Chansons gaillardes* with M Prahl "baryton américain" at the Salle Pleyel.[51]

COMPOSITIONS OF 1927-28: *CONCERT CHAMPÊTRE* AND *TROIS PIÈCES POUR PIANO*

The year 1927 was particularly important because it marked the first time Poulenc completed a concerto. Whereas the *Marches militaires* still languished unfinished, the *Concert champêtre* was written for Wanda Landowska, who was incessantly pestering Poulenc to complete the work. As mentioned earlier, Poulenc had met Landowska at the private performance of Falla's *El Retablo de Maese Pedro* in June 1923 at which time she requested concertos from both composers. Falla's was premiered under the composer's direction in Barcelona on 5 November 1926, before Poulenc even began his. Poulenc continued to see Landowska sporadically over the intervening years, but it was only when Poulenc visited Landowska at her country home in Saint-Leu-la-Forêt, a few kilometers north of Paris, that he was inspired to write ". . . a rustic concerto, appropriate to this forest of Saint-Leu, where Rousseau and Diderot once strolled and where Couperin, like Landowska, once stayed."[52]

> For a lad who until the age of eighteen thought of the country as the Vincennes woods and the hills of Champigny [Poulenc wrote], rustic implies the suburbs. In 1928, Landowska was living at Saint-Leu-la-Forêt, near Ermenonville. It is in a very eighteenth century country atmosphere that I placed my work. This concerto is rustic in the style of Diderot and Rousseau. The countryside is that of *Reveries du promeneur solitaire*, if you wish. This explains the refined aspect of certain melodic shapes. At the time he wrote music criticism, Gabriel Marcel believed that he had discovered scandalous and inexplicable "military bugle calls" in the last movement. That is absolutely right. For me, perennial city-dweller, the Vincennes fort trumpets, heard from the neighboring woods, are just as poetic as Weber's hunting horns. In any case, you see that this concerto has nothing to do with

48 "Lundi" [Nov. 1927] letter to Jeanne Manceaux in Poulenc 1994, 27-10.
49 Schmidt 1995, FP 47, pp. 144-5.
50 Both were premiered on 10 June 1928. The third appears not to survive.
51 *Le Guide du concert et des théâtres lyriques* 14 (4 Nov. 1927), 131. Prahl is listed as being a student of M Decreus at the Conservatoire américain in Fontainebleau.
52 Poulenc 1963a, p. 57 (Poulenc 1978, p. 46).

the Touraine, as it would be easy to imagine. One more time, the slogan "Poulenc the Tourangeau" turns out to be erroneous.[53]

As early as January 1927, while touring the United States, Landowska had discussed the *Concert champêtre* with Boston Symphony Orchestra conductor Serge Koussevitzky. Koussevitzky was interested in a Boston premiere and a New York reprise. She nudged Poulenc to inform her immediately if the work could be ready. "I have suffered too greatly from the tortures of waiting [for Falla's concerto], and from the resulting anxieties, to go through a similar martyrdom."[54] Poulenc failed to meet her initial deadline, at least partially owing to preoccupation with Le Grand Coteau, but by September was again at work, and in November he invited his sister to spread the news that Landowska would premiere the concerto at the "nouvelle salle Pleyel" in June 1928.[55] This date was also aborted and Poulenc was in Paris in July 1928 to work with Landowska on the first movement.[56] Landowska wanted to see him again for several days beginning on 5 or 8 August to review what worried her about the first movement (Plate 10).[57] She complained about delays because she now anticipated that Ernest Ansermet would conduct the first performances on 26 and 28 October. Then, on 12 August, she sent Poulenc several suggested emendations along with explanations.[58] In early September Poulenc dispatched two sections of the Finale, which she found very difficult, but no mention is made of the middle movement.[59] Several days after one of Poulenc's frequent visits in early October, she was diagnosed with an appendicitis and underwent surgery.[60] The premiere canceled, Poulenc departed to bask in the sun at La Lézardière. When finally completed, the concerto was privately premiered at Saint-Leu with Poulenc playing the orchestral accompaniment on the piano shortly before the 3 May 1929 public premiere with the Orchestre Symphonique de Paris, Pierre Monteux conducting (Plate 11).[61] Among the friends for whom he played the work before its premiere only Milhaud disliked it.[62] Later,

[53] Poulenc 1954, p. 78. Marcel spent most of his time as a philosopher and dramatist. Poulenc 1978, p. 46.
[54] Landowska's 19 Jan. 1927 letter to Poulenc in Poulenc 1994, 27-1 (Poulenc 1991, no. 98).
[55] [Sept. 1927] letter in Poulenc 1994, 27-8 and "lundi" [Nov. 1927] letter in Poulenc 1994, 27-10. No performance took place.
[56] "Samedi" [21 July 1928] letter to Ardoin in Poulenc 1994, 28-4.
[57] 2 Aug. 1928 letter in Poulenc 1994, 28-7 (Poulenc 1991, no. 102).
[58] Fragment of Landowska's letter in Poulenc 1994, pp. 292-3, note 2.
[59] 5 Sept. 1928 letter in Poulenc 1994, 28-9 (Poulenc 1991, no. 101).
[60] [Early Oct.] letter to Lecanu in Poulenc 1994, 28-10.
[61] About the private performance see Lacretelle, pp. 104-05, Hell 1978, pp. 91-2, and Schmidt 1995, FP 49, pp. 154-5.
[62] 24 Jan. 1929 letter to Collaer from Paris in Poulenc 1994, 29-1 and Collaer 1996, 29-2.

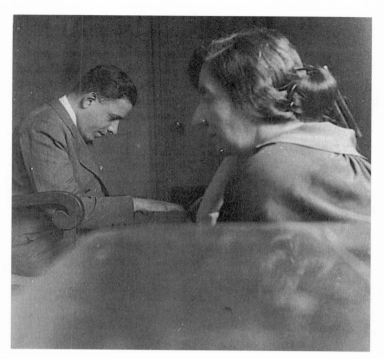

Plate 10: Two photographs of Wanda Landowska and Francis Poulenc taken during work on **Concert Champêtre** (several marked "Poulenc Eté [19]18 on the back; probably taken by Momo Aldrich. Now in the collection of Prof. Larry Palmer and used with his kind permission.)

however, Milhaud reported that the premiere had gone very well and that the first movement was fine, but the rest of the work bored him.[63] The "galant" *Concert champêtre* made a stunning contrast to the rest of the program, which included Robert Schumann's Symphony no. 4, Johannes Brahms' *Variations on a Theme of Haydn,* and Franz Liszt's *Les Préludes.*

Poulenc, who viewed his first concerto as a major accomplishment, was rewarded by an enthusiastic press, which turned out in force to review it. His earliest known interview, given just before the public premiere, is revealing.

> I wrote the *Concert champêtre* between October 1927 and September 1928, or rather I wrote it for the first time. You know what a supreme artist Wanda Landowska is. The way she has as one could say resuscitated or, if you prefer, renewed the harpsichord verges on the prodigious. I worked on the first version of my *Concerto* with her. We took it up bar by bar, note by note. However, we did not change a single bar or melodic line, but the keyboard writing and the choice of accompanying instruments were the subject of our most profound study. We especially clarified the writing, whether by simplifying the chords or by deleting notes. In short, we arrived at a score that will certainly strike you with its simplicity, the effect of which nevertheless remains rich and varied.[64]

Sensitive of the need to justify his choice of the harpsichord to potential listeners, Poulenc continued:

> Above all I wanted to use the harpsichord in a way that was both modern and did not resemble a pastiche. I wanted to show that the harpsichord was not an obsolete instrument, imperfect, of an interest above all retrospective, but that on the contrary it was and always will be an instrument that has reached perfection, with specific characteristics, its own possibilities, accents, and timbres that no other instrument can replace. I also wanted, in a modern language, to be inspired by the purely French style of the seventeenth century, full of majesty and pomp, which has nothing to do — I insist on that fact — with the "pastorales" of the following period.

Whereas Falla's Concerto is scored for harpsichord and five solo instruments, Poulenc's uses a relatively large orchestra. The problem of balance between soloist and orchestra concerned him.

> I decided [. . .] to employ the full orchestra against the fragile harpsichord. If they dialogue, one will not harm the other. Whenever they play together, I extract the requisite parts from the whole and, one by

---

[63] Milhaud's [9 May 1929] and 6 June [1929] letters to Collaer in Collaer 1996, 29-4 and 29-6 respectively.

[64] This and the next two quotations from Chevaillier, p. 856.

one each group emerges, without obliterating the sound of the harpsichord. On the contrary, the result is one of a greater variety of colors.

Reviews of the concerto were numerous, and critics from Europe and the United States were favorably disposed toward a piece for an instrument few were accustomed to hearing in front of a symphony orchestra. In honor of the success, Poulenc's publisher proudly issued a sampling of reviews in a sixteen-page pamphlet that also included pictures of Poulenc and Landowska at work.[65] During the 1930s Landowska played the work with some frequency, but Poulenc later told Stéphane Audel he regretted that it was not played more often.[66]

While working on the *Concert champêtre*, Poulenc was reminded of the old unpublished *Trois pastorales* written in late 1917. Alfredo Casella, who had admired them and owned a manuscript copy, inquired of their fate. Poulenc responded by revising them significantly for the 10 June 1928 Auric-Poulenc concert at the Salle Pleyel, and then offered them to Heugel for publication.[67] His fingers must have been well warmed up for the occasion, because he had performed Stravinsky's *Les Noces* in Brussels on 21 and 22 April at the Théâtre de la Monnaie.[68] The revisions have already been considered in Chapter III. Poulenc thought the new "Hymne" was closely related to *Concert champêtre*, and some material recurred frequently in later works. In particular, the opening dotted figure reappears in

---

[65] *Le Concert Champêtre pour clavecin et orchestra par Francis Poulenc* (Paris: Rouart, Lerolle & Cie, n.d.).

[66] Landowska recorded it with Leopold Stokowski and the New York Philharmonic Orchestra on 19 Nov. 1949 (now available on a Music & Arts CD-821), and Aimée Van de Wiele made the only other recordings during Poulenc's lifetime in 1957 (with the Orchestre de la Société des Concerts du Conservatoire, Pierre Dervaux conducting) and in 1962 (with the same orchestra conducted by Georges Prêtre). Bloch, pp. 56-7. For two recordings by Poulenc as pianist see Appendix 3.

[67] These pieces were renamed *Trois pièces pour piano*. Schmidt 1995, FP 48 and the earlier discussion of FP 5.

[68] In a 24 Mar. 1928 letter to Collaer from Cannes, Poulenc asked for a fee of 2,000 francs to play *Les Noces*. Collaer 1996, 28-6. See also Rieti's 2 Aug. 1927 letter to Collaer and Poulenc's [12 Sept. 1927] letter to Collaer in Collaer 1996, 27-11 and 27-12 respectively. During 1927 and 1928 Poulenc followed Stravinsky's latest offerings. On 29 and 30 May 1927 he heard the *avant première* and premiere of *Oedipus Rex*. In a [30 May 1927] letter he told Stravinsky: "Your art has reached such a height that it would need the language of Sophocles himself to describe it. My goodness, how beautiful it is!" Poulenc 1994. 27-4 (Poulenc 1991, no. 99). He also attended Ida Rubinstein's 27 Nov. 1928 *Le Baiser de la fée* premiere at the Paris Opéra, which he discussed with Collaer in a [24 Jan. 1929] letter in Poulenc 1994, 29-1 and Collaer 1996, 29-2.

the C-major Nocturne (1929) and as the opening gesture of the *Gloria* (1959).[69] Poulenc was an unrepentant self-borrower and those who know his music well invariably find this an endearing characteristic. The "Toccata," placed last in the 1953 edition, was recorded first by Horowitz in 1932 and subsequently by numerous pianists including Emil Gilels, Bernard Ringeissen, Gabriel Tacchino, and Philippe Entremont.[70]

COMMISSIONING AND COMPOSITION OF *AUBADE*: 1928-29

In 1928, with the *Concert champêtre* still incomplete, Marie-Laure and Charles de Noailles asked Poulenc to write music for a fête at their *hôtel particulier* planned for their town house on the Place des États-Unis in Paris.[71] The occasion was a "Materials Ball" scheduled for 18 June 1929

> ... for which costumes were to have been made of cardboard, paper, cellophane, or some other unorthodox substance. [. . .] Guests performed a series of Gothic and heraldic dances, while magic lanterns projected Jean Hugo's drawings.[72]

Auric was commissioned to provide music for the dancing. Poulenc proposed a piece called *Aubade* (FP 51) using eighteen instruments composed mostly of winds to accommodate the outdoor setting.[73] He also agreed to a contract (shared with him by Jean-Michel Frank, creator of the décor) guaranteeing 25,000 francs.[74] *Aubade* is absent from Poulenc's correspondence until early 1929 when he complained that even the waters of Vichy could not heal his malaise while composing it.[75] By March a scenario containing six

[69] Machart, pp. 56 and 61 discusses the motif. This is one of many which recur in Poulenc's music without regard to genre or medium.
[70] Bloch, pp. 154-5.
[71] Sachs 1933, p. 166 wrote flatteringly of Charles: "Who of all the men of society gives most attention to the arts, who is a generous patron, whose collection holds treasures, and who has aided in the production of films new and hardly realizable by commercial enterprise — *L'Age d'or* of [Luis] Buñuel and *Le Sang d'un poète* of Cocteau." Poulenc recalled meeting Marie-Laure in 1920 at a performance of Diaghilev's Ballets Russes when he encountered her in Misia's box. Poulenc's 2 Sept. [1929] letter to Marie-Laure in Poulenc 1994, 29-17. Poulenc acknowledges the commission in a 16 July [1928] letter to Charles in Poulenc 1994, 28-2. According to Rorem, Marie-Louise Bousquet, Marie-Laure de Noailles, and Marie-Blanche de Polignac ". . . were known to upper-crust Paris as *Les trois Maries.*" Rorem 1994, p. 528.
[72] Faucigny-Lucinge 1987, p. 70. Poulenc loved these celebrity balls and in 1928 attended one given by Mme Cardinal at which he attempted to resemble Colette's Chéri. See Cossart, p. 158.
[73] Concerning its genesis see Poulenc 1954, pp. 79-80.
[74] 16 July [1928] letter to Charles de Noailles in Poulenc 1994, 28-2.
[75] Poulenc alludes to the emotional crisis, but blames problems on his liver. "Samedi" [early 1929] letter to Charles de Noailles in Poulenc 1994, 29-2.

Plate 11: *Caricature of Poulenc at the time of* **Concert champêtre**
(Les Nouvelles litteraires, *11 May 1929, 12*).

sections for four dancers (three Coryphées and one star) had been drafted.[76] Later this plan was significantly modified to consist of eight sections. He had also contacted Frank before his departure for America and promised to consult Nijinska about the choreography when she returned from assisting the touring dancer Ida Rubinstein.

At this time Poulenc took a brief respite from thinking about *Aubade* to write *Pièce brève sur le nom d'Albert Roussel* (FP 50) for piano, one of eight *Hommage à Albert Roussel* celebrating the composer's sixtieth birthday.[77] Poulenc was particularly fond of Roussel and did not miss the opportunity to honor his friend. A handful of critics praised the anthology, but Poulenc's offering is mediocre in qual-

---

[76] [Mar. 1928] letter to Charles in Poulenc 1994, 29-4. In a [late Mar. 1929] postcard depicting the fountain in the garden of Diana at Fontainebleau, Poulenc confirmed having consulted Nijinska.

[77] Maurice Delage, Honegger, Alexandre Tansman, Jacques Ibert, Conrad Beck, Arthur Hoérée, and Milhaud also contributed. Lucie Caffaret gave the first performance on 18 Apr. 1929 at the Salle Gaveau.

ity compared to the nocturnes, impromptus, and concerted works he would write in the years to come. Roussel graciously thanked Poulenc the day after the premiere saying he would play Poulenc's piece for himself despite failing fingers, but *under* the prescribed tempo![78] The scores were published in a 1929 supplement to *La Revue musicale*. Twenty years later Poulenc arranged the piece for a chamber orchestra with eight winds, three brass, timpani, harp, and strings.[79]

Music for *Aubade* was composed during May and June 1929, a short time for just over twenty minutes of music.[80] The culminating entertainment on the evening of 19 June, it met with great success. Jean-Louis de Faucigny-Lucinge, a habitué of decades at Parisian costume balls, wrote that the guests included Paul Morand, Max Jacob, Louis Aragon, Max Ernst, the Dalis, and Jacques Février.[81] Poulenc was not only royally entertained at the Noailles' town house, but earlier he stayed with the Princess de Poix (Charles' mother) in Fontainebleau.[82] Afterwards Marie-Laure sent him a silver service from Puiforcat in Paris, which touched him deeply.[83] In appreciation, he penned a one-measure fanfare for them (reprise ad lib: FP 52) for twenty clarinets, ten trumpets, and ten trombones! Later he occasionally visited the Noailles' 1923 Hyères Villa Saint-Bernard that was designed for them by Robert Mallet-Stevens on hills overlooking the Mediterranean.[84]

Poulenc was fond of *Aubade* and performed it often.[85] The public premiere at the Théâtre des Champs-Élysées on 21 January 1930,

[78] Roussel's 19 Apr. 1929 letter to Poulenc in Poulenc 1994, 29-6.
[79] Schmidt 1995, FP 50, p. 158.
[80] Poulenc 1993, p. 40.
[81] Faucigny-Lucinge 1987, pp. 70-5. Distinguished guests included Henri Laurens and his wife, Baroness de Almeida, Lady Iya Abdy, the Count and Countess Etienne de Beaumont, Nabokov, Markevitch, Countess Hélion de Beaumont, Mme Edmond Barrachin, Marquise de Lambertye, Viscountess de La Rouchefoucauld, Mme Blacque-Belaire, Duchess de Vallombrosa, Countess de Ségur, Countess Jean de Vogüé, Parr, Mme Henri Bernstein, Countess Albert de Munn, Mme Suberviel, Mme Bemberg, Countess de Ganay, Jean Bourgoint, Cocteau, Jean Desbordes, Valentine Hugo, Tony Gandarillas, Princess "Baba" de Faucigny-Lucinge, and the Duke di Verdura. Photographs of the host, hostess, and guests in their costumes appear on pp. 71-9. See especially p. 76 for Anna Ludmilova, who danced the role of Diana in *Aubade*. Frank's set design for *Aubade* is reproduced in Ivry, pp. 72-3.
[82] "Mardi matin" [18 June 1929] and [July 1929] letters to the Noailles in Poulenc 1994, 29-12 and 29-13 respectively.
[83] 2 Sept. [1929] letter to Marie-Laure in Poulenc 1994, 29-17.
[84] Descriptions in Hugo 1983, pp. 301-03 and Markevitch, pp. 232-3, and Poulenc's "dimanche" [29 Dec. 1929] letter to Marie-Laure in Poulenc 1994, 29-23.
[85] Partial listing in Schmidt 1995, FP 51, pp. 165-6. Later, Poulenc tried to interest Ansermet in a performance ([early Nov. 1929] letter in Poulenc 1994, 29-19).

however, displeased him because he detested George Balanchine's choreography, which included men in what he considered a quintessentially female ballet. Was this but another reflection of Poulenc's emotional state concerning his sexuality?

On 10 July 1929, less than a month after the "Materials Ball," Poulenc was invited to another *soirée* chez Marie-Laure. After dinner, guests were entertained with a showing of Salvador Dali's and Luis Buñuel's film *Un chien Andalou*, shot the previous year.[86] This important work "was among those adopted by the Surrealists as precursors of their movement."[87] Jean Hugo, present with Valentine, recalled that Poulenc, Cocteau, Mme de Chevigné, and the Etienne de Beaumonts were among the invitees.[88]

Poulenc not only found favor with the Noailles family, he also benefited from his flowering relationship with Marie-Blanche and Jean de Polignac. In summer 1928, he was invited to visit the Polignac's Breton estate called Kerbastic near Guidel. Daughter of Jeanne Lanvin and Emilio di Pietro, Marie-Blanche had first met Poulenc at Jean de Polignac's home in 1918. The artist Jean Hugo wrote about the château, its grounds, music room, and Marie-Blanche's musical talents:

> Through a lane of tall trees, one arrives at a long, low house from the period of Louis XVI. It opens in the middle onto a little horseshoe-shaped courtyard closed on its free side by a wide ditch framed by woods; to the north, the perspective of a meadow which climbs toward the horizon lined by trees. In the morning, in front of the steps, rabbits and peacocks splash about together in the puddles left by the night fog in the hollows of the prairie. [. . .] The small drawing room on the courtyard was cluttered with two interlocked grand pianos. There was the heartbeat of the house. Marie-Blanche, with a voice as pure as a siren, gave to music the best part of her life. She remained for hours at the piano sight-reading the most difficult scores.[89]

Germaine Tailleferre, another visitor, wrote that the château was:

> . . . not particularly imposing. It was composed of a group of large, typically Breton buildings, with sets of windows in white granite. But there was a splendid park in Guidel, next to the sea. . . .[90]

This was the first of many invitations and he excitedly suggested an 11 August arrival date and inquired about the tricky connection

[86] Concerning Buñuel's work see Baxter, pp. 89-101.
[87] Steegmuller 1970, p. 403.
[88] Jean Hugo as mentioned in Steegmuller 1970, p. 403 and Baxter, p. 88.
[89] Hugo 1983, pp. 384-5.
[90] Tailleferre, p. 43. See also the description in Conrad 1997, pp. 161-6 and the photographs in Buckland/Chimènes, plate 13.

by trains and bicycle.[91] Poulenc, at Le Tremblay, had not yet confirmed an arrival time. He wrote again in late July that he would bring a bathing suit, that people would die laughing at his tennis, and that he was proficient at bridge.[92] A manuscript of Poulenc's *Novelette* in C major that he copied for Marie-Blanche on 14 August as a birthday present, confirms the trip was made.[93] She favored him with summer invitations to Kerbastic, and a year later he spent part of August there before going to Le Tremblay in September.[94]

FIRST SOUND RECORDINGS: 1928-30

By 1928 Poulenc was singing the praises of the phonograph, considering several recording projects, and writing criticism of new recordings for *Ars phoniques*, a review established by Jacques Nels.[95] Working through Maurice Lecanu, artistic director of Columbia-Couesnon, Poulenc arranged to record *Trois mouvements perpétuels* and the Trio early in the year, and *Le Bestiaire* and Duparc's *L'Invitation au voyage* (both with Claire Croiza) a little later.[96] In 1929 they added several new recordings to their catalogue including Debussy's "Il pleure dans mon cœur" (from *Ariettes oubliées*) and Fauré's *Claire de lune*, and in 1930 Poulenc recorded *Aubade* with Walter Straram and *Airs chantés* with Suzanne Peignot. Until 1934 he recorded exclusively for French Columbia. Over the years he was an avid listener who frequently delighted friends and guests at Noizay with selections from his extensive personal collection.[97]

[91] [July 1928] letter to Marie-Blanche and Charles in Poulenc 1994, 28-5.
[92] "Mardi" [31 July 1928] letter in Poulenc 1994, 28-6.
[93] Dedication in Poulenc 1994, p. 291, note 2. Born on 15 Aug. 1897, she and Poulenc were close in age and Poulenc frequently presented manuscripts for her birthday, dedicated pieces to her, and occasionally performed with her.
[94] [Aug. 1929] letters to Croiza in Poulenc 1994, 29-15 and 29-16, and 2 Sept. [1929] letter to Marie-Laure from Le Tremblay in Poulenc 1994, 29-17. He was back in the Touraine on 8 Sept.
[95] 16 July [1928] letter to Lecanu in Poulenc 1994, 28-3. For reviews by Poulenc of recordings see Poulenc 1928a, Poulenc 1928c, and Poulenc 1929. In November he also reviewed Alfred Cortot's and Jacques Thibaud's performance of Fauré's Sonata for Violin and Piano in A major (Poulenc 1928c).
[96] [Early Oct. 1928] letter to Lecanu in Poulenc 1994, 28-20. The Trio recording may have coincided with the 3 Mar. 1928 performance, and Poulenc was already speaking about the possible appearance of the *Trois mouvements* on 20 Oct. Letters to Lecanu of "lundi" [5 Nov. 1928] and [late Nov. 1928] in Poulenc 1994, 28-11 and 28-12 respectively clarify that recording sessions with Croiza and of the *Biches* excerpts would occur between 5 and 12 Dec. See Appendix 3 for Poulenc's recordings as piano soloist or accompanist.
[97] Comments in a "dimanche" [29 Dec. 1929] letter to Marie-Laure. Poulenc 1994, 29-23, says his phonograph was playing non-stop and that he adored a new Columbia recording of Stravinsky's *Le Sacre du Printemps*.

FALL 1929 AND THE YEAR 1930

Diaghilev's death in Venice on 19 August 1929 at age fifty-seven overwhelmed Poulenc. The impresario had been responsible for commissioning *Les Biches* and for introducing Poulenc's music to Europe on a grand scale.[98] Through Diaghilev Poulenc had met innumerable artists, critics, patrons, and members of the European aristocracy. From the day they met, Diaghilev's impact had been enormous. The impresario never asked Poulenc for a second ballet after the huge success of *Les Biches*. Was this another example of Diaghilev sensing that a composer did not fit future plans for his company? Fortunately, Poulenc followed other muses and continued to write music for dance.

Compositional time during fall 1929 was divided between the ill-fated *Marches militaires* discussed earlier and Sonata for Violin and Piano [III] (FP 54). Poulenc hoped to see both works progress before his return to Paris in late November. He joked about his poor track record with violin sonatas, telling André Schaeffner: "Its style is very curious. Five linked movements: Largo, Allegro, Sérénade, Presto, Conclusion."[99] Nearly a year later he tantalized Marie-Laure de Noailles: "This winter you will hear the *Marches [militaires]*, a Sonata for Violin and Piano, and a little folly for piano in the spirit of the *Folies françaises* by Couperin. The title is: Le Carnaval de Nazelles."[100] He also told the renowned pianist Marguerite Long that he was going to complete the sonata, and it is last mentioned in October of 1932.[101] Like its earlier siblings, this violin sonata passed into oblivion, never to be heard of again.

The 1929 season also marked the tenth anniversary of *Les Six*. Two concerts were planned: the first on 11 December at the Théâtre des Champs-Élysées with the orchestra of the Concerts Straram and the second on 18 December at the Salle Gaveau.[102] (See programs on facing page.)

Shortly after these festivities, the following anonymous poem entitled "Les Six" (see p. 176) was received by the editor of *Le Guide du concert et des théâtres lyriques:*

[98] 2 Sept. [1929] letter to Marie-Laure in Poulenc 1994, 29-17.
[99] 11 Nov. [1929] letter to Schaeffner in Poulenc 1994, 29-20.
[100] "Mercredi" [1 Oct. 1930] letter to in Poulenc 1994, 30-11.
[101] Unpublished 6 Oct. 1931 letter to Long in F-Pgm (Fonds Marguerite Long) and fragment of his 1 Oct. [1932] letter in Poulenc 1994, p. 329, note 3.
[102] Milhaud's [Paris 21 Nov. 1929] letter in Collaer 1996, 29-12. Désormière, who witnessed the first concert, was uncomplimentary. "Vendredi" [12 Dec. 1929] letter to Collaer in Collaer 1996, 29-13. When *Aubade* was published in 1930, Poulenc sent Collaer a copy knowing he disliked it. (Dedication in Collaer 1996, 30-21.)

WEDNESDAY, 11 DECEMBER 1929 CONCERT[103]

"Le Groupe des Six"

Les Fâcheux	Auric	Auric, conducting
Aubade	Poulenc	Poulenc, piano Honegger, conducting
2ᵉ Suite symphonique	Milhaud	Milhaud, conducting
Neige, Carillons	Durey	Durey, conducting
Concerto for Piano	Tailleferre	Tailleferre, piano Milhaud, conducting
"Mort d'Hippolyte" from *Phaedra*	Honegger	Honegger, conducting
Rugby	Honegger	Honegger, conducting

WEDNESDAY, 18 DECEMBER 1929 CONCERT

"Le Groupe des Six"

Album des Six	Auric, Durey, Honegger Milhaud, Poulenc, Tailleferre	Andrée Vaurabourg, piano
Sonata for Violin and Piano	Tailleferre	Robert Kretly, violin Tailleferre, piano
Huit poèmes de Jean Cocteau	Auric	Suzanne Peignot, soprano; Auric, piano
String Quartet no. 2	Milhaud	Krettly Quartet
Intermède: *La Toisoin d'Or*	Cocteau	Cocteau (first performance)
Sonatine for Flute and Piano	Durey	Marcel Moyse, flute A. Vaurabourg, piano
Sonata for Cello and Piano	Honegger	André Navarra, cello A. Vaurabourg, piano
Trio	Poulenc	Roger Lamolrette, ob. Gustave Dhérin, bsn. Poulenc, piano
Six *mélodies*	Auric, Durey, Honegger Milhaud, Poulenc, Tailleferre	Peignot, soprano the authors, piano

[103] This and the following concert listed in *Le Guide du concert et des théâtres lyriques* 16 (6 Dec. 1929), 289 and (13 Dec. 1929), 321-2.

En cercle académique assis,
Ils forment le conseil des Six:
Durey, Francis Poulenc, Honegre[a]
Milhaud traduit par George [sic] Auric,
Font de la musique pour nègre
Que renierait Satie (Erik).
A ces cinq hommes, je préfère
Leur sœur, Germaine Tailleferre.

[a]Licence poétique. Th. Gautier écrivait à la rime: Wèbre, pour Weber.[104]

At this same time, Poulenc also participated in two other concerts. On 10 December, for a "Jeunes musiciens polonaise" concert at the Salle Pleyel, he accompanied Marya Freund in *Le Bestiaire* and *Poèmes de Ronsard* and played "Hymne" from *Trois pièces pour piano* and *Deux novelettes.* The pair also performed Ildebrando Pizzetti's *Trois poèmes populaires italiens*, Karol Szymanowski's "L'Enfant-Jésus" (from Five Songs, op. 13), and Wieniawski's *Deux chansons populaires polonaises.*[105] Then, for the "12e Soirée musicale" on 14 December, Poulenc and Germaine Tailleferre shared the spotlight as composer-performer. Poulenc and Tailleferre, at two pianos, played his *Concert champêtre* and her Concerto for Piano, and Poulenc also accompanied Suzanne Peignot in *Le Bestiaire.*[106] The concert concluded with Milhaud's Sonata for Clarinet and Piano. For good measure, Poulenc accompanied Suzanne Peignot in a "Concerts pour enfants" at the Théâtre du Vieux-Colombier on 21 Dec. 1929 in his own *Le Bestiaire* and played a group of piano pieces.[107]

In the third week of January 1930 Poulenc played three performances of *Aubade* given by the Nemtchinova Ballet and the Orchestre des Concerts, Walter Straram conducting, at the Théâtre des Champs-Élysées.[108] Then, following Raymonde Linossier's death on 30 January, Poulenc escaped Paris to change a routine that reminded him of his departed friend. For several months we lose track of his activities until he joyfully announced to Manuel de Falla a pending April trip to Spain.[109] Years earlier Falla had tried to lure

[104] *Le Guide du concert et des théâtres lyriques* 16 (17 Jan. 1930), 411.
[105] *Le Guide du concert et des théâtres lyriques* 16 (6 Dec. 1929), 289. Poulenc also played *Trois mouvements perpétuels* and the Sonata for Two Clarinets was performed. I have been unable to identify the Wieniawski pieces "Je longe la route" and "Jean m'a dit" further.
[106] *Le Guide du concert et des théâtres lyriques* 16 (6 Dec. 1929), 291.
[107] *Le Guide du concert et des théâtres lyriques* 16 (13 Dec. 1929), 325.
[108] Schmidt 1995, FP 51, p. 166. The 21, 24, and 25 Jan. performances had décor by Derain and choreography by Balanchine. Milhaud's [Paris 9 Jan. 1930] letter to Collaer in Collaer 1996, 30-2.
[109] [Early Mar. 1930] letter to Falla in Poulenc 1994, 30-3.

him: "We are happily singing your *Chanson à boire* at the Alhambra! Come and direct it for us. The weather is marvelous and the Sierra is covered with snow. You will be pleased with our reception and your visit. . . ."[110] Poulenc's trip featured a "Conference-concert" during which he played the Trio dedicated to Falla, various piano pieces, and *Concert champêtre* (at two pianos). He asked Falla to recommend wind players for the Trio, and a pianist capable of playing the orchestra reduction of the Concerto. The trip afforded a further benefit, time away from Paris to spend with Richard Chanlaire, who joined him after Easter.

Falla's response from Grenada surprised him. Under doctor's care for serious medical problems that precluded writing letters, Falla said he would be away from Grenada for approximately two months beginning in early April, and that they might see each other in Paris when Poulenc returned.[111] Undeterred, Poulenc left France on his lengthiest trip to date.[112] The first part included three lecture-recitals in Madrid (central Spain), Bilbao (north coast), and Málaga (Costa del sol).[113] In addition, he spent a day outside Madrid at Escorial visiting the museum and taking measurements of the gardens for Charles de Noailles. He was frequently entertained at the lavish homes of prominent Spanish nobility, which made delectable reporting to Marie-Laure de Noailles, whom he kept fully informed. Once the lecture-recitals were completed, he stayed in

[110] Falla's 19 Sept. 1923 letter to Poulenc in Poulenc 1994, 23-33 (Poulenc 1991, no. 65).

[111] Falla's 13 Mar. 1930 letter to Poulenc in Poulenc 1994, 30-4 (Poulenc 1991, no. 108).

[112] Information in three letters to Marie-Laure dated "vendredi" [11 Apr. 1930] from the Gran Hôtel Carlton in Bilbao, [21 Apr. 1930] from Seville, and "jeudi" [1 May 1930] from Grenada." Poulenc 1994, 30-5, 30-6, and 30-7 respectively. See also Poulenc's [May 1930] letter from Grenada to Ardoin in Poulenc 1994, 30-8. Poulenc arrived in Madrid early in Apr. (first concert date unknown, but see the 8 Apr. 1930 issue of *El sol de Madrid*), made a day trip to Escorial, had lunch with Carlos Beistegui and his wife on the 10th, arrived in Bilbao on the 11th, gave his 2nd Bilbao concert on the 12th, returned to the Puerta del sol on the 13th, lunched with the Duchesse de Durcal on the 14th, dined with Countess Yebes on the 15th, left for Seville on the 16th, attended a magnificent evening with the Duchess Medinaceli including a concert of Cuadro Flamenco at the Pilatos Palace in honor of the king and queen (thanks to Neña Salamanca) on the 20th, saw Daisy Fellowes on her magnificent yacht, left Seville for Málaga on the 21st where he gave his 3rd concert, left Málaga for Grenada on the 22nd, and returned to Paris on 20 May. While in Madrid Poulenc performed at the Student's Residence with the assistance of the eminent pianist Aurelio Castrillo and the wind players Cabrera and Quintana. See Henri Collet's note in *Le Ménestrel* 92 (9 May 1930), 217.

[113] Poulenc told Ardoin that his arrival in Grenada was the end of his "looping." [May 1930] letter in Poulenc 1994, 30-8.

Grenada, a brief distance from Málaga, to rest and compose. Happily, his "pension anglaise," situated on the heights near the Alhambra, had a piano. Near there, in a kiosk, he found an issue of *Les Nouvelles littéraires* containing Monnier's moving tribute to Linossier.[114] From this year forward Poulenc gave a number of lecture-recitals on a variety of musical subjects.

Back in Paris during late spring 1930, Poulenc showed his puckish side to several important visitors. The renowned cellist Gregor Piatigorsky remembered that after his last recital at the Opéra Vladimir Horowitz remained in Paris at the Majestic Hotel where he entertained friends, especially himself and the Russian-born American violinist Nathan Milstein with whom they had formed a trio.

> While Horowitz relaxed with Piatigorsky one afternoon at the hotel, Francis Poulenc suddenly appeared. Poulenc was given to rushing in unexpectedly, crying "Allo, allo, allo!" and then trotting to the piano to play one of his short, witty pieces—after which he would back out the door throwing kisses.[115]

During Poulenc's short respite in Paris he gave a concert at the École normale de musique on 23 May with Suzanne Peignot. The repertoire was particularly eclectic and included a number of early works that could have been programmed by Nadia Boulanger (Plate 12, see p. 181). At the end of the season, on 30 May, Poulenc made a cameo appearance playing *Deux novelettes* at a Salle Gaveau "Soirée de danses" featuring Emmy Magliani (with Terence Kennedy, Lily Laskine, and Denyse Dixmier).[116] Shortly thereafter he departed for Noizay where he spent the summer and fall, taking jaunts to see friends and family. He visited Charles and Marie-Laure de Noailles in Hyères,[117] the Polignacs at Kerbastic for two weeks,[118] his sister in Normandy for two more, and his elderly, sick nurse in Bourgogne (with side trips to Montjeu, Autun, Avallon, Vézelay, and Auxerre).[119] In Avallon he even bought a fountain for Le Grand Coteau.[120]

Compositional activity during 1930, sandwiched between trips

[114] [May 1930] letter to Ardoin in Poulenc 1994, 30-8.
[115] Plaskin, p. 237.
[116] *Le Guide du concert et des théâtres lyriques* 16 (23 and 30 May 1930), 931 and 944.
[117] "Jeudi" [summer 1930] letter to Ardoin in Poulenc 1994, 30-9.
[118] There he enjoyed the company of Denise and Edouard Bourdet, Emilio Terry, the Chadournes, and someone named Almeida.
[119] "Mercredi" [1 Oct. 1930] letter in Poulenc 1994, 30-11.
[120] Later, Poulenc spoke about his plans for a French garden on a terrace mentioning other purchases and the expense involved. "Mercredi" [1 Oct. 1930] letter to Marie-Laure (but this portion addressed to Charles) in Poulenc 1994, 30-11 and fragment of his 27 Oct. 1930 letter to Marie-Laure in Poulenc 1994, p. 331, note 4. Concerning his nurse see Chapter I, note 17.

or accomplished during them, yielded a sketch of *Les Soirées de Nazelles* (FP 84) and *Épitaphe* (FP 55), a short *mélodie* in Linossier's memory. Work on both was completed by early October. When *Les Soirées de Nazelles* was finally published in 1937, Poulenc described its genesis:

> The variations that form the center of this work were improvised at Nazelles during long country evenings, when the author played musical "portraits" with his friends grouped around the piano. We hope today that these variations, presented here between a Préambule and a Final, will have the power to evoke this game in the frame of a Touraine salon, with a window open to the evening.[121]

Lacking the 1930 sketches, we do not know how the piece evolved. A comparison of titles of the two versions, however, suggests that Poulenc either shortened the work considerably, or combined numbers. He dedicated the final version to Virginie Liénard's memory, evoked in variation 8, who had died in 1935. Later, in a characteristically uncharitable mood toward his piano music, he suggested that variations 4-6 be omitted from performance.

LES SOIRÉES DE NAZELLES

1930 Sketch	1936 Final Version
Ouverture	Préamble; Cadence
Le Contentement de soi	1. Le Comble de la distinction
La Joie de vivre	2. Le Cœur sur la main
L'Instinct	3. La Désinvolture et la discrétion
La Suite dans les idées	4. La Suite dans les idées
Le Comble de la distinction	5. Le Charme enjôleur
Le Charme voulu	6. Le Contentement de soi
Les Points de suspension	7. Le Goût du malheur
Romance	8. L'Alerte vieillesse
Frissons	Cadence; Final
Nerfs	
Soupirs	
L'Alerte vieillesse	
Final	

[121] Preface to the Durand & Cie edition (Paris 1937).

Épitaphe was composed at Noizay in July 1930 at Alice Ardoin's suggestion. It was intended as part of a small volume honoring her sister Raymonde Linossier, which was to include Raymonde's letters, her novel *Bibi-la-Bibiste* (dedicated to Poulenc), and Léon-Paul Fargue's moving poem *Une violette noire* penned in her memory.[122] Poulenc lovingly chose a brief six-line text by François de Malherbe (1555-1628), a favorite of Henri IV and Louis XIII:

Belle âme qui fus mon flambeau	Beautiful soul that was my torch
Reçois l'honneur qu'en ce tombeau	receive the homage that in this tomb
Le devoir m'oblige à te rendre;	duty obliges me to render you;
Ce que je fais te sert de peu,	that which I do serves you but little,
Mais au moins tu vois en la cendre	but at least you see in the ashes
Que j'en aime encore le feu.	that I still love their fire.

Poulenc sent manuscript copies to Raymonde's two sisters on 9 October 1930, but the commemorative volume never materialized. Instead, Rouart, Lerolle & Cie published *Épitaphe* in December, and Poulenc quickly dispatched printed copies with touching dedications concerning his loss to Jeanne Dubost and Suzanne Peignot. He gave additional copies to the beautiful Countess Charles de Polignac (known as "Pata") and Marya Freund.[123]

In 1930 Poulenc also began a set of piano *Nocturnes* (FP 56), which grew to six by 1934.[124] Though these pieces will be discussed later, it is important to note that the C-major Nocturne is dedicated to Suzette Chanlaire, Richard Chanlaire's sister-in-law. On 13 November 1929 Poulenc had offered her a sketch (*brouillon*) of *Aubade* ". . . because this work is a wound, and that wounded yourself you knew, better than anyone, how to heal my broken heart. . . ."[125]

---

[122] Poulenc 1994, p. 329, note 1.
[123] Schmidt 1995, FP 55, p. 171 and Poulenc 1993, pp. 16-17 (Poulenc 1989, pp. 24-5) for Poulenc's suggestions about performing this *mélodie*.
[124] The printed score of the C-major Nocturne gives the date "1929," the manuscript gives "Noizay 1930," and it was first printed on 31 Dec. 1931.
[125] Schmidt 1995, FP 51, p. 161. The dedication probably refers to the emotional turmoil Poulenc felt while composing this work. See the earlier discussion of Poulenc's relationship with Richard Chanlaire.

Plate 12: Suzanne Peignot/ Francis Poulenc concert program 23 May 1930 (gift of Mme Peignot).

SALLE DE L'ÉCOLE NORMALE DE MUSIQUE
78 RUE CARDINET PARIS XVII·

VENDREDI 23 MAI 1930 A 21 HEURES

RÉCITAL
DE
CHANT

SUZANNE PEIGNOT

AVEC LE CONCOURS DE

FRANCIS POULENC

BUREAU DE CONCERTS MARCEL DE VALMALÈTE - 45 RUE LA BOÉTIE - PARIS

PROGRAMME

I

Lasciatemi morire..	C. MONTEVERDE
Star vicino	SALVATOR ROSA
Come raggio di sol	A. CALDARA
Stizzoso, mio stizzoso..	G. B. PERGOLÈSE

II

Lachen und Weinen	SCHUBERT
An Silvia.	SCHUBERT
Weigenlied	SCHUBERT
Klarchens Lied	SCHUBERT

III

Trois Poèmes de Stéphane Mallarmé .. C. DEBUSSY
1. Soupir
2. Placet futile
3. Éventail

Le Promenoir des deux Amants .. .. C. DEBUSSY
1. Auprès de cette tombe
2. Crois mon conseil, chère Climène
3. Je tremble en voyant ton visage

Le Balcon .. .. C. DEBUSSY

IV

Sainte.. .. .. M. RAVEL
Cinq Mélodies populaires grecques .. .. M. RAVEL
1. Le Réveil de la mariée
2. Là-bas vers l'Église
3. Quel galant
4. Chanson des cueilleuses de lentisques
5. Tout gai

V

Les bords de l'Illysus (Socrate). .. .. Erik SATIE
Attributs .. .. F. POULENC
Le Tombeau (poème de Ronsard) .. .. F. POULENC
Quatre Airs chantés .. .. F. POULENC
1. Air romantique
2. Air champêtre
3. Air grave
4. Air vif

P I A N O   G A V E A U

181

VII

A Wealth of Mélodies *and Piano Music: 1931-1935*

RENEWED INTEREST IN *MÉLODIES:* FIRST HALF OF 1931

The opening months of 1931 witnessed Poulenc's embracing of a genre in which he had worked only sporadically. Between 1931 and 1935 he wrote or arranged nearly thirty works for voice and piano. After he began his collaboration with Pierre Bernac in 1935, he composed two-thirds of his total output of songs, many of which they premiered. Poulenc also added significantly to his piano works in 1932 and 1934. Some were the result of pressure from his publisher Jacques Lerolle to provide short works for a receptive public. Later Poulenc looked dimly on many of these piano works, but a few received his blessing.

> I tolerate the *Mouvements perpétuels,* my old *Suite en ut,* and the *Trois pièces.* I like very much my two collections of *Improvisations,* an *Intermezzo* in A flat, and certain *Nocturnes.* I condemn *Napoli* and the *Soirées de Nazelles* without reprieve. I do not think much about the others.[1]

Before turning to composing, Poulenc traveled to Strasbourg for a 9 February 1931 Festival Francis Poulenc sponsored by the Société des Amis du Conservatoire de Strasbourg in the Salle Hector Berlioz. Two-piano versions of the *Concert champêtre* and *Aubade,* played by Poulenc and Alphonse Fœhr, framed the *Airs chantés* sung by Louise

---

[1] Poulenc 1954, p. 35. Inspite of Poulenc's assessment of his piano music, his works were performed by many of the leading pianists of his day. Those listed in *Le Guide du concert et des théâtres lyriques* for the 1920s and early 1930s include: Claudio Arrau, Aline van Barentzen, Marcel Ciampi, Marthe Dron, Juliette Durand-Texte, Jacques Février, Walter Gieseking, Henri Gil-Marchex, Marguerite Long, Marcelle Meyer, Arthur Rubinstein, Magda Tagliaferro, Ricardo Viñes, and Janine Weill, among many others.

Debonte, Trio played by Poulenc, Pierre Fosse, and André Eby, and selected piano solos by Poulenc.[2]

Possessed of a particularly fine ear for poetry, Poulenc had predominantly set poems by Apollinaire and Jacob. For his first 1931 group, composed at Noizay during February, however, Poulenc set three Louise Lalanne poems (FP 57): "Le Présent," "Chanson," and "Hier," which were dedicated to Marie-Blanche de Polignac. But after an encounter with Marie Laurencin at the home of Mme de Castries, the record was set straight.

> In looking at your charming score, I saw that you had also set to music three poems of Louise Lalanne. Of these three poems, two are by me, *Hier* and *Le Présent*. Eugène Montfort, at that time director of *Marges*, had the idea of duping his readers by inventing an imaginary poetess. Naturally Guillaume [Apollinaire], enthralled with this idea, accepted. At the time of going to press, Guillaume, who was laziness itself, had done nothing, and I remember we searched through my childhood notebooks, full of nonsense you understand, and ended by finding those two early efforts, *Hier* [and] *Le Présent*, which I find to be nothing out of the ordinary.[3]

Poulenc later wrote that "Le Présent" was influenced by the unison writing in Chopin's Sonata for Piano in B minor (finale), and that in composing "Hier" he thought both of the actress and singer Yvonne Printemps (1894-1977) and an interior painted by Édouard Vuillard (1868-1940).[4] Throughout his life Poulenc exhibited a deep love for art, frequently visiting art galleries and admiring the possessions of wealthy friends. Paintings influenced his own compositions, and he used analogies with painters to describe his music.[5] Bernac, who later traveled with Poulenc and knew his work habits, explains Poulenc's keen eye for art and its effect on him.

> He was not at all interested in discussing philosophy or politics, but on subjects that appealed to him—music, of course, or literature, and above all, painting—he could explain his very personal views with a zest, a spontaneity and a vitality all his own. He used to say that he liked painting as much as music, and his memory, not at all good musically, was infallible visually, especially for paintings. I had experience of this several times. During our tours we had many oppor-

---

[2] Program in F-Pn (Fonds Montpensier). Poulenc played *Trois mouvements perpétuels*, and *Deux novelettes*.

[3] Laurencin's [1931] letter to Poulenc in Poulenc 1994, 31-6 (Poulenc 1994, no. 111). Laurencin's poems appeared in *Marges* 14 (Mar. 1909).

[4] Poulenc 1993, p. 17 (Poulenc 1989, pp. 26-7).

[5] "It [the first of his *Sept répons*] is more Mantegna than Zurbarán," he might say. "Mercredi" [Sept. 1960] letter to Bernac in Poulenc 1994, 60-25 (Poulenc 1991, no. 320). See the important discussion of Matisse's influence elsewhere in this book.

tunities of visiting museums and galleries together, some of which were among the finest in the world. I remember one occasion, at the Phillips Collection in Washington, when he said to me: "Do you see the green of the dress in this portrait is exactly the same green as the costume of the soldier who holds the lance in the Mantegna of San Zenon in Verona?" And I could believe it. Did he not say to Claude Rostand: "I could match from memory the color of the velvet in *L'Enseigne de Gersaint* of Watteau."[6]

Concurrent with work on the Lalanne songs, Poulenc wrote "L'Anguille" [The Eel] and "Carte postale" [Postcard], on *"ravishing texts"* by Apollinaire.[7] The third and fourth ("Avant le cinéma" [Before the Cinema] and "1904"), composed in March, complete the group called *Quatre poèmes de Guillaume Apollinaire* (FP 58). Poulenc described them as "Atmosphère espadrilles, 'Bébert dit l'anguille. Narcisse et Hubert le Merlan'."[8] In the midst of his work, however, he could not resist making a hasty trip to Paris to hear two Stravinsky concerts at the Théâtre des Champs-Élysées. Sharing duties with Ernest Ansermet, Stravinsky himself conducted French premieres of *Quatre études pour orchestre* on 20 February and *Symphonie de psaumes* on the 24th. After the second concert Poulenc attended a private dinner party for ten at Eugenia Errazuriz's home, with the Picassos, the Stravinskys, Ansermet, and himself.[9] In a review for *Le Mois* Poulenc noted:

> . . . Stravinsky has never disappointed us, but rarely, however, has he offered us such a beautiful surprise. I place this *Symphonie* very high in the long list of masterpieces which go from *l'Oiseau de feu* to the *Capriccio*. [. . .] What is above all to my taste in the *Symphonie de psaumes* is the absence of grandiloquence. . . . It is a work of peace: heaven as one imagines it through Raphaël. [. . .] Such a power of renewal confounds us and fill us with wonder. I salute you, Jean-Sébastien Stravinsky.[10]

By late March the last two Apollinaire songs had reached Paul Rouart, but he retained the last two Lalanne songs for a few days.[11]

6 Bernac 1977a, p. 34 (Bernac 1978, p. 32).
7 [16 Mar. 1931] letter to Marie-Laure in Poulenc 1994, 31-2.
8 [25 Mar. 1931] letter to Marie-Laure in Poulenc 1994, 31-3.
9 [16 Mar. 1931] letter in Poulenc 1994, 31-2. Poulenc saw Jacques Offenbach's *La Vie parisienne* at the Mogador theater, where he met the painter Fréderic de Madrazo and Natividad de Faucigny-Lucinge. Elsewhere he also ran into Jean-Louis de Faucigny-Lucinge and his wife Liliane.
10 Poulenc 1931, pp. 249-50. Poulenc sent his review to Stravinsky with a "jeudi saint" [2 Apr. 1931] letter, and Stravinsky thanked him from Nice on 6 Apr. 1931. Poulenc 1994, 31-9 (Stravinsky 1984, p. 211 and Poulenc 1991, no. 115) and 31-10 (Poulenc 1991, no. 116).
11 "Vendredi" [26 Mar. 1931] letter to Rouart in Poulenc 1994, 31-5. It also re-

Both sets were published by mid-June 1931.[12] To present his new songs, he rented the Salle Pleyel for 1 June, hoping to recreate the atmosphere of the first Auric-Poulenc concert. Suzanne Peignot was asked to sing *Cocardes* with instruments and to premiere the *Trois poèmes de Louise Lalanne*, and the baritone Gilbert-Moryn to sing the *Quatre poèmes de Guillaume Apollinaire.*[13] Poulenc sent letters on special paper to "all the right people"[14] and contracted the finest orchestral players to ensure success.[15] For unknown reasons, the 1 June date was abrogated in favor of 19 June, and the Trio plus premieres of an early version of the Sextet and some unnamed piano pieces completed the program.[16]

TRIBULATIONS AND COMMISSIONS: SECOND HALF OF 1931

All had not been well during the spring, and Poulenc described his tribulations to Marie-Blanche de Polignac. ". . . Poor Poupoule is traversing black days at this time from every point of view." Problems were medical and financial, rather than romantic. He had a sore on his foot which the same surgeon who had repaired his hand following an earlier train accident attended to.[17] His doctor suggested "Two weeks *alone* on a beach by the ocean."[18] He then told Marie-Blanche about his financial misfortunes indicating he had lost

---

veals that Poulenc was to receive 10,000 francs for the *Quatre poèmes* and 5,000 for the *Lalanne*. Poulenc gave the manuscript of *Quatre poèmes* to Laurencin in May 1931. Schmidt 1995, FP 58, p. 182.

[12] Poulenc sent printed copies to Boulanger and Prokofiev. 11 Sept. 1931 letters to Poulenc in Poulenc 1994, 31-15 and 31-16.

[13] [5 Mar. 1931] letter to Peignot in Poulenc 1994, 31-1 (Poulenc 1991, no. 112).

[14] Poulenc 1994, 31-3 (Marie-Laure), 31-4 (Cœuroy), 31-8 (Sauguet), and 31-9 (Stravinsky).

[15] Darrieux, Dhérin, Lamorlette, Cahuzac, etc.

[16] An advertisement for a 1 June 1931 performance appeared in *Le Guide du concert et des théâtres lyriques* 17 (15 & 22 May 1931), 836. The correct 19 June date is confirmed in the (29 May 1931), 882 issue. This work went through various revisions and performances before reaching its definitive state. The only known mention of a "Sextuor pour piano et instruments à vent" before its performance is in a 5 Mar. 1931 letter to Peignot. Chalupt's column for the Nov. 1931 *Chesterian* confirms that a performance actually took place: "Francis Poulenc's muse is not formed on the same model as Honegger's, but it has inspired him in very intelligent and lovely compositions, such as the piano pieces, the *Poèmes d'Apollinaire* and the *Sextet* for piano and wind-instruments which we heard for the first time at the Salle Chopin during a festival." *Chesterian* 13/98 (Nov. 1931), 53 and Schmidt 1995, FP 100, pp. 296-7.

[17] "Mercredi soir" [July 1931] letter in Poulenc 1994, 31-11 (partial translation in Buckland/Chimènes: b, p. 231). The earlier accident is described above.

[18] Poulenc spent two weeks at the Hôtel Morgane in La Baule. Fragment of his [14 Aug. 1931] letter to Marie-Laure in Poulenc 1994, p. 342, note 2. In a "jeudi" [13 Aug. 1931] letter to Countess Charles de Polignac from Noizay, Poulenc gave his La Baule address as "chez Mme Virant, Ker-Vir."

money during the spring due to a failed bank. "I am trying desperately to refloat my boat, which is sinking terribly," he said.[19] Afraid of losing Noizay, he hoped that a planned movie venture with the celebrated singer Damia would bail him out, but that never came to pass.[20] At the end of this doleful letter, Poulenc added:

> I have worked a little. Two cycles of *mélodies* [are] on my desk. *Cinq poèmes de Paul Eluard* for baritone and *Quatre chansons de Max Jacob*, very *Quimper, Guidel, Concarneau* for soprano. [. . .] The *first* is dedicated to you as it should be because it is very Keker.[21]

This is the first mention of the Eluard songs, which were not completed until March 1935, and the Jacob songs ultimately numbering five not four. As was the case in the 1920s, Poulenc was once again projecting works well into the future.

The second Jacob set (FP 59) was composed between July and December 1931 in Nogent and Noizay. Based on Breton poems published under the pseudonym Morven le Gaëlique, the songs were dedicated to five ladies in Poulenc's life: Marie-Blanche de Polignac, Madeleine Vhita, Suzanne Peignot, Suzanne Balguerie, and Eve Curie. Peignot sang the fourth and fifth songs with Poulenc on a 24 May 1932 recital at the Ancien Conservatoire in what were supposed to be premieres. However, a listing for Lucienne Tragin's 20 May recital accompanied by Mlle de Smet indicates all five were on that program.[22]

If Poulenc's year had its down side, the prospect of a commission from Princess Edmond de Polignac changed things dramatically![23]

[19] "Mercredi soir" [July 1931] letter to Marie-Blanche in Poulenc 1994, 31-11 (partial translation in Buckland/Chimènes: b, p. 231). His 15 Oct. [1931] letter to Prokofiev suggests that the bank was the Lyon-Allemand. Poulenc 1994, 31-21 (partial translation in Buckland/Chimènes: b, p. 241).

[20] Poulenc also tried to make some arrangement for a movie with Colette after the deal with Damia collapsed. Colette's [summer 1931] letter to Poulenc in Poulenc 1994, 31-12 (Poulenc 1991, no. 117) and the fragment of Poulenc's 12 Sept. 1931 letter to Marie-Laure in Poulenc 1994, p. 343, note 4 which speaks of a Colette-Poulenc film project. Apparently Poulenc also asked Jacques Ibert about the problems of composing a film score. Ibert's 22 Sept. 1931 response mentioned in note 4. The possibility of this collaboration still existed on 15 Oct. when Poulenc mentioned it to Collaer. Poulenc 1994, 31-20 (Collaer 1996, 31-15).

[21] "Mercredi soir" [July 1931] letter to Marie-Blanche in Poulenc 1994, 31-11. Poulenc sent a copy of "Chanson bretonne" to her as a birthday present. Inscription printed in note 10. Poulenc's references are to cities in Brittany. Guidel is the town in which Kerbastic is situated.

[22] *Le Guide du concert et des théâtres lyriques* 18 (6 & 13 May 1932), 789. We have not located the Tragin program to clarify matters. Concerning Tragin, see Chapter IX.

[23] Poulenc and Milhaud had known the Princess before the name *Les Six* was coined. Cossart, pp. 141-2.

The Countess Charles de Polignac (whose husband was Jean de Polignac's brother and Princess Edmond de Polignac's nephew) discussed the matter with Poulenc before he left for La Baule. His mid-August letter to "Pata," her nickname, clarifies that she was acting on her aunt's behalf and that terms had previously been discussed. Poulenc agreed that the dedication, manuscript, and first performance should all belong to the Princess. Moreover, he suggested a fee based on that received for *Aubade*, eagerly anticipating financial salvation in the form of a chèque once agreement was reached.[24] The Princess sent the formal commission in late August.

> Could this work take the form of a piece for piano, in the same vein as the concerto for Landowska, if possible arranged for three pianos: one solo and two secondary? [. . .] May I propose that for this work you accept the sum of twenty thousand francs, plus five thousand francs for the performance which would take place this winter or next spring at my home in Paris. I would be so pleased to add your name to those of Stravinsky, Fauré, Falla, Satie who accepted to write the beautiful pages which you know for my "collection."[25]

Poulenc responded with the idea of writing a concerto for two pianos.[26] "It must be for two pianos only," she told him.[27] Again Poulenc clarified the situation, and the Princess wrote back: "You are right to give preference to the combination: two pianos and chamber orchestra (or reduction for a 3rd piano). The sonority will be charming, I am sure of it."[28] In the early fall, Poulenc decided on a Concerto for Two Pianos and Chamber Orchestra including pairs of flutes, oboes, and bassoons, plus horn, tuba, violin, viola, violoncello, and contrabass grouped in the shape of a fan around the two pianos.[29] With the work conceived, but unwritten, Poulenc undertook other tasks. He did not return to the concerto until the summer of 1932 at Le Tremblay.

[24] "Jeudi" [13 Aug. 1931] letter to Countess Charles de Polignac in Poulenc 1994, 31-13 (partial translation in Buckland/Chimènes: b, p. 231).

[25] Princess Edmond de Polignac's 24 Aug. 1931 letter to Poulenc in Poulenc 1994, 31-14 (partial translation in Buckland/Chimènes: b, pp. 231-2).

[26] See her 16 Sept. 1931 letter in Poulenc 1994, 31-17. Poulenc's letters to the Princess have not been found. On 12 Sept. he wrote Marie-Laure: "Important commission, I am writing a Sonata for 2 pianos for Princess Edmond [de Polignac] which you will hear this winter." Unpublished letter in F-Pn and Schmidt 1995, FP 61, p. 196.

[27] Stravinsky had not yet written his *Concerto for Two Solo Pianos*, so the Princess could not have had this work in mind.

[28] See her 1 Oct. 1931 letter in Poulenc 1994, 31-18 (partial translation in Buckland/Chimènes: b, p. 232).

[29] "Samedi" [Oct. 1931] letter to Countess Charles de Polignac in Poulenc 1994, 31-19 (partial translation in Buckland/Chimènes: b, p. 232). Poulenc, who had only been in Noizay for ten days, intended to remain for the winter.

In October an attempt was made to have *Aubade* performed in Brussels for the tenth anniversary of the Pro Arte concerts. Poulenc also suggested programming the *Concert champêtre* and asked for a fee of 1,000 Belgian francs to cover expenses. Owing to his economic crisis he could not play gratis.[30] The concert on 12 January included only Milhaud's String Quartet no. 2 plus Poulenc's *Trois poèmes de Louise Lalanne* and *Quatre poèmes de Guillaume Apollinaire.* [31] In late October, Poulenc made one of his quick trips to Paris for the local premiere of Prokofiev's String Quartet no. 1 (commissioned by the American music patroness Elizabeth Sprague Coolidge) at a "Séance privée" she organized on the 26th at the Institut international.[32] While there Poulenc also hoped to attend a second "Séance Coolidge" on the 28th to hear Malipiero's String Quartet no. 3 "Cantari alla madrigalesca." [33]

That fall Poulenc was the beneficiary of still another important commission, from Marie-Laure and Charles de Noailles for a "spectacle-concert" at Hyères on 20 April 1932. In mid-November he decided on a cantata on poems from Max Jacob's *Bal masqué.*[34] The instrumentalists, expected to sing a brief refrain as simple as the *Madelon*, would include players on oboe, bassoon, piston, violin, violoncello, piano, and drum. Little more than a week later he added a clarinet "which *I cannot do without.*"[35] Poulenc's conception was "very Casino d'Hyères." Jacob recommended calling the fifth song "Souric et Mouric" and also authorized the use of "La Dauphine" in *Le Bal masqué.*[36] Despite the fact that the original manuscript indi-

[30] 15 Oct. [1931] letter to Collaer in Poulenc 1994, 31-20 (Collaer 1996, 31-15) and note 1. There was also discussion about possible dates, and Poulenc and Milhaud (whose music was also to be included) could not make 18 Feb. Nor was 1 Mar. good because Poulenc anticipated performing in Cannes late in Feb.
[31] Prokofiev's 22 Oct. 1931 letter to Poulenc in Poulenc 1994, 31-23. Though *Aubade* did not make the program, Prokofiev saw it listed on an advertising poster as scheduled for 23 Apr., his birthday.
[32] Poulenc asked Prokofiev how such commissions were arranged, seeking a way out of his financial crisis. See also Prokofiev's 22 Oct. 1931 response in Poulenc 1994, 31-23 in which the ever resourceful Prokofiev told him about a bridge tournament in New York sporting a $25,000 prize. This was much better than Mrs. Coolidge's modest $1,000 commission, he joked.
[33] 16 Oct. [1931] letter to Malipiero in Poulenc 1994, 31-22. He asked Malipiero to arrange with Coolidge's secretary to have two tickets sent to 24, rue du Chevalier de la Barre, Paris Montmartre. This concert also included a performance of Hindemith's *Concerto for Piano, Brass, and Harp.*
[34] 18 Nov. [1931] letter to Marie-Laure in Poulenc 1994, 31-24 (partial translation in Buckland/Chimènes: b, p. 230).
[35] "Vendredi" [27 Nov. 1931] letter in Poulenc 1994, 31-25 (partial translation in Buckland/Chimènes: b, p. 230). See Schmidt 1995, FP 60, p. 187 for the final instrumentation (which made the drummer into a full-fledged percussionist).
[36] Jacob's 11 Dec. 1931 letter to Poulenc in Poulenc 1994, 31-27.

cates that composition took place in Noizay and Cannes between February and 10 April 1932, Poulenc was already busy composing the music by the end of 1931. He sent the complete text to Marie-Laure outlining the cantata's overall shape, and told her that he had already composed no. 5 "La Dame aveugle."[37] Poulenc probably did not progress much further because he was about to leave Noizay and was also working on the "Concerto de la Tante W[innie]," which had a very Balinese first movement.

Poulenc did not get far with a *Concertino* for piano four-hands promised to Jacques Lerolle. The *Concertino* for elementary players was to have distinct movement titles so each could be sold separately. The initial *Largo,* dedicated to Jacques' son Claude (b. 1925), to be played with one hand and a single finger, was soon abandoned. When he did complete a piano work for children, it was the *Villageoises (petites pièces enfantines pour piano)* which he gave to Salabert in 1933. The impetus to write songs and piano pieces for Lerolle may have come from his need for funds to stem his cash-flow problem.[38] By year's end the Jacob songs were also ready for Lerolle. "Four out of five are ok to engrave," he said, adding "I adore the last one."[39] Earlier he had told Lerolle that one of them was "in the genre of a French Moussorgsky."[40]

Poulenc also became associated with an important new concert series La Sérénade, the brainchild of Yvonne de Casa Fuerte, a violinist from Milhaud's generation at the Paris Conservatoire.[41] Established to support the performance of twentieth-century music, this series featured premieres by both French and foreign composers. It supplemented those by the established Parisian concert associations such as Colonne, Lamoureux, and Pasdeloup. Moreover, financial backing for La Sérénade by several of Paris' most important cultural doyens provided a cachet guaranteeing it would

[37] "Samedi" [12 Dec. 1931] letter in Poulenc 1994, 31-28.
[38] Poulenc wrote on 25 Sept. to Lerolle that he had worked for a week on piano pieces and *mélodies.* Fragment in Poulenc 1994, p. 358, note 1.
[39] "Mercredi" [16 Dec. 1931] letter in Poulenc 1994, 31-29. Poulenc's particular affection for "Souric et Mouric" is also expressed in a 15 Feb. 1932 letter to Falla and a [1 Mar. 1932] letter to Collaer. Poulenc 1994, 32-5 and 32-6 respectively. Poulenc asked Lerolle to send miniature scores of *Aubade* and *Concert champêtre,* along with the *Quatre poèmes de Guillaume Apollinaire* and *Trois poèmes de Louise Lalanne* to André Cœuroy, so he could write about them in *Paris-midi* and *Le Figaro illustré.*
[40] Fragment of Poulenc's 14 Oct. [1931] letter to Lerolle in Poulenc 1994, p. 358, note 3.
[41] Schaeffner 1933, p. 168 described the Société de la Sérénade as a group ". . . formed two years ago, which gives concerts for small and chamber orchestras and represents the neo-classic movement."

not be taken lightly. Poulenc was a member of the musicians' committee that provided artistic advice.[42] Although not included in the
inaugural 1 December 1931 concert, which featured Markevitch,
Rieti, and Sauguet premieres, his music appeared on later concerts.

THROUGH *LE BAL MASQUÉ*: FIRST HALF OF 1932

For Poulenc, 1932 was an exceedingly busy year. Not only did he
have important commissions of *Le Bal masqué* (FP 60) and Concerto
in D minor (FP 61) to complete, but attending and performing concerts drained his time and energy. For the most part he stayed in
Noizay, with frequent Paris forays during the winter and spring,
with trips to Mulhouse in the winter, Le Tremblay in the summer,
and Venice in the late summer and early fall.[43]

Poulenc spent late 1931 and early 1932 in Paris amidst a frenzy of
activity. He attended a revival of the Serge Lifar ballet *Spectre de la
rose* on 31 December at the Opéra, and the premiere of Milhaud's
monumental opera *Maximilien* on 5 January. He found Lifar "very
good," but the scenery of the ballet "impossible;" Milhaud's music
for *Maximilien* "very lifeless, very old" and Pedro Pruna's scenery
"vulgar."[44] Only the singers were praised. A post-performance supper was arranged at the Café de Paris to honor Milhaud. Jane Bathori,
Paul Collaer, Henri Sauguet, the Nabokovs, Vittorio Rieti, and others attended and the assembled guests, according to Poulenc, talked
about everything *but* the opera. After a quick visit to Noizay, where
he was on 12 January, he returned to Paris for the premiere of Ravel's
Concerto in G played by Marguerite Long, with Ravel conducting,
on the 14th and Cocteau's film *Le Sang du poète* at the Théâtre
Ermitage on the 16th. Poulenc had already read Ravel's concerto
with Février at Mme de Polignac's *hôtel,* and their reading of portions of Poulenc's Concerto in D minor pleased her.[45]

On 18 January Poulenc performed in Mulhouse and on the 21st
he accompanied Suzanne Peignot at a "Concerts pour les enfants"
which featured brief commentaries by Roland-Manuel.[46] A proposed
Marseilles engagement on the 29th, however, almost certainly did
not occur. News-filled letters to Nora Auric and Marie-Laure de
Noailles prove decisively that Poulenc needed to escape Paris so

[42] Other committee members included Auric, Désormière, Markevitch, Milhaud,
Nabokov, Rieti, and Sauguet. Founders included Princess Edmond de Polignac,
Countess Jean de Polignac, and Viscount Charles de Noailles.
[43] While in Paris Poulenc stayed at Georges Salles' Montmartre home at 24, rue
du Chevalier de La Barre, behind Sacré-Cœur.
[44] 12 Jan. [1932] letter to Nora Auric in Poulenc 1994, 32-2. Pruna [O'Cerans], a
painter from Barcelona born in 1904, first exhibited during 1919. He also
designed for Diaghilev's Ballets Russes.
[45] 12 Jan. [1932] letter in Poulenc 1994, 32-2.
[46] *Le Guide du concert et des théâtres lyriques* 18 (13 Jan 1932), 371.

inspiration could return.[47] Paris was the catalyst, Noizay the crucible, but getting away was difficult. Poulenc was enslaved by his social involvement, which was absolutely basic to his character. The following partial account of his activities leaves one breathless. He attended the private presentation of Coco Chanel's new *haute couture* collection with Countess Betka; many dinner parties at the Avenue Henri-Martin *hôtel* of Princess Edmond de Polignac (where he saw Stravinsky, Colette, Anna de Noailles, Francis Carco, Max Jacob, Dunoyer de Segonzac, Misia Sert, Marthe Hyde, Solange Lemaître, the François d'Harcourts, and the Pomereus); a cocktail party at the Hôtel Pomereu with Jean Gabriel Domergue and Jean de Gaigneron; Marcel Achard's amusing play *Domino*;[48] Stravinsky's 24 January performance of the *Capriccio* (Jacques Février, piano) with the Orchestre Symphonique de Paris; and a visit to Misia's "very pretty and very agreeable" new apartment. It is almost a miracle that *Le Bal masqué* was also progressing with Sauguet's assistance!

He performed *Aubade* with the Orchestre Lamoureux, Albert Wolff conducting, on Saturday, 20 February.[49] He also participated in the second La Sérénade concert given 22 February, in which his *Trois poèmes de Louise Lalanne* and *Quatre poèmes de Guillaume Apollinaire* were sung by Suzanne Peignot and Roger Bourdin respectively.[50] The second half featured Satie's lyric one-act comedy *La Piège de Méduse* with Henri Sauguet, Pierre Colle, and Madeleine Milhaud in the cast.[51] For March we know only of his brief appearance in an "Amis des Artistes" concert at the Salle Pleyel on the 14th accompanying Mme Blanc-Audra in several of his own *mélodies*.[52]

Work on *Le Bal masqué*, a particularly important work for Poulenc, continued in March and was completed in Cannes on 10 April.[53]

---

[47] 12 Jan. [1932] and 14 Feb. [1932] letters in Poulenc 1994, 32-2 and 32-3 respectively.

[48] In late 1933 Poulenc provided a bit of music for Achard's three-act comedy *Pétrus*. Schmidt 1995, FP 67.

[49] Just before leaving Noizay on the 17th he wrote Falla renewing a suggestion that *Aubade* be performed by the Orchestre Bética and noting that he had arranged with Lerolle to supply parts for a modest rental fee. The Lamoureux concert was broadcast on 21 Feb. at 3:00 pm.

[50] The concert also featured Sauguet's six *Polymètres* and an organ sonata by Milhaud (first performed in Berlin in 1932). Poulenc personally invited Olga Picasso to hear "Avant le cinéma." [Feb. 1932] letter to Olga in Poulenc 1994, 32-4.

[51] Milhaud had conducted the first public performance at the Théâtre Michel on 24 May 1921. Orledge 1990, p. 298.

[52] *Le Guide du concert et des théâtres lyriques* 18 (11 Mar. 1932), 657.

[53] Schmidt 1995, FP 60, p. 188. In a 12 Apr. [1932] letter Poulenc told Boulanger: "Last evening I finished a *Cantate profane* that will be given at the Noailles' in a week. If this work pleases you (you will have the chance to hear it in Paris this

It is one hundred percent Poulenc. To a lady in Katchamka [a peninsula in Siberia] who would write to me inquiring what I was like, I
would send her Cocteau's portrait of me at the piano, Bérard's portrait of me, *Le Bal masqué*, and the *Motets pour un temps de pénitence*. I
think that in this fashion she would get an exact picture of Poulenc-
Janus.[54]

His intention in writing the cantata is best described in a 1935
article entitled "Éloge de la Banalité."

In a familiar atmosphere which evokes the Parisian suburbs, Max
Jacob and I have put in motion a sort of carnival during which Mlle
Malvina, a woman in love, pretentious and unappeased, gives her
hand to a monstrous blind woman who, dressed in a fluffy gown, is
getting drunk with her brother-in-law. We glimpse these characters
from the window of a "charming chalet" on the banks of the Marne,
and we have tried to make them more universal by exaggerating their
characteristics. An *Air de bravoure*, which flows from the "Préambule,"
carries the listener at a wild gallop across the words, which are linked
by pure fantasy. An old violent and dull-witted man, "the repairer of
old automobiles," concludes this gallery of bizarre portraits which
the instrumental interludes serve to frame. Above all, Max Jacob and
I have sought the laugh from surprise, perhaps even from shock, rather
than the ironic smile, tight-lipped, logical, or even with an air of "su-
periority," a facial expression so dear to lovers of refined art.[55]

When Poulenc described *Le Bal masqué* to Henri Hell in 1948 as a
"carnaval nogentais,"[56] he confirmed what he had written earlier
when he said the second and third vocal numbers ("Malvina" and
"La Dame aveugle") were "painted from life."

While writing "La Dame aveugle" I thought a great deal about an
astonishing rotund lady of independent means who, around 1912,
hung around the Île de Beauté at Nogent-sur-Marne. She inhabited a
chalet, half Swiss, half Norman, and spent her days playing solitaire
sitting on her porch clothed in a black silk dress. On a cane armchair
a few steps from her sat a man who looked like [Henri Désiré] Landru
[1869-1922, a famous murderer], with pince-nez and a cyclist's hat,
reading his newspaper. In discovering in *Laboratoire Central* the poem
by Max Jacob, I had the decided impression of having recovered an
old photo in a country album. In writing *Le Bal masqué* I was speaking therefore about things that were familiar to me. Now what was

---

June), I will be happy because very often while working I think of your judgment, one of the rare ones which counts for me."

[54] Poulenc 1993, pp. 33-4 (Poulenc 1989, pp. 58-9).

[55] Poulenc 1935b, p. 25.

[56] Inscription in the score given to Hell in Schmidt 1995, FP 60, p. 190.

necessary was to find the special perspective to put all this carnival on the stage. It is the only one of my works in which I believe I have found a way of heightening the atmosphere of the environs of Paris so dear to me. This is due to the words of Max which are full of unforeseen ricochets, and to the instrumental material that I have used. Here the *color* underscores the bombast, the ridiculous, the pitiable, the terrifying. It is the atmosphere found in the color prints of crimes in the Sunday issues of *Le Petit parisien* during my childhood.[57]

About the time of the premiere Poulenc granted an interview to Nino Franck while a guest at Salles' Montmartre apartment.[58] Poulenc proudly reported that the servants appeared first thing in the morning singing a fragment of the last section![59] Although Franck thought he was describing *"Poèmes de Max Jacob,"* he actually printed a description of Poulenc's *Le Bal masqué*:

> In this work I tried to create a vocal style which would be both hallucinatory, something like photographs of crime scenes or vulgar pulp magazines, and strangely jarring, mixing both vulgar and appropriate harmonies, deforming the words and the sounds. [. . .] I am very fond of this work which will undoubtedly shock the paladins of so-called modern music.[60]

Between the 10th and the premiere at the Hyères theater on the 20th, rehearsals with the baritone Gilbert-Moryn and the orchestra conducted by Roger Désormière took place. No report of the Noailles' fête exists, but a photograph showing ten attendees commemorates the event.[61] Another, on the steps of the Noailles' *hôtel* in Paris, shows Henri Sauguet, Nicolas Nabokov, Marie-Laure de Noailles, Yvonne de Casa Fuerte, Igor Markevitch, Charles Koechlin, Roger Désormière, and Poulenc.[62] When the performance was repeated on 13 June at the fourth La Sérénade concert, the composer

---

[57] Poulenc 1993, pp. 34-5 (Poulenc 1989, pp. 60-1).
[58] Nino Franck, who interviewed Poulenc there in Apr. 1932, described the house: ". . . a large and quiet street, without automobiles between the squat houses, which climbs horrifyingly, straight ahead toward the basilica [of Sacré-Cœur]. In one of these houses, a large and elegant studio; I wait there at 9:00 am for the musician whom someone has gone to awake. A window in a door looks out on a charming small garden, on the flank of the butte: you raise your eyes, and the steeples, curiously carnal, appear whiter than ever in the morning sun."
[59] Although Poulenc reported the final form of the cantata in this letter, it continued to undergo alteration.
[60] Franck in *Comœdia* (28 Apr.) quoted by Daniel, p. 262.
[61] Photograph of Désormière, Poulenc, Auric, Pierre Colle, Alberto Giacometti, Boris Kochno, Nora Auric, Luis Buñuel, Igor Markevitch, and Christian Bérard in Sauguet, between pp. 288/89.
[62] Machart, pp. 70-1. See also Buckland/Chimènes, plate 15 for a different photograph which adds Nora Auric and Vittorio Rieti.

Lennox Berkeley wrote a favorable account:

> There has not been very much new music, but some interesting new things were played at a chamber concert of works written for the Vicomte de Noailles. The composers represented were Auric, Markevitch, Nabokoff, Poulenc, and Sauguet. Sauguet's work for voice and small orchestra was pleasing, and is probably the best thing that he has done so far; Markevitch's "Galop" for piano and small orchestra is clever and strikes a personal note. Poulenc's "Le Bal Masqué" (poem by Max Jacob), for voice and a small number of instruments, was perhaps the most enjoyable work of the evening. It is very typical of Poulenc, tuneful and witty, and carried along with great brio from beginning to end. It is extremely well orchestrated, and one notices particularly the progress that Poulenc has made in this side of his art.[63]

Poulenc quickly got additional mileage from *Le Bal masqué*, a work which he thought might have trouble breaching the French frontiers.[64] He had Rouart, Lerolle & Cie issue the second, fourth, and sixth numbers separately in 1932 as *Intermède pour piano en ré mineur, 1er Bagatelle pour violon et piano en ré mineur*, and *Caprice en ut majeur pour piano*.[65]

THE CONCERTO IN D MINOR: SECOND HALF OF 1932

The Hyères trip completed, Poulenc was extremely pressed to finish the Concerto in D minor. In the solitude of Noizay, interrupted only by a brief visit from the Aurics, the Prokofievs, Rieti, and Sauguet at Pentecost (15 May), Poulenc worked quickly. The last touches were added during three weeks at Le Tremblay.

> I am working like crazy [he wrote Marguerite Long]. I am finishing my *Concerto à 2 pianos et orchestre* which I will play with Février in Venice on 5 September. Brigitte [Manceaux] has helped me a great deal with my work, rehearsing certain passages a thousand times.[66]

In addition to completing the Concerto, Poulenc revised *Rapsodie nègre* in preparation for a new edition.[67] As payment for monies he owed, Poulenc suggested that he compose a novellette, but none was written for Chester until 1959. He also begged Kling to forward his yearly royalties, pleading dire financial straits.

[63] *Monthly Musical Record* 62 (Sept. 1932), 159.
[64] Poulenc 1993, p. 35 (Poulenc 1989, pp. 60-3).
[65] Schmidt 1995, FP 60, pp. 189-91. All the scores were © in the U.S. by 15 June. Although we do not know the dates, Poulenc dispatched copies of the piano pieces to Cortot and Horowitz. A performance of the *Bagatelle* by Françoise Soulé (accompanied by Maurice Faure) occurred in Paris on 30 May 1933.
[66] 16 July [1932] letter in F-Pgm (Fonds Marguerite Long).
[67] Unpublished [early July 1932 letter from Le Tremblay] to [Harry] Kling (who had succeeded his father Otto Marius Kling, deceased in 1924) in GB-Lchester.

In July and August work on the Concerto intensified:

> Above all excuse my silence. I am *crazy* with work. After a month of
> intense labor I am finally finishing the Concerto vénitien (I have no
> more than three days to go). [...] I remain here until the 26th. Jacques
> Février will come on the 21st in order to work with me.[68]

Poulenc had abandoned his initial conception of a Concerto for
chamber orchestra in favor of a normal symphony orchestra. A postcard to Marie-Laure de Noailles from Rouen on the 26th states: "*Concerto* finally finished. I am dead, but not unhappy. I leave Tuesday
for Venice by gondola[!] Very affectionately Francis." To this Février
added: "I am enchanted with my composer. I leave with him...
Jacques."[69] On the way they stopped in Milan to rehearse with the
La Scala orchestra and made a brief excursion to Lake Como. Poulenc
spent two weeks in Italy before returning to Paris for three weeks
and then headed to Noizay where he intended to remain until January.[70]

While in Venice Poulenc and Février were guests of Princess
Edmond de Polignac at the Palazzo Polignac on the Grand Canal.[71]
The new Concerto was performed under the auspices of the Société
Internationale de Musique Contemporaine (ISCM) on 5 September
with Désiré Defauw conducting the La Scala Orchestra. ". . .
Toscanini"s orchestra!!!! It is quite simply a miracle at every mo-
ment," Poulenc said.[72] Nora Auric was told:

> It is true that the Toscanini orchestra played so well as to make all
> other performances pale by comparison. You have no idea what it is
> to hear musicians fascinated by the great shadow of Toscanini. The
> violins are heavenly in the high register, the clarinets loving, the oboes
> sweet and cheerful. It is admirable!!! Jacques was a perfect second,
> and it seems we played very well. We have, moreover, many engage-
> ments for the winter.[73]

He also found Defauw a "remarkable conductor."[74] Disappointed
that his friend "Pata" (Countess Charles de Polignac) could not at-

---

[68] [10 Aug. 1932] letter to Marie-Laure in Poulenc 1994, 32-14. Poulenc later told
Sauguet that he had worked extremely hard in both July and Aug. to complete
the Concerto. Poulenc's "dimanche" [probably 18 or 25 Sept. 1932] letter to
Sauguet from Noizay in Poulenc 1994, 32-16.

[69] Transcription in Poulenc 1994, p. 372, note 1.

[70] "Dimanche" [Sept. 1932] letter in Poulenc 1994, 32-17.

[71] Invitation in Poulenc 1994, p. 372, note 1.

[72] "Dimanche" [probably 18 or 25 Sept. 1932] letter to Sauguet in Poulenc 1994,
32-16.

[73] "Dimanche" [Sept. 1932] letter in Poulenc 1994, 32-17.

[74] 1 Oct. [1932] letter to Collaer in Poulenc 1994, 32-19 (Poulenc 1991, no. 121) and
Collaer 1996, 32-15.

tend the premiere, he nonetheless thanked her for facilitating the commission.[75]

Poulenc's Concerto gave Février's career a boost. They played it frequently together and recorded it commercially in 1958 with Pierre Dervaux and in 1962 with Georges Prêtre.[76] They also made private recordings (1960 with Charles Bruck and 1962 with Manuel Rosenthal), as well as one of Satie's *Trois morceaux en forme de poire* in 1961.[77]

Occasionally we can discover some of the stimuli which lie behind Poulenc's compositions. Such is the case with the first movement of the Concerto, which reflects Poulenc's interest in the Balinese music he first heard at the 1931 Exposition Coloniale de Paris. He also spoke of Mozart 's influence on the second movement.

> In the Larghetto of this Concerto I permitted myself, for the first theme, to return to Mozart, because I have a fondness for the melodic line, and I prefer Mozart to all other musicians. If the movement begins *alla* Mozart, it quickly diverges at the entrance of the second piano, toward a style that was familiar to me at that time.[78]

Poulenc gave one final hint of influence. "Would you like to know what I had on my piano during the two months gestation of the *Concerto?*," he asked Markevitch, "The concertos of Mozart, those of Liszt, that of Ravel, and your *Partita.*"[79]

Venice was also the last place Poulenc saw Manuel de Falla, his friend since 1917, and the two spent much time together.

> I lived that month of September with Falla at the Palazzo Polignac, right on the Grand Canal; Arthur Rubinstein and other artists lived there as well. The large drawing-rooms were full of pianos. [. . .] What music we made in 1932! I remember, among others, a morning when I played *The Nights in the Gardens of Spain* with Arthur Rubinstein for Falla; Arthur, be it understood, taking the solo piano part and I the orchestral part. Falla from the beginning always showed me as much kindness as affection; it was therefore a pleasure to meet again under such circumstances. At that Venice Festival a staged performance of *El Retablo* was being given: Falla and I left early each

[75] "Jeudi" [8 Sept. 1932] letter in Poulenc 1994, 32-15.
[76] That Poulenc recognized this is clear from his "dimanche" [30 Sept. 1934] letter to Peignot. He orchestrated the *Poèmes de Ronsard* to assist her career telling her, "That is why I wish to help you and why I think that the *Ronsard* will be for you what the *Concerto* was for Jacques." Poulenc 1994, 34-8.
[77] Appendix 3.
[78] Poulenc 1954, p. 83 and Machart, p. 84 for links to Mozart's Piano Concertos K. 467 and 503.
[79] Fragment of Poulenc's [Sept. 1932] letter to Markevitch in Poulenc 1994, p. 368, note 1.

morning for rehearsals, because they were preceded for Falla by daily Mass. I would not be telling the truth if I said that I myself was also as faithful to Mass. When I did not go there with Falla to Mass, I would join him at a café near the Teatro la Fenice where he had breakfast after taking Communion.[80]

Apparently Poulenc also met the singer Maria Rota from Milan. He described her as a "very intelligent [Claire] Croiza-[Jane] Bathori," and said he hoped to tour with her, possibly performing some of Sauguet's *mélodies*.[81] No performance with her is known.

YEAR-END EVENTS INCLUDING A *VALSE-IMPROVISATION*

Once returned to Noizay, Poulenc worked on the two-piano transcription of his Concerto for performance without orchestra, corrected various proofs, and tried to complete his Sextet in ten days.[82] At the end of September he arranged performances for the coming season, badgering Paul Collaer to include his music on future Pro Arte concerts. He especially coveted the opportunity to play *Le Bal masqué* there on 8 December.[83] Aware that his new Concerto was being discussed in Belgium, he provided the following analysis:[84]

> You will see for yourself what an enormous step forward it is from my earlier works, and that I am truly entering my great period. You will also understand that this evolution has its origin in the *Concert champêtre* and in *Aubade* which were two *indispensable* steps in my evolution. In these two concertos it is possible that my concern for technical perfection, particularly in the orchestration, might have diverted me from the true nature of my music; but it was necessary, and you yourself will see with what a "precise" pen I have orchestrated *Le Bal* and the *Concerto* which are, I assure you, pure Poulenc.[85]

[80] Poulenc 1963a, pp. 115-16 (Poulenc 1978, pp. 88-9) and Cossart, pp. 185-6.
[81] "Dimanche" [18 or 25 Sept. 1931] letter to Sauguet in Poulenc 1994, 32-16. Poulenc refers to two singers with whom he had worked earlier.
[82] Since Poulenc had already performed the Sextet on 18 June 1932, this must represent his initial revision of the score. In a [Nov. 1932] letter to Marie-Blanche in Poulenc 1994, 32-20 (Poulenc 1991, no. 122), he wrote that he would have hurried to finish the Sextet for the opening of the Salon des Antiques (a request Marie-Blanche must have made to Poulenc) had he not been so busy with multiple projects.
[83] 1 Oct. [1932] letter to Collaer in Poulenc 1994, 32-19 (Poulenc 1991, no. 121) and Collaer 1996, 32-15. In stark contrast to his interest in performance fees during his 1932 financial crisis, Poulenc now offered to play gratis.
[84] Defauw, who conducted the premiere, was the regular conductor of the Orchestre du Conservatoire royal de Bruxelles as well as director of the Conservatoire. As much as anyone, he may have been responsible for discussion of the work in Belgium.
[85] 1 Oct. [1932] letter in Poulenc 1994, 32-19 (Poulenc 1991, no. 121) and Collaer 1996, 32-15 . Poulenc had earlier stated that with *Les Biches* he was entering his great period!

By 8 October Poulenc had finished a "Valse-improvisation sur le nom de Bach" for piano later included as the third of five pieces in *Hommage à J.S. Bach* (FP 62) published in a *La Revue musicale* supplement.[86] Pure Poulenc it was not! Whereas other composers chose fitting genres suchas a ricercar or prelude and fugue, Poulenc wrote an improvisation using the B-A-C-H motive set as a waltz-musette. Toward the middle the motive returns in retrograde motion in fortissimo octaves, and later the "A-C-H" portion of the motif sounds simultaneously as a collection of seconds in a very high register just before the piece ends on what seems like a first inversion triad (minus the root). Even a dedication to the famous Vladimir Horowitz, possibly given to recognize his November 1932 recording of the "Toccata" from *Trois pièces pour piano* and the "Pastourelle" from *L'Eventail de Jeanne*, did little to ameliorate the bizarre wedding of musical styles and concepts contained in this piece.[87]

In November, lacking commissions for new works, Poulenc lamented to Marie-Blanche de Polignac that he would have to write piano works to please his publishers. "I understand," he said, "that one must work for the love of art, but nevertheless there are times when one must think equally about coal and a pork chop."[88] And write he did, completing six *Improvisations* (FP 63) the fifth of which is dated 25 November and the last simply December.[89] These pieces range from one with two contrasting ideas (no. 1) to a chromatic étude (no. 5) with a single theme. In the set there are reminiscences of the Concerto in D minor and harbingers of *Histoire de Babar*. Altogether Poulenc left fifteen *Improvisations:* ten from 1932-34, two from 1941, and three from 1958-59.[90] He occasionally played a few, favoring nos. 2, 3, 5, and 10 in a concert tour of North Africa in 1935, and no. 4 in a tour of the Midi the same year.[91] The *Improvisations* were always among his most cherished piano pieces.

There was also a pending project to record the *Chansons gaillardes* with Bernac for Columbia in early November, and Poulenc planned to be in Paris between the 8th and the 12th for the session.[92] This

[86] Other works were by Roussel, Casella, Malipiero, and Honegger.
[87] V.S.M. DB 2247 recording listed in Bloch, pp. 144 and 154. In a [Sept. 1933] letter to Markevitch in Poulenc 1994, 33-8, Poulenc asked if he could find a copy of the recording in Montreux.
[88] [Nov. 1932] letter in Poulenc 1994, 32-20 (Poulenc 1991, no. 122).
[89] These pieces were all dedicated to different friends and relations: Mme Long de Marliave (Marguerite Long), Durey, Brigitte Manceaux, Claude Popelin, Auric, and Février.
[90] Each *Improvisation* is discussed in Daniel, pp. 179-84.
[91] Schmidt 1995, FP 63, p. 205. He recorded nos. 2, 5, 9, and 10 in 1934. See Appendix 3.
[92] Ultraphone (BP 1531). Poulenc's [Nov. 1932] letter to Marie-Blanche in Poulenc 1994, 32-20 (Poulenc 1991, no. 122).

project was delayed until about 1935, however, when only nos. 3 and 8 were recorded. Auric came to stay at Noizay during the second half of the month, remaining for six weeks until he and Poulenc went to Paris at year's end.[93] Violet Trefusis, Colette, and the writer/ journalist Maurice Goudeket who would become Colette's third husband, were also there for a visit on 20 Nov.[94] He also worked on his schedule for the Lyon visit in February during which he would play his Concerto and, he hoped, give a master class in the interpretation of his *mélodies* and piano music.[95]

COLLABORATIONS WITH JEAN GIRAUDOUX AND LOUIS JOUVET: 1933

Poulenc approached the new year with a burst of energy at least equivalent to that with which he began 1932. Giving concerts, master classes, and lecture-recitals was an ever increasing part of his calendar, and his appetite for concerts and plays was just as voracious. January was extremely busy.[96] On the 12th he attended a concert in Strasbourg at the Salle Hector Berlioz organized by La Sérénade. Not only was his Trio performed, but he and Jacques Février played Auric's *Bibliophilie*, and there were pieces by Milhaud, Rieti, Sauguet, Nabokov, and Markevitch as well. A reviewer noted that "the victor of the evening was without contest M. Francis Poulenc."[97] Four days later he played in *Le Bal masqué* for a private concert conducted by Alfred Cortot,[98] and on the 17th he attended an all-Ravel concert at the Salle Pleyel hearing *Concerto for the Left Hand* played by Paul Wittgenstein accompanied by the Orchestre Symphonique de Paris. The evening of the 20th he heard the second Triton Society concert at the École normale de musique.

For a change of pace, he obtained inscribed copies of Emmanuel Chabrier's *Gwendoline* and *Le Roi malgré lui* at the Hôtel Drouot sale of Vincent d'Indy's library on 20-21 January by bartering a cask of rosé wine with Robert Legouix, director of *Librairie musical Gustave Legouix* and a specialist in rare editions and manuscripts.[99] Then, after seeing Milhaud conduct *Salade* with the Orchestre Symphonique de Paris on the 22nd, Poulenc fulfilled the final obligations of his commission for the Concerto in D minor presenting the original manuscript to Princess Edmond de Polignac and giving a private

---

[93] 31 Dec. 1932 letter to Latarjet in Poulenc 1994, 32-24.

[94] Violet Trefusis' "mardi" 22 Nov. [1932] letter to Poulenc in Poulenc 1994, 32-22 and note 1. Trefusis was Alice Keppel's daughter. Souhami, passim.

[95] 31 Dec. 1932 letter to Latarjet in Poulenc 1994, 32-24.

[96] Information primarily from Poulenc's [23 Jan. 1933] letter to Nora Auric in Poulenc 1994, 33-1 and Chimènes' extensive documentation to that letter.

[97] H. W. in *Revue dernières nouvelles de Strasbourg* (15 Jan. 1933).

[98] Fragment of Cortot's 23 Dec. 1932 letter to Poulenc in Poulenc 1994, p. 383, note 3.

[99] Chabrier's inscriptions to d'Indy in Poulenc 1994, p. 383, note 8.

performance with Février at her Avenue Henri-Martin *hôtel particulier* on 23 January 1933.[100] The recital, originally scheduled for 7 January, was postponed when Poulenc became ill.[101] Poulenc left Paris for London on the 25th to concertize with Sauguet, returning on Monday evening the 30th. Hardly back, Poulenc participated in the sixth La Sérénade concert at the Salle Gaveau on 4 February premiering his *Sept Improvisations* for piano and Sauguet's *Jeux de l'amour et du hasard*, commissioned by Princess Edmond de Polignac, with Sauguet taking the other piano part.[102] But this was not all.

Throughout the barrage of performances and concerts, Poulenc composed incidental music for Jean Giraudoux's three-act comedy *Intermezzo* (FP 64). Very little would be known about this collaboration were it not for Poulenc's own 1953 "Souvenir."[103] One morning in January he received a call from Louis Jouvet: "Tell me, my good man, Giraudoux needs to see you. Come quickly to the theater." Excited, Poulenc went to the Comédie des Champs-Élysées that same afternoon where he found Valentine Tessier and Jouvet rehearsing. Giraudoux appeared and handed Poulenc a copy of the play with only the words "There it is" by way of explanation. When Poulenc asked him what he wanted by way of music, Giraudoux responded "Two country acts and one act of provincial blare."

The next day Poulenc set to work at piano and desk, and after a few days had composed the two "country acts" conceived for chamber orchestra. Giraudoux came to hear the results. "It is ravishing, bravo!" he said: "but I must write a new play in order to use your eclogues. Dear Poulenc, I need music which is not music. It must have the sense of emanating from the décor without giving the impression of a pit orchestra." Chagrined to learn that Giraudoux had already apprised Jouvet of the situation, Poulenc offered to withdraw in favor of someone else. Instead of accepting, Giraudoux invited Poulenc to dinner and it was there that the two got to know each other. At a restaurant on the rue des Saints-Pères, Giraudoux explained that he had been thinking about employing unusual instruments. Poulenc immediately thought of the harpsichord, and between the fruit and cheese courses it was decided that the first two acts would be improvised at the harpsichord and a chamber ensemble including oboe, clarinet, piston, and trombone would be

---

[100] 31 Dec. 1932 letter to Princess Edmond de Polignac in Poulenc 1994, 32-23. Manuscript in the Polignac collection. Poulenc's dedication to the Princess in note 1.

[101] Brooks, p. 428, note 21.

[102] Concerning the number of *Improvisations* performed see Schmidt 1995, FP 63, pp. 204-05.

[103] Based on Poulenc 1953. Parts published in Poulenc 1994, pp. 384-5, note 1 and Schmidt 1995, FP 64, pp. 208-09.

employed for the last. Later, listening to Giraudoux's commands for this or that kind of descriptive music, Poulenc recorded his improvisations.

The opportunity to work in a commercial theater with one of France's premier companies was eye-opening. There were contractual ramifications which Giraudoux broached to Poulenc in late January. It was not a question of having a score of all the incidental music, he wrote, but rather of paying 1/12th of his rights for performances in which Poulenc's recordings of the music were used.[104] Upon his return from London, Poulenc responded that musicians usually received 2/12ths and that he had had to give up two German radio broadcasts as well as work time to comply with the commission. He suggested they split the difference.[105] Whatever the final agreement, the matter was settled amicably because two further collaborations occurred during 1933.

Intermezzo was in rehearsal for much of February with dress rehearsals on the 27th and 28th and the first public performance on 1 March. The comedy ran for 116 performances and press accounts by Pierre Bost, R. De B., René Lalou, Claude Dherelle, Tony Aubin, and Maurice Martin du Gard were most favorable. In several, Poulenc's music was singled out as being exceptionally appropriate.[106] When the comedy later moved to New York under the English title *The Enchanted*, Poulenc was requested to add ten minutes of music which he did. "I improvised poorly," he said.[107] Poulenc's music for *Intermezzo* has been preserved only on records now in the Bibliothèque de l'Arsenal. In February he put together a set of six *Villageoises (petites pièces enfantines pour piano)* (FP 65) based on the incidental music.[108] Dedicated to Giraudoux and Jouvet, these pieces were published by Salabert in May 1933.

OTHER ACTIVITY OF 1933

Poulenc also gave additional performances of the Concerto in D minor during February. On the 12th he played in Lyon with Ennemond Trillat,[109] and later in the month he and Février played at Queen's Hall under the baton of the celebrated English conductor Sir Thomas Beecham.[110] Poulenc also played his *Concert champêtre* with the same orchestra and conductor on the 25th.[111] Some sort of

[104] Giraudoux's "jeudi soir" [26 Jan. 1933] letter to Poulenc in Poulenc 1994, 33-2.
[105] "Lundi soir" [30 Jan. 1933] letter to Giraudoux in Poulenc 1994, 33-3.
[106] Excerpts in Schmidt 1995, FP 64, pp. 206-07.
[107] Blum, p. 64.
[108] Schmidt 1995, p. 209. They are called "little inanities" in the manuscript.
[109] Trillat was a composer and pianist who taught at the Conservatoire de Lyon.
[110] Schmidt 1995, FP 61, pp. 195-6.
[111] Program in GB-Lcm.

concert may have occurred in Marseilles on 5 March,[112] and then, on
the 21st, Février and Poulenc, accompanied by the Orchestre
Symphonique de Paris (Roger Désormière conducting), played the
Concerto in Paris. In April Poulenc traveled to Monte Carlo to hear
Ravel's *Concerto for the Left Hand* played by Paul Wittgenstein, Paul
Paray conducting, at a Ravel Festival on the 12th.[113] That month he
also attended a private performance at the home of Princess Edmond
de Polignac featuring Igor Markevitch's *Hymnes*, which he liked.[114]

Little is known about his late-spring compositional activity except that on 19 May at Noizay he dated a manuscript of *Pierrot* (FP
66), a brief song dedicated to Marie-Laure de Noailles. This is
Poulenc's only work on a poem by Théodore de Banville (1823-91).[115]
As a leader of the so-called Parnassians and a strong advocate of
Richard Wagner's operas, Banville stands apart from most of the
French poets to whom Poulenc turned for texts. Poulenc may have
known the poem from Debussy's ca. 1881 composition on the same
words, which was published in 1926. Unknown to Poulenc's canon
until its discovery in 1991 in the collection of Salabert in Paris, this
song received its public premiere in Paris on 26 March 1996.[116]

Summer activities are poorly documented except for a performance in England of his Sextet presented on a 5 July regional BBC
broadcast.[117] Poulenc told Igor Markevitch the score had been sent
to Hanson for publication.[118] He also mentioned that Princess
Edmond de Polignac had "discovered" his *Le Bal masqué* in London
during the summer, although we do not know for what occasion it
was played, and that an unnamed impresario wanted to present an
evening of his chamber music at the Salle Gaveau during the winter. With that in mind he said he would take up the Sonata for Violin and Piano (III: FP 54) begun eighteen months earlier, and compose a piano work for Marcelle Meyer. Poulenc refers to his *Feuillets
d'album* (FP 68) which eventually contained three pieces ("Ariette,"
"Rêve," and "Gigue") dedicated to Yvonne Martin, Mme A. Bessan,

112 28 Sept. [1932] letter to Jean Witkowski in Poulenc 1994, 32-18.
113 [Apr. 1933] letter to Schaeffner in Poulenc 1994, 33-4.
114 [May 1933] letter to Markevitch in Poulenc 1994, 33-5.
115 Schmidt 1995, FP 66, pp. 215-16. Published in *Intégrale des Mélodies et Chansons publiées aux Éditions Salabert* (Paris, 1996), pp. 74-5.
116 The author thanks Jeremy Drake for his assistance in locating this manuscript and Sidney Buckland for sending a program of the modern-day world premiere performance by François Le Roux and Noël Lee at the Salon Musicora-Audito-rium France Musique.
117 Schmidt 1995, FP 100, p. 297. Robert Murchie, Leon Goossens, Haydn Dra-per, Fred Woods, and Edmund Chapman were members of the London Wind Quintet.
118 [Sept. 1933] letter in Poulenc 1994, 33-8.

and Marcelle Meyer respectively.[119] The set was already in second proofs by 9 November.[120]

Poulenc began his return to Noizay by visiting Tante Liénard for three weeks.[121] On 20 September he and Février left for a 23 September date with the BBC to play the Concerto in D minor.[122] The remainder of the fall was relatively free of performances, allowing Poulenc to devote time to completing an Improvisation in C major (no. 7) in November and correcting proofs of the first six *Improvisations* published collectively in late 1933. Poulenc told Jacques Lerolle he was diligently composing piano pieces and had even begun a longer Intermezzo in C major.[123] Before departing for a Brussels performance of the Concerto, he visited Lerolle's Paris office the morning of 14 November.

Poulenc also contributed music for two other Jouvet productions during 1933: the comedy in five acts, *M. Le Trouhadec saisi par la débauche* by Jules Romains (1877-1972),[124] and *Pétrus* (FP 67) by Marcel Achard (1899-1974).[125] In all probability the commission for *Pétrus* preceded the other because Poulenc gave Achard a copy of *Le Bal masqué* in 1932 inscribed: "to Marcel Achard while waiting for our 'masterpiece' Fr. Poulenc 1932."[126] For *Pétrus* Poulenc wrote a *chanson* first performed with the play on 8 December at the Comédie des Champs-Élysées Theater.[127] Poulenc's music is only mentioned in Colette's 10 Dec. 1933 review.

> The décor of the second act, its atmosphere of encampment and of a voluptuous nursery, its fresh disorder and its luxurious indigence, the beauty of Jeanine Crispin, of Josette and of Arlette makes it worthwhile that we stop there, attentive on the other hand to the chanson written by Francis Poulenc, a chanson which resembles Dorny who cries out of one eye, laughs out of the other and mocks herself with knowing ingenuity. Among the ravishing legs, the cups of hot chocolate, the croissant crumbs and the sounds of the piano accompaniment, Petrus, heroic, pursues his mission.[128]

[119] This piece was © in the U.S. on 20 Dec. 1933 and was probably printed at the end of the year.
[120] [9 Nov. 1933] letter to Lerolle in Poulenc 1994, 33-10.
[121] [4 Sept. 1933] letter to Sauguet from Nazelles in Poulenc 1994, 33-9.
[122] Schmidt 1995, FP 61, p. 196.
[123] "Jeudi" [9 Nov. 1933] letter in Poulenc 1994, 33-10.
[124] First performed at the Comédie des Champs-Élysées 14 Mar. 1923.
[125] *M. Le Trouhadec* was performed at the Comédie des Champs-Élysées beginning on 29 Sept. (répétition générale) and 30 Sept. (premiere).
[126] Schmidt 1995, FP 67, p. 217.
[127] Schmidt 1995, FP 67, pp. 216-17. The chanson and its ritornello appear in Act II, scene 7.
[128] Colette 1989, p. 1050.

Poulenc's contribution to *M. Le Trouhadec saisi par la débauche* was unknown until Myriam Chimènes found a later letter from Jules Romains to Poulenc in which the elderly Académie Française member said he had rediscovered their collaboration while leafing through a long-forgotten program. Romains, it seems, had added several couplets in the form of a final chorus for Poulenc to set that were not in the original 1923 play. The new version was premiered on 29 September 1933 with music (now lost) by Poulenc.[129]

December included both concerts and composition. On the 11th he joined Sauguet, Rieti, Honegger, and Auric in a "Gala de musique moderne" event presented by the Amis de la Bibliothèque Jacques Doucet: Poulenc accompanied Gilbert-Moryn in *Le Bestiaire* and Yvonne de Casa Fuerte in Debussy's Sonata for Violin and Piano.[130] Then, on the 16th, he participated in a La Sérénade concert which included his Sextet.[131] As if a harbinger of piano works to come, Poulenc wrote his nocturne for piano "Bal de jeunes filles" (FP 56) in Paris the day before Christmas. This was his second nocturne and he wrote four more by May 1934.

PIANO WORKS OF 1934

Poulenc worked in Noizay as the new year began and only traveled to Paris to play his Concerto with Février late in the month for a Colonne concert at the Théâtre du Châtelet, Paul Paray conducting.[132] Composition was his primary occupation, however, and in early February he wrote Lerolle concerning financial arrangements for his latest compositions. He expected 1,500 francs each for the Improvisation in D major (no. 9) and Intermezzo in C major, the subject of earlier work, which would remain incomplete until March. Composing and performing continued in February. He spent the 18th in Paris before taking a train to Strasbourg for another performance of the Concerto with Février on the 21st at the Société des Concerts, Fritz Munch conducting.[133] On his return trip, Poulenc saw Lerolle on the 22nd and also consulted with the Polish singer Maria Modrakowska concerning texts for eight Polish songs for soprano and piano he intended to harmonize.[134] Poulenc expected

---

[129] In his 7 Jan. 1953 letter to Poulenc, Romains spoke about his futile search for Poulenc's music. Poulenc's 10 Jan. [1953] response to Romains, from Ouchy-Lausanne where he was recording for Radio-Lausanne, is in Poulenc 1994, 53-4.

[130] *Le Guide du concert et des théâtres lyriques* 20 (8 Dec. 1933), 270.

[131] *Le Guide du concert et des théâtres lyriques* 20 (8 Dec. 1933), 274. Once again the Sextet is listed as a first performance.

[132] Schmidt 1995, FP 61, p. 196.

[133] "Vendredi" [9 Feb. 1934] letter in Poulenc 1994, 34-1. This Palais des Fêtes concert was broadcast live.

[134] Poulenc 1954, p. 89. How Poulenc met Modrakowska is uncertain. Rosenstiel says that: ". . . the slender, blond Polish émigrée singer and writer, was enchanting both Paris audiences and the readers of *Le Monde musical*. She had

6,000 francs for these songs. They were composed between January and July as follows: nos. 1, 2, and 7 at Noizay during January, nos. 3 and 5 in Paris during January, no. 6 in Noizay during February, and nos. 4 and 8 in Paris on the 30th and 29th of April respectively.[135] The *Huit chansons polonaises* (FP 69), each dedicated to an important Polish woman in Poulenc's life, formed the centerpiece of programs given by Poulenc and Modrakowska in early 1935.[136]

Poulenc completed two piano pieces, an Intermezzo in C major (FP 71) and the Nocturne no. 4 (FP 56) in Rome during March.[137] In April he did not miss hearing the world premiere of Stravinsky's *Perséphone* performed by Ida Rubinstein's company at the Opéra on the 30th. "I place *Perséphone* very high among your works . . ." he told Stravinsky.[138] While at Noizay in May, Poulenc completed an Improvisation in A minor (no. 8) and his sixth Nocturne. His activities in June have not been traced, but in July he visited his sister at Le Tremblay where he wrote a brief *Presto in B-flat* (FP 70), which he played during the North African tour. The piece was published in November 1934 and an advertisement noted:

> The *Presto in B-flat* calls for more brilliant performance [than the *Badinage*], as becomes a piece dedicated to Vladimir Horowitz. Although the effect is extremely sparkling, the spirit of simplicity is retained, and first class pianists and teachers of advanced students will enjoy this short work, so simple in structure, yet so vivacious in mood. For all who would know Francis Poulenc at his best these two new pieces are strongly recommended.[139]

---

made her successful debut early in 1931 at a concert of the Association des Jeunes Musiciens Polonais. As an aspiring foreign musician in Paris, Modrakowska naturally gravitated toward the Ecole normale, where she first met Nadia [Boulanger]." Rosenstiel, p. 238. Poulenc may have met her through Marie-Blanche or Croiza, whose course on interpretation she attended. Modrakowska was born in Lwow, Poland and studied piano, chemistry, and botany simultaneously. She is reputed to have been able to sing in ten languages, and by 1933 was a vocal soloist in the first major Hôtel Singer-Polignac gala concert conducted by Boulanger on 30 June. Photograph of Marie-Blanche, Boulanger, and Modrakow-ska taken in June 1934 in Rosenstiel, p. 251.

[135] Schmidt 1995, FP 69, p. 218.

[136] Dedicatees include Ida Godebska, Misia (originally dedicated to Modrakow-ska), Countess Elisabeth Potocka, Freund, Mme Kochanska (originally dedicated to Landowska), Mme Arthur Rubinstein, Landowska, and Modrakowska.

[137] Poulenc composed his Nocturne no. 3 (subtitled "Les Cloches de Malines") in Malines, Belgium (*chez* Collaer). Nocturne no. 5 was also composed in 1934.

[138] [11 May 1934] letter to Stravinsky in Poulenc 1994, 34-2. Stravinsky's $7,500 fee was princely compared to those Poulenc received.

[139] *Chesterian* 16/121 (May-June 1935), 144. In 1937 Heifitz transcribed it for violin and piano. In an 11 Mar. 1935 letter to Poulenc in Poulenc 1994, 35-3, Walter Gieseking said he had already performed the Presto in Berlin (extraordinary success) and during Jan. in Zurich. He planned to play it on his next U.S. tour.

Between 9 and 18 July he was ensconced in the Hôtel Albert Ier, his favorite Vichy retreat.[140] From there he went to Kerbastic on 4 August to visit Marie-Blanche de Polignac for a week before heading to Salzburg on the evening of the 11th in order to be in Austria on the 13th for the Salzburg Festival.[141] While at Kerbastic Poulenc wrote his second of two Intermezzi (FP 71), this one in D-flat major which he dedicated to Marie-Blanche.[142]

EVENTS IN SALZBURG: SUMMER 1934

Poulenc's trip to Salzburg coupled duties as a critic for *Le Figaro* with performance.[143] His reviews of Carl Maria von Weber's *Oberon* and Richard Strauss' *Elektra* were published in Paris on 1 and 4 September respectively, and he also attended Mozart's *Don Giovanni*.[144] In addition, he gave two concerts. The first, at Villa Kummer on 17 August, was organized by a Mrs. Moulton and featured Bernac singing Debussy songs.[145] Apparently Poulenc had not anticipated this event when he left for Salzburg. The second, at the Salle de concerts of the Grand Hôtel de l'Europe, was sponsored by Gabriel Puaux, the French minister to Vienna on 21 August. Arranged by the composer Pierre-Octave Ferroud, this concert featured instrumentalists from the Vienna Philharmonic who joined Suzanne Peignot and Poulenc. Repertory included songs by Debussy, Ravel's *Poèmes de Mallarmé*, a Sonata for Violin and Piano by Robert Soëtens, a Trio for wind instruments by Ferroud, and his own Trio. Poulenc noted that Peignot had sung like an angel, that he had played very well, and

---

[140] Poulenc's unpublished 9 July [1934] letter to Modrakowska. Concerning this and other letters see footnote 167.
[141] "Lundi" [9 or 16 July 1934] letter to Marie-Blanche in Poulenc 1994, 34-3.
[142] When published in Dec. 1934, Poulenc sent it and the first intermezzo to Horowitz with the inscription, "I love these pieces very much. May you share my sentiment dear Horowitz." Chimènes (Poulenc 1994, p. 400, note 1) transcribed the dedication on the manuscript Poulenc gave to Marie-Blanche in remembrance of his visit.
[143] For a fragment of Paul Morand's 13 June 1934 letter to Poulenc establishing payment of 500 francs for each article, see Poulenc 1994, p. 395, note 1.
[144] Poulenc 1934a and 1934b.
[145] For Bernac's brief request that Poulenc accompany him, delivered to Poulenc's hotel three days before the proposed concert, see Poulenc 1994, 34-5 (Poulenc 1991, no. 123). Bernac indicated the proposed fee was handsome and asked for a quick response. If Poulenc actually did not know of this concert before coming to Austria, then his remark to Modrakowska in a letter of 9 July [1934] that "I play exactly on 17 Aug. in Salzburg" must mean that his other concert was rearranged. Unpublished letter. The fact is, however, that Poulenc had heard Bernac sing in the salon of Mme Mante-Rostand on 23 June. Their contact was, thus, renewed before the Salzburg trip. Buckland/Chimènes: b, p. 225 (see p. 226 for a reproduction of the program).

that his Trio had been a great success. No doubt the presence of many wealthy, socially-minded friends buoyed his spirits. A "Lettre de Salzbourg," signed "Anna-Laetitia Pecci-Blunt" for *Le Figaro*, provides a superb glimpse:

> From noon until 1:00 pm, all of Salzburg meets on the terrace of the Bazaar; the French group forms a small compact block. Here François Mauriac reigns, he is ecstatic and in moving terms, sings his praises of Mozart's *Don Giovanni*. Around him, Francis Poulenc, Jacques Février, Mme Homberg, Georges Poupet, and Mme Peignot applaud without reservation the impeccable mastery of Bruno Walter and express their pleasure at being here. The last arrivals come to join the group or to sit a little further away: Nathalie Paley, Baba et Jean-Louis de [Faucigny-]Lucinge, Marie-Laure de Noailles, Edmond de Pourtalès, Louis Gautier-Vignal, Bernard Fay, Dorothée Palffy, Mme de Montsaulnin and Mme de Chabannes. You would think you were in Paris and, in honor of Paris, one is very busy taking photos of each other and running to the post office in order to mail the prints. Elsewhere the Italians are transported by Toscanini, and several English are scattered around. With but few exceptions men and women alike are in local costume. Francis Poulenc owns three regional hats which he wears with assurance, others wear only one; Mauriac wears none.[146]

Whereas Poulenc knew Suzanne Peignot well by the time of their Salzburg collaboration, and the opportunity to be a correspondent was hardly more than an excuse to help pay his expenses, the request to accompany Bernac presaged the future. Bernac had gone to Salzburg to improve his repertoire under Reinhold von Wahrlich, and while there he was asked to sing a concert. Bernac and Poulenc had collaborated on the *Chansons gaillardes* premiere in 1926, but had only seen each other sporadically over the intervening years. Bernac recounted:

> It was not until the spring of 1934, meeting again in the salon of a mutual friend ([Mme Mante-Rostand] the sister of Edmond Rostand), where I had been singing some songs of Debussy, that Francis told me he would like to accompany me in these same songs and some of his own songs. I replied that it would be a joy, but for the moment I was about to leave for Salzburg where I was spending the summer working at my Lieder repertoire with my dear old master, Reinhold von Wahrlich. I suggested we could discuss it again in the autumn, but fate decreed otherwise. That summer in Salzburg there was an American lady who had rented a superb house overlooking the Mirabell Gardens. She was extremely wealthy and, to say the least, original. When requested to call on her, one found her in bed, aiming a toy rifle at you. This lady wanted to organize an evening devoted

[146] *Le Figaro* (28 Aug. 1934), 2.

to the music of Debussy, during the Festival, and she asked me to sing. By a coincidence, the newspaper *Le Figaro* had asked Poulenc to review the Festival. Knowing that he was coming, I left a note at his hotel asking him to accompany me. What a strange event that Debussy evening was!. . . First there was an orchestral concert at the Mozarteum directed by a young conductor, for whom a brilliant future was predicted, Herbert von Karajan. After that the audience went to the Mirabell Gardens, where, in an open air theater, Serge Lifar and the Ballet of the Vienna Opera danced *L'Après midi d'un faune*. Then the audience crossed the garden and climbed over a high wall by a wooden staircase which the American lady had had constructed, and which descended into her garden. There, under a big linden tree, stood a piano. At the stroke of midnight, it was there that Francis Poulenc and I gave a concert which was to be the first of a long series, for we found that our musical accord was such that we decided to form an association dedicated to the idea of bringing to the interpretation of the vocal concert repertoire a care and perfection of ensemble similar to that found in certain team players of instrumental sonatas. From this moment our friendly collaboration began. [. . .] The collaboration was to last 25 years, until, on reaching our sixtieth birthday, I decided to retire from the concert platform.[147]

Poulenc remembered that at the end of the evening guests had a choice between hearing their outdoor performance of Debussy *mélodies*, during which the piano went further out of tune each minute, or retiring inside to a well-heated library for a performance of Debussy *Préludes*. The next day Poulenc told Bernac: "If you want, we can do this again next winter in Paris, in a well-heated room."[148] Later, assessing the true value of their association, he told Stéphane Audel that Bernac was one of three great encounters which profoundly influenced his art: Wanda Landowska and Paul Eluard were the other two. Beginning with the first post-Vienna recital on 3 April 1935 at the École normale de musique, the duo gave numerous recitals in Europe and abroad offering a large repertory enhanced by many first performances. Moreover, Poulenc wrote some of his most important songs especially for Bernac.

COMPOSITIONS AND EVENTS OF LATER 1934

During August and September Poulenc composed a brief "Villanelle" (FP 74) included in a small volume entitled *Pipeaux* which was re-

---

[147] Quoted in Bernac 1977a, p. 27 (Bernac 1978, pp. 21-2). Chimènes prints the account Bernac gave to Gérard Michel for France Culture between 20 Jan. 1970 and 15 Jan. 1971 in Poulenc 1994, pp. 396-7, note 1. Bernac can also be heard recounting this story in an interview with Graham Johnson on "The Essential Pierre Bernac," a set of three compact discs issued by Testament in 1999 (SBT 3161).
[148] Poulenc 1954, p. 91.

quested by its dedicatee Louise B. M. Dyer.[149] This simple collection of *Gebrauchsmusik,* copyrighted in 1934 but published in early 1935, also contains short pieces by Milhaud, Roussel, Ibert, Auric, Ferroud, and Henri Martelli. *Pipeaux* is surely an homage to Dyer's interest in early music. Poulenc's lilting compound meter pastoral melody for one "pipe" can be performed with or without accompaniment.

One other set of pieces was probably begun during the summer months: *Quatre chansons pour enfants* (FP 75) on texts by Jaboune (pseudonym for Jean Nohain).[150] These clever songs bear dedications and places of composition: (1) Marie-Blanche de Polignac (Noizay), (2) Mme H. Ledoux (Besançon), (3) Mario Beaugnies de St Marceaux (Vichy), and (4) Jean de Polignac (Paris). Poulenc was in Vichy later in July and Kerbastic during early August, which may account for two songs, but we cannot document a trip to Besançon, and he was frequently in Paris. He often took Marie-Blanche new music as a gift. This is one of two collections published with Enoch & Cie in Paris, and the only one which had separate voice parts with decorative covers designed by Marianne Clouzot.[151]

As summer ended, Poulenc was contacted by the Princesse de Polignac concerning a suggestion he must have made to her earlier to compose an organ concerto. The Princess was an amateur organist who took lessons from Nadia Boulanger, but Poulenc knew little about the instrument. The matter, dropped earlier because Poulenc's suggestion came at an inopportune time when the Princess was leaving for Canada, was renewed. Blaming President Franklin Roosevelt for having considerably reduced her liquid income available to commission new works, she offered 12,500 francs or precisely half the sum provided for Concerto in D minor.[152] The Princess asked Boulanger, her music advisor, to write to Poulenc reassuring him about the organ on the rue Cortambert.[153] Poulenc worked sporadically on the Concerto over the next several years, thinking he had the work in hand in 1936. Sensing it might be a failure, he only took it up seriously in 1938. This complicated compositional history will

[149] Dyer was an Australian patroness of music who founded The Lyre-Bird Press in Monaco. With her own private funds, she published *Pipeaux* and other prestigious volumes of previously unpublished works from the medieval and renaissance periods. We have found no mention of the date Poulenc actually composed his "Villanelle."
[150] Nohain wrote in excess of a dozen books including a group specifically for children which are listed in Nohain 1980, p. 4. He also wrote chanson texts for Poulenc, Claude Pingault, and Mireille.
[151] This collection is not mentioned in Poulenc's known correspondence.
[152] Princess Edmond de Polignac's 16 Sept. 1934 letter to Poulenc in Poulenc 1994, 34-6 (partial translation in Buckland/Chimènes: b, p. 233).
[153] [Sept. 1934] letter to Poulenc in Poulenc 1994, 34-7 (partial translation in Buckland/Chimènes: b, p. 233).

be reviewed in a subsequent chapter. By October 1934, he knew it would be a Concerto for Organ and Strings.[154]

Poulenc's real September and October project, undertaken in Nazelles where he stayed until 13 October, was the orchestration of five *Poèmes de Ronsard* composed a decade earlier. Nos. 1-3 were completed in September and nos. 4-5 in October. Conceived as a means of advancing Suzanne Peignot's career, Poulenc used a far larger orchestra than was typical for him.[155] He confessed having worried about her since Salzburg, and said that the first performance had already been offered to Jean Morel, conductor of the Lamoureux Concerts.[156] Other conductors in Lyon and Brussels had also been contacted about further performances.[157] Poulenc then raised a troubling issue.[158] While negotiating with the Université des Annales in Paris for a "conférence" the coming year, the director Mme Brisson had expressed a preference for Maria Modrakowska over Suzanne Peignot because the latter sang using music.[159] Poulenc, therefore, scheduled Peignot for a different "conférence" on 17 January at the Vieux-Colombier theater. He also proposed that she and her husband Henri Laubeuf join Monique Haas at Noizay the weekend of 14 October. Poulenc had obtained a French agent, Mme Grignon-Faintrenie, for his "conférence-concerts" and suggested one entitled "French Piano Music of Chabrier and Our Time" that included a twenty-minute lecture and fifty minutes of playing.[160] In October, Poulenc also contemplated revisiting *Les Soirées de Nazelles*, though apparently he did not, and told Marie-Blanche de Polignac how much he had enjoyed J. Desaymard's new book on Chabrier.[161] Later Poulenc wrote his own book on Chabrier.

As the calendar year closed, he composed a brief *Badinage* (FP 73) for piano (dated "Noizay, Décembre 1934"), citing over the first line

---

154 [Oct. 1934] letter to Marie-Blanche in Poulenc 1994, 34-9.
155 Orchestra listed in Schmidt 1995, FP 38, p. 114.
156 [30 Sept. 1934] letter to Peignot from Nazelles in Poulenc 1994, 34-8.
157 One [Oct. 1934] letter to Jean Witkowski in Lyon is in Poulenc 1994, 34-11.
158 Poulenc even forecast a performance in London for the Promenade Concerts (which never took place) as well as one for Geneva.
159 This occurred on 7 Mar. 1935. Printed version in Poulenc 1935a.
160 The playing including five pieces: one each by Chabrier, Debussy, Ravel/Satie, Auric/Milhaud/Sauguet, and Poulenc. See Poulenc's [Oct.? 1934] letter to André Latarjet in Poulenc 1994, 34-10. Poulenc stated Peignot's fee as 1,000 francs. He gave much the same information in a "jeudi" [25 Oct. 1934] letter to Sauguet. Poulenc 1994, 34-12. Discussing the content of one of his "conférences-concerts," Poulenc said he might play two pieces arranged for piano from Auric's ballet *Les Fâcheux*, Milhaud's *Printemps* (op. 25) and the "Tango des Fratellini" from *Le Bœuf sur le toit*, and the "Romance" [= "Rêve"?] from his own *Feuillets d'album*. He asked Sauguet which of his compositions he would suggest.
161 [Oct. 1934] letter to Marie-Blanche and the "jeudi" [25 Oct. 1934] letter to

of music a short verse by his deceased friend Radiguet.[162] Sometime during the year he also wrote *Humoresque* (FP 72), a piano piece dedicated to Walter Gieseking, whose playing he admired.[163] Unlike most of the other piano pieces, this was not written for Lerolle, and had to wait until 1936 when Raymond Deiss published it. The years 1932-34 were his most productive in terms of solo piano works. He wrote five *Nocturnes*, the *Valse-improvisation sur le nom de Bach*, ten *Improvisations*, five *Villageoises*, three *Feuillets d'album*, *Presto in B-flat*, two *Intermezzi*, *Humoresque*, and *Badinage*. Most were published by Rouart, Lerolle & Cie, the remainder by Deiss. Poulenc, as much as he disparaged some of these pieces later in life, was the first to acknowledge that judicious and heartfelt dedications to Vladimir Horowitz and Gieseking, which led to performances and recordings, gained him valuable international exposure and boosted his reputation. A further boost came from his own 1934 records which included *Nocturnes* 1, 2, and 4 and *Improvisations* 2, 5, 9, and 10.[164]

Just before Christmas Poulenc entertained Louise de Vilmorin, a friend of Marie-Blanche de Polignac, at Noizay. On 22 December she wrote a beautiful poem entitled "Musique" in his guest book.[165] Later he set Vilmorin poems in *Trois poèmes* (1937), *Fiançailles pour rire* (1939), and *Métamorphoses* (1943), referring to the first two sets as "feminine songs." In her recollections (1963), Vilmorin mistakenly believed that she and Poulenc first met in 1935 at Kerbastic.[166]

TOURING WITH MARIA MODRAKOWSKA: EARLY 1935

It is hard to underestimate the importance three events had on Poulenc's overall career. During 1935 he took his first extensive concert tour outside of France, composed the first of many vocal works on poems by Paul Eluard, and he and Bernac gave their first full-length joint recital. The major event of early 1935 was a February concert tour of North Africa with Maria Modrakowska followed by one of provincial French towns during April and May. Because we can seldom provide contractual information about Poulenc's concert tours, we take the opportunity here to utilize documents retained by Modrakowska to discuss these tours in detail.[167] Poulenc's memory of dates often faltered in discussions with Claude Rostand and Stéphane Audel. Such is the case concerning Modrakowska for

---

Sauguet in Poulenc 1994, 34-9 and 34-12 respectively. See *Emmanuel Chabrier d'après ses lettres, L'Homme et l'œuvre* (Paris: Fernand Roches, 1934).
[162] Schmidt 1995, FP 74, p. 230.
[163] Schmidt 1995, FP 72.
[164] French Columbia LF 142 and 143. Bloch, p. 213 and Appendix 3.
[165] Transcription in Poulenc 1994, p. 1056.
[166] Poulenc 1994, p. 1054.
[167] Documents, programs, and reviews generously supplied from his archive by Tadeusz Jackowski, Modrakowska's son. I am extremely grateful to him.

he places the tour in the incorrect year, forgets the Université des Annales program and the provincial French tour several months later, and says he never saw her again after the North African tour.

> In March 1934 [*recte* 1935] I had just made a tour of North Africa with Modrakowska. It is for her that I had harmonized the *Huit chansons polonaises* which she had chosen. Alas! these would be her last concerts, because this mysterious Polish woman, incomparably gentle, renounced singing and the world and, since that time, no one has ever known what became of her.[168]

Negotiations for the French tour began in October 1934, but Poulenc and Modrakowska were already planning other concerts before Poulenc left for Salzburg in August. On 9 July 1934 Poulenc had proposed a BBC concert, but his handwriting had been misunderstood as 17 August when he had intended the 27th.[169] Nevertheless, it appears that they planned to rehearse in Paris after the Salzburg trip from which Poulenc returned on the 25th. He had spoken to Charles Kiesgen, the well-known Parisian concert agent, about their performing together and recommended that she too write him so he would not forget.[170] Poulenc was particularly interested in a tour to Bourgogne about which we know nothing more. From Kerbastic in early August 1934 he confirmed repertoire for the proposed BBC concert (*Airs chantés, Vocalise, Huit chansons polonaises*) and said news about Algeria was sparse.[171]

In late October Modrakowska heard from Kiesgen who was checking to be sure she would do concerts with Poulenc for a Société Philharmonique tour "en province."[172] Three days later she received a letter stating, "I have just had a telephone conversation with Poulenc who accepts to tour provincial French towns with you."[173] Another early November letter mentions the North African tour for the first time indicating that agents in Mostaganem were offering 2,000 francs for both performers.[174] Kiesgen had scheduled four concerts in North Africa, and had not yet heard from Mascara, southeast of Oran, about a fifth.[175] Three days later word was received that Radio Algiers wanted a brief performance for the joint fee of

---

[168] Poulenc, 1954, p. 89.

[169] Unpublished 9 July [1934] letter to Modrakowska.

[170] "Bureau international de concert Charles Kiesgen" (252, rue faubourg Saint-Honoré, Paris).

[171] Unpublished [between 4 and 11 Aug. 1934] letter to Modrakowska. This trip had been suggested earlier than the extant correspondence indicates.

[172] Unpublished 27 Oct. 1934 letter. How much in advance of this letter discussions actually began is unknown.

[173] Unpublished 30 Oct. 1934 letter.

[174] Unpublished 5 Nov. 1934 letter.

[175] Unpublished 4 Dec. 1934 letter. Apparently no concert was given in Mascara.

800 francs.[176] Each concert required a separate contract and the one for Tunis in the amount of 4,000 francs to be shared by both participants, for example, was signed on 15 December. A 4 February 1935 letter from the Kiesgen agency included the contract for the Algiers concert and requested a number of program changes. The program had already been accepted in Oran and Mostaganem, but there had been no response from Tunis. The North African tour is summarized in Appendix 2.

Before touring Poulenc was inundated with work preparing his "conférence-concert" entitled "La Mélodie française de Chabrier à nos jours." The first presentation was for the "Conferences Rive Gauche" on 16 Jan. with the assistance of Suzanne Peignot.[177] He planned to be in Paris from 15-30 January so he and Modrakowska could rehearse.[178] Concerned that his solo piano portion would overshadow her, he suggested she add a third group of mélodies even though Kiesgen had already submitted the program. He reminded her to bring double copies of any music she did not intend to sing from memory and suggested she select music for the radio broadcast that would not appear on their concerts.[179] Poulenc was apparently back in Noizay on 3 February, but left the 4th to give a concert in Clermont-Ferrand.[180] The two did not meet again until the boat departed for Africa, probably from Marseilles on 9 February. Once in North Africa, they traveled by train.

Concerts consisted of alternating piano or vocal groups. Although programs varied slightly, Poulenc played his *Improvisations* nos. 2, 3, 5, and 10, *Presto in B-flat, Humoresque,* "Adagietto" and "Rondeau" from *Les Biches, Nocturnes* (nos. unspecified, but probably 1, 2, and 4), *Trois mouvements perpétuels,* and "Valse" from *Album des Six.*[181] Modrakowska sang two old French chansons *Petit Bossu* (1599) and *Inutile défense* (18th century), Schubert's *Gretchen am Spinnrade* and *Das Fischermädchen,* Duparc's *Chanson Triste,* Fauré's *Notre amour,* Debussy's *Chansons de Bilitis,* plus Poulenc's *Vocalise* and *Huit chan-*

---

[176] Unpublished 7 Dec. 1934 letter.
[177] Unpublished [early Jan. 1935] letter to Modrakowska. For a listing of works performed see *Le Guide du concert et des théâtres lyriques* 21 (11 Jan. 1935), 371.
[178] On 27 Jan. Poulenc almost surely attended Pierre Monteux's Orchestre Symphonique de Paris concert featuring what was advertised as the first concert performance of his ballet *Les Biches.* See *Le Guide du concert et des théâtres lyriques* 21 (18 Jan. 1935), 403.
[179] Poulenc suggested Stravinsky's early wordless *Pastorale* and his own "Air champêtre" from *Airs chantés.*
[180] Unpublished "dimanche" [3 Feb. 1935] letter to Modrakowska.
[181] A review by Laurent-Chat in *Le Courier tunisien* (25 Feb. 1935) also indicates that Poulenc played a piece called "Jazz" which was encored. (This may refer to Roussel's *Jazz dans la nuit.*) The bulk of the repertory appears on the program for the Algerian concert.

sons polonaises. In the Tunis concert she added Roussel's *Jazz dans la nuit*. The North African press greeted their concerts with enthusiasm.[182] An interesting sidelight of this tour is that Henri Hell, Poulenc's long-time friend and biographer, attended the first concert in Oran. Reminiscing about Poulenc shortly after the composer's death, Hell wrote:

> I was sixteen [sic] years old when I heard Francis Poulenc's music for the first time. It was at the time of a concert given in Oran by the musician with the assistance of the singer Maria Modrakowska. He had accompanied his *mélodies* and as a soloist played his *Nocturnes*, and his *Improvisations* and — I remember — the *Adagietto* from *Les Biches*. I was immediately conquered by the pianist and by the composer. Since the first contact I felt that Poulenc was going to become forever one of *my* musicians. The following year — or two years later — he returned this time accompanied by Pierre Bernac, the incomparable interpreter of his *mélodies*.[183]

Over the years their friendship blossomed and along with Jean Roy, Hell was Poulenc's principal biographer during the composer's lifetime.

Back at the Dominion Hôtel in Avignon on 25 February, Poulenc reminisced that he had little taste for the Orient (too much couscous) and that everyone had called him "maître."[184] He also became ill after they docked and saw a doctor.[185] The 28th he was in Bordeaux, staying at the Grand Hôtel Montré, probably to give his lecture-recital on French piano music.[186]

Modrakowska and Poulenc were back together briefly in Paris for a new lecture-recital at the Université des Annales on 7 March, invited by Mlle Yvonne Sarcey. Poulenc's "Mes maîtres et mes amis," was printed in the university proceedings.[187] In an autobiographical account of his formative years describing the influence of Viñes, Jane Bathori, and Diaghilev on his development, he interpolated performances of his *Trois mouvements perpétuels* plus "Adagietto" and "Rondeau" from *Les Biches* followed by *Huit chansons polonaises*,

---

[182] References to the Algerian press in Schmidt 1995, pp. 36, 109, 133, 177-8, 205, 221, 225, and 229.

[183] Hell in JournalMF 1963, 3. Hell, born in 1916, was nineteen in 1935.

[184] "Lundi" [25? Feb. 1935] letter in Poulenc 1994, 35-1.

[185] 28 Feb. [1935] letter to Modrakowska in Poulenc 1994, 35-2.

[186] An unsigned review in *La France de Bordeaux* (15 Apr. 1935) states that "Récemment applaudi à Bordeaux au cours d'une causerie qu'il avait faite et agrémentée d'une partie de concert, le compositeur et pianiste Francis Poulenc vient de se produire une deuxième fois, et cette fois au Grand-Théâtre, avec le concours de la cantatrice Maria Modrakowska." [Reference to their Apr. concert.]

[187] Poulenc 1935a. Because of its early date, this account is useful in establishing details of Poulenc's formative years.

Vocalise, and "Air champêtre." The musical portion concluded when the Société des instruments à vent performed his Sextet. Poulenc had mastered the art of eking mileage out of a finite repertoire by repackaging it for presentation in diverse venues.[188] A week later, on 15 March, Poulenc participated in a Triton Society concert at the École normale de musique, playing the piano part in *Le Bal masqué* conducted by M Fendler.[189] Poulenc's March concerts conluded on the 19th when he joined in a "Grande Soirée Artistique" at the Palais de Trocadero in Stravinsky's *Les Noces.*[190]

FIRST SETTING OF POETRY BY PAUL ELUARD

Busy performing from January through the first week in March, Poulenc accomplished little if any composition. He had his 3 April debut concert with Bernac to prepare. Along with music by Chabrier, Debussy, Ravel, and Poulenc to practice, he quickly composed songs on texts by Paul Eluard especially for the occasion.[191] He had met Eluard at Adrienne Monnier's bookstore, and had a fondness for him from the beginning. In 1935 Poulenc came across *A toute épreuve* (1930), a small collection of poems printed on pink paper. Encouraged by Auric, he chose five to set to music which: ". . . opened up for me all the poetry of Eluard. At last I had found a lyric poet, a poet of love, be it human love, or love of liberty."[192] These five *mélodies* became *Cinq poèmes de Paul Eluard* (FP 77). Poulenc composed the first song "Peut-il se reposer?" in Hyères during March. We cannot determine where nos. 2-4 were composed (they are dated only "Mars 1935"), but no. 5 was composed in Cannes where Poulenc was no doubt visiting his ailing Tante Liénard.[193] He later said that they represented a tentative beginning in his quest to set Eluard.

> A searching, groping work. A key turned in a lock. I tried to achieve the *maximum* at the piano with the *minimum* of means. In composing

---

[188] This "Conférence" received most favorable reviews in *Le Temps* (9 Mar. 1935) and *Le Monde musical* (31 Mar. 1935).

[189] See *Le Guide du concert et des théâtres lyriques* 21 (8 mar. 1935), 626.

[190] The soloists were Mmes S. Jacovleff, H. Savoden, MM. d'Ariel, and C. Kaidanoff. The pianists were Beveridge Webster, Jacques Février, Poulenc, and Soulima Stravinsky with Paul-Jean Morel conducting. See *Le Guide du concert et des théâtres lyriques* 21 (15 Mar. 1935), 657.

[191] Poulenc gives conflicting dates as to when this first meeting took place. He told Audel 1917 (Poulenc 1963, p. 61) and 1916 (Poulenc 1963, p. 131; Poulenc 1989, p. 97), and Rostand 1917 (Poulenc 1954, p. 93). Buckland argues persuasively that Eluard's name does not appear in La Maison des Amis des Livres registers until 19 Jan. 1918 and that Poulenc must have conflated events and become confused about when their first meeting took place. See Buckland/ Chimènes: a, pp. 153 and 174-5.

[192] Poulenc 1954, p. 94.

[193] Poulenc's 12 [July 1945] letter to Bernac in Poulenc 1994, 45-13 and p. 407, n. 1.

these *mélodies*, I thought a great deal about an exhibition of Matisse drawings for a Mallarmé edition, in which one sees juxtaposed a first pencil draft, full of crossings-out and corrections, and the final version, retaining only the essential, as if produced by a single stroke of the pen. I regret having burned the *brouillon* of "Peut-il se reposer." A critic from Geneva [Robert Aloys Mooser], who never lets me get away with anything, could [then] see the origin of "my simplistic writing."[194]

Durand & Cie, which published them collectively in August or early September 1935, paid Poulenc 3,000 francs and Eluard 350 francs for non-exclusive rights to the poems.[195]

FIRST FULL RECITAL BY THE NEW BERNAC/POULENC DUO

The Eluard set was premiered by baritone Pierre Bernac and Poulenc at the Salle de l'École normale de musique on Wednesday, 3 April 1935. This was their formal debut, and the duo became a fixture on the European scene until their final concert together in 1959. Bernac, born Pierre Louis Bertin, changed his name to avoid confusion with the actor Pierre Bertin; he had begun his career working at his father's Parisian brokerage house. When Bernac turned to music, he specialized in French repertoire of the late nineteenth and early twentieth century. As already noted, he also studied German Lieder in Salzburg, where he and Poulenc performed together. For the rest of Poulenc's life, Bernac remained a trusted friend whom he consulted about many of his vocal works, particularly the opera *Dialogues des Carmélites* and *Gloria*. Poulenc wrote more than half of his *mélodies* for Bernac, who also premiered them, and he valued their collaboration enormously. Unlike their English counterparts, the tenor Peter Pears and pianist/composer Benjamin Britten, the relationship between Bernac and Poulenc was unequivocally platonic. As will be seen later, when Poulenc's own amorous problems threatened their ability to tour, Bernac did not hesitate to warn Poulenc that his private life must take second place to their artistic integrity. Recordings give ample opportunity for the contemporary listener to judge the extraordinary sensitivity of Bernac's interpretations and of Poulenc's consummate skill as an accompanist. Moreover, Bernac wrote a book about Poulenc's *mélodies* which is full of sage advice for the potential performer.[196] Given the importance of their April debut recital, Bernac and Poulenc must have spent much of March preparing. This can be inferred from their habit in subsequent years

---

[194] Poulenc 1993, pp. 19-20 (Poulenc 1989, pp. 30-3). Concerning the influence of Matisse's working methods on Poulenc see my "Distilling Essences: Poulenc and Matisse" in Buckland/Chimènes: k, where the Matisse drawings are reproduced.
[195] Contracts in F-Pdurand of 3 May 1935 (Poulenc) and 17 May (Eluard).
[196] See Bernac 1977 and Bernac 1978. For an article see Bernac 1965.

of spending weeks in out-of-the-way places rehearsing for concert tours. Reviews of the concert, though hardly numerous, were quite favorable, and the Bernac/Poulenc duo was launched.[197]

Not one to rest for long, Poulenc gave his "conférence-concert" entitled "La Musique française de piano de Chabrier à nos jours" in Paris on 4 April at "Rive Gauche" 28 *bis* rue Saint-Dominique.[198] A day later he and Modrakowska embarked on their provincial tour to Lille (5 April), Lyon (9 April), and Bordeaux (13 April). The Poulenc repertoire was similar to that of the North African tour, but four Schubert songs from *Schwanengesang* and two Fauré songs replaced the early French numbers.[199] Reviews again were extremely favorable, but the concert in Bordeaux was their last together. Modrakowska eventually departed for Poland where she gave up a successful singing career to raise a son. Given her great friendship with Marie-Laure de Noailles and Nadia Boulanger, it is difficult to believe that Poulenc was oblivious to her fate. Contrary to what is stated in his conversations with Claude Rostand, Modrakowska continued to concertize during spring 1935, and on 21 June Kiesgen's agent expressed sorrow that she was ill and that her letter so stating had arrived *while Poulenc was in the office!*[200]

Poulenc left Paris in Soulima Stravinsky's company on 21 April for a brief trip to Rome at Mimi Pecci-Blunt's behest. Two years earlier she, Mario Labroca, and Vittorio Rieti had founded "I Concerti di Primavera," a concert series held at her private theater. Closely allied with La Sérénade, this series sought to showcase foreigners (particularly French) in Rome. She had arranged a 25 April concert of two Roman premieres: Soulima Stravinsky played his father's *Duo concertant* and Poulenc played *Aubade*.[201]

Shortly after the Roman concert, Tante Liénard became seriously ill and Poulenc immediately went to Cannes, staying at the Hôtel des Princes. He tried to comfort the woman of ninety who had been his constant refuge and inspiration since the early 1920s by playing for her and gently teasing her about Noizay. The nobility of her life was an example for them all, he said.[202] Tante Liénard died on 11 May, and Poulenc told his sister that he would send notices to *Le Figaro, Le Jour, L'Echo de Paris,* and *Excelsior* indicating the time of a memorial mass.[203] Her passing touched him deeply.

[197] Schmidt 1995, FP 77, p. 237.
[198] *Comœdia* (6 Apr. 1935). This was the second such event Poulenc had recently given in Paris.
[199] Unlabeled program from Bordeaux.
[200] Unpublished 21 June 1935 letter from Modrakowska.
[201] "Jeudi" [18 Apr. 1935] letter in Poulenc 1994, 35-4.
[202] "Vendredi" [10 May 1935] letter to Jeanne Manceaux in Poulenc 1994, 35-5.
[203] Liénard died at a hotel run by "les dames Buet." I have not located these announcements.

That same spring, Poulenc wrote one of the few aesthetic statements he issued during his lifetime. In "Éloge de la banalité" [In praise of the commonplace] he attempted to defend the concept of simplicity in his music, particularly in respect to *Le Bal masqué*.

> It is my most spontaneous tribute to banality and it is because of the performance it will receive in Geneva this month that I have taken up this topic, not to exonerate myself, but to explain myself better.[204]

He points out that at that moment in time novelty is frequently sought no matter the price; that ears are polarized to accept either tonality or atonality, rhythm or eurythmics; and that Schönberg is largely responsible for this schism. He also believes that art has not been immune to the same phenomena. Out of admiration, Poulenc quotes Picasso's phrase to the effect that "The truly original artist is the one who never tries to copy exactly."[205] In the course of explaining his position, Poulenc pays his respects to the composers Stravinsky and Markevitch, the artist Picasso, and his poet-collaborator Max Jacob.[206]

LA BELLE AU BOIS DORMANT: POULENC'S FIRST FILM MUSIC

During the summer of 1935 Poulenc tried his hand at film music, a genre already tested by Auric, Honegger, and Milhaud. Music for *La Belle au bois dormant* (Sleeping Beauty: FP 76), an animated color publicity film for Vins Nicolas produced by the talented Alexandre Alexeieff, was written and orchestrated in just ten days.[207] No surviving copy is known, nor is any of its music extant in any other form, but the critic Jean-Pierre Liausu wrote an extremely favorable review calling the film a splendid mixture of art and commerce.[208] In fact, the film was so successful that at a private showing attended by Liausu, the audience demanded it be replayed. "The music is by Francis Poulenc" he said; "it is fresh, pretty, exquisite, spiritual; it goes, comes, jumps, laughs, amuses; dancing, humorous. . . ." The critic Émile Vuillermoz added, ". . . the film is sustained from one end to the other by the very pretty quality of Poulenc's score."[209] Although we know little about the score, it included a harpsichord,

[204] Poulenc 1935b, p. 25. The performance actually took place on 28 Oct. at a Carillon concert.
[205] Poulenc 1935b, p. 24.
[206] Other excerpts from this article are translated in Buckland/Chimènes: f, pp. 32-3. Orledge also explains the context of this article involving Poulenc's own writings and those of Ernst Krenek.
[207] "Samedi" [July? 1935] letter to Paul Rouart in Poulenc 1994, 35-6.
[208] Full text under the byline "L'Art et la vie," from an unidentified periodical, in Schmidt 1995, FP 76, pp. 234-6. The author is grateful to Mme Rosine Seringe for having drawn his attention to this article.
[209] Review quoted in Schmidt 1995, FP 76, p. 234.

an instrument used again in *Margot,* one of his next projects.[210]

In July Poulenc was invited to Count Etienne de Beaumont's "Le bal d'Orgel" at which guests dressed as celebrated sculptors or painters. Poulenc adored such occasions and attended them if invited. Claude Mauriac recalled that the numerous guests included Madeleine Le Chevrel, Sauguet, Auric, Poulenc, Max Brusset, Jacques Vallery-Radot, Jacques Février, Paul Morand, Jacques de Lacretelle, Serge Lifar, Lady Abdey, Mme de Carbuccia, Horace de Carbuccia, and la Casati.[211]

Later that summer while at Kerbastic visiting Marie-Blanche de Polignac, he busied himself composing incidental music for Edouard Bourdet's historical play *La Reine Margot* (FP 78).[212] Uncertain how to proceed, Poulenc consulted Nadia Boulanger who suggested that he base his music on Henri Expert's 1908 edition of Claude Gervaise's *Livre de danceries.*[213] Poulenc transcribed Gervaise's works rather than re-composing them (in the sense of Stravinsky's re-composition of models in *Pulcinella*), even retaining the original modes. Each dance begins with borrowed material which is then subjected to expansion. Only the "Complainte" appears to be newly composed.[214] In addition to the dances, the play called for two songs, both of which were for the star, Yvonne Printemps. Auric wrote "Printemps" for Act I and Poulenc "A sa guitare" (FP 79), on a Ronsard text, for the final scene. While at Kerbastic Poulenc presented Marie-Blanche de Polignac with the Interludes from Act II inscribed "For Marie-Blanche, who brought about this music at Kerbastic. Very affectionately. Francis. "Le Poupoule." 3 August 1935."[215]

Poulenc made three arrangements of the *Suite* (FP 80): two in 1935, the first for keyboard, the second for small orchestra consisting of nine winds and brass plus percussion and harpsichord, and the third in 1953 for violoncello and piano.[216] His contract with Durand, signed 21 October 1935, provided payment of 4,000 francs.[217] The two songs were published separately late in 1935 in editions with unsigned color title pages drawn by Christian Bérard.[218] According to Poulenc Printemps recorded his song: ". . . in a version enhanced by several instrumental touches. Unfortunately I lost the orchestral parts. I

[210] During the 1940s and 1950s Poulenc wrote music for three films: *La Duchesse de Langeais* (1942), *Le Voyageur sans bagage* (1943), and *Le Voyage en Amérique* (1951).
[211] Mauriac, pp. 361-2.
[212] Bourdet 1936. The play contains two acts and thirteen scenes.
[213] Poulenc 1994, p. 690, note 1. Gervaise fl. 1540-60.
[214] Daniel, p. 113.
[215] Poulenc 1994, p. 1014. I have been unable to see this manuscript.
[216] Schmidt 1995, FP 80, p. 242. The version for violoncello and piano is dedicated to the cellist Pierre Fournier.
[217] Schmidt 1995, FP 80, p. 247.
[218] Bérard created the décor and most of the costumes for *Margot.*

regret this because it was very pretty."[219] Poulenc's 18 September 1935 contract for his chanson predates that for the *Suite*. It too provided for the sum of 4,000 francs.[220]

Colette, reviewer of numerous Parisian theatrical entertainments, wrote a lengthy review on 1 December 1935 which concluded:

> Interludes, romances, ballet, the inspirations and the jaunty virtues, modern and archaic of the small orchestra are owing to two young celebrated composers, the honor of French musical vineyards: Auric and Poulenc.[221]

Poulenc continued his busy concert schedule through the end of 1935. He was in Geneva to perform *Le Bal masqué* on 28 October,[222] and the play *La Reine Margot* was premiered at the Marigny Théâtre on 26 Nov. 1935, marked by the debut of the eleven year old Charles Aznavour. Poulenc accompanied Madeleine Grey at the Salle Chopin on 5 December,[223] and the small orchestra version of the *Suite* was premiered at an 11 December 1935 Triton concert in the Salle Chopin by the Orchestre de Chambre de la Société Philharmonique de Paris.[224] Poulenc and Bernac gave their second Parisian recital at the Salle de l'École normale de musique on 12 December, reprising the *Chansons gaillardes*, which they had first performed in 1926. They also performed eleven songs from Schubert's *Die Winterreise*, and music by Milhaud, Auric, and Satie.[225] Years later, Bernac gave up performing the *Chansons gaillardes* finding the tessitura too high for his voice. On the 13th of December at Le Havre Poulenc and Suzanne Peignot presented the "conférence-concert" entitled "La mélodie française de Chabrier à nos jours."[226]

Although dating recording sessions for Poulenc's early commercial recordings is difficult, we believe that the Bernac/Poulenc duo recorded nos. 3 and 8 from *Chansons gaillardes* and the first three numbers of *Quatre poèmes de Guillaume Apollinaire* late in the year.[227] After such a busy fall Poulenc no doubt looked forward to the holidays and a much needed rest from the concert stage.

[219] Poulenc 1993, pp. 20-1. See her 20 Dec. 1935 recording (V.S.M. DA 4879) in Bloch, p. 106 and Appendix 3.
[220] Schmidt 1995, FP 80, p. 241.
[221] Colette 1989, p. 1217.
[222] Jean Binet's review in *Présences* 3 (Nov. 1935), 36.
[223] Announcement in F-Pn (Fonds Montpensier). Poulenc accompanied his own *mélodies* and Gilberte Lecompte accompanied the bulk of the program.
[224] Schmidt 1995, FP 80, p. 246. This concert also featured the Paris premiere of Hindemith's chamber opera *Hin und Zurück*.
[225] Program in Poulenc 1993, p. 69.
[226] Pistone, p. 38.
[227] Ultraphone BP 1531. See Appendix 3.

VIII

Of Faith Rediscovered and the Advent of War: 1936-1939

FRENCH POLITICS TO THE END OF THE DECADE

The three years immediately preceding France's collision course to war with Germany on 3 September 1939 saw considerable political and economic instability. French economic fortunes had experienced a downturn throughout the early 1930s, and a succession of governments could not reverse the economic plight. In January 1936 the Pierre Laval government fell partly because the Left succeeded in creating an alliance including the Popular Front, SFIO (Socialist Party), the PCF (Parti Communiste Français), and the radicals. Elections of 1936 showed that the all-male French electorate preferred Communism to Fascism, and Popular Front parties carried the day. When Léon Blum became France's first Socialist Prime Minister in May, his effort to make a new Popular Front rather than a Socialist government, was met by a refusal of the Communists to participate. The confrontation resulted in a series of strikes beginning in late May, and the price to settle them in the first part of June was steep. Employers began to lose confidence in the government and gold was removed from the country at an alarming pace. Blum was forced to devalue the franc despite his promise not to do so. One of Poulenc's aristocratic friends, Marie-Laure de Noailles, was a participant in marches led by the Popular Front in 1936 and a few years later "became notorious as 'La Vicomtesse Rouge'."[1]

The Maison de la Culture welcomed the new government with a 14 July (Bastille Day) gala at the Alhambra Theatre, which Poulenc attended. Symbolism was everything and Roman Rolland's play *Quatorze Juillet*, written in 1902, was performed with music com-

[1] Beevor & Cooper, p. 204 recount an interesting story involving her which took place in 1941.

221

missioned from Milhaud, Roussel, Honegger, Auric, Ibert, Koechlin, and Daniel Lazarus. Picasso designed the curtain.[2] Poulenc and Sauguet were not asked to participate. On 15 August Poulenc expressed some political misgivings in a letter to Marie-Blanche de Polignac.

I curse the difficult times that necessitate my playing the piano in Carcassonne, and I curse Monsieur Blum who terrifies publishers who bury themselves alive in their safes. Marie-Blanche, I do not support the Popular Front. Am I wrong? I am an old French Republican who once believed in liberty. I hate M. de La Rocque [creator of the "Parti social français"], but I used to like M. Loubet [former president of the Republic from 1899-1906] very much. For me, you see, the Republic was men like Clemenceau of whose maxim I think often. On your feet!!!!! Since yesterday, however, I have made peace with the government and am ready for once to embrace Monsieur Zay for his proper and intelligent appointment of Edouard [Bourdet], which makes me jump for joy. At last, a tribute to competence, to taste, and to intelligence. Marie-Blanche, to believe that I have no leftist leanings is to know me poorly. I thought that I had long ago provided proof that popular *fronts* are dear to me and I confess that what pleased me about *Le Quatorze Juillet* was actually the *audience*. This is all very complicated.[3]

Two days later Poulenc commiserated with Sauguet about the directorial reorganization of the Théâtres lyriques nationaux which, like the 14 July gala, excluded their participation.[4] Although Poulenc was miffed, one cannot help but believe that the politics of music interested him far less than its performance and composition.

In July 1936, Spain was wracked by civil war between the elected left-wing government and General Franco's Fascists. Owing to a variety of pressures, Blum refused the Spanish Government's request to purchase arms, adopting a non-interventionist stance. Poulenc worried about the fate of his many Spanish friends in Madrid such as Gustavo Pittaluga, Salvador Bacarisse, Miguel Querol, and Ernesto Halffter. For twenty-four hours Falla's death was rumored, driving Poulenc crazy until it was proven to be unfounded.[5]

As 1937 arrived, the Spanish Civil War, which had drawn little notice from many European nations, suddenly took on new significance. The historian Olivier Bernier writes:

[2] Writing to Sauguet, Poulenc complimented Auric's and Milhaud's music as well as Picasso's curtain, but called the other music "merde." Fragment of his [5 Aug. 1936] leter in Poulenc 1994, p. 421, note 10.
[3] 15 Aug. [1936] letter in Poulenc 1994, 36-15. (Poulenc 1991, no. 130). Bourdet had been appointed director of the Comédie-Française.
[4] [17 Aug. 1936] letter in Poulenc 1994, 36-16.
[5] "Mardi" [25 Aug. 1936] letter to Auric in Poulenc 1994, 36-18. Garcia Lorca died on 19 Aug. 1938.

For Hitler and Mussolini it offered a double opportunity, that of ensuring the triumph of fascism in yet another country, and that of testing their newest weapons while training their soldiers and aviators. [. . .] Before 1936, the increasingly alienated population had come to see the politicians and great industrialists as its chief enemies; briefly, in the summer of 1936, a wave of concord and progress had seemed to sweep away many evils. Now, as 1937 began, the alienation was back, and it took an even more destructive form than before. [. . .] Still, life had to go on, and there were palliatives. For the Tout-Paris, the resumed dance of the ministries provided an ever-renewed fount of gossip; and Paris itself, at the beginning of 1937, was livelier than it had been in a while.[6]

Unable to stabilize the French economy, Blum was forced to ask Parliament for special powers to repay the government debt. However, the majority of Senators did not favor the Popular Front. When the Senate refused him, he abruptly resigned on 21 June 1937 making way for Camille Chautemps, a noted radical, to become Prime Minister.[7] This time the Senate granted the new finance minister Georges Bonnet a variety of powers, though his actions did not always please the Senators, especially his increase in taxation. Eventually, the franc had to be devalued again.

In the shadow of these events the Exposition Internationale des Arts et Techniques officially opened in Paris on 1 May with only three pavilions completed. Ironically they represented Europe's three dictatorships: Germany, Russia, and Italy. Early in 1938 the Chautemps Government resigned and in the interim Hitler's troops reached Vienna on 11 March. Blum returned to power in France, but in less than a month, after a series of confrontations with the Senate and discontent with his appointments, the government fell. Edouard Daladier, previously in power in 1933, was next in the parade of prime ministers. Taking over in April, he too soon had to devalue the franc. While French productivity declined steadily, the Germans produced military hardware (planes, tanks, armored vehicles) at an incredible rate by comparison. The next months were dizzying as Russia, Czechoslovakia, France, and Great Britain all awoke to the voracious German demands for territories and concessions. Recognizing their lack of armament, the finance minister Paul Reynaud sought to raise taxes and reduce the government work force by eliminating numerous jobs.

The vertiginous route to war was swift in 1939. Barcelona fell to the Fascists in January; Hitler invaded Czechoslovakia in March; Mussolini invaded Albania in April; and Hitler invaded Poland on

---

[6] Bernier, pp. 252-3.
[7] Detailed account in Bernier, Chapter X.

1 September. When a British-French attempt to get Germany to honor an agreement with Poland failed, each declared war on Germany two days later. The next day Poulenc wrote to Marie-Blanche de Polignac that he had reported to his barracks five days earlier to await departure orders, but that none had arrived from Paris. He had also heard about a German raid on Paris. "Hitler's witches will one day get coffee dregs in their eyes and zebra dung," he wrote.[8]

Through it all Poulenc persevered, maintaining his career as pianist and accompanist, traveling frequently, and composing some of his most compelling music. Politics was simply not his interest, although when France was threatened in the 1940s, as we shall see, Poulenc created music of great pathos and courage in *Figure humaine*, stuck his musical tongue out at the Germans in his ballet *Les Animaux modèles*, and supported the Resistance with fervor and unflinching determination. In these four years Poulenc wrote another marvelous concerto, his first sacred choral music, numerous songs, and secular choral works. His music reflects events in his personal life far more than the turbulent politics of France.

EARLY 1936: CONCERTS AND *SEPT CHANSONS*

Following a busy December, Poulenc continued a heavy performance schedule during the initial quarter of 1936. His first January engagement was particularly gratifying. Under Cortot's baton, he played *Aubade* at the Salle Gaveau on the 22nd. Five days later he and Bernac performed in Lyon at André and Suzanne Latarjet's home.[9] Noted for their private concerts, this couple hosted great artists including Viñes, Horowitz, Yves Nat, and Février.[10] Early in February Poulenc and Suzanne Peignot presented their joint lecture-recital in Reims and late in the month he and Bernac performed in Avignon at the invitation of the Société avignonnaise de concerts. This was their first engagement offered by Simone Girard in her capacity as secretary of a society over which she later presided. The Bernac/Poulenc duo made an excellent impression and was frequently asked back.[11] Moreover, Poulenc became quite friendly with her not only exchanging many confidences via letters, but presenting her with a manuscript of the *Stabat Mater* and making her the

---

[8] "Lundi" [4 Sept. 1939] letter from Noizay in Poulenc 1994, 39-11.
[9] Suzanne Latarjet was Raymonde Linossier's sister. In 1911 she married Professor André Latarjet. Suzanne was a childhood friend of Jeanne Manceaux.
[10] Poulenc 1994, p. 1033.
[11] In a [May 1936] letter to her from Noizay Poulenc enclosed a promised copy of the *Quatre poèmes de Guillaume Apollinaire* with a handsome inscription. Poulenc 1994, 36-11 and p. 410, note 1. First quarter performances included one with Madeleine Vhita at the Salle Chopin. See René Dumesnil's review in *Mercure de France* (15 Mar. 1936), 119.

dedicatee of "Quem vidistis pastores" from *Quatre motets pour le temps de Noël*.

Poulenc was also busy with a choral work to be called *Sept chansons* (FP 81), which he dedicated "to André and Suzanne Latarjet, with my profound affection; [and] to the Chanteurs de Lyon, with my admiration and gratitude." This was an important departure for Poulenc, who had written only one brief choral piece, a virtually unknown drinking song, nearly a decade and a half earlier.[12]

> A work is often born [Poulenc said] out of a group of circumstances. That is precisely what happened in the case of the *Sept chansons sur des poèmes d'Apollinaire et d'Eluard*. In March 1936, I had attended several performances of Monteverdi motets by Nadia Boulanger's vocal ensemble at the *hôtel* of the princess Edmond de Polignac. Since I owned the complete edition of Monteverdi, I returned home and passionately re-studied these polyphonic masterpieces. At this same time, a remarkable amateur chorale, the Chanteurs de Lyon, under the direction of the late Bourmauck, asked me, through the intermediary of their president, my friend Professor André Latarjet, to write something for them. A volume of Eluard, *La Vie immédiate*, had appeared a little earlier, and I was full of admiration. One poem, "Belle et resemblante," literally bewitched me. [. . .] I had first thought of setting it as a song, but a piano accompaniment could only weigh it down. I then had the idea to set it a cappella and that was the genesis of the *Sept chansons*.[13]

By March, as the composition was being planned, he wrote the Latarjets:

> I have chosen 2 Apollinaire, 3 Eluard, and perhaps 2 Max Jacob [texts]. That will create a choral cycle analogous to my song cycles. I had thought of a keepsake title for the ensemble, but that seemed a little too much like Walter Scott, Scottish fabric so I will simply call them *Chansons pour chœurs a cappella*.[14]

Le Bestiaire, Trois mouvements perpétuels, and *Les Biches* prove that Poulenc could create masterpieces with his initial effort in a genre. Many years later Sauguet wrote:

> With the *Sept chansons* written in 1937 [*recte* 1936] Francis Poulenc took his first steps in a cappella choral writing. He found himself immediately at ease and a worthy successor to the fifteenth- and six-teenth-century masters who had given him the taste to write these

---

[12] See the earlier discussion concerning the Harvard Glee Club in Chapter V.
[13] Poulenc 1954, pp. 98-9.
[14] [Mar. 1936] letter to the Latarjets in Poulenc 1994, 36-2. Concerning Boulanger's relationship to Princess Edmond de Polignac's salon see Brooks, passim.

"chansons" on texts by Guillaume Apollinaire and Paul Eluard, his
two elected poets who inspired him so much and were his fellow
travelers. [. . .] How could we not praise them here underlining the
perfection of their form, their verve, fantasy, emotion, spontaneous
vivacity, and refined sonorities (nearly orchestral, said the critics of
the time).[15]

Monteverdi's influence is evident in the inventive ways Poulenc
juxtaposes voices utilizing concertato techniques familiar to the
revered Mantuan. At least sixteen singers are required because at
the end of "Par une nuit nouvelle" (no. 3) the music divides into
multiple parts. On occasion brief sections for solo voice occur creating a variety of textures. There are also inventive uses of the syllable "ah" (no. 1) or "la" (no. 6).

Poulenc composed "La Blanche neige" (no. 1) in March and by
early April had nearly completed three others.[16] He was still contemplating using a text by Max Jacob, but ultimately abandoned
the idea. Work progressed quickly and he finished the set the morning of 22 April.[17]

Like a peasant who takes his vegetables to the market [Poulenc said],
I am leaving today for two days in Paris in order to deliver to Durand
my seven a cappella choruses on poems by Eluard and Apollinaire
for the admirable Chanteurs de Lyon. I believe they are rather good
and new for me. Our Biquette [Brigitte Manceaux] who has heard
them, has greatly encouraged me.[18]

Reminiscing about Noizay years later, Poulenc said, "It was the
joy of a solitary April here [at Le Grand Coteau] that inspired *Sept
chansons*, to mention only one instance."[19] In May he anticipated
that the scores would not be printed by 4 July because strikes at
Durand had delayed production. Moreover, Poulenc did not want
the work printed until Ernest Bourmauck could read the proofs.[20]
Problems lay ahead. Although contracts had been signed on 22 May
between Poulenc, Eluard, and Durand, permission had not been
granted by Gaston Gallimard to use the two Apollinaire poems.[21]

[15] Program note for the 1972 Erato ERA 9066/67 recording of "Motets & chansons polyphoniques" sung by the "Chorale & ensemble universitaires de Grenoble," Jean Giroud conductor.
[16] [Early Apr. 1936] letter to Suzanne Latarjet in Poulenc 1994, 36-6 and note 2.
[17] 22 Apr. [1936] letter to the Latarjets in Poulenc 1994, 36-8.
[18] [30 Apr. 1936] letter to Marie-Blanche in Poulenc 1994, 36-9 (Poulenc 1991, no. 129).
[19] "Mercredi" [May 1945] letter to Bernac in Poulenc 1994, 45-11 (Poulenc 1991, no. 180).
[20] [May 1936] letter to Latarjet in Poulenc 1994, 36-12.
[21] Schmidt 1995, FP 81, p. 254. Poulenc's was for 6,000 francs and Eluard's for 350 francs for non-exclusive rights to five poems.

Poulenc was still waiting in September when he expected second proofs of the five engraved Eluard settings which he planned to send to Boulanger for correction.[22] Ultimately Gallimard denied permission forcing Poulenc to substitute "La Reine de Saba" and "Marie" by his friend Jean Nohain. Earlier, he had used Nohain poems in *Quatre chansons pour enfants* (1934). The first performance occurred on 21 May 1937 with the Nohain texts; the Apollinaire texts were only restored when the work was reissued in 1943.[23]

PROGRESS ON THE CONCERTO IN G MINOR: 1934-36

Concurrent with composition of *Sept chansons*, Poulenc toiled at the Organ Concerto commissioned by the Princesse de Polignac.[24] First discussed in fall 1934, no further mention is found until 1935, when an announcement in the July-August *Chesterian* reported that "Francis Poulenc is at present engaged upon two new works, a *Grande Suite [Les Soirées de Nazelles]* for piano and a *Concerto* for Organ and Orchestra."[25] In 1936 Poulenc wrote:

> The Concerto is approaching its end. It has given me much difficulty but I hope that such as it is it will please you. It is not the amusing Poulenc of the *Concerto à deux pianos* but more like a Poulenc on the way to the cloister, very XVth [century], if you will. Granted, the other 15th [arrondissement] also has its charm . . . Vaugirard, etc.[26]

Writing from London in early June, the Princess told Poulenc that she had learned from Vere Pilkington and Lennox Berkeley that the Concerto was magnificent and that she hoped to hear some of it upon her return to Paris.[27] Poulenc said the Concerto had cost him many tears because it had been built of new materials.[28] In a September letter to Nadia Boulanger he noted "Here I am returned to the Touraine where I am looking for the 1/6th of the Concerto

---

[22] [Early Sept. 1936] letter to Boulanger in Poulenc 1994, 36-20. Poulenc had earlier expressed his difficulties in a [5 Aug. 1936] letter to Sauguet. Fragment in Poulenc 1994, p. 428, note 1.
[23] Poulenc was finally able to send music for five *Chansons* to Latarjet in Nov. 1936. It was dispatched in *parties séparées*, though no such copies are known to exist. [Nov. 1936] letter in Poulenc 1994, 36-24. Poulenc further suggested that the pieces be rehearsed in the order 5, 7, 2, 4, and 3, though he did not advocate their performance in this order. The definitive version was premiered on 8 Feb. 1943 at a Pléiade concert.
[24] Chapter VII.
[25] 16/122 (July-Aug.), 172. Undoubtedly Poulenc himself was behind the report.
[26] "Jeudi" [30 Apr. 1936] letter in Poulenc 1994, 36-9 (Poulenc 1991, no. 129).
[27] Fragment of Princess Edmond de Polignac's 3 June 1936 letter to Poulenc in Poulenc 1994, p. 415, note 1. Vere, who worked for Sothebys, was a harpsichordist in London. Berkeley, a composer who had read French and philosophy at Merton College, Oxford, had studied with Boulanger in Paris from 1927-33.
[28] "Mercredi" [17 June 1936] letter to Markevitch in Poulenc 1994, 36-13.

bungled this spring."[29] To affirm that he had accomplished substantial work, Poulenc wrote to Nadia Boulanger in November: "Tell
the dear Princess [Edmond de Polignac] that the Concerto is not a
myth, that I am ashamed but that I will not deliver it to her until it is
perfect, in that imperfect perfection that is mine."[30] Myth or not,
much work lay ahead, and completion was several years away.

MID-1936: *LES SOIRÉES DE NAZELLES* AND *PETITES VOIX*

Poulenc was seldom in Paris between 15 March and 1 July, though
as noted he took several works to his publisher as April turned to
May.[31] While there he dined with Misia Sert and Marie-Laure de
Noailles to catch up on gossip missed in Noizay.[32] On 8 May Poulenc,
an inveterate listener to Radio Paris, heard a direct broadcast from
Brussels of Igor Markevitch's *Paradis perdu* (first performance), Jean
Françaix's *Jeu sentimental*, and Albert Roussel's *Aeneas*. He admired
Paradis, but disparaged the others.[33] In later May he was away from
Noizay for three concerts and mired in correspondence to secure
others for the winter season.[34]

An event of great consequence during the late spring was the ac-
quisition of an unfurnished room in his Uncle Royer's apartment
building at 5, rue de Médicis opposite the Luxembourg Gardens
(Plate 13). In his inimitable fashion of pleading poverty to the rich,
Poulenc told Marie-Blanche de Polignac: "The style will be flea market. I have already purchased a bed, an armchair, a piano-stool, a
chair, all for 200 francs."[35] Once ready in September, he no longer
had to rely on the generosity of friends such as Georges Salles for a
place to stay. Ten years later, after his uncle's death in November
1945, Poulenc inherited the apartment where he would eventually
die in 1963.

On 4 July the Bernac/Poulenc duo performed a recital of French
mélodies in the Jeu de Paume at the American School in Fontainebleau
directed by Nadia Boulanger. This was most likely the first of their
recitals at this august French summer institution on the grounds of
the chateau built for François I. A week later Poulenc was in Lon-

---

[29] [Sept. 1936] letter to Boulanger in Poulenc 1994, 36-20 and [11 Sept. 1936] letter
to Nora Auric in Poulenc 1994, 36-22.
[30] "Samedi" [Nov. 1936] letter in Poulenc 1994, 36-26.
[31] 15 Aug. [1936] letter to Marie-Blanche in Poulenc 1994, 36-15 (Poulenc 1991, no.
130). Poulenc was visited at Noizay over the Easter holidays (28 Mar.) by
Edward James, Rieti, Sauguet, and Rostand. Poulenc 1994, p. 452, note 4.
[32] "Jeudi" [30 Apr. 1936] letter to Marie-Blanche in Poulenc 1994, 36-9 (Poulenc
1991, no. 129).
[33] 9 May [1936] letter to Markevitch in Poulenc 1994, 36-10.
[34] [May 1936] letter to Suzanne Latarjet in Poulenc 1994, 36-12.
[35] "Jeudi" [30 Apr. 1936] letter to Marie-Blanche in Poulenc 1994, 36-9 (Poulenc
1991, no. 129).

Plate 13: Doorway to the 5, rue de Médicis Paris building in which Poulenc maintained an apartment (1991 by the author).

don for a National BBC Broadcast with the soprano Madeleine Grey. Late in the summer he tried to finished *Les Soirées de Nazelles* (FP 84), begun in 1930, and work was nearly completed by 10 August when Henri Sauguet wrote congratulating him and asking to be placed on the list for a complimentary copy.[36] A contract was signed with Durand & Cie on 8 Oct. 1936, and when proofs were ready in November, Boulanger was again asked to read them.[37] Their friendship had blossomed over the mid-1930s and in April 1936, still mourning the death of her mother the year before, she had invited Poulenc to her apartment on the rue Ballu to play some of his piano music with which she was only cursorily acquainted.[38]

Poulenc had intended to visit the Polignacs at Kerbastic that summer, but did not go in conjunction with his usual August visit to Le Tremblay. Thus in August he wrote Marie-Blanche de Polignac a melancholic letter lamenting ten days spent alone in his sister's large house pelted by heavy rain "thumping away on a piano that has more fungus than flats."

> I have thought endlessly of the times when I was the spoiled and happy child at Kerbastic. Unfortunately this year 1936, which I detest, is depriving me of what once were *my sole true holidays:* I leave tomorrow for Uzerche where, between the dear Yvonne Gouvernante [Yvonne Gouverné] and the gentle Pierre Gouverné [Pierre Bernac], I have to be a good boy for two weeks.[39]

At Uzerche, a small town in the Corrèze south of Limoges 453 kilometers from Paris, he was to prepare winter repertoire with Bernac under the watchful eye of Yvonne Gouverné, a musicologist who directed the choirs of the French Radio from 1935 until 1960.[40] Bernac had known her since the early 1920s, and he and Poulenc valued her help in shaping their performances.[41] Proposed repertoire included six songs by Weber, four by Liszt, eight by Schubert, a

---

[36] Sauguet's 10 Aug. 1936 letter to Poulenc in Poulenc 1994, 36-14. However, Poulenc told Auric on 25 Aug. that he was still ten days from completion. "Mardi" [25 Aug. 1936] letter to Auric in Poulenc 1994, 36-18. Printed edition gives "Esquissé en 1930, terminé à Noizay le 1er Octobre 1936."
[37] Schmidt 1995, FP 85, p. 263. The contract was for 15,000 francs. See also his "samedi" [Nov. 1936] letter to Boulanger in Poulenc 1994, 36-26.
[38] Boulanger's 19 Apr. 1936 letter to Poulenc in Poulenc 1994, 36-7.
[39] 15 Aug. [1936] letter to Marie-Blanche in Poulenc 1994, 36-15 (Poulenc 1991, no. 130). As noted earlier, Poulenc was disturbed by political problems in France. His comment about being a good boy may refer to his self-confessed custom of seeking casual male company during summer sojourns to the Midi.
[40] Gouverné and Bernac met him at the train station. While there he resided at the Hôtel du Commerce. Gouverné, p. 16.
[41] Poulenc 1994, p. 1028.

Schumann cycle, Debussy's *Trois ballades de Villon*, and Ravel's *Histoires naturelles*.[42]

The sojourn, however, turned out to be infinitely more significant than Poulenc could have envisioned. Two days after he arrived, his friend Pierre-Octave Ferroud was decapitated in an automobile accident at Debrecen in eastern Hungary. A few days later, he asked to be driven to Rocamadour (Plate 14).

> In 1936 [he told Claude Rostand], a significant date in my life and my career, taking advantage of a working holiday with Yvonne Gouverné and Bernac at Uzerche, I asked the latter to drive me in his car to Rocamadour, a place about which I had often heard my father speak. This place of pilgrimage is in fact very near to the Aveyron. I had just learned, several days before, of the tragic death [on 17 August] of my colleague, Pierre-Octave Ferroud. The tragic decapitation of this musician so full of vitality had stupefied me. Thinking about the frailty of the human condition, I was once again attracted to the spiritual life. Rocamadour served to lead me back to the faith of my youth. This sanctuary, certainly the oldest in France (St Louis stopped there upon his departure for the Crusade), completely captivated me. Suspended in full sunlight in a vertiginous rock crevice, Rocamadour is a place of extraordinary peace, which accentuates again the very limited number of tourists. Preceded by a courtyard surrounded by pink laurel trees, a very modest chapel, half constructed in the rock, shelters a miraculous statue of the black virgin, sculpted, according to tradition, from black wood by St Amadour, little Zachée of the Gospel, who had to climb a tree in order to see Christ. The same evening of that visit to Rocamadour, I began my *Litanies à la Vierge noire* for female voices and organ. In this work I tried to depict the "rustic devotion" side that struck me so strongly in this lofty place. That is why one must sing this invocation without pretension. From that day onward, I returned often to Rocamadour, putting under the protection of the Black Virgin such varied works as *Figure humaine*, *Stabat Mater*, dedicated to the memory of my dear friend Christian Bérard, and the *Dialogues des Carmélites* of Bernanos. Now you know, my dear Claude, the true source of inspiration for my religious works.[43]

For Poulenc, the rediscovery of his faith occasioned by a cataclysmic event had both immediate and far-reaching implications. It led to his composing *Litanies à la Vierge noire* (FP 82), a non-liturgical sacred work for three-part women's (or children's) voices and organ which exhibits great emotional character and depth with a cer-

---

[42] 15 Aug. [1936] letter in Poulenc 1994, 36-15 (Poulenc 1991, no. 130). Apparently the Schumann cycle was abandoned to be replaced by the not yet composed *Tel jour telle nuit*.

[43] Poulenc 1954, pp. 108-09.

2. - ROCAMADOUR. - Vue générale de face

Plate 14:
Ca 1905
postcard of
Rocamadour
"Vue génerale
de la face"

tain austerity of sound and simplicity appropriate to the cloister. Compositions such as the Mass in G major (1937) and *Quatre motets pour un temps de pénitence* (1938-39) continue in this vein, while the Concerto in G minor (1934-38) extends it to an instrumental genre.

The *Litanies*, of seminal importance to Poulenc's artistic and emotional development, are based on a pious text he found on a small card containing an image of the Black Virgin on the reverse. He obtained it visiting the chapel at Rocamadour on 22 August, the day the *Litanies* were begun.[44] Poulenc worked quickly, completing the score in a week. "The vocal style is worlds apart from that of the *Sept chansons*, for the strong influences here are chant and fauxbourdon, rather than a complex, quasi-orchestral homophony."[45] Poulenc sought Nadia Boulanger's counsel with the organ part and with proofreading, and offered her the first performance. It is, he

[44] Schmidt 1995, FP 82, p. 255 and Gouverné, p. 21.
[45] Daniel, p. 221.

told her, "certainly one of the two or three of my works that I would take with me to a desert island."[46]

Then, in one of his few written descriptions of his own music, he continued:

> The text (very beautiful) of the *Litanies* is in French, [and] the work lasts seven minutes. It begins with several bars of introduction in D major-minor, followed by numerous modulations in distant keys and then a *lengthy* conclusion in G minor. It is very special, humble, and I believe quite striking. Suddenly fully half of my aveyronnais blood triumphs there over the other nogentais half.

The *Litanies* remain one of Poulenc's most compelling works. Completely unpretentious in conception, *Litanies* have a power and directness unparalleled in his œuvre. Several themes, like some in *Trois pièces pour piano*, recur in other works. Boulanger premiered *Litanies* with women from her small touring ensemble accompanied by Annette Dieudonné (organ), on 17 November 1936 during a BBC regional broadcast. The private Parisian premiere took place in Marie-Blanche de Polignac's salon on 5 February 1937.[47] Poulenc orchestrated *Litanies* on 1 September 1947, but the effect is far less powerful than with organ.[48]

While in Uzerche, Poulenc also visited Nora Auric at the home of Georgette Chadourne in the Dordogne.[49] Before departing on 29 August, he spent three days at the Hôtel Berthier in Espalion (Aveyron),[50] and on his way to Noizay he crossed the Lozère, countryside that he found marvelous in its poverty.[51] Bernac, on the other hand, departed for Hyères to seek Auric's guidance with Emmanuel Chabrier's song *L'Ile heureuse* and several works by Satie which he and Poulenc intended to record. Poulenc immediately composed a series of "Five easy choruses in three-parts for young voices" on poems by the Belgian poet Madeleine Ley entitled *Petites voix* (FP 83). The poems were written between 1915 and 1925, though the illustrated book containing them was not published until 1930.[52] Ley said that when Léon-Paul Fargue and Charles Vildrac had read her book, both suggested that Poulenc set some of the poems.[53] Poulenc, who later wrote other music inspired by verse for children, dedi-

[46] [Sept. 1936] letter to Boulanger in Poulenc 1994, 36-20.
[47] Schmidt 1995, FP 82, p. 256.
[48] The instrumentation requires 12 vn. 1, 10 vn. 2, 8 vla., 6 vc., 4 d.b., and 3 timp.
[49] "Mardi" [25 Aug. 1936] letter to Georges Auric in Poulenc 1994, 36-18 and his remark to Sauguet in a "vendredi" [28 Aug. 1936] letter in Poulenc 1994, 36-19.
[50] "Mardi" [25 Aug. 1936] letter to Auric in Poulenc 1994, 36-18.
[51] [16 Sept. 1936] letter to Nora Auric in Poulenc 1994, 36-22.
[52] Ley. The book was illustrated by Edy Legrand [Édouard Léon Louis].
[53] "Mardi matin" [Sept. 1936] letter to Poulenc in Poulenc 1994, 36-21.

cated each piece to the child of a friend. The use of three voices
echoes his own *Litanies*, but the writing is neither so inspired nor on
a par with that of the *Sept chansons*. *Petites voix*, actually requested
by Paul Rouart to satisfy a financial advance for a violin sonata
Poulenc never completed,[54] was published late in the year by Rouart,
Lerolle & Cie, to whom Poulenc returned for the first time since 1934.[55]

Late in September he put finishing touches on *Les Soirées de
Nazelles*, and the printed scores indicates the work was completed
on 1 October. He corrected proofs of various works for part of October and November, and on 30 November he and Bernac participated in a special Association des amis du Trigintuor concert at the
Salle Molière in Lyon, Ernest Bourmauck conducting. Poulenc
played *Aubade* and Bernac sang song cycles by Debussy and Ravel
for large orchestra. Poulenc, who arrived in Lyon on the 26th, offered to coach the Lyon singers on his *Sept chansons* and practiced
Les Soirées de Nazelles, which he offered to play for Suzanne Latarjet
and friends if she wished. Because of a 1 December London commitment, Poulenc and Bernac departed Lyon by midnight train on
30 November in order to make an early morning flight. That evening
Poulenc premiered *Les Soirées de Nazelles* and Bernac joined him for
a group of *mélodies* on a BBC broadcast. For La Voix de son Maître
the Bernac/Poulenc duo completed three recordings in July, which
were released in early December, and two more during January
1937.[56]

THE ABORTED *PLAIN-CHANT* CYCLE AND COMPOSITION OF *TEL JOUR TELLE NUIT*

In September 1936 Poulenc also began a song cycle on texts from
Cocteau's 1922 *Plain-chant* (FP 85) intended for performance with
Bernac. "I am trying *Plain-chant* but have not yet found their style,"
he confided to Yvonne Gouverné.[57] The struggle continued in No-
vember and eventually four of the six numbers were written, but
Poulenc destroyed them.[58]

> At Christmas in 1936 [Bernac remembered] I was at Noizay for a
> short stay in order to make the most of this free time to prepare the
> programs for our forthcoming tours, and in particular the new songs
> that Poulenc had written and which we were going to perform at our
> annual recital in Paris. They were settings of poems by Jean Cocteau

[54] [11 Sept. 1936] letter to Nora Auric in Poulenc 1994, 36-22.
[55] In an undated letter excerpted in Poulenc 1994, p. 430, note 2, Poulenc told
Rouart that he was delighted to be back.
[56] [Nov. 1936] letter to Latarjet in Poulenc 1994, 36-24 and Bloch, pp. 223-4. See
Appendix 3.
[57] Sept. 1936 letter [date according to Gouverné] in Gouverné, p. 12.
[58] Poulenc 1993, p. 21.

[en]titled "Plain-chant." The evening I arrived Poulenc went to the piano and let me hear them. Frankly I did not feel enthusiastic, and he must have sensed this from my reaction. Suddenly, to my alarm, to my horror, Poulenc took his manuscript and threw it on the big fire that was burning in the grate. He began to laugh and said, "Don't worry, you will have something much better for February 3rd!" It was to be *Tel jour telle nuit* [FP 86].[59]

The demise of the *Plain-chant* cycle, if Poulenc's memory was secure, overlapped the beginning of another song entitled "Bonne journée," which ultimately opened the cycle *Tel jour telle nuit*.

One Sunday in November 1936, I felt very happy. [I was strolling down the Avenue Daumesnil, watching a locomotive in a tree. It was so pretty and so reminiscent of my childhood departures when I went back to Nogent by train from the Bastille. With trains departing from the height of a second story I did not need surrealism to perch a locomotive in a plane tree. Moved by this recollection of my youth] I began to recite the poem "Bonne journée," from the collection *Yeux fertiles*. That evening the music came to me.[60]

In December, still lacking material for the coming season, Poulenc tried again using eight poems drawn from Paul Eluard's *Les Yeux fertiles* (1936) and one from *Facile* (1935).[61] Years later, in an interview by Roland Gelatt, he spoke of his attraction to Eluard's poetry.

He is unique in contemporary French literature as a lyricist and poet of love. Even Baudelaire could not write of love as he does. His "Tel Jour, Telle Nuit" [. . .] is comparable to the best of Heine. [. . .] Eluard is responsible for having bestowed real lyricism on my music. Every composer eventually discovers what he considers to be his own source of greatness. I have found it in the poetry of Paul Eluard and in religious inspiration.[62]

Four of the nine songs, nos. 2, 4, 6, and 7, were composed in Noizay during December.[63] According to the singer Madeleine Vhita, Bernac was pulling the songs from himself one by one, which was making his hair gray.[64] Nos. 1 and 9 were composed in Lyon during one or

[59] Bernac 1977a, p. 98 (Bernac 1978, p. 98).

[60] Poulenc 1993, p. 21.

[61] Eluard had already sent Poulenc copies of *L'Amour la poésie, Capitale de la douleur,* and *Facile,* with a 4 Apr. 1936 letter. We know also that Bernac and Poulenc performed on 13 Dec. at the invitation of the Société Mozart de Nantes, before going to Noizay.

[62] Gelatt, p. 58 (Doda Conrad facilitated the English translation during the interview).

[63] Each song is dedicated to a different friend.

[64] Fragment of Vhita's [Dec. 1936] letter to Poulenc in Poulenc 1994, pp. 440-1, note 1.

both of Poulenc's January 1937 visits. Anecdotal evidence helps us to know how no. 9 was composed:

> As always when we passed through Lyons on one of our tours, we stayed with our friends the Latarjets. I remember during dinner we tried to persuade Poulenc to leave the piano—"Francis, the food will be all cold!" He was composing "Nous avons fait la nuit," one of the most beautiful songs that he had ever written.[65]

Of the remainder, no. 3 is dated "Monte-Carlo 27 Janvier 1937," nos. 5 and 8 "Paris Janvier 1937."[66] Well before the cycle was completed, Poulenc asked Eluard's assistance in providing a title. Eluard suggested four in his own order of preference: (1) "Tout dire," [Saying it all] (2) "Tel jour telle nuit," [As is the day, so is the night] (3) "Aussi loin que l'amour," [As far away as love] and "Paroles peintes" [Painted words].[67] The end result, a cycle called *Tel jour telle nuit*, is arguably Poulenc's finest song cycles and one of the finest cycles composed this century.[68]

Tel jour telle nuit is indebted to Schumann cycles that Poulenc acknowledged in discussions with Claude Rostand. "I endowed this cycle with a piano coda that allows the listener, as in Schumann's *Dichterliebe*, to prolong his own feelings, generated by the songs themselves."[69] Also, he made the greatest effort to unify these nine songs.

> The cyclical elements include: the clear transitional nature of the third, fifth, and eighth songs, which serve mainly to highlight the songs that follow them; the careful balance and juxtaposition of moods, styles, and songs, one about day and the other about night and the lengthy, serene piano coda, recalling the last few bars of the first song.[70]

The final song ("Nous avons fait la nuit") exhibits another interesting characteristic. It reprises material from the first song in the time-honored fashion of Beethoven (*An die ferne Geliebte*) and numerous of his successors, but also shares harmonic and melodic material with two of his own works: *Litanies* and the Concerto in G minor. Poulenc may have been nostalgic about Anost where the *Litanies* were composed when he dedicated it to Yvonne Gouverné.[71] While composing the cycle Poulenc performed the *Concert champêtre*

[65] Bernac 1977a, p. 98 (Bernac 1978, p. 98).
[66] Schmidt 1995, FP 86, p. 264.
[67] Buckland's translations in Poulenc 1991, no. 132 and Buckland/Chimènes: a.
[68] See Barry.
[69] Poulenc 1953, p. 63.
[70] Daniel, p. 265.
[71] Compare "Nous avons fait la nuit" mm. 17-19 with Concerto, rehearsal 35; the end with the end of *Litanies*. There are other more subtle hints of the *Litanies* in "Nous avons" as well.

(on the piano) at a Colonne concert on 10 January under the direction of Paul Paray and gave the Parisian premiere of *Les Soirées de Nazelles* at a La Sérénade concert on 19 January.[72] He also played what was advertised as the premiere of Luigi Dallapiccola's *Hymnes* for three pianos with Jacques Février and A. de Gontaut-Biron.

When the cycle was premiered at the Salle Gaveau on 3 February 1937, it concluded a program featuring lieder by Weber and Liszt, Debussy's *Trois ballades de Villon*, and Ravel's *Histoires naturelles*. Eluard, who was ill but attended anyway, told his wife Gala [Elena Dmitrievna Diakonova] on 14 February 1937: "Since I came back from Cannes I have been constantly in pain. I've only been out once at night to a Poulenc concert featuring 9 of my songs. Great success."[73] A few days after the premiere, Poulenc delivered the manuscript to Durand et Cie and signed a contract for 8,000 francs.[74] In mid-April Eluard received 660 francs for non-exclusive rights to his poems.[75] The cycle was published in early December 1937, and in a copy Poulenc later inscribed to his friend Geneviève Sienkiewicz he referred to "these *mélodies* which I prefer to all others."[76]

Poulenc also had designs on poetry requested from Louise de Vilmorin.[77] In November Vilmorin spent all her time while visiting Marie-Blanche de Polignac writing two poems he had requested. Though she chided him terribly for his complicity in her discomfort, she was nevertheless flattered at his confidence in her poetic ability. Upon returning home she sent him "Le Garçon de Liège" and "Eau-de-vie, au-delà," also enclosing a third poem, "Chevaliers de la Garde blanche," composed earlier at Jean Hugo's home in Fourques.[78] Poulenc set these to music a year later.[79]

Finally, in 1936 Poulenc also paid homage to his old friend from the early twenties Marthe de Kerrieu, Viscountess Louis de La Rochette, by writing the brief preface to a book about her. He had known the Viscountess from the time he spent in Amboise, where her friends included Toulouse-Lautrec, the Médrano Circus clown Footit, and Maurice Barrès.[80] At year's end Poulenc and Bernac performed in the salon of the Princesse de Polignac on 19 Dec.[81]

---

[72] See *Le Guide du concert et des théâtres lyriques* 23 (18 & 25 Dec. 1936 and 1 Jan. 1937), 377 and (15 Jan. 1937), 398 respectively.

[73] Eluard 1989, letter no. 228, pp. 224-6.

[74] 8 Feb. 1937 contract in Schmidt 1995, FP 86, p. 268.

[75] 20 Apr. 1937 contract in Schmidt 1995, FP 86, p. 268.

[76] Schmidt 1995, FP 86, p. 267.

[77] Concerning Vilmorin see Bothorel.

[78] Vilmorin's "mardi," Nov. 1936 letter to Poulenc in Poulenc 1994, 36-27.

[79] Two of the poems were written in the summer of 1937 (Poulenc 1991, p. 23).

[80] Poulenc 1936.

[81] Buckland/Chimènes: b, p. 224.

A PROPOSED COLLABORATION WITH ARMAND LUNEL[82]

During the winter of 1936-37 Poulenc was twice in Monte Carlo where he hoped to find Armand Lunel, a writer and professor of philosophy.[83] When he failed, Poulenc wrote a detailed letter establishing the parameters of a libretto he sought. A comic opera like *Esther de Carpentras* was out of the question. Rather, the work should be a real love story, perhaps, with an erotic atmosphere, alive with action: a real drama! Poulenc suggested the model of Verdi's *Otello*, which Lunel evidently did not know. The libretto, projected in three linked acts, must include grand arias, duos, and ensembles and sustain a work between one and one and a half hours duration. There should also be a soprano role like that of Desdemona in *Otello*. Poulenc had for some time thought of fashioning a stage work out of Honoré de Balzac's *La Fille aux yeux d'or,* but now doubted it would be feasible. Nevertheless, he suggested that Lunel reread *La Fille.*[84]

By late April, thrilled at the prospect of working with Poulenc, Lunel had thought about George Sand's novel *Mauprat,* which he found a bit heavy. This in turn made him think of Théophile Gautier's *Mademoiselle de Maupin,* though he found its rough side less sincere than Balzac's work. Lunel agreed to consider the various novels and respond to Poulenc in May.[85]

On 17 May, vacationing in Italy, Lunel kept his word. He had considered *La Fille aux yeux d'or,* which he thought might be difficult to reshape, and *Splendeurs et misères des courtisanes,* which he disliked. A new proposal, Balzac's *Le Lys dans la vallée,* was too long, and Jacques Cazotte's *Le Diable amoureux* was uninteresting. Furthermore, Stendhal's *L'Abesse de Castro* had the impossible situation

---

[82] Discussion of this project is based on letters located by Chimènes. [Apr. 1937], [late Aug. 1937], and 12 Oct. [1937] letters to Lunel and Lunel's 27 Apr. 1937 and 17 May 1937 letters to Poulenc. Poulenc 1994, 37-3, 37-4 (partial translation in Buckland/Chimènes: l, pp. 253-4), 37-6, 37-14, and 37-17 (partial translation in Buckland/Chimènes: l, p. 255) respectively. A fragment of Poulenc's [winter of 1937-38] letter is published in Poulenc 1994, p. 455, note 2. For a study of Poulenc's search for a libretto see Denis Waleckx's article in Buckland/Chimènes: l.

[83] Lunel had earlier supplied Milhaud with librettos for *Les Malheurs d'Orphée* (1924) and *Esther de Carpentras* (1925-27, but first performed on the radio on 3 Apr. 1937), and it was about such a project that Poulenc sought a meeting. In an [Apr. 1937] letter from Noizay, Poulenc said that the first time he had had to leave the same day by train for Cannes, and the second time Lunel was out of town. This second visit probably coincided with composition of the third song in *Tel jour telle nuit,* which is dated "Monte-Carlo 27 Janvier 1937."

[84] [Apr. 1937] letter in Poulenc 1994, 37-3 (partial translation in Buckland/ Chimènes: l, pp. 253-4). Poulenc also mentioned another Balzac work, *Splendeurs et misères des courtisanes,* as well as Stendhal's *L'Abesse de Castro,* and two operas: Debussy's *Pelléas et Mélisande* and Dukas' *Ariane et Barbe-bleue.*

[85] Lunel's 27 Apr. 1937 letter to Poulenc in Poulenc 1994, 37-4 (partial translation in Buckland/Chimènes: l, pp. 253-4).

of a love affair between an abbess and a priest! Lunel asked Poulenc to read Balzac's *Massimila Doni,* which was the right length and could be reshaped. It also offered the charm of an 1840s Venetian décor, and Lunel knew Poulenc would consider the décor carefully. Lunel prepared Poulenc for the fact that unlike *Otello,* this work lacked a tragic quality and tended toward the comic.[86]

How quickly Poulenc accomplished his assignment is uncertain, because he became involved in other compositional projects including *Sécheresses* and the Mass in G major. At the end of August, with the Mass completed, Poulenc told Lunel that he had enjoyed reading his new novel *Le Balai de la sorcière* and was still interested in the possibility of setting Balzac's *Le Lys dans la vallée.* He suggested further discussions at Noizay after 3 September if Lunel could make it.[87] Apparently Lunel did not visit, because Poulenc wrote that he had just finished rereading *Le Lys dans la vallée,* and had grave reservations.[88] How to conclude a work on this subject eluded him even though he found various moments fascinating. Poulenc also introduced a project connected with Lunel, but which is unmentioned in earlier correspondence: a theatrical work entitled *La Jeunesse de Gargantua* based on Rabelais in three parts each fifteen minutes long with a Te Deum at the end.[89] Poulenc suggested the following plan:

      a. Préambule [Preamble]
      b. La Naissance de Gargantua [The Birth of Gargantua]
      c. La Jeunesse avec les jeux [Youth with Games]
      d. Le Départ pour Paris et le vol des cloches de
            Notre-Dame, La Restitution [The Departure for Paris
            and the peal of the Bells of Notre-Dame, Restitution]
      [e.] Te Deum[90]

Later, he revised the plan as follows:

      I   Court prologue [Short prologue]
      II   La Naissance et le festin [Birth and Celebration]
      III L'Enfance [Childhood]
      IV L'Arrivée à Paris - Vol de cloches - Te Deum (en latin pour
            finir) [The Arrival in Paris - Peal of bells - Te Deum
            (in Latin to conclude)][91]

[86] Lunel's 17 May 1937 letter to Poulenc in Poulenc 1994, 37-6.
[87] [Late Aug. 1937] letter from Anost in Poulenc 1994, 37-14.
[88] 12 Oct. [1937] letter in Poulenc 1994, 37-17 (partial translation in Buckland/ Chimènes: l, p. 255).
[89] [12 Oct. 1937] letter to Collaer: "It is Lunel who is creating the libretto for *La Jeunesse de Gargantua* because I cannot make one work out." Poulenc 1994, 37-18 and Collaer 1996, 37-2.
[90] 12 Oct. [1937] letter in Poulenc 1994, 37-17 (partial translation in Buckland/ Chimènes: l, p. 255).
[91] [Winter 1937-8] letter in Poulenc 1994, p. 455, note 2.

Poulenc's story was drawn from Rabelais' *Gargantua*, written in the early 1530s.[92] Precisely when he became interested in Rabelais' work is unknown, but in an August 1937 letter to Sauguet Poulenc made a fleeting reference to Rabelais.[93] Nothing further is known about this work and neither libretto nor music for it has been found. Several years later thoughts of a Rabelais libretto were superseded by those of one based on Shakespeare.

CONCERTS AND COMPOSITIONS OF MAY-SEPTEMBER 1937

Two spring concerts including Poulenc's works provided high points. The public French premiere of *Litanies à la Vierge noire* was given in Lyon at the Salle Rameau on 3 May 1937 with Poulenc in attendance. The concert was broadcast, and Poulenc hoped Sauguet would review *Litanies* for *Le Jour* since it was as yet unknown.[94] Poulenc then accompanied the Latarjets to their family estate at Saint-Just and to Serrières.[95] The other concert, in Paris on 21 May under the auspices of La Sérénade, was sung by the Chanteurs de Lyon, Ernest Bourmauck conducting. It featured premieres of *Sept chansons* and Milhaud's *Cantique du Rhône* plus music by Monteverdi, Palestrina, Jannequin, and Ravel.[96]

• "Bourrée, au Pavillon d'Auvergne" from *A l'exposition*

In late spring Poulenc finished two minor commissions: a "Bourrée, au Pavillon d'Auvergne," for a collective work entitled *A l'exposition* (FP 87), completed at Noizay on 7 May, and *Deux marches et un intermède* (FP 88) composed in June.[97] Both were written in honor of the Exposition Internationale des Arts et Techniques, a World's Fair that had not only become the pawn of posturing European nations, but also a mirror of political and social problems in France itself.[98] Many descriptions of the Exposition have been written by political historians, but far fewer remain from the pens of artists whose works were central to the many pavilions. One was by Milhaud.

---

[92] The second edition was published in 1535. It has been debated whether the first edition, the only known copy of which lacks its title page, was composed the same year or one year earlier.

[93] [17 Aug. 1936] letter in Poulenc 1994, 36-16.

[94] Fragment of Poulenc's [2 May 1937] letter to Sauguet in Poulenc 1994, p. 441, note 3.

[95] "Vendredi" [probably 7 May 1937] letter to the Latarjets in Poulenc 1994, 37-5.

[96] Schmidt 1995, FP 81, pp. 252-3. The program initially approved by the committee of *La Sérénade* is given in Poulenc's [Nov. 1936] letter to Suzanne Latarjet in Poulenc 1994, 36-25. The program presented is in note 1. Milhaud acknowledged that Poulenc was responsible his having been offered the commission. Milhaud 1953, p. 258 (Milhaud 1987a, p. 207).

[97] Schmidt 1995, FP 87 and 88.

[98] See Bernier, Chapter X concerning political implications of the Exposition.

In spite of the difficult period that followed the adoption of social reforms (forty-hour week, paid vacations, organized leisure), and in spite of the disturbances, lockouts, and sit-down strikes at factories, the International Exposition of 1937 went ahead and was realized. It was an extraordinary accomplishment! However, the sound of sinister threats and forewarnings could be heard. There was to be an Austrian pavilion, yet the evil forces of the *Anschluss* were never very distant. Picasso's *Guernica* [commemorating the Basque town of Guernica attacked and destroyed by German bombers provided to Franco by Hitler] adorned the walls of the Spanish pavilion, but the Republic had been murdered. The pavilions of Germany and Soviet Russia, placed face to face, seemed to defy each other. One evening while we contemplated the sunset behind the huge mass of flags of all the nations which dominated the Pont d'Iéna, Madeleine felt such deep anguish that she clutched my arm and whispered: "This is the end of Europe!" The arts were well represented. Great painters, whether French or foreign, had created panels and frescos; sculptors had the opportunity to exhibit their talents, and architects to demonstrate their new concepts.[99]

Numerous composers including Arthur Honegger and Florent Schmitt were invited to contribute, and others like Milhaud wrote music to accompany the spectacular Festivals of Water and Lights presented after dark.[100]

Poulenc's first contribution, a "Bourrée, au Pavillon d'Auvergne," is one of eight short, descriptive piano pieces published collectively by Raymond Deiss in late 1937.[101] The complete set was premiered at the "Inaug. Pavillon de la Femme et de l'Enfant" by one J. Damasekan, age 9.[102]

•*Deux marches et un intermède*

His second contribution, *Deux marches et un intermède,* is of greater significance. Containing a "Marche 1889," an "Intermède champêtre," and a "Marche 1937," this work was commissioned by Duke François d'Harcourt for a dinner he hosted at the Maison de la Chimie on 24 June to honor the writer Harold Nicolson and other English notables. According to Henri Hell:

The *Marche d'entrée* as well as the music for the sorbet course and after-dinner coffee was commissioned from Georges Auric. The guests ate the pineapple course to the sounds of the "March of the period

[99] Milhaud 1953, p. 255 (Milhaud 1987a, p. 205).
[100] More than twenty scores were commissioned. Milhaud 1953, p. 256 (Milhaud 1987a, p. 206).
[101] Schmidt 1995, FP 87. Others were by Auric, Marcel Delannoy, Ibert, Milhaud, Sauguet, Schmitt, and Tailleferre.
[102] Schmidt 1995, FP 87, p. 269.

1889," by Poulenc, the cheeses while listening to the "Rustic Inter-mezzo" by the same Poulenc, whose "March of the period 1937" concluded the dinner.[103]

Scored for a chamber orchestra of flute, oboe, clarinet, bassoon, trumpet, and strings, these pieces provide a *Rückblick,* an assessment of the present, and a glimpse of the future. "March 1889," indebted to Emmanuel Chabrier, is reminiscent of Poulenc's own ballet *Les Biches.* The more solemn "Intermède champêtre" uses none of the conventions often associated with *musique champêtre* throughout history. If Poulenc was making a pun on rustic music because the dinner course included cheese, one would not know it. The final "Marche 1937" is much the most interesting piece. Stravinsky's influence is unmistakable. Four years later Poulenc reaffirmed that Stravinsky's imprint on his music had not moderated.

> At the age of twenty, I was crazy about Stravinsky's music. Many of my early works bear witness to this passionate veneration; it was a natural influence since, at that time, I often played the overture to *Mavra* or the finale of *Pulcinella* more than twenty times on a single day. Now that I am over forty, and I am controlling, or should be controlling my passions, my fervor for Stravinsky's music is intact, and I continue to owe many of my happiest musical experiences to this master.[104]

This music is the inspiration behind the opening of Act III, scene 4 of *Dialogues des Carmélites.*

•Mass in G major

The crowning achievement of 1937 was Poulenc's composition of an *a cappella* Mass in G major (FP 89) during August. Like *Sept chansons,* the Mass was intended for the Chanteurs de Lyon.

> In arriving at Anost in August 1937, I had decided to write a Mass dedicated to my father's memory. Because I am from Aveyronais stock, that is to say Montagnard and already Mediterranean, the Romanesque style has always been at the root, quite naturally, of my preferences. Thus I tried to write in a rough and direct style, this act of faith called a Mass. This roughness is especially striking in the opening *Kyrie,* but do not forget that at the beginning of the Church, the unbaptized could also sing this hymn with the priests. It is what explains the almost savage style of my *Kyrie.* For the *Sanctus,* I thought of the heads of angels intermingled in the frescos of Gozzoli in the Riccardi Palace in Florence. It is a carillon of voices. As for the con-

[103] Hell 1978, p. 144 (Hell 1959, p. 54).
[104] Poulenc 1941a, p. 195.

cluding *Agnus*, sung by a solo soprano in a high register, it symbolizes the Christian soul, confident of a life after death.[105]

Anost seems to have been chosen because Poulenc enjoyed the
Morvan region (Plate 15).

> We are staying in a little country house with a superb view of the
> Morvan valley. We take our meals at the hotel where the cooking is
> noteworthy and the company ideal, small businessmen from Paris
> on vacation with their wives and children etc. [. . .] The male element
> is very good, but thank heavens nothing is tempting me. (However,
> in Saulieu there is a marvelous young man aged 22 about whom I
> sometimes dream. . . .)[106]

Poulenc had still deeper ties to the Morvan.

> It is not by chance that I discovered this corner of the Morvan. My
> nurse was born and interred there. Few towns appeal to me more
> than Autun, few mountains reflect the "evening fire" with greater
> mellowness than the hills of the Morvan. It is the gateway to Bur-
> gundy, but with a lighter atmosphere. As a reward for our days of
> work, Bernac and I would dine at Saulieu or Arnay-le-Duc.[107]

If he proved one thing to himself between 1936 and 1939 it was
that he could compose vocal music quickly. *Tel jour telle nuit*, born
of adversity, was accomplished with dispatch, and composition of
the Mass also progressed rapidly. On 17 August Poulenc reported:
"I have recopied the Kyrie, the Benedictus, and the Agnus, the remainder is sketched. I am unable to figure out why choral music is
easy for me."[108] Two days later only the Gloria remained to be written.[109] It is noteworthy, however, that Poulenc chose not to set the
Credo, the central confession of faith, in his Mass. He and Bernac,
under Yvonne Gouverné's watchful eye, also rehearsed Debussy's
complete *mélodies* for BBC performances during the coming season.[110]

• *Sécheresses*

Over the summer months Poulenc also corresponded with Edward James, the eccentric British poet, collector of surrealist art, and

[105] Poulenc 1954, pp. 155-6.
[106] [17 Aug. 1937] letter to Nora Auric in Poulenc 1994, 37-9.
[107] Poulenc 1993, p. 26 (Poulenc 1989, pp. 46-7).
[108] [17 Aug. 1937] letter to Nora Auric in Poulenc 1994, 37-9. Poulenc also had
sketched parts of his cantata *Sécheresses*, discussed below, and the opening of the
letter seems to indicate that Auric had sent Poulenc music for some other Masses.
[109] 19 Aug. [1937] letter to Jeanne Manceaux in Poulenc 1994, 37-10.
[110] "Vendredi" [27 Aug. 1937] letter to Marie-Blanche in Poulenc 1994, 37-12.
Shortly before departing Anost he sent a touching letter of condolence to Mme
Albert Roussel on the death of her husband Albert on 23 Aug. "Vendredi soir"

Plate 15: Poulenc seated on a carousel lion at a village fair in Anost, 1937. (Private collection of Francis Poulenc used with the kind permission of Rosine Seringe.)

godson of King Edward VII.[111] The close friend of Yvonne de Casa Fuerte, James asked Poulenc to compose a cantata first called *Quatre sécheresses* (FP 90) for mixed chorus and orchestra intended for the

[27 Aug. 1937] letter in Poulenc 1994, 37-13. Poulenc lunched with the Latarjets at St Just before taking the train from Bourg-en-Bresse to Paris, where he spent a week before returning to Noizay. 19 Aug. [1937] letter to Jeanne Manceaux in Poulenc 1994, 37-10. He made much the same report to Sauguet adding that the "team" was also working on a divine piece by Gounod. [20 Aug. 1937] letter to Sauguet in Poulenc 1994, 37-11.

111 Concerning James see Lowe, passim.

Chanteurs de Lyon.[112] James himself wrote the poems, which he revised as the summer progressed. Initial agreement was acknowledged by Poulenc in July and on the 21st James sent a new version of the texts planned in four movements: (1) "Les Sauterelles" [The Grasshoppers], (2) "Le Village abandonné" [The Abandoned Village], (3) "Le Faux avenir" [The False Future], and (4) "Le Squelette de la mer" [The Skeleton of the Sea].[113] By 17 August he had sketched the first movement, described as "music in the style of giraffes in heat," and was relying on thoughts of Salvador Dali for guidance.[114] At the end of the month James telegraphed a title for the work suggesting *Les Pays de la Sécheresse*.[115] In the end Poulenc shortened this to *Sécheresses*. James also continued to alter the text, always soliciting Poulenc's opinion. Composing continued from September to December 1937, and the orchestration was completed at James' home in London on 3 March 1938.[116] When Poulenc wrote Paul Collaer in October 1937 about his recent works, he indicated that *Sécheresses* would not be available before March 1938 because James himself was doing the English translation.[117] However, the published piano-vocal score includes no such translation, nor is one in the 1952 published orchestral score.[118]

During the last quarter of 1937 Poulenc wrote a very direct letter to his dear friend and frequent collaborator Suzanne Peignot, for whom he had written various *mélodies*.[119] Concerned that her career was flat, he advised her to practice her singing diligently, like Bernac, and to join Nadia Boulanger's coterie of singers, which already included Paul Derenne, Marie-Blanche de Polignac, Doda Conrad, and Hugues Cuénod. Above all, she must abandon amateur behavior,

---

[112] In 1933, James had commissioned three ballets for his wife to dance from Kurt Weill *(The Seven Deadly Sins)*, Sauguet *(Fastes)*, and Milhaud *(Les Songes)*. See Nichols 1996, pp. 84-5.

[113] 10 July [1937] letter to James and James' 21 July 1937 reply to Poulenc in Poulenc 1994, 37-7 (partial translation in Buckland/Chimènes: b, p. 236) and 37-8 respectively. Poulenc also makes clear that James commissioned the work.

[114] [17 Aug. 1937] letter to Nora Auric in Poulenc 1994, 37-9. When James' poems were published in *Minotaur*, Dali illustrated them. See *Minotaur*, pp. 53-7.

[115] James' "mardi matin" [31 Aug. 1937] letter to Poulenc in Poulenc 1994, 37-15.

[116] Schmidt 1995, FP 90, p. 273.

[117] [12 Oct. 1937] letter in Poulenc 1994, 37-18.

[118] Doda Conrad prepared a literal translation for Robert Shaw. See Schmidt 1995, FP 90, p. 273. On 24 Jan. 1938 Poulenc signed a contract with Durand for 10,000 francs to publish his *Trois poèmes de Louise de Vilmorin* and *Sécheresses*. Contract in Schmidt 1995, FP 90, p. 276. James authorized Poulenc to use his poetry in a 29 Dec. 1937 letter to Poulenc, and signed a 400 franc contract with Durand on 23 Feb. 1938 for non-exclusive rights to his poems. The premiere was sung from separate choral parts published by Durand in 1938.

[119] [12 Oct. 1937] letter to Peignot in Poulenc 1994, 37-16 (Poulenc 1991, no. 133).

making excuses for not having enough time to spend on her art, and become the consummate professional, completely devoted to duty.[120] At the same time, Poulenc extolled Marie-Blanche's progress as a singer, chiding Peignot:

> Although it might seem incredible to you, Marie-Blanche has worked much harder than you for the past two years. If you need to be convinced, you have only to listen to her Monteverdi recordings. Pierre was astonished by them.[121]

In addition to projects already mentioned, Poulenc was contemplating a ballet for Léonide Massine on La Fontaine fables in which Jacques Rouché, Director of the Paris Opera, had tried to interest him.[122] Poulenc postponed writing the ballet in question, eventually called *Les Animaux modèles*, until 1940.

During December, however, Poulenc revisited poems Vilmorin had written for him a year earlier, turning them into *Trois poèmes de Louise de Vilmorin* (FP 91) dedicated to Marie-Blanche de Polignac.[123]

> Few people move me as much as Louise de Vilmorin: because she is beautiful, because she is lame, because she writes French of such innate purity, because her name reminds one of flowers and vegetables, because she loves her brothers like a lover and her lovers like a sister. Her lovely face recalls the seventeenth century, as does the sound of her name. I can imagine her as a friend of "Madame" or painted by Ph. de Champaigne, as an abbess, a rosary in her long hands. [Marie Laurencin is often restricted by her "Bibliothèque rose" side, she who was so much better equipped to paint *Les Biches*.] Louise always escapes childishness despite her country house where they play on the lawns. Love, desire, joy, illness, exile, financial difficulties, were at the foundation of her genuineness.[124]

Whereas most songs of the period 1937-39 were for Bernac, this set was for the pure soprano voice of Marie-Blanche with whom Poulenc premiered them at a La Sérénade concert in the Salle Gaveau on 28 November 1938. As the year concluded, Poulenc wrote to the "irascible diva" Madeleine Grey agreeing to a recording session in January.[125] The pair had given at least two earlier concerts on 3 May 1927 and 5 December 1935. Particularly renowned for her perfor-

[120] Peignot did not take Poulenc's advice concerning Boulanger's group.
[121] [12 Oct. 1937] letter to Peignot in Poulenc 1994, 37-16 (Poulenc 1991, no. 133).
[122] [12 Oct. 1937] letter to Collaer in Poulenc 1994, 37-18 and Collaer 1996, 37-2. Serge Lifar finally took over the project.
[123] Vilmorin's 1 Dec. 1937 letter to Poulenc granted him rights to set the poems, and she was paid 300 francs for non-exclusive rights (signed 10 Feb. 1938 receipt).
[124] Poulenc 1993, pp. 22-3 (Poulenc 1989, pp. 36-8).
[125] [Dec. 1937] letter in Poulenc 1994, 37-19 (Poulenc 1991, no. 134).

mances of Ravel and Canteloube, Grey had learned Ravel's *Don Quichotte à Dulcinée* for her annual recital.[126] Aware it was written for a man's voice, she and Poulenc auditioned it for Ravel to see what he thought. Ravel's only comment concerned her taking a slight unnotated rallentando.[127] When Poulenc heard the test pressing of their recording in 1938, however, he found it unflattering (it lacked joy) and advised her not to permit its release: "This is why six sides of Bernac-Poulenc performing Fauré have just been relegated to the dust bin," Poulenc told her.[128]

COMPOSITIONS AND CONCERTS OF EARLIER 1938

In 1938, a year before political events made travel in Europe problematic, the Bernac/Poulenc duo toured with abandon. Their extensive sets of concerts included: five in early March in London, during which they performed Debussy's complete *mélodies* on the BBC; four in late March in Italy; a group in Holland in mid-October; and another group in Eastern France in late October-early November. In addition, Poulenc appeared in Amsterdam, Avignon, and Venice. His compositions were also numerous. Six *mélodies*, the Concerto in G minor, and two penitential motets were drafted or completed.

As the year progressed, Poulenc worked tirelessly to fill gaps in his concert schedule first pestering Mimi Pecci-Blunt for an invitation to Rome, reminding her the Bernac/Poulenc duo would already be in Florence on 25 March. Hoping to reinterest her in the lecture-recital "Souvenirs de mes 20 ans" canceled the previous year, Poulenc proposed a two-part scenario:

1. Présentations. Excuses	1. Presentations. Apologies
1ers souvenirs. Viñes. Satie.	Early memories. Viñes, Satie.
Engueulade Vidal	Bawling out by Vidal
Satie intime. Arcueil.	Satie close up. Arcueil.
La boutique du père Demets.	Father Demets' shop.
Nos réunions. Elaborations.	Our meetings. Elaborations.
Les Programmes	The Programs
Groupe des Six	*Les Six*
Rue Huyghens — atmosphère	Rue Huyghens — atmosphere
Pièces de Satie, Poulenc.	Pieces by Satie, Poulenc.

---

[126] Nichols 1996, pp. 84-5. The article originated in *Le Guide musical*.

[127] Nichols 1996, pp. 84-5. Grey indicates the year as that of Ravel's death (1937).

[128] 7 June [1938] letter in Poulenc 1994, 38-7 (Poulenc 1991, no. 137). In Jan. 1937 he and Bernac recorded six Fauré *mélodies* of which only two were issued. During 1937 Poulenc also recorded Satie's *Parade* and *Trois morceaux en forme de poire* with Auric. See Appendix 3.

2. Les Ballets russes
  Parade. Elaboration. Première
  atmosphère 1917. Esprit d'une
  époque. Picasso. Lecture
  Apollinaire. Je connais Diaghilev
  Stravinsky. Rencontre chez
  Valentine Hugo. Commande des
  Biches

2. The Ballets Russes
  Parade. Elaboration. Atmosphere
  of the 1917 premiere. The *Zeitgeist.*
  Picasso. Reading
  Apollinaire. I know Diaghilev
  Stravinsky. Meeting at Valentine
  Hugo's house. Commission for
  Les Biches

Exemple de Stravinsky
  Souvenir sur *Les Noces*
  Première de *Mavra*
  J'écris *Les Biches*
  Musique de mes 20 ans
  Marie Laurencin
  Je joue *Les Biches.*

The example of Stravinsky
  Recollection of *Les Noces*
  Premiere of *Mavra*
  I write *Les Biches*
  Music when I was in my twenties
  Marie Laurencin
  I play *Les Biches.*[129]

Bernac and Poulenc began the year with an Amsterdam Concertgebouw recital on 25 January that was followed by their major Parisian winter concert at the Salle Gaveau on 7 February. They performed four Mozart songs, Schumann's *Sechs Gedichte*, op. 90, as well as works by Gounod, Roussel, Ravel, and Debussy. They were already in England by 19 February for a Haslemere Chamber Music concert shared with violinist Antonio Brosa and pianist Franz Reizenstein.[130] The results of their intense work of the previous summer are best seen in the five BBC broadcasts embracing the complete *mélodies* of Debussy. Presented between 28 February and 4 March, these concerts were broadcast either regionally or internationally.[131] Hardly more than a week later they gave their second Avignon recital sponsored by the Société avignonnaise de concerts at Simone Girard's request.

The first completed piece of the year was *Le Portrait* (FP 92) one of five *mélodies* for the Bernac/Poulenc winter 1938-39 recitals.

[129] 26 Jan. [1938] letter to Mimi Pecci-Blunt in Poulenc 1994, 38-1 (Poulenc 1991, no. 135). Poulenc requested a 3,000 lira fee. According to Poulenc the 1937 *conférence* was canceled, but the 27 Mar. 1937 issue of *Les Nouvelles littéraires*, p. 10 indicates that Poulenc was in Rome at that time: "He [Poulenc] has just given in Rome, at the *Sabati di primavera*, . . . under the direction of the Countess Pecci Blunt, a *conférence-concert* which had a great success. *Memories of my twenties* was the subject he chose."
[130] Program in GB-Lcm (featured *Tel jour telle nuit, mélodies* by Fauré and Debussy, as well as five piano pieces played by Poulenc).
[131] While in London, they may have stayed at James' 35 Wimpole Street home. James' letterhead prefaces a 3 Mar. [1938] letter Poulenc sent to Wiéner in Poulenc 1994, 38-2 (Poulenc 1991, no. 136).

Envisioned Order of Program   Place/Date of Composition

Deux poèmes de Guillaume Apollinaire

    1. "Dans le jardin d'Anna"   Anost, August 1938
    2. "Allons plus vite"   Noizay, May 1938

Le Portrait   Paris, March 1938

Miroirs brûlants

    1. "Tu vois le feu du soir"   Anost, August 1938
    2. "Je nommerai ton front"   Noizay, 7 January 1939

Poulenc composed *Le Portrait* to a poem by Colette, whom he had known from at least the early 1930s.[132]

> For years Colette had been promising me some poems. One day sitting by her bedside with Thérèse Dorny and Hélène Jourdan-Morhange, I implored her for some. "Here, take this," she said to me, laughing, as she threw me a quite large gauze handkerchief on which this pretty poem was transcribed in facsimile. I must confess that my music expresses quite inadequately my admiration for Colette. It is a very ordinary song, useful nevertheless in the present group because it prepares marvelously well for "Tu vois le feu du soir."[133]

Poulenc completed these *mélodies* between March 1938 and January 1939, though they were not composed in the order he imagined them performed.[134]

COMPLETION OF THE CONCERTO IN G MINOR: MARCH-AUGUST 1938

The Bernac/Poulenc duo departed on 12 March for a tour of Italy which took them to Milan, Turin, Lugano, and Florence.[135] Apparently, however, Poulenc's hope to present a lecture-recital in Rome was dashed. In April he was back composing the Concerto in G minor (FP 93) which had occupied him intermittently between 1934-36.[136] Under pressure from the Princesse de Polignac to complete

---

[132] Poulenc and Colette, the famous novelist, exchanged letters at least as early as mid-July 1931. Poulenc 1994, 31-12 (Poulenc 1991, no. 117). The more precise date is established after Richardson, pp. 145-6. In 1932 she visited Noizay. Poulenc 1994, p. 1017.

[133] Poulenc 1993, p. 26 (Poulenc 1989, pp. 44-5).

[134] Poulenc 1993, p. 24 (Poulenc 1989, pp. 40-1).

[135] 12 Mar. [1938] letter to the BBC from the Kiesgen agency in GB-Rbbc (Francis Poulenc Artists file 1a (1937-1945)) and his 26 Jan. [1938] letter to Mimi Pecci-Blunt in Poulenc 1994, 38-1 (Poulenc 1991, no. 135). Although the dates of these concerts have not been determined, Poulenc and Bernac were in Turin on 18 Mar. (postcard to Boulanger from Turin cited in Schmidt 1995, FP 93, p. 282). They arrived in Florence on the 25th.

[136] See above.

"her" Concerto, Poulenc toiled through August, when it was finally finished. The Princess had desired a 1938 performance together with the premiere of Jean Françaix's chamber opera *Diable boiteux*, but Poulenc was unable to finish in time. Françaix's opera was performed on 30 May without the Concerto.[137] At the end of May, Poulenc wrote that the Concerto was nearing completion, but begged the Princess not to press for the 29 June date. He complained that this work above all others had given him great difficulty in finding his means of expression, and blamed delay on the need to consult the touring Nadia Boulanger about registrations and other compositional details.[138] Several days later the Princess acquiesced to a postponement.[139] Perhaps to mollify his friend, Poulenc offered her the manuscript of his Mass.[140]

Poulenc finally read the Concerto on the piano for the Princess in July[141] and immediately spread the news of its completion to Auric, Sauguet, and his Uncle Royer. The Princess had been moved by the music, and Poulenc gave her the score in Venice during his visit for a performance with Bernac.[142] She in turn passed it on to Boulanger in early December and the organist Maurice Duruflé rehearsed the Concerto on 15 December.[143] The first private performance followed in the Hôtel Singer-Polignac with Boulanger conducting on 16 December 1938. The public premiere at a La Sérénade concert in the Salle Gaveau, Roger Désormière conducting, was delayed until 21 June 1939. Again, Duruflé was the soloist, and he, not Boulanger, is acknowledged in the printed score for having assisted with the registration. In a post-premiere letter to Boulanger Poulenc lamented that Désormière gave a perfectly correct reading, but one which lacked the heart and lyricism evident in her conducting of the private premiere.[144]

---

[137] Brooks, pp. 460-2 and Princess Edmond de Polignac's 24 May 1938 letter to Poulenc in Poulenc 1994, 38-5.

[138] [25, 26, or 27 May 1938] letter to Princess Edmond de Polignac in Poulenc 1994, 38-6 (translated in Buckland/Chimènes: b, pp. 234-5).

[139] See the fragment of the Princess' "vendredi" [27 May 1938] letter to Poulenc in Poulenc 1994, p. 464, note 4 (translated in Buckland/Chimènes: b, p. 235). Poulenc wrote to Jeanne Manceaux the same day saying that he was recopying the Concerto that was written with a technique which was new for him. Fragment in Poulenc 1994, p. 464, note 4.

[140] Poulenc 1994, p. 464, where the dedication to the Princess is printed. Poulenc dated his dedication "année du *Concerto*!!!!"

[141] "Mercredi" [July 1938] letter in Poulenc 1994, 38-8 (Poulenc 1991, no. 139).

[142] [Aug. 1938] letter to Milhaud, [16 Aug. 1938] letter to Sauguet, and "dimanche" [4 Sept. 1938] letter to Royer in Poulenc 1994, 38-9, 38-10, and 38-12 respectively.

[143] Princess Edmond de Polignac's 10 Dec. 1938 letter to Poulenc in Poulenc 1994, 38-18.

[144] "Lundi" [July 1938] letter in Poulenc 1994, 39-4.

OTHER EVENTS: MAY-AUGUST 1938

The first few days of May saw a heavy concentration of Poulenc concerts. The Chanteurs de Lyon were the principal chorus for each occasion: on 1 May the *Sept chansons* were performed at the Salle Gaveau, on 2 May the Mass in G major was premiered at the Chapelle des Dominicains, and also on 2 May *Sécheresses* debuted at a Colonne concert, Paul Paray conducting.[145] The first two concerts were highly successful and Poulenc told Boulanger weeks before that "The Chanteurs de Lyon sing the Mass miraculously."[146] The first two concerts were repeated in Lyon, and Suzanne Latarjet thought the choir had never sung better. "What enchanted me," she said, "was the *complete, unanimous,* and *triumphal* success of your choruses."[147] Poulenc's Mass was also performed on 2 December 1938 over Radio flamande in Belgium thanks to Paul Collaer.[148]

The first performance of *Sécheresses,* however, was jinxed. Delayed in Sweden by the breakdown of his airplane, Paray arrived forty-eight hours late and had only one inadequate rehearsal with the performers. Poulenc called the performance a "disaster" and the reception "glacial." Upon exiting the hall he told Auric: "No one will ever perform *Sécheresses* again, it is a failed work. I am going to destroy it." Auric responded with his customary insight: "You can destroy your *Poèmes de Ronsard* or *Les Soirées de Nazelles* without harm, but on no account this."[149] Several good performances, including one by Charles Munch on 16 February 1941 with the Chorale Yvonne Gouverné and the Orchestre de la Société des Concerts du Conservatoire, convinced Poulenc that Auric was right.[150] He studied the score carefully when revising it for publication about the time the *Stabat Mater* was written in 1950-51.[151]

With the concerts completed, Poulenc returned to Noizay where he composed "Allons plus vite," the second of his *Deux poèmes de*

---

[145] Transcription of the little card printed to announce performance of the Mass in Schmidt 1995, FP 89, p. 271.
[146] Fragment of Poulenc's 13 Mar. 1938 postcard from Turin in Poulenc 1994, p. 458, note 2.
[147] Latarjet's [May 1938] letter to Poulenc in Poulenc 1994, 38-3.
[148] Collaer's 3 Dec. 1938 letter to Poulenc in Collaer 1996, 38-4. The soloists were Germaine Teugels (S.) and Flore Moulaert-Mass (MS.).
[149] Poulenc 1954, p. 101. Keith Daniel, writing about Poulenc's choral works with orchestra, considers *Sécheresses* a failed work. He believes that Poulenc had not yet found his orchestral "voice." See Buckland/Chimènes: c, pp. 50-4.
[150] sent Gouverné an important set of "Observations pour *Sécheresses*" in a "lundi" [May 1938] letter anticipating this performance. The letter also describes significant revisions which Poulenc made. Poulenc 1994, 38-4 (Poulenc 1991, no. 138). Gouverné's piano-vocal score, containing copious performance indications, is in a private collection. Schmidt 1995, FP 90, p. 275.
[151] Poulenc 1954, p. 101.

Guillaume Apollinaire (FP 94).[152] The first number was not composed until his August visit to Anost. Poulenc gives considerable insight into how he approached setting a poem in his discussion of "Allons plus vite."

> There are few poems which I "lusted after" more intensely and for a longer time. As early as 1935 I had prepared a sketch, later burned and, thank goodness, completely forgotten. Suddenly, in 1938, the music for "sur le Boulevard de Grenelle" came into my mind. Rarely do I begin a song at the beginning. One or two lines, chosen at random, take hold of me and very often provide the tonality, the secret of the rhythm, the key to the work. The poem by Apollinaire begins like Baudelaire: "Et le soir vient et les lys meurent." Then, abruptly, after taking flight with a few noble lines, returns to earth on a Parisian sidewalk. After an opening in A minor I have jealously saved the major key to illuminate this effect of surprise. I have so frequently loitered at night in Paris that I think I know better than any other musician the rhythm of a felt slipper gliding along the asphalt on a May evening. If one does not understand the sexual melancholy of the poem, it is useless to sing this *mélodie*.[153]

The link between events or physical objects and Poulenc's musical settings of poetry is no better illuminated than in this account.

As discussed earlier, the late spring was predominantly devoted to finishing the Organ Concerto. Work continued into summer, but Poulenc did not disturb his customary summer routine. In July he visited Marie-Blanche de Polignac at Kerbastic, before returning to Tours.[154] Then it was off to Paris to play the Concerto for the Princesse de Polignac and socialize, dining with friends of the Princess such as Anthony Chaplin and his wife Alvide, Marie-Laure de Noailles, Auric, and Paul Eluard.[155] Still in July, Poulenc left for a week at Le Tremblay. His Touraine neighbor Suzanne Lalé, who later drove him to Venice, was also there.[156] At one point during his stay he had lunch with Antoinette d'Harcourt, Auric, and Madeleine Le

---

[152] Concerning revision of *Sécheresses* see Poulenc's "lundi" [May 1938] letter to Gouverné in Poulenc 1994, 38-4 (Poulenc 1991, no. 138). The concert was postponed until 16 Feb. 1941.

[153] Poulenc 1993, p. 25 (Poulenc 1989, pp. 42-3).

[154] "Mercredi" [July 1938] letter to Marie-Blanche from Le Tremblay in Poulenc 1994, 38-8 (Poulenc 1991, no. 139).

[155] See note above.

[156] In 1935 Poulenc inscribed a copy of his *Cinq poèmes de Paul Eluard* "à Suzanne très tendrement Francis Noizay 1935" and gave her the holograph manuscript inscribed "à Suzanne Lalé très tendrement et avec toute la force de ma vive reconnaissance. Francis Paris juin 1935." I am extremely grateful to Roger Gross for this information. Poulenc frequently referred to Mme Lalé as "Voisine" in his correspondence.

Chevrel.[157] From Le Tremblay he returned to Paris before going south to Anost on 31 July where he and Bernac stayed until 28 August.[158] There they prepared their winter concert repertoire which included works of Schumann and Weber to be given on Brussels Radio.[159]

During July Poulenc began a project conceived during Holy Week 1938 following a concert by the Petits Chanteurs à la Croix de Bois, Abbé Maillet director. After hearing the first performance of Milhaud's cantata *Les Deux Cités,* Poulenc decided to write some Lenten motets for Maillet.[160] The result was *Quatre motets pour un temps de pénitence* (FP 97) written between July 1938 and January 1939. Poulenc first composed the third motet, "Tenebrae factae sunt," in July, dedicating it to Nadia Boulanger.[161] By August he had composed two of the projected four Lenten motets.[162] Though he may have drafted a second motet, the extant motet manuscripts indicate that the next motet was no. 4, composed in November. Could "Plange quasi virgo plebs mea," which is listed as the title of the second motet in the manuscript of no. 3, be the missing piece?[163] A mid-August letter states that he had written only one motet.[164]

While at Anost Poulenc composed the first Apollinaire *mélodie* "Dans le jardin d'Anna" and Eluard's "Tu vois le feu du soir," the first of what would become *Miroirs brûlants* (FP 98). Summarizing work there for his Uncle Royer, Poulenc said everything had come very well and easily.[165] "Dans le jardin d'Anna" was originally intended to be part of *Quatre poèmes de Guillaume Apollinaire* (1931). "As in all poems that concern an enumeration of mental images," Poulenc said, "a *tempo* that is continuous and strict is essential." He had failed to understand that in 1931.[166] In 1938 he reapproached the poem at pains to avoid a repetition of his earlier problems." ... The last lines [. . .] evoke for me the end of a September day somewhere in Seine-et-Marne, towards Chartrette, with a view of the river and the forest of Fontainebleau."[167] Considering "Tu vois le feu du soir," Poulenc later remarked:

[157] "Mercredi" [July 1938] letter to Marie-Blanche in Poulenc 1994, 38-8 (Poulenc 1991, no. 139).
[158] 24 Aug. 1938 telegram to Boulanger in Schmidt 1995, FP 93, p. 282. The trip was initially jeopardized because Bernac's father was ill.
[159] [Aug. 1938] letter to Milhaud from Anost in Poulenc 1994, 38-9 and [16 Aug. 1938] letter to Sauguet from Anost in Poulenc 1994, 38-10.
[160] Poulenc 1954, p. 157.
[161] He presented her with the *brouillon* of this work. Schmidt 1995, FP 97, p. 289.
[162] [Aug. 1938] letter to Milhaud in Poulenc 1994, 38-9.
[163] Schmidt 1995, FP 97, p. 289.
[164] [16 Aug. 1938] letter to Sauguet from Anost in Poulenc 1994, 38-10.
[165] "Dimanche" [4 Sept. 1938] letter to Royer in Poulenc 1994, 38-12.
[166] Poulenc 1993, p. 24 (Poulenc 1989, pp. 40-1).
[167] Poulenc 1993, p. 25 (Poulenc 1989, pp. 40-3).

No one will ever sing this *mélodie* like Pierre Bernac. This is why I dedicated it to him. I wonder at the silly game of "desert island recordings" if this might not be the song of mine I would choose to take.[168]

Poulenc had found Eluard's poems in the 15 July 1938 issue of *Mesures*, a literary magazine which his concierge probably bought for him at Librairie José Corti just below his rue de Médicis apartment.[169] At approximately four minutes, "Tu vois le feu du soir" is one of Poulenc's longest *mélodies*.[170] Poulenc also began the second *mélodie*, "Je nommerai ton front," but could not complete it at Anost because news that Bernac's father was dying caused them to break off their working vacation.[171]

SEPTEMBER-DECEMBER 1938

Shortly after returning to Paris Bernac and Poulenc left with his neighbor Suzanne Lalé who drove them to Venice for the VIᵉ Festival International de Musique Contemporaine de la Biennale de Venise, scheduled between 5 and 13 September. They were already in Venice at the Hotel Monaco et Grand Canal on the 4th.[172] He and Bernac performed *Tel jour telle nuit* on the 7th at the Palazzo Giustiniani and headed home the next day passing through the Aveyron on the way to Noizay.

Poulenc composed little during September and October. However, on 29 September he read Charles d'Orléans poem "Priez pour paix doulce Vierge Marie," in "Les prières pour la paix," a regular column of *Le Figaro*.[173] One of his few vocal works which lacks a dedication, it was influenced by the *Litanies à la Vierge noire*, his first religious work. Poulenc described it as a "prayer to be spoken in a country church," and immediately composed the music dating the manuscript Noizay 29 September 1938.[174] *Priez pour paix* (FP 95) is also one of the few *mélodies* he permitted to be printed in more than one key. Nadia Boulanger chose Doda Conrad to sing it at Canterbury Cathedral on 27 August 1939, the week before France declared war on Germany.[175]

---

[168] Poulenc 1993, p. 26 (Poulenc 1989, pp. 44-5).
[169] The date may well have been 31 July when he left for the Morvan. See details of Poulenc's conflicting testimony on this purchase in Schmidt 1995, FP 98, p. 293.
[170] Daniel, p. 267 refers to it as "this quintessential Poulenc song."
[171] Poulenc 1993, p. 27 (Poulenc 1989, pp. 46-9).
[172] "Dimanche" [4 Sept. 1938] letter to Royer in Poulenc 1994, 38-12. He excused his brief note saying there was much to see in just four days.
[173] In Poulenc 1993, p. 27 (Poulenc 1989, pp. 48-9) Poulenc mistakenly gives the date as 28 Sept. Article set in the holograph manuscript at F-Psalabert.
[174] Poulenc 1993, p. 27 (Poulenc 1989, pp. 48-9).
[175] 6 Oct. 1939 letter to Poulenc in Poulenc 1994, 39-17.

In October Poulenc also wrote *La Grenouillère* (FP 96), a brief *mélodie* dedicated to Marie-Blanche de Polignac, probably in anticipation of their November concert together.

> My friend, Countess Jean de Polignac, this marvelous musician to whom I have dedicated numerous *mélodies*, often under her given name of Marie-Blanche, having told me that for Christmas her mother, Mme Jeanne Lanvin, had given her a magnificent Renoir, I decided to offer her one of my own doing. And that is how my modest *mélodie* *La Grenouillère*, on a poem by Apollinaire, came to be a musical evocation of a landscape by Renoir.[176]

The poem appealed because of its nostalgic evocation of a small island in the Seine not far from Paris with its restaurant that attracted artists and painters. *La Grenouillère* is the counterpart of Pierre Auguste Renoir's painting *The Boatman's Luncheon*.[177] Poulenc also acknowledged a debt to Modeste Moussorgsky noting:

> Two measures recall Moussorgsky. It would be childish to hide this influence; such subterfuge would be repugnant to me. I disdain sons who blush at resembling their father.[178]

Poulenc gave Marie-Blanche de Polignac a manuscript inscribed: "Noizay, October 1938, Dear Marie-Blanche, evidently a Renoir would be more beautiful. Accept, however, this small present from your old Francis."[179] He presented the compositional sketch called a *brouillon* to the singer known as Madame Donalda that same month.[180]

Poulenc also returned his attention to the Eluard set which contained "Tu vois le feu du soir." Having written the second piece, "Je nommerai ton front," he asked Eluard to provide a suitable title for the pair.[181] Initially nothing came to Eluard, but by November he sent Poulenc several suggestions including *Miroirs brûlants*.[182] Precisely when Poulenc completed the song in the form we know is uncertain, but the printed score is dated 7 January 1939.

The third week of October was devoted to a concert tour with

---

[176] Poulenc 1954, p. 174.

[177] Poulenc 1993, p. 28 (Poulenc 1989, pp. 48-51).

[178] Poulenc 1993, p. 28 (Poulenc 1989, pp. 50-1). Poulenc refers to mm. 14-15 (where he sets the line "Petits bateaux vous me faites bien de la peine") which is reminiscent of the song cycle *The Nursery*.

[179] Dedication in Poulenc 1994, p. 475, note 2.

[180] Schmidt 1995, FP 96, p. 287. Mme Donalda was the pseudonym for Pauline Lightstone.

[181] Eluard's "lundi" [Oct. 1938] response in Poulenc 1994, 38-15 (Poulenc 1991, no. 140).

[182] Eluard's 1 Nov. 1938 letter to Poulenc in Poulenc 1994, 38-17 (Poulenc 1991, no. 141).

Bernac which took them north to The Hague, Amsterdam, Hilversum, and Rotterdam. On the 14th at The Hague they premiered *Deux poèmes de Guillaume Apollinaire, Le Portrait,* and "Tu vois le feu du soir." Poulenc's decision to premiere these *mélodies* outside of France is unusual. Not long after returning home in late October-early November they toured east to Metz, Nancy, and Besançon, and then back across France to Nantes. Again, contrary to custom, the French premieres occurred during this tour rather than in Paris.[183]

The compositions of 1938 were completed with the addition of two motets to the penitential cycle begun in July. "Tristis est anima mea" (no. 4) was composed in Paris during November and "Vinea mea electa" (no. 2) in Noizay during December.[184] Like no. 3 they are dedicated to choral conductors, Ernest Bourmauck and Yvonne Gouverné respectively.

Poulenc's last known concert of 1938 occurred in Paris under the auspices of La Sérénade on 28 November at the Salle Gaveau.[185] In the only full-length public recital he is known to have given with Marie-Blanche de Polignac they premiered *Trois poèmes de Louise de Vilmorin.* This was a prestigious solo recital for a woman who had worked hard in Nadia Boulanger's ensemble.

FRANCE ENTERS WORLD WAR II: 1939

As the year France entered the war with Germany began, Poulenc was occupied with his usual routine juggling composition and concerts. During January he completed two works adding "Timor et tremor" (dedicated to Abbé Maillet) to the three completed numbers of *Quatre motets pour un temps de pénitence,* and "Je nommerai ton front" to *Miroirs brûlants.* The latter (see above) was actually written and tried out earlier, but Poulenc had been unhappy with it. His concert season began in London where he and Bernac gave a recital on 26 January for "The Anglo-French Art & Travel Society" at Seaford House in Belgrave Square. On a program containing vocal works by Gounod, Fauré, Schumann, Liszt, Poulenc, Ravel, Satie, and Chabrier, Poulenc also played seven piano selections by Satie, Chabrier, and himself. The duo probably also performed in Dublin on the 30th.[186] The season continued at the Salle Gaveau on 16 Feb-

---

[183] Concerning these tours see Poulenc 1994, p. 471, note 1. In a 15 Oct. 1938 letter to Dallapiccola from The Hague, he wrote that the concert had gone well and that this was the first time he had warmed the Dutch to modern French vocal repertoire. Poulenc 1994, 38-16.

[184] Schmidt 1995, FP 97.

[185] Speaking about the year 1938, Thomson, p. 284 remarks that "Les Concerts de la Sérénade are dead or dying, the only music series in the world to have expressed the thirties."

[186] Ibbs and Tillett financial ledger at GB-Lcm.

ruary with a recital of selections by Haydn, Schumann, Poulenc, André Caplet, and Fauré. *Deux poèmes de Guillaume Apollinaire, Le Portrait*, and *Miroirs brûlants* were given their Parisian premieres. The Bernac/Poulenc duo was back in England and Ireland for a more extensive tour in mid-February (see Appendix 2).

Poulenc had to cut short plans to perform in Italy due to a severe case of flu contracted "in glacial Ireland," as he wrote the Marquise Elisabetta Barbey de Piccolellis from his sick bed at the London home of his long-time friend Audrey Parr.[187] Half a decade later he set Apollinaire's poem "Hyde Park," nostalgically dedicating it to Parr's memory.[188]

The deteriorating European political situation weighed more and more heavily on Poulenc as time progressed. To Marie-Blanche de Polignac, one of the few friends with whom he discussed such matters, Poulenc wrote: "it is well-known that the country only suits me when my mind is free. When things are not so rosy, I have far greater need for my Bou-le-vard de Grenelle than for the 'meandering of the Loire'."[189] Nevertheless in April he read proofs and wrote the lovely *Ce doux petit visage* (FP 99) dedicated to Linossier's memory. The dedicatee of *Les Biches*, Raymonde Linossier was on Poulenc's mind because in May he reorchestrated half of the ballet, the orchestral score having been buried with her in 1930.[190] Poulenc was particularly fond of this short song based on an Eluard poem.

While at Noizay in April he also contemplated a possible theatrical project with Edouard Bourdet based on Shakespeare's *The Tempest* or *Pericles, Prince of Tyre*.[191] Recently discovered letters reveal that this project still interested Poulenc in 1942 when the field had been narrowed to *Périclès*.[192] No music was ever written, however, and it is not mentioned again in the known correspondence. Instead, after the war, Jean-Louis Barrault suggested that Poulenc provide incidental music for Molière's *Amphitryon* which was composed in 1947.

Little else is known about Poulenc's activities of May and June, but he attended the 21 June Paris premiere of his Concerto in G mi-

---

[187] [Feb. 1939] letter in Poulenc 1994, 39-1. Parr (née Margotine Audrey Manuella Enriqueta Bapst), allied with Milhaud from his days in Brazil, had created the décor for his *L'Homme et son désir*. She resided at 24 Hyde Park Gardens.
[188] Schmidt 1995, FP 127. Poulenc visited the Marquise, an amateur singer, in 1940.
[189] "Lundi" [17 Apr. 1939] letter in Poulenc 1994, 39-3 (Poulenc 1991, no. 143).
[190] He continued orchestrating through Jan. 1940. Schmidt 1995, FP 36, p. 101.
[191] "Lundi" [17 Apr. 1939] letter in Poulenc 1994, 39-3 (Poulenc 1991, no. 143).
[192] Barrault's 16 May 1942 letter to Poulenc and fragment of Poulenc's [12 Sept. 1939] letter to Brianchon in Poulenc 1994, p. 475, note 4. See also Brianchon's 24 Aug. 1942 letter to Poulenc in Poulenc 1994, 42-9.

nor at the Salle Gaveau. In July, while taking a cure at Vichy, he expressed displeasure at what he viewed as the French dislike of the organ as an instrument.[193] Poulenc spent ten days (ca. 6-16 August) at Kerbastic with Marie-Blanche de Polignac, fearful that war would break out at any moment. In *Journal de mes mélodies*, which Poulenc began in 1939, one entry deals with the very real crisis he experienced.

> In August, for lack of anything better to do, I had taken with me to Brittany Louise's [de Vilmorin] small volume *[Fiançailles pour rire]*. Failed vacations. Subdued certainty of the next war. I do not like the sea and still less Brittany. The charm of my numerous stays at Kerbastic at the home of my friends the Polignacs has nothing to do with the countryside. I only understood that well the evening that I took up residence in a sinister room at Pouldu. Crisis of a bad mood such as I had not suffered from in a long time. Kerbastic takes me back. I go each day to work with Bernac. But for what result? I do not know what awaits us. From morning to evening I ask myself if, at Anost, I would better profit from these last days of peace to work. I believe so. I return to Noizay 16 August, stashing away in a corner *Fiançailles* and *les Mamelles de Tirésias*, these barely sketched. Anguish. I am taking up again my *Sextuor* and the instrumentation of *Cocardes*.[194] War arrives. I count my friends in my heart: no surprise, those I think about are well. But, good heavens!, what will become of Loulou [Louise de Vilmorin]? My "feuillet bleu" requires me to remain at home for the moment. I need to work on a human basis. I decide to compose a cycle, the feminine match of *Tel jour telle nuit*. First I write "La Dame d'André," not knowing where I will go next, but with the clear intention to compose the first *mélodie*. Anyway, I have promised it to Marie-Blanche for her birthday on 15 August. I draw up the following plan: (1) "Dame d'André," (2) solemn *mélodie*, (3) fast *mélodie*, (4) "Mon cadavre," (5) happy *mélodie*. I write "Mon cadavre" and "Il vole." I think about using "Fleurs" for my second *mélodie*. Quickly I realize my error: "Fleurs" will close the cycle in choosing for the next to last *mélodie* a distant key which will give value and rarefy the D-flat of "Fleurs." This is then how I write "Violon," a slow but rhythmic *mélodie* which contrasts with "Mon cadavre" and "Fleurs." The cycle becomes, therefore, six *mélodies*.[195]

His stay began in an "uninhabitable" inn at Pouldu,[196] "a small bathing-place on the right bank of the Laïta."[197] The Polignacs then

---

[193] "Lundi" [July 1939] letter to Boulanger in Poulenc 1994, 39-4.

[194] Concerning the revised instrumentation of *Cocardes* see Schmidt 1995, FP 16, p. 45. For the Sextet see Schmidt 1995, FP 100.

[195] Poulenc 1993, pp. 31-2.

[196] "Mardi" [29 Aug. 1939] letter in Poulenc 1994, 39-10 (Poulenc 1991, no. 146).

[197] Baedecker North.Fr., p. 249. Le Pouldu, today known as Guidel-Plage, is only

took him in for ten days and he stayed with them through Marie-Blanche's birthday, leaving on the 16th to return to Noizay.

> I worked a great deal, nothing new, as I have not felt much like it, but I have thoroughly revised my entire Sextuor for Chester (now very good) and corrected much music, etc. I had started working on *Les Mamelles de Tirésias*, enthralled by my libretto, but slightly modified. You know that nothing in Apollinaire embarrasses me.[198]

Poulenc thanked the Polignacs for their kindness: "How happy, pleasant, and gentle Kerbastic was and how good you were to gather me in. Without you what would have become of the Master of Amboise, quite sad on his beach."[199] Later he fondly recalled two evenings of music they shared together, having asked that "Tu vois le feu du soir" be sung at the end of the second because he knew he would not hear it again for some time.[200]

During the summer Poulenc had also decided to write an opera based on Apollinaire's *Les Mamelles de Tirésias*.[201] He had been experimenting with the text, making sketches and discussing them with his neighbor (Suzanne Lalé) until late in the evening. Work on the opera continued sporadically over the next few years, but was taken up in earnest between May and October 1944.

Sometime in later 1939 Poulenc also joined with Auric, Marcel Delannoy, Honegger, Maurice Jaubert, Milhaud, Roland-Manuel, and Tailleferre in requesting that André Boll organize a series of theatrical performances in a new format. A portion of their *communiqué* notes:

> The lyric theater is undergoing a particularly grave crisis. At the present time, between the subsidized stages and stages for light music, there no longer exists any intermediate stage, which could attract a lyric work with a limited orchestra, free of the traditional formulas. We think that *sung theater* can no longer stay away from the dramatic

---

a few kilometers from the Polignac château at Kerbastic.

[198] "Mardi" [29 Aug. 1939] letter in Poulenc 1994, 39-10 (Poulenc 1991, no. 146).

[199] "Samedi" [late Aug. 1939] letter to Marie-Blanche in Poulenc 1994, 38-11. Chimènes dates this letter [20 août 1938], but it must date from a year later. In Aug. 1939 the 19th and 26th were Saturdays, and the similar letter to Sauguet mentioned above is dated "mardi" which Chimènes determines to be [29 août 1939]. Most likely it was written on the 26th because Poulenc wrote again to Marie-Blanche on "lundi" [4 Sept. 1939] concerning his military orders saying he was *still* at Noizay. In Oct. Poulenc told Jean de Gaigneron that Aug. had been infernal. [Oct. 1939] letter in Poulenc 1994, 39-21.

[200] "Lundi" [28 Aug. 1939] letter to Marie-Blanche in Poulenc 1994, 39-9 (Poulenc 1991, no. 147).

[201] Apollinaire wrote this work in 1903 adding to it in 1916. Poulenc attended the first performance of the play in 1917.

evolution realized, thanks to theaters of the cartel, over the course of these past twenty years. The time seems to have come for us to attempt an effort of this same type. This is why we have asked **André Boll**, who seems to us just right as much for his personality as for his musical and theatrical qualifications, to prepare immediately a first series of performances which, in our opinion, could give a new impetus to lyrical theater.[202]

The advent of World War II, of course, not only put a near hold on new theatrical ventures, but made it difficult for existing theaters to maintain their normal schedules. Nothing is known about any response to this joint entreaty.

SEXTET FOR WINDS AND PIANO COMPLETED

The Sextet (FP 100), which Poulenc first mentioned in 1931, finally attained its definitive version in 1939. Because of the difficult political situation, Poulenc retained the manuscript until he could be assured of its safe passage to Hansen in Copenhagen at the end of the war.[203] It was finally performed on 9 December 1940 at the Salle Pleyel for an Association de Musique Contemporaine concert featuring the Quintette à vent de Paris with Poulenc and was published in 1945.[204] Thus ended one of the more complicated compositional sagas of Poulenc's career.

YEAR-END WORK ON MÉLODIES WHILE AWAITING MOBILIZATION

By 15 July Vilmorin had given Poulenc proofs for the yet unpublished Gallimard edition of *Fiançailles pour rire* containing her handwritten corrections. Poulenc recalled her reading various poems to him from her sick bed in an ugly room at the Hôtel Crillon and her promise to send other poems from Hungary.[205] As indicated above, Poulenc took the poems with him to Kerbastic where he planned the cycle. First, since the cycle was intended for Bernac, he needed some less feminine poems. Second, he and Auric both intended to set Louise de Vilmorin poems but Poulenc had preempted Auric by writing *Trois poèmes de Louise de Vilmorin* in December 1937. Therefore, he let Auric choose first so as not to offend his friend a second time. Among others, Auric chose "La Jeune Sanguine," a poem Poulenc particularly coveted. In spite of what he wrote in *Journal de mes mélodies*, Poulenc was still uncertain just how many *mélodies*

[202] Account by R[obert] B[ernard] in the special 28 Dec. 1938 issue of *La Revue musicale* entitled *Hommage à Maurice Ravel*, issued on the first anniversary of his death, p. vi.
[203] "Mardi" [26 Sept. 1939] letter to Boulanger in Poulenc 1994, 39-14.
[204] The Quintet included F. Caratgé, L. Gromer, A. Vacellier, G. Grandmaison, and R. Blot.
[205] Poulenc 1993, p. 30.

Fiançailles pour rire (FP 101) would contain when he wrote Nadia Boulanger in September that he had sketched six, but had yet not found a seventh.[206] Only six were written, and Geneviève Touraine, not Bernac, sang the premiere at the Salle Gaveau on 21 May 1942.[207]

What unsettled Poulenc most was waiting to receive military orders. He had been a reservist in the 1st regiment of the Défense contre avions domiciled at Noizay since 1934. He had then been assigned to the Tours subdivision.[208] Bernac was called up on 3 September 1939 and Poulenc was assigned a special classification with the *Education nationale, administration des Beaux-Arts* on 19 November. The wait wore on his nerves and caused him to envision numerous morbid scenarios. He told Simone Girard that he would gladly sacrifice a leg or two if his hands were spared;[209] he informed Nadia Boulanger that a letter was waiting for her in case something happened to him;[210] and he assured Marie-Blanche de Polignac that he had promised his guardian angel he would write religious music.[211] While waiting in September Poulenc read Jacques-Bénigne Bossuet, Jean de La Fontaine, and Charles Baudelaire "for the various needs of my heart," and composed as well.[212] What made him particularly melancholic was the conviction that World War I had deprived him of his musical education.[213] Boulanger tried to be reassuring, telling him that Doda Conrad had sung his moving *Priez pour paix* at Canterbury Cathedral during a 27 August 1939 concert and had repeated it a week later for a friend, the son of the architect William Bowens van der Boijen.[214] During this period, as artists tried to buoy each other's spirits, Poulenc again established contact with many friends including André Gide, Paul Eluard, and Paul Valéry.[215]

---

206 "Mardi" [26 Sept. 1939] letter in Poulenc 1994, 39-14.

207 A 7 Nov. 1939 entry in *Journal de mes mélodies* reveals that the first performance was for soprano Germaine Teugels, professor at the Conservatoire in Brussels.

208 Poulenc 1994, pp. 479-80, note 1.

209 14 Sept. [1939] letter to Girard in Poulenc 1994, 39-12.

210 "Mardi" [26 Sept. 1939] letter in Poulenc 1994, 39-14.

211 [23 Sept. 1939] letter in Poulenc 1994, p. 488, note 2.

212 [End of Sept. 1939] letter to Paul Valéry in Poulenc 1994, 39-15, and the fragment of his [23 Sept. 1923] letter to Marie-Blanche in note 3.

213 "Mardi" [26 Sept. 1939] letter to Boulanger in Poulenc 1994, 39-14.

214 Boulanger's 6 Oct. 1939 letter to Poulenc in Poulenc 1994, 39-17. The identification of William Bowens van der Boijen is by Chimènes. Oddly enough, Poulenc ended up riding out the war in France whereas Boulanger left France for the United States, arriving in New York on 6 Dec. 1940. For whatever reasons, Poulenc had less frequent interaction with Boulanger after World War II. He did attend some of her classes at rue Ballu and gave master classes and recitals with Bernac at Fontainebleau, but did not ask her to review proofs or do other more mundane tasks.

215 Letters in Poulenc 1994, 39-7 (to Gide), 39-15 (to Valéry), and 39-18 (Eluard's reply to Poulenc).

Moreover, during September his Noizay house had been completely full of refugees. As Robert Paxton has observed, "Frenchmen had gone to war in the first place, in September 1939, with anything but enthusiasm." [216]

Poulenc remained at Noizay awaiting mobilization. In October he was visited by his Uncle Royer, traveled briefly to Paris,[217] and composed *Bleuet* (FP 102), a *mélodie* on a war-time text by Apollinaire. The day he began setting the poem, which he described as "very sober and humane,"[218] he learned of the death of André Bonnélie, whom he had first met in Amboise when Bonnélie was a young boy.[219] No sooner had he completed the music than a letter from the young man arrived announcing his wedding! Delighted by this reversal of fate, Poulenc dedicated the *mélodie* to him. On 27 October he signed a contract with Durand et Cie in the amount of 1,000 francs for its publication, with Apollinaire's heir receiving 120 francs.[220]

In November Poulenc wrote several entries in *Journal de mes mélodies* which illuminate his state of mind. "My piano pieces are often massacred," he said, "but never to such an extent as my songs and, lord knows, I value the songs more highly."[221] Four days later, still smarting from hearing some of his songs bungled on a radio broadcast, he wrote, "If I were a singing teacher I would oblige my students to *read the poems attentively* before working on a *mélodie*."[222] To this he added, "The 'accompaniment' of an art song is as important as the piano part of a sonata."

During 1939 Poulenc composed two other works which cannot be dated precisely. The first, a simple piano piece entitled *Française d'après Claude Gervaise (16ème siècle)* (FP 103), is dated "No[i]zay 1939" and dedicated to Luigi Rognoni, a friend who lived in Milan. Published only in an anthology in mid-1940, it is spiritually close to the October 1935 *Suite française*. The second, an orchestration of three piano pieces by Satie, is entitled *Deux préludes posthumes et une gnossienne* (FP 104).[223]

---

[216] [27 Nov. 1939] letter to Collaer in Poulenc 1994, 39-22 and Collaer 1996, 39-9, and Paxton p. 11.

[217] [Oct. 1939] letter to Jean de Gaigneron in Poulenc 1994, 39-21.

[218] [27 Nov. 1939] letter to Collaer in Poulenc 1994, 39-22 (Collaer 1996, 39-9) and Paxton, p. 11.

[219] See the account in Poulenc 1993, p. 33.

[220] Schmidt 1995, FP 102, p. 302.

[221] Poulenc 1993, p. 13 (Poulenc 1989, pp. 18-19).

[222] Poulenc 1993, p. 14 (Poulenc 1989, pp. 18-19).

[223] In an undated letter, fragment in Poulenc 1994, p. 507, note 3, Poulenc wrote Sauguet: "I am working like a slave. I am completing the orchestration of pieces by Satie for Munch and I have written a large portion of my ballet *[Les Animaux modèles]*, the Waltz scherzo variations of the Grasshopper and the Ant."

As the year ended Poulenc reported to Paul Collaer that Milhaud was not doing well, that Henri Sauguet was in a sad state because his friend the theater designer Jacques Dupont was in the infantry, and that Paul Eluard was a lieutenant stationed near Paris.[224] Bernac, who had written Poulenc in September that he was leading the miserable life of a soldier "second class," was reassigned so that he could join Poulenc in December for a three-month tour of duty under the auspices of the "Ministère des Beaux-Arts pour la propagande musicale."[225] A way had been found to reunite the Bernac/Poulenc duo in spite of the war.

[224] [27 Nov. 1939] letter to Collaer in Poulenc 1994, 39-22 and Collaer 1996, 39-9.
[225] Poulenc 1994, p. 488, note 1 and p. 490, note 2.

IX

The War Years
1940-1944

THE MONTHS BEFORE MOBILIZATION: JANUARY-EARLY JUNE 1940

French confidence that the Germans could be dealt with using military force eroded quickly as the first half of 1940 progressed.[1] When the USSR launched an attack against Finland at the end of November 1939, the French thought about helping the Finns, but did not. Inaction forced Edouard Daladier to resign, though he was almost immediately moved to the Ministry of Defense by Paul Reynaud, his successor. In April 1940 the Germans attacked Denmark and Norway, a fact the French government only learned from a Reuters news dispatch, and the British-French force sent to assist the Scandinavians was defeated by the Germans leading to the fall of the Prime Minister Neville Chamberlain, and Winston Churchill's assumption of his post. Hitler's troops soon moved swiftly through the Low Countries. Having met little resistance, German armies outflanked the Maginot Line and continued through Northern France to occupy Paris on 14 June. In anticipation of the occupation, Benito Mussolini declared war on France and Britain on 10 June. Six days later, the new government formed by Marshal Philippe Pétain (the hero of Verdun who was now 84) asked what the German terms for an armistice would be.[2] When terms were received on 21 June:

> It was resolved that about two-fifths of France—in the southern half, but excluding the Atlantic coast—should remain a free zone, but that

---

[1] Details in large part from Tint, pp. 90-3. See also Burrin, Chapter XXII concerning artists.

[2] General Charles de Gaulle left the country and arrived in London on 17 June. A day later, he made his famous speech on the BBC calling for Frenchmen to join his resistance. See Beevor and Cooper, p. 13.

even in the rest of the country the German Army would not interfere with the administration, except to guarantee its own security.[3]

An armistice was also arranged with the Italians by the 23rd. Pétain's government was installed at Vichy on 1 July, and on 10 July the Assemblée nationale voted the new government full powers. Paris became a pawn, occupied as it was by German soldiers. Whenever the Vichy government displeased the Germans, the threat to create its own government was quickly renewed. Against this backdrop, Poulenc made several tours with Bernac during the first five months of the year beginning with one to Portugal from 2-10 January 1940. Speaking about his war experiences, Bernac noted that he had driven a truck in September 1939 and thereafter had entertained soldiers by singing a program of light music in numerous small villages and large cities, accompanied by the director of the Conservatoire in Belfort.

> Suddenly a few days before Christmas [1939] I received a note saying that I was to leave the army, and resume my concert tours to make artistic propaganda. And thus a few days after leaving behind the uniform, the truck, the snow, and the cold of a terrible winter, I found myself in tails, giving a recital with Francis on the stage of the opera house in Lisbon! One of the most extravagant adventures of my life.[4]

On the return trip by train to Paris, they missed their connections. Poulenc remembered how the day was spent.

> In January 1940 while returning from Portugal, held up in Saint-Jean-de-Luz for a day due to faulty connections, I, a fervent pilgrim, sought the spirit of Ravel in the solitude of a city emptied by war and winter. I evoked him, sitting on a wall of the port looking toward that Spain so dear to him, as the sun was setting on the Pyrénées. When the sea turned emerald green and the mountain peaks turned purple, I entered the church where the little Maurice was baptized. In this Basque church, decorated with wooden balconies, where the nave takes back its true maritime meaning, it was already completely dark. Several candles burned on the altar of the Virgin. At that time, Ravel, I prayed for you; don't smile, dear skeptic, because if I am sure that you had a heart, I am even more certain that you had a soul.[5]

Once returned to Paris, Bernac and Poulenc performed for a "matinée poétique" organized by Edouard Bourdet at the Comédie-

---

[3] Tint, pp. 92-3 and see the map in Burrin, p. xiii.
[4] Radford, p. 774. I am extremely grateful to Sidney Buckland who not only drew my attention to this article, but provided me with materials concerning Bernac-Poulenc performances in England. Though the itinerary of this tour has not been determined, Poulenc saw Olga Cadanal in Cintra. [20 Feb. 1940] letter to Vilmorin in Poulenc 1994, 40-2.
[5] Poulenc 1941b, p. 240.

Française on 13 January.[6] Following the theme "Writers who died for France" they performed Fauré *mélodies* on texts by Jean de La Ville de Mirmont and Poulenc's own *Le Bestiaire* and *Quatre poèmes de Guillaume Apollinaire*, both on texts by Apollinaire, the poet of World War I. They gave a concert in Rome on the 14th of February before performing in Florence on the 17th at the Sala Bianca of the Pitti Palace.[7] On or about the 20th they departed for Trieste and were in Milan by the 23rd. After returning to France for several weeks, they performed Schumann, Debussy, Duparc, Fauré, Poulenc, and Ravel in Zurich on 14 March.[8]

Still awaiting word of his mobilization, Poulenc complained to Auric from Noizay that in ten minutes here and twenty minutes there he had sketched a piece called *Dimanche de mai*.

> I believe that the form is good because it is strict and because I have avoided the rambling of the Final of *Napoli* or of *Soirées [de Nazelles]*. I must look after the *realization* because the melodic lines are at the limit of bad taste.[9]

Bernac and Poulenc also gave a recital to benefit the Red Cross in Avignon on 30 April 1940. The program, probably sponsored by Dr. Pierre Girard, included French *mélodies*.[10] During the war years the Bernac/Poulenc duo performed French works almost exclusively, though the Zurich concert contained four Schumann lieder.

MOBILIZATION: 2 JUNE-18 JULY 1940

Poulenc was finally mobilized into the 72nd Batterie of the Centre d'organisation de l'artillerie de défense contre avions (C.O.A. de D.C.A.) at Bordeaux on 2 June, just two weeks before the armistice. He served only until 18 July because of the treaty arranged between Pétain and Hitler in mid-June.[11] What little we know about his ap-

---

[6] [Dec. 1939] letter to Bourdet in Poulenc 1994, 39-23. Though *Bleuet* is not mentioned in the program, it may have had its first performance at this concert.
[7] While in Florence they stayed with the Marquise Elisabetta Barbey de Picco-lellis. [20 Feb. 1940] letter to Louise de Vilmorin (which gives the Marquise's address) in Poulenc 1994, 40-2.
[8] Program in Poulenc 1993, p. 72.
[9] [1940] letter in Poulenc 1994, 40-4. This piece has not been found.
[10] Poulenc 1994, p. 500, note 3. Poulenc had known the Girards since 1936 when Simone Girard engaged him to give a concert.
[11] Information concerning Poulenc's military record from Poulenc 1994. Chi-mènes has examined his official military record and commented upon it. The story recounted by O'Conner, p. 186 in his life of Maggie Teyte, is difficult to date precisely. "France fell on the day Charles Munch was to have conducted the first concert of a Festival of English and French Music at the Queen's Hall, under the patronage of the French Ambassador, and of Duff Cooper, erstwhile

proximately six weeks in the army, predominantly spent near Cahors, is contained in a few letters to friends.[12]

[To Bernac] I make a ravishing soldier in my khaki uniform. [. . .] Thanks to the Marshal [Pétain] we were not taken prisoner in Bordeaux like our pals from Lyon. We were left to retreat in a southerly direction. After days in cattle trains we have now put down roots in an ideal village in Lot, three kilometers from Cahors, where I sleep in a barn right out of [the Fables of] La Fontaine. I have unearthed an old Philemon and Baucis couple, with whom three of my pals and I eat each night. Divine food, exquisite Cahors wine. Philemon is a former lion tamer who married his Baucis forty years ago in Turin where she was a snake charmer. They adore me and I speak to them about Italy. In a word I am *happy*. *Yes*, "I have my hands," which is what I kept telling myself all day long, deliriously. Paris is intact. I would quickly sacrifice all of Noizay for it. It is in fact quite odd what little store I put in things. I have confidence in the future of our team; moreover I feel full of music. I have found numerous themes and the whole color of my ballet *[Les Animaux modèles]*. The lack of a piano has even been fortuitous. I like this locale. The air is light. I live with peasants who give me confidence.[13]

By 18 July he had learned that Le Grand Coteau was only slightly the worse for wear, although his wine cellar had been invaded and there had been drinking in the house, damage was minimal.[14] In letters from Cahors, Poulenc was quick to transmit news regarding the welfare of friends, and equally quick to express concern for those such as Georges Salles, about whom he lacked news. His five weeks in the military had done him enormous good and he declared himself ready to plunge into his "after-war" production. During his mobilization Poulenc also did a little composing, because on 18 July he told Marie-Blanche de Polignac, "I am actually composing a Sonata for Two Pianos destined for America and, of course, for *us*."[15] How much work was completed is unknown, nor do we know if

---

British Ambassador in Paris. Thomas Russell, manager of the London Philharmonic, had been in Paris to engage Poulenc: "Suddenly Poulenc burst into the room, made the briefest apologies, explaining almost breathlessly that he and Pierre Bernac, who was waiting below in a car, were leaving at once to rejoin their regiment at Tours."

[12] See the following letters: [10 July 1940] to Marie-Blanche, 10 July [1940] to Bernac, [Cahors, July 1940] to Girard, and 18 July [1940] to Marie-Blanche in Poulenc 1994, 40-5, 40-6 (Poulenc 1991, no. 152), 40-7, and 40-8 respectively.
[13] 10 July [1940] letter in Poulenc 1994, 40-6 (Poulenc 1991, no. 152).
[14] 18 July [1940] letter to Marie-Blanche in Poulenc 1994, 40-8. Ivry, p. 117 claims that Poulenc's statement about damage is false.
[15] 18 July [1940] letter in Poulenc 1994, 40-8.

this piece is connected with the sonata he wrote in 1952-53 for the American piano duo of Arthur Gold and Robert Fizdale.[16]

DEMOBILIZATION: 19 JULY-9 SEPTEMBER 1940

Once demobilized, Poulenc went north 100 kilometers to Brive-la-Gaillarde where his family had taken refuge. There, on 22 July, he joined his Poulenc and Villotte cousins, Uncle Royer, sister Jeanne Manceaux, and niece Rosine Manceaux (later Rosine Seringe), staying until 9 September 1940 when he returned to Paris in a cattle train.[17] His address in Brive was *chez Madame Villotte quai des Tournis*, quite close to the Corrèze River, and he used a piano belonging to his friend, the amateur pianist Marthe Bosredon.[18] In August he completed "un grand morceau de piano" entitled *Mélancolie* (FP 105) begun in Talence, near Bordeaux, in June. He also sketched what later became *Histoire de Babar, le petit éléphant* for narrator and piano.[19]

> In order to amuse my cousin's five children [Poulenc said], I have sketched a series of musical commentaries after the adventures of Babar. I am thinking about writing them with the hope of amusing grown up children as well.[20]

As is often the case with works Poulenc composed in proximity, there is at least one passage in *Mélancolie* that is similar to one in *Babar*.[21] Poulenc's largest project at this time was a ballet on some La Fontaine fables later called *Les Animaux modèles*, mentioned in several quotations already cited, which will be considered below.

While in Brive Poulenc dined at the Chadournes with Yvonne Printemps and Pierre Fresnay, who were already contemplating reopening the Théâtre de la Michodière in Paris at year's end with a production of Jean Anouilh's *pièce rose* entitled *Léocadia*. He wondered if the political situation in Switzerland would be stable enough to permit his performing there in November, and even considered invoking the assistance of the famous pianist Walter Gieseking, who was "Kommendantur" in the occupied zone, if he had problems with visas.[22] Poulenc was also astonished to learn the details of Madeleine and Darius Milhaud's difficult trip to America, a journey that took them through France and across Spain to Lisbon, their ultimate point of embarkation.[23]

---

[16] The Gold and Fizdale duo did not form until the mid-1940s.
[17] 9 Sept. 1940 letter to Milhaud in Poulenc 1994, 40-12 (Poulenc 1991, no. 154).
[18] Poulenc 1954, pp. 57-8.
[19] Schmidt 1995, FP 129.
[20] "Jeudi"[Aug. 1940] letter to Girard in Poulenc 1994, 40-9. Schmidt 1995, FP 129.
[21] *Babar* also shares a passage with *Chansons villageoises*. "Hôtel" from *Banalités* is quoted at the end of *Babar* as Babar and Céleste gaze at the starry night.
[22] [20 Aug. 1940] letter to Auric in Poulenc 1994, 40-10.
[23] Details in Milhaud 1953, Chapter XXXIII (Milhaud 1987).

RETURN TO PARIS AND NOIZAY: FALL 1940

With his return to Paris on 9 September imminent, Poulenc had concerns. He intended to spend the winter composing in the Touraine in spite of the cold, and to travel to Argentina with Bernac in June 1941. His ballet *Les Animaux modèles* had to be orchestrated by January, and he hoped Serge Lifar would mount it at the Paris Opéra. He also thought of asking George Balanchine and Nijinska to produce it and *Les Biches* in North America should he be able to go there during 1941-42.[24] Picasso's return to Paris preceded that of Poulenc. As Picasso's biographer and friend Roland Penrose notes, Picasso had declined opportunities to ride out the war in the United States and Mexico.

> It is significant that Picasso was forbidden throughout the occupation to show his works in public. The most serious attacks that were made on him came not directly from the Nazis but from those collaborationist critics who under the new régime found places of authority and ample encouragement for their very reactionary thoughts. [. . .] "To the ashcan with Matisse!" and "To the loony-bin with Picasso!" were the fashionable cries.[25]

Poulenc saw Picasso often during the war years, and Picasso was the dedicatee of his important 1943 cantata *Figure humaine*.[26]

In October Poulenc composed music for Jean Anouilh's *Léocadia* (FP 106) which was premiered on 3 November and ran through the week of 2 May 1941.[27] He composed overtures for five acts, a "final," and a "valse chantée" for Yvonne Printemps entitled "Les Chemins de l'amour."[28] Poulenc's other October project was the commencement of five songs on Apollinaire texts entitled *Banalités* (FP 107). Numbers 2 and 4 were completed that month, and nos. 1, 3, and 5 in November. Poulenc's choice of Apollinaire's poem entitled "Voyage à Paris" for no. 4 (see below) captures his unequivocal joy at having returned to the city he so treasured.

Ah! la charmante chose	Ah! how charming
Quitter un pays morose	to leave a morose place
Pour Paris	for Paris
Paris joli	delightful Paris
Qu'un jour dut créer	that one day
L'Amour.	Love must have created.

---

[24] 9 Sept. 1940 letter to Milhaud in Poulenc 1994, 40-12 (Poulenc 1991, no. 154).
[25] Penrose 1981, p. 333.
[26] Dedicated "To Pablo Picasso whose work and life I admire."
[27] Schmidt 1995, FP 106, pp. 306-07.
[28] The score, which calls for cl., bsn., vn., d.b., and pn., was published by Eschig in 1961. It is among the few published scores of music Poulenc provided for plays or films. Moreover, Printemps' popular song was published separately in 1942 with her likeness on the cover, and a recording of her singing the waltz was

Early in *Journal de mes mélodies* Poulenc wrote at length about his choice of Apollinaire poems and the composition of this cycle.

> [October 1940] It is once more to Guillaume Apollinaire that I turned for this cycle. Much earlier I had chosen "Sanglots" and the curious "Fagnes de Wallonie." I have already noted here my propensity for putting certain poems aside in advance. When I returned to Noizay in October 1940, upon perusing my library, I turned the pages once again, and with what emotion, of those literary reviews that, from 1914 to 1923, had enchanted my adolescence. This time the series of issues of *Littérature* particularly held my attention. How was it possible for so many beautiful poems to have appeared in such a modest publication. But that is the small privilege of this type of review. All of a sudden one comes across a poem by Valéry, now the pride of every anthology. In the present case, as far as Apollinaire was concerned, I chose only the delicious verses of doggerel grouped under the title of *Banalités* ("Voyage à Paris.") When one knows me, it will seem quite natural that I should open my mouth like a carp to snap up the deliciously stupid lines of "Voyage à Paris." For me Paris often brings tears to my eyes and music to my ears. "Hôtel" is still Paris; a room in Montparnasse. Nothing else was necessary to persuade me to start a cycle in which "Sanglots" and "Fagnes" would appear. I still had to find an opening rhythmical *mélodie* since "Sanglots" would conclude the cycle with gravity. It was then that I remembered a song, quite Maeterlinck in style, that Apollinaire had inserted in a strange and beautiful prose work entitled *Onirocritique*. In June 1940, marching as a soldier on the way to Cahors, I began to sing, I don't know why, "Dans la ville d'Orkenise." In *Banalités* I did not make a marching song of it, nor, besides, was I recalling the banks of the Lot where I had initially remembered this first line. Nothing is more confusing for me than the influence of visual impressions. Orkenise is a road in Autun leading to the Roman gate. As for the interpretation, all that I have suggested here concerning "La Grenouillère" holds for "Voyage à Paris," all that I have written about "Le feu du soir" holds for "Sanglots."[29]

On 9 November the Bernac/Poulenc duo gave another full-length Salle Gaveau recital featuring Chausson, Debussy, Fauré, Ravel, and Poulenc's *Tel jour telle nuit*. Just over a month later, on 14 December, they performed their last Parisian recital of the year at the Salle Gaveau, this time including *mélodies* by Charles Bordes, Debussy, Duparc, Roussel, and the premiere of *Banalités*. *L'Information musicale* covered the event printing a fine pre-concert article by Paul

---

made in Paris during the initial performance run. See Bloch, p. 98. The recording was reissued in 1995 by EMI France (243 5 65494 2 5).

[29] Poulenc 1993, pp. 36-7 (Poulenc 1989, pp. 64-7).

Landormy and a review by André Himonet.[30] A few days earlier, on 9 December, Poulenc also performed his Sextet at the Salle Chopin, for an Association de Musique Contemporaine concert.[31] During December the Bernac/Poulenc duo recorded several works including Chausson's *Le Colibri* and *Soupir*, and Fauré's *Après un rêve* and *Lydia*. These were their last recordings until 1945.[32]

In Paris during December Poulenc set to music a poem written by Paul Valéry in 1920, but not published until it appeared in *La Nouvelle Revue française* (1 June 1939). *Colloque* (FP 108), for soprano and baritone, is the only duet among Poulenc's *mélodies*. He rejected it after the first performance on 4 February 1941, and it was not published in his lifetime.

The end of the year found him in good spirits.

> I have good news to tell you: the *brouillon-esquisse* of my ballet *[Les Animaux modèles]* is finished. That is a great weight off because I am *very happy* with it. Add to that the two motets for the marriage of Georges [Salles] which have left for the engravers and an article on Chabrier for the N.R.F. and you will agree that I have not been wasting my time. [. . .] I will be coming to Paris on the 20th for Marcelle [Meyer's] concert. Try to bring everyone. I do not know how long I will stay. I must see Munch and Gouverné for different projects.[33]

These motets, *Exultate Deo* (FP 109) and *Salve regina* (FP 110), are both dated "Noizay Mai 1941" in the printed scores;[34] the Emmanuel Chabrier article is a brief piece commemorating the composer's centennial;[35] and the projects with Charles Munch and Yvonne Gouverné consisted of an upcoming concert on 16 February 1941 in which Poulenc played the *Concert champêtre* under Munch's direction and Gouverné prepared the choruses for a new performance of *Sécheresses*.

Sometime during 1940 Poulenc also penned a brief thirteen-measure "morceau" for solo flute (FP 114) included in an album entitled "Ruines de Tours 1940" by his artist friend Marie-Thérèse Mabille. Poulenc used this brief piece on at least two greeting cards: one addressed "Pour Monsieur Charles" (1941) and the other "Pour Madame Paul Vincent-Vallette" (1942).[36]

---

[30] Schmidt 1995, FP 107, p. 309.

[31] This performance, the first of the definitive version, was with the Quintette à vent de Paris.

[32] V.S.M. DA 4928 and V.S.M. DA 4931 respectively. See Appendix 3.

[33] [Dec. 1940] letter to Jeanne Manceaux from Noizay in Poulenc 1994, 40-13.

[34] FP 109 (dedicated to Georges Salles) and 110 (dedicated to Hélène de Wendel).

[35] Poulenc 1941c.

[36] See Schmidt 1995, FP 114. Concerning the album, which at one point belonged to a Doctor Chauvin, see Boulet, no. 22.

CONCERTS AND COMPOSITIONS: JANUARY-JULY 1941

As the new year began Poulenc was in Noizay, but in mid-month he left for Paris, arriving on the 18th. Involvement in at least nine different concerts within two months made this one of the busiest periods in his career. The concerts (see Appendix 2), often including other artists, featured Poulenc as soloist in two of his concerted works as well as in *Les Noces*, and as accompanist for Bernac and other singers. The diverse repertory must have kept Poulenc extremely busy rehearsing. Concert activity then slackened, and until the fall season only a 10 June "Séance Francis Poulenc" at the Théâtre des Mathurins, during which he accompanied Bernac and Ginette Guillamat, and a 25 July concert with Bernac in Biarritz at the Casino municipal, are known. Little is known about his April-May activity as well except that in May he finished the *Exultate Deo* and *Salve regina* and continued a series of Improvisations, completing no. 11 in G minor (dedicated to Claude Delvincourt) in Paris during June.[37] Prior to this, his most recent Improvisation (no. 10) had been written in September 1934.

LES ANIMAUX MODÈLES: AUGUST 1941-AUGUST 1942

In 1940 Poulenc started a ballet based on the following fables by La Fontaine:

1	Le Petit Jour	Dawn
2	L'Ours et les deux compagnons	The Bear and His Two Friends
3	La Cigale et la Fourmi	Grasshopper and Ant
4	Le Lion amoureux	The Amorous Lion
5	L'Homme entre deux âges et ses deux Maîtresses	An Elderly Man with Two Girlfriends
6	La Mort et le Bûcheron	Death of the Woodcutter
7	Les Deux Coqs	Two Roosters
8	Le Repas de midi	Noonday Repast[38]

By mid-August he had sketched all the numbers and was very pleased because the orchestration had also been conceived (though not yet written down).[39]

> We were, Auric and I, like twin brothers. We threw ourselves into musical careers greedily. We gorged ourselves on music up to the limit, if you can say so, whereas when I began to compose *Les Animaux modèles* [FP 111], during the most somber days of the summer of 1940 I wanted to find, no matter the cost, a reason to hope for the destiny of my country. Jacques Rouché had long ago asked me for a ballet for

[37] Schmidt 1995, FP 113. Delvincourt was an important figure in the Resistance.
[38] English translations by Grant Johannesen.
[39] [20 Aug. 1940] letter to Auric from Brive in Poulenc 1994, 40-10.

the Opéra. I thought about drawing a libretto from several fables of La Fontaine. In August 1940, I set to work at Brive-la-Gaillarde, where I found myself after my demobilization. A friend [Marthe Bosredon . . .] lent me her piano, [and] it is there that I began my ballet. I chose among the fables those which did not especially require animal costumes, or those which one could transpose symbolically, like *Le Lion amoureux*, whom I made into a blackguard, which explains the *Java* in the pas-de deux. [. . .] The ballet was premiered on 8 August 1942, the occupation having singularly modified the theatrical calendar. You can imagine the public of German officers and of secretaries in "dull gray" attending such a typically French spectacle. I had allowed myself the luxury, which only a few orchestral musicians recognized, of introducing the chanson *Non, non, vous n'aurez pas notre Alsace-Lorraine* into the combat between the two roosters. Each time that the trumpet announced the theme, I could not help but smile.[40]

Later, in a 1946 article Poulenc added:

As I dislike animal costumes on the stage, I chose only those fables that do not contain animals (with the exception for the famous fable of the two merchants and the bear), or I substituted for the animals their human symbols. [. . .] The grasshopper became an old ballerina, the ant an old maid from the provinces, the amorous lion a "maquereau." Death is an elegant woman, a sort of duchess in a mask.[41]

During the spring of 1941 Poulenc wrote Eluard, who had supplied titles for several earlier works, requesting that he name the ballet. A loyal friend with a distinct dislike for La Fontaine, Eluard reluctantly agreed to try.[42] By summer he was able to suggest five titles including: *A la lueur de l'homme* [In the light of man]; *Les Animaux modèles* [Model animals]; *Mouvements animaux* [Animal movements]; *À la mode animale* [Animal fashion]; and *Mille pattes* [Centipede].[43] Although his personal preference was *À la mode animale*, Marie-Blanche de Polignac, Valentine Hugo, and Eluard's daughter Cécile all thought *Les Animaux modèles* would make a better impression. They prevailed! Poulenc now attempted to complete the score. In July 1941 he thanked Robert Bernard, editor of *L'Information musicale*, for an article about *Fiançailles pour rire* blaming his delay on the need to finish a piano reduction of his ballet for Eschig.[44] During the

---

[40] Poulenc 1954, pp. 57-8.

[41] Poulenc 1946d, pp. 57-8.

[42] Poulenc's letter to Eluard does not exist. For Eluard's "jeudi" 22 May [1941] reply see Poulenc 1994, 41-4.

[43] Translations by Buckland in Poulenc 1991, no. 156. For Eluard's French titles see his "vendredi" [summer 1941] letter to Poulenc in Poulenc 1994, 41-9.

[44] [July 1941] letter in Poulenc 1994, 41-5. Bernard also wanted Poulenc to write an article about piano pedaling.

second week of September he wrote Jacques Rouché of his intention to deliver six of the eight numbers to Eschig and asking if he (and possibly Serge Lifar) would like to hear the entire ballet on the afternoon of the 17th.[45] Still anticipating an April 1942 premiere at the Opéra, Poulenc began orchestrating in September.[46] The performance, however, was moved back to 8 August, and Poulenc did not finish until June.

As late as December 1941 the décor and costumes were assigned to André Derain, but in January 1942 Derain informed Poulenc that he was abandoning the project and would pay any expenses caused by removing his name from posters or programs.[47] Maurice Brianchon, well-known for other productions at the Paris Opéra, replaced Derain.[48] While in Meknès, Morocco in April 1942 Poulenc drafted a lengthy scenario for the ballet which he adorned with his own drawings.[49] By June the full score and parts were finished, and unofficial rehearsals had begun with various "étoiles."[50]

When the ballet was finally performed, reviews were numerous and on the whole favorable.[51] Poulenc was stung, however, by Koechlin's criticism in a private letter.[52] Invited to the premiere, he praised the orchestration as more masterly than that in *Les Biches*, but preferred *Biches* to *Animaux*, disapproving of the length of some numbers and preferring the burlesque sections to the serious parts. He was particularly hurt by Colette's *Comœdia* article "A Propos d'un ballet."[53] She criticized his collaborators, and Poulenc was quick to tell her that they had been carrying out his instructions, not acting on personal initiative.[54] He issued a public response a week later.[55]

[45] "Samedi" [13 Sept. 1941] letter in Poulenc 1994, 41-11.
[46] Apr. date appears in his [4 Sept. 1941] letter to Girard in Poulenc 1994, 41-10.
[47] Fragment of Derain's 10 Jan. [1942] letter to Poulenc in Poulenc 1994, p. 512, note 1.
[48] Article in *Le Figaro* (12 Dec. 1941), 4 transcribed in Schmidt 1995, p. 315. See also the 3 Oct. 1941 article in *L'Information musicale*, 115. Maquettes for Brianchon's costumes and décor are in F-Po (D 216 [97] and (Esq. O 1942) respectively.
[49] Manuscript now in US-NH, not US-NYpm. Schmidt 1995, FP 111, p. 312. Poulenc was back in Paris by 22 Apr. when Mauriac reports having had lunch with him and Février at Marie-Laure's. Mauriac, p. 108.
[50] For his work Poulenc requested a fee of 10,000 francs, 5,000 in advance and 5,000 the day of the premiere. 4 June 1942 letter to Rouché in Poulenc 1994, 42-4.
[51] Schmidt 1995, FP 111, p. 316.
[52] Koechlin's 19 Aug. 1942 letter to Poulenc see Poulenc 1994, 42-6; for Poulenc's 18 Aug. 1942 reply see Poulenc 1994, 42-7 (Poulenc 1991, no. 159). Cocteau entered a devastating remark in his diary, 23 Mar. 1943: "Monumentally foolish choreography for Poulenc's ballet by Serge [Lifar]." Cocteau 1989a, p. 292.
[53] 22 Aug. 1942 issue of *Comœdia*. Part of this article is reprinted in Poulenc 1994, pp. 522-3, note 1.
[54] 22 Aug. [1942] letter to Colette from Noizay in Poulenc 1994, 42-8.
[55] Poulenc 1942b.

He and Brianchon discussed her article and Poulenc's response in letters exchanged during late August and early September.[56] On the other hand, Adrienne Monnier's article 'Une soirée à l'Opéra avec Francis Poulenc" pleased Poulenc immensely.[57] Monnier not only attended the premiere, but was present at George Salles' home when Poulenc previewed *Les Animaux* for Salles and Sylvia Beach. Monnier sent him a copy of her 1953 memoirs and he found her article "by far one of the very rare *precise* things written about this work."[58] The following reveals her thorough understanding.

> Poulenc is not, up to now, an innovator, but he is a perfectly original composer. In his review of *Les Animaux modèles*, Arthur Honegger correctly writes that the influences that have worked upon him, Chabrier, Satie, Stravinsky, are now completely assimilated. Listening to his music you think—it's Poulenc. If I had to describe Poulenc's style, I would speak about the particular nuances of his playfulness, of his piety, of his melancholy. Besides these qualities that belong so essentially to our composer, we should note, in *Les Animaux modèles*, the presence of a remarkable vigor. The episode of "Les Coqs rivaux" ["The Rival Roosters"] shows a brilliance, a violence that go far beyond the resources of the minor masters.[59]

Poulenc was very pleased with the production: "Everything went very well for *Les Animaux*, which was, I think, a complete success. Lifar and Brianchon helped me marvelously."[60] He was upset at the reduced orchestra that performed the ballet. The string section, due to the absence of Jews and others taken prisoner, consisted of only ten first and seven second violins, six violas, six violoncellos, and five contrabasses.[61] His attachment to the work led him to dedicate it to Raymonde Linossier's memory. Alice Ardoin, invited to the premiere, was quite moved by both the dedication and the music.[62]

When Eschig published the piano score in 1942, Poulenc sent copies to friends inscribed "ami" or "amie modèle."[63] One presented to

---

[56] Brianchon's 24 Aug., 28 Aug., and 1 Sept. 1942 letters to Poulenc and Poulenc's 24 Aug. [1942] letter to Brianchon in Poulenc 1994, 42-9, 42-11, 42-14, and 42-10 respectively. The Brianchons were also Poulenc's house guests at Noizay for the weekend of 24 Sept. 1942. Poulenc 1994, p. 529, note 1.

[57] 12-13 Sept. 1942 issue of *Figaro littéraire*. Reprinted in Monnier 1953 and translated in Monnier 1976.

[58] "Mardi" [29 Dec. 1953] letter to Monnier in Poulenc 1994, 53-35 (Poulenc 1991, no. 243).

[59] Monnier 1976, p. 244 (translation by Richard McDougall).

[60] English translation from the postcard to Hélène Casella offered for sale in Macnutt, Lot 198 and Schmidt 1995, FP 111, p. 316.

[61] 18 Aug. [1942] letter to Koechlin in Poulenc 1994, 42-7 (Poulenc 1991, no. 159).

[62] Ardoin's [Paris, Aug. 1942] letter to Poulenc in Poulenc 1994, 42-5.

[63] See those listed in Schmidt 1995, FP 111, p. 314.

André Dubois, a chief of police, included a note clarifying the significance *Les Animaux modèles* had for his love of country.

> *Les Animaux modèles* are the tribute of admiration and of tenderness that for many years I have held for La Fontaine and for the Bourgogne. Why place the *Fables* in Bourgogne someone objected?[64] Because they are as at home there as at Château Thierry, each verse of La Fontaine finds its perfect resonance in the four corners of France. Bourgogne and the Morvan—countryside of my nurse—represented for me *Earthly paradise,* so it is quite natural that I should make the celebrated animals which this time serve as models for men dance there. The realization of the libretto cost me *one* year of work; the score two. After this long gestation I hope that nobody will call to mind the fable of *La Montagne qui accouche,* which I did not take into account.[65]

INCIDENTAL MUSIC FOR FILMS AND PLAYS: OTHER PROJECTS OF 1941

As the year continued, Poulenc contemplated projects which took him in new directions. During his summer residence at Noizay he began a String Trio (FP 115) destined for the Trio Pasquier but never finished.[66] The next two projects were designed to bring him much-needed income. He agreed to compose incidental music for Charles Exbrayat's three-act play *La Fille du jardinier* (FP 112).[67] Charles Dullin disliked using recorded music for his plays, preferring live sound.[68] Little is known about this work except that his old friend Valentine Hugo designed the costumes for the 8 October 1941 Théâtre des Mathurins premiere.

The third project was incidental music for a Jean Giraudoux film after Balzac entitled *La Duchesse de Langeais* (FP 116).[69] Earlier he had contributed to Alexandre Alexeieff's animated film *La Belle au bois dormant* to advertise Vins Nicolas, but *La Duchesse* was a feature film by a noted playwright making his film debut. The thought of composing a film score especially pleased him, and he quickly shared

---

[64] Reference to Colette's article.

[65] From the score in F-Pbodin as cited in Schmidt 1995, FP 111, p. 314. *La Montagne qui accouche* [The Mountain in Labor] concerns the birth of a mountain. It was thought that something larger than Paris would result from the reverberations and groans, but in the end the striking monstrosity was a mouse!

[66] This work is first announced in his [July 1941] letter to Bernard in Poulenc 1994, 41-5. Poulenc indicates the work is sketched, but will require much more patience. See also his "vendredi" [1 Aug. 1941] letter to Marie-Blanche in Poulenc 1994, 41-7 and *L'Information musicale* (26 Sept. 1941), 64.

[67] Charles Dullin's 30 Aug. 1941 letter to Poulenc in Poulenc 1994, 41-8. The letter begins "I am happy that Exbrayat's play pleases you and I'm delighted to work with you."

[68] Dullin's 30 Aug. 1941 letter to Poulenc in Poulenc 1994, 41-8. Dullin directed Exbrayat's play.

[69] [July 1941] letter to Bernard in Poulenc 1994, 41-5.

the news with both Marie-Blanche de Polignac and Simone Girard.[70] In an interview granted at the time, Poulenc said:

> I had always refused to work for the movies and no doubt I would have refused again this time if the collaboration of Giraudoux, Baroncelli, and Edwige Feuillère, an intelligent artist whom I greatly admire, had not proved to be an effort with which I am now happy to have been associated. To be sure, film music can hardly be but an illustration. The role of the musician there is necessarily passive, subordinated to the pictures and even to the action. To take *La Duchesse de Langeais* as an example, we find two elements in it: a style particular to the epoch, a modern commentary in sound which permits greater liberty... In the first part, we will have danced waltzes, among others *Le Fleuve du Tage,* celebrated at the time, and that I hardly transposed. [. . .] Our conversation took place in a large empty studio where the composer himself had recorded the film music on the piano.[71]

By 4 September, still at Noizay, Poulenc was too busy with *Les Animaux modèles* to mention *La Duchesse.*[72] Instead he anticipated Bernac's week-long visit to prepare an upcoming concert and a visit from photographers to shoot a feature on his house for the Christmas issue of *Images de France.*[73] Poulenc was in Paris in mid-September, carrying major portions of *Les Animaux modèles* to the publisher.

Once committed to write for Dullin's production, Poulenc was apparently asked by Louise de Vilmorin to compose music for a film of her novel *Lit à colonnes.*[74] Poulenc begged off saying he lacked enough time and tried to pass the work to Jean Françaix whose name he suggested to Vilmorin and her great friend Marie-Blanche de Polignac. He also told Françaix that he was busy helping to organize a bi-monthly concert series at the Théâtre des Mathurins. One concert was to be shared by Olivier Messiaen and Françaix, so Poulenc asked Françaix if he had twenty-five minutes of new chamber music for the occasion.[75]

While in Paris during November he composed his twelfth Improvisation in E-flat minor entitled "Hommage à Schubert" (FP 113)

---

[70] "Vendredi" [1 Aug. 1941] and [4 Sept. 1941] letters in Poulenc 1994, 41-7 and 41-10 respectively.

[71] Interview by Pierre Allan in *Ciné-Mondial* (19 Dec. 1941) reprinted in Poulenc 1994, p. 511, note 5.

[72] [4 Sept. 1941] letter to Girard from Noizay in Poulenc 1994, 41-10.

[73] Baschet, pp. 41-4. This article includes photographs of Poulenc at his piano and work table, the Noizay gardens and terrace overlooking the Loire valley, and his living room, dining room, and bedroom.

[74] Unpublished and undated letter from Poulenc to Jean Françaix kindly communicated by Frédéric Cellier from the Archives Jean Françaix.

[75] Poulenc also indicated that the concert would include Messiaen's *Quatuor pour la fin du temps* and would probably be broadcast by Radio Vichy.

and performed a full-length 15 November Salle Gaveau recital with Bernac including airs by Jean-Baptiste Lully, lieder by Liszt, the premiere of Honegger's *Trois poèmes de Claudel*, and *mélodies* by Poulenc and Ravel. Three weeks later, on 9 December, Poulenc participated in a commemorative "Festival Albert Roussel" at the Salle de l'École normale de musique. Just before Christmas, he had a relatively rare opportunity to hear his Concerto in G minor for organ performed at the Palais de Chaillot in Paris by Maurice Duruflé and the Orchestre de la Société des Concerts du Conservatoire, Charles Munch conducting.[76]

THE WAR DURING LATER 1940 AND 1941

By the middle of 1940 tightening German control of the country made life for French citizens increasingly difficult. Germany had annexed Alsace and Lorraine, "pillaged the French treasury and French industry,"[77] and rendered the Vichy government impotent. As the year concluded the relationship between Pétain and Laval, heads of rival factions, became so strained that the former dismissed the latter. Pétain simply could not abide Laval's interest in a French-German collaboration to defeat England. Pétain then became so bold as to decline an invitation from Hitler to attend a reinterment of the Duke of Reichstadt's remains in Paris. Quick to retaliate at this rebuke, the Germans closed off travel between the free and occupied zones of France to men between the ages of 18 and 45.[78] This probably accounts for why Poulenc, then in his early 40s, traveled much less during 1942 than in 1941. On 3 December 1942, Poulenc wrote Ernest Ansermet that he had made his first trip into the free zone since June 1940, and could write to him from there without fear of censorship.[79] By year's end Erwin Rommel was retreating in North Africa, and the Americans had entered the war after the humiliation at Pearl Harbor. With German victory in Europe far from assured, Pétain was requested to supply 150,000 French workers for factories in Germany. He refused.

French artists were in a quandary: to abide by the letter of German occupational policy, or to become members of the Resistance. Cocteau's biographer Francis Steegmuller considers this issue.

> The Occupation of Paris by the Germans from 1940 to 1944 was a period so macabre as to defy description even by those who were there, and to baffle understanding by those who were not. It was

---

[76] Schmidt 1995, p. 281, where the date is mistakenly given as 1942. In a "jeudi soir" [Apr. 1947] letter to Munch (Poulenc 1994, 47-3) he fondly remembered this occasion.

[77] Tint, p. 97.

[78] Discussion based on Tint, pp. 99-100.

[79] 3 Dec. [1942] letter from Brive-la-Gaillarde in Poulenc 1994, 42-21.

possible, it has to be said, to avoid "collaboration" with the conquerors in only one way—by refusing any activity that required licensing. But almost any activity did require licensing, and no license was given without German approval. To refuse to ask for a license meant, for artists, no publication of books, no production of plays, no showing of films, no concerts, no exhibitions. One became a "collaborator" merely by legally exercising one's profession.[80]

Although Poulenc lent his hand to theatrical events which could not have been presented without the requisite licenses, he was in no way a collaborator. In fact, as will be shown, he actively opposed restraints placed by the Nazi occupation force.

CONCERTS OF EARLIER 1942

On 25 January Poulenc played his *Concert champêtre* in the Théâtre du Châtelet at the Concerts Gabriel Pierné under the direction of Gaston Poulet. There may have been another in Marseilles during March, and we know that in April he was in Morocco.[81] Late in May he participated in three different concerts including a 19 May recital at the Salle Gaveau with Bernac and the great French pianist Marguerite Long in a "Festival Fauré." Bernac and Poulenc performed eight *mélodies* plus *La Bonne Chanson,* while Long played Nocturnes nos. 2 and 6 plus Valse-Caprice no. 3. Four days later, Poulenc accompanied Geneviève Touraine at the École normale in works by Giovanni Battista Pergolesi, Francesco Cavalli, Giulio Caccini, Charles Gounod, and Albert Roussel. After these unusual works, the concert ended with the first performance of *Fiançailles pour rire.*

The flurry of May recitals concluded on the 23rd when the Bernac/Poulenc duo participated in an "Initiative musicale" at the Salle du Conservatoire performing Roussel and Robert Bernard's *Trois poèmes de Paul Fort.* This preceded one of the most ambitious recitals the pair ever attempted. On 5 June at the Salle de l'École normale de musique, they gave a "Récital de mélodies contemporaines" which included first performances of music by six composers: Jolivet's *Trois airs de Dolorès,* Louis Beydts' *La Lyre et les Amours,* Claude Delvincourt's *D'un paravent de laque,* Jean Françaix's *L'Adolescence clémentine,* Henri Sauguet's "Le Chat" and *Deux poèmes de Tagore,* and Marcel Delannoy's *Noël.*[82]

Less than a month later, on 1 July at the Salle Gaveau, the string of premieres continued at an "Association de Musique Contemporaine"

[80]Steegmuller 1970, pp. 439-40.
[81] 1 Jan. [1942] letter to Sophie Milhaud in Poulenc 1994, 42-1. A scenario with some drawings for *Les Animaux modèles* in Poulenc's hand is dated April 1942 from Meknès (Morocco). See Schmidt 1995, p. 312.
[82] "Le Chat" (from *Six mélodies sur des poèmes symbolistes*) may have been a Parisian premiere, but it had been given in London in 1939. See Chapter VIII.

concert forming part of the "Semaine Honegger" (25 June-3 July), given in conjunction with Éliette Schenneberg and the Quatuor Gabriel Bouillon. The Bernac/Poulenc duo presented *Trois psaumes*[83] and *Petit cours de morale* (texts by Giraudoux),[84] as well as the early *Six poésies de Jean Cocteau*.[85] Bernac also sang *Pâques à New York*.[86] Then, on 3 July at the Palais de Tokyo, they performed works by Gounod, Chabrier, Auric, Poulenc, and Ravel plus the premiere of Sauguet's *Deux mélodies lyriques sous des textes frivoles*.

COMPOSITIONS OF 1942:

• *Chansons villageoises*

During the war years concerts provided Poulenc with a much more reliable income than royalties from publications, with the exception of plays and films. So, while the steady gait of concerts continued in 1942, the number of new compositions dropped off dramatically. Early in the year his primary concern was completing *Les Animaux modèles* for its August premiere. As noted earlier, Poulenc attended rehearsals and was thoroughly occupied with bringing to fruition a work he deeply loved. The sole new composition, *Chansons villageoises* (Village Songs: FP 117), a cycle of six orchestral songs on texts by Maurice Fombeure, was finished between October and December.[87] He resumed work on his Sonata for Violin and Piano (V) during the summer, but did not finish it until Easter, 1943.[88]

Henri Hell cites a plausible reason for Poulenc's use of Fombeure rather than his beloved Apollinaire or Eluard:

Fombeure's poetry, willingly lightened with humor and fantasy, evokes, without the least hint of pastiche, the old popular folksongs of France. It is the same gracious simplicity, the same charm, the same rhythm. And the same wisdom of the peasant emerges. Touching, quizzical or grave, happy or sad, these songs hide, beneath their nonchalant facade, beneath their apparent simplicity, considerable art: an art that is skillful, subtle, and delicate. Popular songs, to be sure, but more highly wrought poetically than they first appear. They

[83] Spratt, p. 558. Halbreich, p. 293 gives the date as 28 June, but this disagrees with *L'Information musicale* (29 May 1942), 955.
[84] Spratt, p. 559.
[85] Spratt, p. 520. These were probably in Hoérée's arrangement for voice and string quartet.
[86] Spratt, p. 511 (for voice and string quartet).
[87] Each song is dedicated to a friend: (1) Louis Beydts [composer and friend of Reynaldo Hahn and a correspondent with Poulenc during the war], (2) Jean de Polignac, (3) Roger Bourdin, (4) André Schaeffner, (5) André Lecœur, and (6) André Dubois.
[88] Poulenc 1993, pp. 39-40 (Poulenc 1989, pp. 70-1).

have this in common with Poulenc's art. Similarly the latter [Poulenc] has been able to avoid the danger of true folksong.[89]

Poulenc described the inspiration which lay behind the *Chansons*:

Written in September 1942, shortly after the first performance of *Les Animaux modèles*, the *Chansons villageoises* sprang directly from that work in terms of orchestration and even in their harmonic style ["C'est le joli printemps," end of "Mendiant"—"Petit jour," "Deux coqs")]. I conceived them as a symphonic song cycle for a strong Verdi baritone (Iago). [Bourdin, who created them, was excellent but lacked chest and shoulders. Too much jabot—the word "jabot" taken in the eighteenth-century sense and not the animal sense, as I would have wished. Bernac could not sing the *Villageoises* except with piano. The ideal interpreter remains to be found. For the piano version it is definitely Bernac.] Fombeure's texts evoke for me the Morvan where I have spent such wonderful summers! It is out of nostalgia for the surroundings of Autun that I composed this collection [at Noizay. . .]. In the Morvan portable ballrooms with polished floors, crocheted curtains, velvet benches, and copper candelabras are used. All that, in my memory, serves as a frame for "Les Gars qui vont à la fête" "shaved to the underskin" and danced at Julien the fiddler's. [. . .] "Le Mendiant" is quite influenced by Moussorgsky, something that sprang very naturally from the subject.[90]

He left unmentioned still another link because, like Stravinsky, he seldom alluded to borrowing. A comparison of the opening of "Le Mendiant" with music for Babar's ride on his mother's back from *Histoire de Babar, le petit éléphant* shows that direct borrowing took place.[91] A blatant case, the opening of the song is transposed a third higher than the similar passage in *Babar*. While working on this cycle Poulenc alluded to another influence:

I am also working on six songs for voice and orchestra, based on "folk poems" by Maurice Fombeure. Imagine a sort of *Pribaoutki* [a set of pieces for male voice and nine instruments by Stravinsky] from the Morvan. I think they will be quite good and very striking in both style and instrumentation.[92]

Later Poulenc noted that the title "chanson" as used here represents a clear distinction with the term *"mélodie"* applied to the vast majority of his solo vocal works.

You will notice straight away the difference between my chansons

[89] Hell 1978, p. 178. Quoted in part in Bernac 1977a, p. 170 (English) and Bernac 1978, pp. 158-9 (French).
[90] Larche, 20 July 1945 entry in Poulenc 1993, pp. 39-40 (Poulenc 1989, pp. 70-1).
[91] *Babar*, p. 4, last two braces. Daniel, pp. 271-2.
[92] [Oct. 1942] letter to Schaeffner in Poulenc 1994, 42-20 (Poulenc 1991, no. 160).

and my *mélodies*. In my opinion, the word *chanson* implies a style which, without actually being folkloric, nevertheless suggests a total freedom with regard to the text. I repeat words, cut them up, even use ellipses, as at the end of "Les Gars qui vont à la fête" [from *Chansons villageoises*]. Maurice Chevalier's singing style taught me a great deal about this.[93]

•Sonata for Violin and Piano (V)

Although he found the summer "odious and detestable,"[94] Poulenc resumed work on the Sonata for Violin and Piano (FP 119), a work that shared some musical ideas with one he had written in the mid-1930s.[95]

> I have revised and finished the rough draft of a Sonata for Piano and Violin. The "monstre" is now ready. I am going to begin the realization. It is not bad, I believe, and in any case very different from the endless *violin line melody* sonatas written in France in the nineteenth century. How beautiful Brahms' sonatas are! I did not know them very well. One cannot achieve a proper balance between two such different instruments as the piano and the violin unless one treats them absolutely equally. The prima donna violin over an arpeggio piano accompaniment makes me vomit. Debussy, somewhat breathless in his Sonata, has nevertheless succeeded in turning it into a masterpiece by sheer instrumental tact.[96]

After numerous aborted attempts, Poulenc completed a string sonata that was both performed and published. Of the four earlier attempts in 1918, 1924-25, 1929, and 1932-35 only the first reached a single performance. Because no music remains for the first three, we cannot say whether they are musically related, but that is unlikely. However, a short fragment of music included in a 1935 letter clarifies that the 1932-35 sonata contains a theme found in the Intermède of the 1942-43 sonata.[97] The narrative quality of this phrase is no doubt linked to the primary reason why this work was composed:

> Having always wished to dedicate a work to the memory of Lorca, [...] I was inspired by one of his most celebrated verses: "The guitar makes dreams cry" (even translated it is pretty). At first I composed a sort of vaguely Spanish *Andante-cantilène*. Then, I imagined as a

[93] Poulenc 1947c, p. 513.
[94] "Samedi" [26 Sept. 1942] letter to Brianchon in Poulenc 1994, 42-17.
[95] Chimènes suggests that Poulenc sketched this Sonata in 1940, which would substantiate his claim that he was revising and finishing a rough draft, but I can locate no period documentation. Poulenc 1994, p. 533, note 2.
[96] [Oct. 1942] letter to Schaeffner from Noizay in Poulenc 1994, 42-20 (Poulenc 1991, no. 160).
[97] [30 Dec. 1935] letter to Jacques Lerolle in Poulenc 1994, 35-8.

finale, a *Presto tragico* of which the rhythmic and vital spirit would suddenly be broken by a slow and tragic coda. An impetuous first movement must set the mood. All that, despite some technical innovations by Ginette Neveu, despite her genius of interpretation, did not amount to much.[98]

Just before the premiere, Poulenc wrote, "This intermezzo is a melancholic improvisation in memory of a poet whom I love equally with Apollinaire or Eluard."[99] Poulenc and Ginette Neveu gave the premiere at the Salle Gaveau on 21 June 1943 to benefit imprisoned writers and musicians. Several months later, Poulenc remarked: "My colleagues have not given me good press for the Sonata, but praise the *Chansons villageoises* to the skies. Happily violinists are impatient to see the Sonata published."[100] Eschig published it early in 1944, but this version was later withdrawn because Poulenc thought the piece flawed.[101] In 1949 he revised the finale to address what he considered the most pressing problem.

REMAINING EVENTS OF 1942

One further development was the organization in July of a group of French musicians called the "Comité National des Musiciens." According to Roland Penrose :

> They published a clandestine newspaper, *Le Musicien d'Aujourd'hui*, which exposed the activities of traitors in the musical world, pointed out the tendencious nature of musical events organized by Vichy and Radio-Paris and endeavoured to safeguard the essential values of French music, which were becoming submerged beneath a flood of a certain type of German music specially favoured by the Nazis. Their desire was to save French music and her musicians from being stolen from them by the Germans who had laid claim on racial grounds to several French composers such as Berlioz, and banned all who could be suspected of Jewish origins.[102]

Penrose names Roger Désormière (president), Poulenc, Auric, Claude Delvincourt, Manual Rosenthal, Roland-Manuel, Durey, and Elsa Barraine as members.[103] That year, dozens of clandestine news-

[98] Poulenc 1954, p. 120
[99] Letter in *Comœdia* (19 June 1943). Poulenc 1943b.
[100] 17 Aug. [1943] letter to Bernac in Poulenc 1994, 43-4 (Poulenc 1991, no. 161).
[101] Poulenc gave the original manuscript to Brigitte Manceaux. It is inscribed: "For Brigitte, with the best of my heart, this manuscript which is not my best work. Francis. Le Tremblay Aug. 46." Schmidt 1995, FP 119, p. 330.
[102] Penrose 1945, p. 33.
[103] Penrose 1945, p. 34. Penrose further points out that a Resistance center was set up at the Conservatoire Nationale de Musique under Delvincourt's direction and that Roland-Manuel gathered a group of musicians and radio-technicians in a clandestine Paris studio to record poems by poets of the underground (Eluard,

papers also appeared, whose collective goal was to disseminate information which could not appear in the "approved" press. Often these publications, like Eluard's poems, were distributed by a network of street workers who slipped them in mail slots or under doors at the risk of life and limb if discovered by the Germans.[104]

During the autumn Poulenc took time off from practicing and composing to reflect about the state of music in France and to replay compositions written between the wars. He was disturbed by what he saw, calling it "worthless drivel," and felt that the names which counted were still "Stravinsky, Prokofiev, Satie, Hindemith, Falla, etc."[105] He chided his peers saying that except for younger composers such as Jean Françaix and Olivier Messiaen, all the rest were quite content with what had been composed before 1914. In conclusion, he wrote:

> I know very well that I am not the sort of musician who makes harmonic innovations, like Igor [Stravinsky], Ravel, or Debussy, but I do think there is a place for *new* music that is satisfied with using other people's chords. Wasn't this the case with Mozart and Schubert? And in any case, with time, the personality of my harmonic style will become evident. Wasn't Ravel for a long time regarded as nothing more than a *petit maître* and imitator of Debussy?

Almost immediately after returning to Paris for the winter he and Bernac gave a 7 November Salle Gaveau recital featuring excerpts from André Campra stage works, Schumann's *Sechs Lieder* op. 90, Debussy's *Trois chansons de France* and Ravel's *Trois poèmes de Mallarmé*, Stravinsky's *Trois histoires pour enfants*, and a reprise of Poulenc's venerable *Chansons gaillardes*. They rarely performed in German. Since the 14 March 1940 recital in Zurich, the Bernac/ Poulenc duo had tried to showcase only repertoire in French.

They also gave a series of concerts in Cannes, Marseilles, and Lyon immediately before 3 December. At the end of the year Poulenc spent five days with his friend, the amateur pianist Marthe Bosredon in Brive where he reestablished communication with Ansermet. Assessing the current scene for his friend, Poulenc wrote:

Aragon, etc.) and music by banned musicians (Milhaud, Hindemith, Schönberg, etc.). The account by Parrot, which differs slightly, indicates that the Comité de Front National (pour musique) was organized in Sept. 1941 by Désormière, Barraine, and Roland-Manuel. They were soon joined by Auric, Poulenc, Munch, and Rosenthal. Parrot, pp. 182-3. Barraine, who has not been mentioned here before, was a composer who studied with Dukas, Noel Gallon, and Georges Caussade at the Paris Conservatory.

[104] Simon, pp. 101-03.
[105] For this and the next quotation see his [Oct. 1942] letter to Schaeffner in Poulenc 1994, 42-20.

Parisian musical life is intense. Munch is giving very beautiful concerts and each one [of us] tries to preserve the spiritual atmosphere of our good city. Picasso paints solitarily and superbly, Braque likewise. Eluard writes masterpieces.[106]

Poulenc's last known public performance of 1942 was for the two hundredth concert of "Le Triptyque" at the Salle de l'École normale on 22 December. He and Bernac were joined by Aline van Barentzen, Suzanne Demarquez, André Navarra, Olivier Messiaen, Robert Bernard, André Pascal, and the Quintette Instrumental Pierre-Jamet. The Bernac/Poulenc duo performed Honegger's *Trois poèmes de Claudel* and Sauguet's *Quatre mélodies* ("Le Souvenir," "Le Pélerin," "L'Apparition," "Les Guides de la vie").[107] Their advocacy of contemporary French *mélodies* continued.

DESPAIR AND HOPE IN 1943: OF WAR AND THE FRENCH RESISTANCE

On 8 November 1942, under the code name "Torch," the allies launched a multipronged invasion of northwest Africa in territory still loyal to the Vichy government of Marshal Pétain. The French resistance to these landings was swiftly overcome and agreements were concluded with Pétain. In retaliation German and Italian forces overran southern France on 11 November. From that date forward there was no longer any difference between Vichy territory and Occupied territory. Penrose describes the effect this had on the French Resistance:

All Frenchmen, wherever they lived, were directly under Nazi domination. Nothing could have been more valuable to the resistance than this unification of France. No one could now imagine that they would be able to escape the control of the Nazi rulers or the attention of the Gestapo. The result was a widespread increase of underground activity strengthened by the great hope that came from the news of the victories of the Allies, and increased in vigour in spite of the growing brutality of Nazi oppression.[108]

In late summer 1943, Mussolini fell, and in September the Allies landed in Sicily. Although disheartened by the effect of the war around him, especially the murder of Parisian intellectuals by the Vichy police or the Gestapo, Poulenc was able to keep up much of his usual activity. In addition to the customary complement of concerts, including six in Paris during May and June, he had finished the Sonata for Violin and Piano (V), wrote an Intermezzo in A-flat major (FP 118), and completed the cantata *Figure humaine* (FP 120)

---

[106] 3 Dec. [1942] letter in Poulenc 1994, 42-21.
[107] Concerning *Trois poèmes* see Spratt, pp. 556-7. *L'Information musicale* 3 (19 Dec. 1942), 143.
[108] Penrose 1945, pp. 31-2.

during the summer.[109] Later he wrote three *mélodies* entitled *Métamorphoses* (August-October: FP 121) and *Deux poèmes de Louis Aragon* (September-October: FP 122). Finally, *Le Voyageur sans bagage* (FP 123), music for a film of Jean Anouilh's play first produced in 1936, was composed in late 1943 or early 1944. These works owe their composition to aspects of the political situation described above.

WINTER AND SPRING OF 1943: THE CONCERTS

In February and March at the Salle Gaveau, Poulenc, Bernac, and the pianist Nicole Henriot-Schweitzer participated in a "Festival Maurice Ravel."[110] The Bernac/Poulenc duo performed *Deux épigrammes de Clément Marot, Histoires naturelles,* and *Don Quichotte à Dulcinée,* Henriot-Schweitzer played "Oiseaux tristes" and "Alborada del gracioso" from *Miroirs* and joined Poulenc for *Ma mère l'oye.* Poulenc had hoped to visit Brussels twice during the winter with Bernac and Henriot-Schweitzer respectively, but plans collapsed at the last minute.[111] Poulenc also may have played a concert in Lyon during March[112] and was in Bordeaux early that month to review a performance of Fauré's opera *Pénélope.*[113] Then, on 5 April at the École normale, Poulenc joined pianist Bernadette Maire and soprano Geneviève Touraine for the 235th concert of "Le Triptych." Repertory included works by fifteen composers. Poulenc accompanied music by Bach, Lully, Antonio Caldara, Debussy, Julien Tiersot, Fauré, and himself.

During the winter he attended screenings of films arranged by Henri Langlois in a small projection room at 44, Champs-Élysées. One he viewed on 26 February is described by Claude Mauriac: "All the customary 'Tout-Paris' was there, Misia Sert in ruins, Bichette (Poulenc), Marcel Achard, his wife and his mistress, Marie-Laure [de Noailles], [Denis] Marion, [Georges] Geffroy, the Duchess of Harcourt, [Robert] Piguet, [Christian] Bérard, etc."[114]

Additional concerts occupied him on 24 and 28 May as well as 11, 21, 23, 24, and 28 June. The 24th of May he and Suzanne Balguerie gave a full-length recital including three Duparc *mélodies,* Fauré's *La*

---

[109] The Intermezzo is dedicated to Juliette Mante-Rostand, Edmond Rostand's sister, who organized a *matineé musicale* that Bernac and Poulenc participated in on 23 June 1934.

[110] 6 Feb. concert repeated on 27 Mar.

[111] 20 Aug. 1943 letter to Collaer in Poulenc 1994, 43-6 and Collaer 1996, 43-4.

[112] Interview with Poulenc in *Ce Soir* (25 Nov. 1944).

[113] Poulenc 1943a. Though he liked the music of Fauré's opera, he thought Koechlin should rework the orchestration. See also the commentary in Buckland/Chimènes: f, pp. 38-9.

[114] Claude Mauriac was François Mauriac's son. See Mauriac, p. 237 and pp. 257-8. Also quoted in Cocteau 1989a, p. 258. Films of Cocteau and others were shown here. See also Tual, pp. 198-200.

Bonne Chanson, Debussy's *Ariettes oubliées,* and his own *Fiançailles pour rire.* Four days later he joined Jacques Février for a Concerts du Conservatoire performance of his Concerto in D minor, Charles Munch conducting. The first June concert, featuring a *pot-pourri* program in which Poulenc accompanied Balguerie in Debussy's *Trois mélodies de Verlaine* and *Trois ballades de Villon,* also included the *Motets pour un temps de pénitence* performed by the Chorale Passani.

During 1943 "La Pléiade," a new concert series was founded. It was financed by the publisher Gaston Gallimard under the auspices of *La Nouvelle Revue Française* (N.R.F.). The inaugural Galerie Charpentier concert benefited imprisoned writers and musicians.[115] Poulenc, probably involved with the series from its inception, attended the 10 May 1943 performance when Olivier Messiaen's *Les Visions de l'Amen* was premiered by the composer and his student Yvonne Loriod. Paul Valéry, Claude Mauriac, Cocteau, Jean Paulhan, Georges Henri Rivière, Roland-Manuel, Charles Dullin, and Pierre Boulez were also in attendance.[116]

Poulenc's music was included on two late-season concerts; the first, at the Salle Gaveau on 21 June, presented the premiere of his Sonata for Violin and Piano (V) played by Ginette Neveu and the venerable *Sept chansons.*[117] Also featured were Debussy's *Le Promenoir des amants* sung by Bernac, and Debussy's *Chansons de Charles d'Orléans* as well as Ravel's *Trois chansons* performed by the Chorale

[115]Chimènes, Poulenc 1994, p. 535, note 1, suggests a 22 Mar. date. The composer Michel Ciry (b.1919) wrote, in his diary on 8 Feb. 1943, that the first Pléiade concert was performed that day. See Ciry, pp. 48-50. Ciry, a student of Nadia Boulanger, had asked Poulenc to recommend a singer to perform his cycle *Madame de Soubise,* and later diary entries indicate that Poulenc made some alterations in the score. Poulenc suggested the tenor Paul Derenne rather than Pierre Bernac, whose voice did not suit the tessitura. See also Ciry's entries of 2 Feb. (when he telephoned Poulenc) and 26 Feb. (when he met Poulenc chez Marie-Blanche de Polignac). At that *soirée,* Poulenc entertained the guests by reading a risqué letter, and played his *Chansons villageoises* (which Ciry thought Poulenc played like a god, but sang atrociously). After the reprise of his Ravel recital with Bernac on 27 Mar., Poulenc asked Ciry to come to his rue de Médécis apartment on the 30th to hear him rehearse with Derenne. The 30 Mar. entry indicates that Poulenc understood the music so well that he needed no pointers whatsoever from Ciry, but a 22 Apr. entry indicates Poulenc found the accompaniment difficult. The final rehearsal was at Poulenc's apartment on 2 May with the dress rehearsal and performance a day later. At the concert Poulenc also played his own *Cocardes* and accompanied Soulima Stravinsky in his father's Piano Concerto.

[116]Tual, p. 197. Poulenc was probably present at the second concert on 2 Apr. (Mauriac, p. 289) and that of 3 May at which his *Cocardes* were performed (Mauriac, p. 302).

[117]The goal of these concerts, organized by Tual and Schaeffner, was to present works by composers whose music had been banned by the Germans. It is through this concert series that Poulenc became better acquainted with Denise

Passani. Two days later, he joined violinist Renée de Saussine and pianist Nadine Clado at the Salle Pleyel for the second. We are uncertain precisely which works Poulenc accompanied, but he may have played the violin-piano transcription of his own *Presto* and performed four hands with Clado. That day Poulenc also recorded Pierre Vellones' *A mon fils* with Bernac for Voix de son Maître.[118] On 24 June, Poulenc participated in the 250th concert of the series "Le Triptyque" joining ten other artists and the Trio Pasquier. He may have accompanied Geneviève Touraine in *Fiançailles pour rire*. Finally, on 28 June, his *Chansons villageoises* was premiered by the baritone Roger Bourdin at a Pléiade concert. This was a fitting conclusion to an exceptionally busy season, and Gallimard personally thanked Poulenc for his assistance in launching the Pléiade series.[119]

SUMMER 1943: *FIGURE HUMAINE*, POULENC'S "PIÈCE DE RÉSISTANCE"

This spate of concerts concluded, Poulenc turned to summer projects which required solitude away from Paris. Accordingly, he rented a two-room apartment containing an excuse of a piano "Chez Madame Marchand" in Beaulieu-sur-Dordogne, Corrèze, 532 kilometers south of Paris.[120] Poulenc referred to Beaulieu as "An ideal town with thousands of décors out of *Animaux modèles* in every corner of the street."[121] Lacking inspiration, Poulenc considered writing a quartet dedicating one pair of instruments to Marie-Blanche de Polignac and the other to her husband Jean. Nothing came of this or of a violin concerto for Ginette Neveu.

> During the occupation a few privileged people, of whom I was one, had the solace of receiving with the morning mail wonderful typed poems, at the bottom of which, despite the use of pseudonyms, we recognized the signature of Paul Eluard. This is the manner in which I received the majority of the poems contained in *Poésie et Vérité 42*. During the summer of 43, I had rented a two-room apartment in Beaulieu-sur-Dordogne. "With piano," the agency said, but what a piano!!! I went there to compose a violin concerto for Ginette Neveu, but I soon gave up this project. The idea of composing a clandestine work which could be prepared and printed in secret and then performed at the so-long-awaited time of liberation had come to me at

---

and Roland Tual. See Tual, pp. 192-7. Michel Ciry, having spent the afternoon with Marie-Blanche de Polignac, accompanied her to the Salle Gaveau for the Poulenc premiere. Ciry, entry for 21 June 1943 (he detested the Poulenc).

[118] Bloch, p. 227 and Appendix 3.

[119] Gallimard's 30 June 1943 letter to Poulenc in Poulenc 1994, 43-1. Michel Ciry also attended this concert and spoke favorably of Poulenc's work in his diary entry for 28 June 1943.

[120] Account in Poulenc 1954, p. 103.

[121] [July 1943] letter to Marie-Blanche in Poulenc 1994, 43-2.

the end of a votive pilgrimage to Rocamadour, quite near to Beaulieu. I enthusiastically began *Figure humaine*, which I completed by the end of the summer [of 1943]. My publisher and friend Paul Rouart agreed to publish this cantata secretly. Thanks to him, at the time of the liberation the music could be sent to London, and before the end of the war, in January 1945 [sic], under the direction of Leslie Woodgate, the choirs of the B.B.C. gave the first performance of it. Thanks to the English Ambassador to Paris, His Excellency Duff Cooper, I was able to take a place on board an English military plane and attend the last rehearsals. Dear Benjamin Britten most graciously accepted at this time to play my Concerto for Two Pianos with me at Albert Hall.[122]

Jeannie Chauveau's interview with Poulenc reveals the genesis of the cantata.

It was following a concert of La Pléiade, at which my *Sept chansons* were performed, five of which were written on poems by Eluard and two on verses by Apollinaire, that Mr. Screpel, the director of the Compagnie des Discophiles, asked me to set to music, in order to make a record, the poem *Liberté*, which opens Eluard's *Poésie et Vérité 1942.* [. . .] This took place in March 1943. At the time I was frightened by the difficulty of the task. I departed then to play a concert in Lyon, where I found, at a bookstore, the small Swiss edition of these poems. I reread them. I was impressed by the different presentation of the work and noticed it anew. Suddenly I had the idea to set to music not only *Liberté*, but a cantata of which *Liberté* would be the culmination. During the entire spring, I reflected on this project, already eager to realize it but not knowing what form the work would take. Then in July 1943 I departed for Beaulieu-sur-Dordogne, and there, in six weeks, wrote this cantata for double chorus *a cappella*. I forgot to tell you that in the meantime, the Antwerp Chorale, having heard about this project, let me know that they would like to sing it in Belgium immediately after the Liberation.[123]

Before beginning the cantata he made a pilgrimage to Rocamadour to pray for its success.[124] *Figure humaine*, which he imagined as a choral work in the spirit of *Tel jour telle nuit,* is often said to be his most important score.[125] Wilfred Mellers explains both the connection of the two works and the relation of *Figure humaine* to the French Resistance.

In relation to the Eluard song-cycle *Tel jour, telle nuit* we noted that

[122] Poulenc 1954, pp. 103-04. The cantata was not performed until 25 Mar. 1945 in English and 2 Dec. 1946 in French (in Brussels).
[123] *Ce Soir* (25 Nov. 1944). I am grateful to Sidney Buckland for identifying the source of this interview. See also Poulenc 1994, p. 537, note 2.
[124] Guth 1952, p. 4. Reprinted in Poulenc 1994, pp. 537-8, note 2.
[125] [July 1943] letter to Marie-Blanche in Poulenc 1994, 43-3.

although the nine poems are all short, Poulenc's settings produce in sequence an effect of some grandeur. *Figure humaine* also consists of short poems, with the difference that they were intended to form a sequence, and are capped by an epilogic poem of some length. Poulenc, with his experience as a writer of song-cycles, finds no problem in making the cantata's short sections cumulative, and sustains momentum through the long consummatory poem, being resourceful in dealing with the refrain, "J'écris ton nom". The name proves to be "liberté." . . .[126]

Louis Parrot, who studied the dissemination of French thought via clandestine means, confirms that copies of Eluard's *Liberté* were not only transmitted to Switzerland and Algeria, but were passed among cells by prisoners.[127] The Royal Air Force also dropped thousands more from planes flying over occupied territories, and the poem was read over the BBC.[128]

Before leaving Beaulieu, Poulenc wrote to friends about the cantata with Bernac receiving the most detailed account. By mid-August he was pleased with his completed rough draft. Calling *Figure humaine* the most powerful of his choral works to date, he predicted that two hundred singers would be required for its performance and delighted in discussing the modulations suggested by the poem.[129] Though Poulenc's letter to Eluard is lost, Eluard's response indicates he was queried about a title but could think only of *Je suis né pour te nommer* [I was born to name you].[130] Picasso was asked if the work could be dedicated to him.[131] Finally, Poulenc discussed performances of his music and plans for the future with Paul Collaer, indicating that he had written a cantata destined for Louis De Vocht's Chorale Sainte-Cécile d'Anvers.[132] "*Liberté*, which concludes the work is, I believe, quite sensational" [he told Roland-Manuel]. "Thus I would have the greatest joy to show it to you as well as to our friends."[133] When the cantata was published, Poulenc expressed his happiness.

Raymond [Destouches] brought me a copy of the Cantata. The others rest well-wrapped at friend Paul's [Rouart]. How comforted I am by this work in my hours of despondency. I implore heaven to let me hear it at least once in my lifetime. When I received it, I did not

[126] Mellers, p. 84.
[127] Parrot, p. 111.
[128] Penrose 1945, p. 44.
[129] 17 Aug. [1943] letter in Poulenc 1994, 43-4 (Poulenc 1991, no. 161).
[130] Eluard's 23 Aug. 1943 letter in Poulenc 1994, 43-7 (Poulenc 1991, no. 162).
[131] [20 Aug. 1943] letter in Poulenc 1994, 43-5.
[132] 20 Aug. 1943 letter in Poulenc 1994, 43-6 and Collaer 1996, 43-4.
[133] [8 Nov. 1943] letter in Poulenc 1994, 43-13.

wish, as happens frequently with my other compositions, after an evil glance, to revise it. It succeeds both in its inspiration and in its craftsmanship which invigorates me. Too bad it is so difficult to perform. Yet this is also one of its strengths. Paul E[luard] mysteriously sent me a typewritten poem inscribed: "My dear Francis . . . Paul." The tone of the poem, quite beautiful, moreover, and the terseness of the writing, touched me deeply. It is really Eluard who has brought out my best.[134]

SUMMER 1943: *MÉTAMORPHOSES* ON POEMS BY VILMORIN

While composing *Figure humaine* in August, Poulenc also wrote two of the three *mélodies* entitled *Métamorphoses:* (1) "Reine des mouettes," dedicated to Marie-Blanche de Polignac, and (2) "C'est ainsi que tu es," dedicated to Marthe Bosredon.[135] At Noizay in October he completed the remaining *mélodie* "Paganini," dedicated to Jeanne Ritcher. The set was born, in part, out of Bernac's frustration.

> Bernac [Poulenc said], a great admirer of Louise de Vilmorin, envious of these *mélodies [Fiançailles pour rire]*, which were impossible for him to sing, solicited some masculine poems from the poetess. So it was that Louise de Vilmorin wrote *Les Métamorphoses*. [. . .][136]

When they were written he noted, "I evoke with emotion Louise de Vilmorin's salon at Verrières[-le-Buisson] where I played them for him [Jean de Polignac] in August 1943."[137] Jean de Polignac had died on 23 October 1943. Throughout the war Poulenc was concerned about Vilmorin's isolation and about her safety. After the conclusion of hostilities, Vilmorin gave Poulenc a typescript of the poems used in this collection entitled "LE SABLÉ DU SABLIER Miroir du sort", which is dated "31 janv. 1945" and inscribed "A mon Francis chéri son amie Louise de Vilmorin."[138]

In September Poulenc made the acquaintance of Jacques Leguerney at Bernac's home.[139] A student of Samuel-Rousseau and Nadia Boulanger, Leguerney had begun in earnest to compose

---

[134] 24 June [1944] letter to Bernac in Poulenc 1994, 44-4 (Poulenc 1991, no. 164). Poulenc first met Raymond Destouches in the early 1930s and the two were close friends until Poulenc died. Destouches was a chauffer by occupation who lived in the Touraine. Their relationship was complex and varied, ranging from love to paternal sentiments. Destouches was twice married, the second time to Céline in 1952. Poulenc dedicated several pieces to Destouches including the Concerto for Piano (co-dedicated to Denise Duval) and *Mélancolie*, and dedicated "Le Hérisson" from *Petites voix* to Raymond's son Jean.
[135] Schmidt 1995, FP 121.
[136] Poulenc 1947c.
[137] Poulenc 1993, p. 40.
[138] Schmidt 1995, FP 121, p. 339. Vilmorin crossed out words 2-4 of the title.
[139] Poulenc 1994, p. 1033.

mélodies, many set to Ronsard poems, but also to those of Apollinaire and Laurencin. Leguerney *mélodies* were "distinguished by a courtly elegance of line and supple, sophisticated harmony. At the time they were regarded as second only to those of Poulenc."[140]

COMPOSITIONS AND CONCERTS: FALL 1943

Poulenc remained in Beaulieu until 20 August before going to Brive for five days.[141] He then returned to the Paris region, making a pilgrimage to Nogent-sur-Marne, which he found devoid of the pleasures such as accordion bands and open-air dance halls that he recalled from his youth.[142] Once returned to Noizay, he wrote *Deux poèmes de Louis Aragon*. Though he had first met Aragon at Monnier's Parisian bookstore during World War I, he had never set any of his poetry to music. At summer's end a friend brought back *Les Yeux d'Elsa* from Switzerland. Two poems conformed precisely with his state of mind. Within one week he wrote "C" and "Fêtes galantes."[143]

> This poem ["C" Bernac wrote] evokes the tragic days of May 1940, when a large part of the French population was fleeing before the invading armies. In this horrible exodus, the poet himself, at the Ponts-de-Cé close to Angers, had crossed the Loire, filled with 'overturned vehicles' and 'discarded weapons,' in the total confusion of a 'forsaken France.'[144]

The other poem, "Fêtes galantes," is a sequence of twenty lines, nineteen of which begin with the words "On voit . . ." [You see]. Though cheerful on the surface, underneath Aragon has hidden a poignant description of occupied Paris. Poulenc set the repetitive text in the style of a cabaret song with extremely rapid declamation. As such it makes a remarkable contrast with the tragic and pensive tone of "C." Having heard both *mélodies* in 1945, Koechlin said that "the intense and noble emotion of 'Ponts-de-Cé' breathes the very soul of our wounded country."[145]

Poulenc went to Paris on 25 November to rehearse with Bernac for their 8 December Salle Gaveau recital.[146] The program contained his *Métamorphoses* and *Deux poèmes de Louis Aragon* plus music by Pierre-Alexandre Monsigny, Schubert, Fauré, and Chabrier. The

[140] Griffiths, p. 619.
[141] 17 Aug. [1943] letter to Bernac from Beaulieu in Poulenc 1994, 43-4 (Poulenc 1991, no. 161).
[142] "Mercredi; 5 heures"[Aug. 1943] letter in Poulenc 1994, 43-8 (Poulenc 1991, no. 163).
[143] Poulenc 1947c, p. 512. These poems had been printed clandestinely.
[144] Bernac 1977a, p. 187 (Bernac 1978, p. 172).
[145] Koechlin's 30 Apr. 1945 letter to Poulenc in Poulenc 1994, 45-6 [final version] (Poulenc 1991, no. 176 [first version]).
[146] [Oct. 1943] letter to Jolivet in Poulenc 1994, 43-9.

Germans in the audience apparently failed to grasp the implications of Aragon's poems.[147]

At year's end Poulenc may have traveled to Brussels on 9 December with Charles Munch to join a Belgian pianist for a performance of his two-piano concerto.[148] Neveu also wanted Poulenc to perform his violin sonata with her in Reims, but it is unclear if he accepted.[149] Finally, he continued his study of French scores and read Heinrich Strobel's "noteworthy" 1940 book *Claude Debussy*.[150] During 1943 Poulenc made three recordings of Debussy *mélodies* with soprano Lucienne Tragin featuring selections from *Ariettes oubliées* including "Aquarelles no. 2," and *Le Martyre de Saint Sébastien*.[151]

DARKEST DAYS OF THE WAR: JANUARY 1944 TO THE LIBERATION OF PARIS

The Allies pressed their way up the Italian peninsula to Rome during the first part of 1944, but their progress was slow. The French Colonial Corps, the United States 5th Army, the Polish Corps of the 8th Army, and other groups moved inexorably toward Rome, which fell to the Allies on 4 June. Florence, 256 kilometers to the north, fell on 12 August before autumn rains further slowed the advance. Major developments also took place in France. Though planned for May, "Operation Overlord," the Allied invasion of northern France, finally began on 6 June "D-Day" when 156,000 men landed on the Normandy coast. By 31 July the Americans had breached German defenses at Avranches, the Normandy gateway to Brittany. By 17 August, operating near the Loire River, Americans took Orléans, and on 24 August a French division liberated Paris. Troops also landed in southern France on 15 August taking Marseilles on the 23rd and Lyon in September. Other forces drove north into Belgium, entering Brussels on 29 August, and crossing the Moselle near Metz on 5 September.

Throughout the winter and spring, Poulenc rode out the war at Noizay, sheltering refugee friends from Amboise and Tours. It was an alarming period which the historian Matila Simon called "a time

---

[147] Daniel, p. 272 and Penrose 1945, p. 33.
[148] [Oct. 1943] letter to Jolivet in Poulenc 1994, 43-9.
[149] Excerpt from Neveu's 16 Oct. 1943 letter to Poulenc in Poulenc 1994, p. 544, note 2. Neveu also sent corrections to proofs of the Sonata for Violin and Piano.
[150] [8 Nov. 1943] letter to Roland-Manuel in Poulenc 1994, 43-13.
[151] French Columbia (LFX 650 and LFX 651) and Voix de son Maître (COLC 317) respectively. See Appendix 3. Tragin made her Paris debut on 5 Mar. 1932 advertised as a "Soprano léger de La Monnaie de Bruxelles." She was back in Paris assisting Titta Ruffo in a program of duets at the Salle Gaveau on 24 Mar. 1933 during which she also sang something by Poulenc. See *Le Guide du concert et des théâtres lyriques* 18 (26 Feb. 1932), 597 and 19 (17 Mar. 1933), 669 respectively. It is likely, therefore, that Poulenc had known her for about a decade.

of hope and a time of dying."[152] Jean Cocteau, whom Poulenc visited on 2 February, reported in his diary that Poulenc's best friend [Raymond Destouches?] had been arrested a week earlier.[153] Poulenc's concert schedule slowed dramatically. Moreover, the chaotic scene at Noizay, where Poulenc lodged displaced friends, sometimes caused him to abandon composing altogether.

> I am taking further advantage of a small lull in the domestic storm to tell you about things other than power failures, the lack of water, missing keys, refugees, etc. It is not amusing day after day, I assure you, and a week ago I even reached the point of envying you your precarious nocturnal electricity while here we were going to bed in complete darkness and carrying water from the foot of the garden. Moreover, the house is full. After the bombardment of Amboise, I went to gather in old mother La Rochette and then the group from Tours—Raymond's [Destouches'] mother, father, and sister. The elderly prima donna is at our table. The others eat in the outside kitchen. As I was taxed by four refugees, I prefer it this way, but things are not going smoothly and the situation is rather delicate, as always when the social levels are not the same. [. . .] I dream of nothing more than a long cure of solitude after the war.[154]

Though Poulenc felt claustrophobic during these dark days at Le Grand Coteau before the Liberation, he was able to escape to Paris for a few concerts. On 5 March he performed his Concerto in D minor with Mme Mercenier at a "Société des Concerts" event in the Salle du Conservatoire under the Belgian conductor Franz André.[155] The day before, Poulenc's friend Louis Laloy, a champion of modern French music and a man of great intelligence and vast culture, died in Dôle. The 31 March issue of *L'Information musicale* contained an "Hommage à Louis Laloy (1874-1944)" for which Poulenc contributed a short letter.[156] Poulenc also may have traveled to Brussels to perform the Concerto in D minor (with André?).[157] Then, on 4 April in the same hall, he performed *Aubade* as part of the "Pléiade" series under André Cluytens.[158] Claude Roy, a member of the Resistance and a communist sympathizer, wrote Poulenc a touching let-

---

[152] Simon, p. 116.

[153] Cocteau 1989a, p. 462.

[154] 24 June [1944] letter to Bernac in Poulenc 1994, 44-4 (Poulenc 1991, no. 164).

[155] *L'Information musicale* 4 (25 Feb. 1944), 208.

[156] Poulenc 1944. Others paying homage include Henri Rabaud, Paul Mazon, Romain Rolland, Pierre de Bréville, Paul-Marie Masson, Cocteau, Gabriel Grovlez, Dupré, Gustave Samazeuilh, René Peter, Jean Chantavoine, Poueigh, Lifar, and Hoérée.

[157] 11 Mar. 1944 letter to Koechlin from Collaer in Koechlin, pp. 120-1.

[158] *L'Information musicale* 4 (31 Mar. 1944). Michel Ciry also wrote of this concert in his diary. Ciry, entry for 5 Apr. 1944.

ter telling him how much his music meant, particularly the fine performance of *Aubade*.[159] Poulenc probably also heard the April reprise of *Les Animaux modèles* at the Opéra.

Although he composed little during this period, Poulenc did complete music for Jean Anouilh's play *Le Voyageur sans bagage* performed
at the Théâtre de la Michodière and adapted for an Éclair-Journal
film production.[160] We know virtually nothing about this work except that the first public screening took place on 23 February 1944.
Michel Ciry had a chance encounter with Poulenc at the Concorde
métro station on 21 January.[161] Poulenc said he was exhausted from
having just recorded the score. Had Milhaud been in France, the
music he wrote when the play was first produced at the Théâtre des
Mathurins on 16 February 1937 might have been used. However,
Milhaud was living in the United States and his unpublished music
was not available.[162] The few concerts and compositions of early
1944 were but a pale prologue to the real work of the May-October
period during which Poulenc completed *Les Mamelles de Tirésias*.

LES MAMELLES DE TIRÉSIAS: HOMAGE TO APOLLINAIRE AND MILHAUD

As is frequently the case with Poulenc, *Les Mamelles* was in his mind
years before its serious composition was undertaken. Precisely what
place these seemingly dormant works occupied in Poulenc's psyche
cannot be guessed, but when he moved them from the contempla-
tive realm to his work table he often did so with great energy and
consuming devotion. Such was the case with *Les Mamelles*.

Apollinaire revised his play for production in 1917, a time when
Europe was fully involved in World War I, and the message he delivered proclaimed "the need to repopulate and re-establish
France."[163] Surely Poulenc was sympathetic to Apollinaire's advice
when he took up the work during World War II. The plot is as bizarre as the music is witty, and Poulenc made a point of explaining
why he had made a few changes to Apollinaire's original.

> Since Apollinaire's play, except for the Prologue and the last scene,
> dates from 1903, I consider that I have a perfect right to place the
> action in an epoch that is for me typically Apollinarian, to wit the
> years 1910-1914 (*Alcools* appeared 20 April 1913). I think that exoti-
> cism also has nothing to do with the story, so I have preferred to lo-

---

[159] Roy's 10 Apr. [1944] letter in Poulenc 1994, 44-2.
[160] See Schmidt 1995, FP 123.
[161] Ciry, entry for 21 Jan. 1944.
[162] Milhaud's version was originally scored for pn., vn., and cl. Collaer 1988, p. 327.
[163] Sams 1992, p. 173. See also the mention of the play at the end of Chapter III.

cate Apollinaire's Zanzibar somewhere between Nice and Monte Carlo, where the poet grew up.[164]

In the prologue, sung before a draw curtain, the Director (baritone) exhorts the audience to take what follows seriously. "Have children, you who have scarcely made any," he pleads. When the draw curtain rises Thérèse (soprano) rails against her husband declaring that she is bored with a woman's lot and prefers to be a soldier, waiter, or even president of the republic. She grows a beard, opens her bodice to release her breasts (two colored balloons), and completes her disguise by adding a mustache. Her Husband assumes she has been the victim of an assassin. The metamorphosis complete, she sets off to make her fortune in a masculine world. Two clowns, Lacouf (tenor) and Presto (baritone), enter and argue about whether or not they are in Paris or Zanzibar. Drawing guns, they kill each other only to return at the end of Act I on roller-skates. As the act closes, in a reversal of roles, Thérèse has become Tirésias and the Husband laments "her" desertion of bearing children, resolving to find a way to accomplish the task unilaterally! Accordingly he promises a policeman (baritone), who has arrived on the scene, that he will show him how to assume responsibility for repopulating France.

Act II opens with an entr'acte followed by a couples dance in the style of a syncopated sarabande played by a music-hall band. "The band is asked to sing a yowling chorus portraying the 40,049 children that the Husband has produced in one day."[165] When a journalist arrives to interview him about his prowess, and suggests that the Husband must be rich, he is told that in fact the children are supporting him. One is a successful journalist who has already written a best seller. The journalist is dispatched after greedily asking for a loan and the Husband makes a journalist of his own by pouring ink and glue into one of the incubators adorning the stage. The resulting son, however, is a master of yellow journalism and tries to blackmail his father on the next day's news before leaving to work. To feed his numerous children, the Husband enlists the aid of a Cartomancer (Thérèse/Tirésias in further disguise) to supply ration cards. Arrested by a policeman, the Cartomancer strangles him before revealing her true identity. The policeman is revived and Thérèse's true identity is restored amidst the fetching of balloons which she releases. The *opéra bouffe* ends with a jovial nonsense chorus of exhortation linked with the Prologue.

---

[164] Translation and facsimile of Poulenc's original French in the program booklet accompanying the recording (Angel 35090).
[165] Sams 1992, p. 174.

Hear, ye French, the lessons of war, and have children, you who have scarcely made any. Scratch yourself if you itch, love black or white. It is merrier when it changes. It suffices to see it right. Dear audience, go make children.

As would later be the case with *Dialogues des Carmélites,* Poulenc relied on Bernac's guidance concerning vocal range and tessitura. They must have discussed such matters in May because on 6 June ("D Day") Bernac wrote a detailed letter containing his opinions.[166] Their letters reveal that roles were conceived in terms of other operas or singers: "Aria à la Iago for Beckmans or Etcheverry..."[167] or "Tirésias' aria (with grateful thanks to *Manon*)."[168] He studied various operatic scores for inspiration carefully reading Ravel's *L'Heure espagnole.* Poulenc also had Bernac's voice in mind, and his Uncle Royer once remarked, "Oh! I can just hear Bernac singing that." Poulenc acknowledged other influences.

> There are many scenic details which have suggested the music to me. I think the situations themselves will be enough, because in the theater I hardly ever rely much on the power of words. (It would be difficult to imagine "Fêtes galantes" on the stage.)

By 24 June the Act I division had been determined and he was close to finishing a sketch of the Prologue and Scene 1. Events at Noizay over the next month, however, were hardly conducive to continued composing.[169] He summoned a doctor from Asnières (calling those from Amboise quacks) to treat his "rheumatism" which was spreading to his shoulder. The new diagnosis, however, led to treatment for an attack of acute arthritis. The opera was still on his mind, but he had problems.

> Touraine is killing me, as you said. It exasperates me that each evening I become feverish, just as I did in Rome. Between seven and eight in the evening I literally suffocate, and the remainder of the time I curse this place, its domestic problems, and my own anxiety. For three weeks I have done no work because all this is enough to curdle the milk of my *Mamelles.* I do not know what to think of this work and I prefer to let it rest. Obviously, give me a room near Autun and some solitude and inspiration would return quickly. Yet everyone must pay his share

---

[166] Fragment in Poulenc 1994, p. 555, note 1 (Poulenc 1991, no. 164, note 2).

[167] "Vendredi soir" [9 June 1944] letter to Bernac in Poulenc 1994, 44-3. Henri-Bertrand Etcheverry, who debuted at the Paris Opéra in 1932, was especially noted for his interpretation of Russian roles such as Boris Godunov.

[168] 24 June [1944] letter in Poulenc 1994, 44-4 (Poulenc 1991, no. 164). The next two quotes are also from this letter.

[169] "Vendredi 30" [June 1944], 14 July [1944], and "samedi" [22 July 1944] letters to Bernac in Poulenc 1994, 44-6, 44-7 (Poulenc 1991, no. 165), and 44-8 (Poulenc 1991, no. 166) respectively.

and mine is pretty thin. I try to escape from here in thought. A photo album of Paris charms and numbs me like a shot of morphine.[170]

A visit from Jacques Février and Claude Rostand,[171] who came to Noizay by bicycle, and another from Paul Rouart helped take his mind off his complaints.[172]

In spite of protestations to the contrary, Poulenc plugged away at his opera, and by late July it was drafted except for the two finales and the entr'acte. He wrote Sauguet that the work was dedicated to Milhaud to celebrate his return to France.[173] Early in August Poulenc told Bernac that *Les Mamelles* would not surprise him, since its antecedents included "Dans le jardin d'Anna," from *Deux poèmes de Guillaume Apollinaire*, and *Banalités*.[174] Three weeks later the unfinished opera was being recopied; its length exceeded fifty minutes.[175] Precisely when Poulenc completed the two finales and the entr'acte is unknown, but Michel Ciry reports that he played, mimed, and sang the opera at the Tuals' home on 24 November 1944 and that by May 1945 he was orchestrating, a task he completed by 9 August.[176] Roger Désormière told Paul Collaer that he hoped to conduct it during the next season.[177] Discussion of these aspects of the opera, as well as its ultimate performance, are reserved for Chapter X.

OTHER ACTIVITIES AND COMPOSITIONS TO THE END OF THE YEAR

While working on *Les Mamelles* Poulenc also devoted time to *Montparnasse* and *Hyde Park* (FP 127), two *mélodies* on Apollinaire texts. His interest in setting *Montparnasse* had first been piqued in 1941 when he composed music for lines 10-11. Then, during 1943, music for lines 8-9 came to him. Much of the end of the *mélodie* was composed in 1943 and the opening lines in Paris during 1944.[178] Setting *Montparnasse* was a lengthy struggle.

---

[170] 27 July [1944] letter to Marie-Blanche in Poulenc 1994, 44-9 (Poulenc 1991, no. 167).

[171] "Samedi" [22 July 1944] letter to Bernac in Poulenc 1994, 44-8 (Poulenc 1991, no. 166).

[172] "Samedi" [29 July 1944] letters to Bernac in Poulenc 1994, 44-13 and [26 July 1944] to Agathe Rouart-Valéry in Poulenc 1994, 44-10 (Poulenc 1991, no. 168).

[173] 28 July [1944] letter to Sauguet in Poulenc 1994, 44-12 (Poulenc 1991, no. 170). Milhaud himself learned of this fact from Poulenc's 1 July 1945 letter in Poulenc 1994, 45-12 (Poulenc 1991, no. 181).

[174] "Dimanche" [6 Aug. 1944] letter in Poulenc 1994, 44-15.

[175] "Dimanche" [27 Aug. 1944] letter in Poulenc 44-16 (Poulenc 1991, no. 169).

[176] Ciry, entry for 24 Nov. 1944. Paul Derenne, André Schaeffner, and the Gallimards were also present for Poulenc's impromptu reading of the score.

[177] 16 Nov. 1944 letter in Collaer 1996, 44-5. He did not.

[178] Poulenc 1993, p. 42 (Poulenc 1985, pp. 74-5). "Le Pont" was also cobbled together over a period of years. Schmidt 1995, FP 131, p. 370 and Chapter X.

I took four years to write *Montparnasse*. I do not regret the care I lavished on it because it is probably one of my best songs. [. . .] After this I let these fragments macerate and drew everything together in three days, in Paris in February 1945. This manner of working by fits and starts, may be surprising. It is, however, quite customary for me when it comes to songs. [. . .] Because I *never* transpose music which I have just thought of for a certain line, or even for several words, into another key to make it easier for myself, it follows that the piecing together is often difficult and I need to stand back in order to locate the exact place where I am obliged to modulate.[179]

The two *mélodies* [Poulenc added], *Montparnasse* and *Hyde Park* by Apollinaire, are nearly finished except for a word here or there. Given that, in some strange prescient way, the second of the two is presently impossible to sing, there is no hurry.[180]

Once again, Poulenc's recollection of when these *mélodies* were finished is at odds with the extant manuscripts and printed versions issued by Eschig in late 1945. The sources suggest a January 1945 completion date.[181] Although he praised *Montparnasse* as one of his best *mélodies*, he dismissed *Hyde Park* saying that like "Paganini" it functions merely as a bridge to something else, not as a fitting conclusion.

While working on *Les Mamelles de Tirésias* in June 1944 Poulenc became increasingly interested in the music of Olivier Messiaen and asked Bernac about possible performances he might have heard.

24 June [1944] to Bernac:

Did the Messiaen performances take place and did you hear the *Liturgies*? I have been through much of his music again. When he remains faithful to his own methods *Visions* is truly remarkable; in other more contrived pages Dukas' influence is annoying.[182]

Nearly a year later on the 27th of March 1945, Poulenc wrote to Milhaud in California.

The ascension of Messiaen has been the most significant musical event. You will, in fact, find a fanatical sect surrounding this musician who, for all the impossible literary jargon, is nevertheless remarkable. Messiaen's followers are quite against Stravinsky's "last period." For

---

[179] Poulenc 1993, p. 42 (Poulenc 1989, pp. 74-5).
[180] 24 June [1944] letter to Bernac in Poulenc 1994, 44-4 (Poulenc 1991, no. 164).
[181] Manuscripts and prints cited in Schmidt 1995, FP 127, pp. 356-7.
[182] Poulenc 1994, 44-4 (Poulenc 1991, no. 164). The pieces in question are *Trois petites liturgies de la présence divine* and *Les Visions de l'Amen*. On 14 July [1944] Poulenc thanked Bernac for having sent one of Messiaen's scores. Poulenc 1994, 44-7 (Poulenc 1991, no. 165).

them, Igor's music ends with *Le Sacre.* They booed *Danses concertantes,* which I love. But this makes things lively. This is what it is all about.[183]

While in Noizay during the late summer of 1944, Poulenc developed near paranoia about the fate of Paris and his many friends. Often without electricity, deprived of newspapers, and with unpredictable deliveries of mail by private trucks, he fell victim to rumors. He heard that one hundred thousand had been killed in Paris alone, that the Opéra had burned, that Les Invalides and other buildings had been destroyed, that the Luxembourg Gardens had been heavily shelled, and that Maurice Chevalier had been shot. He recounted the liberation of his zone by Americans sweeping east from Rennes and proudly proclaimed Raymond Destouches' heroism in guiding American tanks against sniper attacks in Amboise, crediting him with convincing the Americans not to fire at the Chateau itself. "The day the Americans arrived," Poulenc said, "I triumphantly placed my Cantata *[Figure humaine]* on the studio desk, under my flag, at the window."[184]

In late October or early November the BBC dispatched Véra Lindsay, one of their Radio Newsreel producers, to meet with Poulenc and to discuss the English premiere of the cantata. Poulenc sent a score back with her, and Victor Hely-Hutchinson, Director of Music at the BBC, responded enthusiastically offering a studio performance during February or early March with Leslie Woodgate conducting approximately sixty professional singers.[185] Hely-Hutchinson, himself a pianist and composer, was most anxious to learn how to obtain scores and how much rehearsal time would be required. Poulenc's answer nearly a month later stressed the difficulty of the music and requested that sufficient time be allowed for its mastery. Moreover, some sections were in twelve parts and sixty performers would be too few. Eighty-four performers or seven to a part would be better. He was also concerned about the singer's French diction because no English translation existed. Poulenc said he would be coming to England with Bernac in January 1945 and lobbied for a performance of his Sonata for Violin and Piano (V).[186] His publisher Paul Rouart wrote to Hely-Hutchinson on 6 December stating Paul Eluard's wish that Roland Penrose do the English singing translation and Poulenc's desire that his old friend Rollo Myers view the results to make sure the translation fit the music.[187] On 27 November Poulenc played two favorite works for his friends:

[183] Poulenc 1994, 45-4 (Poulenc 1991, no. 175).
[184] [27 Aug. 1944] letter to Bernac in Poulenc 1994, 44-16 (Poulenc 1991, no. 169).
[185] Hely-Hutchinson's 6 Nov. 1944 letter to Poulenc in Poulenc 1994, 44-17.
[186] Letter to Hely-Hutchinson [received on 1 Dec. 1944] in Poulenc 1994, 44-18.
[187] Fragment of Rouart's 6 Dec. 1944 letter in Poulenc 1994, p. 576, note 2.

Five o'clock at Marie-Laure de Noailles' home, with Picasso, Eluard. Poulenc played *Les Mamelles de Tirésias* and Eluard's poem *[Figure humaine]* sung *a cappella*. What strikes us in *Mamelles* is the grace, pungency, and exquisite freshness of the text. Picasso said to me: "It is perhaps due to Poulenc that we notice it." The distinctiveness of Poulenc is to place the text in the foreground. Eluard's poem "Liberté" wins out. We wonder if the text sung in this manner is not the sole possible form of declamation for a poem. The actor distorts the text or recites it dryly. Even Francis' singing showed us how his musical intelligence heightens both the harshness and the charm of a text.[188]

Figure humaine was also heard at the Tuals' home on 21 December 1944.[189] Poulenc played it with Bernac turning pages in the company of the Eluards, Cocteau, Albert Camus, Max-Pol Fouchet, the Albert Olliviers, Lise Deharme, Jacques Parsons, Christian Bérard, and Marcel Herrand. Eluard inscribed a score "To Denise and Roland Tual in gratitude for the first performance at their home, with a heart full of friendship, 21 December 1944."[190]

As the year came to an optimistic close, Poulenc gave a recital with Suzanne Peignot in late November and completed two other compositions: incidental music for James Barrie's play *La Nuit de la Saint-Jean* (FP 124)[191] and *Un soir de neige* (FP 126), a six-minute chamber cantata for six mixed voices or chorus a cappella in four sections. Little is known about the former, which was apparently in production at the Comédie des Champs-Élysées from 11 December 1944 through early February 1945. None of Poulenc's music survives, and it attracted scant notice in the French press. The brief cantata, set to Eluard poems from *Poésie et Vérité 1942* and *Dignes et vivre* (1944),[192] was composed between 24-26 December. It is dedi-

[188] Cocteau 1989a, pp. 576-7.

[189] Earlier in the month, Poulenc heard a 4-hand reduction of Michel Ciry's Symphony together with Paul Collaer and Roland Bourdariat. Ciry, entry of 1 Dec. 1944. He was also at the Polignac's on 22 Dec. for an evening of music, at which he appeared to doze occasionally. When some of Ciry's own songs were brought out, Ciry sensed mild jealousy on Poulenc's part. Ciry, on 22 Dec. 1944, mentions that Louise de Vilmorin and François Valery (both of whom left early), Annette Dieudonné, Prince Pierre de Monaco, Pierre Souvchinsky, André Zwoboda, Léo Préger, Bourdariat, Sauguet, Julius Katchen and Nora Auric were also present.

[190] Tual, p. 223. I have been unable to locate the sketches drawn by Cocteau that Tual indicates were done that evening.

[191] Concerning the recital see Auric's review "Œuvre de Paul Hindemith," *Les Lettres françaises* (2 Dec. 1944), 7. Barrie's play was originally entitled *Dear Brutus*. Reviews indicate that décor by J.-A. Bonnaud was not in harmony with the text.

[192] Eluard was paid 2,000 francs for use of the poems. [Spring 1945] letter to Eluard in Poulenc 1994, 45-10 (Poulenc 1991, no. 179).

cated to Marie-Blanche de Polignac.[193] *Un soir de neige* closed a period in which Eluard's works were a source of comfort for Poulenc. Grateful that his life and property had been spared, he wrote: "When I think that Noizay is so completely untouched I almost feel ashamed. I trust that *Figure humaine* and *Les Mamelles* will be a sufficient tribute from a Frenchman."[194]

Writing from abroad in later 1944 as part of a forum on the plight of musicians in Europe during World War II, Milhaud summarized events in Paris as French musicians reacted to German occupation.

> I have just had very interesting news from Paris about the magnificent participation of the musicians in the "Resistance." During these four years I have sometimes had news from Francis Poulenc who managed to reach me by people who escaped from France and sent me a letter from Spain. He wrote about the magnificent activity of the French musicians, writing and performing for the French public. I know now that Poulenc, Louis Durey, Georges Auric and Roger Désormière were active in the Resistance. Paul Paray, the conductor of the Concerts Colonne refused to direct orchestras from which the Jews had been expelled. Claude Delvincourt was offered the post of Director of the Paris Conservatoire by the Vichy government. He accepted because he knew he could help the Resistance. He became one of the important persons in the clandestine movement in which he was known as Monsieur Julien. His office was transformed into a counterfeiting headquarters. None of the Conservatoire students was deported to Germany and during the last weeks they all enlisted in the French Forces of the Interior or in the Maquis for the battle of the liberation of Paris. During these days of fighting in the capital, Roland-Manuel was in the building of the French National Radio. He was with Manuel Rosenthal (former conductor of the Radio Orchestre National who, being a Jew, was ousted), Herman Moiens and Roland Bourdariat. All around this building there were shooting, barricades, fires; at the peril of their lives, they managed to take down, by dictation through the Moscow radio, the music of the new Soviet anthem, to orchestrate it and to copy the parts so that it could be performed with the other allied national hymns at the very moment of the liberation of Paris.[195]

---

[193] Chimènes found the manuscript in the Polignac collection and printed its inscription in Poulenc 1994, p. 590, note 3.
[194] [27 Aug. 1944] letter to Bernac in Poulenc 1994, 44-16 (Poulenc 1991, no. 169).
[195] Milhaud 1944, p. 6. At least some of Milhaud's information came from a 17 Jan. 1945 letter from Koechlin in Paris. Koechlin, pp. 128-30.

X

The Post-War Years
1945-1949

A RETURN TO LONDON WITH BERNAC: JANUARY 1945

"I have been in London since yesterday. You can imagine my delight and what this means in terms of freedom refound."[1] With these lines, penned to Milhaud on 3 January 1945 and carried abroad by a military officer departing for New York, Poulenc expressed his joy as travel limitations eased even if passage remained difficult and unpredictable. London was particularly important because Chester had published his earliest works, the BBC had advanced his international reputation during the later 1930s, and critics and the public alike had enthusiastically acknowledged his concerts.[2] Stimulated by friends, conversation, and locales he loved, Poulenc was particularly moved by his London reception as was Bernac. Years later Bernac told an interviewer for *France Culture:* "Imagine our joy at finally being able to leave France. Stepping out on the Wigmore Hall stage, the entire audience rose and my emotion was such that instead of beginning to sing, I began to weep. . . ."[3]

Remaining in London for approximately two weeks, Poulenc gave a barrage of concerts and made various appearances. The 5 January *London Times* reported how his visit began.

[1] 3 Jan. [1945] letter to Milhaud in Poulenc 1994, 45-1 (Poulenc 1991, no. 172). Poulenc gave Milhaud a summary of this own recent compositional activity as well as that of Auric, Sauguet, Honegger, Ibert, Françaix, and Messiaen.
[2] Poulenc 1954, p. 104: "Very graciously, dear Benjamin Britten accepted to play my *Concerto for Two Pianos* at Albert Hall. You can imagine, after four years of occupation, my pleasure at seeing England again to which I owe, thanks to Stravinsky, my first publisher, Chester, and my most faithful public in Europe."
[3] Excerpt of Bernac's interview with Gérard Michel, 20 Nov. 1970-15 Jan. 1971, in Poulenc 1994, p. 579, note 5 (Poulenc 1991, no. 174, note 1).

The committee of the London Philharmonic Orchestra gave a reception at 53, Welbeck Street yesterday evening [4 Jan. 1945] to M. Francis Poulenc. Among those present were: Mme. Renée Massigli, M. and Mme. Ja[c]ques Emile Paris, M. Pierre Bernac, Mr. Thomas Russell, M. and Mme. Louis Roché, Professor and Mme. Paul Vaucher, General Flipo, the Hon. Anthony and Mrs. Chaplin, Sir Kenneth Clark, Lady Colefax, Mr. Leslie Boosey, Mr. Benjamin Britten, Mr. Peter Pears, Mr. Scott Goddard, Mr. Edwin Evans, and Professor E. J. Dent.[4]

Poulenc's first performance of the Concerto in D minor, assisted by Benjamin Britten, was at Royal Albert Hall on 6 January.[5] This began a lasting friendship between fellow composers. The critic W. H. Haddon Squire wrote:

> Time has not staled the easy wit and charm of a composition that seems to have flowed from the pen with the naturalness and inevitability that mark a work by Mozart. Here the elegance is that of the aristocratic Faubourg-Saint-Honoré, far, to borrow another Cocteau phrase, from "the kind of novelty which thinks that novelty necessarily walks on its head, because the public looks at it and listens to it upside down." This concerto is certainly original, but it keeps on its feet and moves with grace and distinction. Poulenc and Britten are both excellent pianists; and aided by the London Philharmonic Orchestra under Basil Cameron, they achieved a performance that must have pleased the composer as much as it did the audience.[6]

On the 7th the Bernac/Poulenc duo performed works of Duparc, Fauré, Debussy, and Poulenc at Wigmore Hall, and they were busy again on the 8th recording Fauré, Debussy, and Poulenc for the BBC. An internal BBC memorandum suggests that after the recording session Poulenc was invited to an informal dinner attended by Victor Hely-Hutchinson [Director of Music], J.L. Herbage [Deputy Director of Music], Edward Lockspeiser [Assistant in Overseas Music Department], Leslie Woodgate, Rollo Myers, Elizabeth Poston [European Music Supervisor], and Véra Lindsay [Radio News Reel Producer]. After dinner he played his cantata *Figure humaine*.[7] On the 9th *mélodies* by Fauré, Debussy, and Poulenc were performed at the National Gallery. His link to England reestablished, Poulenc's return to France was duly noted by the press:

[4] See p. 6b.
[5] Basil Cameron conducted Mendelssohn's *Ruy Blas* overture, Poulenc's Concerto, and Tchaikovsky's Symphony no. 5; Britten conducted his own *Sinfonia da Requiem*. For a fresh assessment of the Poulenc-Britten association, particularly as it relates to Aldeburgh, see Buckland/Chimènes: i.
[6] Review in F-Pn (Fonds Montpensier).
[7] 5 Jan. 1945 memorandum entitled "Entertainment of Poulenc and Bernac" in Francis Poulenc Artists file 1a (1937-1945) GB-Lbbc.

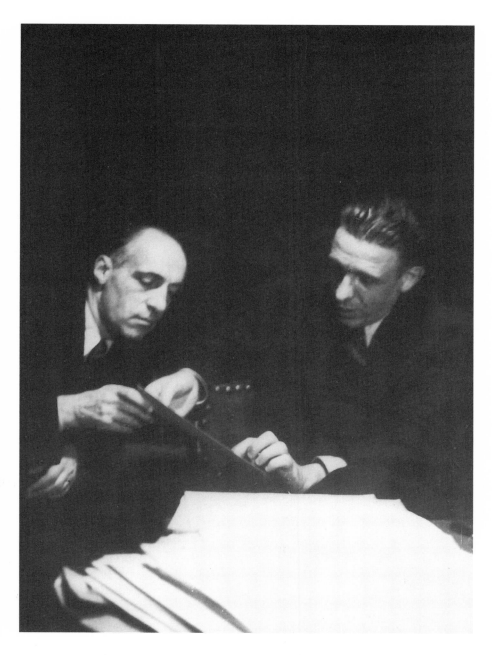

Plate 16: Bernac and Poulenc in Brussels 1945 taken at St. Bernard's Palace, home of Rose and Auguste Lambiotte. (Collection of Rosine Lambiotte-Donhauser and used with her kind permission.)

PARIS BOAT-TRAIN LEAVES

The first civilian boat-train from Britain to the Continent since May 1940, left a London station of the Southern Railway yesterday [15 Jan. 1945] morning as arranged. Until a few hours before the several hundred passengers did not know from what station and port they would leave or at what port on the other side they would arrive. Detectives checked the credentials of all passengers, who were mainly representatives of firms whose goods are needed by the French Government in carrying out their reconstruction programme. The final destination of most of the passengers is Paris. They included M. Francis Poulenc, the French composer, and M. Pierre Bernac, the singer.[8]

PARIS CONCERTS IN FEBRUARY

Early in February Poulenc joined Geneviève Joy, Monique Haas, and Pierre Sancan in a performance of *Les Noces* at a Stravinsky festival. They were accompanied by the Orchestre National de la Radiodiffusion française, Manuel Rosenthal conducting.[9] On the 18th he privately recorded *Trois mouvements perpétuels*, Sonata for Violin and Piano (with André Asselin), *Poèmes de Ronsard* (nos. 1 and 4) and *Cinq poèmes de Max Jacob* (with Suzanne Peignot).[10] Performing preoccupied him, and except for touching up *Hyde Park* and *Montparnasse* in January he had only a String Quartet (FP 133) on his desk.[11] He did little composing until summer, because March and April were filled with concerts in England and France.

RETURN TO ENGLAND IN MARCH: CONCERTS AND THE *FIGURE HUMAINE* PREMIERE

Poulenc and Bernac spent much of March in London staying at the Hyde Park Hotel. In addition to concerts accompanying Bernac, Poulenc performed with the English soprano Maggie Teyte, and the French violinist Ginette Neveu in forums ranging from BBC broadcasts to benefit recitals.[12] His repertoire included English premieres, the most important being that of *Figure humaine* on a 24 March BBC broadcast. Those recitals and broadcasts that are known are listed in Appendix 2.

---

[8] *London Times* (16 Jan. 1945), 4g.

[9] Bloch, p. 217 lists the recording made on this occasion. The performance was on 5 Feb.

[10] Bloch, pp. 214, 193, 164, and 162 respectively. See Appendix 3.

[11] 27 Mar. 1945 letter to Milhaud from London in Poulenc 1994, 45-4 (Poulenc 1991, no. 175). The quartet will be discussed below.

[12] After his return to France, Poulenc thanked Edward James for a package containing among other things chocolate and cheese. He told James to return quickly to Europe, saying that he had passed nostalgically by James' Wimpole Street address. Poulenc 1994, 45-8 and note 5.

Several concerts are of particular interest. On the 20th Poulenc joined august company to honor the renowned British critic Edwin Evans, who had died in London on 3 March. An article in *The Musical Times*, for which Evans wrote in 1919-20, describes the occasion.

> At the Fyvie Hall (Regent Street Polytechnic) on Mar. 20 a representative gathering of musicians paid tribute to Edwin Evans. The principal speakers were Arthur Bliss who presided, Prof. E. J. Dent, Francis Poulenc and Marie Rambert. Harriet Cohen played piano pieces by [Arnold] Bax, Debussy and Falla. Maggie Teyte and Pierre Bernac, accompanied by M. Poulenc, sang the closing scene from "Pelléas et Mélisande."[13]

Another was the 27 March Wigmore Hall performance with Bernac featuring English premieres of cycles by Maurice Jaubert, Jean Françaix, and Poulenc. During their English sojourn the Bernac/Poulenc duo also recorded Fauré's *La Bonne Chanson*.[14]

The highlight of Poulenc's second post-war London visit, however, was the BBC performance of *Figure humaine* conducted by Leslie Woodgate. The composer was disappointed that it was sung in English.[15] He recorded a twelve-minute script on his cantata for later broadcast and expressed interest in attending some rehearsals.[16] According to a 5 March internal BBC memorandum from the concerts manager Miss M. E. Crewdson, rehearsals of the BBC Revue Chorus augmented by 28 extra Bedford choristers were scheduled to begin on 8 March and continue through Saturday, 24 March.[17] It was suggested that Poulenc be invited to attend the final rehearsals beginning on 21 March. An Elizabeth Poston memorandum states that *Figure humaine* embodied France's fortitude and sufferings and was, therefore, a very important work for the BBC to disseminate. At the conclusion of the broadcast, Victor Hely-Hutchinson spoke to the guests, who were entertained in the Council Chamber with coffee and sandwiches. He noted that the BBC was exceedingly grateful to Charles Munch, Nicole Henriot, Paul Paray, Yvonne Lefébure, Roger Désormière, and Ginette Neveu, who had all given BBC broad-

---

[13] *The Musical Times* 86 (Apr. 1945), 108. Poulenc also published a tribute in the literary monthly *Adam*. Poulenc 1946f.

[14] His Master's Voice (DB 8931/3).

[15] 27 Mar. 1945 letter to Milhaud in Poulenc 1994, 45-4 (Poulenc 1991, no. 175).

[16] Documents at GB-Lbbc indicate that Alec Robertson made the local arrangements with Juilian Herbage. Francis Poulenc Artists File 1a (1937-1945).

[17] Memorandum at GB-Lbbc Francis Poulenc Artists File 1a (1937-1945). Other rehearsals were scheduled for 14 and 15, 21, 22 and 23, and 24. The final rehearsal and recording took place from 6:15-9:15 pm at St. Hilda's Convent, Sheldon Road, Maida Vale. The run-through and balance test was at 7:30 pm and the transmission from 8:30-9:00 pm on 25 Mar., both at the Concert Hall, London.

casts in the previous five months. He also lauded the Bernac/
Poulenc duo especially thanking Poulenc for the opportunity to
premiere *Figure humaine*. In response, the French Ambassador and
Poulenc praised the BBC for their excellent performance and the
suitability of having the premiere of a work of liberation written in
captive France performed in England.

When the broadcast took place, a technical glitch developed.
Transmission lines were needed for military purposes and so it was
arranged for Radio France to receive and retransmit the broadcast
from the BBC Home Service. Inexplicably, the plan was not carried
out and only those French who could pick up the direct BBC broadcast were able to enjoy the work.[18] Unable to hear the broadcast,
Georges Auric wrote an article on the cantata for *Les Lettres françaises*
which ended with the fervent hope that another broadcast could
take place.[19] The invited but absent Paul Eluard sent Poulenc a marvelous poem inscribed "A Francis Poulenc" which said that he did
not listen to himself, but rather heard himself through Poulenc.[20]
Performances of *Figure humaine* were few during Poulenc's lifetime,
and no Parisian performance took place until 1947.[21]

POULENC'S INAUGURAL "FESTIVAL DE MÉLODIES"

Poulenc next prepared for the first "Festival de Mélodies" exclusively featuring his songs and attended the premiere of *Un soir de
neige* at a La Pléiade concert in the Salle du Conservatoire on 21
April 1945.[22] This concert also featured Olivier Messiaen's *Trois petites liturgies de la présence divine* and the premiere of Milhaud's *Quatrains valaisans* for a cappella chorus.[23] According to Messiaen "the

[18] Hely-Hutchinson's 26 Mar. 1945 memorandum in GB-Lbbc Francis Poulenc
Artists File 1a (1937-1945). A separate guest list contains approximately fifty
typed names and six handwritten additions. W. R. Anderson noted that "This
was the first time that listeners in freed France had heard the B.B.C. on their own
wave-lengths: a heartening occasion certainly, even if the music conveyed little
to some of us." *The Musical Times* (May 1945), 144. One listener, Michel Ciry, said
the transmission was so bad that it was difficult to judge the cantata. Ciry, entry
for 26 Mar. 1945.
[19] 31 Mar. 1945, 3. Auric also staunchly applauded Poulenc for his devotion to
France in paying no heed to Berlin or Vichy.
[20] Poulenc 1994, 45-9 (Poulenc 1991, no. 178) and his [spring 1945] reply in
Poulenc 1994, 45-10 (Poulenc 1991, no. 179).
[21] Concert de La Pléiade 22 May 1947. Another performance at the Salle Gaveau
on 27 May 1959 honored Poulenc's 60th year. Schmidt 1995, FP 120, p. 336.
[22] Poulenc had earlier played his new cantata and accompanied Bernac in some
of his songs at a Marie-Blanche de Polignac *soirée* after most of the guests had
departed. Ciry, entry for 7 Feb. 1945. A more formal presentation, before invited
guests including Poulenc and Sauguet, was given at her rue Barbet-de-Jouy *hôtel*
on 9 Apr. 1945. Ciry, entry for 9 Apr. 1945.
[23] In a [26 Apr. 1945] letter to Collaer Poulenc called Messiaen's work marvelous

hall was full to overflowing—and the audience was composed in large part of the greatest names in music, painting, and literature."[24] Poulenc had first discussed a recital of his songs in a 24 June [1944] letter to Bernac.

> I have created the program for a Festival of Poulenc *mélodies* which I submit to you (this in order to take my mind off things and to give me hope). I have harbored this idea for a long time.
>
> I. *Bestiaire* (1919). *Quatre poèmes Apoll[inaire]* (1932) - you
> II. *5 Max Jacob* (1932) - Suzanne Balg[uerie]
> III. *Tel jour* (1937) - you
> IV. *Fiançailles* (1939) - Suzanne
> V. "[Dans le] Jardin d'Anna" (1938) - you
> "Allons plus vite "(1944)
> *Montparnasse, Hyde Park* (1943)
> 2 *Aragon.*
>
> Not bad, eh, with *Villageoises* for an encore, thereby rendering homage to Apoll[inaire], Max [Jacob], Eluard, Aragon, Loulou [Louise de Vilmorin]. Festival of Songs by Fr. Poulenc with the assistance of Mme. S.B., M P.B. and the composer. Pretty poster.[25]

When the recital took place on 27 April 1945, the program was illustrated with a guitar designed by Picasso, and the Salle Gaveau was completely full. *Banalités* replaced *Bestiaire* and *Quatre poèmes de Guillaume Apollinaire*, and *Fiançailles pour rire* was placed second.[26] *Montparnasse* and *Hyde Park* were premiered, and *Priez pour paix* was the encore.[27]

Armand Pierhal's review for *La Nef* was very complimentary.

> Francis Poulenc is our Mozart. We are convinced that his reputation will not cease to assert itself and that posterity will place him very high among the musicians of our epoch. With the assistance of M.

---

and said it should be performed next season. Fragment in Poulenc 1994, p. 587, note 2. Concerning *Quatrains valaisans*, op. 206, written in 1939 to Rainer Maria Rilke poems, see Collaer 1988, p. 304. The premiere is incorrectly dated 1948.

[24] Mayer, p. 131 and Schmidt 1995, FP 126, p. 355. Messiaen had written Poulenc on 19 Apr. 1945 indicating his pleasure at the prospect of hearing *Un soir de neige* and saying that his own *Liturgies* were "a work full of love." Poulenc 1994, 45-5. Messiaen also invited Poulenc to a 29 Apr. concert featuring his *Vingt regards sur l'Enfant Jésus* "chez Mme Sivade" to be played by Loriod, saying "I would be happy and proud for your presence."

[25] 24 June [1944] letter in Poulenc 1994, 44-4 (Poulenc 1991, no. 164).

[26] 30 July [1945] letter to Casa Fuerte in Poulenc 1994, 45-18 (partial translation in Poulenc 1991, p. 367). Poulenc said he intended to repeat the performance in Brussels during the coming winter.

[27] Marc Pincherle's review in *Les Nouvelles littéraires* (10 May 1945), 6.

Pierre Bernac and Mme Suzanne Balguerie, he offered us a selection
of his most recent songs, in one of his concerts of which we cherish a
luminous memory. Simple art, dealing only with the essential, which
knows how to attain a rare expressive power; art made of distinction, of the highest sense of the word, of refinement, of classical measure, of finesse, also of humor, which permits him to render a range
of quite varied sentiments. The maturity of his works composed after 1940 is striking, with their moving sobriety, their strength, their
grandeur. Here prosody attains perfection. With Poulenc, the vocal
part always holds the place which it deserves, sustained by a piano
with a marvelous efficiency, but which refuses to play the role of a
miniature orchestra. Praising Mme Balguerie is no longer necessary.
As for M. Bernac, by the beauty of his sound, his power, and his
purity, impeccable diction, expression so precise and measured, the
depth of emotion, he remains, as he was ten years ago, our best singer
of lieder.[28]

Other critics were equally quick to express their approbation of
this auspicious concert. Roland-Manuel and Clarendon [Bernard
Gavoty] sang Poulenc's praises and Claude Rostand noted, "This
evening confirms for those who might still have any doubt that his
place is in the front ranks of the great modern French composers."[29]
Charles Koechlin, however, was not so unequivocal in his praise.
He had not liked all the songs equally, though he particularly praised
Tel jour telle nuit and the first of the Aragon songs. He reserved his
greatest applause for Poulenc as accompanist and for Bernac, who
displayed "a prodigious diversity of vocal color, a precision of accent, an impeccable diction, an accomplished mastery which remains
discrete and which I find clearly superior [compared to Balguerie]."[30]

A RETURN TO COMPOSING FROM MAY-SEPTEMBER:

After the emotional stress of this concert, Poulenc returned to Noizay
leaving behind a concert season which he described to Milhaud in
America as not particularly brilliant with the possible exception of
works by Olivier Messiaen.[31] May was spent at Noizay, and June
saw a return to Paris on the 7th where he may have given a radio
performance of his *Deux poèmes de Louis Aragon* with Bernac on the
9th. Whether or not he stayed there through 1 July, when he began

[28] June 1945, pp. 152-3.
[29] Portions of these reviews in Hell 1978, pp. 207-08.
[30] Koechlin's 30 Apr. 1945 letter to Poulenc in Poulenc 1994, 45-6. The English
translation in Poulenc 1991, no. 177 is from the initial draft written at midnight
shortly after the performance. (For a translation of the revised 30 Apr. version
see Buckland/Chimènes: f, pp. 39-40.) Poulenc thanked Koechlin for his letter.
[May 1945] letter in Poulenc 1994, 45-7 (Poulenc 1991, no. 177).
[31] 1 July 1945 letter to Milhaud in Poulenc 1994, 45-12 (Poulenc 1991, no. 181).

a letter to Milhaud from his 5 rue de Médicis address, is unknown.[32] By the 8th he had visited Rocamadour and on the 9th he left for Larche (Corrèze), where he intended to spend two months. Enthralled by his lodgings at "La Chatoine" in Larche, which even included a piano, he wrote Bernac:

> As for me, I've found *paradise*. In a charming little spot on the banks of the Vézère, I am living like the lord of a quite small château that was made into a restaurant four months ago. There are only three rooms, the owner's, her son's, and mine. Raymond [Destouches] is sleeping in a small room in the farmhouse. . . . I have a room with bath, and a ravishing view.[33]

Only the proprietress' decision to close the restaurant and evict Poulenc several days into his stay made for momentary anxiety. The discovery that Destouches had known her late husband in 1926 and that they had friends in common saved the day and Poulenc was invited to the owner's table. Except for a two-day visit with his friends Paul and Georgette Chadourne in late July, Poulenc remained in Larche through August.[34] He returned to Paris on the 26th, spent a week with Jean Anouilh and Armand Salacrou, and then went to Noizay on 1 September.[35]

His concentration on the orchestration of *Les Mamelles de Tirésias*, completed in late July or early August, was broken only by discussions with Bernac about future concerts. By the 16th of August a corrected score was ready for his copyist M. Gunst.[36] He also worked on a string quartet, several numbers of *Chansons françaises* (FP 130), incidental music for Salacrou's *Le Soldat et la Sorcière* (FP 128), and *Histoire de Babar, le petit éléphant* (FP 129).

•*Histoire de Babar, le petit éléphant*

Poulenc's contemporary Jean de Brunhoff, author of *The Story of Babar (Histoire de Babar)*, came from an illustrious family. His father published the monthly Parisian review *Comœdia illustré* (which dealt

---

[32] Poulenc originally told Bernac that he would depart for the South, making a pilgrimage before his actual vacation, on 28 or 30 June. "Mercredi" [May 1945] letter in Poulenc 1994, 45-11 (Poulenc 1991, no. 180).

[33] 12 [July 1945] letter in Poulenc 1994, 45-13 (Poulenc 1991, no. 182). See also his 1 July 1945 letter to Milhaud in Poulenc 1994, 45-12 (Poulenc 1991, no. 181) and 22 July [1945] letter to Marie-Blanche in Poulenc 1994, 45-15, and July [19]45 letter to Collaer in Collaer 1996, 45-3.

[34] 30 July [1945] letter to Casa Fuerte in Poulenc 1994, 45-18.

[35] Poulenc 1994, 45-19 (Poulenc 1991, no. 184) and unpublished "dimanche" [after 16 Aug. 1945] letter to Bernac in US-NH.

[36] Poulenc spoke fondly of *Les Mamelles* to various friends, and in Sept., when he suffered "a very tragic end of the month," he asked Paul Rouart to advance him 15,000 francs which he had loaned to a man named Capdeville. 2 Oct. [1945] letter to Rouart in Poulenc 1994, 45-26.

with the contemporary theatrical scene), books on the Russian artist Léon Bakst, and splendid programs for Diaghilev's Ballets
Russes.[37] An inveterate theater goer Poulenc was acquainted with
the senior Brunhoff's work. The *Babar* series was inaugurated in
1931 with the very story Poulenc set to music. Six more books,
through *Babar and Father Christmas,* were completed by 1941. Jean's
brother Michel de Brunhoff, editor of *Jardin des Modes* and the Paris
edition of *Vogue,* was also Poulenc's friend. Poulenc mentioned *Babar*
in various summer 1945 letters from Larche where he stayed at "La
Chatoine."

To Bernac 22 July [1945]

I have finished the rough draft of my *Babar* which I am going to begin to recopy. I think that it will be very funny. The difficulty is to
avoid making a series of little sections but to make a sort of mosaic
between the texts. At the beginning of September I will give you the
words so that you can practice them. In concerts where more piano
music is required, this work could be quite amusing.[38]

To Sauguet [3 Aug. 1945]

At the request of the BBC and of His Master's Voice, I have again
taken up an old project for which I have just finished a sketch. It is
The Story of Babar, the Little Elephant, set to music for speaker and
piano in the manner of Prokofiev's *Peter and the Wolf,* but with a
much funnier and unpredictable text. I will make recordings in French
with Bernac and in English with a children's specialist from the BBC.[39]

To Paul Rouart [Aug. 1945]

I believe that it is amusing and in any case very "radiophonique"
and "phonogénique."[40]

To Bernac "dimanche" [Aug. 1945]

It is much better than I thought and the text, of unequal length, read
between musical numbers of unequal length, is also very well done.
The end came very well in the poetic style: chaste evening of love
according to children's usage.[41]

To André Schaeffner [Aug. 1945]

If *Babar* contains nothing new musically (it is very close to *Animaux*

[37] Weber, passim.
[38] Poulenc 1994, 45-14 (Poulenc 1991, no. 183).
[39] Poulenc 1994, pp. 596-7, note 1.
[40] Fragment in Poulenc 1994, p. 597, note 1.
[41] Fragment in Poulenc 1994, p. 597, note 1.

[*modèles*]) the writing for piano is clearly an evolution, and for the first time approaches the piano writing in my *mélodies*.[42]

To Bernac "samedi" [8 Sept. 1945]

I am working like an angel. In four days *Babar* will be completely finished. You will see, harmonically, it is very curious. I am sending the text to you today. You must *absolutely* learn it by heart in order to obtain the tone and the freedom of the contents.[43]

Problems arose in 1947 concerning literary rights, so Poulenc suggested that his publisher Robert Douglas Gibson of J. & W. Chester, Ltd. contact Michel de Brunhoff to forge an agreement.[44] When published in 1949 it sported a cover drawn by Laurent de Brunhoff, Jean's son, who continued writing the adventures of Babar from 1946 on, adding approximately thirty illustrated books to the series. In remarks to Sauguet and others Poulenc referred to his own setting of *Babar* as "eighteen glances at the tail of a young elephant," a reference to Olivier Messiaen's *Vingt regards sur l'Enfant Jésus*, then something of an item in Parisian musical circles.[45]

Bernac and Poulenc premiered *Babar* during a *Chaîne nationale* broadcast at 9 pm on 14 June 1946, and Poulenc performed it frequently on radio transmissions. Although he and Bernac never recorded *Babar*, Poulenc recorded it with Pierre Fresnay on 2 July 1954, Bruce Belfrage on 8 February 1949, and Noël Coward ca. 1957. Bernac did finally record *Babar* with Graham Johnson for the BBC on 27 November 1977 and in Jean Françaix's orchestration with the O.R.T.F. conducted by Edgar Cosma on 24 April 1966.[46]

• *Chansons françaises pour chœur a cappella*

Poulenc also arranged three of a proposed ten choruses for mixed voices which became *Chansons françaises pour chœur a cappella*.[47] Bernac had supplied the original chanson settings for this "commercial" enterprise from which Poulenc expected 5,000 francs.[48] Poulenc retained the original words and melodies, altered the rhythms and meters, and added his own harmony and counterpoint. The problem of monotony was avoided through skillful use of varied repetitions for the strophic texts. Two further choruses were

---

[42] Fragment in Schmidt 1995, FP 129, p. 363.
[43] Fragment in Poulenc 1994, p. 596, note 1.
[44] List of letters outlining these negotiations in Schmidt 1995, FP 129, p. 363.
[45] 9 Aug. [1945] letter in Poulenc 1994, 45-19 (Poulenc 1991, no. 184).
[46] Bloch, pp. 87-9. The version with Johnson is recorded on Testament SBT 3161.
[47] Nos. 1, 3, and 7: "Margoton va t'a l'iau avecque son crochon" [Margoton to the well had brought her pail along],"Pilons l'orge," and "Ah! mon beau laboureur."
[48] Fragment of the unpublished [8 Sept. 1945] letter to Bernac in Schmidt 1995, FP 130, p. 369.

added at Noizay in September, and the final three were composed there during April 1946.[49] He dedicated his "anthology" to Henri Screpel, director of the Compagnie des Discophiles, who had originally suggested setting Eluard's poem "Liberté" in 1943.[50] These unpretentious pieces remained unpublished until 1948. Years later, Norman Luboff's English translations made them readily accessible to American choruses.

• *Le Soldat et la Sorcière*

Upon returning to Paris Poulenc discussed with Armand Salacrou his incidental music for *Le Soldat et la Sorcière*, the last of the stage plays or films for which he supplied music between 1940 and 1945. Back at Noizay in September he wrote: "I am actually writing the music for Salacrou, which will add nothing to my œuvre, but you understand why I am doing it. It will be, in any case, proper."[51] A week later the music was finished: "As I told you, Saturday I sent my *musique de scène* for Salacrou."[52] Playwright and composer also exchanged letters in September concerning various details. Poulenc wanted a textual alteration for the song of Simon Favart, which he found "too pompous to be sung by an *actor* accompanied by a few instruments."[53] Salacrou hastily responded that the text "is not mine: *it is by Favart* and *it is the historic song* by which Maurice de Saxe announced the battle for the next day."[54] Finally Poulenc objected to the proposed title of the play, *Les Amours de Chambord*. Salacrou accepted Poulenc's suggestions and, in the matter of the chanson, agreed to dispense with the repetition of two lines. Poulenc described how the chanson would work vis à vis his use of instruments assuring Salacrou that he would be returning to Paris on 15 September and put everything in good order by October.[55]

When performed at the Théâtre Sarah-Bernhardt, Salacrou's play garnered plaudits from Parisian critics. André Alter called it "a most

---

[49] Nos. 2 and 4: "La Belle se sied au pied de la tour" and "Clic, clac, dansez sabots" and nos. 5, 6, and 8: "C'est la petit' fill du prince qui voulait se marier," "La Belle si nous étions dedans," and "Les Tisserands sont pir' que les évèques."
[50] Poulenc also wrote Screpel on 24 July 1946 pointing out the necessity to determine a publication order for the chansons. Fragment in Poulenc 1994, p. 646, note 3.
[51] Fragment of Poulenc's unpublished "samedi" [8 Sept. 1945] letter in US-NH.
[52] Unpublished [before 15 Sept. 1945] letter to Bernac in F-Pn. The Saturday was probably 8 Sept.
[53] 10 Sept. [1945] letter to Salacrou in Poulenc 1994, 45-22.
[54] Salacrou's [Sept. 1945] letter to Poulenc from Courval in Poulenc 1994, 45-23.
[55] [Before 15 Sept. 1945] letter to Salacrou in Poulenc 1994, 45-24. He also requested 1/6 of the royalties (the same arrangement negotiated with Anouilh for *Léocadia* and *Voyageur sans bagage*) and said he had suggested to Charles Dullin that Chapelain-Midy be retained to design the décor and costumes.

agreeable spectacle and worthy of a long success;" Gabriel Marcel wrote "Le théâtre Sarah-Bernhardt has finally attained a great and lasting success;" and Kléber-Haedens concluded "Of all the new plays which were presented this season, that of M. Salacrou is by far the best and the most exciting for the spirit."[56] Critics also praised Poulenc's music, Philippe Hériat calling it "most agreeable."[57] Unfortunately Poulenc's music has not been preserved. The play enjoyed a successful run and was still being advertised in May 1946.

COMPOSITIONAL ACTIVITY FROM OCTOBER TO DECEMBER:

• String Quartet (II)

Poulenc occasionally struggled with compositions over an extended period of time. The most extreme case, that of *Marches militaires*, occupied him for more than a decade, but he also had difficulty writing for particular instruments. It took four aborted attempts before he wrote a violin sonata that he allowed to enter the repertory. He made several attempts to write a string quartet, the second of which occupied his thinking from July 1943 through late 1946. Over these forty months he frequently picked the piece up and put it down, as can be ascertained from numerous letters.[58] On 8 May [1946] he wrote Nadia Boulanger:

> I am a prisoner face to face with my quartet. How difficult it is. There are days when we embrace each other, others when we slap each other in the face. In any case, I am writing what seems good to me, even if it is not a quartet like those of Schönberg or Bartók.[59]

He accomplished his most significant work in late summer of 1945, and late spring and summer of 1946. Once completed in late 1946, Poulenc heard it played by the Calvet Quartet. He recalled the occasion with horror.

[56] *L'Aube* (Dec. 1945); *Les Nouvelles littéraires* (10-11 Feb. 1946); and *L'Epoque* (date uncertain) respectively.

[57] *Bataille* (13 Dec. 1945).

[58] See the following letters: [July 1943] to Marie-Blanche (Poulenc 1995, 43-2); "jeudi soir" [28 Oct. 1943] to Marie-Blanche, 43-12; 27 Mar. 1945 to Milhaud, 45-4 (Poulenc 1991, no. 175); 1 July 1945 to Milhaud, 5-12 (Poulenc 1991, no. 181); 12 [July 1945] to Bernac, 45-13; 22 July [1945] to Bernac, 45-14 (Poulenc 1991, no. 183); [3 Aug. 1945] to Sauguet, 45-12, note 8; 6 Aug. [1945] to Marie-Blanche, 45-20; 10 [Sept. 1945] to Bernac, 45-21 [no. 185]; [Sept. 1945] to Bernac, 45-25 (partial translation in Buckland/Chimènes: l, pp. 256-7); 2 Oct. [1945] to Paul Rouart, 45-26; unpublished [undated Noizay, 1945] to Boulanger in F-Pn; 8 May [1946] to Boulanger, 46-4; 4 June [1946] to Milhaud, 46-6; unpublished [undated, mid-1946] to Virgil Thomson in US-NH; [Aug. 1946] to Sauguet, 46-9; 21 Aug. 1946 to Casa Fuerte, 46-12; 21 Aug. 1946 to Collaer, 46-12, note 1; 23 Aug. 1946 to Bernac, 46-13; [Sept. 1946] to Collaer, 46-14 and Collaer 1996, 46-11; 28 Dec. 1946 to Milhaud, 46-16; 5 Jan. 1947 to Gibson, 46-16, note 2.

[59] 8 May [1946] letter in Poulenc 1994, 46-4.

This quartet is the disgrace of my life (Joseph Calvet was kind enough to read three movements of it for me one morning in 1947 [*recte* 1946]). My cheeks flush with shame just thinking about it. From the first measures, I said to myself: "That would in any case be better on an oboe, here one must have a horn, there a clarinet." Wasn't this work condemned with a single blow? I had only one thought: flee. With joy, leaving the Calvets, I threw my manuscript down a sewer in the place Péreire! Next I entered a café and I called Auric: "You know, I threw my quartet down the sewer." That's idiotic! "There were only three pretty themes and only if played by wind instruments. Then, you have done well, but try not to forget the three themes. These motifs figure today in my *Sinfonietta,* which in memory of this call, I dedicated to Auric.[60]

• *Casanova:* **An Unrealized Project**

In September Poulenc also considered setting to music Apollinaire's *opéra bouffe* libretto *Casanova.* Enthusiastic, he could think of nothing but the libretto, which had been carefully copied for him by Jacqueline Apollinaire. "It is Guillaume's last work," he said, "(June-October 1918) 4 acts which take place in Venice with Casanova as the hero and made specially to be set to music."[61] Apollinaire had written it for Henri Defosse, a Diaghilev conductor who composed music only for the first act by the time of the poet's death.[62] Poulenc also spoke of this project to Paul Rouart in early September, but it was quickly forgotten, and he abandoned opera until the early 1950s when he turned ever more passionately to Georges Bernanos' *Dialogues des Carmélites.*[63]

FINAL CONCERTS OF 1945 AND PLANNING FOR THE 1946 SEASON

As early as 22 July Poulenc was planning future concerts. He sent six projects for a festival to Kiesgen in Paris, told Bernac that he wanted to spend February 1946 in Switzerland, that their presence was requested in Rome, and that he had asked Henri Hoppenot in Berne to see if he could arrange for a performance of *Figure humaine* at the Lucerne Festival.[64] He agreed to perform in Reims before Brussels, wrote Paul Collaer about a possible performance of *Figure humaine* and a radio engagement, worked on going to Dublin, agreed to perform in Besançon and Mulhouse, and inquired about a con-

---

60 Poulenc 1954, p. 125.
61 [Sept. 1945] letter to Bernac in Poulenc 1994, 45-25 and note 3 (translation in Buckland/Chimènes: l, pp. 256-7). Apollinaire finished the text on 5 Aug. 1918.
62 Waleckx indicates that Defosse may have had an interest in seeing his own music performed as late as 1951. See Buckland/Chimènes: l, p. 257.
63 2 Oct. [1945] letter to Rouart in Poulenc 1994, 45-26.
64 22 July [1945] letter to Bernac in Poulenc 1994, 45-14 (Poulenc 1991, no. 183).

cert in Strasbourg before going to Switzerland.[65] When coal supplies at Noizay allowed him to stay there in colder months, he considered resuming his pre-war schedule: seven months of concerts, three months of composing, and two months of vacation as follows:

October	Noizay
November	Concerts
December	Noizay
January-March	Concerts
April-May	Concerts
June	Concerts (possibly London)
July-August	Vacation
September	Noizay

He had suggested that Kiesgen make reservations for England, Sweden, Denmark, Holland, Belgium, Switzerland, Italy, and Spain—insisting that the last two at least be included for the 1946-47 season. Looking ahead Poulenc expressed interest in composing a piano concerto for the same season.[66] He also contemplated an autumn Milhaud Festival for the Salle Gaveau, but eventually joined with the Radiodiffusion française to organize such a concert at the Conservatoire.[67] The Festival, held on 14 December in the Salle de l'ancien Conservatoire, was broadcast.[68]

Poulenc resumed his own performance schedule in October. "It is without joy that I am going to leave Noizay on the 14th of October," he told Paul Rouart. "Truly I only want to compose and my terrible winter of concerts does not fill me with joy."[69] Bernac and Poulenc gave concerts in Reims on 24 October and Brussels on the 31st; then, Poulenc returned to Noizay after which they performed in England between 29 November and 9 December. (See Appendix 2.) Of special note was their first performance in London of "Tu vois le feu du soir," *Le Portrait, Montparnasse,* and *Hyde Park* on 2 December at Wigmore Hall. The English trip was brief, however, and Poulenc was back in Paris by 18 December.[70]

While away from home during November, Poulenc's "Uncle

---

[65] "Lundi 10" [Sept. 1945] letter in Poulenc 1994, 45-21 (Poulenc 1991, no. 185).

[66] Poulenc actually composed his Piano Concerto between May and Oct. 1949. Schmidt 1995, FP 146.

[67] Fragment of Poulenc's 10 Sept. [1945] letter to Milhaud in Poulenc 1994, p. 600, note 2.

[68] Chimènes indicates that String Quartet no. 12, *Bal martiniquais, La Cheminée du Roi René,* and Sonata no. 1 for Viola and Piano wereperformed. (Poulenc 1994, p. 616, note 5.) Manuel Rosenthal also presented the first Paris radio performance of the cantata *La Sagesse* on 18 Nov. 1945.

[69] 2 Oct. [1945] letter to Paul Rouart in Poulenc 1994, 45-26.

[70] [18 Dec. 1945] letter to Collaer from Paris in Poulenc 1994, 45-30 and Collaer 1996, 45-6.

Papoum" (Marcel Royer) died of cardiac arrest in Paris.[71] Shortly thereafter Jeanne Manceaux moved into Royer's apartment at 5, rue de Médicis, and Poulenc moved out of the maid's quarters into a new apartment on the seventh floor of the building, which overlooked the Luxembourg Gardens.[72]

At this time Poulenc was invited to respond to four questions on aesthetics for the inaugural issue of *Contrepoints*, a new music review directed by Frederick Goldbeck.[73] Poulenc had known Goldbeck since the 1930s when he worked for *La Revue musicale*, and Goldbeck was married to the well-known pianist Yvonne Lefébure. Aesthetic pronouncements were not Poulenc's forte, and his stunningly brief answers contrast markedly with the more verbose comments of Charles Koechlin, Dynam-Victor Fumet, Roland-Manuel, André Jolivet, Claude Delvincourt, Daniel-Lesur, and others. The questions included:

(1) What is the "canon" of your esthetic and of the technique which serves as the foundation of your style?

(2) Is there some general, stylistic principle which informs in your work the overall procedure (harmony, counterpoint, form, choice?)

(3) Are there writing methods that you apply systematically or that you avoid systematically?

(4) In works of art there is the element called "work" and the element called "art": the technical side and the expression and meaning side; there is the musical architecture of which you are the architect, and there is a musical inspiration that you subject everything to in giving it form. For your music, how do you see the relationship of these elements?

In response, Poulenc wrote with exceptional terseness.

I understand nothing about surveys. I would have said to your readers:

(1) that my "rule" is instinct;
(2) that I have no principles and I'm proud of the fact;
(3) that I have no system for writing music, thank God (for, to me, "system" means "gimmick");
(4) that inspiration is such a mysterious thing that it is better not to attempt to explain it.

Don't count, therefore, on a long-winded speech from me...[74]

---

[71] 28 Dec. [1945] letter to Milhaud in Poulenc 1991, 45-31.
[72] 4 June [1946] letter to Milhaud in Poulenc 1994, 46-6.
[73] Poulenc 1946a.
[74] English adapted from Bernac 1965, p. 315.

The January 1946 issue also contained his assessment of Milhaud's most recent work sent from America in mid-1945.[75] Poulenc declared Milhaud's muse intact after pouring over nearly a dozen works including string quartets, compositions for orchestra, a clarinet concerto, songs, Latin prayers for voice and organ, and two viola sonatas. Stravinsky also sent some of his own music late in the year.[76] Finally, Poulenc renewed his correspondence with Dallapiccola, which had lapsed since the late 1930s.[77]

In December Bernac and Poulenc made five recordings for His Master's Voice including single discs of Gounod and Duparc as well as two devoted entirely to Poulenc's songs.[78] These were the first commercial recordings made by the Bernac/Poulenc duo since June 1943; more would be made in mid-1946.

CONCERTS AND *CHANSONS FRANÇAISES*: FIRST HALF OF 1946

The entire first half of 1946 was devoted to concerts in France, Belgium, Switzerland, Holland, and England as Poulenc and Bernac carried out the plans made in September 1945.[79] He completed the final three numbers of *Chansons françaises* written at Noizay during April, but the major work was his continued struggle with the string quartet described above. The year began, however, with word that Poulenc had been named "Chevalier de la Légion d'Honneur" by an 18 January 1946 decree. Requiring a sponsor for the presentation, he wrote his old friend François Mauriac (a grand officer of the Légion d'Honneur) from Amsterdam on 15 March requesting assistance. Mauriac agreed, and the ceremony took place on 17 June.[80]

The Bernac/Poulenc duo performed in Mulhouse on 22 January, Strasbourg (25th), Besançon (26th), and then moved into Switzerland for concerts in Vevey (1 February), and Winterthur (3rd). Poulenc, who probably spent part of February back in Paris, then departed for Holland on 4 March and was still there on the 18th when he wrote Nadia Boulanger, who had returned to Paris during

---

[75] This music is mentioned in Poulenc's 1 July 1945 letter to Milhaud in Poulenc 1994, 45-12 (Poulenc 1991, no. 181). Poulenc assessed each work and indicated what he had done with the copy. The majority were entrusted to the publisher Deiss. Unfortunately Deiss, a member of the Resistance, was murdered by the Gestapo. Many of Milhaud's manuscripts were in Deiss' possession at the time, and Poulenc discusses their removal from Deiss' house, which the Nazis had commandeered, in a letter to Milhaud dated 4 June [1946] in Poulenc 1994, 46-6.
[76] 28 Dec. [1945] letter to Stravinsky in Poulenc 1994, 45-32 (Poulenc 1991, no. 187).
[77] 15 Oct. 1938 and [Nov. 1945] letters to Dallapiccola in Poulenc 1994, 38-16 and 45-27, and Dallapiccola to Poulenc of 24 Nov. 1945, 45-28.
[78] Bloch, 226. See Appendix 3.
[79] "Lundi 10" [Sept. 1945] letter to Bernac in Poulenc 1994, 45-21, and above.
[80] Poulenc 1994, p. 620, note 1.

January 1946 from her years of war exile.[81] Poulenc wasted no time
trying to interest her in conducting the first French performance of
Figure humaine.[82] He also wrote Edward Lockspeiser at the BBC to
arrange performances in French (with Bernac) and English (with a
native English narrator) of *Babar* during a late June London trip.[83]
Before returning to Paris, he and Bernac performed in Brussels on
27 March staying with the industrialist and collector Auguste
Lambiotte and his wife Rose in their mansion at 25, rue Saint-Bernard (Plate 17). Poulenc was exceedingly fond of the Lambiottes
and their daughters Claudine and Rosine, dubbing them "my Belgian family."[84]

He returned to Paris around 30 March and then headed to Noizay.[85]
"After a winter of incessant trips," he subsequently told Milhaud, "I
have plunged myself into work since April."[86] Noizay remained his
base through early June at which time he returned to Paris for the
premier broadcast of *Babar* on 14 June and the "Légion d'Honneur"
ceremony. He and Bernac then crossed the Channel to fulfill various engagements. They performed a recital at Brighton on the 23rd
and Poulenc performed *Babar* for the BBC "Children's Hour" on 24
June, probably with Robert Irwin as narrator. At Mayflower Barn,
Jordans on 29 June they gave a full recital including Debussy, Fauré,
and Poulenc as well as works in English by John Dowland and German by Schubert. The concert concluded with Poulenc playing several of his own piano pieces. On 30 June and 3 July the Bernac/
Poulenc duo was joined by oboist Leon Goossens for chamber concerts on the BBC, Bernac had brief BBC solo appearances on the 3rd
and 4th, and Poulenc was interviewed for fifteen minutes by Cecil
Madden at the Alexandra Palace on 9 July. Poulenc enjoyed these
short, hectic trips basking in the English limelight.

[81] 18 Mar. [1946] letter in Poulenc 1994, 46-3; see Rosenstiel, p. 334.
[82] See also his 8 May [1946] letter in Poulenc 1994, 46-4. Chimènes has documented much of Poulenc's saga leading to the first performance of *Figure humaine*
in Paris on 22 May 1947 at the Théâtre des Champs-Elysées conducted by Collaer.
Poulenc 1994, pp. 621-2.
[83] Unpublished 18 Mar. [1946] letter to Lockspeiser. Poulenc had written on 30
Dec. [1945] to wish him a happy new year and suggested that the French pianist
Lazare Lévy perform on the BBC. Lockspeiser responded on 3 Jan. 1946 with
questions about *Babar*. On 8 Jan. 1946 he said that the American organist E. Power
Biggs had broadcast the Concerto in G minor from Harvard University (WABC of
the CBS network) and that the BBC had a copy. See also Lockspeiser's 26 Mar.
1946 response to Poulenc's 18 Mar. letter. All correspondence in GB-Rbbc.
[84] Unpublished "lundi" [2 Nov. 1951] letter in US-NYlambiotte-donhauser and
Poulenc 1994, p. 1032.
[85] 15 Mar. [1946] letter to François Mauriac in Poulenc 1994, 46-2.
[86] 4 June [1946] letter in Poulenc 1994, 46-6.

Plate 17: Poulenc at the piano in Brussels in 1946 taken at St. Bernard's Palace, the home of Rose and Auguste Lambiotte. (Collection of Rosine Lambiotte-Donhauser and used with her kind permission.)

SUMMER 1946

Bernac and Poulenc spent a three-week working vacation at Le Tremblay in late July and early August before returning to Noizay on 10 August where Poulenc was joined by Raymond Destouches.[87] At Noizay he completed two *mélodies* on poems by Apollinaire: "Le Pont" and "Un poème" (FP 131). He recalled that their composition spanned several years:

> "Le Pont" is surely one of the most tricky of Apollinaire's poems to set to music. It is these that generally attract me the most. That is why for my personal use I always prefer the collection *Il y a* to *Alcools*. In 1944, while working at Noizay, I found the music for the line "qui vient de loin qui va si loin," in 1945 at Larche (Corrèze), "Et passe sous le pont léger de vos paroles". In May 1946 I worked again at the whole song and completed it in one fell swoop in Normandy during a working vacation with Bernac.[88]

Although the printed edition of "Le Pont" is dated only "Le Tremblay juillet 46," "Un poème" carries the precise date "Le Tremblay 27 Juillet 46." Poulenc told Bernac in September 1945 that he was working on "Le Pont" but that he had little desire to write *mélodies*.[89]

During July he also composed *Le Disparu* (FP 134) on poetry by Robert Desnos, one-time member of the surrealist group whose Resistance activities led to his arrest by the Gestapo.[90] Poulenc dedicated the piece to Sauguet, acknowledging that this sad waltz is a cousin to *Les Forains*.[91] While at Noizay during August, Poulenc wrote *Paul et Virginie* (text by Radiguet: FP 132) and *Main dominée par le cœur* (text by Eluard: FP 135).[92] When he mailed *Paul et Virginie* to Bernac he recalled originally setting the poem in 1920. Unable to write a song without modulation, he had abandoned the project.[93]

---

[87] 27 July 1946 letters to Audel from Le Tremblay and [Aug. 1946] to Sauguet in Poulenc 1994, 46-8 and 46-9 respectively.

[88] Poulenc 1993, p. 48 (Poulenc 1989, p. 81).

[89] [Sept. 1945] letter in Poulenc 1994, 45-25 (partial translation in Buckland/ Chimènes: l, pp. 256-7).

[90] Desnos died of typhus in the Terezin concentration camp in Czechoslovakia on 8 June 1945.

[91] [Aug. 1946] letter to Sauguet in Poulenc 1994, 46-9. Sauguet's ballet was premiered on 2 Mar. at the Théâtre des Champs-Élysées.

[92] A copy of the manuscript of *Main dominée par le cœur* given to Marie-Blanche for her birthday is inscribed "Fr. Poulenc, Noizay, 14-18-19 août 46." Poulenc 1994, p. 628, note 1. Bernac 1977a, p. 125 (Poulenc 1978, p. 120) is mistaken when he suggests that Poulenc wrote this *mélodie* in 1947, the date on the printed score. The first printed edition was dated "Imp. A. Mounot — Paris. Juillet 1947."

[93] "Dimanche" [Aug. 1946] letter in Poulenc 1994, 46-10 (Poulenc 1991, no. 189). Poulenc also told Bernac that he had been thinking a lot about Radiguet and "Le Pont" was dedicated to his memory.

Poulenc suggested using the piece as a second encore and *Main dominée par le cœur*, of which he was particularly fond, as the first.

While composing new *mélodies* Poulenc studied and was stimulated by the works of others. In a 28 August entry to his *Journal de mes mélodies* he called Bizet's song "Les Adieux de l'Hôtesse Arabe" divine, and in another of 8 September he said he never tired of re-playing Moussorgsky's *Children's Songs*.[94] During August Poulenc also penned a culinary response to *Harper's Bazaar*, which was published in November. Preferring not to write on a musical subject, Poulenc proffered recipes for *Eau Clairette, Lait de Poule, Poulet à l'Aveyronnaise*, and *Crème Bachique*.[95]

THE CLOSE OF 1946

In the remaining fall months the Bernac/Poulenc duo rehearsed for their 1946-47 season. One piece that gave them particular difficulty was Luigi Dallapiccola's *Rencesvals: Trois fragments de la Chanson de Roland*, which Poulenc first sent to Bernac on 23 August. Poulenc promised Paul Collaer the world premiere for Brussels in December.[96] Poulenc also struggled to arrange a performance of *Figure humaine* in Brussels. The major event of November, their Salle Gaveau recital on the 6th, included particularly eclectic repertory by André-Ernest-Modeste Grétry, Schumann, Debussy, Hindemith, and Poulenc. "Le Pont" and *Le Disparu* were premiered and *Main dominée par le cœur* may have been an encore. The Hindemith pieces, listed as first performances, included "On a Fly Drinking out of his Cup," "Echo," "Sing on there in the Swamp," and "The Moon."[97] With the recital concluded, Poulenc turned his attention to Brussels for the performance of *Figure humaine*. Originally scheduled for 8 December, the actual radio performance was advanced to 2 December and accomplished with 140 singers under Paul Collaer's direction.[98] Poulenc thanked Collaer on 4 December and told Milhaud

---

[94] Poulenc 1993, p. 52 (Poulenc 1989, pp. 86-9).

[95] Poulenc 1946e. The *Newsweek* reviewer of Poulenc's 7 Nov. 1948 Town Hall recital noted that Poulenc wrote this 1946 letter of recipes for his friend Carmel Snow, editor of *Harper's Bazaar*. *Newsweek* (15 Nov. 1948), 85.

[96] Fragment of Poulenc's [10 Oct. 1946] letter to Collaer in Poulenc 1994, p. 629, note 2 and 23 Aug. 1946 letter to Bernac, 46-13. Poulenc's 25 Sept. 1946 letter to Collaer from Noizay promising *Rencesvals* also indicates the Bernac/Poulenc duo would be performing in Liège on 17 Dec. Collaer 1996, 46-12.

[97] A 12 Nov. 1947 program lists the work as a first performance.

[98] Letters of [Sept. 1946] to Collaer and the fragment of his 22 Oct. 1946 letter to Milhaud in Poulenc 1994, p. 631, note 4. An unpublished letter in US-NH dated 25 Sept. 1945 from the director of the Association Française d'Action Artistique to Poulenc requested his London programs for 1 and 2 Dec. The rescheduling of *Figure humaine* changed these dates. Poulenc's [22 Oct. 1946] letter to Collaer said he would return to Paris on 23 Oct. Collaer 1996, 46-13. Michael Ciry heard this

on the 28th that the performance had been sensational.[99] While in Brussels he also performed *Babar* in Collaer's Flemish translation and heard *Alissa* (op. 9), Milhaud's early suite for voice and piano performed by Mariette Maertens and Collaer at the Lambiottes.[100]

As 1946 concluded Poulenc performed once more in Paris, playing his Sextet with the Quintette à vent de Paris at the Conservatoire on 16 December,[101] before heading to Monte Carlo where living conditions had improved and money was easier to make. He cited Auric as a model saying: "Our Auric is covered with glory and gold. Vice president of SACEM, a Legion of Honor recipient, and winner of the Cannes music prize. . . ."[102] Sometime during 1946 Poulenc also revised an arrangement for nine instruments of his *Trois mouvements perpétuels* originally completed in 1944.[103]

For Poulenc 1946 held two other significant events. On 13 September Frédérique ["Freddy"] gave birth to a little girl, Marie-Ange, naming Poulenc as the father.[104] The mother, whom Poulenc had known since the 1920s, was the dedicatee of "Une ruine coquille vide," the second *mélodie* of *Tel jour telle nuit* composed in December 1936 and "Dans l'herbe," the second mélodie of *Fiançailles pour rire* composed in September-October 1939. In a charming letter written just prior to Marie-Ange's second birthday, Poulenc referred to himself as her godfather rather than her father.[105] This was the way he characterized their relationship for the rest of his life: concerned yet distant. When years later Marie-Ange aspired to be a ballet dancer, Poulenc tried to accommodate her wish. He asked Georges Hirsch, General Administrator of the Paris Opéra, for assistance and later appointed Lycette Darsonval as her dance instructor.[106] Unfortunately her physiognomy was not suitable to a professional career. Madeleine Milhaud remembers that on trips to the United States

---

this performance and his rather unfavorable comments about the cantata itself are found in Ciry, entry for 4 Dec. 1946.

[99] Poulenc 1994, 46-15 (Collaer 1996, 46-16) and 46-16 respectively.

[100] In a [Sept. 1946] letter to Collaer, Poulenc asked his friend to translate the text. Poulenc 1994, 46-14. In a 5 Jan. 1947 letter to Gibson, Poulenc said the speaker was marvelous. Unpublished letter in GB-Lchester.

[101] *Le Guide du concert et des théâtres lyriques* 27 (13 Dec. 1946), 168.

[102] Fragment of Poulenc's 22 Oct. 1946 letter to Milhaud in Poulenc 1994, p. 633, note 6.

[103] Schmidt 1995, FP 14, pp. 31-3. The arrangement is scored for fl., ob. (c.a.), cl., bsn., hn., vn., vla., vc., and d.b.

[104] For conjecture concerning this liaison see Rorem 1983, p. 54.

[105] 8 Sept. [1948] letter to Marie-Ange in Poulenc 1994, 48-5. During her childhood Poulenc's true relationship to Marie-Ange was never revealed. Out of respect to the family, I have chosen not to identify her further.

[106] Poulenc 1994, p. 857, note 2.

Poulenc delighted in buying presents for Marie-Ange.[107] During his lifetime he always provided for her and in his will assigned copyright renewals of his music in her name.[108]

Poulenc completed *Les Mamelles de Tirésias* in 1945 but its production was postponed for several years for a variety of reasons including the difficulty of locating a soprano for the dual role of Thérèse-Tirésias. Finding a suitable soprano was the second significant event of 1946. He told Claude Rostand that "Up until February 1947 I had not found this rare bird" and that it was his friend Max de Rieux at whose suggestion he came to the Opéra-Comique to audition a young woman who had worked at the Folies-Bergères.[109] The young woman was Denise Duval, a Parisian soprano who had debuted at Bordeaux in 1943 as Lola in *Cavalleria rusticana* (Plate 18). Poulenc's meeting with Duval must have taken place earlier than he told Rostand because in early January he wrote her an impatient letter anticipating their work together upon his return to Paris on 22 January, and offering advice about the role she would create. He concluded: "Bernard [Gavoty] came for the weekend. We spoke of you incessantly. The whole of Touraine speaks of nothing but *our* marriage!!!!!"[110] Poulenc quickly developed a deep affection for Duval and told Rose Lambiotte, "If Thérèse loses her breasts, me, I have lost my head for my interpreter who is as beautiful as the day, the most 'chic' on earth, [has] a golden voice etc. . . ."[111] Immediately after the premiere Poulenc wrote: "I have an unbelievable Thérèse who is stunning Paris with her beauty, her gifts as an actress, and her voice. She is a new [Fanny] Heldy."[112] Duval and Poulenc maintained a close personal and professional relationship until the composer's death and it was for her that he wrote the roles of Blanche de la Force in *Dialogues des Carmélites*, Elle in *La Voix humaine*, and *La Dame de Monte-Carlo*.[113] When the Bernac/Poulenc duo retired from the stage, Poulenc occasionally toured with Duval even taking her to the United States.

CONCERTS AND THE PREMIERE OF *LES MAMELLES DE TIRÉSIAS*, 1947

Building on his postwar success in England, Poulenc's engagements with the BBC in February, March, May, June, October, and Decem-

[107] Private conversation with Madeleine Milhaud, summer 1992.
[108] Schmidt 1995, passim.
[109] Poulenc 1954, p. 149. She was then rehearsing *Madame Butterfly*, not *Tosca* as suggested by Poulenc.
[110] "Lundi" [13 Jan. 1947] letter in Poulenc 1994, 47-1 (Poulenc 1991, no. 191).
[111] "Samedi" [10 May 1947] letter in Poulenc 1994, 47-4 (the reference is to his opera *Les Mamelles de Tirésias*).
[112] 11 June 1947 letter to Milhaud in Poulenc 1994, 47-5 (Poulenc 1991, no. 192). Heldy was a famous French soprano of Belgian birth.
[113] Berenguer, pp. 66-8.

Plate 18: Denise Duval (Bex, Switzerland, summer 1991 by the author)

ber dominated performance activity during 1947. The first half of the year also centered around preparations for the 3 June premiere of *Les Mamelles de Tirésias*. Much of the summer and fall was occupied with composing *Trois chansons de F. Garcia-Lorca* (FP 136) and *Mais mourir* (FP 137), incidental music for Jean Anouilh's *L'Invitation au château* (FP 138) and Molière's *Amphitryon* (FP 139), and two commissions, one from the BBC for *Sinfonietta*, and the other from an Amsterdam choir for an orchestration of *Litanies à la Vierge noire*. Late in the year three new commercial recordings were made with Bernac, and a private recording of the early *Rapsodie nègre*. In 1947 Poulenc was also made an officer of the International Society for

Contemporary Music (I.S.C.M.). He served with Edward J. Dent (President), Alois Haba, Douglas Moore, Paul Sanders, and Edward Clark (Honorary Secretary).[114]

From 9 February through 6 March Bernac and Poulenc performed in and around London. Once again Ibbs and Tillett acted as agents arranging BBC performances as well as one for Poulenc of his *Aubade* and Sextet in Chelsea Town Hall with the Leighton Lucas Orchestra. (See Appendix 2 for what is known about this tour.)

On 20 March, with Bernac's assistance, Poulenc gave a lecture entitled "Mes mélodies et leurs poètes" at the Université des Annales in Paris featuring performances of Schubert's "Soleil d'Hiver" [Die Nebensonnen] from *Winterreise* and his own *Montparnasse, Tel jour telle nuit, Métamorphoses*, and *Chansons villageoises*.[115] On 7 May, for a "Concert Public Radio," Bernac and Poulenc performed Dallapiccola's *Rencesvals*, three Eluard songs by Poulenc, and "4 Mélodies anglaises" by Hindemith.[116] On 12 May he accompanied Françoise Soulé in his Sonata for Violin and Piano (V) at the Conservatoire for the Société des Concerts, and on 22 May he attended the long delayed French premiere of *Figure humaine* at the Théâtre des Champs-Élysées under Paul Collaer's direction.[117] Several weeks later, on 3 June, the much-anticipated premiere of *Les M Mamelles* took place at the Opéra-Comique.

Not much is known about the rehearsal schedule for *Les Mamelles de Tirésias*, but it added to the hectic nature of Poulenc's winter.[118] As delighted as he was with Duval's preparation and performance, the production itself was not without problems. He had originally counted on Christian Bérard for the décor and costumes, but in the end Erté (Romain de Tirtoff), one of this century's most talented and prolific artist-designers, created them.

> Since returning to Paris [Poulenc remarked to Lockspeiser in early April] I have led a crazy life because of *Mamelles*. After a thousand misadventures I have finally found a divine Thérèse, who acts wonderfully, a very ingenious designer, and an outstanding producer. I hope that the orchestral side will be as good. I have my first reading the 15th.[119]

---

[114] *The Musical Times* 88 (1947), 10.

[115] Text of this talk in Poulenc 1947c.

[114] *The Musical Times* 88 (1947), 10.

[116] *Le Guide du concert et des théâtres lyriques* 27 (2 May 1947), 408.

[117] Poulenc thanked Boulanger for having published kind words about *Figure humaine* in a 16 June 1947 letter in Poulenc 1994, 47-7.

[118] 11 June 1947 letter to Milhaud in Poulenc 1994, 47-5 (Poulenc 1991, no. 192).

[119] Unpublished ca. 10 Apr. 1947 [stamped received 14 Apr. 1947] letter to Lockspeiser in GB-Rbbc.

Entrancing Muse

Erté first met Max de Rieux, producer of *Les Mamelles de Tirésias*, in 1944 when Rieux asked him to design *Don Pasquale* produced at the Palais de Chaillot. The veteran of other theatrical collaborations, Erté designed what he himself later referred to as "my greatest success" in opera.[120] Poulenc commented on his collaboration just before the premiere:

> I have asked for costume and set designs from Erté, the prestigious magician of the Tabarin [a famous Parisian music-hall], for whom 1912 was not merely a memory but a significant date, for at that time Erté was a dress designer with a great Paris fashion house. *Les Mamelles* having its "faerie" side, I needed a man of the theater who had surmounted the snares of the backstage machinery. Erté exceeded my expectations in giving nobility and style to a period which is usually ridiculed by the younger generation.[121]

Erté warmly remembered his collaboration with Poulenc:

> Oddly enough, Poulenc and I had never met at the Tabarin. It was Max de Rieux who first brought us together. From the moment we first met, there was a bond of sympathy and understanding between us. I have always admired Poulenc's music in all its forms—opera, ballet, instrumental works, songs, and religious music. . . . At the dress rehearsal, which took place before an extremely elegant audience of VIPs and press representatives, the opera was a tremendous success. But at the public opening there was a scandal. The middle-class audience, which constituted the chief clientele of the Opéra-Comique, was shocked by the outspoken language of Apollinaire's text. A fight broke out in the theater, and a number of seats were broken. . . . After the dress rehearsal Poulenc gave a dinner at the Grand Véfour. The atmosphere was exhilarating. I sat beside Jean Cocteau, whose brilliant conversation had always cast a spell on me. . . . I have never enjoyed working on a production more than I did on *Les Mamelles de Tirésias*. Collaborating with Poulenc was a pleasure, for we shared much the same tastes and views.[122]

Olin Downes, critic for *The New York Times*, printed an account based on the review published in *Carrefour* by the drama critic Palamède II:

> When this piece was produced at the Opéra-Comique the "steady patrons" objected to a work which in the estimate of the conservatives, was fit only for the burlesque stage—if for that—and not for this famous theatre. "Decadent!" cried an old gentleman, projecting

---

[120] Erté, p. 142. Erté also designed the cover of the printed piano-vocal score.
[121] Translation from Erté, pp. 146-7. Poulenc 1947b.
[122] Erté, p. 147. An unsigned announcement in *Carrefour* (24 June 1947), 8 adds a few more details.

himself from his seat in the gallery. "But it's horrible," yelped a lady in a loge. "Doubtless," rejoined a Poulencophile in a box near by, in cutting and icy tones, "You refer to yourself!" In the intermissions, on the staircase, the members of the "opposing camps" glared savagely at each other, "eyes full of hatred." They did not come to blows, but it was cheerfully observed that they might be expected to do this at future performances.[123]

In spite of the ruckus, the press was favorably disposed toward Poulenc's work, which shared billing with a now forgotten ballet in three tableaux entitled *La Rose rouge* after a tale by Oscar Wilde.[124] Numerous reviews appeared in French newspapers written by notables such as Marc Pincherle (*Les Nouvelles littéraires*), Maurice Brillant (*L'Aube* and *L'Epoque*), Claude Rostand (*Carrefour*), Roland-Manuel (*Combat*), Paul Le Flem, Louis Beydts, and others.[125] A week after the premiere, Poulenc told Milhaud:

> Erté, whose amusing program cover you have seen, has created a very amusing production in the style of the Folies Bergères. Only one drawback: your absence. I would very much have liked the performance of this work—dedicated to you—to coincide with your return.[126]

A RETURN TO COMPOSING AT NOIZAY DURING SUMMER AND FALL 1947

At the conclusion of the Paris season Poulenc left with Bernac for an eight-day trip to England where they performed an ambitious recital at Mayflower Barn, Jordans, on 7 June which included music by Grétry and Debussy as well as Schumann's *Dichterliebe*, Ravel's *Don Quichotte à Dulcinée*, and Poulenc's own *Tel jour telle nuit*. They recorded for the BBC on the 8th and 13th, and may also have performed at a private party at 3 Belgrave Place.[127] While in London

---

[123] Olin Downes (24 Aug. 1947), II, 5. Original in *Carrefour* cited above. Palamède II's review was "Un opéra démographique ou les mamelles de discorde."
[124] Music by Pierre Auclert, choreography by Jean-Jacques Etchevéry. After the production of Poulenc's opera, Apollinaire's play was revived in 1949 at the Théâtre des Noctambules with "une musique de percussion de Dino Castro." One wonders what Poulenc would have thought of this production in the event he saw it. See *Le Guide du concert et des théâtres lyriques* 29 (29 Apr. 1949), 193.
[125] Poulenc so enjoyed Le Flem's article that he thanked him in a 16 June 1947 letter (see Poulenc 1994, 47-6): "You *alone* have understood the exact sense of the Prologue." Hélène Jourdan-Morhange began her review with the words, "It was a catastrophe or a triumph."
[126] 11 June 1947 letter in Poulenc 1994, 47-5 (Poulenc 1991, no. 192). Milhaud's telegram to Poulenc, sent the day after the premiere, is quoted in Poulenc 1994, p. 639, note 3.
[127] All these concerts, including the private party (which may have been at an

Poulenc met Paul Hindemith and heard several of his works including *Variations for Piano and Strings*, which he liked very much, and
Hérodiade, which he found "always against Mallarmé."[128] Following this trip Poulenc returned briefly to Paris before taking a short
vacation. "After a more than hectic spring I have come to rest in the
Corrèze and to cleanse my soul at Rocamadour," he told Rose
Lambiotte.[129] Poulenc returned to Paris at the end of July before going to Noizay on 1 August for a period of intense composition.

• *Sinfonietta:* A BBC Commission (1947-48)

The history of this commission is detailed in various internal
memoranda and letters between Edward Lockspeiser at the BBC,
his superiors, and Poulenc. In a 24 February 1947 memorandum
Lockspeiser reported that he had discussed various possibilities with
Poulenc for a commission for "the Third Programme anniversary."[130]
What most interested Poulenc was a work for small orchestra, possibly a sinfonietta, modeled after Prokofiev's *Classical Symphony* and
lasting 14-16 minutes. Lockspeiser asked a Mr. Lowe what fee should
be suggested and said that Poulenc wished payment to be made
only upon completion of the work. In a follow-up memorandum
Lockspeiser reported that Poulenc would accept £100, which could
be offered to him while he was still at the Piccadilly Hotel in London, and that the offer would include the BBC's right to give the
first performance and to receive the manuscript full score.[131]

By mid-April, before orchestral rehearsals of *Les Mamelles de
Tirésias* began, Poulenc wrote Lockspeiser that he was thinking about
a *Sinfonietta* (FP 141) and hoped to have it ready for the October
anniversary, but would make no promises because they created anxiety.[132] Poulenc reiterated his fear of not being able to finish in time.[133]
Subsequently he told Milhaud that he was going to write a *Sinfonietta*
using a modest orchestra of winds in pairs (no trombones).[134] He

---

embassy), are listed in Ibbs and Tillett ledgers. There is also a dubious pencil
entry for a concert in Sheffield.

[128] 11 June 1947 letter to Milhaud in Poulenc 1994, 47-5 (Poulenc 1991, no. 192).
Poulenc writes this phrase in English.

[129] 17 July [1947] letter from Rocamadour in Poulenc 1994, 47-9.

[130] Lockspeiser's unpublished 24 Feb. 1947 memo to Mr. Lowe in GB-Rbbc (Francis
Poulenc Composer File 1).

[131] Lockspeiser's unpublished 28 Feb. 1947 memo to Mr. Lowe and Miss Candler in
GB-Rbbc (Francis Poulenc Composer File 1).

[132] Unpublished ca. 11 Apr. 1947 (stamped as received 14 Apr. 1947) letter to
Lockspeiser in GB-Rbbc. An [Aug. 1947] letter from Poulenc to Sauguet indicates
that the score was due in London on 4 Oct. Fragment of Poulenc's letter in
Poulenc 1994, p. 640, note 2.

[133] Unpublished 29 Apr. 1947 letter to Lockspeiser in GB-Rbbc.

[134] 11 June 1947 letter to Milhaud in Poulenc 1994, 47-5 (Poulenc 1991, no. 192).

also wrote to Bernac, André Schaeffner, Robert Douglas Gibson, and Doda Conrad sharing details about his intense work in August and September.[135] To Schaeffner Poulenc confided that the thematic material of the *Sinfonietta* came from the String Quartet destroyed the summer before.[136]

Poulenc must have worked diligently on the *Sinfonietta* over the summer because on 18 August he wrote to Lockspeiser that the *Sinfonietta* had grown catastrophically and had become a symphony, the first three movements lasting over nineteen minutes with the finale still to be written. Moreover, he had orchestrated two of the three movements. Since he lacked the speed of Hindemith, Falla, or Ravel, Poulenc was sure he could not possibly finish the commission on time.[137] He expressed this fear again on 5 September.[138] It was self-fulfilling prophesy for he did not complete the work until 8 September 1948 when he reported that he had added the last barline that morning.[139] Poulenc feared that his inability to produce on time had ruptured his relationship with Lockspeiser and the BBC. He proposed taking only £50 in exchange for the first performance and asked there be no agreement concerning either the dedication or the transfer of the full score.[140] Poulenc arranged with Roger Désormière to conduct the *Sinfonietta*, and in a brief note dated Paris, 1 October [1948] he wrote: "I offer to the BBC my heart and the world premiere performance of my *Sinfonietta* in exchange for a simple kiss of peace."[141] The correspondence ended on 13 September when Poulenc informed Lockspeiser that Désormière had delivered the last movement to the copyist.[142] Désormière also conducted the world premiere on 24 October 1948 with the Philharmonic Orchestra.[143]

[135] Relevant excerpts in Schmidt 1995, FP 141, pp. 389-91.

[136] Unpublished 23 Aug. [1947] letter to Schaeffner in F-Pgm; excerpt in Schmidt 1995, FP 141, p. 390.

[137] 18 Aug. [1947] letter to Lockspeiser in Poulenc 1994, 47-11. Similar information was conveyed to Schaeffner in an unpublished 23 Aug. [1947] letter. See F-Pgm (Fonds Schaeffner, no. 217).

[138] Unpublished 5 Sept. [1947] letter (fragment in Poulenc 1994, p. 643, note 1) in GB-Rbbc.

[139] Unpublished 8 Sept. [1948] letter to Lockspeiser (fragment in Poulenc 1994, p. 643, note 1) in GB-Rbbc. See also his letter to Sauguet in Poulenc 1994, 48-4 in which he says he would be working with Désormière on the 11th.

[140] Poulenc then dedicated the work to Auric, upon whose advice he retained themes from his destroyed String Quartet (II).

[141] 1 Oct. [1948] letter in Poulenc 1994, p. 643, note 1. Lockspeiser's amenable 7 Oct. reply is also printed in note 1.

[142] Schmidt 1995, FP 141, p. 387. In the holograph manuscript (in a private collection) Poulenc indicates that the movements were written: (1) "Noizay Août 47", (2) "Noizay — Avril 48", (3) "Noizay Septembre 47," (4) "Achevé le 8 Septembre 1948."

[143] Unpublished 13 Sept. [1948] postcard to Lockspeiser in GB-Rbbc. On 18 Oct.

• *Trois chansons de F. Garcia-Lorca* and **Orchestration of** *Litanies*

While wrestling with the *Sinfonietta* Poulenc set three Federico Garcia Lorca texts in "excellent" French translations by Félix Gattegno and orchestrated *Litanies à la Vierge noire*.[144] Correspondence with Bernac and André Schaeffner clarifies that Poulenc struggled with these *chansons,* and on 1 September he wrote Bernac: "The third ('Chanson de l'oranger sec') is a sarabande!!!! The second a jota rather Plaza Clichy as Satie would have said."[145] Poulenc dedicated each to a friend: (1) and (3) to the singers Geneviève Touraine and Gérard Souzay, and (2) to Mme Auguste Lambiotte. He intended that Souzay, then Bernac's voice student, sing the cycle. "The group is not written too high so that Gérard can sing them," he said.[146] The dedication of a song to Mme Lambiotte stems partially from the hospitality she and her husband showed him during visits to Brussels, and partially from the fact that she had sent him two poems for consideration. Poulenc told her that he felt no symbiotic relationship with the poetry of Paul Verlaine or Stéphane Mallarmé and even less with that of Paul Valéry.[147] On 10 August, however, he had a solution: "I have finally found a poem for you. It is by Lorca 'Adelina à la promenade.' It is sort of your portrait as a gypsy."[148] In February 1948 Poulenc gave her a printed score with an inscrip-

---

1949 a performance of the *Sinfonietta* by the Orchestre de Toulouse (Le Conte conductor) was broadcast on French Radio. See *Le Guide du concert et des théâtres lyriques* 30 (14 Oct. 1949), 14. George Szell performed the American premiere of *Sinfonietta* in Cleveland on 13 and 15 Oct. 1949, and Poulenc used this fact to press Gibson to publish it. To that end, Poulenc arrived in London on 15 Dec. 1950 with corrections in hand, and during spring 1951 continued his lobbying, inquiring why the score was not yet printed. (Unpublished "samedi" [early Dec. 1950] postcard to Gibson and unpublished 18 May [1951] letter to Gibson both in GB-Lchester.) By 17 June he had received proofs for several movements and was delighted with what he saw. (Unpublished 17 June [1951] letter to Gibson in GB-Lchester.) In Aug. Poulenc sent a list of metronome markings to be added to the score. (Unpublished 19 Aug. [1951] letter to Gibson in GB-Lchester.) He was concerned about shopping the work around to conductors for potential performances, thus the need for a printed score. One finally appeared in later 1951.
144 Unpublished 23 Aug. [1947] letter to Schaeffner in F-Pgm (excerpt in Schmidt 1995, FP 136, p. 377). Garcia Lorca was an important Spanish poet and writer killed at the start of the Spanish Civil War.
145 1 Sept. [1947] letter to Bernac in Poulenc 1994, 47-12.
146 Bernac's [Aug. 1947] letter partially transcribed in Poulenc 1994, pp. 643-4, note 1. A further [Sept. 1947] letter to Bernac quoted in the same note, indicates that Poulenc had sent copies of two chansons to Souzay and was upset at the lack of any acknowledgment.
147 17 July [1947] letter in Poulenc 1994, 47-9.
148 Fragment of Poulenc's [10 Aug. 1947] letter to Rose Lambiotte in Poulenc 1994, p. 641, note 1.

tion noting how much Adelina resembled a certain "dame rose."[149] When considering this cycle in *Journal de mes mélodies*, Poulenc lamented the difficulty he had always had expressing his passion for Garcia Lorca.

> My sonata for piano and violin, dedicated to his memory, is, alas, quite mediocre Poulenc, and these three songs are of small import among my vocal works. The last song has the defect of being "nobly" French while it should be "gravely" Spanish.[150]

Poulenc was asked by the Choir of St Graal [sic] in Amsterdam to orchestrate his *Litanies à la Vierge noire*, originally composed for voices and organ in August 1936.[151] The manuscript, dated 1 September, is scored for strings (12 first violins, 10 second violins, 8 violas, 6 violoncellos, 4 doublebasses) and 3 timpani.[152]

•*L'Invitation au château* and *Amphitryon*

In July 1947 Poulenc was requested to provide incidental music for two plays: Jean Anouilh's new *L'Invitation au château*, first performed 5 November 1947 at the Théâtre de l'Atelier (direction and décor by André Barsacq), and Molière's venerable *Amphitryon*, first performed 5 December 1947 at the Théâtre Marigny by the Compagnie Madeleine Renaud-Jean-Louis Barrault (direction by Barrault, décor and costumes by Christian Bérard).[153] Anouilh told Poulenc that the only requirement was to write a very funny waltz using a single theme in minor mode which would be reprised frequently. On the other hand, if Poulenc preferred to write an *opéra bouffe* he stood ready to recast the text and to spend two or three weeks together with Poulenc and a piano![154] In the end, the former plan obtained, and Poulenc supplied a score for clarinet, piano, and violin. He told André Schaeffner:

> I have completed a *musique de scène 1900* for Anouilh (. . .) without great importance (pretty waltzes [. . .] that's all) and am beginning something much more difficult and *grave* (in every sense of the word) for Molière's *L'Amphitryon* [. . .].[155]

Barrault mentioned that he wanted to meet Poulenc in Paris between 24 July and 1 August to discuss the project and to settle pre-

---

[149] Dedication in Schmidt 1995, FP 136, pp. 376-7 and Poulenc 1994, p. 641, note 1.
[150] Poulenc 1993, p. 53 (Poulenc 1989, pp. 90-1) and Mellers, pp. 72-3.
[151] 1 Sept. [1947] letter to Bernac in Poulenc 1994, 47-12.
[152] Schmidt 1995, FP 82, p. 255.
[153] Schmidt 1995, FP 138 and 139 respectively. The complete music (nearly seventeen minutes) for *L'Invitation*, minus a few "vamps," has been recorded on CALA (CACD 1018, disc A) ©1994.
[154] Anouilh's [July 1947] letter to Poulenc in Poulenc 1994, 47-10.
[155] Unpublished 23 Aug. [1947] letter to Schaeffner in F-Pgm.

cise timings for the musical selections.[156] "I saw Barrault at length,"
Poulenc told Bernac, "All his ideas are striking and we reached agreement about everything."[157] Composing the score was difficult and
demanding, but by 23 September he reported that "*Amphitryon* will
be *very special*. If I have succeeded it will surely be my best incidental music. It was horribly difficult to do, but there, finally, I have a
pit orchestra."[158]

After a brief trip to England for a BBC broadcast with Bernac on 3
October, Poulenc went to Paris to record four radio broadcasts and
to see Barrault, Anouilh, and Charles Kiesgen, before returning to
Noizay for two weeks.[159] A month later *L'Invitation au château* began
its run which continued through the first half of 1948.[160] Critics spoke
most favorably of the production, and André Alter noted:

> In any case, André Barsacq has mounted one of his best productions.
> Everything is perfect in the mechanism which he has regulated, ev-
> erything is a celebration for the eye and royal for the spirit. Francis
> Poulenc's music allies itself perfectly with the ironic grace of the décor
> and costumes.[161]

Amphitryon followed *L'Invitation* by a few weeks, opening on 5
December. Again Alter reviewed the production, concluding that
"The décor and costumes of Christian Bérard are charm itself; Francis
Poulenc's music is ravishing."[162]

•...Mais mourir

Poulenc's only other composition of the fall was a *mélodie* entitled
...Mais mourir dedicated to Nusch Eluard's memory. She died on 28
November 1946 of a cerebral hemorrhage.[163] Poulenc, who had dedi-

---

[156] Barrault's 12 July 1947 letter to Poulenc in Poulenc 1994, 47-8.

[157] Fragment of Poulenc's 4 Aug. [1947] letter to Bernac in Poulenc 1994, pp. 640-1, note 2.

[158] Fragment of Poulenc's "samedi" [Oct. 1947] letter to Bernac in Poulenc 1994, p. 640, note 2.

[159] Partially unpublished "samedi" [Oct. 1947] letter in US-NH. An article by Scott Goddard, "London Letter," in the *Chesterian* 22, no. 152 (Sept. 1947), 44 indicates that the Bernac/Poulenc duo also performed at Wigmore Hall.

[160] Schmidt 1995, FP 138, p. 379. The 150th performance took place the week of 31 Mar. 1948, and the last listing in *Le Monde* was published on 10 July. A contract from the Théâtre de Bruxelles before 31 May 1948 between Lejeune and Gobert (directors) and Anouilh and Poulenc (author and composer) was on sale at Galerie d'autographs Jean-Emmanuel Raux (Saint-Germaine-en-Laye) in 1998.

[161] *L'Aube* (9 Nov. 1947), 2. Schmidt 1995, FP 138, p. 379.

[162] *L'Aube* (7 Dec. 1947), 2. Lengthier passage in Schmidt 1995, FP 139, p. 381. Other Bérard productions took place in New York City on 20 Nov. 1952 and in Paris at the Théâtre National de l'Odéon on 25 Oct. 1961.

[163] Concerning the sudden death of Eluard's second wife see Gateau, pp. 307-08. Appropriately, the text was by Eluard.

cated "Le Front comme un drapeau perdu" (no. 3 of *Tel jour telle nuit*) to her in 1937, greatly admired her beauty (particularly her hands) and mourned her passing.[164] Work was completed at Noizay by 21 October 1947 when he wrote Robert Douglas Gibson that it and the three Garcia Lorca chansons would be published by Heugel. The Garcia Lorca songs were first printed on 3 November 1947 (in an edition of 500 copies) and *...Mais mourir* on 13 February 1948 (in an edition of 1,000 copies).[165] On 21 October, when he sent Gibson corrected proofs for another printing of *Trois mouvements perpétuels*, Poulenc was still concerned about getting *Babar* published.[166]

YEAR-END EVENTS

The Bernac/Poulenc duo also gave its customary fall recital at the Salle Gaveau on 12 November featuring diverse offerings by Rameau, Schubert, Stravinsky, and Ravel, and the premiere of *Trois chansons de F. Garcia-Lorca*. A review suggests that Poulenc's *Le Portrait* was sung as an encore.[167]

In September Poulenc began recording a series of programs under the title "A Bâtons rompus" for French Radio.[168] Between September 1947 and late April or early May 1948, the first series was recorded. Each thirty-minute program, which contained equal portions of commentary and recorded music, was broadcast over *Chaîne nationale*. A second series of twelve installments was recorded after he returned from his first trip to America in 1949. Information about both series appears in Appendix 2.

Finally, in early December, the Bernac/Poulenc duo went to England for various engagements. They appeared for BBC Television on 3 December, on the 4th they gave a recital, and on the 7th they performed music by Debussy and Ravel for a BBC Third Programme.[169] During their stay they recorded Fauré's *Soir, Le Secret, L'Automne,* and *Les Berceaux* for Voix de son Maître/His Master's Voice. They did not record again until February-March 1950 during their second North American tour.

---

[164] Several Man Ray photographs of Nusch in Buckland/Chimènes, plates 11-12.
[165] Schmidt 1995, FP 136, p. 376 and FP 137, p. 378 respectively.
[166] Unpublished 21 Oct. [1947] letter to Gibson from Noizay in GB-Lchester.
[167] P.V.'s review in *Le Guide du concert et des théâtres lyriques* 28 (28 Nov.1947), 143.
[168] Lucie Kayas has studied Poulenc's broadcasts and published her findings in Kayas 1999 and Buckland/Chimènes: e. Transcripts of the commentary portions of the broadcasts in Poulenc's hand exist at F-Pn (Rés. Vmc. ms. 125; Rés. Vmc. ms. 126 (1-5); and Rés. Vms. ms. 131). Tape recordings of some are in the Institut national de l'audiovisuel, Paris.
[169] They may have been in London as early as 3 Dec., the date suggested in Poulenc's unpublished 21 Oct. [1947] letter to Gibson from Noizay in GB-Lchester.

EVENTS LEADING TO THE FIRST NORTH AMERICAN TOUR: 1948

By 1948 Poulenc was an inveterate concertizer as accompanist or soloist. Having toured from Seville to Amsterdam, Marseilles to Warsaw, Europe held few new challenges for the composer as he neared fifty. Moreover, after the war he had settled into a routine similar to that described to Bernac: seven months of concerts, three of work at Noizay, and two of vacation.[170] For Poulenc, the July-August period meant a working vacation. The focus of his 1948 touring with Bernac was their first trip to the United States from late October through mid-December. *Calligrammes,* a song cycle on poems by Apollinaire, was composed for it.

Poulenc's activities during the first part of 1948 are not well documented, except for a fifteen-concert tour to Holland with Bernac.[171] The pair traveled to Amsterdam by train on 19 January and were in The Hague on 2 February.[172] Poulenc was at Noizay during April and May, notwithstanding brief trips to Paris, where he made preliminary sketches of two Apollinaire *mélodies* which would become part of *Calligrammes.*[173] In April he wrote Henry Barraud, director of music for the national radio, concerning a possible conducting engagement for Luigi Dallapiccola, the first performance of the orchestral version of *Litanies* by Roger Désormière on 27 May, the engagement of Yvonne Gouverné to prepare the chorus for *Litanies,* and the premiere of *Chansons françaises;* he also asked if Désormière could be engaged for a performance of the *Sinfonietta* which Poulenc longed to hear before his 22 October departure for America.[174]

In the spring Poulenc met the American piano duo of Arthur Gold and Robert Fizdale, who were making their first European visit after an enormously successful debut recital at New York's Town Hall on 15 February 1946. The meeting, at a party given by Germaine Tailleferre, is described by Gold and Fizdale:

> Our boat train reached Paris at midnight. Early the next morning we telephoned Germaine Tailleferre, the only woman member of *Les Six.* We told her that friends had sent her a package from New York, and she asked us to lunch. When we arrived there was an animated party in progress. It was our first taste of the life that Misia knew: that par-

---

[170] "Lundi 10" [Sept. 1945] letter to Bernac in Poulenc 1994, 45-21 (Poulenc 1991, no. 185).

[171] *Le Guide du concert et des théâtres* 27 (10 Jan. 1948), 202.

[172] Ciry, entry for 19 Jan. 1948 (Ciry was on the same train from Paris to Amsterdam), and fragment of Poulenc's 2 Feb. [1948] letter to Denise Bourdet from The Hague in Poulenc 1994, p. 656, note 3.

[173] 18 July [1948] letter to Bernac from Le Tremblay in Poulenc 1994, 48-2 (Poulenc 1991, no. 193).

[174] [Apr. 1948] letter to Barraud in Poulenc 1994, 48-1.

ticularly Parisian mixture of worldly elegance, artistic cultivation, caustic wit, and superb food. The package we were carrying was the score of Virgil Thomson's opera *The Mother of Us All*. After lunch Georges Auric sat at the piano, carefully turned the music upside down, and improvised a Thomsonesque accompaniment while Francis Poulenc "created" the roles. He sang a nonsense-syllable imitation of Gertrude Stein's English in a hilarious falsetto, and was especially compelling in the role of America's pioneer suffragette Susan B. Anthony.[175]

Poulenc's attachment to this pair resulted in three works: *L'Embarquement pour Cythère*, Sonata for Two Pianos, and *Elégie*.[176] In later trips to France this attractive couple became a favorite in many Parisian salons and was welcomed by some of Paris' most influential patronesses such as Marie-Blanche de Polignac.

Poulenc and Bernac were in London for a BBC Third Programme devoted to music by Mozart and Poulenc on 1 June and during the month they discussed *Calligrammes* (FP 140).[177] Immediately after London, Poulenc participated i the Strasbourg Festival, playing his *Bal Masqué* on 12 June.[178] In July Poulenc made his customary trip to Le Tremblay.[179] As usual, his time there was fruitful. "Music keeps flowing out of me, flowing and it is a joy," he said, "Quite often my winter uneasiness is the result of my lack of creativity." The principal new composition was *Calligrammes*, but he also worked on a Sonata for Cello and Piano and the finale of the *Sinfonietta*.

Quickly some good news [he wrote Bernac]: you will have, for our second New York recital, a beautiful new cycle which I already love as much as *Tel jour telle nuit*. In *Calligrammes* I have truly found just what I required. What I do not owe to Apollinaire! I have already written four *mélodies* (two having been vaguely sketched in Noizay in May); there will be seven altogether and I know precisely what they will all be like. Even more carefully crafted than *Tel jour*, this cycle has a true internal structure. All these poems of 1913-15 conjure up a flood of memories from my Nogent past and from the time of the 1914 war. Thus the dedications to my childhood friends.[180]

[175] Gold, p. 306.
[176] Schmidt 1995, FP 150, 156, and 175 respectively. Poulenc first speaks of meeting "les boys" in a 15 Sept. [1948] letter to Thomson in Poulenc 1994, 48-6. He also referred to them as "kiddies."
[177] Fragment of Poulenc's unpublished [June 1948] letter to Bernac in Poulenc 1994, p. 648, note 5. The Ibbs and Tillett ledgers indicate that Poulenc played *Aubade* with the BBC on 1 June.
[178] *Le Guide du concert et des théâtres lyriques* 28 (16 and 23 Apr. 1948), 279.
[179] By the 18th he had already spent a week.
[180] 18 July [1948] letter in Poulenc 1994, 48-2 (Poulenc 1991, no. 193). Poulenc dedicated the seven songs to Simone Tilliard, Pierre Lelong, Jacqueline Apolli-

Four years after completing the cycle, Poulenc elaborated on what lay behind his conception.

> Since for me, inspiration (pardon the use of this word) always springs
> from an association of ideas, *Calligrammes* will always be connected
> with that spring of 1918 when, before leaving for the front, I bought
> the volume of *Le Mercure* at Adrienne Monnier's. (To tell the truth, I
> believe that it was Raymonde Linossier who offered it to me.) I was
> then in an antiaircraft section stationed at Tremblay. Once again chance
> led me to the banks of the Marne of my childhood. When we were
> not jumping on the nearest Vincennes tram taking make believe leave,
> I would end each day in one of the little bistros in Nogent. It was
> actually in one of these that I first made contact with the volume of
> Apollinaire, thus melding what I was going to live through with the
> poetic fictions of *Calligrammes*.[181]

During his last few days in Paris Poulenc went to Vincennes and other nostalgic places where the cycle took shape in his mind. By this time he knew the precise key structure of the cycle even if he misrepresented the first song as being in F-sharp minor rather than F minor. Poulenc said that if he succeeded, one *mélodie* would be broken up with very long piano interludes.[182] Progress was steady, and by 22 July five *mélodies* were completed.[183] At the end of July he spent a week in Paris and by the 31st had completed all seven.[184] Poulenc expressed great satisfaction with this cycle and called "Voyage" one of the two or three songs he valued the most. He felt his North American tour, during which *Calligrammes* was premiered, would represent him as "the master of contemporary song."[185]

From sketches made between 1940 and 1942, Poulenc worked on the Sonata for Cello and Piano at Le Tremblay while finishing the *Sinfonietta*.[186] By 18 July two movements were finished and he hoped to complete the finale that week. Work slowed, however, because on 8 September two more weeks were required.[187] It is dedicated jointly to Marthe Bosredon, at whose home it was begun, and Pierre

---

naire, the memory of Emmanuel Faÿ, Jeanne Manceaux, Jacques Soulé, and the memory of Raymonde Linossier.

[181] Poulenc 1993, p. 54 (Poulenc 1989, pp. 92-5).

[182] "Jeudi" [July 1948] letter to Bernac in F-Pn. Excerpt in Schmidt 1995, FP 140, p. 385.

[183] "Jeudi 22" [July 1948] letter to Bernac in F-Pn. This excerpt in Schmidt 1995, FP 140, p. 386 and Poulenc 1994, p. 648, note 4.

[184] 31 July [1948] letter to Bernac in F-Pn. Excerpt in Schmidt 1995, FP 140, p. 386.

[185] 8 Sept. 1948 letter to Lockspeiser in GB-Rbbc and Schmidt 1995, FP 140, p. 386.

[186] The manuscript indicates that the Sonata was written between Apr. and Sept. 1948. Schmidt 1995, FP 143, p. 393.

[187] 8 Sept. [1948] letter to Sauguet from Noizay in Poulenc 1994, 48-4.

Fournier, who assisted with various technical aspects such as bowings and with whom Poulenc premiered it in Paris on 18 May 1949.

In late summer Poulenc was asked by his nephew Frère Jérôme Poulenc to compose for a chorale directed by Père Jean-Joseph Buirette at the convent of Carrières-sous-Poissy (northwest of Paris).[188] While at Noizay in August he wrote *Quatre petites prières de Saint François d'Assise* (FP 142) for male choir a cappella, the texts taken from a small pamphlet published by the Franciscans.[189] A minor work, it is dedicated in part to the memory of his uncle Camille, one of a very few dedications to members of his own family.[190]

As summer waned, Poulenc enjoyed working through Sauguet's new song cycle *Visions infernales* with Doda Conrad and spent evenings listening to the radio.[191] Poulenc was particularly delighted by performances from the Venice Festival of Arnold Schönberg's Violin Concerto (Schönberg at his best) and Paul Hindemith's opera *Cardillac* (some remarkable pages, but lacking in contrast), and he looked forward to future broadcasts of Luigi Dallapiccola's one-act ballet *Marsia* and Béla Bartók's opera *Bluebeard's Castle*.[192] Poulenc announced his return to Paris for 29 September. Just before embarking on 22 October, he and Bernac attended a *soirée* on the 16th at the home of Marie-Blanche de Polignac (rue Barbet-de-Jouy) to perform some of the New York repertoire. Here *Calligrammes* received its unofficial premiere.[193]

FIRST TOUR WITH BERNAC TO THE UNITED STATES

In place of the customary November Salle Gaveau recital, Bernac and Poulenc made a six-week coast-to-coast tour of North America. Given the repertoire, much time must have been devoted to rehearsals immediately preceding departure. Poulenc planned this tour

---

[188] Fragments of Frère Jérôme Poulenc's 15 Aug. 1948 letter to Poulenc in Poulenc 1994, p. 649, notes 1 and 2. Frère Jérôme was born Gérard Poulenc. Poulenc told John Gruen, "I had a great uncle, the Abbé Joseph Poulenc who was the curé of Ivry-sur-Seine, so that a strong religious tradition is firmly tied to my work." Gruen 1960, p. 6.

[189] Schmidt 1995, FP 142, p. 392 for more information. In Poulenc 1954, p. 159 Poulenc reported the pieces were composed in Sept., but the holograph manuscripts give Aug. for all four numbers. In an 8 Sept. [1948] letter to Sauguet Poulenc reported the work complete. Poulenc 1994, 48-4.

[190] Mellers, pp. 138-9.

[191] It was premiered by Conrad at New York's Town Hall in 1949.

[192] 8 Sept [1948] letter to Sauguet in Poulenc 1994, 48-4.

[193] Conrad 1983, p. 71 and Buckland/Chimènes: b, p. 223. Included among the guests were Freund [Conrad's mother], Arthur Rubinstein, Long, Chalupt, Peignot, Conrad, Robert Veyron-Lacroix, and Jacques Leguerney.

with the assistance of the bass Doda Conrad, a member of Nadia Boulanger's entourage in the 1930s, who had lived abroad for years, becoming an honorary U.S. citizen in 1942. Conrad's superb command of English, numerous contacts, and penchant for organization made him an invaluable asset.[194] Coppicus & Schang Inc. of Columbia Artists Management Inc. in New York City became their official U.S. agents. The Bernac/Poulenc duo played in everything from New York's Town Hall to hotel ballrooms and humble high school auditoriums (Plate 19). Poulenc also carefully paved the way with the influential New York composer-critic Virgil Thomson. "Tell everybody that Poupoule is a Parisian type, who speaks English poorly, is sometimes unsociable, but full of good will. In any case I play the piano well."[195]

Once settled in New York City Poulenc could not wait to share news with his niece.

> Everything is going wonderfully. I am vanquished by New York and divinely accommodated. I have a two-room apartment at the Saint-Moritz [Hotel] with a piano supplied by Baldwin and a heavenly view out on [Central] Park. Think of me at the [Hotel] Meurice! It is very expensive but everyone advised me to do this and, anyway, I am so relaxed here that I have been able to complete the *Hymne* [FP 144] for Doda Conrad in excellent form.[196]

The tour began with concerts in the east before wending its way to Los Angeles. From there they went to Salt Lake City before returning to New York. Poulenc made many new acquaintances and renewed others. (See Appendix 2 for a tour overview.)

When Poulenc arrived in New York he was feted by friends old and new. The famous Metropolitan Opera soprano Lily Pons sent flowers to his hotel, hosted a dinner party at which Vladimir Horowitz was a featured guest, and threw an immense cocktail party in his honor.[197] Poulenc also dined with his old friend Christian Dior, who had just opened a new boutique called "Dior New York" at 730 Fifth Avenue,[198] and by the end of two weeks he had spent time with other old friends including Yvonne de Casa Fuerte, Vittorio Rieti,

---

[194] He arranged Boulanger's first tour of England with her group. I am most grateful to Conrad for a lengthy interview in 1991 at his home near Blois, France.
[195] 15 Sept. [1948] letter to Thomson in Poulenc 1994, 48-6.
[196] 3 Nov. 1948 letter to Manceaux in Poulenc 1994, 48-8 (Poulenc 1991, no. 194). Brigitte took some of the publicity photographs Poulenc used during his American tour. According to the manuscript, *Hymne* was composed in "New-York 2-8 Novembre [19]48"; the printed edition incorrectly says "New York, Jan. 1949." By then Poulenc had returned to France. See also Schmidt 1995, FP 144, pp. 396-7.
[197] 3 Nov. 1948 letter to Manceaux in Poulenc 48-8 (Poulenc 1991, no. 194).
[198] 10 Nov. [1948] letter to Manceaux from Boston in Poulenc 1994, 48-9 (Poulenc 1991, no. 195).

**Plate 19: Caricature of
Bernac and Poulenc by
James House (14 Dec.
1948, The Evening Bul-
letin, Philadelphia, PA.)**

Natalie Paley, and Nicky de Gunzbourg.[199] Their first performance
on 4 November in the music room at Dumbarton Oaks, the estate of
Ambassador and Mrs. Robert Woods Bliss in Washington D.C., was
a prelude to the Town Hall recital three days later. Both featured
three *mélodies* by Debussy, three excerpts from Jean-Baptiste Lully
stage works, plus Poulenc's *Tel jour telle nuit* and *Chansons villageoises*.
In Town Hall their entrance was greeted by a three-minute ovation,
and seven curtain calls followed *Tel jour telle nuit*. Press accounts
were most flattering and under the headline "TWO FRENCHMEN WIN
CHEERS" the *New York World-Telegram* critic wrote:

> The baritone happened, however, to be the French Pierre Bernac, an
> artist of astonishing power, and since Mr. Poulenc turned out to be
> one of the smartest accompanists in Town Hall annals, the occasion
> was well worth two hours of any music gourmet's time.

Noel Straus, writing in the 8 November edition of *The New York
Times*, concluded:

> Poulenc was not only to be admired as composer at this concert, but
> also as an unusually talented accompanist. His technical proficiency
> made it possible for him to take some of his own songs at an exceed-

[199] Poulenc had known Paley (formerly married to the couturier Lucien Lelong)
since the early 1930s. She was now married to the theater producer John Wilson.
Nicky de Gunzbourg was an editor of the American magazine *Vogue*. Poulenc
had known Rieti since 1922 when they met in Vienna. See Chapter V.

ingly high rate of speed and yet keep his playing expertly clean and transparent. Like M. Bernac, he exhibited flawless taste and refinement of style, and there was an uncommonly sympathetic merging of every detail of the interpretations on the part of the two artists.[...] Whether viewed from the standpoint of M. Bernac's accomplishments, or those of M. Poulenc, this was a recital long to be remembered.[200]

The day after Poulenc reported being bombarded by telephone calls from publishers and recording companies.[201] One interview in French, with lapses into English, was granted to Olin Downes of *The New York Times*.[202] In it Poulenc named Milhaud as the greatest living French composer and called Messiaen "extremely gifted," adding:

> The outside world has never affected Messiaen. He lives wholly within himself. War or peace, he would be just the same. He is apart from his fellow creatures. This is his strength, also his problem. Clarification, objectivity are things necessary, I think, for his free and complete expression.

Downes quoted Poulenc's opinions of some French musical icons:

> I have the deepest respect and affection too for the music of Franck. What I cannot stand is the perfect polish and sentimentality, the beautiful breeding of the fashionable drawing room, in the music of Fauré. I cannot help it. [...] No, I cannot help it, even though Nadia Boulanger considers him a god.

Further conversation revealed that "Poulenc had other enthusiasms unfashionable in modern French musical circles." He admired the music of Tchaikovsky (particularly the Symphony no. 6, "Pathétique"), greatly admired Richard Strauss (*Till Eulenspiegels lustige Streiche, Tod und Verklärung, Don Quixote,*and *Don Juan;* but he disliked the *Sinfonia domestica* and *Also sprach Zarathustra*), agreed with Ravel's words to him just before he died to the effect that "Richard Strauss and myself are among our contemporaries the great masters of instrumentation," extolled Stravinsky (*Oedipus Rex*) and Paul Hindemith (*Mathis de Maler*), and paid homage to Arnold Schönberg (Violin Concerto) though he preferred the music of Berg. The interview closed with Poulenc's thoughts on composing.

> But a truce to composing by theory, doctrine, rule. Above all, let not a composer seek to be in the mode. If you are not à la mode today, you may not be out of the mode tomorrow. [...] It is the alpha and omega of the creative artist, it is his only title to recognition or such

---

[200] See p. 24.
[201] 10 Nov. [1948] letter to Manceaux in Poulenc 1994, 48-9 (Poulenc 1991, no. 195).
[202] *The New York Times* (7 Nov. 1948), II, 7.

measure of reputation as he achieves. And his only protection against destruction.

After three performances of the *Concert champêtre* with Mitropoulos on 11, 12, and 14 November and a recital at Smith College in Northhampton, Massachusetts, Bernac and Poulenc gave their second Town Hall concert on 20 November before a packed house. The world premiere of *Calligrammes* received seven curtain calls and earned five encores. Their program of music by Gounod, Schumann, Fauré, Ravel, and Poulenc garnered twenty-three curtain calls.[203]

Sometime during his New York stay Poulenc also dined with the violinists Nathan Milstein and Zino Francescatti and saw a thriller entitled *The Rope*, which had been showing for months.[204] This Alfred Hitchcock production, released by Transatlantic Warner Brothers in 1948, was the "macabre story of two young men who give a tea party over a chest which contains the body of a boy they have murdered. . . ."[205] Poulenc realized that the only music used in the film was a three-fold repetition of his *Trois mouvements perpétuels*. Following the advice of George Middleton in New York, Poulenc asked Robert Douglas Gibson at Chester for the appropriate letter so that he could collect royalties. Mme Salabert granted him 50% of moneys accrued from films, and he suggested Gibson do likewise.

Immediately following the second New York concert Bernac and Poulenc left for a two-week tour to Québec, Detroit, Chicago, Los Angeles, Oakland, Salt Lake City, Denver, Pittsburgh, and Philadelphia. The complete itinerary of the tour is not known, but contracts for their Chicago engagement indicate that they received $750 for a 28 November recital at The Fortnightly (120 East Bellevue Place).[206] On this occasion Poulenc included four of his own short piano works as the fifth segment of the concert. While in Chicago Poulenc met the violinist Louis Kaufman who would give the American premiere of his Sonata for Violin and Piano with Erich Itor Kahn at Carnegie Hall in New York on 10 December 1948. A year later he and Poulenc played the Sonata "as a memorial broadcast [for Ginette Neveu] for the French National Radio."[207]

---

[203] 21 Nov. [1948] letter to Marie-Blanche in Poulenc 1994, 48-10 (Poulenc 1991, no. 196).

[204] *The Rope* is described in unpublished letters of 3 and 19 Nov. [1948] from Poulenc to Gibson (originals in GB-Lchester).

[205] Kenneth MacGowan's review in *Script* (Sept. 1948), 42. The film starred James Stewart.

[206] Copies of the 26 May 1948 contract, program, newspaper clippings, and other advertising materials in US-Cn (The Arts Club Papers).

[207] Annette Kaufman's liner notes for the 1972 recording on Orion (ORS 7292) of the Sonata with Hélène Pignari. The cover of this recording reproduces a page of

While in California, he visited the Stravinskys in Los Angeles and the Milhauds at Mills College in Oakland.[208] According to Vera Stravinsky she and Igor attended the Wilshire Ebell Theater recital and on 2 December entertained Bernac and Poulenc for lunch.[209] Albert Goldberg, in the *Los Angeles Times*, noted that this concert:

> . . . was not to be gauged by conventional standards. Mr. Bernac's voice is not one which would pass muster if it were to be put to the usual tests, it is probably past its prime, and possibly it never boasted the sonority or the sensuous quality that is required for an easy success by current notions. But, Mr. Bernac is a superb artist, and in Mr. Poulenc he had an extraordinary accompanist, one who made the piano part of each song, a sensitive and integral part of its structure in a way that one had almost forgotten existed.[210]

On the return trip East, they stopped in Salt Lake City, which Poulenc called a "very curious city."[211] Once back east, one final New York concert remained on 11 December at the Museum of Modern Art. Sponsored by the League of Composers, it was entirely devoted to Poulenc's music, including *Le Bestiaire, Banalités,* Trio, *Le Bal masqué* (with Poulenc at the piano), "Dans le Jardin d'Anna," "Allons plus vite," *Le Portrait,* and "Tu vois le feu du soir."[212] The tour ended with engagements in Pittsburgh and Philadelphia crammed in before their departure.

In the course of his tour Poulenc also made new friends. One was Rose Dercourt, an American soprano of Polish birth who had lived in Paris between the two wars, and studied voice with Marya Freund.[213] Eventually she married Fred Plaut, noted photographer and engineer for Columbia Records. Rose Dercourt made repeated visits to France beginning in 1951 to coach with Poulenc, who later dedicated a song to her which they recorded. Fred took more than five hundred photographs of Poulenc and he delighted as much in sending new prints to Poulenc as Poulenc did in receiving them.[214]

---

the sonata inscribed by Poulenc "Pour Louis Kaufman qui joue si bien cette Sonate avec un grand merci. Francis Poulenc [rule] Chicago 49 [rule]," as well as a photograph of Poulenc, Kaufman, and an unidentified woman [probably Annette Kaufman].

[208] In a 5 Dec. [1948] letter to Sauguet (partially transcribed in Poulenc 1994, p. 655, note 2), Poulenc said that he was leaving Milhaud, who seemed well and happily situated.

[209] StravinskyV, p. 145.

[210] 5 Dec. 1948, III, 7.

[211] 5 Dec. [1948] letter to Denise Bourdet in Poulenc 1994, 48-11.

[212] Program reconstructed from R[obert] S[abin]'s review in *Musical America* 69 (Jan. 1949), 10.

[213] Poulenc 1994, p. 1021.

[214] Negatives and letters at US-NH.

The Plauts' relationship with Poulenc is revealed in the nearly fifty letters Poulenc wrote to them between 1951 and the month of his death. Another new friend was the young conductor and composer Leonard Bernstein. Although the precise circumstances of their meeting are unknown, their friendship grew over the years. Not only was Bernstein in large part responsible for a Lincoln Center commission of Poulenc's *Sept répons des ténèbres*, but he also premiered Poulenc's Sonata for Clarinet and Piano with Benny Goodman shortly after the composer's death. They exchanged a number of letters, and Poulenc was a great admirer of *West Side Story*.

Gold and Fizdale, who entertained Poulenc in New York, wrote an anecdotal account of several events:

> Poulenc and the baritone Pierre Bernac [. . .] looked us up when they arrived in New York. We spent an amusing evening together—at least, they seemed to be amused when the restaurant we went to served veal kidneys with bérnaise sauce. Stimulated by this unorthodox combination, they agreed to be taken down to Chinatown, then up to the Savoy Ballroom in Harlem to watch the jitterbugging and listen to the jazz. "*La trompette est parfaite!*" Poulenc shouted in approval. The Poulenc-Bernac concerts across America were received with an enthusiasm that was matched by Poulenc's reaction to every aspect of American life. "*J'adore Hollywood!*" he announced to the assembled reporters who met his train. "I want to marry Greta Garbo and live here for the rest of my life."[215]

The first North American tour was a grand success and the adoring public buoyed his spirits. Although he missed his dear Place de la Concorde, he wanted future North American tours and wasted little time before planning the next one which took place in 1950.

Now Poulenc had captivated two English-speaking countries, both of which rewarded him with their love and affection from the moment of conquest! Upon his return to Paris, he told Marcel Landowski that he had given fifteen recitals with Bernac. When asked "In short: did you like America?" he responded, "More exactly it fascinated me, because I did not feel at home as in Paris."[216] He also paid an immediate visit to Misia Sert.

> Many years later Denise Mayer told us [Gold and Fizdale] that she had happened to call on Misia at the same time and found her helpless with laughter at Poulenc's stories. "You must listen to this," Misia said. "He's just discovered America."[217]

---

[215] Gold, p. 308.
[216] Landowski.
[217] Gold, pp. 308-09.

CONCERTS AND TOURS THROUGH JUNE 1949

As the decade of the 1940s closed, Poulenc temporarily lost his compositional muse. 1949 was a throwback to 1947: repeated trips to England, yet this time he managed to write only one relatively unimportant *mélodie* for Doda Conrad, whom Poulenc admired more for his tour-planning abilities than his voice, and the Piano Concerto to be premiered in Boston on his second North American tour. He was occupied by tours, radio broadcasts, and related activities.

Poulenc did a January broadcast concerning Yvonne Printemps' recordings and resumed his "A Bâtons rompus" series of broadcasts for Chaîne nationale begun in 1947. In these twelve broadcasts (see Appendix 2) Poulenc emphasized, among other things, recordings purchased in the United States.

After his return Poulenc also prepared with Bernac for concerts in England to be given in the second and third weeks of February (see Appendix 2).[218] While he was away, his close friend and neighbor Christian Bérard died suddenly on 12 February of a cerebral embolism. Profoundly moved, Poulenc composed one of his finest choral works, a *Stabat Mater* "to entrust his soul to Our Lady of Rocamadour" during the summer of 1950.[219]

In March, which he again spent mostly in Paris, Ricardo Viñes' niece Elvira Viñes Soto enlisted his cooperation in reissuing recordings made by her uncle in 1930 and in providing the preface for a book on Viñes being prepared by Ignacio Sanuy.[220] Poulenc was willing, but the project apparently never materialized. Late in the month he and Bernac performed in Perpignan on 29 March and then spent two weeks in Spain visiting Madrid and Barcelona. He found the "artistic climate dead except for Barcelona where Mompou [Halffter?] and his group are doing good work."[221]

One important project of 1949 and early 1950 was helping to mount Milhaud's *Bolivar* at the Paris Opéra.[222] Although Milhaud

[218] Fresnay requested a transcript from Poulenc. [Feb. 1949] letter to Fresnay and Fresnay's 14 Feb. 1949 response in Poulenc 1994, 49-1 and 49-2 respectively. Oblivious that he had already thanked Poulenc, Fresnay wrote another letter on 28 Mar. 1949. Poulenc 1994, 49-4.
[219] Schmidt 1995, FP 148, p. 407.
[220] Letter in Poulenc 1994, 49-3 (Poulenc 1991, no. 197).
[221] *Le Guide du concert et des théâtres lyriques* 29 (25 Mar. 1949), 165 and 25 July [1949] letter in Poulenc 1994, 49-10 (Poulenc 1991, no. 199). Chimènes gives "Monpou" and Buckland "Hälffter." (I have not been able to see the original.) Poulenc was still at the Astoria Hotel in Madrid on 9 Apr. when he wrote to Fresnay. Poulenc 1994, 49-5.
[222] Milhaud had first composed incidental music for a production of Jules Supervielle's play *Bolivar* at the Comédie-Française in 1936.

had returned to Paris in 1947, he divided his time between Mills College (Oakland, California), the Aspen Summer Music Festival (Colorado), and teaching duties at the Paris Conservatory. During early 1949 Poulenc wrote Milhaud about securing an appropriate director, designer, and conductor for the opera.[223] By 25 July only the conductor remained to be named, and Poulenc advised Milhaud to write Georges Hirsch at the Opéra adamantly requesting André Cluytens.[224] When the opera opened on 12 May 1950, not only was the cast of singers stellar (Janine Micheau, Roger Bourdin, Jean Giraudeau, etc.), but the production staff was extraordinary (Max de Rieux producer, Fernand Léger designer, and Cluytens conductor).[225] Poulenc was so emotionally involved with this work that he sent a spirited defense of *Bolivar* to *Le Figaro* taking issue with a review written by their critic Clarendon [Bernard Gavoty].[226]

He devoted time in April to preparing for a Salle Gaveau recital with Pierre Fournier at which he accompanied his new Sonata for Cello and Piano (FP 143) and the Debussy Sonata. Poulenc was delighted with the rehearsals and told Marie-Blanche de Polignac, "He is so precise, I have the impression of playing with Bernac."[227] As he had done before with Ginette Neveu for the Violin Sonata, Poulenc gave an *avant-première* performance at Marie-Blanche's *hôtel particulier*.[228] Fournier and Poulenc played it again during tours to England (1949) and Italy (1953). Unhappy with aspects of the last movement, Poulenc revised it, making several cuts, and Heugel printed the revised version in 1953.[229] Although Claude Rostand reviewed the work favorably, Henri Hell found only the Cavatine worthy.[230] Subsequent critics have expressed mixed feelings, though few rank it with the wind sonatas.

---

[223] From Poulenc's 10 Jan. 1949 letter to Milhaud in Poulenc 1994, p. 665, note 5.
[224] 25 July [1949] letter to Milhaud in Poulenc 1994, 49-10 (Poulenc 1991, no. 199). Milhaud had wanted Désormière, but he was having a dispute with the Opéra.
[225] Claude Baignères' review clarifies that *Bolivar* was a grand opera in every respect requiring numerous ballets (choreographed by Serge Lifar), an on-stage orchestra, and various scene changes. He points out that Léger designed seven hundred costumes inspired by historic engravings at the Bibliothèque Nationale. *Le Figaro* (12 May 1950), 6. Later critics felt this was Léger's masterpiece of stage design. Léger, pp. 166-85 includes color reproductions of the sets and costumes.
[226] *Le Figaro* (15 May 1950), 6 (rpt. in Gavoty, p. 77) and Poulenc 1950b for the 6 June response.
[227] Mercredi" [May 1949] letter in Poulenc 1994, 49-6.
[228] Poulenc personally requested that the Countess invite his companion Raymond Destouches, who was not accustomed to such circles, and Duval. The precise early May date is unknown.
[229] Schmidt 1995, FP 143, pp. 394-5. See also Poulenc 1954, pp. 123-4.
[230] *Carrefour* (1 June 1949) and Hell 1958, p. 154 (Hell 1959, p. 74), Hell 1978, p. 214.

He spent some time at Noizay in May, but by mid-June Poulenc was in London where he and Fournier repeated the Salle Gaveau concert for a BBC broadcast on 15 June, playing it again three days later at Mayflower Barn, Jordans.[231] Both performances were praised by Frank Arnold.[232] The brief English tour concluded with a final BBC recital on the 19th.[233]

In June Poulenc also attended a concert by Gold and Fizdale during which he announced to them his definite decision to write a new work.

> When we returned to give our first public concert in Paris in June 1949 [Gold and Fizdale remembered], Poulenc appeared backstage. *"Je vous couvre de merde,"* he said in an exaggeratedly extravagant version of the French "Good luck." To our great delight he re-appeared at the intermission and announced that he would write a two-piano sonata for us.[234]

He kept his word completing a Sonata for Two Pianos in spring 1953. Before relinquishing the stage for summer activities, he participated in two concerts: a Chausson Festival sponsored by the Société nationale at the Salle Gaveau on 25 June for the fiftieth anniversary of Chausson's death, and a recital at the thirteenth-century Abbaye de Royaumont a day later. In the former he accompanied Janine Micheau and Bernac in *mélodies* and duets; in the latter he accompanied Bernac in André Jolivet's *Poèmes intimes*, his own *Calligrammes*, and the premiere of Jean Françaix's *Huit anecdotes de Chamfort*. Recapping the Paris season Poulenc commented:

> Although the spring in Paris has been very brilliant from a social and entertainment standpoint, I cannot say as much with regard to music; as for ballet and theater there have been nothing but repeats. They have been living off of old stock. Lifar mounted a ballet by Leguerney; nice, but!!! The virtuosos have been playing Chopin and Beethoven. Only your lovely town [Aix-en-Provence] is triumphantly in vogue.[235]

Shortly before leaving Paris Poulenc received his first visit from Ned Rorem, who had just arrived in France.[236] The twenty-six year

[231] Poulenc told Gibson he would be at Noizay until 15 May. Unpublished 13 Apr. [1949] letter from Madrid in GB-Lchester.
[232] *Sunday Times* (19 June 1949). See also the anonymous review in *Music Review* 10 (1949), 211.
[233] Ibbs and Tillett ledger entry.
[234] Gold, p. 309.
[235] 25 July [1949] letter to Milhaud in Poulenc 1994, 49-10 (Poulenc 1991, no. 199).
[236] Rorem had arrived aboard the SS Washington, which sailed from New York on 25 May 1949. Over a year later he would receive a Fulbright to study with Honegger. Rorem wrote frequently about Poulenc in later years, referring to him

old Rorem idolized Poulenc, and José Hell (as Rorem referred to Henri Hell) arranged a meeting at tea time on 6 July at Poulenc's apartment. When they arrived, Poulenc, "garbed in a peignoir," informed Hell that he could not receive them and implored them to return on the 8th. Rorem remembered the Friday meeting "would be the first of a dozen visits over the years whereat Poulenc and I, with José as cheering section, played for each other."[237]

A RETURN TO COMPOSING IN SUMMER 1949:

• "Mazurka" from *Mouvements du cœur*

Poulenc's summer began in July with his customary three-week visit to Le Tremblay. By the 16th he had written a "Mazurka" for *Mouvements du cœur* (FP 145), a collective work conceived by Doda Conrad to celebrate the 100th anniversary of Chopin's death.[238] A day later he wrote Conrad:

> Your *mélodie* has been finished since yesterday. I am going to let it rest after such anguish caused by all these wicked "font, font, font" [. . .] It is a "Mazurka" that one could dance at the ball in the Grand Meaulne[s].[239] [Written in the] middle register, neither low, nor high. When I come through Paris at the beginning of August, I will give it to Heugel for engraving, which will make things easier for you.[240]

Conrad recounted events leading up to the creation of the work.

> I asked Louise de Vilmorin to write a series of poems whose titles would be "Prélude", "Mazurka", "Waltz", "Scherzo impromptu", "Study", "Nocturnal Ballad", and "Polonaise Postlude". I suggested to her a sort of fabrication which [would] evoke episodes in Chopin's life: Warsaw, Vienna, Paris, Majorca, Nohant, his nostalgia for the country of his birth, his ardent patriotism. I went to find Philippe and François Heugel. They "strode"—as if one. I approached Sauguet, Poulenc, Auric, Françaix, Milhaud, and a very gifted composer who died shortly after: Léo Préger. Admirably exact, and having fulfilled her task with marvelous precision, Louise de Vilmorin released the seven poems to me at the beginning of 1949. Without delay I sent no. 2—the "Mazurka"—to Poulenc. He quickly set it to music and I got

---

as "the twentieth-century composer to whose work I feel most akin." Rorem 1994, pp. 387 and 406.

[237] Rorem 1994, p. 408. Rorem's account, in his inimitable fashion, also devotes attention to Poulenc's homosexual proclivity.

[238] 25 July [1949] letter to Milhaud in Poulenc 1994, 49-10 (Poulenc 1991, no. 199).

[239] A reference to Alain Fournier's novel.

[240] 17 July 1949 letter in Poulenc 1994, 49-7. Concerning problems of prosody, see also Poulenc's 19 July [1949] letter to Vilmorin in Poulenc 1994, 49-8 (Poulenc 1991, no. 198).

his manuscript to Auric without delay, with the third poem: the "Waltz". He too returned his composition to me in record time. I proceeded similarly with no. 4—the "Scherzo impromptu", which I entrusted to Jean Françaix, in submitting to him the two compositions already completed. So followed no. 5—the "Study" and no. 6 —the "Ballad nocturne"—which, respectively, Préger and Darius Milhaud had accepted to set to music. [. . .] It is to Henri Sauguet that I owe the title "Mouvements du cœur" by which the "Homage to the memory of Fryderyk Chopin" was published in time to be placed on sale, in New York, the same day as the first performance—at Town Hall—19 October 1949, the day after the anniversary.[241]

Before the collection was printed, Poulenc objected to the proposed order of pieces, and Conrad changed it.[242] He also disparaged "Mazurka" calling it, "in the style of Poulenc by a Poulenc who was bored by an affair such as this."[243]

• Concerto for Piano and Orchestra

Poulenc's only major orchestral composition of 1949 was a Piano Concerto (FP 146) commissioned by the Boston Symphony Orchestra. He had contemplated such a piece as early as October 1943, and intentions turned to action during the spring of 1949.[244] Spurred by the possibility of centering his next North American tour around this commission, he began his Concerto at Noizay during May, completing it there in October. Later, Poulenc stated his intent.

> As opposed to the famous concertos of the past, which require great virtuosos, I decided to write a light concerto, a sort of souvenir of Paris for pianist-composer. I had no fear that such a thing would be poorly received, so that is why I interjected into the *rondeau à la française* the rhythm of the maxixe and a Negro spiritual derived from an old song sung by La Fayette's sailors. I was amused and pleased by this handshake with a country that, right now, contains my most numerous and loyal audience.[245]

[241] Conrad 1983, p. 72.

[242] Unpublished [autumn 1949] letter from Noizay to Conrad in US-NYwurlitzer-bruck. Partially transcribed in Schmidt 1995, FP 145, p. 400. Poulenc also suggested that he would like to play the piece for Marie-Blanche and Vilmorin on 2 Aug. at the latter's estate in Verrières-le-Buisson. Poulenc's letters of 19 July [1949] to Vilmorin in Poulenc 1994, 49-8 (Poulenc 1991, no. 198) and [July 1949] to Marie-Blanche in Poulenc 1994, 49-9.

[243] Poulenc 1993, p. 55 (Poulenc 1989, pp. 96-7).

[244] [Oct. 1943] letter to Jolivet in Poulenc 1994, 43-9.

[245] Poulenc 1954, p. 133. The program for the Boston premiere (unsigned notes, p. 592) discussed the tune Poulenc used: "The theme (which the composer uses in the piano part, in the middle of the [last] movement) comes from a traditional song of France, traced back to the beginning of the eighteenth century, which made its way to French Canada, and there became a patriotic song of revolt in

He did significant work in July at Le Tremblay. With the "Mazurka" completed, he told Milhaud "now I have made some progress with my Concerto for Boston (first movement completed, second movement sketched)."[246] By 13 August two movements were finished and he began orchestrating. The last movement remained to be found.[247] Before going to Aix-en-Provence on 29 August he said his Concerto was coming along and that he was happy with it.[248]

> I am completing the orchestration of my first movement [he told Bernac]. Then it will be the Andante's turn and finally I will write and orchestrate the rondo finale. I do not count on returning to Paris before 20 October. The best definition of the Concerto is that it is raked like my terrace [at Le Grand Coteau]. The orchestration is quite carefully done and varied, and the piano part brilliant—my forte. In any case, even if it is not a triumph, it will not be a flop because it is good work.[249]

Progress continued in September.

> After my nervousness of early August [. . .] I took the bull by the horns and I am proud to announce that I finished the orchestration of my Andante this morning. Here are 2/3 of the Concerto, ready for the copyist. Between us, I am very content with myself. What I showed to Brigitte [Manceaux] pleased her very much. If it is raked, it is very rich in music which is not disordered. I believe that the Andante is one in a thousand. I gave myself until the 15th, thus I am two days ahead. I estimate that the Finale, for which I have all the elements, will be finished by 15 October. You see that I will not feel the panic of the last minute. I have all the themes for it and then some. Regular work here is the only good thing for me, even if I curse about the climate.[250]

> The *Concerto* progresses. I truly believe that. Provided that the Final succeeds. In any case, the orchestration is very good.[251]

1837. Having undergone many changes in text and notation, it is now called 'A la claire fontaine.' The 'Negro Spiritual' referred to in the opening refrain: 'Way down upon the Swanee River' of Stephen Foster."

[246] 25 July [1949] letter to Milhaud in Poulenc 1994, 49-10 (Poulenc 1991, no. 199).
[247] Fragment of Poulenc's "samedi" [13 Aug. 1949] letter to Brigitte Manceaux in Poulenc 1994, p. 662, note 3.
[248] 25 July [1949] letter to Milhaud in Poulenc 1994, 49-10 (Poulenc 1991, no. 199).
[249] Partially transcribed "mardi" [30 Aug. or more likely 5 Sept. 1949] postcard in Poulenc 1994, p. 663, note 3.
[250] Partially transcribed "lundi" [19 Sept. 1949 letter in Poulenc 1994, pp. 662-3, note 3]. Chimènes gives 12 Sept., but the MS of Poulenc's Concerto indicates orchestration of the Andante was finished on Monday, 19 Sept.
[251] Poulenc's "lundi" [19 Sept. 1949] letter to Bernac from Noizay in Poulenc 1994, 49-14 (Poulenc 1991, no. 200)

Poulenc gave the two completed movements to Rouart for engraving on 28 September[252] and boasted to Doda Conrad that "I found the coda to the rondo in the French style [...] of my Concerto for Boston."[253] He added: "My trip to America, now that I know the 'monstre' [of my Concerto] enchants me. Certainly the 31st together. The Concerto is being copied."

The Concerto is dedicated to Denise Duval and Raymond Destouches who "are truly like children to me."[254] Before going to America, Poulenc played a two-piano version with Jacques Février chez Mme Salabert in Paris for a host of composers including Honegger, Milhaud, Sauguet, Landowski, Auric, Daniel-Lesur, and Jean Rivier.[255] He also attended "a swanky reception" in honor of Copland given by Rosamond "Peggy" Bernier on 27 October. *Le Tout Paris* was there including Auric, Messiaen, Nadia Boulanger, Marie-Laure de Noailles, and others. Aaron Copland recalled that: "Messiaen seemed very self-concentrated and looked somewhat seedy, but poetic. Auric was friendly, Poulenc amusing."[256]

CLOSE OF THE DECADE: PREPARATIONS FOR THE SECOND AMERICAN TOUR

When Gold and Fizdale returned to Paris from their summer in Provence they stopped to visit Poulenc at his Noizay estate. They played his venerable Concerto in D minor for him and "Between the magnificent lunch and the superb dinner, Poulenc sang for us his *Huit chansons Polonaises (Eight Polish Songs).*"[257] Later, when Poulenc visited America, the piano duo returned his hospitality by showing him around New York.

The remaining days of 1949 were predominantly devoted to preparing for the grueling three-month American concert tour. Bernac and Poulenc gave their only recital before departing for America at the Salle Gaveau on 8 December. Bernac, who played a vital role in their programming, had already chosen the program by 19 September when Poulenc pronounced it *"perfect."*[258] Three early English songs were followed by works of Fauré, Schumann, Chabrier, Poulenc (*Calligrammes*), and Ravel's *Trois chants hébraïques*. Bernac

---

[252] 29 Sept. 1949 letter to Gibson in GB-Lchester. This excerpt in Schmidt 1995, FP 146, p. 404.

[253] Excerpt from Conrad's [autumn 1949] letter in US-NYwurlitzer-bruck in Schmidt, 1995, FP 146, p. 404.

[254] 10 Mar. [1950] letter to Casa Fuerte in Poulenc 1994, 50-17 (Poulenc 1991, no. 207).

[255] *Musique et Radio* (Jan. 1950), 21 quoted in Schmidt 1995, FP 146, p. 402.

[256] Copland 1989, p. 147.

[257] Gold, p. 308.

[258] "Lundi" [19 sept. 1949] letter to Bernac from Noizay in Poulenc 1994, 49-14 (Poulenc 1991, no. 200).

questioned his vocal ability during the summer of 1949, but Poulenc reassured him that his summer concerts had been excellent and that he had at least six good years ahead of him.

Their next American tour benefited from two fortuitous events. First, Wanda Landowska played three performances of his *Concert champêtre* with Leopold Stokowski and the New York Philharmonic on 17, 18, and 20 November, and Richard Burgin (assistant conductor and concertmaster of the Boston Symphony Orchestra) conducted his Concerto in G minor in Boston on 29 October 1948 with E. Power Biggs as organ soloist.[259] Biggs expected to record it with Charles Munch and wrote to Poulenc concerning interpretation. Poulenc answered Bigg's letter from Paris on 22 July 1949 saying how happy he was to learn of Biggs' intentions.[260] Poulenc and Biggs had met in New York during his first tour, and he was keen that Biggs record with Munch and the Boston Symphony. Poulenc offered several suggestions and wrote in some depth concerning his own conception.[261] Biggs' biographer Barbara Owen relates the story.

Poulenc was delighted with the idea ("Quelle joie pour moi d'apprendre que vous avez l'intention d'enregistrer mon Concerto pour Orgue et orchestre . . ."), especially if the conductor was to be Charles Munch, whom Poulenc felt would provide the necessary pungency and lyricism ("le mordant et le lyricisme necessaire"). While Biggs did in fact record Poulenc's work that year, for some reason it was not with Munch and the Boston Symphony, but with Richard Burgin and a smaller group dubbed the "Columbia Symphony Orchestra." The solo timpanist, violist, and cellist were all members of the Boston Symphony Orchestra, however. In response to Biggs's request, Poulenc wrote twice giving his suggestions for performance. The second letter went into considerable detail, but the first gave a nice overview of Poulenc's concept: "Forget Haendel —play very much in the French style, pompous, gay, and pungent (pompous in the introduction)— the two andantes shouldn't drag, strictly in time, no rubato — the solo cadenza should be very allegro and sprightly—Land squarely on the big chords (G minor) with an extreme violence (timpani dry and firm)—the final Allegro should be very rhythmic (very fast) and sprightly, in contrast to the serene and poetic conclusion—but why do I tell you all this—I am sure that it will be marvelous."[262]

[259] Honegger, pp. 194-5. Biggs had played the American premiere in 1939 with the Harvard University Orchestra. He also played it under Munch on 14 Nov. 1949 for the inauguration of the new Aeolian-Skinner organ at Symphony Hall.
[260] Transcript and translation in Hunt, p. 121. The original letters, as well as numerous press clippings and programs, are in US-But (Biggs correspondence).
[261] Undated letter and that of 23 Aug. [1949], both from Paris, in Hunt, pp.122-4.
[262] Owen, p. 53. Translation of Poulenc's letter by Eileen Hunt. Biggs recorded

Preparations for his tour, however, did not proceed without incident. On 28 October the brilliant young French violinist Ginette Neveu and her brother were killed in a plane crash in the Azores.[263] The tragic loss of a superb player just thirty years of age touched Poulenc deeply, and in the summer of 1950 he participated in a memorial concert in her honor.

Shortly before his departure Poulenc had a dream at Noizay which he related to the pianist Irène Aïtoff.

> I had just played the first movement of my Concerto in Boston. Twenty American ladies could not prevent themselves from crying out in admiration. After the Andante we had to carry away on a stretcher about a hundred of them who passed out overcome by the voluptuous aspect of my music. After the Final, all the remaining women were shouting "down with Poulenc! Don't fool around with a public like that. This French Rondo is the image of a true Parisian brothel." As no men attended this concert it is impossible to defend the reputation of our brothels. Look in what state my Rondo puts me.[264]

Poulenc's Concerto on 11 Dec. 1950. In 1961 Biggs had planned to record it with Ormandy and the Philadelphia Orchestra, but a strike forced cancellation of the session, which was recheduled for the next season. Shortly after, Biggs wrote to Poulenc: "Would you perhaps consider adding to the Concerto parts for woodwinds and brasses?![. . .] This, I know, is a daring suggestion to make to a composer. I hope you will forgive me!" (See Poulenc's undated letter in Hunt, pp. 126-7.) On 11 Nov. 1961 Poulenc responded "Alas! I cannot agree to your request because I simply do not want to hear wind instruments in my concerto because they will create a redundancy with the sound of the organ."

[263] Ronze-Neveu 1952 and 1957.

[264] [End of 1949] letter to Aïtoff in Poulenc 1994, 49-16. Concerning Aïtoff see Poulenc 1994, p. 1009.

XI

North American Tours Two and Three: 1950-1952

The years 1950-52 were framed by the second and third tours Poulenc and Bernac made to America. These were the last relatively calm years before the stress of work on *Dialogues des Carmélites*, and his stormy relationship with Lucien Roubert, a traveling salesman from Toulon, led to crises affecting his health. Poulenc met this young man during the spring of 1950 while Roubert was living in Marseilles, and the two maintained a close relationship until the latter's death on 21 October 1955 from cancer.

SECOND AMERICAN TOUR: 28 DECEMBER 1949-29 MARCH 1950

Poulenc flew to New York from Paris on 28 December 1949 and after a two-day respite went directly to Boston to prepare the premiere of his Concerto. (See Appendix 2 for a synopsis of this tour.) Writing to Brigitte Manceaux after the first rehearsal, he pronounced his orchestration excellent, saying that Charles Munch and the orchestra, which included some thirty Frenchmen, were delighted with it.[1] He premiered the Concerto on the 6th of January and played it again on the 12th in Washington D.C. and the 14th in New York City (Carnegie Hall,) both with the Boston Symphony Orchestra.[2] Robert Sabin reviewed the New York performance for *Musical America*.

> It is a work of considerable length, and rich, sometimes massive, sonority, but it is essentially blithe in spirit. Mr. Poulenc is the most

---

[1] 3 Jan. 1950 letter in Poulenc 1994, 50-1 (Poulenc 1991, no. 201). Bernac, who came to America after Poulenc, phoned him on the 3rd from New York to say he had arrived.

[2] On 15 Feb. [1950] Poulenc thanked Munch for his work with the Concerto. Poulenc 1994, 50-7 and Honegger 1992, p. 202.

eclectic of contemporary masters. He pays his respects to Debussy, Ravel, Rachmaninoff, and Stravinsky in this concerto, yet the style, the flavor and the format of the work are unmistakably his own. It is a witty and beautiful musical discourse, enhanced by piquant orchestration. [. . .] Mr. Poulenc played his concerto with delightful nonchalance and refinement of accent, and the audience was charmed.[3]

Writing in a diary of his trip, Poulenc expressed concern about reception of the last movement, although he thought the actual performance had been credible.

The concerto went well. Five recalls, but more friendliness on the audience's part than genuine enthusiasm. The *Rondeau à la Française*, with its deliberate impertinence, was something of a shock. I was aware while playing of the audience's dwindling interest. I had hoped that this musical portrait of Paris, the Paris of La Bastille rather than of Passy, would amuse them. In fact, I think they were disappointed.[4]

Their Town Hall recital on 22 January was repeated in Toronto on the 24th. The baritone was in good form, and Poulenc commented that "as soon as Bernac reached the New World, he regained his youthfulness."[5] Early in the tour Poulenc recorded piano music by himself and Satie.[6] He and Bernac also visited Samuel Barber to hear two songs on French poems by Rainer Maria Rilke. Barber wrote to William Strickland, "Poulenc and Bernac were here Sunday and I played them for them to check on French prosody (o.k.) and they want the first performance in Paris."[7] These songs were later incorporated into *Mélodies passagères*, a cycle premiered by the duo at Dumbarton Oaks in Washington D.C. two years later.[8]

On 2 February, during a ten-day late January-early February trip to Canada,[9] Poulenc teamed with his old conductor-friend Désiré Defauw for a performance of the new Concerto in Montreal.[10] Then

---

[3] "Poulenc Performs New Piano Concerto," 70 (15 Jan. 1950), 59.
[4] Poulenc 1950c, p. 68. Poulenc wrote back to Paris that "The work is in a 'mouvement très léger,'very Parisian, very Toulouse-Lautrec." *Le Guide du concert et des théâtres lyriques* 30 (July 1950), 157.
[5] 12 Jan. [1950] letter to Brianchon in Poulenc 1994, 50-2.
[6] 12 Feb. [1950] letter to Sauguet from New York in Poulenc 1994, 50-6 (Poulenc 1991, no. 204). This record was released as Columbia ML 4399. See Appendix 3.
[7] Heyman, p. 324.
[8] See below.
[9] "I was delighted with my stay in Canada," he reported in an unpublished 16 Feb. [1960] letter to Mme Lambiotte. See US-NYlambiotte-donhauser.
[10] 12 Feb. [1950] letter to Sauguet in Poulenc 1994, 50-6 (Poulenc 1991, no. 204). Poulenc called this journal "the sacrosanct paper of American concert societies." Throughout his life he was keenly aware of what the press said about his music and performances.

he and Bernac recorded some of his songs and those of Ravel for Columbia Records.[11] Poulenc hoped to record *Aubade* with Leonard Bernstein, but this project was abandoned. Bernac and Poulenc continued to work out of New York City until the end of the second week of February when they embarked cross country by train. From Toledo on 23 February, Poulenc reported that he had given his seventeenth concert and that, *fortunately*, the last thirteen lay under the warmth of the sun on the Pacific coast.[12] From the charming seaside town of Carmel, California on the 28th, he noted that twenty-seven concerts had been given and that nine lay ahead.[13] Mathematics was clearly not his forte!

Once returned to New York on 18 March, Bernac and Poulenc spent their remaining days recording for Columbia, seeing old friends, and making new ones. The recordings of music by Satie, Chabrier, Poulenc, and Debussy were taped on the afternoons of 25 and 27 March.[14] Their later release, along with Robert Shaw's 1950 recording of the Mass in G major and E. Power Biggs' 1951 recording of the Concerto in G minor, helped Poulenc's U.S. reputation.[15]

He was already looking ahead in early March to the winter concert season with Bernac and planning a song cycle based on Eluard's poem "Vue donne vie" published in *Le Livre ouvert I* (1940). "The new Eluard cycle that I have started; very special: a long poem in five sections tied together by pianistic episodes."[16] Poulenc took this piece up again in April. Anticipating his return to New York, and always seeking opportunities to socialize, Poulenc encouraged Yvonne de Casa Fuerte to arrange a dinner with Christian Dior for 21 March, the day he returned to the St Moritz Hotel. Firmly estab-

---

[11] ML 4333. Precisely when the duo recorded *Banalités, Chansons villageoises*, plus Ravel's *Histoires naturelles*, and *Trois chants hébraïques* is unknown, but Poulenc told Marie-Blanche it would be after their return from Canada in early Feb. (25 Jan. [1950] letter in Poulenc 1994, 50-3). See Appendix 3.

[12] 23 Feb. [1950] letter from Toledo, Ohio to Daniel-Lesur in Poulenc 1994, 50-10. There had been snow, wind, and cold in the east.

[13] 28 Feb. [1950] letter to Jolivet in Poulenc 1994, 50-13. On 1 Mar., still in Carmel, Poulenc wrote Roland-Manuel that Californians had been extremely generous to him lending cars, houses, planes, etc. He found the climate divine and the flowers admirable. Poulenc 1994, 50-14.

[14] 10 Mar. [1950] letter to Casa Fuerte in Poulenc 1994, 50-17 (Poulenc 1991, no. 207). These pieces were contained on Columbia ML 4484.

[15] R.C.A. Victor LM 1088 and Columbia MM 951 respectively. The first Poulenc recording issued in the U.S. was of his Concerto in D minor played by Arthur Whittemore and Jack Lowe under Dimitri Mitropoulos (R.C.A. Victor 120366/8) in 1948. Details in Bloch.

[16] Fragment of Poulenc's 2 Mar. [1950] letter to Collaer in Poulenc 1994, p. 689, note 2 and Poulenc's 10 Mar. [1950] letter to Casa Fuerte in Poulenc 1994, 50-17 (Poulenc 1991, no. 207).

lished in the United States, Dior offered a winter 1950 collection of
evening gowns bearing the names of venerable composers such as
Schubert and Mozart. Particularly applauded were those named
for Poulenc and Sauguet.[17] Earlier in his trip, Poulenc had dined
with the singers Jenny Tourel and Doda Conrad, spent days with
Vladimir Horowitz and Wanda Landowska, and met the renowned
German-born American soprano Lotte Lehman, who attended one
of his California concerts. He also saw Vittorio Rieti and the pianists Gold and Fizdale, who played Sauguet's *Valse brève* for him.[18]

While touring Poulenc kept abreast of events in France through
letters from friends and relatives.[19] In return, he sent back news of
his accomplishments overflowing with pride at the successful 17
February first American performance of *Figure humaine* by Hugh
Ross at Carnegie Hall.[20] Unfortunately he could not attend, having
already departed for the midwest. Poulenc also conducted business by letter, setting up future events or looking after bookings
already in progress. One was the planned June 1950 production of
Aubade at the Opéra-Comique with décor and costumes by Maurice
Brianchon and choreography by Jeanine Charrat.[21] He envisioned
touring England in November, Holland in December, and Italy after 15 January 1951.[22] His views on music were also shared with
correspondents such as Yvonne de Casa Fuerte, whose approval he
coveted:

> As for Stravigor I agree, although I do not share your enthusiasm for
> *Orpheus*. It is remarkable, but more deliberate than inspired and a
> little bit "contrived" in its grandeur. Enough of mythology, of Greece,

[17] Poulenc 1994, p. 687, note 1 (Poulenc 1991, no. 207).
[18] Information partially from Poulenc's 12 Feb. [1950] letter to Sauguet in Poulenc
1994, 50-6 (Poulenc 1991, no. 204).
[19] See, for example, his 23 Feb. [1950] letter to Daniel-Lesur in Poulenc 1994, 50-10
in which he says that his secret police have told him of the success of his new
collaboration with the singer Noémie Pérugia; his 28 Feb. [1950] letter to Jolivet
congratulating him for the success of his *Concerto pour ondes Martenot* which had
been performed on 4 Feb. 1950 (Poulenc 1994, 50-13 and note 1); and his 9 Mar.
[1950] letter to Dutilleux in which he speaks about performances of Dutilleux's
music in Paris as reported by Brigitte Manceaux (Poulenc 1994, 50-16). Poulenc
also kept tabs on Duval's activity as his 1 Mar. [1950] letter to Roland-Manuel
attests (Poulenc 1994, 50-14).
[20] He wrote of the success to Eluard in a "dimanche" [June 1950] letter in Poulenc
1994, 50-19 (Poulenc 1991, no. 208).
[21] 12 Jan. [1950] letter to Brianchon and Brianchon's 6 Mar. [1950] letter to Poulenc
in Poulenc 1994, 50-2 and 50-15 respectively. The performance did not occur until 20 Nov. 1952, and then the choreography was by Marcel Berge. See also
Poulenc's 7 Dec. [1950] card to Maurice Lehmann, general administrator of the
Réunion des Théâtres lyriques nationaux, in Poulenc 1994, p. 671, note 1.
[22] 2 Feb. [1950] letter to Girard in Poulenc 1994, 50-4 (Poulenc 1991, no. 202).

of antiquity, otherwise we shall be verging on "the bombast of the seventeenth century, late Corneille." Orpheus' variation is a very poor theme, and the conclusion does not approach the toe of *Apollon*. This is why, at heart, I condone the young Europeans looking for new emotion in the not yet ossified twelve-tone system and why I find pitiable that they are still buzzing like flies around Hindemith and Igor, venerable though their old age may be. Pay attention to what I say (and believe me when I tell you that the young Europeans do not like me at all): one more time it is from Europe that new ideas will spring. This said, Igor remains my passion, to be sure, although I would prefer to have written Bartók's last quartets than [Stravinsky's] most recent works.[23]

In a 20 February letter to Stravinsky, he spoke differently.

It is truly sad for me to miss you everywhere. I was overjoyed to find you again in America, [but] we are playing hide-and-seek, unless by some miracle you will be in New York from March 21 to 30. I cry at the thought that I will not see *Orpheus*, whose every bar I love, and not hear the new *Firebird*, and not even glimpse the [score of the] opera. This is really too sad.[24]

Poulenc was in luck! The Stravinskys *were* in New York: on the 18th they were together and on the 28th they shared a box at a Carnegie Hall concert featuring Virgil Thomson's Concerto for Violoncello and Orchestra. Poulenc also saw Gian Carlo Menotti's opera *The Consul* on the 22nd before returning to Paris on the 29th. The tour was an unquestionable success in spite of his qualms about the reception of his Concerto.

COMPOSITIONS OF 1950:

• *La Fraîcheur et le feu*

After America, Poulenc immediately headed for Noizay to compose and recover from months of traveling. He wrote a program note for the July Festival d'Aix-en-Provence performance of his Concerto, and took up *La Fraîcheur et le feu* [The Coolness and the Fire] (FP 147), the song cycle begun during the North American tour.[25] Little is known about his work on this cycle, except that it was composed in "Noizay-Brive Avril-Juillet 1950."[26] In 1950 he wrote:

---

[23] "Dimanche" [26 Feb. 1950] letter from San Francisco in Poulenc 1994, 50-11 (Poulenc 1991, no. 205).
[24] Letter hand delivered by Casa Fuerte in Stravinsky 1985, p. 213, misdated 1948 by Craft. Fragment in Poulenc 1994, p. 681, note 2.
[25] 18 Apr. [1950] letter to Marc Pincherle (General Secretary of the Aix Festival) in Poulenc 1994, 50-18.
[26] Manuscript in CH-Bsacher. Poulenc dedicated the work to Stravinsky and gave him the holograph manuscript.

Indisputably the most highly planned of my song cycles. I have written so many songs up till now that I have lost my taste for them, and without a doubt I shall write less and less of them. If these are successful, and I believe they are, it is because a technical problem has stimulated my appetite. In reality it is not so much a cycle as *one single poem* set to music in separate sections exactly as the poem is printed. A rhythmic unity (two tempi: one fast, one slow) is the foundation of the construction. [. . .] These *mélodies* are dedicated to Stravinsky. I owe them to him because in a fashion they stem from him. The third one, in fact, borrows the tempo and the harmonic progression from the final cadence of his *Serenade in A* for piano.[27]

Poulenc had already been influenced by the *Serenade*, borrowing a dotted rhythmic progression for "Hymn" (from *Trois pièces* and later the opening of *Gloria*). But Stravinsky is not the only debt Poulenc acknowledged. He ascribed to Henri Matisse, an artist he greatly admired, the economy of the difficult piano writing.

I cannot tell you how much the exhibition of his sketches for Mallarmé's poems impressed me several years ago. You could see in them the same subject, especially a swan, in three or four stages, which always went from the more complex and thick (sketches of charcoal or soft lead pencil) to the most ideally simple and pure pen strokes. I often tried, especially in the accompaniments to my *mélodies,* to take this lesson into account.[28]

Pleased with this cycle, Poulenc thought that the tessitura suited Bernac perfectly.[29] Bowing to Marie-Blanche de Polignac's advice, Poulenc changed the end of the cycle.

But above all her musical judgment was infallible. I have no better proof of this than the coda for piano of the last song of *La Fraîcheur et le feu,* which in Poulenc's original version ended rather lamely. It was she who, when we performed the cycle for her, suggested to Poulenc that he should repeat the first bars of the cycle, thus giving a logical conclusion and a unity to the whole.[30]

Poulenc played the first European performance of his Concerto for Piano on 24 July in Aix-en-Provence under Charles Munch.[31] A

[27] Poulenc 1993, p. 56 (Poulenc 1989, pp. 96-9).
[28] Poulenc 1954, p. 172. Poulenc refers to *Poésies de Stéphane Mallarmé; eaux-fortes originales de Henri-Matisse* (Lausanne: Albert Skira & Cie, 1932). Poulenc had viewed an exhibition of Matisse's drawings for this book in 1933. See Chapter VII and my article in Buckland/Chimènes: k.
[29] [Early Aug. 1950] letter to Bernac from Le Tremblay in Poulenc 1994, 50-24.
[30] Bernac 1977a, p. 130 (Bernac 1978, pp. 124-5).
[31] A day later he heard the first French performance of Messiaen's *Turangalîla* symphony, Désormière conducting. In a 1 Aug. [1950] letter to Messiaen in Poulenc 1994, 50-22, he acknowledged disliking the work.

number of friends either traveled south to hear it or listened to the simultaneous radio broadcast. Numerous congratulatory letters arrived, especially from followers of Honegger, and while Claude Rostand's review was quite favorable, Bernard Gavoty's was not.[32] His old nemesis Robert Aloys Mooser excoriated it. Poulenc played the Paris premiere on 26 November at the Théâtre des Champs-Élysées with the Orchestre de la Société des Concerts du Conservatoire, André Cluytens conducting.

After completing *La Fraîcheur et le feu* Poulenc took a sabbatical from writing songs, composing only three others until 1956. He did, however, write large-scale vocal works such as *Stabat Mater* and *Dialogues des Carmélites*.

• *Stabat Mater*

For Poulenc, the decision to write a piece in memory of Christian Bérard, or "Bébé" as he was familiarly known, was inevitable. The two had been acquainted for years and had worked together on theater projects, enjoyed costume balls, and shared numerous friends. Precisely what shape to give his memorial, however, perplexed Poulenc. Paul Guth gave the most detailed account of the *Stabat Mater's* genesis.

> We come now to the *Stabat Mater*, which has just opened the *Festival of Works of the Twentieth Century* in Paris. Francis Poulenc had decided to write music in memory of his friend Christian Bérard. "—A requiem would have looked like a funeral service for Bérard the grandson of the undertaker of Borniol. A *Stabat Mater*, as a prayer of intercession, seemed to me more suitable. I thought about it for a long time, but I wrote it very quickly during the summer of 1950, just after writing a piano concerto in a very irreverent style, which provoked a lot of biting criticism." The *Stabat Mater* does not constitute an apology but rather Poulenc's habitual jumping from the profane to the sacred. He chose the classic form typical of Pergolesi. He divided the gory poem of Jacopone de Todi in twelve verses: *Stabat Mater dolorosa/Juxta Crucem lacrimosa/Dum pendebat Filius*. "The Mother of sorrows, streaming with tears, was standing at the foot of the cross where her son was suspended." "—The *Agnus dei* of my Mass was a soprano solo in a disembodied style. The soprano solos of my *Stabat* are, to the contrary, in a very human style, very expressive, which, if one does not have the luck of obtaining Mme Moisan [*recte* Moizan] as the interpreter, would necessitate a warm voice, Italian... There are many conceptions of a choral work with orchestra. What I have cho-

---

[32] 22 Aug. [1950] letter to Jourdan-Morhange in Poulenc 1994, 50-25. On 30 Aug. [19]50 he sent Long a copy of the Concerto. Schmidt 1995, FP 146, p. 402 and Poulenc 1994, 50-27.

sen is a veritable setting in the orchestra of a choir which, even when
it sings with the orchestra, has the harmonic structure of an *a cappella*
chorus."[33]

In July, with the *Stabat Mater* (FP 148) on his mind, Poulenc went
to Rocamadour.[34] Almost immediately after performing his Concerto in Aix, he spent three weeks at Le Tremblay.[35] Before leaving
on 16 August, the *Stabat* was underway. "Now I am attacking the
Stabat with patience and calm [he told Bernac]. I already see the
first four versets—that is to say sections. La Danco [Suzanne Danco]
will enter in the 4th."[36] A few weeks later, from Noizay, he added:

> The *Stabat* is going at such a speed that it is certainly a miracle of
> Rocamadour. Out of 12 numbers 3 are done, 2 nearly done, 1 sketched
> and all this in 10 days. I believe I have returned to the period of the
> Mass at Anost. You will see that it is full of music without formulas
> and rehashing. The first aria for la Danco, which one has to await for
> a long time (N° 6) is, I believe, "very good." There will be a second
> one (N° 9) and some interjections. That will strengthen the tragedy
> of the venture.[37]

In the midst of reports to Bernac, Poulenc also told Marguerite
Long, "I feel very much at home with it, and I hope I can touch
those who like prayers."[38] Finally, in October, he wrote: "The *Stabat*
is finished. I am going to recopy it now, but ten days in 'no-man's
land' were indispensable."[39] The *Stabat* was finished on the 3rd,
and though composed with uncharacteristic dispatch, the orchestration took time.[40] A late December letter to Virgil Thomson suggests that he had finished orchestrating,[41] but the holograph manuscript states the orchestration was not completed until 22 April 1951.[42]

[33] Guth 1952.

[34] 6 Sept. [1950] letter to Casa Fuerte in Poulenc 1994, 50-29.

[35] 6 Sept. [1950] letter to Milhaud in Poulenc 1994, 50-28.

[36] [Early Aug. 1950] letter in Poulenc 1994, 50-24. Poulenc was fond of the Belgian
soprano and admired her voice and the versatility of her repertory.

[37] 29 Aug. 1950 letter to Bernac in Poulenc 1994, 50-26 (the first three sentences are
translated in Poulenc 1991, p. 381, where the letter is dated 19 Aug.). Poulenc
told Bernac that he would return to Paris from Le Tremblay on 16 Aug. and then
go to Noizay with Destouches on the 19th. In a 6 Sept. [1950] letter to Milhaud in
Poulenc 1994, 50-28 he said that he had been in Noizay since 15 Aug.

[38] 30 Aug. [19]50 letter in Poulenc 1994, 50-27 (partial translation in Dunoyer, p.
130).

[39] [Early Oct. 1950] letter to Bernac in Poulenc 1994, 50-31 (Poulenc 1991, no. 213)
and Poulenc's unpublished [postmarked 4 Oct. 1950] letter to Mme Lambiotte
during which he says he is finishing the *Stabat*. US-NYlambiotte-donhauser.

[40] 5 Oct. [1950] letter to Sauguet in Poulenc 1994, 50-30.

[41] Unpublished [28 Dec. 1950] letter in US-NH.

[42] Schmidt 1995, FP 148, p. 407. In Poulenc's unpublished "samedi" [7 Apr. 1951]

While in London during November 1950, he played the *Stabat* for the staff of the BBC. An internal memorandum circulated by Lockspeiser was disparaging. "The work lasts about 35 minutes and left the impression from this performance on the piano of being a little bitty."[43]

RETURN TO THE CONCERT STAGE: FALL-WINTER 1950-51

Poulenc returned to Paris for the fall season on 15 October. Beginning in November he intended to play the piano for four and a half months.[44] In reality, his season began on 28 October when he accompanied Rose Dercourt-Plaut in *Fiançailles pour rire* at the Salle Gaveau. Irène Aïtoff accompanied the balance of the varied program of music in Italian, German, French, and English.[45] A few days later Bernac and Poulenc crossed the Channel beginning their tour in Birmingham where they premiered *La Fraîcheur et le feu*. On the 6th they participated in a BBC Third Programme broadcast and stayed in London through the 18th. Poulenc's season featured numerous performances of his new Concerto including the first one in England on 8 and 9 November at Royal Albert Hall with the BBC Symphony Orchestra, Basil Cameron conducting.[46] Before concluding their English stay the Bernac/Poulenc duo performed music by Verdi, Brahms, Mompou, Debussy, Poulenc, and Stravinsky at Wigmore Hall on the 15th, and Poulenc may have been on the BBC Light Programme "Stanford Robinson Presents" on the 18th.[47]

From London it was straight back to Paris where most of the Wigmore Hall recital was repeated at the Salle Gaveau on 22 November. The month closed with Poulenc playing his Concerto at the Théâtre des Champs-Élysées on the 26th with the Orchestre de la Société des Concerts du Conservatoire, André Cluytens conducting. After such a busy month Poulenc's schedule inevitably quieted down. The duo's stay in Brussels on 6 December probably preceded a concert in Holland. Late in the year or early in 1951 he played his Concerto with the celebrated German conductor Otto Klemperer in Amsterdam.[48]

Just before leaving Paris in January, he was invited to Marie-

letter to Mme Lambiotte he says he was swamped with work including orchestrating the *Stabat*. US-NYlambiotte-donhauser.
[43] 20 Nov. 1950 in GB-Rbbc quoted in Schmidt 1995, FP 148, p. 409.
[44] 6 Sept. [1950] letter to Milhaud in Poulenc 1994, 50-28.
[45] Concerning Poulenc's relationship with Aïtoff see Poulenc 1994, p. 1009.
[46] At least some reviews were highly critical including *The Musical Times* (Dec. 1950), 477 and C. M.'s review on p. 482.
[47] Unpublished [4 Oct. 1950] letter to Mme Lambiotte in US-NYlambiotte-donhauser.
[48] 6 Mar. [1951] letter to Milhaud from Agadir in Poulenc 1994, 51-3 (Poulenc 1991, no. 215).

Blanche de Polignac's for a Sunday evening dinner honoring the visiting Samuel Barber. Poulenc played a recording of *Dover Beach* sung by Barber himself and then encouraged Barber to sing until he was exhausted.[49] He also attended a special costume party at Marie-Laure de Noailles' during the third week of January. Susan Marie Alsop, whose husband worked for the State Department at the U.S. Embassy in Paris, was included among the guests. She wrote:

> There were side shows; in one, Daisy de Cabrol was the armless and legless woman, and there was a touching little beach scene in which [Baron Alexis de] Redé, [Arturo] Lopez, and Daisy Fellowes lolled in the sand eating caviar. Cocteau, Poulenc, and Février did a cabaret. How strange and unreal these Paris parties are—not one deputy, not one member of the government or one newspaperman. Trade was represented by the Rothschilds and the dressmakers. I think that if it had been announced that the President and the whole Cabinet had been assassinated, not one man out of all those present would have turned around, except for the Rothschilds, David Bruce, Duff Cooper, [Carl] Burkhardt, and Bill [Blair]. And the pansies now outnumbered the men at all parties.[50]

On the road again in mid-January, Poulenc arrived in Aix-en-Provence from Lyon on the 22nd. While there he expressed interest in playing his new *Stabat Mater* for Simone Girard, Vincent Laugier, and several others.[51] He left Aix for Cannes on 23 January and then began a solo tour of Italy featuring his new Concerto. He played in Rome with Clemens Krauss; Florence; Turin with Arturo Basile on 2 February; Milan, where he played the old *Concert champêtre* with Gallera; and Bologna.[52] From Turin Poulenc told Bernac that the Italian trip had been going very well.[53]

After Bologna Poulenc probably returned to the Hôtel des Négociants in Cannes before going to Morocco and Algeria.[54] Little

---

[49] Heyman, p. 321 quotes from Barber's 8 Feb. 1951 letter to his family.
[50] 20 Jan. 1951 letter to Marietta FitzGerald in Alsop, p. 164. Evangeline and David Bruce, Marie-Louise Bousquet, Christian Dior, Mr. and Mrs. Carl Burkhardt, and Mrs. Harrison Williams also attended.
[51] 9 Jan. [1951] letter to Simone Girard in Poulenc 1994, 51-1. Laugier was a businessman who had some talent as a painter and musician. He conducted the Chorale Vincent d'Indy in Avignon at this time and was a friend of Simone Girard.
[52] 6 Mar. [1951] letter to Milhaud from Agadir in Poulenc 1994, 51-3 (Poulenc 1991, no. 215).
[53] Unpublished "vendredi" [2 Feb. 1951?] letter in US-NH.
[54] In Poulenc's 3 Feb. [1951] letter to Doctor Claudine Escoffier-Lambiotte from Turin in Poulenc 1994, 51-2 he told her that she could write to the Hôtel des Négociants in Cannes (before 10 Feb.) after which he would be at M Morette 4, rue de Madrid, Casablanca.

is known about where Poulenc performed, but he told Bernac that a Concerto performance had been successful in Algiers. He stayed at the Hôtel d'Angleterre, eating very well at a nearby restaurant.[55] Bernac joined him later as he had on their second North American tour. After this tour Poulenc intended to become a composer again until 30 October 1952.[56]

COMPOSITIONS OF 1951: A LEAN YEAR

Early in 1951 Poulenc planned one of two compositions completed that year, a film score for *Le Voyage en Amérique* (FP 149). Films were never such high priorities for him as they were for Georges Auric. He told Paul Guth: "At the theater, let's hope that there is dust, an armchair, a curtain which rises, I can see anything... I am happy. At the most beautiful film, I am bored."[57] Poulenc had been persuaded to compose this music by Dr. Claudine Escoffier-Lambiotte, a friend of Pierre Fresnay and Yvonne Printemps and of the film's director Henri Lavorel, who had asked him personally.[58] Since the film was slated for completion by 20 May, and Poulenc suspected that work might take longer, he decided to create the score after returning from the *Stabat Mater* premiere in June. Exactly when he did finish is unknown, but he recorded the two-piano score with Jacques Février on "vendredi," presumably 13 July.[59] Poulenc described the music as being "in a popular dance-hall style, Max Linder silent cinema." Although the film score has neither been located nor published, Poulenc had Eschig issue a "Valse-musette pour deux pianos" from it entitled *L'Embarquement pour Cythère* (FP 150).[60]

The other completed composition was *Thème varié* (FP 151), a theme and eleven variations for solo piano, dated "Noizay Février-Septembre 1951". A draft was finished by 15 August: "I have just completed my *Thème varié* for piano, a serious work but I hope not boring. The coda of the final variation is strictly the theme backwards. You see, Mr. Leibowitz, that we too. . . . ", Poulenc chided.[61] He also told Doda Conrad, "I have finished a *Thème varié* for piano

---

[55] Unpublished 14 Feb. [1951] letter to Bernac in US-NH.

[56] 6 Mar. [1951] letter to Milhaud from Agadir in Poulenc 1994, 51-3 (Poulenc 1991, no. 215).

[57] Guth 1952, p. 4.

[58] Poulenc answered her request in his 3 Feb. [1951] letter from Turin in Poulenc 1994, 51-2.

[59] "Lundi" [9 July 1951] letter to Sauguet in Poulenc 1994, 51-9 (Poulenc 1991, no. 217).

[60] The dedication reads: "To Henri Lavorelle [sic], this evocation of the banks of the Marne, so dear to my childhood. Very affectionately, Francis Poulenc. October [19]51."

[61] 15 Aug. [1951] letter to Sauguet in Poulenc 1994, 51-11 (Poulenc 1991, no. 218). Poulenc was poking fun at René Leibowitz, a noted writer on twelve-tone music. See also Poulenc's 31 Aug. [1951] letter to Souvtchinsky in Poulenc 1994, 51-14.

that I am going to let rest before the final retouching."[62] In November 1951 he presented a copyist's manuscript to Vladimir Horowitz, "the pianist of my *heart*, and of my music." The manuscript contained numerous variants and an extended coda which differed from the printed edition.[63] Signed copies of the printed score (July 1952) were given to Marguerite Long, Horowitz, André Dubois, and Henri Hell. Février played the premiere at the Salle Gaveau on 15 December 1952, and Poulenc dedicated the score to Geneviève Sienkiewicz.[64]

Toward the end of 1951 Poulenc also began a series of *Quatre motets pour le temps de Noël* (FP 152), counterpart to the austere *Quatre motets pour un temps de pénitence* written in 1938-39.[65] Composition was not complete until mid-May 1952. These popular motets are frequently performed by choirs around the world.

No.	Title	Date of Composition	Dedicatee
3	Videntes stellam	Aix-en-Provence, November 1951	Madeleine Bataille
2	Quem vidistis pastores	Marseilles, December 1951	Simone Girard
1	O magnum mysterium	Noizay, April 1952	Félix de Nobel
4	Hodie Christus natus est	Paris, 18 May 1952	Marcel Couraud

MISCELLANEOUS EVENTS AND THE REMAINDER OF 1951

Early in June Poulenc sat on the jury of the prestigious Concours Marguerite Long-Jacques Thibaud in Paris. Among the twenty-three piano jury members were Henry Barraud, Nadia Boulanger, Claude Delvincourt, Roger Désormière, Samson François, Sergiu Celibidache, Edward Lockspeiser, Gian Francesco Malipiero, Georges Enesco, Ernesto Halffter, Pierre Agostini, and Nicole Henriot. Jacques Ibert presided with Louis Aubert vice president.[66]

Poulenc attended the 13 June 1951 *Stabat* premiere in Strasbourg where Fritz Munch led the choirs of Saint-Guillaume and the Orchestre Municipal de Strasbourg with Geneviève Moizan as soprano soloist. Various friends came while others listened to the direct broadcast. Henri Hell called the work *"profoundly moving;"*[67]

---

[62] Undated [Sept. 1951] letter in Poulenc 1994, 51-15 (Poulenc 1991, no. 220).

[63] Schmidt 1995, FP 151, p. 416.

[64] Fragment of Sienkiewicz's 27 Feb. 1961 letter to Poulenc in Poulenc 1994, p. 1051. In a later thank-you letter to Poulenc Sienkiewicz referred to herself as "Your oldest and dearest friend."

[65] "Lundi" [10 Dec. 1951] letter to Girard in Poulenc 1994, 51-16 (Poulenc 1991, no. 221).

[66] "Lundi" [9 July 1951] letter to Sauguet in Poulenc 1994, 51-9 (Poulenc 1991, no. 217) and Dunoyer, pp. 138-9. French pianist Jeanine Dacosta won the grand prize.

[67] Hell's "vendredi" [15 June 1951] letter to Poulenc in Poulenc 1994, 51-6.

Suzanne Latarjet was "carried away" by it;"[68] and Simone Girard said it was "purely and simply *superbe.*" [69] *Stabat* was reviewed by numerous critics including Bernard Gavoty in *Le Figaro* (15 June) and René Dumesnil in *Le Monde* (16 June), and Poulenc quickly wrote to Wanda Landowska, "My *Stabat Mater* [. . .] has just had a triumph in Strasbourg"[70] and to Robert Douglas Gibson "The *Stabat* had an *extraordinary* success in Strasbourg."[71] To Bernac he wrote:

> And then, I had a *great joy* in Strasbourg. Fritz Munch, with great calm, great seriousness, found the *Stabat* superb. I had the impression that he is the first person who realized the choral novelty of this work. I am assured of a magnificent performance because we understand each other. (Praise God he does not have the half-drugged, half-paradisical side of his brother [Charles Munch].) He has marvelously defined his work. "It is a perfectly written work which will give vocal joy to my choristers, but it is a *demanding* work." I find this word perfect.[72]

On the 18th Poulenc wrote a "secret" letter to Girard expressing concern about Bernac's state of mind. Bernac, disappointed by his last trip to America, was seriously considering giving up singing. Poulenc reasoned that quitting would lead to the conclusion he had no more voice and that his student Souzay had edged him out.[73] From the 14th to the 23rd he was in Brive after which he visited Hyères in southern France where Marie-Laure de Noailles had an estate.[74] Ned Rorem, who was staying there wrote in his diary:

> Lunched with Poulenc who, with Auric, becomes less and less sure of himself and manifests this by speaking of the inadequacies of others: they both want to change, whereas if they stayed the same they might become great. (I am sure that each of "Les Six" dreads the day when one of them will die: the others will say, "Ah! at least it wasn't me this time; nevertheless it's beginning!" Moral: If death worries you, don't associate yourself with others). . . .[75]

[68] Fragment of her [June 1951] letter to Poulenc in Poulenc 1994, p. 706, note 2.
[69] Fragment of her 14 June [1951] letter to Poulenc in Poulenc 1994, p. 709, note 1.
[70] 18 June [1951] letter in Poulenc 1994, 51-8.
[71] 17 June [1951] letter in GB-Lchester (fragment in Schmidt 1995, FP 148, p. 410). According to the 1951 Ibbs and Tillett ledger Poulenc and Bernac were originally scheduled to perform the 16th in Bournemouth. Poulenc must have realized that the trip to England was too close to his Strasbourg premiere and so Gerald Moore took his place.
[72] Fragment of Poulenc's "mercredi" [24 Jan. 1951] letter to Bernac from Cannes in Poulenc 1994, pp. 703-04, note 8.
[73] 18 July [1951] letter in Poulenc 1994, 51-10 (Poulenc 1991, no. 216).
[74] In his "lundi" [9 July 1951] letter to Sauguet, Poulenc speaks of his intention to be in Brive between these dates. Poulenc 51-9 (Poulenc 1991, no. 217).
[75] Rorem 1966, p. 40.

Having spent most of August at Noizay, Poulenc wrote Sauguet:

I will spend the summer here, except for a week in Edinburgh with Bernac. I am giving up Venice where I had momentarily dreamed of making a hop from London on 8 September, because it is awfully expensive and besides I must work.[76]

While in Edinburgh Poulenc performed *mélodies* by Debussy and himself with Bernac and Nina Milkins on 2 September, did a pre-recording for the BBC at 12 noon on the 3rd, and played a symphonic engagement in Bournemouth on the 6th.[77]

In Noizay, Pierre Souvtchinsky asked him for an article on Prokofiev's piano music. Poulenc expected to finish it by early October 1951, but couldn't until November while in Aix-en-Provence.[78] An appearance with Bernac, Jean Françaix, and the cellist Maurice Gendron on 31 October for an "Amis de la musique de chambre" concert at the Salle Marceau-Chaillot in Paris was one of the interruptions.[79] Eventually published in 1953, the essay shows that Poulenc was fond of this repertoire and intimately acquainted with it.[80] Sometime in late October or early November he heard an Igor Markevitch concert in Paris also attended by Boulanger and Stravinsky.[81] The reason for the Aix-en-Provence trip was a concert arranged by Simone Girard.[82] While there he finished the third of his Christmas motets; the second was completed in Marseilles during December. He was also in Brussels briefly on 2 November for a performance of *Stabat Mater*.[83]

Poulenc lost several close friends during 1951 including his neighbor Georges Poupet (shortly after 9 July) and the actor/director Louis Jouvet (15 August).[84] He also had to have his pet terrier "Mickey"

---

[76] Poulenc's 15 Aug. [1951] letter from Noizay in Poulenc 1994, 51-11 (Poulenc 1991, no. 218). See also Poulenc's unpublished 8 Aug. [1951] letter to Gibson in GB-Lchester. He said he would be in Edinburgh on 1 Sept., record *Babar* for the BBC on the 3rd, and pass through London on both the 4th and 7th when he hoped they could lunch together. Had Poulenc gone to Venice, he would have attended the La Fenice theater premiere of Stravinsky's *The Rake's Progress*.

[77] Unpublished 5 Sept. [1951] letter to Mme Lambiotte in US-NYlambiotte-donhauser and the 1951 Ibbs and Tillett ledger.

[78] 31 Aug. [1951] letter in Poulenc 1994, 51-14.

[79] *Le Guide du concert* 32 (19 Oct. 1951), 22.

[80] Poulenc 1953b.

[81] Rorem 1966, p. 68.

[82] "Lundi" [10 Dec. 1951] thank-you letter to Girard in Poulenc 1994, 51-16 (Poulenc 1991, no. 221). Poulenc reported that Bernac was in particularly good form and that they were preparing for their next trip to America.

[83] Unpublished 5 Sept. [1951] letter to Mme Lambiotte in US-NYlambiotte-donhauser.

[84] 15 Aug. [1951] letter to Sauguet from Noizay in Poulenc 1994, 51-11 (Poulenc

(or "Toutou" as he familiarly referred to him) put to sleep and later told Marie-Blanche de Polignac that he cried his eyes out when he kissed the dog for the last time.[85]

THIRD AMERICAN TOUR: JANUARY-MARCH 1952

In mid-January 1952 the Bernac/Poulenc duo traveled to New York on the steamship De Grasse for a tour which was shorter and less hectic than the previous two.[86] This one was primarily centered around New York City with a trip to Caracas, Venezuela instead of Canada. Also, there was no transcontinental foray to California.[87] Following their 1950 plan, the initial concert was given on 21 January in Washington D.C. at Dumbarton Oaks. Although the program contained music from their extensive repertoire, the inclusion of Samuel Barber's *Mélodies passagères* was innovative. On previous American tours they had not included music by American composers. Barber spoke of the occasion in an interview with the composer-pianist-writer Phillip Ramey:

> P.R.: Poulenc [and Bernac] recorded *Mélodies Passagères*. Was he enamored with those songs?
>
> S.B.: Francis was a darling man, but he was enamored only with his own songs. However, when I played *Mélodies Passagères* for him he liked them and did not suggest any changes in the French prosody. But he did say that while there were no mistakes in the French setting he thought that a sensitive French musician would nonetheless know the songs were not written by a Frenchman. Probably because the musical style is my own—I certainly didn't try for a French tone. Actually, I don't think that Francis knew my music all that well. I do remember that Horowitz played my Piano Sonata and Poulenc enthused about it, terming the fugue "a knockout." But Francis and I were very friendly—in fact, I've rarely been that close to another composer. I dedicated *Mélodies Passagères* to him, and he dedicated to me his "Capriccio d'après *Le Bal Masqué*" for two pianos. He used to visit me in Mount Kisco and I him in Paris. The last time I saw Francis was in Paris, at Les Halles: he was rushing off on the back of a motorcycle and waved an extravagant goodbye. I know Poulenc would be very happy that this record has finally been released after so many

---

85 4 Feb. [1952] letter from Caracas in Poulenc 1994, 52-4 (Poulenc 1991, no. 225). Various photographs of Poulenc and his dog have been published. Hell 1958, cover; Poulenc 1978, 190/1; Ivry, pp. 92-3.

86 Poulenc 1994, p. 1020. On this trip Poulenc met Prof. Paul Delmas-Marsalet, with whom he would spend time during the summer of 1954.

87 See Appendix 2 for a synopsis of the tour.

[Note: the top footnote fragment begins: "1991, no. 218). For Sauguet's account of the days after Jouvet's death, see his 20 Aug. 1951 letter to Poulenc in Poulenc 1994, 51-12 (Poulenc 1991, no. 219)."]

years, for he often asked me why it had been held up. (I never knew. Incidentally, I was present at the recording session.)[88]

Barber, present at both the Dumbarton Oaks and Town Hall performances, was very pleased and wrote to William Strickland, "Bernac and Poulenc did the Rilke songs so well, especially in New York."[89]

Commenting on his first week there Poulenc said: "Delectably lazy week in my sumptuous suite at the Wyndham Hotel, bedroom, room with piano (only eight dollars)."[90] Thirsting for news, he was pleased to receive his niece's letter, his first from Paris in four days! He also enjoyed seeing the Bulgarian-born Austrian soprano Ljuba Welitsch at the Metropolitan Opera in Richard Strauss' *Salomé* and anticipated Robert Shaw's performance of Bach's Mass in B minor on the 27th. Yvonne de Casa Fuerte was his constant companion, but he missed Vladimir Horowitz, who was touring Cuba. Sometime before 27 February Poulenc played his Concerto in Cincinnati.

Poulenc and Bernac left for Caracas in late January or early February giving their first recital there on the 2nd. He played the *Concert champêtre* with Sergiu Celibidache's Berlin Philharmonic on Sunday the 3rd and gave two additional recitals with Bernac on the subsequent Monday and Wednesday before returning to New York on the 7th.[91] He disliked Caracas, finding it deadly dull, although Bernac seemed to have been rejuvenated twenty years.[92]

Once returned to New York the major focus was a 10 February Town Hall reworking of the Dumbarton Oaks recital with the addition of four *mélodies* by Duparc and Ravel's *Don Quichotte à Dulcinée*. Though the recital was well reviewed in *The New York Times*, the critic found fault with Poulenc's accompanying, saying "his pianism was little more than adequate." This is one of the rare criticisms of Poulenc's accompanying. His songs, on the other hand, "formed the evening's apex, for no living composer can match their deft evocation, their freshness of spirit, their strange sense of completion even when they are the merest fragments."[93] Bernac was much praised, the same critic adding, "M. Bernac's voice may not be what

---

[88] Ramey, p.2

[89] Quoted in Heyman, p. 327.

[90] 26 Jan. 1952 letter to Brigitte Manceaux in Poulenc 1994, 52-2 (Poulenc 1991, no. 224).

[91] 4 Feb. [1952] letter to Marie-Blanche in Poulenc 1994, 52-4 (Poulenc 1991, no. 225). In a 13 Feb. [1952] letter to Rouart, Poulenc expressed his fascination with Celibidache, a fascination which apparently went beyond the conductor's musical gifts. Fragment in Poulenc 1994, p. 720, note 1.

[92] 4 Feb. [1952] letter to Marie-Blanche in Poulenc 1994, 52-4 (Poulenc 1991, no. 225). According to Poulenc this was the result of getting away from Paris.

[93] C[arter] H[ayman's] review (11 Feb. 1952), 21.

it once was, but his interpretations had such conviction that they swept aside such limitations and brought his listeners deep into the heart of the music." Robert Sabin was less kind to Bernac, finding him "in poor vocal form at the beginning of the evening." His overall conclusion, however, was much more favorable.

> [It was] as fine a vocal program as New York has heard in many a day. The accompaniments were superb; and Barber, who was present, had every reason to feel happy about the performance, as well as about the reception, of his songs.[94]

Reporting to Doda Conrad from Wanda Landowska's Lakeville, Connecticut home Poulenc said that Town Hall had been full and that there had been six curtain calls and excellent press.[95] During Poulenc's visit to Landowska she shared portions of her latest Bach recording with him and he told Conrad:

> What I like about Wanda is that she does not suffer from the musical bulimia of our Nadia [Boulanger]. After four preludes and fugues she stopped the phonograph saying that that sufficed [and] that we could no longer listen very well.

Poulenc said there would be additional concerts and recordings, and indeed they did record Barber's cycle. Poulenc took time to answer letters including one written from Edith Borroff, a music historian, who suggested that she come to New York for advice on composition. Poulenc politely advised her not to make the long trip. Since he had no pedagogical gift he never gave compositional advice; to make matters worse he told her he understood little English and spoke even less![96] On 5 March the duo returned to France.

SPRING AND SUMMER 1952

Once back, Poulenc spent a week in Paris and then headed south to relax and recover.[97] His time was divided between Marseilles,

[94] *Musical America* 72 (Feb. 1952), 224.
[95] 13 Feb. [1952] letter to Conrad from Lakeville in Poulenc 1994, 52-6. He thanked Landowska in a 21 Feb. [1952] letter in Poulenc 1994, 52-7. After this concert, the duo was entertained by Elsa Maxwell for dinner and sent a collective card to Vilmorin signed by Poulenc, Nine Nyan [*recte* Nin Ryan?], Franz Osborne, Casa Fuerte, Bernac, Menotti, and Sacha de Manziarly. See also Chimènes reference to this letter at F-Psg (Doucet) in Poulenc 1994, p. 718, note 4.
[96] Unpublished letter (postmarked New York: 16 Feb. 1952) in US-Cn.
[97] On 8 July [1952] Poulenc told Landowska: "After America: one week in Paris— one week in the Midi with agreeable loves—one week in Munich—three weeks , of work in Noizay— one month of the Festival du XXᵉ siècle—two weeks more of work at Noizay—two weeks of touring in England and finally a little peace in Normandy at my sister's house." Poulenc 1994, 52-18. He was in Noizay on 25 Aug. when he wrote Collaer that he had heard his radio performance of Stravinsky's *Rake's Progress*. Collaer 1996, 52-1.

Cannes, and Monte Carlo, in part to be with his new friend and lover Lucien Roubert. Poulenc was already thinking about future compositions, especially one for Gold and Fizdale.[98] His homecoming was marred by news that his friend, the noted conductor Roger Désormière, had suffered a catastrophic cerebral hemorrhage while touring Italy, an attack which sadly left him paralyzed until his death eleven years later.[99] After a week in Munich, Bernac and Poulenc journeyed to London, where they performed at Goldsmith's Hall on the 27th, made a pre-recording for the BBC on the 28th, and gave a recital at Wigmore Hall on the 30th.[100] Their repertoire was entirely French including Milhaud's early *Quatre poèmes de Léo Latil* (1914), Jacques Leguerney's *La Solitude* (1951), and works by Ravel, Roussel, and Poulenc. Though the duo performed throughout the spring, Poulenc's thoughts turned increasingly to composing.

As noted earlier, he completed the *Quatre motets pour le temps de Noël* begun in November 1951. Finally, in April he gave serious thought to Marc Pincherle's request for a contribution to the collective work *La Guirlande de Campra* (FP 154).[101] Pincherle spoke to Poulenc about this project before he left for America, but we do not know precisely when initial contact was made.[102] The original concept is described in the dedication to Roger Bigonnet which prefaces the printed score:

> In homage to a much neglected composer and to the city of his birth: Aix-en-Provence, seven of today's musicians have assembled this *Guirlande de Campra* [*Garland of Campra*], a series of variations or meditations on a theme from his 1717 opera *Camille*.[103]

Poulenc advised Pincherle that Auric should write the overture followed by Daniel-Lesur, Roland-Manuel, Tailleferre, Poulenc, Sauguet, and Honegger. His order was adopted with the exception that Honegger's "Toccata" was placed first and Auric's "Ecossaise" last.[104] Poulenc's own contribution went through a quick metamorphosis because in April he had drafted a "Matelote provençale" in

[98] 21 Mar. [1952] letter to Casa Fuerte from Cannes in Poulenc 1994, 52-8.
[99] Poulenc wrote Milhaud on 10 July 1952 that this event left him close to tears whenever he thought of it. Fragment in Poulenc 1994, p. 724, note 1 and Wiéner 1966, p. 24.
[100] 1952 Ibbs and Tillett ledgers.
[101] Pincherle, a noted critic and musicologist who had been associated with Landowska's famous course on interpretation at Saint-Leu-la-Forêt in 1950, became secretary general of the Aix-en-Provence Festival.
[102] 16 Apr. [1952] letter to Pincherle in Poulenc 1994, 52-10. It may have been as early as late 1951, because Honegger's piece was written in November 1951.
[103] Printed score (Paris: Salabert, 1954). Schmidt 1995, no. 153, p. 421.
[104] 16 Apr. [1952] letter to Pincherle in Poulenc 1994, 52-10.

the mold of François Couperin's piece of a similar name.[105] He sent
Pincherle his manuscript on 11 June earmarking the fair copy for
Bigonnet and the sketch, which he customarily burned, for
Pincherle.[106] *La Guirlande* was premiered by the eminent Austrian
conductor Hans Rosbaud and the Orchestre de la Société des Con-
certs du Conservatoire at Aix on 31 July 1952.[107]

He spent May in Paris attending a *Works of the Twentieth Century*
Festival established by Nicolas Nabokov.[108] The festival opened with
Stabat Mater at the Church of Saint-Roch on 28 April with the com-
poser in attendance.

> For this first Parisian hearing, Francis Poulenc did not want any per-
> formers other than the Chorale Saint-Guillaume, directed by Fritz
> Münch, with Mme Moisan [*recte* Moizan] as principal interpreter. "—
> The Chorale Saint-Guillaume, celebrated for its execution of Bach Pas-
> sions, has brought a true fervor to the performance of my work. It is
> even curious that a Protestant chorale could assimilate so well the
> style of a long prayer to the Virgin." Churches lend themselves poorly
> to orchestras. The vaults push away those brasses and profane strings.
> The Church of Saint-Roch is one of those whose acoustic proves some-
> what less forbidding. Francis Poulenc also chose it by inclination.
> "—-The Bossuet style of Saint-Roch adapts itself to my aesthetic.
> Corneille, Le Nôtre are buried there. When I enter Saint-Roch, I also
> think of 'the end of Ferragus' where the Thirteen listen to a funeral
> service in each of the chapels. I am an old Balzacian. There are parts
> of town which I detest. I only go to Neuilly to visit sick people. As
> little as possible to the Plaine-Monceau, very rarely to Passy, never to
> the rue de Prony. Paris, for me, begins at l'Etoile and goes toward the
> east. Saint-Roch, that is my Paris. . . ."[109]

The Festival presented a number of visiting companies, who performed Berg's *Wozzeck* (Vienna State Opera), Britten's *Billy Budd*
(Royal Opera Covent Garden; Poulenc left after Act II), Stravinsky's
Le Sacre du Printemps (at which he could not greet Stravinsky because Robert Craft and Nabokov kept everyone away), Vittorio
Rieti's opera *Don Perlimplin* (which he attended twice), and ballets
by Auric (*Coup de feu*) and Sauguet (*Cordélia*).[110] Virgil Thomson's

[105]18 Apr. [1952] postcard to Pincherle in Poulenc 1994, 52-11.
[106]11 June [1952] letter to Pincherle in Poulenc 1994, 52-16 and Schmidt 1995, FP
153, p.421.
[107] For Poulenc's account of this minor work see his 20 Aug. [1952] letter to Bernac
(Poulenc 1994, 52-21). See also the program for the Ve Festival international de
musique Aix-en-Provence in F-Po (PRO.C.8), p. [44].
[108] Tual, p. 253 summarizes the activities, which took a year to plan.
[109] Guth 1952/
[110] 8 July [1952] letter to Casa Fuerte from "Le Neubourg" in Poulenc 1994, 52-17.
Rieti's opera was first performed on 7 May 1952.

Four Saints in Three Acts opened on 30 May. Stravinsky conducted *Oedipus Rex* with Cocteau as narrator, and the New York City Ballet (of which George Balanchine was the director) presented works unfamiliar to Parisian audiences. Toward the end of the festival Bernac and Poulenc gave a recital on 23 May at the Château de Brède in Bordeaux for the "Festival de musique." Poulenc also entertained Thomson and Hell at Noizay for a weekend before beginning his summer activity.

The last few weeks of June were spent with Bernac in England for a 20 June BBC recital, a 22 June recital of music by Rameau, Fauré, Wolf, Debussy, Poulenc, and Ravel in Hampstead (North London), and an appearance at Britten's Aldeburgh Festival on the 27th.[111] Early in July Poulenc visited his sister and accomplished a lot of work in "the calm, the freshness, the peace" of Le Tremblay. One project on his mind was a ballet commissioned by La Scala and Ricordi for the winter of 1953-54. He wrote about this commission to Yvonne de Casa Fuerte, Wanda Landowska, Milhaud, and Simone Girard during the second week of July reporting that he had had the most amiable visit from the director of Ricordi, who was no doubt in Paris because of the festival.[112] Poulenc was thinking of a ballet on the life of a martyred saint, telling Landowska he had in mind a *ballet sacré*. Eventually, unable to find a suitable saint to portray, Poulenc abandoned this idea, turning instead to Georges Bernanos' *Dialogues des Carmélites*.

Though bedeviled by a persistent eye problem at Noizay during August, he completed a brief *Ave verum corpus* (FP 154) for women's voices commissioned by the Howard Heinz Foundation for performance at the Pittsburgh International Contemporary Music Festival.[113] The work, which sets a sequence hymn for Corpus Christi by Pope Innocent VI (d. 1342), was premiered on 25 November in Pittsburgh at Carnegie Music Hall by the Pennsylvania College for Women Choir, Russell G. Wichman conducting.

Poulenc also entertained various friends at Le Grand Coteau. Goddard Lieberson and his wife Vera Zorina came on 19 August for a lengthy discussion about various matters including a future

---

[111] 1952 Ibbs and Tillett ledger.
[112] 8 July [1952] letters to Casa Fuerte and Landowska in Poulenc 1994, 52-17 and 52-18; and his 10 July [1952] letters to Milhaud and Girard in Poulenc 1994, p. 733, note 2 (fragments only).
[113] 20 Aug. and 2 Sept. [1952] letters to Bernac in Poulenc 1994, 52-21 and 52-22 respectively. On 20 Aug. Poulenc told Bernac, "Fortunately in two days I have just completed a very simple *Ave Verum*, very pure and, I believe, very successful." See also his unpublished note [postmarked 23 Oct. 1952] to the Lambiottes in US-NYlambiotte-donhauser.

American tour.[114] Nadia Boulanger was there for the first time on 10 September,[115] and, following another pleasant visit by Rose Dercourt-Plaut and her husband Fred that month, Poulenc completed a *Capriccio d'après Le Bal masqué* (FP 155) for two pianos which he dedicated to Samuel Barber. At one point he put it away in favor of a flute sonata which came suddenly to mind at the Austerlitz station in Paris. This is the first-known mention of a flute sonata, which may or may not be connected to the 1957 sonata dedicated to Jean-Pierre Rampal.[116] The end of the summer, however, was awful: he could not work effectively, he was disturbed over poor Roger Désormière's fate, and his eye problem irritated him. Nevertheless, he completely sketched the sonata for Gold and Fizdale and worked on one for flute and piano.[117] The Sonata for Two Pianos (FP 156), which first occurred to Poulenc in June 1949, advanced during stays in Marseilles and Ouchy-Lausanne and was completed at Noizay in spring 1953. This work will be discussed in the following chapter.

FALL 1952

Poulenc and Bernac may have performed a charity concert in Nazelles the weekend of 21 September to benefit Poulenc's parish priest.[118] During the fall Poulenc spent October in Lyon and Avignon and made several trips to Marseilles where Simone Girard's son-in-law Guillaume Bonnasse arranged a room with piano at the Hôtel Beauveau.[119] He was there between 20 November and 20 December and spent January in Ouchy-Lausanne.[120] Poulenc planned his winter 1952-53 tour of England (February) and Italy (March), brokered concerts at Aix and other venues in southern France, and considered trips to the Dutch West Indies and a fourth American tour.[121]

The year ended sadly. In November the literary world suffered a severe blow when Paul Eluard died suddenly of a heart attack at Charenton.[122] Poulenc was profoundly touched by the passing of a man he had first seen more than thirty years earlier and whose poetry had provided him with such inspiration. Eluard was interred at Le Père Lachaise cemetery at 2:00 pm on 22 November with Poulenc among the mourners.[123]

---

[114] 20 Aug. [1952] letter to Bernac in Poulenc 1994, 52-21.
[115] Boulanger's 30 Sept. 1952 letter to Poulenc in Poulenc 1994, 52-24.
[116] 2 Sept. [1952] letter to Bernac in Poulenc 1994, 52-22.
[117] 3 Oct. [1952] letter to Casa Fuerte in Poulenc 1994, 52-26.
[118] 20 Aug. [1952] letter to Bernac in Poulenc 1994, 52-21.
[119] Fragment of Poulenc's 30 Sept. [1952] letter to Bonnasse in Poulenc 1994, p. 741, note 1.
[120] 3 Oct. [1952] letter to Casa Fuerte in Poulenc 1994, 52-26.
[121] [Sept. 1952] letter to Girard in Poulenc 1994, 52-23.
[122] Gateau, p. 362.
[123] In a 22 Nov. [1952] letter to Dr. Maurice Delmas-Marsalet, written hours before

As the year closed, *Aubade* was revived in November at the Opéra-Comique.[124] Poulenc also worked diligently at his Sonata for Two Pianos, no doubt sharing some of the composition with Gold and Fizdale during their three-day visit to Marseilles in late November or early December.[125] Now nearly fifty-four, Poulenc enjoyed southern France and anticipated his move to the Hôtel Beau-Rivage in Ouchy-Lausanne from which he would prepare a series of twenty radio interviews with Rostand and continue work on his Sonata. On 6 December Poulenc wrote the preface to Gabriel Laplane's *Albéniz, sa vie, son œuvre*, a book which was not published until 1956.[126] He spent Christmas day with Bernac as he prepared for his departure.[127] The stage was now set for one of the most eventful years of his life; the year in which transforming George Bernanos' *Dialogues des Carmélites* into an opera would become a consuming passion.

---

the interment, Poulenc sent along an Eluard memento at the doctor's request. It was one of the poems mysteriously delivered to his door by courier during the somber mornings of the Occupation in 1944. Poulenc 1994, 52-27.
[124] Décor by Maurice Brianchon with Diana danced by Mlle Paule Morin in Marcel Berge's choreography. See the reviews by André Warnod and Clarendon in *Le Figaro* (22-3 Nov. 1952).
[125] 8 Dec. 1952 thank you note to Poulenc in Poulenc 1994, 52-28. One of the many photographs of this visit, showing the three, is reproduced as no. 31.
[126] Poulenc 1956c.
[127] Fragment of Poulenc's 28 Dec. 1952 letter to Girard in Poulenc 1994, p. 748, note 2.

XII

Obsession with Dialogues des Carmélites: *1953-1957*

The years 1953 through 1957 were dominated by the composition and performance of *Dialogues des Carmélites* (FP 159). Before, during and after the writing of this opera Poulenc worked on other compositions among which only the song cycle *Le Travail du peintre* (FP 161) and the Sonata for Flute and Piano (FP 164) are of particular significance. From time to time during this period Poulenc gave concerts as the Bernac/Poulenc duo wound down its lengthy association. But these were five difficult years for Poulenc; in spite of a consuming passion for *Dialogues,* his life was marred by emotional turmoil. Deep depression sometimes led him to the edge of a mental breakdown, and on one occasion in November 1954 his shaky emotional state curtailed a tour with Bernac in Germany. Two real problems contributed to Poulenc's emotional depression. First, he was frustrated in his attempt to obtain literary rights to *Dialogues,* leading him to believe the project might be stillborn. Second, he witnessed the declining health of Lucien Roubert, with whom he had had a six-year relationship. Ironically, Roubert died of cancer on 21 October 1955 at the precise hour Poulenc finished composing *Dialogues.*[1] The second problem weighed as heavily on Poulenc as the first.

This period also witnessed Poulenc's first significant attempt to document the fascinating story of his life through radio conversations with his friends the actor Stéphane Audel and the critic/writer Claude Rostand. Audel recorded three series of conversations for Swiss Radio in 1953, 1955, and 1962, and a fourth series was to begin

---

[1] 31 Oct. [1955] letter to Girard in Poulenc 1994, 55-16 (Poulenc 1991, no. 269).

377

the day Poulenc died in 1963.[2] Rostand recorded his interviews, which Poulenc actually prepared in written form, between 13 October 1953 and 16 February 1954 for broadcast over Paris Inter.[3] As Poulenc may have realized, however, the wealth of letters written since his teens would ultimately provide far more useful information than formal interviews.

SWITZERLAND, ITALY, AND THE "DISCOVERY" OF *DIALOGUES:* EARLY 1953

Poulenc went to Switzerland on 4 January and was royally ensconced at the Hôtel Beau-Rivage overlooking Lac Léman in Ouchy-Lausanne. Diana Vreeland, noted fashion editor for *Vogue* and *Harper's Bazaar* and an occasional hotel guest, had been enraptured by the spectacular view of Mont Blanc.[4] Poulenc was equally taken with the location and wrote enthusiastically to Bernac:[5]

> My arrangement here is pure paradise. Room on the 4th floor overlooking the lake. Salon with [an Erard] grand piano nearby, detached from a "royal suite" and totally soundproof. [. . .] How calm it is here! It is doing me a world of good. And what weather for working! Today I am beginning the interviews with Rostand, which will be published by Julliard, like those of Darius.[6]

Having passed his fifty-fourth birthday there, he described his daily routine to Simone Girard:

> I get up at 6 am because I go to bed at 9:30 pm. I read in bed [and] get dressed at 7 am. Breakfast (sublime tea and jams) at 7:30 am. From 8 to 9:30 am I prepare my twenty chats with Rostand. At 9:30 am I walk in the garden [and at] 10 am one hour of music. I have a piano isolated in a little private salon. At 1 pm lunch. From 2 to 3 pm I walk along the lake. From 3 to 6 pm music. From 6 to 7:30 pm a brief tour of Lausanne. At 8 pm a light dinner and bed at 9:30 pm.[7]

Poulenc was eating very carefully, drinking only water, and going out very little. During his first evening foray he heard Paul Sacher

[2] Poulenc 1994, p. 746, notes 2 and 3.
[3] Poulenc 1954 [Rostand] and Poulenc 1963a [Audel] respectively. The interviews with Rostand have been released as two compact disks entitled *Francis Poulenc ou l'Invité de Touraine: Entretiens avec Claude Rostand* by the Archives Sonores INA (no. 211734, © 1995: includes prefatory notes by Renaud Machart). The aural version contains musical excerpts impossible to reproduce in the printed book.
[4] Vreeland, p. 83.
[5] Unpublished 29 Dec. [1952] letter to Rose Dercourt-Plaut in US-NH.
[6] "Mardi" [6 Jan. 1953] letter in Poulenc 1994, 53-1 (Poulenc 1991, no. 229). The hotel contained only about 100 guests including the King and Queen of Jordan, and Charlie Chaplin and family.
[7] 8 Jan. 1953 letter to Girard in Poulenc 1994, 53-3 and fragment of his [11 Jan. 1953] letter to Bernac in Poulenc 1994, p. 748, note 1.

and the Orchestre de la suisse romande in a program featuring Hindemith's 1951 symphony *Die Harmonie der Welt*. He was also visited by Henri Hell, was working on the Sonata for Two Pianos for Gold and Fizdale, and had decided to write *Le Travail du peintre*. The cycle, to be dedicated to Bernac "in letters of gold," was for the Bernac/Poulenc twentieth anniversary concert. Poulenc envisioned this concert as also containing Fauré, Schumann or Schubert, as well as Ravel's *Trois chants hébraïques*, and Debussy's *Fêtes galantes*.[8] He remained in Switzerland until 28 January writing to Igor Markevitch just before departure that he had tried in vain to contact him during his stay. An orchestral score of *Sécheresses* had finally been published for Roger Désormière's upcoming Paris performance, but Poulenc had to ask Markevitch to step in for the incapacitated conductor. He also rejoiced that his *Stabat Mater* had won the prestigious New York Music Critic's Circle award for the best choral work of 1952.[9]

In September 1952, Poulenc told Simone Girard that he planned to be in England later in February 1953 and would return to Paris (at the latest) on the 27th.[10] After Switzerland Poulenc spent three weeks in Paris and anticipated two in the Midi before leaving for Italy.[11] Bernac and Poulenc were in Avignon for a recital on 2 March, but we are unsure if any of the other concerts envisioned for Southern France materialized.[12] Some time in early March was spent with Pierre Fournier preparing for their forthcoming Italian tour. Fournier and Poulenc debuted in Turin on 18 March and, as Cocteau wrote in his diary about Poulenc, "He played last night before a public of chilly old ladies."[13] They garnered two encores, one more than recently accorded Robert Casadesus, Arthur Rubinstein, or Walter Gieseking, but only because twenty young auditors demanded a second after everyone else had departed! Poulenc wrote:

> We caused a sensation with the Debussy, which was worthy of *Fêtes galantes*, played the Schubert very well, the Schumann less well, the Poulenc quite well, and the Stravinsky *very well*. Tonight in Bergamo

[8] [11 Jan. 1953] letter to Bernac in US-NH. Fragment in Poulenc 1994, p. 820, note 3.
[9] 24 Jan. [1953] letter in Poulenc 1994, 53-5. He learned of the award on the 12th from Charlie Chaplin's secretary Anthony Chaplin and subsequently by cable. Fragment of Poulenc's 12 Jan. 1953 letter to Girard in Poulenc 1994, p. 750, note 5.
[10] [Sept. 1952] letter in Poulenc 1994, 52-23.
[11] Unpublished "lundi" [postmarked 11 Feb. 1953] letter to Mme Lambiotte in US-NYlambiotte-donhauser.
[12] One in Cannes was proposed for 6 Mar. See his [Sept. 1952] letter to Girard in Poulenc 1994, 52-23.
[13] Cocteau 1988, p. 63 (Cocteau 1985, p. 80).

everything should go well. At any rate, it is very easy to play with Fournier. Like Pierre I [Bernac], he never falters.[14]

Poulenc told Fournier's wife Lydia, in a postcard sent upon arrival in Bergamo, that the program included "Locatelli, Schubert, Poulenc, interval, Debussy, [and] Stravinsky."[15]

After Bergamo, they performed in Assisi, spending the day, before traveling to Rome.[16]

> We are beginning to play very well together. The recording for the radio is good, I think. [. . .] Rome very amusing and very mundane. Sam[uel Barber] is there. [Nicolas] Nabokov as well!!!!![17]

Fournier and Poulenc were sought after everywhere, but Poulenc said that their appearances would be of great rarity and very expensive.[18] Moreover, their Roman triumph was such that he was obliged to guarantee two weeks for the coming March.[19] Not withstanding such successes, the trip's real significance was Poulenc's meeting with Guido Valcarenghi, Director of Ricordi editions, while passing through Milan. Balking at composing a ballet concerning a martyred saint, Poulenc expressed his apprehension to Valcarenghi. Valcarenghi countered by suggesting an opera on Georges Bernanos' screen play *Dialogues des Carmélites*. Bernanos had based his work on Gertrud von le Fort's 1931 *Die Letzte am Schafott (The Last on the Scaffold)*, but the project for a film remained unrealized at his death in 1948.[20] Poulenc recollected the chain of events leading to his consideration of Bernanos' play.

> I had vaguely thought about a half-profane, half-sacred topic concerning Saint Marguerite of Cortona, but I could not come to grips with my project (I have always written the arguments for my ballets). [. . .] I revealed to Mr. Valcaranghi [sic], director of Ricordi Editions, which had commissioned the ballet, my lack of enthusiasm for the project. Ah! I added, in the midst of a charming lunch, why don't you ask me to write an opera. — There's no problem with that, I will

---

[14] [Mar. 1953] letter to Girard in Poulenc 1994, 53-6 (Poulenc 1991, no. 230).

[15] Quoted from the English translation of his 1 June [1953] letter in Hughes 1998, p. 82.

[16] Unpublished card to Rose Dercourt-Plaut in US-NH. It is the same card from Ostia as Poulenc sent Thomson (also in US-NH).

[17] [26 Mar. 1953] postcard to Bernac from Assisi in Poulenc 1994, 53-7 (Poulenc 1991, no. 231).

[18] [Mar. 1953] letter to Girard in Poulenc 1994, 53-6 (Poulenc 1991, no. 230).

[19] Fragment of Poulenc's "vendredi" [3 Apr. 1953] letter to Girard in Poulenc 1994, p. 751, note 4.

[20] Concerning Bernanos' association with von le Fort's novel, which he first saw in 1938, and the history of his own setting, see Speaight, pp. 262-8. The most detailed history of Poulenc's opera is in Buckland/Chimènes: d.

commission one from you right away, replied my host. But the libretto? —Since you are looking for a mystical topic, why not write an opera on *Dialogues of the Carmelites* by Bernanos. I was stupefied by this proposition. What would the public say about an opera lacking a love intrigue? Having always given credit to the innate theatrical sense of the Italians, I dismissed this objection, but needed time to consider... Oh! how much! To be sure, I knew Bernanos' play which I had read, reread, and seen twice, but I had no idea of its verbal rhythm, a most important point for me. I had decided to examine it later, upon my return to Paris, when, two days later, right in the middle of the window of a Roman bookstore, I saw *The Dialogues* which seemed to await me. I had left my hotel early in order to stroll from church to church, as I like to do when I am in Rome. The weather was so nice that I could think of nothing other than to savor the beauty of a spring morning, and here, in spite myself, I was led on a great adventure which would haunt me for three years. I bought the book and decided to reread it. In order to do so I installed myself in the Piazza Navone, on the terrace of the café *Tre Scalini*. It was ten in the morning. At noon I was still there having had a coffee, an ice cream, orange juice, and a bottle of Fuggi water in order to excuse my lengthy stay. At twelve thirty, I was drunk with enthusiasm but decisive proof was needed: would I find the music for such a libretto. I opened the book at random obliging myself, to translate *instantly* into music the first sentences that I was reading. Luck did not spare me. You judge: Mother Superior [First Prioress]. "Do not believe this chair that I use is mine through rank and position, like the footstool of a Duchess. Alas! this is the wish of my loving daughters who take such good care of me, and insist that I revel in comfort. But it is not always easy to revive all those former habits that one has long ago discarded. And I can see that what should have been a remarkable pleasure will forever remain for me only a dire necessity." As unbelievable as this may appear, I immediately found the melodic curve of this lengthy response! The die was cast. At two o'clock, I telegraphed Mr. Valcarenghi, the true dowser, that I would write *Dialogues*. I pondered at length the division into scenes and then, in June of 1953, on the train between Paris and Brive, I suddenly realized it.[21]

Poulenc's restructuring of Bernanos' play is interesting (see p. 382).

Albert Béguin, Bernanos' literary executor, was most complimentary about the way Poulenc adapted the film script.

It seems to me you have accomplished a veritable tour de force in adapting his [Bernanos'] text of *Dialogues des Carmélites* to the exigencies of a musical composition, while remaining absolutely faithful all the time to his spirit and to the major lines of a very delicate architect-

---

[21] Poulenc 1957, pp. 15-17 and Allorto.

Correspondence Between Bernanos' Script and Poulenc's Libretto				
Bernanos' Script	*Poulenc's Final Libretto (3 Acts)*[22]			*Poulenc's Original Libretto (2 Acts)*[23]
Tableau 1 Scenes 1-4	Act I	Scene 1		Act I
Tableau 2 Scenes 1-5		Scene 2		
Scene 6		Scene 3		
Scenes 7-10		Scene 4		
Scene 11	Act II	Scene 1		
Tableau 3 Scene 1			Interlude 1	
Scene 2		Scene 2		
Scene 7			Interlude 2	
Scene 8		Scene 3*		
Scenes 12, 13, 16		Scene 4		Act II
Tableau 4 Scene 12	Act III	Scene 1		
Tableau 5 Scene 5			Interlude 1	
Scene 8		Scene 2		
Scene 9			Interlude 2	
Scenes 12, 13, 14		Scene 3		
Scene 16			Interlude 3	
Scene 17		Scene 4		
*tenez-vous fière				

ture. It was not an easy thing to transpose into an opera this frame-work nourished by profound ideas and sustained by a continuous meditation. I find *all* of Bernanos in your presentation, and if I had not known that you had to sacrifice many lines I have the impression that I would not notice it.[24]

Poulenc quickly shared his news with friends. Performances were assured, he told Bernac, for La Scala (Milan), Teatro Colon (Buenos Aires), San Carlo (Naples), Covent Garden (London), the Berlin Op-

[22] Poulenc cut more than two thirds of Bernanos' lines.
[23] In Poulenc 1954, p. 213 Poulenc noted: "There will be two main acts, the first containing eight scenes, the second seven. Two very brief scenes will take place before the special curtain containing the insignia of the Carmel de Compiègne. The first act contains the scenes before the Revolution. The second those of the Revolution." On 8 June [1954] he told Honegger that he had finished Act I (1 hour 40 minutes) and hoped to finish the second and last act (1 hour). Poulenc 1994, 54-18.
[24] Hell 1958, p. 175 and Hell 1978, p. 250.

era, and maybe even Paris.[25] Rose Dercourt-Plaut learned about the commission via postcard from Ostia while the tour was still in progress,[26] Yvonne Gouverné on 3 April, and Leonard Bernstein on 24 July.[27]

CLEARING THE WAY FOR *DIALOGUES*

Before Poulenc became seriously engrossed in *Dialogues*, however, he had miscellaneous commitments to finish. On 3 April, while staying at Marie-Blanche de Polignac's estate in Antibes, he heard a broadcast of his *Stabat Mater*. He sat in Marie-Blanche's large American car that was parked in the garden and listened to the radio. Poulenc was exceedingly pleased with the performance prepared by Yvonne Gouverné, which featured soprano soloist Geneviève Moizan and Manuel Rosenthal conducting the Orchestre national and the choirs of the R.T.F.[28] He stayed in Antibes until 11 April, traveling to Monte Carlo on the 10th to play *Aubade* and the Concerto in a "Festival Poulenc," which also featured his *Sinfonietta* and *Les Biches*.

As the spring advanced he read Henry Barraud's study of Moussorgsky, which had appeared in Pierre Souvtchinsky's two-volume *Musique russe*, complimenting Barraud on his *"remarkable"* effort. Poulenc maintained a life-long fascination for Moussorgsky, which he acknowledged once more in the dedication of *Dialogues*.[29] Finally, Poulenc put the finishing touches on his Sonata for Two Pianos. In late April he claimed to be completing the piece, but the holograph manuscript indicates that it was completed at Le Tremblay on Sunday, 23 July.[30] Samuel Barber took the three movements to Gold and Fizdale, who thanked Poulenc in early July calling the Sonata "truly a masterpiece."[31] Preparing to confront writing *Dialogues*, Poulenc told Marc Pincherle that the Aix-en-Provence Festi-

---

[25] [26 Mar. 1953] letter from Assisi in Poulenc 1994, 53-7 (Poulenc 1991, no. 231).
[26] Unpublished [ca. 30 Mar. 1953] postcard in US-NH.
[27] 3 Apr. [1953] letter written from Marie-Blanche's estate Bastide du Roy and 24 July [1953] letter in Poulenc 1994, 53-8 (Poulenc 1991, no. 232) and 53-13.
[28] 3 Apr. [1953] letter to Gouverné in Poulenc 1994, 53-8 (Poulenc 1991, no. 232). See also the fragment of his [23 Apr. 1953] letter to Marie-Blanche in Poulenc 1994, p. 753, note 2. *Stabat* was performed on 7 May 1953 at the Saint-Pierre church in Avignon by the Chorale Vincent d'Indy and the Orchestre de l'Opéra d'Avignon with soprano Arlette Clairgeon, Vincent Laugier conducting. Poulenc was unable to attend, but sent words of encouragement to the performers. "Samedi" [May 1953] letter to Laugier and Poulenc 1994, pp. 753-4, note 1.
[29] 1 June [1953] letter to Barraud in Poulenc 1994, 53-10. Poulenc also spoke of Pierre Boulez's "mixed up" study of Stravinsky's *Le Sacre du Printemps*.
[30] Unpublished 23 Apr. [1953] letter to Gibson in GB-Lchester and Schmidt 1995, FP 156, p. 427.
[31] Gold's and Fizdale's 6 July 1953 letter to Poulenc in Poulenc 1994, 53-11. Poulenc also told Sauguet that he finished the work on 23 July [1953]. Fragment

val was not in his plans opting instead to settle down at Le Tremblay during July. Although he intended to spend time with "these 'Carmelite ladies'," it went to complete other projects.[32]

By 1 July he had transcribed his venerable *Suite française* for violoncello and piano, intending the transcription for an upcoming tour with Pierre Fournier.[33] And, when Fournier was decorated with the Légion d'Honneur the same month, he congratulated him by letter from Noizay and invited him to lunch with Mimi Pecci-Blunt and Gold and Fizdale on the 24th.[34] He also exercised his fingers for performances of *Aubade* at Deauville on 2 August and a recital on the 11th with Fournier at the Menton Festival dusting off music by Luigi Boccherini, Schubert, Debussy, Stravinsky, and Poulenc they had performed on their 1952 Italian tour. Only a paltry seventy people attended the Deauville concert, but he had a pleasant stay in Lyon before a *"very brilliant"* concert with Fournier at Menton.[35] Poulenc flew north from Nice on the 14th and was driven to Noizay by the surgeon Daniel Morel-Fatio. His sister Jeanne Manceaux then joined him on the 18th for the remainder of the month. Just as composition of *Dialogues* began he saw a fine performance of Stravinsky's *The Rake's Progress* in Tours, after which he hosted a wine reception for fifty students sent by Nadia Boulanger from the Conservatoire américain at Fontainebleau. Immersing himself in operas, he told Bernac: "My phonograph is not lying idle. Operas, operas, operas."[36]

DIALOGUES DES CARMÉLITES: AN OVERVIEW

Poulenc began *Dialogues* on 15 August at Noizay and finished the final scene two years later. Orchestration, begun at Noizay in 1954, was finished at Cannes in April 1956. The completion dates of the music appear in the manuscript piano-vocal score.[37]

---

of Sauguet's unpublished letter in Poulenc 1994, p. 755, note 2. Barber apparently also brought with him a copy of the *Capriccio d'après Le Bal masqué*. Gold and Fizdale received the final movement of the Sonata in early Aug. They thanked Poulenc in a [10 Aug. 1953] letter. Fragment in Poulenc 1994, p. 757, note 2. Poulenc's 2 June [1955] letter to Alice Esty clarifies that Gold and Fizdale had been unable to pay Poulenc the $1,000 commission for the Sonata. Subsequently Esty bailed them out by paying $750. Poulenc reminded her of the outstanding balance, which she paid. Letter in Poulenc 1994, 55-5 (Poulenc 1991, no. 262).

[32] Fragment of Poulenc's 28 May [1953] letter in Poulenc 1994, p. 757, note 1.

[33] 31 July [1953] letter to Girard in Poulenc 1994, 53-15 and Schmidt 1995, FP 80, p. 242. The cello transcription was revived by Cecylia Barczyk (cello) and Reynaldo Reyes (piano) at the World Cello Congress II in St Petersburg, Russia, 4 July 1997. See their CD on IC Records 12193.

[34] Fragment of his 1 June [1953] letter in Hughes 1998, p. 83.

[35] 22 [Aug. 1953] letter to Bernac in Poulenc 1994, 53-16 (Poulenc 1991, no. 233).

[36] 22 [Aug. 1953] letter in Poulenc 1994, 53-16 (Poulenc 1991, no. 233).

[37] F-Po Rés. A. 895(1-4).

***Poulenc's Compositional Progress on* Dialogues**

	Final Division		*Date Music Completed* [38]
Act I	Scene 1		"Noizay 18 Septembre [19]53"
	Scene 2		"3 Octobre [19]53 Noizay"
	Scene 3		"Paris Octobre 1953"
	Scene 4		"Lausanne Décembre [19]53"
Act II	Scene 1		"Cannes Janvier [19]54"
		Interlude 1	"Cannes — Mars 1955"
	Scene 2		"Cannes, 12 Février 1954"
		Interlude 2	"Noizay — Avril [19]54"
	Scene 3		"Alexandrie Mars — [19]54"

——a

	Scene 4		"Cannes Mars [19]55"
Act III	Scene 1		"Cannes, Mars Avril [19]55"
		Interlude 1	"Cannes Avril [19]55"
	Scene 2		"Cannes Avril-Mai [19]55"
		Interlude 2	Undated
	Scene 3		["Le Tremblay — Tourrettes-sur-Loup Juillet-Août [19]55"] [b]
		Interlude 3	Undated
	Scene 4		"Tourrettes-sur-Loup Août [19]55"

aAll of Poulenc's letters from 1953-54 use his old division into two acts. Original Act I is above the line and original Act II below.

bNot in F-Po. This date appears in a later printed score.

From the inception, Bernac lent him scores and recordings of other operas, advised him about tessitura and vocal details, and acted as a sounding board for technical and artistic problems.

> *Les Carmélites* are begun and literally I cannot sleep because of them. I think it will be ok, but there are so many problems. You should expect to receive a series of questions because I want it to be more than vocal. I have the sense of the great scene involving the Prioress and Blanche, and a very good plan: calm at the start, fierce in the middle (rules of the Order), renewed calm at the end. If I am to succeed with this work it will only be because the music identifies completely with the Bernanos *spirit.* Very light orchestration in order to permit the text to be understood.[39]

---

[38] Information from the F-Po piano-vocal score.
[39] "Samedi 22" [Aug. 1953] letter to Bernac in Poulenc 1994, 53-16 (Poulenc 1991, no. 233). Poulenc expressed similar sentiments about not sleeping to Girard in a letter of the same date. See 53-17.

COMPLETION OF ACT I: FALL 1953[40]

Less than ten days later Poulenc told Stéphane Audel, "Mother Marie will not permit me the slightest distraction," adding, "I do not go out, do not see anyone. [...]"[41] Writing at the rate of approximately one scene per week, Poulenc was so absorbed by his subject that he believed he actually knew his characters. By early September the first three scenes were drafted, and Poulenc discussed the Prioress' tessitura with Bernac. Music flowed out of him, and he noted, "I am so passionately involved with my work that the slightest outing seems like a waste of time."[42] Only the role of Mother Marie, which he thought of in terms of soprano Suzanne Danco worried him. Suzanne Balguerie was his model for the Second Prioress.

Poulenc's dialogue with Bernac resumed in early September.[43] Bernac advised that the First Prioress be permitted a few high 'A's, telling him to check the roles of Amneris and Azucena in Verdi's *Aida* and *Il Trovatore*. Bernac was concerned that the two Prioresses and Mother Marie would share approximately the same tessitura and that Poulenc might deprive himself of low tessitura for the entire second act. He counseled Poulenc to think of Mother Marie as being sung by a Tosca. Lamenting that he could not persuade Poulenc of his position, he said that if he were contemplating Renata Tebaldi for the Second Prioress there would not be enough contrast.

The allure of *Dialogues* was so strong that Poulenc decided not to go to Paris for the mid-September first recording of *Mamelles de Tirésias* by André Cluytens and the orchestra and chorus of the Opéra-Comique.[44] He had intended to be present, but not even Bernac could persuade him to go. Bernac thought his presence might result in a more definitive performance, one in which tempi would not drag as was Cluytens' custom.[45] Instead he wrote a detailed list for Cluytens which contains a multitude of suggestions and begins:

Above all take all the tempi quickly, *very quickly* because recordings

[40] Act I as it appears in the final division into three acts.
[41] 31 Aug. [1953] letter in Poulenc 1994, 53-18 (Poulenc 1991, no. 234).
[42] 1 Sept. [1953] letter in Poulenc 1994, 53-19 (Poulenc 1991, no. 235). Jeanne Manceaux had just spent two weeks at Noizay to be followed by Brigitte Manceaux.
[43] Bernac's 5 Sept. [1953] letter to Poulenc in Poulenc 1994, 53-20 (Poulenc 1991, no. 236).
[44] Ultimately, in a "vendredi" [11 Sept. 1953] letter to Bernac, Poulenc said that he was not going because he had not been asked, because Berthe Schmitt would supervise things, and because Mother Superior would not let him leave the cloister! Poulenc 1994, 53-21 (Poulenc 1991, no. 237).
[45] Bernac's 5 Sept. [1953] letter to Poulenc in Poulenc 1994, 53-20 (Poulenc 1991, no. 236) and his 13 Sept. [1953] letter to Conrad in Poulenc 1994, 53-23 (Poulenc 1991, no. 238). Dated from original in US-NYwurlitzer-bruck.

always slow down. Bernac and I will never get over a "Ballade des femmes de Paris" which lags. Don't hesitate to conduct all the lyrical passages as you would *Thaïs*. Paradoxically, that will bring out the comical nature of the work.[46]

Poulenc was thrilled with the result calling it sensational, and saying that he was so full of emotion when he heard it he had cried.[47]

Refocusing on the problem of tessitura in his opera, Poulenc said that irritating as it was, Bernac was correct about the three lyric sopranos. He agreed that Constance should be a light soprano, the Second Prioress a lyric soprano, Blanche a soprano, and Mother Marie a mezzo.[48] Poulenc thanked Bernac for the course in *Aida* and for his excellent advice.[49] He also hoped to have the first four scenes of Act I completed by the time he came to Paris in mid-October.[50] Bernac visited Noizay on the 20th and Poulenc refused to play him what he had written, preferring to let Bernac read the score himself. To his relief, Bernac approved both the prosody and tessitura.[51]

Once in Paris Poulenc divided his time between *Dialogues* and other duties. On 1 September he was promoted to the rank of Officer of the Legion of Honor, and the decoration was awarded on 31 October by his friend Colette, herself a Grand Officer, at her Palais-Royal apartment. The Aurics, Marie-Blanche de Polignac, André Dubois, and Brigitte Manceaux witnessed the brief ceremony.[52] Poulenc invited Henri Hell to hear the broadcast of his first conversation with Claude Rostand,[53] and a day later wrote Landowska describing his work on *Dialogues* and saying he would spend his "Carmelite winter" in Lausanne, in Cannes, and a bit in Italy.[54] Gold

[46] Original directions in F-Pbodin. A Philips recording by Seiji Ozawa (PHCP 11028), © 1997, has been issued.
[47] 4 Dec. [1953] letter to Girard in Poulenc 1994, 53-30. He wrote of his pleasure in a 9 Dec. [1953] letter to Leguerney in Poulenc 1994, 53-32 and "vendredi" [18 Dec. 1953] letter to Hell in Poulenc 1994, 53-33 (Poulenc 1991, no. 241), but told Hell he was disappointed that reviews had been uncomplimentary and few.
[48] As Buckland points out (Poulenc 1991, p. 389), the roles were finally distributed: Blanche (soprano), First Prioress (contralto), Second Prioress (soprano), Mother Marie (lyric soprano), Sister Constance (light soprano), Mother Jeanne (contralto), and Sister Mathilde (mezzo).
[49] Letter in US-NH, excerpts in Poulenc 1994, p. 764 (note 6) and p. 764 (note 3).
[50] 13 Sept. [1953] letter to Conrad in Poulenc 1994, 53-23 (Poulenc 1991, no. 238). Poulenc indicated his return for 15 Oct., but in an unpublished 1 Oct. letter to Mme Lambiotte from Noizay he cited the 13th. US-NYlambiotte-donhauser.
[51] 22 Sept. [1953] letter to Auric in Poulenc 1994, 53-25.
[52] See Poulenc 1994, p. 769, note 6. Rorem also heard Poulenc play and discuss parts of *Dialogues*, probably during October. Rorem 1966, p. 129.
[53] "Lundi" [12 Oct. 1953] letter in Poulenc 1994, 53-27.
[54] 13 Oct. [1953] letter in Poulenc 1994, 53-28. Poulenc said he and Brigitte Manceaux had been listening to her recordings of Bach's *Well-Tempered Clavier*.

and Fizdale, who premiered the Sonata for Two Pianos at Wigmore Hall on 2 November, arrived in Paris around the 18th. Poulenc could not go to London because he attended a concert devoted to *Les Six* at the Théâtre des Champs-Élysées on 4 November.[55] Cocteau called this Concert des Six "a great success," noting "Poulenc triumphs with his orchestra and chorus [in *Sécheresses*]."[56] Poulenc heard Gold and Fizdale play the Sonata on the 24th at the Salle Gaveau.

By early December Poulenc had abandoned Paris for the austere and empty Hôtel Beau-Rivage in Ouchy-Lausanne. There he installed himself in a room with two windows overlooking the lake and a studio with piano and radio looking back toward the countryside.[57] As in his trip to Switzerland the year before, Poulenc not only composed, but performed and attended concerts. He played his *Concert champêtre* with the Orchestre de chambre de Lausanne on 7 December and *Aubade* on 11 December in Nyon with the Orchestre de la Radio.[58] Pierre Dervaux conducted both performances. In spite of two slight mishaps, the *Concert champêtre* had an extraordinary success (seven curtain calls): his memory was good, Dervaux was an enjoyable conductor with whom to work, and the payment of 600 Swiss francs for the *Concert champêtre* and 400 for *Aubade* most welcome.[59] Sunday the 13th was spent with Wanda Landowska's former student Isabelle Nef,[60] and on the 14th he attended a performance by the Orchestre de la suisse romande.[61] Poulenc also told Bernac that on 8 December he and the Swiss tenor Hugues Cuenod planned to rehearse "Chansons d'Orkenise," *La Grenouillère*, "Voyage à Paris," *Bleuet*, "Avant le cinéma," and "A sa guitare" in preparation for a recording session on the 9th which also included the *Rapsodie nègre*.[62] Poulenc had known Cuenod since the early 1930s when Cuenod sang in Nadia Boulanger's ensemble.

---

[55] This concert, which featured an overture by Tailleferre, Durey's *Le Printemps au fond de la mer*, Auric's orchestral suite *Phèdre*, Poulenc's *Sécheresses*, Honegger's *Prélude, fugue et postlude*, and Milhaud's Symphony no. 2, all conducted by Georges Tzipine, was recorded in an album entitled *Hommage au Groupe des Six* (French Columbia FCX 264/5 and U.S. Angel 3515B). Poulenc had earlier heard a broadcast of *Sécheresses* under Eugène Bigot's direction by the Paris Orchestre radio-symphonique on 28 Sept. 1953. Gouverné prepared the R.T.F. choirs.
[56] Cocteau 1987, pp. 277-8.
[57] 4 Dec. [1953] letter to Girard in Poulenc 1994, 53-30.
[58] 8 Dec. [1953] letter to Bernac in Poulenc 1994, 53-31.
[59] 9 Dec. [1953] letter to Leguerney in Poulenc 1994, 53-32.
[60] Unpublished "dimanche" [13 Dec. 1953] letter to Bernac in US-NH.
[61] Poulenc 1994, 53-31. The concert featured Beethoven's Symphony no. 8 and Debussy's *Le Martyr de St Sébastien* with Danco, Ansermet conducting.
[62] This session was released on CD in 1997 by Dante Productions (LYSD 254). I am grateful to Sidney Buckland for this information.

All the while Poulenc worked steadily on *Dialogues* finding the going arduous.

> The fourth scene is coming along [he told Bernac], but it has given me more difficulty than I would have thought. Although Mother Marie has only responses, it was necessary from the outset to delineate her personality clearly, which despite its obvious good allows her pride to show through. Her theme which rings out in the vow of martyrdom (2nd act) [Poulenc prints two bars of music] is rhythmically suggested here softly.[63]

By the 13th he had finished two thirds of the fourth scene and sketched the remaining third. "It is horrifying with austerity, dread, pity, [and] misery," he told Bernac, "I put all of my heart into it."[64]

During the third week of December Poulenc attended a concert by the Geneva Chamber Orchestra to hear Cuenod and Flore Wend sing Stravinsky's 1952 Cantata. He found it a crashing bore. It was, he felt, one of Stravinsky's most oriental compositions, the music of which had absolutely nothing to do with the Elizabethan poems.

> It is terrifying to imagine that from now on Stravinsky will be composing in English and that his whisky will forever have the smell of vodka. Oh! the dangers of America. In Paris he would have remained a cosmopolitan. It is sad.[65]

In the week before Christmas Poulenc completed the fourth scene of *Dialogues* . . .

> She took her last breath at seven o'clock last evening, after a most horrible agony. Mother Marie, more ambitious than ever, was unbelievably hard, poor Blanche completely crazy, and that great lump of a doctor completely silent. As for me, I am exhausted, but quite content at having completed the whole scene here. It is *definitely* the most beautiful. You will see that with orchestra it will be thrilling and vocally one can let one's self go.[66]

Early in December, however, storm clouds were on the horizon. Poulenc was having trouble obtaining rights to Bernanos' text which he prayed he could surmount with the assistance of St Anthony of Padua and Ste Teresa.[67] The problem was actually with Emmet

[63] Fragment of Poulenc's "lundi"[7 Dec. 1953] letter in Poulenc 1994, p.773, note 1.
[64] Fragment of Poulenc's "dimanche" [13 Dec. 1953] letter (US-NH) in Poulenc 1994, p. 774, note 1. Fragment of Poulenc's [7 Dec. 1953] letter to Bernac in Poulenc 1994, p. 775, note 2.
[65] "Vendredi" [18 Dec. 1953] letter to Hell from Geneva in Poulenc 1994, 53-33 (Poulenc 1991, no. 241).
[66] 19 Dec. [1953] letter to Bernac in Poulenc 1994, 53-34 (Poulenc 1991, no. 242).
[67] Part of Poulenc's 6 Dec. [1953] letter to Conrad in Schmidt 1995, FP 159, p. 443.

Lavery, who had obtained exclusive rights to von le Fort's play, and who had written his own English version *The Last on the Scaffold*. Lavery refused to permit anyone access to von le Fort's text or to Bernanos' screen play based on it. This problem continued to plague Poulenc in 1954.

Poulenc intended to take a breather before completing Act I and beginning Act II and to return to Paris just before Christmas. December letters to Bernac suggest repertoire for their March 1954 Egyptian tour including a program entitled "French *mélodies* from Chabrier to Poulenc" featuring Chabrier, Fauré, Debussy, Ravel, Roussel, Satie, Milhaud, and Poulenc. He recommended they take a train called the "Comète" on 26 February 1954 in order to rest for several days before their 1 March concert in Alexandria.[68] As 1953 closed, Poulenc received a copy of Adrienne Monnier's *Les Gazettes d'Adrienne Monnier 1925-1945* which pleased him enormously.[69] It contained a transcript of the obituary she wrote for Raymonde Linossier and an article on *Les Animaux modèles*.[70]

Act II Begun: January-February 1954[71]

In Paris Poulenc socialized and attended concerts and went to a rehearsal of Honegger's *Une cantate de Noël*, which was performed at the Théâtre des Champs-Élysées on 10 January. Honegger, ill in Switzerland, could not attend, so Poulenc wrote him a moving account of the rehearsal and of his personal pleasure with the composition.[72] He also attended a Domaine Musical concert on the 13th in which music by Bach, Luigi Nono, Karlheinz Stockhausen, and Stravinsky (*Renard*) was presented. Poulenc would have preferred to have heard Pierre Boulez's *Soleil des eaux*, but wanted to hear more Nono.[73] The performance of *Renard* was scandalously inadequate and at its conclusion the percussionists told him they could not follow Hermann Scherchen's beat.

He went to Cannes during the third week of January and stayed at the Hôtel Majestic until 15 February.[74] His first week was less than fruitful because, reminiscent of the King of the Elephants in *Histoire de Babar*, Poulenc had gotten food poisoning from eating a

---

[68] 19 Dec. [1953] letter in Poulenc 1994, 53-34 (Poulenc 1991, no. 242).

[69] Monnier 1953.

[70] "Mardi" [29 Dec. 1953] letter in Poulenc 1994, 53-35 (Poulenc 1991, no. 243). An excellent (but poorly known) photographic portrait of Poulenc, probably taken in late 1953 or early 1954 by Jean-Marie Marcel, appears in Guth 1954, plate 34.

[71] Act II as it appears in the final division into three acts.

[72] "Samedi 9" [Jan. 1954] letter in Poulenc 1994, 54-1.

[73] 27 Jan. [1954] letter to Souvtchinsky in Poulenc 1994, 54-4 and fragment of his [27 Jan. 1954] letter to Hell in Poulenc 1994, p. 781, note 1.

[74] Unpublished 2 Feb. [1954] letter to Mme Lambiotte in US-NYlambiotte-donhauser.

"julienne de légumes".[75] Always a social animal at heart, he lamented that there was absolutely no one staying in gray, misty, rainy Cannes, and that the week of *Les Six* concerts would surely play to empty houses. Poulenc inquired if Paris was becoming "dodecanised" noting that his poor Carmelites could only sing in tune.[76] This would assure good working conditions, but afford little distraction. Early in his stay, however, he did enjoy the 24 January broadcast of *Les Mamelles de Tirésias* with Daniel-Lesur's commentary.[77]

The stream of letters to Bernac slowed to a trickle while Poulenc was in Cannes. Tracking the progress of *Dialogues* thus becomes more difficult. In his only January letter to Bernac, Poulenc mentioned that he had completely revised the first four scenes, fifty-five minutes in length, and that the entire act would take one hour and twenty-five or thirty minutes.[78] A 27 January letter to Henri Hell indicates that work was going very well, and that the fifth scene (Act II:1) was completed. The problem of how to write for the Second Prioress was also solved. Moreover, the formula of the prayer for the deceased Prioress and the Ave Maria had been found.[79] Satisfied that his January work was excellent, he told Brigitte Manceaux the fourth scene was "overwhelming, terrifying, and sublime," and the fifth scene was "icy and horrible." The sixth scene (Act II:2) "will surely be finished for my return," he said.[80] Bernac arrived in Cannes on 3 February for two pre-tour concerts.[81]

Poulenc returned to Paris on the 15th and before his departure for Egypt played selections from his opera for friends.[82] He also enjoyed an evening playing *Dialogues* for Marie-Blanche de Polignac and hearing the pianists Nikita Magaloff, Alexis Weissenberg, and Lili Kraus (whom he complimented profusely).[83] Finally, Poulenc accompanied a performance of Satie's *Socrate* sung by the seventy-eight year old Marya Freund. After she overcame a bout of stage fright, everything went well, and the death of Socrates was superb.

---

[75] 23 Jan. [1954] letter to Marie-Blanche in Poulenc 1994, 54-2.

[76] "Jeudi" [28 Jan. 1954] letter to Sauguet in Poulenc 1994, 54-5 (Poulenc 1991, no. 244).

[77] Letter of 25 Jan. [1954] to Daniel-Lesur in Poulenc 1994, 54-3.

[78] Fragment of Poulenc's unpublished [Jan. 1954] letter to Bernac in Poulenc 1994, p. 784, note 1.

[79] Fragment of Poulenc's [27 Jan. 1954] letter to Hell in Poulenc 1994, p.785, note 1.

[80] "Lundi" [1 Feb. 1954] letter in Poulenc 1994, 54-7. See also the fragment of Poulenc's [12 Mar. 1954] letter to Girard in Poulenc 1994, p. 786, note 1 to 54-9.

[81] Unpublished 2 Feb. [1954] letter to Mme Lambiotte in US-NYlambiotte-donhauser.

[82] For example, he played for Manceaux and Hell on the 16th. "Dimanche" [14 Feb. 1954] letter to Hell in Poulenc 1994, 54-9 (Poulenc 1991, no. 245).

[83] "Mercredi" 17 Mar. [1954] letter to Conrad in Poulenc 1994, 54-12 (Poulenc 1991, no. 246).

TOUR OF EGYPT AND THE ORIENT: MARCH 1954

Bernac and Poulenc spent March touring the Orient and Egypt, a country in which an army led by General Mohammed Naguib had overthrown King Farouk in 1952, replaced him with the infant Fouad II, and instituted an Egyptian republic in 1953.[84] At the outset of the tour, Poulenc and Luigi Dallapiccola presided over the jury at the Cairo Conservatory. One winner was the town's champion cyclist who not only received a diploma in piano, but a medal in solfège.[85] Then, during his ten days in Alexandria, the French Consul lodged Poulenc at the Consulate where he was fortunate to have both a piano and the calm necessary to finish Act I (then the first eight scenes) of *Dialogues*. Bernac and Poulenc gave their first recital on 9 March—all Poulenc featuring *Le Bestiaire*, *Aubade*, and *Le Bal masqué*. Three days later they performed *mélodies* by Fauré, Debussy, Ravel, Duparc, Milhaud, Roussel, and Poulenc.

They returned to Cairo to present a 19 March recital for the Société de Musique d'Egypte. Always planning, and aware that Jacques Leguerney would be in Rome when he was, Poulenc wrote ahead requesting that he bring a number of items including Chabrier's *Trois valses romantiques* for Marcelle Meyer (then living in Rome), André Cluytens' recording of *Les Mamelles de Tirésias* (a present for Mimi Pecci-Blunt), and proofs of his *Entretiens avec Claude Rostand*.[86] He told Simone Girard that their trip had ended with a visit to the austere and beautiful Luxor, which he found ravishing.[87] Poulenc, however, disliked Egyptian funerary art which reminded him of tombstone sellers at Le Père Lachaise cemetery in Paris. Egyptian tombs gave him "visual claustrophobia." "This art based solely on death depresses and bores me," he said, "and I often have the desire to bite an Egyptologist (they are generally quite ugly!!!). [...]"[88]

When the Egyptian tour was complete, he and Bernac enjoyed forty-eight hours of relaxation in Greece on 27-28 March. They rented a large Packard for 12,000 francs each and toured Salonique, Corinth, and Mycena. From Greece they flew to Rome and stayed with Mimi Pecci-Blunt in rooms overlooking various churches.[89] Poulenc, de-

---

[84] While on tour Poulenc sent Rose Dercourt-Plaut a postcard entitled "Le Charmeur de Serpents." Once home Poulenc wrote again saying he had been on tour five weeks. Unpublished postcard from Marrakech and letter from Noizay in US-NH.

[85] "Mercredi 17" [Mar. 1954] letter in Poulenc 1994, 54-11.

[86] 19 Mar. [1954] letter to Leguerney from Cairo in Poulenc 1994, 54-13. Poulenc and Meyer recorded Chabrier's *Valses* in 1955.

[87] Fragment of Poulenc's postcard to Girard in Poulenc 1994, p. 787, note 2. See also Poulenc's 24 Mar. 1954 postcard to Gouverné from Luxor in Gouverné, p. 13 (misdated 1952).

[88] "Mercredi 17" [Mar. 1954] letter in Poulenc 1994, 54-11.

[89] 30 Mar. [1954] letter to Brigitte Manceaux in Poulenc 1994, 54-15.

lighted to find letters from Doda Conrad and Robert Fizdale awaiting him, learned that his Sonata for Two Pianos had been given its
American premiere at Town Hall and that Jay Harrison, the *New
York Herald Tribune* critic, had called it a masterwork from a master
hand. Poulenc attended the Festival Nicolas Nabokov, Renata
Tebaldi's performance of Verdi's *Otello* on the 30th, and corrected
proofs of *Entretiens.* They returned home, possibly visiting Antibes
to see Marie-Blanche de Polignac from 7-9 April.[90] In Poulenc's esti-
mation, this trip accomplished something very important: it helped
take his mind off domestic worries and sentimental problems.

REMAINDER OF 1954

Once more, Poulenc settled down in Noizay putting aside *Dialogues*
after completing Act II, Interlude 2 except for orchestrating Act I
and conceiving the music for the extreme end of the opera. He did
not take it up again until he visited Cannes in March 1955.[91] In April
and May 1954 Poulenc turned back the clock and wrote three *mélodies:*
the first two were set to poems from Max Jacob's 1921 *Le Laboratoire
central*, last visited in *Le Bal masqué* (1932), and the third one by
Apollinaire.[92]

> At the time of *Le Bal masqué* I had been thinking of introducing the
> poem "Jouer du bugle" into the cantata, but I had to give up the idea
> because it would have duplicated "La Dame aveugle." Coupled with
> the absurd "Vous n'écrivez plus," so typically Max Jacob, in 1954 I
> gave it the overall title *Parisiana* [FP 157], which situates the work in a
> Parisian ambiance. There is nothing special to say [about these two
> *mélodies*] that I have not already said about this kind of fantasies.
> "Jouer du bugle" is more musical than "Vous n'écrivez plus" because
> of its gently moving ending. The third *mélodie* is written on a poem
> by Apollinaire taken from *Alcools:* "Rosemonde" [FP 158]. It is a *mélodie*
> of no great import with a quite pretty final ritornello.[93]

All three pieces were premiered in Amsterdam on 12 October 1954.
Poulenc hoped that Bernac would finally be awarded a professor-
ship at the Paris Conservatory, but hopes were dashed when Bernac

---

[90] Poulenc asked if she would be there and could lodge him in a "mercredi 17"
[Mar. 1954] letter in Poulenc 1994, 54-11. While in Rome Poulenc met Allen
Hughes, who reports that Poulenc was actually there for a performance of
Litanies. Hughes 1963, p. 29.

[91] In a 26 May [1954] letter to Leguerney from Noizay Poulenc said, "I practice my
piano without break, having retired these ladies [the Carmélites] to the cupboard
behind my piano in Paris; to tell the truth I miss them terribly, but it is better this
way." Poulenc 1994, 54-17 (Poulenc 1991, no. 249).

[92] The *mélodies* are dedicated to the memory of Pierre Colle, to Paul Chadourne,
and to Countess Pastré.

[93] Poulenc 1993, pp. 57-8 (Poulenc 1989, pp. 99-101).

was passed over again early in 1954.[94] Lacking a secure source of income, Bernac had to continue giving concerts and master classes.

Poulenc had a concert in Brussels on 5 May, and asked if he could stay with the Lambiottes.[95] He intended to leave Noizay on 2 May, spend the 3rd in Paris, and arrive in Brussels by train the morning of the 4th.[96] *Entretiens avec Claude Rostand* was published in late April or early May, and he sent copies to his friends. One of them was Honegger, with whom he enjoyed a renewed relationship. He also attended the May recital at the Salle Pleyel given by Pierre Fournier and Wilhelm Kempff, their first together.[97]

By mid-June Poulenc expressed concern about his physical health to Robert Douglas Gibson.[98] Cancellation of plans to participate at Britten's invitation in the June Aldeburgh Festival foretold the future.[99] He was having problems with his gall-bladder which in the end did not require surgery.[100] His state of mind was also poor when he went south under the care of Professor Paul Delmas-Marsalet, whom he had met on the steamship De Grasse during a 1952 trip to the United States.[101] The two stayed in Arrens, a small town nestled 1878 meters up in the Pyrénées, twenty-four kilometers from the pilgrimage center of Lourdes. Poulenc blamed his troubles on too much work, but felt that his health was improving.[102] The truth is more complex: his concern for the ailing Roubert and the uncertainty of rights to Bernanos' script weighed heavily on him. Moreover, his performing career with Bernac was winding down after almost twenty years. Letters to his sister Jeanne Manceaux and niece Rosine Seringe tell of corresponding with a Father Griffin of the Discalced Carmelite Fathers at Mount Carmel Seminary in Dallas, Texas.[103] Poulenc had written Griffin:

[94] Fragment of Delvincourt's 27 Jan. 1954 letter to Poulenc in Poulenc 1994, p. 785, note 1, and Poulenc's "samedi" [6 Feb. 1954] letter to Roland-Manuel in Poulenc 1994, 54-8.

[95] Unpublished 9 Feb. [1954] letter to Mme Lambiotte in US-NYlambiotte-donhauser.

[96] Unpublished 23 Apr. [1954] letter to Mme Lambiotte in US-NYlambiotte-donhauser.

[97] English translation of Poulenc's 31 May [1954] letter to Fournier in Hughes 1998, p. 85.

[98] Unpublished 17 June [1954] letter in GB-Lchester.

[99] Chimènes indicates that Britten's invitation is dated 21 Jan. 1954 and that he wrote again on 14 July [1954] expressing regret that Poulenc could not come. Poulenc 1994, pp. 814-15, note 3.

[100] Fragment of 17 June [1954] letter to Gibson in Poulenc 1994, p. 794, note 2.

[101] Poulenc 1994, p. 1020. Poulenc later presented Delmas-Marselet with a manuscript score of *Dialogues* which is not mentioned in Schmidt 1995.

[102] "Mercredi" [21 July 1954] letter to Manceaux in Poulenc 1994, 54-19.

[103] "Mercredi" [21 July 1954] and [July 1954] letters in Poulenc 1994, 54-19 and 54-20 respectively. Griffin, p. 539 wrote: "Everyone knew Poulenc by sight during

My God, you cannot know the anguish. God knows if I shall ever complete *dialogues des carmélites* because I am very ill. It is my stomach. Cancer. In spite of my doctors' reassurances that there is nothing wrong with me, I fear that I will never be able to work again. Will you ask the Carmelite Fathers of Dallas to make a novena that I recover my health and that I may be able to glorify God and the blessed martyrs of Compiègne with my music? I am in terrible fear. Will God take into account my poor efforts—the Mass, the religious motets? Will He at least see them and me kindly, as another bungler, a *jongleur de Notre Dame?* Please locate a good peasant priest to help me. The priests who are considered "intelligent" exhaust me.[104]

His unsubstantiated claim that he had cancer paralleled Roubert's medically diagnosed condition. Poulenc secretly copied Griffin's response in which he promised to obtain the assistance of *all* the Carmelites in the United States for Rosine Seringe![105] His anguish reached a fever pitch in late July when he told Bernac why he had never been able to "tutoyer" either him or Raymonde Linossier, two of his dearest friends.[106]

At the conclusion of his stay in the south, Poulenc visited Rocamadour where he had found rejuvenation before. Secretly he must have harbored doubts about whether supplication to the Black Virgin could extricate him from his present physical and emotional problems.[107] His faithful friend Raymond Destouches came to get him in Poitiers for the return to Noizay. Poulenc, who had always said he would give up Le Grand Coteau without even blinking rather than renounce Paris, told Bernac, "It is there that I can work again

---

the prewar years in Tours. He wore an odd green hat at all times, and it was rumored he never removed it, even in the house. We schoolboys would remark with distaste that he was *très bizarre* but a great pianist, which, of course, excused everything. After the war, I was back in Tours, in a room in Jacques Duthoo's *Château de Belles Ruries* where I practiced on an old pedalless Pleyel piano that had been desecrated by the Nazis. Poulenc was to come for lunch that day. None of us looked forward to it. He was too cloying, too precious. He hovered about one with an air of solicitude, almost tenderness, like a puppet being manipulated by a Cupertino or a Neri; as an unfortunate joke that never came off. It left one with an oversweet taste and always an undercurrent of panic, of suspected tragedy under all of this — of some man helplessly trapped behind a mask."
[104] Griffin, p. 538.
[105] [July 1954] letter in Poulenc 1994, 54-20.
[106] "Mercredi" [28 July 1954] letter in Poulenc 1994, 54-21 (Poulenc 1991, no. 250). Georges Auric, another very close friend, was also concerned about his mental stability. See his "mercredi" 28 July [19]54 letter to Poulenc from Hyères in Poulenc 1994, 54-22.
[107] Entry in Maurice Delmas-Marsalet's diary quoted in Poulenc 1994, p. 795, note 3. Poulenc visited Rocamadour the evening of 7 Aug. immediately before returning to Noizay the next day.

because I have always worked there and then I have my books there, my music, my phonograph, my records, [and] my radio."[108] He implored Bernac to visit him at length in September to prepare their October recitals in Holland, and said he had asked Jeanne Manceaux to be at Noizay to greet him upon his return. Delmas-Marsalet, however, wondered if Poulenc could manage at Noizay given his depressed state.[109] The only good that came of this stay was Poulenc's discovery of the final scene for his opera.

> In a moment of extraordinary emotion and confusion (before Delmas), I found the very end of the *Carmélites*, the arrival of Blanche and her ascent of the scaffold. In looking coldly on this music I believe I am able to say that it is heartrending in its simplicity, resignation, and ... peace. There is a modulation to the major which is far and away one of my best and which struck the dear Doctor though he was unable to explain why.[110]

In spite of Delmas-Marsalet's fears, the security of Noizay had its healing effect. Poulenc wrote Milhaud that he did not plan to spend much time in Paris the coming winter season and Simone Girard that he "was *intact*."[111] He had begun orchestrating *Dialogues* on August 16th and was content with the first twelve pages.[112] "Auric was right," Poulenc said, "the weight of a work forces the doors open."[113] His problems with the literary rights for the opera remained, however, and Poulenc anticipated meeting with Lavery in Paris, possibly in September. Before the end of the month scene 1 was done and by the first week of September half of Act I was orchestrated.[114]

Stéphane Audel was scheduled for a lengthy stay at Noizay from 1-25 September, but in the midst of the visit, his nerves still frayed, Poulenc went to Paris possibly to see Emmet Lavery concerning rights for *Dialogues*.[115] In late September or early October he made a

[108] "Mercredi" [28 July 1954] letter in Poulenc 1994, 54-21 (Poulenc 1991, no. 250).
[109] Entry in Dr. Delmas-Marsalet's diary quoted in Poulenc 1994, p. 798, note 8. Dr. Delmas-Marsalet is Prof. Dalmas-Marsalet's son.
[110] "Mercredi" [28 July 1954] letter to Bernac in Poulenc 1994, 54-21 (Poulenc 1991, no. 250). Poulenc reminded Prof. Delmas-Marsalet of these events in a 28 June [1957] letter written after the Paris performance of *Dialogues*. Poulenc 1994, 57-21.
[111] [Aug. 1954] letters to Milhaud and Girard in Poulenc 1994, 54-23 and 54-24 respectively.
[112] The date is given in the manuscript full score.
[113] "Mardi" [Aug. 1954] letter to Bernac in Poulenc 1994, 54-25 (Poulenc 1991, no. 251).
[114] "Lundi" [6 Sept. 1954] letter in Poulenc 1994, 54-26 (Poulenc 1991, no. 252).
[115] Letters to Bernac of "mardi" [Aug. 1954] to Bernac in Poulenc 1994, 54-25 (Poulenc 1991, no. 251) and Milhaud of 8 Sept. [1954] in Poulenc 1994, 54-27. Poulenc told Hell (10 Sept. [1954] letter) that his nerves were almost as bad as in

brief trip south taking "Le Mistral" to Marseilles. During a stay in Avignon with the Girards he wrote his old friend Denise Bourdet:

> God be praised my cancerphobia has disappeared, but this abomi-
> nable state of nerves from which I have suffered for months has not.
> This *Carmélites* problem has really floored me. Just imagine, I am still
> waiting for the Bernanos agreement. My lawyer promises it within
> two weeks. Maybe then I will regain my composure. Admittedly it's
> a horrible adventure.[116]

On 12 October Bernac and Poulenc performed at a small hall of the Amsterdam Concertgebouw, giving first performances of *Parisiana* and *Rosemonde*.[117] The trip to Holland was brief, but a longer German tour was planned for November, and Bernac felt compelled to write Poulenc a strong letter before the two met explaining his grave reservations about Poulenc's preoccupation with Lucien Roubert and his ability to complete the tour. Bernac worried that Poulenc would talk at all hours about Roubert thereby destroying Bernac's ability to focus on singing. "I *fear* this tour and these conditions," he concluded.[118] Bernac's fears were well-founded. Poulenc's collapse in mid-tour forced his return to Paris.[119] Clearly Poulenc had overestimated his ability to maintain his emotional stability. He was taken to a clinic at L'Haÿ-les-Roses by the conductor Manuel Rosenthal and placed under Dr. Maillard-Verger's care.[120] Poulenc, who had been unable to sleep, spent a week sleeping eighteen or nineteen hours daily, heavily sedated with barbiturates. He told Simone Girard that he was leaving the clinic on Monday the 20th to fly to Cannes, thus avoiding Marseilles and Toulon, the source of his torments. Poulenc hoped that time in the sun spent predominantly with Marie-Blanche de Polignac at Antibes, would speed his

---

July (see 54-28). Claude Gendre (see Buckland/Chimènes: d, p. 302) states that Poulenc went to Paris on 16 Oct. to consult his neurologist. In a 1984 letter Lavery told Gendre that they met that same day quite by accident. Gendre also prints a 1 Oct. 1954 letter from Lavery to Gertrude von le Fort indicating he had *already* come to agreement with Poulenc. The chronology is inconsistent and additional documents gathered by Gendre indicate that Lavery was not always honorable in representing the facts. See p. 304 for a 30 Mar. 1955 agreement and information about another dated 23 Dec. 1955.

[116] Fragment of Poulenc's [4 Oct. 1954] letter to Bourdet in Poulenc 1994, p. 809, note 2. (Original in F-Psg (Doucet).)

[117] Poulenc 1994, p. 803, note 4.

[118] Bernac's 4 Nov. [1954] letter to Poulenc in Poulenc 1994, 54-34 (Poulenc 1991, no. 256).

[119] [Late Nov. 1954] letter to Marthe Bosredon in Poulenc 1994, 54-35 (Poulenc 1991, no. 257) and his 20 Dec. [1954] letter from Paris to Rose Dercourt-Plaut in Poulenc 1994, 54-37.

[120] Saudinos. Poulenc was supposed to stay three weeks in the clinic, but only stayed one.

recovery.[121] Ten days into his stay Poulenc wrote Alice Ardoin that he was still living in hell because the requisite authorizations for *Dialogues* were unsecured. He hoped 1955 would bring respite from the vicious circle of emotional turmoil and insomnia relievable only by drugs.[122] As the most trying year of his life concluded, he wrote Benjamin Britten about their anticipated joint performance of the Concerto in D minor on 16 January 1955.[123]

Virgil Thomson and Bernac were quite concerned about his physical and mental health. Responding to Thomson's questions, Allen Hughes, later a New York critic, told him what he knew.

> The question you raise about Poulenc is really a grave one, and one that cannot be answered satisfactorily at the moment. Whatever the confusion about the rights to the book may have had to do with the beginning, it seems to be irrelevant now, since the problem is supposed to be settled satisfactorily. But Poulenc is still in a bad state. Perhaps you know that he and Pierre went to Germany for a tour that they were forced to cancel almost before it had begun. Poulenc had a real nervous collapse, and he went into a clinic as soon as they got back to Paris. He stayed for about three weeks, but the treatment consisted only of continuous sedation.[124] There seems to be no basic improvement in his condition. He has just returned from two weeks at Biot, where he spent the holiday season with Marie-Blanche, and he seems to want to do the concerts in England that he and Pierre have scheduled for this month. Also, he wants to go through with the Paris recital on Feb. 2. Pierre is terribly pessimistic about it all, and he has a right to be, since he has borne the brunt of all this business. Poulenc is remarkably enthusiastic about my labors, and he was quite cheerful when I called him this morning. I am going to spend the day with him tomorrow [9 January 1955]. He seems to get along much better now with relative strangers, like me for example, than with people he has known for years, especially his sister, etc. If he is mad, he has a madness that is very lucid at the moment. What is to come of it all? No one seems to know. I, being optimistic by nature, feel that all this will pass, but I have no scientific basis for my belief. Just how much Poulenc's Catholicism keeps him from getting the

[121] "Samedi" [18 Dec. 1954] letter in Poulenc 1994, 54-36 (Poulenc 1991, no. 258). P Poulenc, who shows estrangement from Roubert in this letter, asked she write to the Hotel Majestic in Cannes, where he took a room. Concerned about Poulenc's mental and physical health, Sauguet wrote a detailed account to Collaer from Paris on 22 Nov. 1954. Collaer 1996, 53-2.
[122] 30 Dec. [1943] letter to Ardoin in Poulenc 1994, 54-39 and similar letter to Bosredon of 30 Dec. [1954], 54-40 (Poulenc 1991, no. 259).
[123] [Late Dec. 1954] postcard from Nice in Poulenc 1994, 54-41 (Poulenc 1991, no. 260).
[124] As shown above, Poulenc actually stayed only one week.

full benefit of psychiatric assistance, I don't know. I do feel, however, that this possibility has not been thoroughly enough investigated. In any event, I think it a bit early to say that he is finished. Only the future will tell, and I shall keep you informed.[125]

Hughes wrote Thomson again after his meeting with Poulenc saying he suspected "sentimental complications" were contributing to Poulenc's condition, but that "I don't think he's mad."[126]

ACT II COMPLETED AND ACT III BEGUN: FIRST PART OF 1955[127]

Partially recovered Poulenc arrived in London with Bernac on 13 January and immediately set to work. Their recital was recorded on the 15th for broadcast the 16th, and the Concerto was performed with Britten that evening at Royal Festival Hall with the Liverpool Philharmonic Orchestra, John Pritchard conducting. Bernac and Poulenc also performed *mélodies* at Carlisle (Cumberland) on the 18th and at Newcastle-Upon-Tyne on the 20th before returning to France.[128] By 1955 Poulenc had a regular circuit of concerts within a short radius of London which allowed him easy access to the BBC and its schedule. Poulenc wrote Mme Lambiotte from the Crown and Mitre Hotel that his tour had gone very well and that he would return to Paris on the 23rd a little less poor.[129] He also planned to go to Brussels on the 26th and return to Paris for Denise Duval's debut in *Manon* on the 27th. While on the road Poulenc sent a letter to Christiane Manificat (dedicatee of Bernanos' version of *Dialogues*), pleading for intervention on his behalf concerning the still unresolved literary rights.[130]

Bernac and Poulenc presented their 20th-anniversary concert devoted to Fauré, Debussy, Roussel, Ravel, and Poulenc on 2 February at the Salle Gaveau, but the number of concerts in 1955 decreased dramatically as *Dialogues* and other projects demanded more time. "Grand success, magnificent press, Pierre in form as always," Poulenc wrote Milhaud.[131] Stanley Lock, Thomson's Fulbright piano student studying at the Conservatoire with Jean Doyen, heard

---

[125] Unpublished 8 Jan. 1955 letter to Thomson in US-NH.

[126] Unpublished 11 Jan. 1955 letter to Thomson in US-NH. Hughes now notes that only 7/8ths of the rights problem had been resolved. There remained, he said, some question about signage of posters advertising the opera. Hughes' suspicions were correct, but it is unclear what if anything he may have known about Lucien Roubert.

[127] Acts II and III as they appear in the final division into three acts.

[128] Poulenc 1994, p. 814, note 2. All these concerts are listed in the Ibbs and Tillett ledgers.

[129] Unpublished "mercredi" [19 Jan. 1955] letter to Mme Lambiotte in US-NYlambiotte-donhauser.

[130] 24 Jan. [1955] letter mentioned in Buckland/Chimènes: d, p. 304.

[131] 5 Apr. [1955] letter in Poulenc 1994, 55-2.

the concert and said that the performers "outdid themselves" and that the overflow audience was even seated on the stage.[132]

Early in the year Poulenc learned that Jean Giraudoux's *Intermezzo* (first produced in 1933) would be revived by the Renaud-Barrault Company with his music at the Théâtre du Petit-Marigny.[133] The financial windfall from rights permitted him to repay an outstanding debt to Auguste Lambiotte.[134] All was not well, however. In mid-February his lover Roubert developed pleurisy and was transported to Cannes for observation before he could return home to Toulon. Poulenc hoped the problem was tubercular in origin and not cancerous.[135] Roubert's illness and Poulenc's composition of *Dialogues* paralleled each other in uncanny ways.

His own health improved and Poulenc departed for Cannes on 1 March to resume work on his opera interrupted in March 1954. While staying at the Hotel Majestic he completed scenes 3 and 4, and on 5 April he finally received authorization to use the libretto.[136] Only two fifths of the score remained to be composed and Poulenc felt himself again. Enjoying hotel life away from home, he attended the Cannes Film Festival and welcomed visits from friends.[137]

In the interim between April 1954 and March 1955, although we do not know precisely when, Poulenc invited Hervé Dugardin, Guido Valcaranghi, and Margarita Wallmann (who would later direct the La Scala *Dialogues* performance in Milan) to his Paris apartment to hear the first act of *Dialogues*.[138] When Poulenc finished singing and playing he awaited their reaction. Wallmann reports the reception as "magnificent" and "overwhelming" but notes that she told Poulenc he had already written two acts, not one. When she

[132] Lock's unpublished 4 Feb. [1955] letter to Thomson in US-NH.
[133] Pierre Boulez, who conducted, informed Poulenc that additional performances would take place in Lyon on 6 and 7 June. [Apr. 1955] letter to Poulenc in Poulenc 1994, 55-3.
[134] Unpublished 19 Feb. [1955] letter to Mme Lambiotte in US-NYlambiotte-donhauser. The debt was 17,220 francs. In a 24 Mar. [1955] letter to Denise Bourdet in Poulenc 1994, 55-1, he said he was pleased with *Intermezzo's* success and that his music was not outdated. Because of *Dialogues*, he could not attend any performance.
[135] 5 Apr. [1955] letter to Milhaud in Poulenc 1994, 55-2.
[136] 5 Apr. [1955] letter in Poulenc 1994, 55-2. See also Buckland/Chimènes: d, p. 304.
[137] Two of these were Pears and Britten, who gave a poorly attended concert in Cannes. Rorem, who was also in Cannes at this time, wrote: "Poulenc was in Cannes, quite recovered from his long illness, but looking old and smothered in pimples. As he's always been rather *le cher maître* in my eyes, I was chilled by his talk of sexual success." Rorem 1966, p. 211.
[138] Wallmann, p. 151. For an English translation of this passage see Buckland/Chimènes: d, p. 305.

suggested a new division into three acts Poulenc was overjoyed and reacted by whirling her around the room in his arms. So it was that the opera was suddenly transformed into three shorter acts and the previous division into before the revolution and during the revolution abandoned.

Poulenc returned to Paris on 12 April to prepare for a charity concert on the 18th,[139] and he and Bernac performed in Toulouse the 19th. He intended to spend three weeks in Noizay, but went back to Cannes in order to be closer to Roubert.[140] Before leaving he completed Act III:1 and began scene 2. By 12 May he was back in Paris for a recital with Bernac. With *Dialogues* now two scenes from completion, he turned to a work contemplated before Eluard's death in November 1952, a work originally intended for the Bernac/ Poulenc duo's February 1955 20th-anniversary concert.

COMMISSIONING OF *LE TRAVAIL DU PEINTRE AND* LATER 1955

September 1956: Nevertheless I did write this cycle, *Le Travail du peintre,* about which I had already spoken to Paul Eluard a few months before his death!! The seven poems which comprise this collection are taken from the volume *Voir* [written to the glory of the painters]. I thought that it could stimulate my work to *paint musically:* Picasso, Chagall, Braque, Gris, Klee, Miró, Villon. When I spoke to Eluard about my project, I asked him for a poem about Matisse, whom I adore. Paul half promised me. I say "half promised" because he did not share my passion for this painter. In my opinion, "Matisse" should have concluded the cycle in joy and sunshine. Today, "Villon" closes it lyrically and somberly. "Gris" is the first *mélodie* I sketched several years ago. I always very much admired this painter and very much liked him as a man, this worthy and unfortunate Juan who is only today beginning to take the place he merits. "Picasso" opens the collection: "honor to whom honor is due." Its first theme, also found a long time ago, served as stock for Mother Marie's theme in *Dialogues des Carmélites.* Here, as in my opera, it takes on a tone of pride appropriate to the subject. This *mélodie,* in C major, very distantly recalls the opening of *Tel jour telle nuit;* but many years have elapsed since then, and for the musician, C major no longer means peaceful happiness. It is the progress of the prosody, with its long run-on lines, that gives a lofty tone to this *mélodie.*[141]

---

[139] This concert, requested by Dr. Robert Debré, Prof. Jean Hamburger (husband of the pianist Annette Haas), and Lucien de Gennes, may not have been given. 5 Apr. [1955] letter in Poulenc 1994, 55-2.

[140] 5 May 1955 letter to Britten from Cannes in Poulenc 1994, 55-4 (Poulenc 1991, no. 261).

[141] Poulenc 1993, pp. 58-9 (Poulenc 1989, pp. 100-03).

In May, once again thinking about Eluard's poems, Poulenc conceived a plan to have Alice Esty, Bernac's wealthy American acquaintance, commission *Le Travail du peintre* for one thousand dollars.[142] On 2 June he wrote reminding her of their Noizay engagement on Monday the 6th to work and have dinner. Once Bernac paved the way, she was offered the opportunity to commission *Le Travail*, which included the dedication, manuscript, first performance, and a recording accompanied by Poulenc.[143] It was Poulenc's intention to compose during the early summer, but work on *Dialogues* changed his plan, and the cycle was not complete until August.[144]

By 17 June Poulenc had traveled to the Hotel Beau-Rivage from where he took a cure at Evian-les-Bains, staying until 3 July.[145] Not only did the water cure his body, but he admitted that the music he heard there by such turn-of-the century composers as Paul Lacome d'Estalenx, Paul Wachs, Francis Thomé, Louis Ganne, Ernest Gillet, Ernest Guiraud, Cécile Chaminade, and Ernest Reyer cleansed his mind of "dodécacas," Poulenc's term for twelve-tone music. Next he headed for Le Tremblay dividing his time in July between there and Aix-en-Provence.[146] August found him in Tourrettes-sur-Loup "an adorable village 30 kilometers northwest of Nice. . . 400 meters up in the mountains."[147] Thanks to his old friend Richard Chanlaire, he had a room with piano at the Hotel "Grive Dorée" which he preferred to Hyères, where Marie-Laure de Noailles had invited him to stay.[148] There he completed Act III, scene 3, begun at Le Tremblay, and the final scene 4. He also settled on a poem for a *mélodie* promised to Rose Dercourt-Plaut.[149] The waning summer was compli-

[142] Concerning Esty's extensive commissions of works by Rorem, Thomson, Paul Bowles, Marc Blitzstein, Ben Weber, Quincy Porter, John Gruen, Daniel Pinkham, Charles Jones, and others, see Rorem 1983, pp. 230-1 and Chapter XIV. Esty had studied with Florence Kimball.

[143] 2 June [1955] letter in Poulenc 1994, 55-5 (Poulenc 1991, no. 262).

[144] At least one *mélodie* had been begun years earlier.

[145] [June 1955] letter to Sauguet in Poulenc 1994, 55-6, his unpublished 17 June [1955] and undated letters to Gibson in GB-Lchester, and his 2 July [1955] letter to Rose Dercourt-Plaut in Poulenc 1994, 55-7 (Poulenc 1991, no. 263).

[146] The most noteworthy outcome of his time in Aix was reported in a 17 Aug. 1955 radio interview with Micheline Banzet. He had met Menotti at the festival and they had joked about working on an opera together, Menotti writing the libretto and Poulenc the music. See Buckland/Chimènes: l, p. 258.

[147] 12 Aug. [1955] letter to Rose Dercourt-Plaut in Poulenc 1994, 55-10 (Poulenc 1991, no. 264).

[148] Fragment of Poulenc's 8 Aug. [1955] letter to Sauguet in Poulenc 1994, p. 825, note 1. About Poulenc's earlier relationship with Chanlaire see Chapter VI. A scarf hand painted by Chanlaire, dated "Tourrettes, Tarentelle, Août 1955, Francis Poulenc" was once owned by a Mme Aubert. See Boulet, no. 48.

[149] 12 Aug. [1955] letter from Tourrettes-sur-Loup in Poulenc 1994, 55-10 (Poulenc 1991, no. 264). The poem turned out to be "Nuage" by Laurence de Beylié.

cated by the worsening of Roubert's condition which required that Poulenc take him to Cannes on 16 August.[150] Lucien recovered quickly from this temporary setback, although he was nearing the end of his life.

> I have entrusted him to my sixteen blessed Carmelites [Poulenc told Bernac]: may they protect his last days since he has been so closely involved with their story. In effect, I began this work happily at his side in Lyons in August 1953. After all the torment, which I don't need to describe to you, I have just completed the work, at his side, during the last days of his life on earth. As I already wrote to you, Bernanos' phrase "We do not die for ourselves alone . . . but for, or instead of, each other" haunts me. If Raymond [Destouches] remains the secret of *Les Mamelles* and *Figure humaine*, Lucien is certainly that of the *Stabat* and the *Carmélites*.[151]

In August Poulenc also learned that the 19 June 1954 death of Adrienne Monnier was a suicide. Maurice Saillet requested he contribute a short homage for an issue of *Mercure de France*. Poulenc wrote "Lorsque je suis mélancolique" ("When I Am Melancholic") which was finally published in January 1956.[152]

He intended to return to Paris on 15 August, but he didn't travel to Noizay until 1 September.[153] There were only details left to complete on the piano-vocal score of his opera. These included several issues of prosody in the last four lines of the *Veni Creator* sung by Blanche as she mounts the scaffold, and phrasing for the final march, as well. The finished score was also copied at Noizay. In August Poulenc boldly grew a mustache. He reported: "I'm as fit as the Pont neuf, I sleep, I look ravishingly well, and... I've grown a mustache which is driving all the women crazy about me. At last!!!"[154] He polled friends concerning whether or not they liked it: only five were against (including Bernac) with nine in favor (among them Denise Bourdet, Richard Chanlaire, Georgette Chadourne, and Simone Girard).[155]

---

[150] "Vendredi" [19 Aug. 1955] letter to Bernac from the Hotel Majestic in Cannes in Poulenc 1994, 55-11 (Poulenc 1991, no. 265).

[151] Poulenc 1994, 55-11 (Poulenc 1991, no. 265).

[152] Saillet's 11 Aug. 1955 letter to Poulenc (Poulenc 1994, 55-9 and Poulenc 1956a).

[153] 12 Aug. [1955] letter to Rose Dercourt-Plaut and "vendredi" [19 Aug. 1955] letter to Bernac in Poulenc 1994, 55-10 and 55-11 (Poulenc 1991, nos. 264 and 265).

[154] English translation of Poulenc's 16 Sept. [1955] letter to Fournier in Hughes 1998, p. 85 [misdated 1954].

[155] "Vendredi" [9 Sept. 1955] letter to Bernac in Poulenc 1994, 55-13 (Poulenc 1991, no. 267). Expecting a Noizay visit from Rose Dercourt-Plaut, Poulenc told Mme Lambiotte he had grown a mustache. Unpublished "jeudi"[15 Sept. 1955] letter in US-NH. Rorem curtly reported,"Poulenc has grown a mustache: his pimples disappear." Rorem, 1966, p. 224.

By September, back in form, his desk was overflowing with projects.[156] There were recordings of Chabrier, *Histoire de Babar*, and a two-record set of songs to prepare, accompaniments for Schumann's *Liederkreis* and *Dichterliebe* to practice, an article to write about the Ballets Russes for *La Pléiade*,[157] and a brief description of the Sonata for Two Pianos for the Gold and Fizdale recording.[158]

Poulenc's dear friend, Lucien Roubert, age forty-seven, finally succumbed to lung cancer on 21 October in Toulon without too much suffering.[159] "It was a tragic fall of the curtain after six years of liaison," Poulenc confided to Milhaud from Noizay.[160]

> Lucien [was] delivered from his martyrdom ten days ago, the final copy of *Dialogues* completed (take note) at the same moment the poor boy took his last breath. I rose from the table and said to my faithful Anna: "I have finished: Monsieur Lucien will die now." Who will ever know what is at the secret heart of certain works?[161]

Late in the year, Bernac and Poulenc returned to the concert stage presenting Schumann's *Dichterliebe* and *Liederkreis* in memory of the deaths of Schumann (d. 1857), Heine (d. 1856), and Eichendorff (d. 1857) at Chaumont on 16 November and the small hall of the Amsterdam Concertgebouw on 13 December. Poulenc also recorded a group of Satie piano pieces on 21 November with Marcelle Meyer, gave a concert in Tours on the 28th with Bernac,[162] and published a brief "Hommage à Béla Bartók" in *La Revue musicale*.[163]

On 27 November of this year, Arthur Honegger passed away at the age of sixty three, the first member of *Les Six* to die. During Honegger's last three years he and Poulenc had grown closer than before. Poulenc recalled one encounter in conversations with Stéphane Audel.

> I believe that Arthur has had a sort of presentiment of the brevity of his life, his illness, and impending death. I am sure of that because

---

[156] Poulenc was visited for two weeks by Hell, who was finishing his Poulenc biography, and on the 23rd by Rose Dercourt-Plaut. Unpublished 12 Sept. [1955] letter to Sauguet in F-Pn.

[157] Poulenc 1963c and "vendredi" [9 Sept. 1955] letter to Bernac in Poulenc 1994, 55-13 (Poulenc 1991, no. 267).

[158] 17 Sept. [1955] letter from Noizay to Gold and Fizdale in Poulenc 1994, 55-14 (Poulenc 1991, no. 268). The recording is U.S. Columbia ML 5068.

[159] Gendre prints Poulenc's special supplication to the Carmel of Compiègne, dated 27 Sept. 1955, asking that they pray for his sick friend. See Buckland/ Chimènes: d, pp. 306-07.

[160] "Vendredi 28" [Oct. 1955] letter in Poulenc 1994, 55-15.

[161] 31 Oct. [1955] letter in Poulenc 1994, 55-16 (Poulenc 1991, no. 269).

[162] See a listing of the program in Boulet, no. 23.

[163] Poulenc 1955.

one day, ill myself, I said to him: "You, with your marvelous health!" and, he melancholically replied: "Ah, who knows who will die first!" Especially at the end I think that he had no illusions about his illness, and as a matter of fact I have a very upsetting memory.[164]

Honegger had given him an empty spiral notebook identical to Poulenc's own, telling him to use it because he himself would not be writing any more music. Incapable of writing in it, Poulenc retained it as a memento of their friendship. Reflecting on their relationship at the end, Poulenc noted that they had developed:

> A very great tenderness, indeed, for tenderness is the word which should be used, and I must say it was during the last three years of his life that we really understood each other, that we talked about everything.[165]

He was particularly proud of one of the last letters he received from Honegger sent on 10 May 1954 from Basle. Honegger had just read Poulenc's *Entretiens avec Claude Rostand* and penned a letter which praised Poulenc to his embarrassment. After noting numerous differences between himself and Poulenc, he concluded:

> All these differences, far from separating us, on the contrary, seem to bring us together. Is not variety the most beautiful thing in life and in art? Do not find me too presumptuous if I put myself beside you to say: "We are two 'honorable men'."[166]

Sometime during 1955 Poulenc also assisted with the first recording of his beloved *Stabat Mater*. The performance, by the Orchestra de l'Association des Concerts Colonne and the Chœurs de l'Alauda assisted by soprano Jacqueline Brumaire, was under the direction of Louis Frémaux.[167] Henri Hell wrote the notes for this recording, which won the Grand Prix du Disque de l'Académie du Disque français for 1956, and the cover states, "Recording realized under the artist direction of Francis Poulenc."[168]

CONCERTS AND HONORS: FIRST HALF OF 1956

Little is known about Poulenc's activities during early 1956 except that he met with members of Jeunesses Musicales de France at the request of the journalist Claude Samuel, who had founded a record

---

[164] Poulenc 1978, p. 112 (Poulenc 1963a, p. 152).

[165] Poulenc 1978, p. 112 (Poulenc 1963a, p. 153).

[166] Poulenc 1994, 54-16 (Poulenc 1991, no. 248).

[167] Frémaux, a member of the French Resistance, had studied conducting at the Paris Conservatory from which he graduated in 1952 with a first prize. This recording contract was an honor for such a young conductor.

[168] See Bloch, p. 195 (Véga C-35 A 1). I am grateful to Roland John Wiley for informing me of Poulenc's direct connection with this recording.

club.[169] Perhaps it was then that he and Bernac recorded *Le Bal masqué* with Louis Frémaux conducting.[170] Bernac and Poulenc flew to Greece in early March for concerts after which Poulenc went to Italy, stopping briefly in Rome on the 16th, before departing for Milan on the 17th.[171] He returned to Paris on the 21st and then went on to London and Liverpool at the end of the month. Whereas Greece was business as usual, in Italy Poulenc was lavished with honors. While staying in Rome with Mimi Pecci-Blunt, he was named an honorary member of the venerable Academy of St Cecilia, along with Aaron Copland, Dmitri Shostakovitch, and Olivier Messiaen; Gian Carlo Menotti was made a regular member.[172] "Rome was charming, quite social," Poulenc wrote. "Grand dinners and lunches every day. My reception at the Academy was very kind and very cordial."[173] The Milanese sojourn provided the opportunity to play his opera for Victor de Sabata, music director at La Scala. Sabata, enormously enthusiastic about the score, memorized it in a week. Poulenc's reception was such that he told his sister, "I was treated like Richard Wagner!!" Sabata suggested that he would need thirty orchestra rehearsals to prepare the opera. While in Milan Poulenc attended Stravinsky's *Apollon* and Falla's *Retablo* at the Piccola Scala, hobnobbed with Herbert von Karajan and Elisabeth Schwartzkopf at the Biffi restaurant, and thoroughly enjoyed the limelight.

Back in Paris on 21 March he saw a Domaine Musical performance at which Pierre Boulez's *Le Marteau sans maître* received its Parisian premiere. Poulenc was especially complimentary about the score, though he thought the prosody resembled "the toothed edge of a saw, which made the text unintelligible."[174] Poulenc had been a staunch supporter of the Domaine Musical series, and attended its concerts regularly.[175] His brief respite in Paris concluded, Poulenc went to England where he and Jean Françaix gave a concert in Liverpool on 27 March playing the Concerto in D minor.[176]

---

[169] 20 Jan. 1956 letter thanking Samuel for the gift of two bottles of wine in Poulenc 1994, 56-1.

[170] Made with members of the Théâtre National de l'Opéra on Véga C 35 A 35 (U.S. release on Westminster XWN 18422). See Appendix 3.

[171] 21 Mar. 1956 letter to the Collaers from Paris in Poulenc 1994, 56-3 and Collaer 1996, 56-2.

[172] *The New York Times* (6 Mar. 1956), 27.

[173] These and subsequent details in his 28 Mar. 1956 letter to Manceaux in Poulenc 1994, 56-4 (Poulenc 1991, no. 271). By special dispensation, Meyer and the Countess were permitted to attend the customary all-male induction reception.

[174] 28 Mar. 1956 letter in Poulenc 1994, 56-4 (Poulenc 1991, no. 271).

[175] For a fitting tribute paid Poulenc at the first concert after his death (13 Feb. 1963), see Poulenc 1994, p. 836, note 7.

[176] Listed in the Ibbs and Tillett ledgers.

Things settled down a little during April when he returned to his favorite room at the Hotel Majestic in Cannes. There, following a repeat of the Liverpool concert with Françaix on the 5th, Poulenc finished orchestrating Act II of *Dialogues*. Once returned to Noizay he hastily composed "Bucolique" (FP 160), an orchestral movement dated "Noizay, 5 mai 56," which formed the seventh section of a collected work honoring the renowned pianist Marguerite Long. Jean Françaix, Henri Sauguet, Milhaud, Jean Rivier, Henri Dutilleux, Daniel-Lesur, and Auric also contributed. The work, celebrating the 50th anniversary of Long's 1906 appointment at the Paris Conservatory, was premiered at the Grand Amphitheater of the Sorbonne on 4 June 1956, with Charles Munch conducting the Orchestre National.[177] By mid-month he was in Brive from where he dispatched the full score of Act III of *Dialogues* on the 18th. He also corrected the piano score and prepared the concert and lecture he would give in London on 22 June and Aldeburgh at the Britten Festival on the 24th.[178] Several bars for his *mélodie* "Nuage" also came to him.

In mid-June he outlined his summer plans:

> . . . from 26 June to 12 July, Evian. From 12 to 20, Milan. From 20-23, Aix. From 24 to 28, American Conservatory in Fontainebleau, where I am teaching a course with Bernac on my music. From 28 July to 14 August, Normandy, at my sister's. Then Noizay.[179]

While at the Hôtel Splendide in Evian Poulenc disclosed that he was thinking about fashioning a libretto from Jean Anouilh's *Le Bal des voleurs*, a project he quickly abandoned.[180] Poulenc and his new boyfriend left for Venice on 8 July by car, then went on to Milan to prepare for the premiere of *Dialogues*.[181] The centerpiece of his visit to the American Conservatory in Fontainebleau was a recital with Bernac on 24 July in the Salle du Jeu de paume.[182] During Poulenc's

[177] Details in Dunoyer, pp. 185-7.
[178] Poulenc played *Aubade* under Paul Sacher. [24 June 1956] report to Girard from the Wentworth Hotel, Aldeburgh, Suffolk in Poulenc 1994, 56-8 (Poulenc 1991, no. 273). His one and a half hour talk, entitled "Propos à bâtons rompus sur la musique" dealt with his own musical evolution.
[179] 16 June [1956] letter to Rose Dercourt-Plaut from [Brive] in Poulenc 1994, 56-7 [Poulenc 1991, no. 272]. In a [24 June 1956] letter to Girard, Poulenc wrote that he would stay at the Hôtel Splendide in Evian where his nice boyfriend would join him. (It is uncertain who this is, but it could be a certain "Claude" referred to in several letters.) Poulenc 1994, 56-8 (Poulenc 1991, no. 273).
[180] 3 July [1956] letter to Leguerney in Poulenc 1994, 56-9. Poulenc also spoke of this project in a 26 Aug. 1956 letter to Collaer excerpted on p. 841, note 4.
[181] Poulenc's new companion was a young man named Claude who worked for Citroën. 7 July [1956] letter to Denise Bourdet and 17 Aug. [1956] letter to Bernac in Poulenc 1994, 56-11 and 56-15 (Poulenc 1991, no. 275) respectively.
[182] Poulenc 1994, p. 843, note 2.

stay at Le Tremblay he finished *Le Travail du peintre,* which he considered to be as important as *Tel jour telle nuit,* and spoke of it to
Nadia Boulanger and Doda Conrad.[183] *Le Travail* was composed under the influence of *Dialogues,* with which it shares themes.

Occupied by his work, Poulenc stayed longer at Le Tremblay than
he intended.[184] He left on 19 August with Brigitte Manceaux and
Henri Hell, who visited with him at Noizay.[185] No doubt Hell was
there to work on his Poulenc biography published by Plon in 1958.

COMMISSIONING OF THE SONATA FOR FLUTE AND PIANO

On 3 April, while he was still working on *Dialogues,* Poulenc was
approached by Harold Spivacke of the Library of Congress in Washington on behalf of The Elizabeth Sprague Coolidge Foundation.[186]
The Foundation sought a piece for two pianos, but offered the alternative of a chamber work for no more than six instruments for a 19-
21 October 1956 festival. Poulenc declined because he was still orchestrating *Dialogues.* Biding his time, Spivacke reoffered the commission in early May, suggesting a flute sonata.[187] Poulenc finally
expressed interest in August stating the following conditions:

1. The work will be dedicated to the memory of Madame Coolidge
2. The manuscript will belong to the Library of Congress
3. The Foundation will control the first American performance
4. The world premiere performance will be reserved for himself at
   the Strasbourg Festival
5. The fee will be $750 (below his customary fee).[188]

Poulenc may have been banking on resurrecting a flute sonata
begun in late August 1952 heralded by the *Chesterian* at the time.

> Francis Poulenc is at present writing a Sonata for Flute and Piano
> which, it is hoped, will be ready for publication early next year. The
> work is being specifically composed for a well known American flau-
> tist, who will introduce it in the United States.[189]

[183] Unpublished [Aug. 1956] letter to Boulanger from Le Tremblay in F-Pn. This
and the reference to Conrad are cited in Schmidt 1995, FP 161, p. 453.
[184] 16 June [1956] letter to Rose Dercourt-Plaut in Poulenc 1994, 56-7 (Poulenc
1991, no. 272).
[185] 17 Aug. [1956] letter to Bernac in Poulenc 1994, 56-15 (Poulenc 1991, no. 275).
[186] Schmidt 1995, FP 164, p. 460. This and other letters regarding the Sonata for
Flute and Piano are in US-Wc. Unless otherwise noted, they are all unpublished,
but many are excerpted in Schmidt 1995.
[187] 9 May 1956 letter in Schmidt 1995, FP 164, p. 460.
[188] [Aug. 1956] letter to Spivacke in Poulenc 1994, 56-13.
[189] 27/172 (Oct. 1952), 40. For a more detailed history of the sonata and its
sources see Francis Poulenc, *Sonata for Flute and Piano,* ed. by Carl B. Schmidt,
Patricia Harper, contributing editor (London: Chester Music Ltd., 1994), ii-xxi.

How much of this earlier sonata was written is unknown; nevertheless, Poulenc tantalized Robert Douglas Gibson in London in letters dated 1953, 1955, and 1956. Poulenc began work on this "new" flute sonata in Cannes during December 1956, composing through March 1957 as annotations on the holograph manuscript indicate.

PREPARATION FOR THE PREMIERE OF *DIALOGUES*: FALL 1956

The rest of 1956 was devoted to thoughts about the Italian-language premiere of *Dialogues* in Milan on 26 January 1957, about which Poulenc had little direct input, and the 21 June 1957 French-language performance in Paris about which he had a good deal to say.[190] Early fall was predominantly spent at Noizay with occasional weekend trips to the Hotel Royal at La Baule-sur-mer and elsewhere.[191] During September he wrote "La Souris" and "Nuage" published as *Deux mélodies 1956* (FP 162).[192] The first was requested by Doda Conrad to celebrate the eightieth birthday of his mother Marya Freund, and the second was Poulenc's present to Rose Dercourt-Plaut.[193]

He wrote Stravinsky and Boulanger lamenting that he could not attend the Venice premiere of *Canticum sacrum ad Honorem Sancti Marci Nominis* at St Marks Cathedral on 13 September,[194] and told Sauguet "How I would love to be in Venice . . . even in an empty gondola!!!"[195] After hearing the broadcast, however, he expressed consternation and blamed Robert Craft for having been a bad influence.[196] In late August at Noizay he recopied *Le Travail du peintre* and mailed it to Alice Esty in New York.[197]

Poulenc returned to Paris on 8 October for the fall season and took a more extended trip with Bernac in November.[198] They played in Birmingham on the 6th, Oxford on the 8th, and recorded a BBC

---

[190] The Italian translation by Flavio Testi entitled *Dialoghi delle Carmelitane* was published in a small booklet issued by G. Ricordi & C. - Milano (1957).

[191] "Dimanche" [16 Sept. 1956] letter to Hell from La Baule-sur-mer in Poulenc 1994, 56-20.

[192] The holograph of the second *mélodie* is dated 13 Sept. Poulenc used a Laurence de Beylié poem sent to him a year earlier by Countess Pastré. Poulenc 1993, p. 60 (20 Sept. 1956 entry).

[193] Poulenc 1993, p. 60 (Poulenc 1989, pp. 104-07).

[194] 7 Sept. [1956] letter to Stravinsky from [Noizay] and undated letter to Boulanger in Poulenc 1994, 56-18 and p. 851, note 1 (excerpt only) respectively. Concerning his opinion about the work see the "dimanche" [16 Sept. 1956] letter to Hell in Poulenc 1994, 56-20.

[195] Unpublished 12 Sept. [1957] letter to Sauguet in F-Pn.

[196] 15 May [1957] letter to Milhaud which ends, "I decidedly do not like the St Marc of Igor. Miserable Craft!!" Poulenc 1994, 57-19.

[197] "Dimanche" [16 Sept. 1956] letter to Hell in Poulenc 1994, 56-20. In an unpublished "mardi soir" [21 Aug. 1956] letter to Bernac in US-NH, Poulenc reported that he would finish the task of recopying in ten days.

[198] 12 Sept. [1956] letter to Hirsch in Poulenc 1994, 56-19.

Third Programme recital on the 10th for future broadcast before going to Berlin on the 25th.[199] After another brief stay in Paris Poulenc headed south to Cannes to compose at the Hotel Majestic from 1-25 December. On the 26th he returned to spend the holidays with his family before leaving for Milan on 4 January 1957.[200]

Poulenc had little input into preparations for the Italian-language world premiere performance of *Dialogues* at La Scala. Though he would have preferred that Denise Duval sing the role of Blanche, which he created for her, powers in Milan gave it to the Rumanian soprano Virginia Zeani instead.[201] He was also not consulted about the *mise en scène* or the décor.

> Speaking of Milan [Poulenc told Bernac], they are busy *making* the sets for Act I and preparing the others. Wake [Wakhevitch] went to see Wallmann in Venice. I have not seen any of it but it is better this way. I have decided to agree to everything with my *eyes closed*, so to speak. I still do not know who is singing but I will leave it to them. There is quite enough to keep me busy with the Paris production.[202]

Poulenc also had an important meeting with Georges Hirsch and Emmanuel Bondeville of the Paris Opéra on the 20th or 21st of August to discuss preparations for the Paris production. Questions centered around the potential production team: director, costume and scenery designer, conductor, and cast. As a potential director, Albert Béguin recommended Alexandre Balachova, and Poulenc felt that Marcelle Tassencourt (who had already directed Bernanos' version as a play) was unacceptable because she knew nothing about music and might use ideas from mounting the work as a play.[203] After the meeting Poulenc wrote Bernac that he had spent two hours with Bondeville and had also played for Régine Crespin the scenes in which she would sing the role of Mme Lidoine.[204] He listed most

---

[199] Fragment of Poulenc's 17 Nov. [1956] letter to Girard in Poulenc 1994, p. 854, note 1 and "samedi matin" [10 Nov. 1956] letter to Dugardin in Poulenc 1994, 56-22. See also his unpublished 25 Nov. [1956] card to Georges Hirsch in F-Po (Lettres autographes Poulenc, no. 15). In a 28 Nov. 1956 entry in *Journal de mes mélodies*, Poulenc noted that he had tried to explain to a German music critic how the flavor of Parisian suburbs was evoked in his music. Spotting a reproduction of Raoul Dufy's "Canotiers aux bords de la Marne" in a shop window, he suggested that this was his Nogent music. Poulenc 1993, p. 61 (Poulenc 1989, pp. 108-09). Dufy's 1925 painting is reproduced in Buckland/Chimènes, plate 1.
[200] Unpublished 22 Dec. [1956] letter to Rose Dercourt-Plaut in US-NH.
[201] Fragment of Poulenc's 30 June [1956] letter to Valcarenghi in Poulenc 1994, p. 848, note 9. Sets for Act I were already being constructed by mid-August 1956.
[202] 17 Aug. [1956] letter in Poulenc 1994, 56-15 (Poulenc 1991, no. 275).
[203] Béguin, Bernanos' literary executor, oversaw the publication of *Dialogues*, and had it produced at the Théâtre Hébertot in 1952 with Tassencourt's assistance.
[204] Unpublished "mardi soir" [21 Aug. 1956] letter in US-NH. For the Milan and

of the cast for Bernac happily reporting that Pierre Dervaux would conduct and that he and Bondeville favored Max de Rieux as set designer. Poulenc had written much the same to Claude Rostand, but added that he was intoxicated at the idea of having Suzanne Lalique design the sets and costumes.[205] By October Poulenc's old friend Jean Hugo was being considered as a potential designer, but Hugo declined so Lalique was retained.[206] Poulenc held out for Maurice Jacquemont as director, who must have been offered the position by 25 November.[207] He noted that Jacquemont would be meeting Lalique and that this combination pleased him.[208] In December from Cannes, Poulenc reaffirmed that he was very pleased with Jacquemont who fitted well with Lalique. Finally Jacquemont wrote to Poulenc about Lalique, and Poulenc responded granting Jacquemont carte blanche for everything concerning *Dialogues*.[209]

During his stay in Cannes Poulenc sent the third act of *Dialogues* to Guido Valcarenghi, worked on his Sonata for Flute and Piano, and composed a "solemn" *mélodie* on a Robert Desnos text *Dernier poème* (FP 163).[210] Desnos had died of typhus on 8 June 1945 not long after the liberation of the concentration camp at Terezin, Czechoslovakia where he had been imprisoned.

MILAN: PREMIERE OF *DIALOGUES* IN 1957

After the holidays Poulenc arrived in Milan on 7 January to witness preparations for the premiere of *Dialogues*.[211] Lodged at the Hotel Continental, he worked from 10:00 am to midnight.[212] Once he had

---

Paris distributions see Schmidt 1995, FP 159, p. 438. Crespin, who did not sing the role of Mme Lidoine after 1974, sang Mme de Croissy in the 1977 Metropolitan Opera performance. See L'Avant scène 1983, pp. 104-07 for Crespin's recollections.

[205] 16 Aug. 1956 letter to Rostand partially transcribed in Poulenc 1994, p. 849, note 10 and L'Avant scène 1983, p. 87.

[206] Hugo's 30 Oct. 1956 letter to Poulenc in Poulenc 1994, 56-21 (Poulenc 1991, no. 277): "But I cannot design sets any more. I feel absolutely incapable of having a single theatrical idea."

[207] Unpublished 4 Oct. [1956] letter in F-Po (Lettres autographes Poulenc, no. 11).

[208] Unpublished 25 Nov. [1956] letter in F-Po (Lettres autographes Poulenc, no. 15). See also his 25 Nov. [1956] letter to Jacquemont in Poulenc 1994, 56-23 and the unpublished "jeudi" [Dec. 1956] letter from Cannes in F-Po (Lettres autographes Poulenc, no. 21).

[209] Fragment of 12 Dec. 1956 letter to Poulenc in Poulenc 1994, p. 856, note 1, and 15 Dec. [1956] letter from Poulenc to Jacquemont, 56-26.

[210] What prompted Poulenc to set this text in 1956 is unknown, but he may have been familiar with the poem from a 1945 article by Henry Serouya recounting Desnos' death. Desnos' poem was also published in this same issue. See Serouya and Poulenc's unpublished 21 Dec. [1956] letter in US-NH.

[211] "Mardi soir" [8 Jan. 1957] letter to Dugardin in Poulenc 1994, 57-2.

[212] [Jan. 1957] postcard to Marie-Ange from Milan in Poulenc 1994, 57-1.

been presented to the cast and heard some rehearsals, Poulenc informed Bernac that he had a "sen-sa-tion-nelle!!!" cast, that what he had seen of Margarita Wallmann's *mise en scène* was excellent, but that he had reservations about the visual aspects.[213] Poulenc exclaimed to Claude Rostand, "There will be about forty rehearsals altogether, of which *thirty* à l'Italienne with orchestra!!!"[214] Earlier in December he had asked Hervé Dugardin, then director of Ricordi in Paris, to invite five French critics — Claude Rostand, Jacques Bourgeois, Henri Hell, Clarendon [Bernard Gavoty], and Antoine Goléa — to review the premiere.[215] Rostand and Hell both wrote laudatory reviews.[216] Poulenc summed up his own opinion of the production saying, "The Italian musical execution was sublime, but the spectacle will be much truer and more beautiful in Paris."[217] Among others, Poulenc invited Simone Girard and Bernac to the *répétition générale* and both sat in his box at the premiere. Afterwards, Countess Crespi gave a sumptuous reception for special guests.

Before leaving Milan Poulenc spent an entire day

> . . . at the RAI listening to a lot of electronic and serial music. Very good Sonata for Flute and Piano by Boulez although a bit too long, but by a *true* musician. Compared with that, what a lot of twelve-tone *stale things* by so many musicians!!!! There is already a frightful [surfeit of] clichés in this genre. The orchestration of Puccini's *Manon Lescaut* last evening was richer in surprises.[218]

PREPARATIONS FOR THE PARISIAN *DIALOGUES* AND THE FLUTE SONATA

Poulenc returned to Paris on 7 February, exhausted from a month of constant activity, and completed arrangements to publish the piano-vocal score of *Dialogues*.[219] He then traveled south to his beloved Hotel Majestic in Cannes to recover from the nervous condition which followed him from Milan to Paris. With *Dialogues* fresh in his mind he quickly modified the score, especially the conclusion of Act II, and the finale to Act III, which were dispatched to Ricordi at

---

[213] "Jeudi" [probably 10 Jan. 1957] letter in Poulenc 1994, 57-3. Earlier, Poulenc had noted there would be 229 costumes. "Vendredi" (7 Dec. 1956) letter to Jacquemont in Poulenc 1994, 56-24.

[214] [Jan. 1957] letter in Poulenc 1994, 57-5 (Poulenc 1991, no. 278).

[215] "Mercredi" [12 Dec. 1956] letter to Dugardin in Poulenc 1994, 56-25.

[216] 2 Feb. [1957] and [early Feb. 1957] letters to Rostand and Hell respectively in Poulenc 1994, 57-6 and 57-7 (Poulenc 1991, nos. 279 and 280).

[217] Fragment of Poulenc's 8 Mar. 1957 letter to Collaer in Poulenc 1994, p. 863, note 5.

[218] [Early Feb. 1957] letter to Hell from Milan in Poulenc 1994, 57-7 (Poulenc 1991, no. 280).

[219] Unpublished 3 Mar. [1957] letter to Valcarenghi from Cannes in I-Mr.

month's end.[220] He also shared suggestions for the upcoming Paris production with Maurice Jacquemont.[221]

Poulenc's most pressing task, however, was completion of his Sonata for Flute and Piano. Work went well enough that by 8 March two of the three movements were finished.[222] Haste was necessary because the first performance was scheduled for 18 June in Strasbourg. He also agreed to accompany Alice Esty's premiere of *Le Travail du peintre* and planned to fly to Basle on 3 April for the first performance in German of *Les Mamelles de Tirésias (Die Wandlung des Tirésias)* before returning to Paris on the 6th.[223] In early March Poulenc asked Henri Hell about progress on the Poulenc biography at the same time telling him that the Flute Sonata is closely allied to Debussy's work in this genre. "The writing is simple but subtle, and the harmony reminds one of Sister Constance."[224]

Heading north on "Le Mistral" Poulenc stopped to see Simone Girard on 15 March, hopscotched to Marseilles the 16th, and to Paris the 17th.[225] Once back Poulenc viewed a Picasso Exposition organized by Daniel-Henry Kahnweiler at the Galerie Louis Leiris on the rue de Monceau and prepared the premiere of *Le Travail du peintre* which took place at the École normale de musique on 1 April.[226] Poulenc only accompanied *Le Travail;* the other works by Thomas Ford, Philip Rosseter, Henry Purcell, Claude Debussy, and Paul Bowles, were accompanied by David Stimer, her regular accompanist. The premiere accomplished, Poulenc was now free to perform the cycle in Edinburgh with Bernac on 5 September 1947.

[220] "Jeudi" [28 Feb. 1957] letter to Dugardin in Poulenc 1994, 57-8 and the unpublished 3 Mar. [1957] letter from Cannes to Valcarenghi in I-Mr.
[221] 28 Feb. 1957 letter in Poulenc 1994, 57-9.
[222] Unpublished 8 Mar. [1957] letter to Gibson in GB-Lchester.
[223] 8 Mar. [1957] letter to Bernac in Poulenc 1994, 57-11.
[224] Constance is in *Dialogues.* 9 Mar. [1957] letter to Hell in Poulenc 1994, 57-12.
[225] "Mercredi" [6 Mar. 1957] letter to Girard in Poulenc 1994, 57-10. His last days in the south were enjoyed with Louis Gautier, a handsome infantry sergeant aged 29 with whom he shared such poetic moments that he forgot everything including *Dialogues.* Fragment of Poulenc's "samedi" [3 Mar. 1957] letter to Dugardin in Poulenc 1994, p. 864, note 2. In a 13 July [1957] letter to Girard, Poulenc remarked that "The Sonata for Flute is proof of the French Army's generosity to the morale of an old maestro." Fragment in Poulenc 1994, p. 864, note 2. Poulenc mentions Louis Gautier with some frequency over the last six years of his life. Gautier, with whom Poulenc had an intimate relationship, built a house in Bagnols-en-Forêt during 1958-9, and he and Poulenc occasionally traveled together. In 1962, Gautier moved to Cannes where he bought a bar.
[226] [27 Mar. 1957] letter to Picasso in Poulenc 1994, 57-13 and note 1. Poulenc had seen Picasso during his recent stay in Cannes at which time Picasso drew his portrait (dated 13 Mar. 1957) for the cover of Hell's biography. A photograph was substituted, and the portrait is conserved in the Musée Picasso in Paris. (See Rostand 1970, p. 177 and Zervos, vol. 17, no. 317.)

Upon hearing *Les Mamelles de Tirésias* in Basel Poulenc wrote Sauguet that the performance was "sensationnelle!!!," and complimented another performance of Stravinsky's *Petrouchka* with choreography by Wazlaw Orlikowski and décor which was "very Chagall."[227] Poulenc made one other quick trip at Guido Valcarenghi's invitation to see Maria Callas in Donizetti's *Anna Bolena* at La Scala on 12 April, remaining in Milan until the 15th at his favorite Hotel Continental.[228] He thoroughly enjoyed his stay.[229]

With the *Mamelles* performance past, Poulenc devoted full attention to the 18 June Strasbourg premiere of his Sonata for Flute, the 21 June Paris production of *Dialogues*, and the recitals with Bernac. Harold Spivacke's 24 April letter reminded him of his obligations, including a request for Poulenc's presence at the first American performance. Poulenc wrote on 7 June that the completed Sonata had been mailed to Washington.[230] He also suggested a possible program of chamber music involving Esty and a flautist to be named.[231]

The Strasbourg premiere with Jean-Pierre Rampal was previewed the day before for Arthur Rubinstein who sat alone in the middle of the front row. Rubinstein could not remain in Strasbourg, so Poulenc arranged for him to hear the piece anyway.[232] Further Poulenc-Spivack correspondence revealed that Poulenc's payment could not legally be channeled through Rose Dercourt-Plaut in New York and that he would not be coming to the United States after all. Poulenc suggested that Rampal and the noted French pianist and harpsichordist Robert Veyron-Lacroix be engaged and their performance took place in the Coolidge Auditorium at the Library of Congress on 14 February 1958. Since its publication by J. & W. Chester in 1958, this Sonata has become a pillar of the repertoire.[233] After

---

[227] "Vendredi" [5 Apr. 1957] letter from [Basle] in Poulenc 1994, 57-16. The performance was reviewed in the *Basler Nachrichten* (8 Apr.), and the paper printed a photograph of Poulenc, conductor Silvio Varviso, and others at the dress rehearsal. Another review appeared in the *National Zeitung Basel* of the same date.

[228] Poulenc traveled to Milan on a morning Air France flight. It is probably during this trip that Hervé Dugardin, while watching Callas take bows after a La Scala performance, said to Poulenc: "But what you ought to set for her is *La voix humaine*, since it's written for just one woman, and then she could have *all* the applause." Quoted by Waleckx in Buckland/Chimènes: l, p. 268.

[229] Unpublished 13 Apr. [*recte* 13 May 1957] letter to Valcarenghi in I-Mr.

[230] Copy of Spivacke's letter in US-Wc and Schmidt 1995, FP 164, p. 462.

[231] Copy of Poulenc's letter in US-Wc and Schmidt 1995, FP 164, p. 462. Fragment in Poulenc 1994, p. 871, note 4. This realization of the premiere never took place.

[232] Goll-Wilson, p. 10 and Rampal, p. 128. For Rampal's account of working with Poulenc during composition of the sonata, see Rampal, pp. 125-6. The two recorded it in 1959 for Véga C 35 A 181 and a copy of the world premiere performance is in Paris at the Phonothèque of the Bibliothèque Nationale.

[233] A new edition of this sonata, the first critical edition of a Poulenc work, was published by Chester in 1994 (order no. CH01605).

Poulenc's death Lennox Berkeley transcribed the piano part for orchestra, but performances in this version have been sporadic.[234]

As for *Dialogues*, Poulenc invited Alice Ardoin to come to one of the Paris performances on 21, 24, 28 June or 1 July and encouraged Rose Dercourt-Plaut as well.[235] Trying to entice Dercourt-Plaut, Poulenc said that while Milan had been extraordinary, Paris would be overwhelming. In particular he singled out Denise Duval, whose characterization of Blanche he found superb. "She is really a great actress and Bernac, with whom she has been working over the past six weeks, has made unimaginable progress with her."[236] Duval was "overwhelming" and Régine Crespin "an admirable Second Prioress."[237] The Paris production was a huge success with most favorable press.[238] Ned Rorem remembered a rather unsuccessful party fter the Paris premiere:

> The party afterward was at the Dugardins' comfortable mansion on the rue de l'Université. There was a buffet for a hundred, though I recall only twenty or so heads — none of the cast — and a mood of cool civility. [239]

SUMMER 1957

Poulenc made his yearly pilgrimage to Rocamadour in early July, staying, as usual, at the Hotel Sainte-Marie.[240] "I thanked the Virgin Mary for *Carmélites*, for the meeting with Louis [Gautier] (she [the Virgin Mary] understands everything), and prayed for our Pierre [Bernac], for our dear departed ones of tragic days, and for all our friends," he told Simone Girard.[241] Before departing the Midi, Poulenc wrote "O Jésu perpetua lux," the first of four *Laudes de Saint Antoine de Padoue* (FP 172). No. 2 was written in Brive during June 1958 and Nos. 3 and 4 in Cannes during March 1959.[242] After Salabert had these modest pieces, predominantly scored for three-part men's

---

[234] Schmidt 1995, FP 164, p. 458.

[235] 25 Apr. [19]57 letter to Ardoin in Poulenc 1994, 57-17 and 1 May [1957] letter to Rose Dercourt-Plaut in Poulenc 1994, 57-18 (Poulenc 1991, no. 281).

[236] 1 May [1957] letter to Rose Dercourt-Plaut in Poulenc 1994, 57-18 (Poulenc 1991, no. 281).

[237] Unpublished 13 Apr. [*recte* 13 May 1957] letter to Valcarenghi in I-Mr.

[238] Several reviews reprinted in L'Avant scène 1983, pp. 122-3.

[239] Rorem 1977, p. 15.

[240] From there he wrote a complex nine-page letter to Valcarenghi dated 4 July [1957] in which he poured out a story of intrigue involving the Milan versus Paris *Dialogues*. Poulenc referred to this letter in later unpublished correspondence with Valcarenghi in I-Mr.

[241] [4 July 1957] postcard in Poulenc 1994, 57-22. Poulenc often took her into his confidence concerning his male companions.

[242] Schmidt 1995, FP 172, pp. 480-1. St Anthony of Padua, the most celebrated disciple of St Francis of Assisi, was his favorite saint.

chorus, engraved, Poulenc presented the original manuscripts to the Lambiottes.[243]

From the Midi Poulenc traveled to Cologne for the first performance of *Dialogues* in German on 14 July. Two days before the performance Poulenc wrote Bernac that he was *very happy* with the production, which he called perfect in more ways than one. He was particularly pleased that the stage director had gracefully consulted him about numerous details and was receptive to his every wish.[244] The audience accorded the performance seventeen curtain calls, but with the critics he fared poorly.[245] Poulenc thought some sort of schism existed between him and German critics, adding, "If the *Carmélites* had been orchestrated with 10 pianos, 20 vibraphones, 40 celestas, [and] 80 xylophones then these messieurs would be delighted . . ."[246] Following his Cologne visit with Claude Rostand, the pair went "to spend two days with Hervé [Dugardin] wallowing in Darmstadt dodécaca"[247] Poulenc headed to Aix on the 19th where he stayed at the Hotel de la Mule noire[248] before going to Avignon for a few days. The charming Le Prieuré Hotel in Villeneuve-les-Avignon, he said, had beautiful gardens.[249]

While Poulenc was traveling, Benjamin Britten wrote inquiring if he had been serious in suggesting to cellist Maurice Gendron that he would love to go to Aldeburgh to give *Les Mamelles de Tirésias* during the 1958 festival.[250] Britten sought a two-piano version, and Poulenc responded with a resounding *"Yes, Yes, Yes."*[251] He also confided to Robert Douglas Gibson that he had begun a Sonata for Bassoon and Piano (FP 166) and envisioned writing others for oboe and piano, and clarinet and piano.[252] No trace of the bassoon sonata has been found, but the others were surely written during the summer of 1962.

[243] Inscription transcribed in Schmidt 1995, FP 172, p. 481.

[244] 12 July [1957] letter to Bernac from the Touring-Hotel-Bristol in Cologne in Poulenc 1994, 57-23 (Poulenc 1991, no. 283).

[245] 26 Aug. [1957] letter to Boulanger in Poulenc 1994, 57-25.

[246] Unpublished 29 July [1957] letter to Valcarenghi in I-Mr.

[247] Unpublished 29 July [1957] letter to Valcarenghi in I-Mr.

[248] 12 July [1957] letter to Bernac in Poulenc 1994, 57-23 (Poulenc 1991, no. 283) from Cologne, written after witnessing a dress rehearsal.

[249] Unpublished 29 July [1957] letter to Valcarenghi in I-Mr.

[250] Fragment of Britten's 2 July [1957] letter in Poulenc 1994, p. 876, note 1.

[251] 1 Aug. [1957] letter to Britten in Poulenc 1994, 57-24 (Poulenc 1991, no. 284). As will be seen later, Poulenc fulfilled the request, but was unable to be present to play the performance. Poulenc also suggested that Pears sing the role of the Husband (which existed in a version for tenor). A photograph of Pears in this role is in Buckland/Chimènes, figure 13.1, p. 358.

[252] Unpublished 23 Aug. [1957] letter in GB-Lchester. He mentioned the bassoon work in a 26 June [1959] letter to Gibson, but it was never written.

In August Poulenc first composed a series of musical interludes, or "anticipations" as he called them, to rectify timing problems in *Dialogues*. Bernac and Henri Hell liked what he wrote and Poulenc himself was particularly pleased with the addition of music that permitted the crowd to show its agitation before the last entrance of the Carmelites during the finale.[253] By September the new music had been finished and mailed to Dugardin.[254] Poulenc also sent a detailed list of his "Modifications pour les *Dialogues des Carmélites*" to Maurice Jacquemont at about the same time explaining the intention of each interlude, and providing useful directions for the upcoming 8 November 1957 reprise of *Dialogues* at the Opéra.[255] Poulenc's 25 September letter to Guido Valcarenghi also included the following note:

> Now - - - - let's speak about the future - - - I definitely believe that I am going to write *La Voix humaine* !!!! [Hans Werner] Henze has relinquished it. I see this as a providential sign. . . I hope to be ready for 58-59. Cocteau accepts to create the décor and *mise en scène* for the Paris premiere. Given her qualities as an actress and her experience with my music, it is understood that Duval will create this "Voix" if it comes out of me.[256]

Dugardin had suggested that Poulenc compose an opera on this text and when he did, he dedicated it to Hervé and Daisy Dugardin. Poulenc did not actively begin writing music, however, until February 1958.[257]

Poulenc was also looking ahead to new productions of *Dialogues* at Covent Garden in London, again with Margarita Wallmann, and at the Metropolitan Opera in New York. He knew that the New York production was scheduled to be televised and was considering seriously the possibility of flying over for the event. The Covent Garden production premiered on 16 January 1958, but Rudolph Bing of the Met, annoyed that his U.S. premiere would be pre-empted by a 20 September 1957 San Francisco Opera production, refused to produce *Dialogues* for the duration of his tenure as head of that august house.

---

[253] Relevant passages to Valcarenghi in Schmidt 1995, FP 159, p. 447.
[254] Piano transcriptions of the Interludes, first printed separately for insertion into the piano-vocal score, were incorporated in later editions.
[255] [Sept. 1957] letter in Poulenc 1994, 57-28 and Poulenc's letter to Hirsch on this subject, partially transcribed in Poulenc 1994, p. 882, note 1. Before the Paris reprise, *Dialogues* was also given its American premiere in Joseph Machlis' English translation by the San Francisco Opera on 20 Sept., Erich Leinsdorf conducting.
[256] Unpublished 25 Sept. [19]57 letter from Noizay in I-MR.
[257] Schmidt 1995, FP 171, p. 474.

NADIA BOULANGER'S SEVENTIETH BIRTHDAY CELEBRATION

Poulenc, who enjoyed remembering the birthdays of his friends, wrote to Nadia Boulanger in August:

> For your birthday [16 Sept.] I am confectioning an "Ave Maria" [FP 165] for the morning, with *a very modest* organ accompaniment. It is sketched but I do not think I will be able to finish it before my departure (the 1st, return the 9th) for Scotland with Bernac. If I am not ready in time don't think anything about it because alas I do not have the facility of a Milhaud or a Hindemith, and the more I write simple music the more time it takes.[258]

It was Boulanger's seventieth birthday, and Igor Markevitch had grandiose plans. While vacationing in Switzerland she was invited to dine with Igor and Topazia Markevitch at their home in Villars-sur-Ollon (Canton of Valais), a popular health resort with views of the Mont Blanc region. When she arrived, one hundred twenty-five friends from around the globe were waiting for her; the guests included Mr. and Mrs. Robert Woods Bliss from Washington D.C., numerous Polignacs including Marie-Blanche, Yehudi Menuhin from England, Hugues Cuenod and Doda Conrad, Mr. and Mrs. Arthur Sachs from California, and Pierre de Monaco.[259] There were special gifts for her. Pathé-Marconi reissued Boulanger's famous Monteverdi recording from the 1930s, and the invited guests contributed over five thousand dollars with which Conrad purchased a magnificent diamond.[260] There were various musical tributes including one by Jean Françaix, and Poulenc wrote a five-bar fanfare to the text "Vive Nadia, la chère Nadia Boulanger, la très chère Nadia. Alleluia" (FP 167) for piano and voice.[261] Conrad distributed copies to the guests who sang it collectively in her honor, and Poulenc presented the original manuscript to Boulanger. On it, among other words, he wrote: "God be praised, dear Nadia, the Ave Maria is truly better. Be patient. I embrace you tenderly."[262] Poulenc never completed the Ave Maria.

---

[258] 26 Aug. [1957] letter in Poulenc 1994, 57-25.
[259] Spycket 1992, pp. 133-4.
[260] Claire Brook learned from Conrad that he had actually discussed her gift with Boulanger. Conrad asked if she would like "a little Renoir?" "Je ne suis pas une visuelle," she replied. How about a small Mozart manuscript? She thought the printed edition was easier to read. Conrad threw his hands up in dismay. "What *would* you like," he asked. "A diamond would be nice," she replied.
[261] Reproduced in Poulenc 1994, p. 875.
[262] Full inscription in Schmidt 1995, FP 167, p. 468. Poulenc refers to the piece he had promised Boulanger in his 26 Aug. letter. He was unable to be present. Fragment of his 3 June [1957] letter to Topazia Markevitch in Poulenc 1994, p. 877, note 1.

FALL 1957

Early in September he and Bernac went to Edinburgh, on the way stopping at Chester in London on 3 September to drop off his Sonata for Flute and Piano.[263] In Edinburgh they performed three times at the Edinburgh Festival, giving what were misadvertised as first performances of *Le Travail du peintre* and *Deux mélodies* on the 5th, and recording a concert of Gounod *mélodies* on the 6th.[264] White at Noizay later in September, Poulenc started an *Elégie* (FP 168) for horn and piano dedicated to the memory of Denis Brain, the British horn virtuoso, who had been killed in an automobile accident on 1 September.[265] October had been a wicked month. His faithful cook Anna had been quite ill, and Christian Dior's death (24 October in Italy) was a terrible blow for Poulenc, who had known him for thirty years.

In November, Queen Elizabeth of Belgium asked him to serve on the jury of the competition bearing her name. Accordingly, he wrote Mme de Chapdelaine (c/o M Lambiotte) asking for a room at their home for the nights of 2-4 November.[266] Poulenc always enjoyed judging competitions. Once returned from Brussels he attended the reprise at the Paris Opéra of his *Dialogues des Carmélites* and then left on the 11th to spend a month at the Hotel Majestic in Cannes.[267] While there he proposed a revision of his two contributions to *Les Mariés de la Tour Eiffel*, composed in 1921. Because the orchestral score was missing, Poulenc reorchestrated his two numbers dating his work on "Discours du général" as Cannes, November 1957 and "La Baigneuse de Trouville" simply as 1957.[268] Three days after his arrival, however, suffering from some undisclosed malady, he took a plane back to Paris "on the double" as he told Picasso.[269] Poulenc wrote Robert Douglas Gibson from Cannes:

> Actually I am finishing my Elégie for horn and piano which, of course,
> I intend for you. You know that I must play it at the beginning of

[263] Unpublished 23 and 30 Aug. [1957] letters to Gibson in GB-Lchester. He requested £250 for the Sonata from Gibson.
[264] 12 Sept. [1957] letter to Markevitch in Poulenc 1994, 57-27. The actual premiere of *Le Travail* had been given on 1 Apr. 1957.
[265] Schmidt 1996, FP 168. The *Elégie* experiments briefly with a twelve-note row.
[266] Unpublished 29 Sept. [19]57 and 18 Oct. [1957] letters addressed to "Mme. de Chapdelaine, secrétariat de Mr. Lambiotte" (and signed jokingly "Isabelle La Note secrétaire du maitre Fr. Poulenc").
[267] Unpublished 1 Nov. [1957] letter to Rose Dercourt-Plaut in US-NH. On 14 Nov. he wrote Gibson stating he would remain until 16 Dec. Unpublished 15 Nov. [1957] letter in GB-Lchester.
[268] Schmidt 1996, FP 23, pp.71-2. Poulenc became reinvolved with this work in 1959.
[269] 16 Dec. [1957] letter to Picasso in Poulenc 1994, 57-31: "dare-dare." Poulenc had hoped to visit Picasso to see Picasso's portrait. See above.

January on the BBC. Since the *Carmélites* will be performed on 16 January, I will make a two-week stay.[270]

He chaffed at the slow pace Chester took printing the Sonata for Flute and Piano and *Elégie*, complaining that both were in demand by performers.[271] It is not surprising that Poulenc wilted emotionally after such a grueling time.[272]

RECORDINGS DURING THE *DIALOGUES* YEARS

The *Dialogues* years (1953-7), though not particularly conducive to recording projects, nevertheless yielded several of note. Along with private recordings of actual performances made with Bernac, Rampal, and others, Poulenc released the following commercial recordings:

Composers	Works	Performers	Date/Label
Debussy, Roussel, & Poulenc	*Mélodies & Chansons*	G.Touraine/ Poulenc	1954: Boîte à musique
Satie	Piano Music	Poulenc	1955: Boîte à musique
Chabrier	Piano Duets	M. Meyer/ Poulenc	1955: Discophiles français
Poulenc	*Le Bal masqué*	Bernac/Poulenc Frémaux, conducting	1956: Véga
Poulenc	*Histoire de Babar*	P. Fresnay/Poulenc	1957: Discophiles français
Poulenc	*Mélodies*	R. Dercourt-Plaut/ Poulenc	1957: Turnabout[273]

* * *

Poulenc's parting shot of 1957, contained in a post-Christmas card to Boulanger reads: "I detest the piano music of Stockhausen!!! And you?"[274]

[270] Unpublished 14 Nov. [1957] letter to Gibson in GB-Lchester. The work was not actually premiered until 17 Feb. 1958.

[271] Excerpts from Poulenc's unpublished letters to Gibson in Schmidt 1995, FP 168, p. 470.

[272] One further saga, an exchange with Pierre Souvtchinsky concerning the Paris revival of *Dialogues*, is discussed in Poulenc 1994. See Poulenc's 15 Nov. [1957] letter to Souvtchinsky from Cannes (57-30) and the several excerpts of other letters in note 1.

[273] Details in Appendix 3.

[274] [27 Dec. 1955] card to Boulanger in Poulenc 1994, 57-32.

XIII

In the Wake of Dialogues des Carmélites, *Equilibrium Regained: 1958-1960*

ENGLAND AND COMPOSITION OF *LA VOIX HUMAINE:* JANUARY-MARCH 1958

January 1958 began with a flurry of activity in London of performances, broadcasts, and the Covent Garden production of *Dialogues des Carmélites*. It also began with an acrimonious exchange between Poulenc's English agent Ibbs and Tillett Limited (represented by Audrey Hurst) and Norman Carrell, Esq. (representing the BBC). The dispute concerned Poulenc's performance fee. Early in his career he received twenty-five guineas for a BBC performance, which was raised to thirty-five in 1946. Unchanged for years, the fee no longer matched Poulenc's position and prestige. A BBC offer to raise the fee five guineas was resoundly rejected in a 1 Jan. 1958 letter suggesting that fifty (not forty) would be appropriate for a solo performance.[1] Remaining contracts for 1958, however, all reflect the original thirty-five guinea fee.

On 5 January Poulenc and Février played the Concerto in D minor with the London Symphony, Alexander Gibson conducting.[2] Poulenc then recorded several chamber works on the 16th (Sonata for Flute and Piano with Gareth Morris) and 18th (*Elégie* with Neill Sanders in the afternoon; Sextet with the Brain Wind Ensemble in the

---

[1] Unpublished letter from Hurst to Carrell in GB-Lbbc. The contract for a Light Programme on 12 Jan. was also returned.
[2] Contract in GB-Lbbc (Francis Poulenc Artist file 1b) which called for two three-hour rehearsals on the 5th.

evening).[3] Some performances were aired on the 17th. Poulenc also attended rehearsals for the English premiere of *Dialogues*, which took place on the 16th. This production, with *mise en scène* by Margarita Wallmann, décor and costumes by Georges Wakhevitch, was the same as that at La Scala except that it was sung in English. It featured Elsie Morrison (Blanche), Jean Watson (Mme de Croissy), Joan Sutherland (Mme Lidoine), Sylvia Fisher (Mère Marie), and Jeanette Sinclair (Sœur Constance), with the Czech-born Swiss conductor Rafaël Kubelik on the podium. Poulenc's thoughts about this production are unknown, but Edward Sackville-West, consultant to Covent Garden, was thrilled.[4]

Dialogues was also honored by the Music Critics Circle of New York as the best opera performed in New York City during the past year.[5] It won over his own *Les Mamelles de Tirésias* and Britten's *Albert Herring*.[6]

Once returned from a Milan conference, some of February was spent in Cannes.[7] To Poulenc's sorrow, his old friend Marie-Blanche de Polignac died on the 14th. She had played an important role in both his and Boulanger's careers, and the two commiserated with each other.[8] On a more positive note, Poulenc seriously contemplated setting *La Voix humaine* (FP 171), Jean Cocteau's forty-minute monologue, written in 1927 and originally created in 1930 by the Belgian actress Berthe Bovy at the Comédie-Française.[9] He had earlier set Cocteau texts in *Toréador* (1918-32), *Cocardes* (1919), and *Le Gendarme incompris* (1920), but had not been attracted to any other Cocteau text except *Plain-chant*. Shortly after returning from Milan Poulenc told Hervé Dugardin: "They are waiting for *La Voix*. We will have [Maria] Callas in Milan and Glyndebourne, [Denise] Duval in Paris."[10]

Poulenc continued to worry about his health in the aftermath of *Dialogues*, but his creativity was unaffected. Acupuncture treatments

[3] Contract in GB-Lbbc (Francis Poulenc Artist file 1b).
[4] 29 Jan. 1958 letter to Poulenc in Poulenc 1994, 58-2 (Poulenc 1991, no. 286).
[5] Performed in New York by the N.B.C. Television Opera Theatre.
[6] *New York Times* (15 Jan. 1958), 23. *Mamelles* had been given at Town Hall on 26 Feb. 1957 by the American Opera Society with a cast featuring Duval, Martial Singher, and Paul Franko.
[7] Unpublished 6 Feb. [19]58 letter to Mme Lambiotte from Cannes in US-NYlambiotte-donhauser.
[8] [18 Feb. 1958] letter from Poulenc in Poulenc 1994, 58-3.
[9] The premiere of *La Voix humaine* in Paris created a scandal involving shouts from the audience, the ejection of Paul Eluard, and words between Cocteau and Eluard. Later actresses who championed the work include Ingrid Bergman, Jo Ann Sayers, and Lillebil Ibsen. See Steegmuller 1970, pp. 400-01.
[10] See the fragment of Poulenc's [Feb. 1958] letter in Poulenc 1994, p. 888, note 2. From the 22nd to the 25th he was in Brussels to play a concert with Paul Collaer.

in Cannes did some good, but he was still terribly nervous.[11] Nevertheless, in only a few days he amazed his old friend Richard Chanlaire by sketching a plan and some music for *La Voix*.[12] He particularly fretted over the possibility that he sounded like Edith Piaf in one section, a slow waltz in C minor, where "Elle" recounts attempting to poison herself. Poulenc told Bernac that he was leaving for Rome on a Monday (10 March?) and that "in theory" he would be staying in Rome for two weeks with Mimi Pecci-Blunt. He also asked Bernac's opinion of Henri Hell's new biography and said he would be dining with Pierre Fournier that evening in Cannes and hearing him play.[13]

The reason for Poulenc's Roman sojourn was another production of *Dialogues*, opening on 17 March.[14] Like the January performance in London, it was a Wakhevitch-Wallmann collaboration conducted by Franco Capuana.[15] Poulenc found the performance a splendid success but said he had felt like a sleep walker. He intended to return to the Hotel Majestic in Cannes on the 21st.[16] Progress on *La Voix* was swift after his return. By late March, having thrown all his medications (except the sedatives Soneryl and Equanil) out the window, the entire opera was sketched.[17] Poulenc wrote about its erotic and autobiographical qualities:

> I found, and this is the secret, *all* my themes. Two are extravagantly *erotic* (Goléa, Goldbeck, and Souvtch[insky] plug up your ears!). They smell of sperm, of between the thighs. When Elle notices that he is calling from some "Ox on the roof" [bar] there is a whiff of incredible 1920s Parisian jazz. The theme of the lie (If you were lying out of kindness) is horrible (that weighs a ton). Fundamental: I found all the end, coming from a distance, when they no longer have anything to say to each other, before and after ("I have the cord around my neck"). Everything will be ready to write when I leave Cannes. I think I will compose it very quickly at Noizay in May. Blanche was me, and Elle is me again, and ... Louis [Gautier], by anticipation, be-

---

There is a reference to his having played Satie in Brussels in Poulenc's "Saint-Raphaël, Pâques 1958" [6 Apr.] letter to Bernac in Poulenc 1994, 58-8 (Poulenc 1991, no. 288).

[11] "Jeudi" [probably 6 Mar. 1958] letter to Bernac in Poulenc 1994, 58-4 (Poulenc 1991, no. 287).

[12] For a comparison of Cocteau's play and Poulenc's libretto see Buckland/Chimènes: m, pp. 325-8.

[13] Hell's biography is Hell 1958.

[14] [17 Mar. 1958] postcard to Marie-Ange in Poulenc 1994, 58-5.

[15] All the early performances in Italy were sung in Italian.

[16] [21 Mar. 1958] letter to Girard in Poulenc 1994, 58-6.

[17] "Dimanche" 30 Mar. 1958 letter to Dugardin in Poulenc 1994, 58-7. He also reduced his dosages of both these drugs.

cause life will take him from me in one way or another, that angel. I am writing to you from his sheepfold while he prunes his olive trees. He is charming to me and (except at *certain moments!*) a tender, polite, and deferential son.[18]

Poulenc also outlined the instrumentation for Milan: fifteen winds and brass, harp, percussion, and nineteen strings (6, 4, 3, 4, 2) which would have to be cut to 5, 4, 3, 3, 2 to make the Milan limit of thirty-four players.[19]

> Cocteau approves of my entire plan [he told Bernac] which struc-
> tures the text into "phases". (Phase of the dog, the lie, the overdose.)
> I have already found many ideas. Two themes, among others, which
> *these messieurs* will find quite scandalous: one amorous and the other
> erotic. For the responses, I found the rhythm quite instinctively. I
> have no fears about the orchestral volume (medium). The ensemble
> is horrific. "Elle" tells of her overdose to the rhythm of a sad waltz in
> the style of Sibelius.[20]

Poulenc's compositional method for *La Voix* differed from that of most of his other works. It resembled the way he worked when he was younger and sought Landowska's advice constantly while com-posing *Concert champêtre*. Now, it was Denise Duval who watched the opera grow day by day.

> *La Voix humaine* was an astonishing experience for me [Duval noted]
> because I saw Francis Poulenc write it page by page, bar by bar, for
> me, with his flesh, but also with my heart wounds: we were then
> both in the midst of sentimental drama, we were crying, and this *Voix
> humaine* has been like a diary of our tears. I was working then with
> my friend Janine Reiss, who is the most marvelous professor, and
> who is a midwife not only of the voice but of the soul. Each day
> Francis Poulenc brought us one or two new pages of his score, the ink
> hardly dry, and, straight away Janine and I threw ourselves at it. We
> worked detail by detail, in front of Poulenc who stayed to listen to us.
> Occasionally I asked him to alter a note or a passage, in order to find
> something more suitable for my voice. This was a unique experi-
> ence, participating in the gestation and very birth of a work.[21]

Despite his preoccupation with *La Voix humaine* even as he at-tended performances of *Dialogues* in Rome, Poulenc composed three

---

[18] "Dimanche" 30 Mar. 1958 letter to Dugardin in Poulenc 1994, 58-7. The themes, several of which first appeared in *Dialogues des Carmélites*, are printed in Buckland/Chimènes: m, pp. 336-8. Concerning Gautier and Bagnols-en-Forêt see fn. 87.

[19] See fn. 30 below for the final instrumentation.

[20] "Saint-Raphaël, Pâques 1958" [6 Apr.] letter in Poulenc 1994, 58-8 (Poulenc 1991, no. 288).

[21] L'Avant scène 1983, p. 134.

other pieces during March visits to the Hotel Majestic: *Une chanson de porcelaine* (FP 169) for Jane Bathori's eightieth birthday, and piano Improvisations 13 and 14 (FP 170), dedicated to Mme Lambiotte and Henri Hell respectively.[22] The Bathori *mélodie*, Poulenc's last setting of an Eluard text, was fittingly drawn from *A toute épreuve* (1930) the source of his first Eluard set in 1935. Bathori, the constant champion of generations of French composers, received the following tribute when Poulenc sent her the manuscript:

> Here, finally, is your *mélodie*. I hope that you will like it, because I created it with tenderness for you, while thinking about our wonderful past. Presently I am composing *La Voix humaine*. I hope that it will be as horrific as one can wish. Who would have thought back then that I would become a somber musician.[23]

In April *Dialogues* had Poulenc "on the road" again. He spent three days in Lisbon, Portugal where the opera was performed at the San Carlo theater on the 18th. From the Hotel Tivoli he updated Rose Dercourt-Plaut on the past few months.[24] Complaining about constant travels occasioned by his opera, and about his dependency on barbiturates or tranquilizers, he said he would fly back to Paris on the 21st and go immediately to Noizay. While in Lisbon Poulenc played a portion of *La Voix* for Casa Fuerte and a friend. Both were reduced to tears, he said, noting that the opera was already being sought by numerous opera houses.

Once in Noizay Poulenc worked hard to complete *La Voix*.[25] By the beginning of June he cabled Hervé Dugardin that the opera was finished.[26] Similar announcements were sent to Paul Collaer,[27] Stéphane Audel,[28] and Rose Lambiotte, who was told: "It is the saddest opera, the most heartrending, the most moving . . . that one could hear. Prepare a pile of handkerchiefs for the premiere."[29] He wrote Valcarenghi that he had completed *La Voix* in record time and set aside the *brouillon* until July when he would recopy the opera.[30]

Poulenc also looked forward to launching a new vocal partnership now that he and Bernac were only occasionally performing to-

[22] Improvisations 11 and 12 were written years earlier in 1941.
[23] Undated postcard reproduced in Cuneo-Laurent, p. 150. "La Souris" was written for Marya Freund's eightieth birthday.
[24] 20 Apr. [19]58 letter in Poulenc 1994, 58-9.
[25] "Mardi "[May 1958] letter to Girard. Poulenc 1994, 58-10 (Poulenc1991, no. 289).
[26] [2 June 1958] telegram in Poulenc 1994, 58-11 and the unpublished 2 June 1958 telegram to Valcarenghi in I-Mr.
[27] [4 June 1958] letter to Collaer in Poulenc 1994, 58-12 and Collaer, 1996, 58-3.
[28] 9 June 1958 letter from Paris in US-TUshapiro and Schmidt 1995, FP 171, p. 479.
[29] Unpublished 4 June [1958] letter to Mme Lambiotte in US-NYlambiotte-donhauser, which erroneously indicates the opera was finished on the 3rd.
[30] Unpublished 13 June [1958] letter in I-Mr. Poulenc included the instrumenta-

gether. "The Duval-Poulenc team loses its virginity in Bordeaux on the 15th," he told Simone Girard, "Denise in top form."[31] The recital actually took place on the 16th at the Château de Labrède, and included operatic arias by Gounod, Chabrier, and Poulenc as well as *mélodies* by Debussy, Ravel, and Poulenc.[32] This new team performed in Europe and for his penultimate American tour in 1960.

During the second week of June, he composed "O proles Hispaniae," the second of four *Laudes de Saint Antoine de Padoue* while in Brive. From Paris, he wrote Benjamin Britten on 13 June, the Feast of St Anthony and the day Charles Mackerras conducted the two-piano version of *Les Mamelles de Tirésias* at Aldeburgh with Britten and Viola Tunnard (substituting for Poulenc) at the two pianos. He excused his absence saying that his doctor had forbidden him to go near the sea.[33] Poulenc, however, did go to Oxford, England to receive the degree Doctor *honoris causa* on 25 June. On the way he stayed with his friends Honor and Vere Pilkington at 28 Hamilton Terrace the evening of the 23rd, and on his return he stopped in London for several days lunching with his publisher Robert Douglas Gibson on the 27th.[34]

Summer took on a familiar pattern: a cure at Evian, a brief stay in Aix-en-Provence, three weeks in Tourrettes-sur-Loup followed by almost a month at Noizay.[35] Paramount in his mind was copying out and completing the piano-vocal score of *La Voix*. Providentially, this task was completed precisely at noon on Thursday, 7 August. The number seven had played an important role in his life (he had been born on the 7th (but not at noon like Mélisande), and he had used precisely the number of pages existing in his spiral notebook, not one more or less.[36] He played the opera for Nice Radio that

---

tion, which was the same as he had listed before (see above) except that the strings included 8 vn., 4 vla., 4 vc., and 2 d.b. for a total of thirty-five instruments.
[31] "Mardi [May 1958] letter in Poulenc 1994, 58-10 (Poulenc 1991, no. 289).
[32] Recorded and commercially released on CLIO 001. See Appendix 3. Concerning the date see Berenguer, p. 67 and the record liner notes.
[33] 13 June [1958] letter to Britten in Poulenc 1994, 58-13 (Poulenc 1991, no. 290) and unpublished 13 June [1958] letter to Gibson in GB-Lchester. Poulenc shared an aversion to the sea with Serge Diaghilev.
[34] Unpublished 13 June [1958] letter to Gibson in GB-Lchester. Honor worked for Sotheby and was an amateur harpsichordist who appeared on recitals in and around London from at least the early 1930s. Later, after they moved to Portugal, Vere was killed in a tragic automobile accident, which her husband survived.
[35] Unpublished 25 July [1958] letter to Rose Dercourt-Plaut from Aix-en-Provence in US-NH, his [July 1958] letter to Ardoin from Evian in Poulenc 1994, 58-14, and his 11 Aug. [1958] letter to Bernac in Poulenc 1994, 58-16 (Poulenc 1991, no. 291). Poulenc was in Aix from about 21-5 July, in Tourrettes until 21 Aug., in Paris that same evening (having arrived by plane), and then in Noizay until 19 Sept.
[36] "Samedi" [9 Aug. 1958] letter to Dugardin in Poulenc 1994, 58-15.

afternoon, on the 11th for Cocteau, and the 13th for Daisy Dugardin (she cried and was unable to talk for five minutes), who carried *La Voix* to her husband in Paris.[37] From Tourrettes Poulenc occasionally went to the Menton summer festival. By 11 August he had heard two concerts, one of Vivaldi concerti by I Musici, which bored him considerably, and one of Schubert quartets by the Hungarian Quartet, which he found admirable.[38] He sent the manuscript of *La Voix* to someone named Astrof to be photocopied, and noted that Jean Cocteau was delighted with the score and had already prepared décors for Paris, Milan, and Duval's tours. He hoped to play the score for him at the Villa d'Este during his Italian trip. "I thirst for Italy," Poulenc said, "and I think that October there is delicious."[39]

With the piano score dispatched to Ricordi in Paris, where Burchardt would engrave it using the printed libretto to decipher his poorly written text, Poulenc began orchestrating on 25 August and completed work on 19 September. He wanted to be free of *La Voix* by his departure to serve on a Ricordi jury convened to choose an opera for La Scala.[40] The day he finished his orchestration he mailed corrected proofs of the Sonata for Flute and Piano and the *Elégie* to Robert Douglas Gibson in London. His health improved and he felt the time at Noizay had been most fruitfully spent![41]

Poulenc asked Guido Valcarenghi to arrange for a car from the airport, to have lunch with him, to purchase a first class train ticket on the 4:00 pm train to Venice, and to withdraw 300,000 liras from his account.[42] Poulenc often kept accounts with publishers or friends which he tapped when traveling.[43] His stay in Venice at Lili Volpi's marvelous palace pleased him enormously and he heard the premiere of Stravinsky's *Threni: id est lamentationes Jeremiae Prophetae* at the Sala della Scuola Grande di San Rocco under the composer's

---

[37] "Mercredi" [13 Aug. 1958] letter to Girard in Poulenc 1994, 58-17.
[38] 11 Aug. [1958] letter to Bernac in Poulenc 1994, 58-16 (Poulenc 1991, no. 291) and "mercredi" [13 Aug. 1958] letter to Girard in Poulenc 1994, 58-17.
[39] Unpublished 17 Aug. [1958] letter to Valcarenghi from Tourrettes in I-Mr. On 6 Dec. 1958 Cocteau sent Poulenc a drawing and description of Duval's costume. Cocteau's letter in Poulenc 1994, 58-20 (Poulenc 1991, no. 292).
[40] Inscription on Poulenc's holograph manuscript quoted in Schmidt 1995, FP 171, p. 474. Poulenc sent Valcarenghi a telegram from Noizay on 20 Sept. indicating his arrival in Milan at noon on 22 Sept. via an Italian plane. (In I-Mr.)
[41] Unpublished 19 Sept. [1958] letter to Gibson in GB-Lchester and his unpublished 19 Sept. 1958 letter to Mme de Chapdelaine (c/o M Lambiotte) in US-NYlambiotte-donhauser. Poulenc included a picture of himself in his Oxford doctoral gown and three newspaper clippings about his honors.
[42] Unpublished 13 Sept. [1958] letter to Valcarenghi from Noizay in I-Mr.
[43] Such accounts were kept by Chester in London, Ricordi in Milan, his friends Rose Dercourt-Plaut and Franco Colombo (a Ricordi representative) in New York, and Zavarini-Foetish in Lausanne, among others.

direction.[44] From Venice he was driven in Volpi's car with the composer Goffredo Petrassi to the Villa d'Este in Cernobbio on Lake
Como, arriving on 28 September. There the Ricordi jury—
Ildobrando Pizzetti, Frank Martin, Goffredo Petrassi, and Poulenc
—reviewed what Poulenc called "123 stupid scores, the majority of
which were revoltingly amateurish. . . ."[45] The jury sheet, also signed
by Eugenio Montale and Werner Egk, awarded no prize. Poulenc
returned to Venice with Louis Gautier by car on Monday the 6th,
expecting to be in Florence the next Saturday. The pair did not arrive back in Paris until 21 October.

From St Raphaël on 16 October he wrote Rose Dercourt-Plaut a
letter filled with news. The winter season of operatic performances
was shaping up nicely with *La Voix humaine* opening in Paris at the
Opéra-Comique on 6 February 1959 and at La Piccola Scala in Milan
on the 18th. Also, a spate of *Dialogues* performances were scheduled
for Barcelona (January), Vienna (12 February), Ghent (13 February),
Naples (mid-February), Catania (early April), Genoa (23 April),
Palermo, and Geneva, with a reprise in London (23 June). He also
planned to go to Barcelona on 8 November 1958 for a *Stabat Mater*
performance (airfare and Ritz Hotel paid!).[46] Like 1957, 1958 also
closed with personal tragedies. "Much sadness at the end of the
year (death of Marcelle Meyer and of Duval's husband). . . ."[47]

ENCORE *DIALOGUES:* JANUARY-APRIL 1959

The new year began with high honors and serious problems. On 7
January, *The New York Times* announced Poulenc's election as an honorary member (along with François Mauriac, Marc Chagall, and Sir
Harold Nicolson) of the American Academy of Arts and Letters
and its affiliated National Academy of Arts and Letters.[48] Since
Poulenc considered America his best audience, the honor pleased
him enormously. On the home front, however, Cocteau was too ill
to come to Paris so Poulenc had to take Denise Duval to Nice for a
week's work on *La Voix*.[49] He then attended the first *Dialogues* of
the new year in Barcelona.

I came here for the *Carmélites*, of which they have given a pathetic
performance. Disgraceful orchestra. Duval, Scharley, and Crespin

---

[44] "Samedi" [4 Oct. 1958] letter to Bernac from Villa d'Este in Poulenc 1994, 58-19.
Poulenc said Stravinsky conducted badly, but he had found the work moving.

[45] "Samedi" [4 Oct. 1958] letter to Bernac in Poulenc 1994, 58-19.

[46] "Samedi" [4 Oct. 1958] letter to Bernac in Poulenc 1994, 58-19.

[47] Unpublished [late 1958] letter in US-NH. Concerning Duval's loss see also his
unpublished 17 Dec. [19]58 letter to M Lambiotte in US-NYlambiotte-donhauser.

[48] See p. 66. Induction ceremonies were reported in the 21 May 1959 issue, p. 28.

[49] "Mercredi" letter to Valcarenghi (received by Ricordi on 28 Jan. [1959]). For
Duval's recollections of her work with Cocteau see L'Avant scène 1983, p. 134.

remarkable, but all the others (quite crude) 36th rate. Fortunately I will have the *Carmélites* on 12 February in Vienna with Zeefreed [Irmgard Seefried] and all the great ladies.[50]

From Barcelona he returned to Paris and then went to Nice because Cocteau was still too ill to travel. Poulenc spent a day with him finalizing production details for *La Voix humaine*.[51] The opera received excellent notice from the Parisian press. Milhaud, among others, thought the orchestration marvelous and Duval sublime.[52] Milan was to be conquered next. Poulenc laid out his February travel plans to Guido Valcarenghi. He and Duval planned to arrive in Milan by air on Monday, 9 February and then Poulenc would depart for Vienna on the 12th returning to Milan the evening of the 14th for the first two performances of *La Voix*. Then he intended to go to Naples for the performance of *Dialogues*, returning to Milan before flying back to Paris.[53] One casualty of his busy schedule was the 13 February Ghent performance of *Dialogues*, which he could not attend.[54]

Poulenc found the Naples performance of *Dialogues*, the first with Rosanna Carteri as Blanche, sensational.[55] From Naples he went to Nice on 7 March and then on the 9th he and Bernac performed in Avignon at the Société avignonnaise de concerts. The Bernac/ Poulenc duo also gave a Marseilles recital during which Poulenc played his Trio with oboist Pierre Pierlot and bassoonist Maurice Allard, and his Sonata for Flute and Piano with Maxence Larrieu.[56] While in Cannes during early March he completed the last two *Laudes de Saint Antoine de Padoue*: "Laus Regi plena gaudio" and "Si quaeris."

[50] 30 Jan. [1959] letter from the Hotel Ritz in Barcelona in Poulenc 1994, 59-1 (Poulenc 1991, no. 294).
[51] [1 Feb. 1959] letter to Aragon in Poulenc 1994, 59-2 (Poulenc 1991, no. 295). Aragon published this letter in lieu of the article he had requested of Poulenc about *La Voix*. The letter appeared in the 6 Feb. 1959 issue of *Les Lettres françaises*.
[52] Fragment of Milhaud's [Feb. 1959] letter in Poulenc 1994, pp. 909-10, note 1. Duval prevailed on Poulenc to let her omit one section of the text which dealt with the dog. She felt its inclusion hindered the dramatic flow. Her description of this passage, during an interview with this author, sent her into paroxysms of laughter.
[53] Poulenc also arranged to purchase a ticket for Louis (Nice-Milan 14 Feb., Milan-Nice 19 Feb.).
[54] Unpublished 17 Dec. [19]58 letter to M. Lambiotte in US-NYlambiotte-donhauser. He received a copy of a 27 Feb. 1959 letter from M R. Desprechind who had attended the performance which called the performance exceptional. Copy in US-NYlambiotte-donhauser.
[55] "Mercredi" [4 Mar. 1959] letter to Manceaux in Poulenc 1994, 59-4 (Poulenc 1991, no. 296). He also complimented the tenor and the orchestra. Poulenc intended to get back to work, but returning to Paris was out of the question.
[56] Unpublished [28 Mar. 1959] letter to M Lambiotte from Cannes in US-NYlambiotte-donhauser and Poulenc 1994, p. 900, note 2.

He went to Rome for a week with Mimi Pecci-Blunt but was again in Cannes on the 28th before going to Catania on the 29th.[57] During this period he had given some thought to setting Cocteau's *La Machine infernale*, but abandoned the idea, finding the work "a little too literary."[58]

Poulenc attended the 8 April performance of *Dialogues* in Catania, which he found admirable; the cast was the best he had heard.[59] "As for Carteri (Blanche) she is as miraculous as Denise in *La Voix*," he told Bernard Gavoty, "Certainly don't say this to Duval."[60] While there he was presented with the Bellini Centenary Medal.[61] Poulenc was so delighted with Capuana's conducting that he vowed to attend the 23 April Genoa production, which he would also conduct.[62] After that he contemplated going to Geneva on 8 May and to Vienna on 1 June. But important concerts lay ahead in May.

SWAN-SONG OF THE BERNAC/POULENC DUO IN MAY 1959

On 14 May Poulenc accompanied Jean-Pierre Rampal in the Sonata for Flute and Piano, and Duval in excerpts from *Mamelles*, *Dialogues*, and *La Voix* at the Salle Gaveau. The concert, for Jeunesses Musicales de France, was televised, and Poulenc was interviewed by Bernard Gavoty. Two weeks later, on the 27th, he celebrated his sixtieth birthday with a concert at the Salle Gaveau joined by Bernac, Rampal, Pierlot, Allard, and the French Radio Choir directed by Yvonne Gouverné. The ambitious all-Poulenc program included the Trio, *Sept chansons*, Sonata for Flute and Piano, *Le Travail du peintre*, and *Figure humaine*. Aware that this would be their final performance together, Bernac had earlier implored Poulenc to "Come back [from Cannes] in time . . . because it is imperative this concert be a success."[63] A remarkable twenty-four year span, begun formally on 3 April 1935 in Paris, was finally at an end.

Yesterday [Poulenc wrote] I appeared on the stage with Bernac for

[57] Unpublished [28 Mar. 1959] letter to M Lambiotte in US-NYlambiotte-donhauser.
[58] 10 Mar. [1959] letter to Milhaud in Poulenc 1994, 59-5 and 13 Apr. [1959] letter to Dugardin in Poulenc 1994, p. 910, note 5. Poulenc mentioned this project to Munch in a 23 May 1959 letter in Poulenc 1994, 59-10 (Poulenc 1991, no. 298).
[59] Apparently he stayed only for the first performance before returning to the Midi. See Poulenc's unpublished 13 Apr. [1959] letter to Valcarenghi in I-Mr.
[60] 18 Apr. [1959] letter from Bagnols-en-Forêt in Poulenc 1994, 59-6.
[61] Unpublished 8 Apr.and 13 Apr. [1959] letters to Valcarenghi in I-Mr.
[62] Poulenc was in Bagnols-en-Forêt on 17 Apr. Unpublished postcard to M Lambiotte in US-NYlambiotte-donhauser. He did attend the Genoa performance as his 23 May 1959 letter to Charles Munch from the Hôtel Bristol Palace in Genoa attests. Poulenc 1994, 59-10 (Poulenc 1991, no. 298).
[63] Bernac's 23 Apr. [1959] letter in Poulenc 1994, 59-7 (Poulenc 1991, no. 297).

the last time. He sang better than ever at this concert at the Salle Gaveau on the occasion of my sixtieth birthday!!! The public accorded a *triumph* to this exemplary artist. My fingers trembled a little in beginning *Le Travail du peintre*. Then I regained control of myself. The end of such a fraternal association is very sad.[64]

Immediately after the recital, Poulenc was again on the road seeing "a splendid *Siegfried*, by Herbert von Karajan, a memorable *Wozzeck*, and an impeccable *Carmélites*."[65] There had been eleven Viennese performances of *Dialogues* that season and fourteen more were projected for the 1959-60 season. After *Dialogues* Poulenc went to Bagnols-en-Forêt before returning to Paris on the 16th to see André Jolivet's *La Vérité de Jeanne* at the Théâtre des Champs-Élysées.[66]

Reflecting in mid-June on the May concert, performances of *La Voix* and *Dialogues*, and the positive effect all this had had on his own psyche, Poulenc wrote:

I must tell you that the success of *La Voix*, of *Les Carmélites* in Vienna (I will tell you more later) and finally of the concert, have put me at peace with myself, that is to say with Monsieur Poulenc. What memories I treasure of 27 May! And if my heart was full of tears, what joy Pierre's triumph was for me. There was not a single person who did not salute, hat doffed, that *great* artist. I sense that he is so profoundly happy, notwithstanding his pretense at detachment, that I think this has contributed to his revival. The day before yesterday he told me on the telephone, "I feel better and better." As for me, old hustler— God knows how much care I took of every detail—that concert was of great significance in setting things straight. Not because I am intoxicated with the idea of being a *grrrrrand musicien*, but it exasperates me nevertheless that so many people think of me as nothing more than a *petit maître érotique*. [. . .] Well, Vienna was marvelous, not the sublime blaze of Catania but a very cold yet *impeccable* performance (post mortem) of a standard work, and all this before a full and enthusiastic house, with not a friend among them!!![67]

The last sentence confirms Poulenc's constant need for the approbation of friends.

---

[64] Poulenc 1993, p. 62 (Poulenc 1989, pp. 108-09), May 1959 entry.
[65] 4 June [1959] letter to Rouart in Poulenc 1994, 59-11 (Poulenc 1991, no. 294). See also the [June 1959] letter to Rostand in Poulenc 1994, 59-12 (Poulenc 1991, no. 299). According to his 21 May [1959] letter to Milhaud in Poulenc 1994, 59-8 he left for Vienna on 30 May.
[66] [June 1959] letter to Rostand and "samedi" [13 June 1959] letter to Girard in Poulenc 1994, 59-12 and 13 (Poulenc 1991, nos. 299 and 300) respectively.
[67] "Samedi" [13 June 1959] letter to Girard from Bagnols-en-Forêt in Poulenc 1994, 59-13 (Poulenc 1991, no. 300).

A KOUSSEVITZKY FOUNDATION COMMISSION: *GLORIA*

Two other projects occupied Poulenc in March 1959: a Koussevitzky Foundation commission and a recording of *Les Mariés de la Tour Eiffel*. At first, his sole aim was to get back to work.[68] In the midst of the hubbub surrounding *Dialogues,* he thought about a long-standing offer from the Koussevitzky Foundation for a commission. Mme Koussevitzky first wanted a symphony, which was not Poulenc's forte and he knew it. "I am extremely touched by the Koussevitzky Foundation commission, unfortunately, for the moment, a symphonic work is not in my intentions," he replied.[69] Next they proposed an organ concerto, but composing a second one interested him not at all.[70] Finally they proposed a work of his own choosing. On 13 April Poulenc wrote to Hervé Dugardin: "I am trying to think about a *Gloria* (FP 177) before definitively proposing it to Boston. I am rusty, but it is always thus. Today for the first time I found four worthwhile bars."[71] Five days later he told Bernard Gavoty that he was working on a *Gloria* for choir, one soloist, and orchestra in the style of Vivaldi.[72] Margaret Grant in Washington DC informed him on 7 July that the Advisory Board had approved a $2,000 commission.[73] Poulenc accepted the terms and started writing the *Gloria.*[74] Following past practice, he requested Bernac's assistance with the text.[75] Work on the piano-vocal score lasted from May through December 1959, with the orchestration extending into June 1960.

In May 1959 Mica Salabert and the record company Véga rekindled their interest in recording *Les Mariés de la Tour Eiffel* with Milhaud conducting.[76] Earlier the original manuscripts had been located in Rolf de Maré's collection in the Stockholm Dance Museum. Poulenc had already reorchestrated his two numbers in November 1957, and Auric was anxious to reorchestrate his. Poulenc invited Germaine Tailleferre to participate, asking her to complete work by October if she was interested.[77] Later, Marius Constant reorchestrated the ballet for chamber orchestra and performed it in New York.[78]

---

[68] "Mercredi" [4 Mar. 1959] letter to Brigitte Manceaux in Poulenc 1994, 59-4 (Poulenc 1991, no. 296).
[69] Schmidt 1995, FP 177, p. 490.
[70] 21 May [1959] letter to Milhaud in Poulenc 1994, 59-8.
[71] Fragment of Poulenc's letter in Poulenc 1994, p. 911, note 3.
[72] 18 Apr. [1959] letter in Poulenc 1994, 59-6.
[73] Schmidt 1995, FP 177, p. 491. Poulenc's request that half the fee be paid in advance was rejected as contrary to Foundation guidelines.
[74] Schmidt 1995, FP 177, p. 491.
[75] Bernac's 23 Apr. [1959] letter to Poulenc in Poulenc 1994, 59-7 (Poulenc 1991, no. 297). Bernac returned the text and translation to Poulenc with this letter.
[76] The work was finally recorded in 1966 and issued as Adès 14007.
[77] [May 1959] letter in Poulenc 1994, 59-9.
[78] Schmidt 1995, FP 23, p. 72.

COMPOSITIONS FROM BRIVE IN JUNE

After the brief respite in Bagnols-en-Forêt, no doubt to see Louis Gautier, he was off to Brive to compose for two weeks, and at the end of June he wrote a short piano *Novelette* (FP 173) on a theme of Manuel de Falla which he dedicated "To my dear friend Gibson." The *Novelette*, on a theme from *El Amor Brujo*, is mentioned first in a 26 June letter to Gibson:

> Your idea of celebrating the centenary of Chester is excellent but I believe that variations by [Arthur] Bliss, Lennox [Berkeley], Igor [Stravinsky], [Gian Francesco] Malipiero and myself would make a disparate ensemble, hardly tempting for a pianist. [. . .] If I were you, I would ask from each of us a piece of his choice to compile a sort of Keepsake. The idea of associating Falla's name is excellent. That has carried me away so much that I am in the act of finishing a *Novellette* in E minor, on the theme from Manuel de Falla's *Amour sorcier*.[79]

A facsimile of the manuscript was published in 1960 in *The House of Chester 1860-1960: Centenary Album*, which also included pieces by Lennox Berkeley, Eugene Goosens, John Ireland, and Gian Francesco Malipiero, each in the composer's autographs.[80]

While in Brive Poulenc must also have worked on the "Lamento" movement from a proposed Sonata for Clarinet and Piano dedicated to Honegger's memory.[81] He had mentioned his intention to write such a sonata in August 1957, but this is the first tangible reference to its actual composition. Sporadic work took place during the summer, and by August he had composed the Andante and was trying to complete the work.[82] *Gloria*, however, got in the way.[83] By 25 October work had gone no further, and Poulenc fatalistically told Gibson that if he never finished to publish it under the title "Andantino tristamente."[84] There were further excuses in 1960, and serious work had to wait until summer 1962.[85]

After two weeks in Brive, which had been fertile compositional territory since the 1930s, he spent ten days at Le Tremblay.[86] On 20 July he was back in Paris working out details for a 1960 American tour with Duval, asking her to think about potential repertoire, be-

---

[79] Poulenc 1994, 59-17. See also Schmidt 1995, FP 173, p. 482.
[80] Poulenc sent his *Novelette* to Gibson with a 10 Aug. [1959] letter. Seethe unpublished letter in GB-Lchester (fragment in Schmidt 1995, FP 173, p. 482).
[81] [3 July 1959] letter to Girard from Rocamadour in Poulenc 1994, 59-18.
[82] This movement was renamed "Romanza."
[83] Unpublished 10 Aug. [1959] letter to Gibson in GB-Lchester.
[84] Unpublished 25 Oct. [1959] letter to Gibson in GB-Lchester.
[85] Unpublished 2 Apr. [1960] letter to Gibson in GB-Lchester.
[86] 19 July [1959] letter to Duval in Poulenc 1994, 59-19 (Poulenc 1991, no. 302).

fore heading back to Bagnols-en-Forêt on the 21st.[87] He arrived in Aix on the 29th to present a conference the next day on "La poésie et la musique" as part of conferences organized by André Jolivet at Maynier d'Oppède's mansion.[88] "Yes, I was very brilliant in Aix," Poulenc told Bernac.[89] The early part of August was spent in Bagnols-en-Forêt which he left to play his Concerto in D minor in Monte Carlo with Jacques Février conducted by Louis Frémaux on the 29th.[90] He returned to Bagnols-en-Forêt on the same day, went north to Paris on the 30th, and to Noizay on 1 September.

While in Bagnols-en-Forêt Poulenc worked assiduously on his *Gloria*. Sketching had begun by 24 July and Poulenc said that it would have nothing in common with the *Stabat Mater*.[91] He was thinking of the "Laudate" [*recte* "Laudamus te"] in terms of Gozzoli frescos in the Ricardi Palace in Florence. By 4 August he confessed that he was having problems dividing the text into movements. Ultimately the original seven sections became six when the last two, "Qui sedes" and "Quoniam/Amen," were combined. He had also determined key schemes for a number of movements, though he was still uncertain about no. 5. Poulenc posed numerous questions and clarified that he heard the "Domine Deus" in terms of Rosanna Carteri.[92] Bernac accepted the plan and expressed no concern for the proximity of the solo numbers.[93] By 10 August Poulenc was working nonstop and felt that the six or seven sections composed were closely related to *La Fraîcheur et le feu*.[94] He was so pleased that he told Milhaud, "Now, God be praised, with the *Gloria* I have taken up again the Poulenc style of [19]37."[95] As his six-week stay in Bagnols-en-Forêt concluded, he wrote Bernac that although *Dialogues* and *La Voix* had brought him international acclaim, he needed to return to his Anost style of the late thirties.[96] Work on the *Gloria* continued

---

[87] Poulenc spent much time in Bagnols because his companion Louis Gautier had for several years been building a house there, not only designing it himself, but also constructing it alone. The house, nearly completed, was finished in August.

[88] Poulenc 1994, p. 925, note 5 and the fragment of Girard's 28 July [1959] letter in the same note.

[89] 4 Aug. [1959] letter to Bernac in Poulenc 1994, 59-21.

[90] Unpublished 28 July [1959] letter to Rose Dercourt-Plaut in US-NH and his 20 Aug. [1959] letter to Bernac in Poulenc 1994, 59-27 (Poulenc 1991, no. 306).

[91] Fragment of Poulenc's "vendredi" [24 July 1959] letter to Bernac in Poulenc 1994, p. 927, note 8.

[92] Carteri, who had sung in *Dialogues*, sang in the European premiere in Paris on 14 Feb. 1961.

[93] Fragment of Bernac's 11 Aug. [1959] letter in Poulenc 1994, p. 928, note 9.

[94] "Lundi" [10 Aug. 1959] letter to Bernac in Poulenc 1994, 59-24 (Poulenc 1991, no. 304).

[95] 13 Aug. [1959] letter in Poulenc 1994, 59-25.

[96] 20 Aug. [1959] letter in Poulenc 1994, 59-27 (Poulenc 1991, no. 306).

during the fall and was finished on 21 December. He went to Noizay on 2 January 1960 to recopy it.[97] There remained only the task of orchestrating the piano-vocal score.

The *Gloria* was not the only work to occupy Poulenc during six weeks in Bagnols-en-Forêt. On 24 July he told Bernac that he was going to write an *Elégie pour deux pianos* (FP 175), very Chabrier in style for Gold and Fizdale, dedicated to Marie-Blanche de Polignac's memory.[98] Eleven days later the *Elégie* was conceived and he commit it to paper at Noizay in September.[99] When published it bore the direction: "This Elegy should be played as if you were improvising it, a cigar in your mouth and a glass of cognac on the piano."[100]

Poulenc completed two other pieces during his weeks in Bagnols-en-Forêt: an inconsequential Fancy (FP 174) for unison voices and piano on words from Shakespeare's *Merchant of Venice* (III:2), dedicated to Miles and Flora (the two children in Britten's opera *The Turn of the Screw*), and his fifteenth and final Improvisation in C minor (FP 176), an homage to Edith Piaf. The first work was a request from Marion Harewood that he contribute to a collection of children's choruses written by Benjamin Britten, Zoltan Kodály, and others. Bernac was consulted about the English prosody, and the setting was complete by 10 August.[101] Bernac thought Poulenc's English was excellent and that there was no problem with accentuation in such short words as those found in the text. As masterful as Poulenc was at setting the French language, the English setting was awkward, Bernac's opinion notwithstanding.[102]

Little is known about the composition of the final Improvisation and it is not mentioned in Poulenc's voluminous correspondence. When it was published in early 1960, Poulenc faithfully gave it to Salabert, who had published Improvisations 13 and 14 and who had earlier acquired the firm of Rouart, Lerolle & Cie, publisher of the first twelve. The end of his Bagnols-en-Forêt season was saddened

---

[97] "Lundi" [21 Dec. 1959] letter to Sienkiewicz in Poulenc 1994, 59-36 (Poulenc 1991, no. 310). Other letters unmentioned here which consider the *Gloria* are excerpted in Schmidt 1995, FP 177, pp. 490-4.

[98] Fragment of Poulenc's 24 July [1959] letter in Poulenc 1994, p. 927, note 7 and Schmidt 1995, FP 175.

[99] 4 Aug. [1959] and 20 Aug. [1959] letters to Bernac in Poulenc 1994, 59-21 and 59-27 (Poulenc 1991, no. 306) respectively.

[100] Poulenc told Gold and Fizdale that Rose Dercourt-Plaut would deliver the manuscript on 15 Oct. See his [28 Sept. 1959] letter in Poulenc 1994, 59-29 (Poulenc 1991, no. 307).

[101] 4 Aug. [1959] letter in Poulenc 1994, 59-21 and fragment of his "jeudi" [10 Aug. 1959] letter to Girard in Poulenc 1994, p. 928, note 10.

[102] Fragment of Bernac's 11 Aug. [1959] letter to Poulenc in Poulenc 1994, p. 928, note 10.

by news of Wanda Landowska's death on 16 August. Poulenc had planned to visit her in Lakeville, Connecticut during his 1960 American tour as he had on the previous one.[103]

THE FIFTIES AT A CLOSE

Several friends visited Noizay in September: Marie-Thérèse Mabille (a photographer/artist from Tours)[104] was there for the first two weeks, his sister Jeanne Manceaux followed, and Rose Dercourt-Plaut and her husband Fred came on the 19th.[105] Poulenc prolonged his Noizay stay to orchestrate the *Gloria* and write a book on Chabrier.[106] Significant time away included two weeks in Bagnols-en-Forêt during the first half of October and two trips to Belgium. The first Brussels trip was for two conferences on 9 October with Bernard Gavoty and Denise Duval,[107] the second to hear *Dialogues* in Ghent.[108] He had always cherished Chabrier and, as noted earlier, had purchased a group of Chabrier letters at auction. The work went quickly, because in early December he wrote: "I have written a book on Chabrier that I believe is successful and amusing. My *Gloria* also is nearing completion and then I must practice the piano—for America."[109] Poulenc left Noizay for Paris on 13 November to discuss his new recordings in Paris at a Club des Trois Centres event organized by Pierre Vidal.[110] He probably also made a recording with Bernac for Columbia records at this time, having written Bernac earlier in the fall: "In all likelihood we will record between 10 and 25 November.

---

[103] 19 Aug. [1959] letter to Girard in Poulenc 1994, 59-26 (Poulenc 1991, no. 305).

[104] Poulenc had written a "morceau" for flute to accompany her illustrated album "Ruines de Tours 1940" (see Boulet, no. 22) and she had made drawings of Noizay, one of which is reproduced as Plate 11.

[105] 20 Aug. [1959] letter to Bernac in Poulenc 1994, 59-27 (Poulenc 1991, no. 306), and his unpublished [18 Aug. 1959] letter to Rose Dercourt-Plaut in US-NH. It also appears that Poulenc flew to Tunis during this period because in an unpublished "samedi" [mid-Sept. 1959] letter to Bernac in US-NH he speaks about an eye infection which resulted from an airplane descent "Tunis[-]Paris."

[106] 20 Oct. [1959] letter to Peignot in Poulenc 1994, 59-30.

[107] Unpublished 19 Aug. [1959], 12 Sept. [1959], and 21 Sept. [1959] letters to Mme de Chapdelaine (Mme Lambiotte), and his 12 Oct. [1959] letter to Mme Lambiotte in US-NYlambiotte-donhauser. Poulenc planned to fly to Brussels on the 8th and return to Nice the 10th.

[108] Concerning Bagnols see Poulenc's 20 Oct. [1959] letter to Peignot in Poulenc 1994, 59-30; concerning Ghent see his unpublished 22 Oct. [1959] letter to Rose Dercourt-Plaut in US-NH. He left for Brussels on 26 October. He asked if Hervé Dugardin could stay at St. Bernard's Palace. Two 20 Oct. [1959] letters to Mme Lambiotte and Mme de Chapdelaine in US-NYlambiotte-donhauser.

[109] Unpublished 5 Dec. [1959] letter to Rose Dercourt-Plaut in US-NH.

[110] This was the first of four such engagements between 1959 and 1962. At the first one on 16 Nov. Poulenc discussed his not-yet released recording of *La Voix humaine.*

I would love to have you here for three days around All Saint's Day [1 November] in order to rehearse."[111]

In late November Poulenc was again at Bagnols-en-Forêt, his base until 28 December when he returned to Paris before going to Noizay on 2 January and then to the Midi.[112] His only significant trip was a much anticipated foray to Milan to hear "La Tebaldi" at La Scala. He flew there on 8 December, heard Mario Del Monaco in Verdi's *Otello* on the 10th and Puccini's *Tosca* with Renata Tebaldi, Giuseppe Di Stefano, and Tito Gobbi on the 11th. He returned to Bagnols through Nice on the 12th delighted with what he had heard and how he had been treated.[113]

A surprise honor ended the year on a high note. Poulenc received a cablegram from Leonard Bernstein and David M. Keiser, Music Director and President, respectively, of the New York Philharmonic:

NEW YORK PHILHARMONIC ASKING TEN INTERNATIONALLY PROMINENT COMPOSERS TO WRITE SYMPHONIC WORKS FOR OPENING SEASON OF PHILHARMONIC HALL AT LINCOLN CENTER, NEW YORK, AND WE HAVE THE HONOR TO INVITE YOU TO WRITE MAJOR WORK FOR THIS INAUGURAL SEASON 1961-62. HOPE YOU WILL BE ABLE TO ACCEPT. KINDEST REGARDS.[114]

Poulenc willingly accepted in December saying he was flattered to be among the ten prominent composers asked.[115] At the conclusion of his American tour in early 1960, Poulenc and the Philharmonic agreed on the commission which ultimately became *Sept répons des ténèbres.*

FOURTH NORTH AMERICAN TOUR: EARLY 1960

The new year began with preparations for a five-week North American tour in February and March. On this, his fourth tour, he was accompanied by Duval and assisted by Georges Prêtre, a distinguished conductor who had just recorded *La Voix humaine* with

[111] Unpublished "samedi" [mid-Sept. 1959] letter in US-NH. This could be U.S. Columbia XLP 9280/81, which was not issued and belonged to Bernac. Bloch, p. 231.
[112] "Lundi" [21 Dec. 1959] letter to Sienkiewicz in Poulenc 1994, 59-36 (Poulenc 1991, no. 310).
[113] Unpublished 5 Dec. [1959] letter to Rose Dercourt-Plaut in US-NH; his unpublished "vendredi" [11 Dec. 1959] letter to Bernac from the Grand Hotel Continental in Milan in US-NH; and his "lundi" [21 Dec. 1959] letter to Sienkiewicz in Poulenc 1994, 59-36 (Poulenc 1991, no. 310). Fragments of letters to Bernac ("vendredi" 11 Dec. 1959) and Rose Dercourt-Plaut (5 Dec. [1959]) in Poulenc 1994, p. 938, note 2.
[114] Unpublished 20 Nov. 1959 cablegram in US-NYpa.
[115] 13 Dec. [1959] letter to Bernstein in Poulenc 1994, 59-34.

Duval. Poulenc intended to go to Lisbon, Portugal in early February to hear her sing *La Voix*, but didn't because the San Carlo Theater management failed to invite him.[116] The performance resulted
in fifteen curtain calls for Duval.[117]

Despite "a very bad month of January" which included a liver
complaint, flu, and nervous anxiety, Poulenc persevered arranging
his American tour and trying to work out a February concert in Brussels with Mme Lambiotte.[118] He had already asked Rose Dercourt-
Plaut to arrange for rooms at the Wyndham Hotel, his locus on an
earlier trip.[119] Initially Prêtre was supposed to arrive on February
14th, Duval and Poulenc on the 16th via Air France.[120] On the 17th,
however, Poulenc cabled the Plauts that he would not arrive until
the 18th.[121]

The tour opened with semi-staged productions of both *Les
Mamelles de Tirésias* and *La Voix humaine* at Carnegie Hall on 23 February. (See Appendix 2 for a synopsis of the tour.) The hall was full,
the evening a triumph, and Martial Singher's staging—the orchestra occupied half the stage, the singers the other—pleased him as
did the musical presentation. Printed reviews were equally favorable with *The New York Times'* Howard Taubman reporting:

> It is difficult to imagine a more convincing and more affecting perfor-
> mance [of *La Voix*] than Miss Duval's. [. . .] Miss Duval, who also
> played it at Milan's Piccola Scala last year, has turned singing and
> acting into a total characterization. [. . .] "Les Mamelles de Tirésias"
> and "La Voix humaine" reveal contrasted aspects of France's most
> lyrical composer. They speak for a man who knows just how high to
> aim, and who does not press his gifts beyond his estimate of them.[122]

[116] Two letters to Ardoin provide information: one written [21 Dec. 1959] indicates
he would attend. A second dated 3 Feb. [1960] informs her he would not.
Poulenc 1994, 59-37 and 60-1, respectively.
[117] Unpublished 6 Feb. [1960] letter to Rose Dercourt-Plaut in US-NH.
[118] Unpublished 6 Feb. [1960] letter in US-NH and unpublished "jeudi" [8 Jan.
1960] letter to Mme Lambiotte in US-NYlambiotte-donhauser. Poulenc suggested 10 Feb., but we do not know if any concert actually took place.
[119] Unpublished 23 Dec. [1959] letter to Rose Dercourt-Plaut in US-NH.
[120] 6 Feb. [1960] letter to Thomson in Poulenc 1994, 60-2. Thomson had earlier
written Poulenc asking if he and Duval could do a concert at the Maison
française. Poulenc preferred an illustrated discussion of his music with examples
sung by Duval plus the Sonata for Flute and Piano if Thomson could find an
appropriate flautist. Duval, he said, had had a very busy fall and did not have a
large repertoire. 20 Oct. [1959] letter in US-NH. Fragment in Poulenc 1994, p.
941, note 2. This event took place on 3 Mar. in a quite different format.
[121] 17 Feb. 1960, 7:18 am telegram in US-NH. The change resulted from a mistake
by Poulenc's agent, who was late securing a required visa. Unpublished 1 Dec.
[19]60 letter to Burkat in US-NH.
[122] 24 Feb. 1960.

When the production was repeated in Philadelphia on 25 February at the venerable Academy of Music, the critics Max de Schauensee and Samuel Singer wrote laudatory reviews.[123] Duval and Poulenc flew to Ithaca, NY on the 27th for a concert; then on to Chicago for a return engagement at the Arts Club where Poulenc had performed on his first tour. Rehearsals were scheduled for 29 February and 1 March with the concert that evening. In addition to *La Voix*, they also performed an air from Debussy's *L'Enfant prodigue*, two numbers from Ravel's *Shéhérazade*, an air from Ravel's *L'Heure espagnole*, and Poulenc's "A sa guitare" and "Air champêtre."[124] Poulenc sang Duval's praises to both Bernac and Stéphane Audel.[125]

From Chicago it was back to New York where Poulenc was presented with the New York University Medal by Dr. George D. Stoddard, chancellor and executive vice president of NYU in the University's Maison française.[126] Following the ceremony Duval sang selections from *La Voix* accompanied by Poulenc. His activities for the next week are undocumented except for a concert in Detroit on the 6th, but they must have included preparation for the Town Hall recital on 10 February. Poulenc was a veteran at Town Hall, but this was Duval's first appearance on one of the world's most prestigious stages. By all accounts it was a grand success.[127]

Poulenc may have been in Washington D.C. on the 13th,[128] but his last known major activity on this tour was to make a recording of his Sextet on 17 March with five members of the Philadelphia Orchestra.[129] The recording, accomplished from 6:00-11:00 pm, went very well and the instrumentalists remember that working with Poulenc was both enjoyable and easy. He made a big impression by appearing at the session in bedroom slippers![130] He also held out

---

[123] *The Evening Bulletin* and *The Philadelphia Inquirer* (both 26 Feb. 1960).
[124] Information from the program and documents in US-Cn (Arts Club papers). The contact indicates the fee for this concert was $1750.00. Poulenc and Duval stayed at the Ambassador Hotel.
[125] "Mercredi" [2 Mar. 1960] and [Mar 1960] letters in Poulenc 1994, 60-4 and 60-5 (Poulenc 1991, nos. 312 and 313) respectively.
[126] 1 Mar. 1960 press release: "The circular bronze medal, which is suspended from a chain, bears on its face the NYU seal. On the reverse side is a reproduction of the Hall of Fame for Great Americans, located at the University, and the name of the recipient. M. Poulenc is the nineteenth person to receive the award since it was established in 1956 to honor distinguished visitors to the University."
[127] Poulenc's 11 Mar. [1960] letter to Bernac in Poulenc 1994, p. 945, note 1.
[128] 13 Mar. 1960 letter to Bernac written on stationary from the French Embassy (Washington).
[129] De Lancie (ob.), Anthony Gigliotti (cl.), Sol Schonbach (bsn.), and Mason Jones (hn.). The recording was released on U.S. Columbia MS 6213. See Appendix 3.
[130] Private correspondence with former members of the Philadelphia Orchestra who played in this recording.

hope that he could record *Aubade,* but no recording was made. While in New York he wrote a brief Sarabande (FP 179) for solo guitar, first mentioned in October 1959, which he dedicated to Ida Presti.[131] The G. Ricordi printed score states "New York, marzo 1960." This trip made him feel ten years younger. "Decidedly, I love America and America loves me," he said.[132]

LATER 1960

When Poulenc returned to France he went briefly to Noizay, then headed south to Bagnols-en-Forêt to orchestrate the *Gloria.*[133] By 25 April five of six movements were complete, though the sixth had to wait until after his Italian trip.[134] Sometime after his return Poulenc also wrote introductions to three articles on Chabrier, Ravel, and Satie for the *Enciclopedia Ricordi,* and asked to have payment put in his Rome Ricordi account in anticipation of an upcoming visit.[135] He traveled to Rome on 30 April for a 5 May concert, returning to France the 7th. By the 17th he had all but finished orchestrating the *Gloria,* but apparently he did not put the final touches on it until July when he completed the last eight pages.[136]

During the spring Poulenc also agreed to a request from Mario Bois, Director of Boosey & Hawkes in Paris and French agent for Chester, to write a brief piece for a memorial book honoring the renowned artist Raoul Dufy.[137] He set a quatrain from Apollinaire's *Le Bestiaire* entitled *La Puce* [The Flea].[138] Although this quatrain was among the rejected numbers of his original 1919 twelve-number set, we do not know if the two versions had anything in common because the earlier one does not exist. The piece was finally dispatched to Bois in late 1960.[139]

Apparently Poulenc was also approached to write a motet for performance in Poitiers.[140] He inquired about what text he should

---

[131] Unpublished 22 Oct. [1959] and 25 Apr. 1960 letters to Valcarenghi in I-Mr.

[132] [Mar. 1960] letter to Audel in Poulenc 1994, 60-5 (Poulenc 1991, no. 313).

[133] This task is mentioned in his 2 Apr. [1960] letter to Britten, Poulenc 1994, 60-7 (Poulenc 1991, no. 315), and unpublished 2 Apr. [1960] letter to Rose Dercourt-Plaut in US-NH. He also spent time at Noizay during April.

[134] 25 Apr. 1960 letter to Conrad in US-NYwurlitzer-bruck (Schmidt 1995, FP 177, pp. 492-3). The orchestral manuscript lists the termination date as May.

[135] Poulenc 1963-64 and unpublished 5 Apr. [19]60 letter to M Bai in I-Mr.

[136] Unpublished 17 May [19]60 letter to Rose Dercourt-Plaut in US-NH, "lundi" [July 1960] letter to Bernac in Poulenc 1994, 60-10 (Poulenc 1991, no. 316), and unpublished 26 Apr. [19]60 letter in US-NYlambiotte-donhauser.

[137] 2 Apr. 1960 response to Bois reporting his intentions in Poulenc 1994, 60-9.

[138] Music in Oury, p. 195.

[139] 10 Nov. 1960 letter to Bois from Noizay in Poulenc 1994, 60-30.

[140] Unpublished 16 May [19]60 letter [to Roger Lecotte?] in F-Pn musique (L.A. Vol. 86, no. 247).

set and requested that two or three be sent from which he could choose. By November he had not composed the work and in late December he was too engrossed with *Sept répons des ténèbres* to be bothered.[141] The 22nd of May Poulenc went to Brussels for a week to serve on the Queen Elizabeth Competition jury and then spent four days in early June in London.[142] Later that month he and Bernac recorded *Banalités, Tel jour telle nuit, Calligrammes,* and *Le Travail du peintre* for Véga.[143] "I am certain the recording will be superb," he told Girard later.[144] It would be their last recording together. Subsequently, he intended to present a 10 June conference in London and go to Aldeburgh a day later for the premiere of Benjamin Britten's *A Midsummer Night's Dream.*[145] A conflict with the Belgian premiere of *La Voix humaine,* however, caused him to cancel his plans.[146]

As usual, Poulenc was in Brive during early July thinking about what he referred to as his *Office des Ténèbres* (later *Sept répons des ténèbres*) and a cycle of "children's songs" (later *La Courte Paille* [The Short Straw]: FP 178).[147] Although he began the songs almost immediately, serious work on *Sept répons* waited until 1961. In Aix on 15 July Poulenc presented a sequel to his 1959 offering in a series given by André Jolivet at Maynier d'Oppède's mansion. This time he spoke about "La musique française dans le théâtre lyrique."[148] His main purpose, however, was to hear Duval and Prêtre perform *La Voix humaine* on the 16th and 24th.[149] Their performance and Cocteau's décor delighted him.[150] At the conclusion of his stay in Aix, Poulenc also saw Purcell's *Dido and Aeneas* in Britten's realization.

[141] Unpublished 4 Nov. [19]60 and 27 Dec. [1960] communications to [Roger Lecotte] in F-Pn musique (L.A. Vol. 86, nos. 246 and 248 respectively).

[142] Unpublished 26 Apr. [19]60 and "mercredi" [19 May 1960] letters to Mme de Chapedelaine (Mme Lambiotte) in US-NYlambiotte-donhauser.

[143] (Véga C 30 A 293) unpublished 17 May [19]60 letter to Rose Dercourt-Plaut in US-NH.

[144] Fragment of Poulenc's "lundi" [probably 4 July 1960] letter in Poulenc 1994, p. 947, note 5.

[145] 2 Apr. [1960] letter to Britten in Poulenc 1994, 60-7 (Poulenc 1991, no. 315).

[146] Fragment of Poulenc's "jeudi" [1960] letter to Britten in Poulenc 1994, p. 945, note 3.

[147] Schmidt 1995, FP 181 and his "lundi" [July 1960] letter to Bernac in Poulenc 1994, 60-10.

[148] Poulenc 1994, p. 950, note 2. Poulenc was assisted by Gavoty. For his account of a significant "scandale" at the conference, see his 28 July 1960 letter from Bagnols-en-Forêt to Bernac and Girard in Poulenc 1994, 60-14.

[149] Poulenc said that the second performance was the best ever done. 8 July 1960 letter from Bagnols-en-Forêt to Bernac and Girard in Poulenc 1994, 60-14.

[150] See Poulenc's 19 July 1960 letter to Duval in Poulenc 1994, 60-11 (Poulenc 1991, no. 317) and [July 1960] letter to Prêtre in Poulenc 1994, 60-12. Duval performed the work again in Edinburgh on 30 Aug. and at the Farnese Palace (residence of the French Ambassador in Rome) on 9 Sept. with Prêtre.

By late July Poulenc had chosen the texts for his *Sept répons:* two from the Thursday service, three from Friday, and two from Saturday. He was also busy writing *La Courte Paille* on poems by the Belgian poet Maurice Carême, which he dedicated to Duval and her husband Richard Schilling in the hopes that she would sing them to their young son.[151] In early August he asked Carême to provide an overall title for the work (as Eluard had done before), and requested permission to change the titles of several selected poems.[152] All seven songs were completed by 11 August when Poulenc thanked the poet for his cooperation in selecting the last text.[153] "As for the title," Poulenc said, "*La Courte Paille* symbolizes my little musical game exactly."[154] Poulenc originally intended that Duval premiere the cycle during their November Italian trip. When this was aborted he suggested a Gavoty-Poulenc conference in Charleroi on either 31 January or 1 February, 1961.[155] Duval disliked the music, however, and never did sing the cycle. Instead, Colette Herzog and Février gave the premiere at the 1961 Royaumont Festival.[156]

After a summer spent in Bagnols-en-Forêt, Poulenc left on 24 August for Noizay to resume work on *Sept répons.*[157] He intended to return to Paris on 26 September before going to Italy on 3 October to peruse twelve one-act operas for Ricordi at the Villa d'Este on Lake Como.[158] Poulenc also expected to complete his Chabrier book during October. Éditions Seuil found the manuscript too short, so he considered Plon, which he preferred to Julliard or Gallimard.[159]

---

[151] Duval had remarried on 14 Apr. 1960. Unpublished 26 Apr. [19]60 letter to Mme de Chapedelaine (Mme Lambiotte) in US-NYlambiotte-donhauser.

[152] 1 Aug. 1960 letter in Poulenc 1994, 60-16. At this writing Poulenc had not yet selected a seventh poem. He told Carême that the songs were arranged in a slow-fast sequence. Carême had been sending Poulenc his poetry collections since 1953. In Carême's 5 Aug. [1960] and 7 Aug. 1960 letters he told Poulenc he would aid his search for a seventh song. Poulenc 1994, 60-17 and 60-18.

[153] 11 Aug. [19]60 letter in Poulenc 1994, 60-19 and [Aug. 1960] letter to Bernac in Poulenc 1991, 60-21 (Poulenc 1991, no. 318).

[154] 11 Aug. [19]60 letter to Carême in Poulenc 1994, 60-19.

[155] Unpublished 4 Sept. [19]60 letter in US-NYlambiotte-donhauser.

[156] Schmidt 1995, FP 178, p. 496.

[157] 9 Aug. [19]60 letter to Rose Dercourt-Plaut in US-NH and [Aug. 1960] letter to Bernac in Poulenc 1994, 60-21 (Poulenc 1991, no. 318), with different dates, and his 22 Aug. 1960 letter to Denise Bourdet in Poulenc 1994, 60-22. Poulenc told Rose Dercourt-Plaut that if the Destouches inquired as to his whereabouts that he was actually in Tourrettes-sur-Loup and not in Bagnols-en-Forêt. This was part of the deception which kept them from learning about his relationship with Louis Gautier.

[158] See also the "vendredi"[19 Aug. 1960] letter to Audel in Poulenc 1994, 60-20 and unpublished 10 Sept. [19]60 postcard to Valcarenghi in I-Mr.

[159] 22 Aug. 1960 letter to Denise Bourdet in Poulenc 1994, 60-22.

Before the book was finally published by La Palatine, Sauguet sent Poulenc a Chabrier manuscript letter and photograph.[160]

As fall progressed, he spent time in Milan during October (where it rained all the time),[161] at Noizay in November (where he finished his *Chabrier*), in Paris (where he arrived on 14 Nov.),[162] and in Bagnols-en-Forêt in late November and/or early December. Poulenc had planned to fly to Milan with Duval arriving the afternoon of 6 December for a concert in Turin the next day and a return to Milan for "la grande première" on the 8th.[163] For unknown reasons, however, Duval withdrew and the tour was canceled. Poulenc told Guido Valcarenghi he would miss seeing Verdi's *Don Carlo* and Donizetti's *Polyeucte (Poliuto)* and having lunch together.[164] He did go to Rome on the 16th to serve on the Santa Cecilia jury from the 17th-22nd and to give several concerts.[165]

PREPARATIONS FOR THE FIFTH NORTH AMERICAN TOUR

From July on Poulenc planned his fifth North American tour, at first thinking in terms of combining the premiere of the *Gloria* with a March tour accompanying Duval.[166] This would have meshed with the originally suggested 24 February date, but when the date was changed to 20 January, Poulenc said he could not afford to go unless he was also engaged as a soloist.[167] Leonard Burkat, artistic administrator of the Boston Symphony Orchestra, responded positively and Poulenc, overjoyed, suggested that he play his Concerto in D minor. For the second pianist Poulenc suggested a young American pianist whose touch would resemble that of Ronald Turini, whom he had heard in the Queen Elisabeth competition, or Malcolm

<hr>

[160] 8 Nov. 1960 acknowledgment to Sauguet in Poulenc 1994, 60-29. See also his 12 Dec. 1960 letter to Sauguet in Poulenc 1994, 60-32.

[161] Unpublished 21 Oct. [19]60 letter to Rose Dercourt-Plaut in US-NH. Poulenc had bought several new suits during his visit.

[162] 10 Nov. 1960 letter to Bois from Noizay in Poulenc 1994, 60-30.

[163] Unpublished 13 Nov. [19]60 letter to Valcarenghi in I-Mr.

[164] Unpublished 8 Dec. [19]60 letter in I-Mr. A live recording of this production (which featured Maria Callas and Franco Corelli) was issued in 1997 on EMI CDMB 7243 5 65448 2 6).

[165] 12 Dec. 1960 letter from Bagnols-en-Forêt to Sauguet in Poulenc 1994, 60-32 and unpublished 29 Nov. [19]60 letter to Gibson in GB-Lchester.

[166] The majority of letters concerning arrangements were exchanged between Poulenc and Leonard Burkat; another group was exchanged with Rose Dercourt-Plaut, and several others went to Charles Munch, then the BSO conductor.

[167] 28 July 1960 letter to Burkat in Poulenc 1994, 60-13. He also expressed regret that Leontyne Price, the soprano solo, would have to be replaced by Adele Addison. Price had written Poulenc on 3 July 1960 expressing the hope that she could perform and record the *Gloria*. Fragment of her letter in Poulenc 1994, p. 949, note 2.

Frager.[168] During September and early October Poulenc tried to locate Charles Munch to confirm which concerto he would play, but was unsuccessful catching a "shooting star."[169] More desperate by 17 October, he wrote Munch that if the Concerto in D minor was not acceptable, he would only agree to the *Concert champêtre*.[170] Poulenc also expressed concern about rehearsals, performance dates, and his fee.[171] In late November he learned that Evelyne Crochet, winner of the 1958 Tchaikovsky Competition, would play the second piano part so the Concerto "situation" was now settled.[172] As the year closed, Poulenc wrote Burkat that he would arrive in New York on 15 January before going to Boston for the first rehearsal.[173] Poulenc's numerous letters and cables arranging the Boston trip betray an obsession with details, but in spite of it all, Poulenc happily told Munch, "I have found my equilibrium."[174]

[168] 5 Sept. [19]60 letter to Burkat in Poulenc 1994, 60-24. Poulenc's early correspondence with Burkat was via telegrams, none of which have survived in the Boston Symphony Archives.

[169] Unpublished 12 Oct. [19]60 letter to Burkat in US-NH.

[170] 17 Oct. 1960 letter to Munch in Poulenc 1994, 60-27. He specifically ruled out the solo concerto premiered in 1950.

[171] Unpublished 17 Oct. [19]60 letter to Burkat in US-NH. He suggested a fee of $1,000 and said he would see that choral parts and the piano reduction of the *Gloria* were dispatched to Alfred Nash Patterson, who was preparing the chorus, and a full score directly to Munch.

[172] Unpublished 1 Dec. [19]60 letter to Burkat in US-NH. Poulenc also asked for a Steinway piano and that all arrangements be made directly with him because he had no agent.

[173] Unpublished 27 Dec. [19]60 letter from Cannes in US-NH.

[174] 17 Oct. 1960 letter to Munch in Poulenc 1994, 60-27.

XIV

The Final Years: 1961-1963

The pace of Poulenc's last twenty-five months was decidedly slower than that of his earlier years. Performances of *Dialogues des Carmélites* no longer dominated his calendar, nor was his touring schedule as hectic. Work on his last compositions was more deliberate and mirrored that of his countryman Claude Debussy, who tended to write sonatas at the end of his life. Poulenc's final *Sept répons des ténèbres,* which completes his trilogy of major accompanied sacred choral works, has received but a fraction of the attention accorded the *Gloria* and *Stabat Mater,* although it deserves more.[1] The last two sonatas, for Oboe and Piano and Clarinet and Piano, though the work of a master craftsman, are overshadowed by the earlier Sonata for Flute. As for theatrical collaborations, Poulenc himself called his incidental music for a Baalbeck Festival performance of Jean Cocteau's *Renaud et Armide* "several inconsequential things."[2] Nor were songs of much interest after Duval's rejection of *La Courte Paille.* With Bernac retired, Poulenc no longer felt the kind of symbiosis that led to so many of his earlier vocal works.

On the other hand, Poulenc's earlier music retained its vitality in France, England, and the United States, engaging new audiences and continuing to delight those more venerable. Moreover, there was a growing interest in Poulenc's music in the Soviet Union, where unauthorized editions appeared with increasing frequency.[3] Through it all, Poulenc the performer was still in demand for lecture-recitals and tours with Duval, though new tours were short.

[1] Writing about Poulenc's choral works with orchestra, Keith Daniel makes a strong case for why this work deserves more attention than it has received. See Buckland/Chimènes: c, pp. 72-84.

[2] Schmidt 1995, FP 183 and 26 Mar. 1962 letter to Bernac in Poulenc 1994, 62-4 (Poulenc 1991, no. 337): literally "several farts."

[3] Schmidt 1995, passim.

Poulenc must have sensed his own mortality. Letters to friends illuminate ever more clearly his hypochondria, his inability to see future directions, his awareness that his personal life would significantly change when Louis Gautier sold his Bagnols-en-Forêt house to buy a bar in Cannes, and his avowed desire to put his musical affairs in order. In May 1962, following Casa Fuerte's two-day visit to Noizay, Poulenc wrote:

> You told me that they [*Sept répons*] are very good. I dare to hope so, but why must I be so little interested in my music. I have the impression that my great success is unwholesome. The other day, while listening to my *mélodies*, I said to myself that this was quite obviously good, but where to go now? Don't speak to anyone about this, but it does me good to open my heart to you. Does too much lucidity perhaps paralyze me at the present time?[4]

At the close of his life he left no unfinished compositions, though death prevented him from correcting proofs of his last sonatas. It is ironic that we know more about Poulenc's earlier career than we do about his last years. He grew increasingly reticent about sharing information concerning his private life, as the letter to Casa Fuerte quoted above suggests. His sudden death in January 1963 stunned the musical world, but his passing failed to dim his star which continues to be visible well above the horizon.

NEW YORK-BOSTON-NEW YORK: JANUARY 1961

In early 1961 Poulenc embarked on yet another cherished trip to the United States where an adoring public awaited him. His celebrity status, cemented by prestigious New York performance awards, guaranteed favorable advance publicity and full houses. Out-of-state newspapers sent critics to his concerts, and he was often reviewed in national publications.

Poulenc flew to New York City on 13 January wishing to adjust to the Eastern time zone before beginning rehearsals with the Boston Symphony.[5] (See Appendix 2 for a synopsis of this tour.) Rose Dercourt-Plaut had again booked his room at the Wyndham Hotel, and arranged much of his social calendar. After resting, he went to Boston on 15 January for the first rehearsal of the *Gloria* on the 17th with Charles Munch and Alfred Nash Patterson's chorus. Poulenc's uncomplimentary appraisal of the rehearsal, at which he arrived

---

[4] "Jeudi" [10 May 1962] letter in Poulenc 1994, 62-9.

[5] Unpublished 26 Dec. 19[60] letter to Rose Dercourt-Plaut in US-NH. The BSO paid 66,000 francs for a 17-day ticket. In New York Poulenc wrote of his disappointment that, according to Rouart, Munch had renounced plans to perform *Gloria* at the Strasbourg Festival in June 1961. Munch incorrectly assumed that his would be the first performance in France, but *Gloria* had already been promised to French Radio."Dimanche" [15 Jan. 1961] letter in Poulenc 1994, 61-2.

late, was immediately dispatched to Bernac with a request that it be read to Brigitte Manceaux.[6] He found the chorus fine, Patterson not the equal of Robert Shaw, the women sharp and shrill, the fill-in soloist with the voice of an out-of-tune goat, and the accompanist unable to play the score properly. Moreover, "The dear, adorable, exquisite Charlie [Munch] had understood precisely *nothing*." Poulenc held his tongue until the break. Then he suggested that the singing should have a Maurice Chevalier quality, took over the piano, had the substitute soloist desist, and slowed Munch's precipitous tempi. Everything came together, and Poulenc wondered what the *Gloria* might have sounded like had he been absent! He also thought that Evelyne Crochet, the second pianist in his Concerto in D minor, was excellent.

By the 19th, Munch had mastered the *Gloria* and Poulenc was delirious about soprano Adele Addison's heavenly voice.[7] That evening he took Rose Dercourt-Plaut to hear Marlene Dietrich, who later posed with him for pictures. Unfortunately, however, the vicissitudes of New England winter weather forced the Friday concert to be rescheduled for Sunday the 22nd, making the Saturday concert the premiere. According to Poulenc the *Gloria* had triumphed, Addison was *"unimaginable,"* there were ovations upon ovations, and the press was excellent.[8] Describing his work Poulenc noted, "The colors are very clear, primary colors—rude and violent like the Provence chapel of Matisse."[9] Robert Taylor wrote:

> Friday's blizzard will pass; but yesterday afternoon's Symphony concert—put over because of the storm—proved one of those rare and precious events that may very well make enduring musical history. [. . .] . . . but I shall merely content myself this morning with the memory of the whole, an exceedingly lovely score and the finest of the Symphony season to date. The performance of the Chorus Pro Musica in the Gloria equaled the resplen[den]ce of the music. Alfred Nash Patterson has trained this group into the outstanding choir of the area; the dynamic level was never less than crystalline. Miss Addison, again, sang superbly; and the partnership of Mr. Poulenc and Miss Crichet [sic], Dr. Munch and the orchestra during the exhilarating Mozartesque concerto was close-knot [*recte* knit].[10]

[6] "Mardi" [17 Jan. 1961] letter in Poulenc 1994, 61-3 (Poulenc 1991, no. 323).

[7] Poulenc inscribed Addison's piano-vocal score "For Adela [*sic*] Addison who sings this GLORIA for soprano solo, chorus, and orchestra "miraculously," with great thanks. Francis Poulenc 61, Boston." *Time* (27 Jan. 1961), 43 quotes Poulenc as stopping the rehearsal to shout, '*Parfait! Parfait! La perfection!*'

[8] "Lundi" [23 Jan. 1961] letter in Poulenc 1994, 61-6 (Poulenc 1991, no. 326) and "lundi" [23 Jan. 1961] letter to Girard in Poulenc 1994, 61-7.

[9] *Time* (27 Jan. 1961), 43.

[10] Review entitled "Poulenc's Gloria Rare, Precious" (source undetermined).

Poulenc returned to New York on the 23rd to spend a week greeting friends, going to parties, and visiting the Metropolitan Opera. Among the names Poulenc mentioned are Leontyne Price (whose New York premiere in *Il Trovatore* with Franco Corelli he attended), Laurence Olivier (in *Becket*), Vladimir Horowitz, Arthur Rubinstein, and Rosine Lambiotte-Donhauser. Such social activity delighted Poulenc. Allen Hughes remembered an amusing evening he spent with Poulenc (probably on the 23rd):

> During his last visit to New York, he was enchanted by the bustling atmosphere of McGinnis' on Broadway at dinner and by a shopping tour of the cheap stores that line Times Square. He bought neckties with nude girls painted on the underside and charmed salespeople with his gleeful enthusiasm, though they did not understand a word he said.[11]

Poulenc was also invited by his friend Barry Brook, a professor at Queens College, to address the music department. Claire Brook, who drove with Poulenc to and from the event, remembers it vividly:

> Barry had invited him to come out to address the music department at Queens College; I don't remember a thing about the trip out but the one back was unforgettable. Poulenc pretended he had no English and Barry had to translate for him; actually, he understood a great deal, for when my husband, basically an 18th-century man, in introducing Poulenc said he was born on January 7, *1799*, Poulenc corrected him instantly. And on the trip home, we had a long conversation—he and I—about prosody and it certainly was not in French! I asked him about Britten's ability to handle French in *Les Illuminations*. He said that Britten had sent him the manuscript before the first performance or the publication to check that he hadn't committed any terrible *bêtise*. Poulenc said he gave him—Britten— dix-sept sur vingt [seventeen out of twenty]. When I asked him why, he said that Britten did not *breathe* like a Frenchman! We were back in Manhattan and heading for his hotel when we stopped for a red light. Looking out the window, Poulenc saw an enormous black man behind the wheel of a huge truck that had pulled up alongside and was also waiting for the light to change. Poulenc gazed up at the bulging muscles and the shining skin and said, in crooning tones: "Comme j'adore les nègres!"[12]

In this last week in New York Poulenc also took time to thank Munch for an "admirable performance" of the *Gloria*, diplomatically adding his hope that Munch would reconsider his decision not to

---

[11] Hughes 1963, p. 29.
[12] I am most grateful to Claire Brook who related this story to me verbally and kindly agreed to write it down so it could be shared here.

play the *Gloria* at the Strasbourg Festival.[13] Poulenc looked forward to exchanging the cold snowy weather of the eastern United States for the warm sun of the Midi. Another concert tour to New York and Chicago, planned for April 1964, never took place.

WINTER SEASON OF 1961

Shortly after returning to France Poulenc got food poisoning from eating a duck paté.[14] This was not his only complaint: he told Stéphane Audel that he still experienced occasional whistling in his ears from the return flight in late January on a Boeing plane.[15] Poulenc attended the European premiere of *Gloria* featuring soprano Carteri, the choirs of the R.T.F. prepared by Gouverné, and the Orchestre National conducted by Prêtre.[16] Signs of the same extreme anxiety he ex-perienced during the composition of *Dialogues* temporarily re-appeared when the Parisian press failed to report the unqualified success acknowledged by their American counterpart. By early March, nerves frazzled, he had already consulted his Cannes acupuncturist and Dr. Chevalier, his physician. Imploring Henri Hell to be more of a leading critical voice in Paris, Poulenc wrote:

> That is why, after the definite success of Boston (I will show you the reviews) Paris has caused me the greatest anxiety. Thank the Lord the *Gloria* was considered *important*. I know full well that I am not considered in vogue but at least I need to be recognized. And this has happened. Besides I think that in the future I will be played more frequently than [Jean] Barraqué or [Henri] Pousseur. Just the same, my music is not all that bad, although at times I ask myself why I continue composing and for whom? It is at times like these that friends like you and Richard [Negrou] grab me by the sleeve when I flounder. I lack pride . . . or a Madame Jolivet . . . I don't deny the talent of this composer but he is definitely not Stravinsky. I think there is a lot of confusion right now. Take note that I am not jealous (there is a place for everyone), but when I read that Messiaen and Jolivet are the two most *important* composers, I wonder.[17]

Poulenc was encouraged that Georges Prêtre was about to record *Sinfonietta* and *Aubade* (with Poulenc as soloist); he preferred to set his stock in works that had stood the test of time, works that were

---

[13] 27 Jan. 1961 letter to Munch in Poulenc 1994, 61-8.

[14] Unpublished 10 Feb. [19]61 letter to Rose Dercourt-Plaut in US-NH.

[15] "Mercredi saint" [29 Mar. 1961] letter to Audel in Poulenc 1994, 61-13 (Poulenc 1991, no. 329) and unpublished 6 Apr. [19]61 letter to Rose Dercourt-Plaut in US-NH.

[16] Premiered 14 Feb. He also attended Prêtre's 17 June performance at the Théâtre municipal de Strasbourg. 24 June 1961 letters to Prêtre and Rouart in Poulenc 1994, 61-19 and 61-20 (Poulenc 1991, no. 332).

[17] 2 Mar. 1961 letter [from Bagnols-en-Forêt] in Poulenc 1994, 61-9 (Poulenc 1991, no. 327 with omissions).

played again and again.[18] Poulenc found Prêtre an excellent interpreter of his music and was pleased to have been present at Maurice
Duruflé's February recording conducted by Prêtre of his Concerto
in G minor at the church of St Etienne du Mont.[19] He also enjoyed
the complimentary comments from friends to whom he had sent
copies of his *Emmanuel Chabrier*, published in February.[20]

In December 1960 Valcarenghi suggested that Poulenc attend an
Athens performance of *Dialogues*. Though interested, Poulenc said
he could go only in late February or early March.[21] While in New
York in late January Poulenc had received word from Valcarenghi
erroneously stating that the Athens performance would take place
on 10 February with rehearsals on the 12th and 14th. Poulenc, who
inquired about the error, said he could make a performance on the
20th, but the 16th would be impossible because six months earlier
he had arranged a concert for the 18th.[22] Extant letters do not indicate if Poulenc attended, but it is unlikely.

Poulenc arrived at the Grand Hotel Continental in Milan the
evening of 6 March to hear Duval sing Jean-Pierre Rivière's *Don
Quichotte* on the 7th even though he disliked this opera, which had
won the Ricordi prize.[23] He returned to Bagnols-en-Forêt, but did
present a conference with Bernard Gavoty in Charleroi on the 27th.[24]

The first New York performance of *Gloria* with the Boston cast
also occurred that month.[25] Such was the *Gloria*'s success that
Poulenc received still another Music Critics Circle Award, announced in *The New York Times* on 19 April.[26] The *Gloria*, however,

[18] Poulenc told Hell that he had to practice *Aubade* for a recording session with
Prêtre and the Orchestre de la Société des Concerts du Conservatoire. This
recording (Véga C 30 A 303) was probably made in March 1961.
[19] French Columbia FCX 882 (released in the U.S.A. as Angel 35953).
[20] Letters to Poulenc from Sienkiewicz of 9 Mar. 1961, Auric of 8 Apr. 1961, and
Cocteau of 7 July 1961 in Poulenc 1994, 61-10, 61-14, and 61-21 respectively. An
exemplar signed to Inghelbrecht is now in US-Bchristie.
[21] Unpublished 27 Dec. [19]60 letter to Valcarenghi in I-Mr. Poulenc said that all
his expenses would have to be paid including airfare and lodging at the Hotel
d'Angleterre.
[22] Unpublished 26 Jan. [19]61 letter to Valcarenghi from New York in I-Mr.
[23] 2 Mar. 1961 letter to Hell in Poulenc 1994, 61-9 (Poulenc 1961, no. 327) and
unpublished 24 Feb. [19]61 letter to Valcarenghi from Bagnols-en-Forêt in I-Mr.
See also his 10 Mar. [1961] letter to Fournier in Poulenc 1994, 61-11 and Hughes
1998, p. 127 (both misdated 1962).
[24] 15 Mar. 1961 letter to Pierre Vidal in Poulenc 1994, 61-12 (Poulenc 1991, no.
328).
[25] Poulenc hoped that Rose Dercourt-Plaut would attend the 8 Apr. concert.
[26] The award covered a fourteen-month period. For Poulenc there was good
news and bad news: although his *Gloria* won decisively over Frank Martin's *Le
Vin herbé*, his opera *La Voix humaine* failed in the opera category. Critics also

received much harsher treatment at the hands of BBC reviewers. A 1 May 1961 internal memo written by Leonard Isaacs, the chief orchestral and choral assistant, states that after examination by three staff members, the work was found unworthy of its dignified text and the BBC should not place its resources behind a work which could not enhance the reputation of its composer.[27] After such a long relationship with the BBC, Poulenc would surely have been appalled had he been privy to this memorandum, which more than thirty-five years of performance history have proved ill-founded.

COMPOSITION OF *LA DAME DE MONTE-CARLO:* APRIL 1961

Perhaps it was the advent of spring, for Poulenc's compositional productivity returned in full flower during April. He picked up work on *Sept répons,* and was attracted to still another Cocteau work by "a phantom [which] invaded my music! Monte Carlo! Monte Carlo, the Venice of my twenties!!"[28] In mid-March while in Cannes visiting his Chinese acupuncturist, he happened across a Théâtre de poche edition of Cocteau's *La Dame de Monte-Carlo,* originally written for Marianne Oswald in 1946.[29] Cocteau's monologue centers around an aging, lonely woman making a final trip to Monte Carlo in hopes of finding fortune at the gaming tables. When she fails to win and cannot even steal successfully, she ends her dismal life by leaping into the sea. Convinced that it would be an excellent vehicle for Duval, Poulenc immediately set it to music (FP 180). He wrote for a similar though slightly smaller orchestra than in *La Voix humaine.* Rose Dercourt-Plaut was among the first to learn of this project; he told her that the monologue was seven minutes long.[30]

The monologue presented a major problem: how to avoid monotony in the musical setting. Hell points out that Poulenc had to juxtapose "melancholy, pride, lyricism, violence, and sarcasm" in a very short piece.[31] Ever the dramatist, Poulenc thought it needed to be sung like the prayer in *Tosca.*[32] Duval sang the premiere in November at Monte Carlo, repeating it in Paris on 5 December 1961 at the Théâtre des Champs-Elysées accompanied by the Orchestre de la Radio-Télévision Française, Prêtre conducting.[33] It was not as suc-

---

considered two other operas, Werner Egk's *The Inspector General* and Stanley Hollingsworth's *The Mother,* but no opera was judged worthy of the award.
[27] Memorandum in GB-Rbbc.
[28] 3 Apr. 1961 entry in Poulenc 1993, p. 63 (Poulenc 1989, pp. 110-11).
[29] Edited by Paul Morihien (1949). Cadieu, p. 179.
[30] Unpublished 6 Apr. [19]61 letter in US-NH. Later Poulenc gave the length as 6'30".
[31] Hell 1978, p. 299.
[32] "Vissi d'arte." Poulenc 1993, p. 63 (Poulenc 1989, pp. 112-13).
[33] At the time of the premiere, Poulenc's friend Denise Bourdet, whom he had known since 1917, interviewed him for *Le Figaro littéraire* (see Bourdet 1961). In

cessful as *La Voix humaine;* Poulenc's last work for Duval has been infrequently sung over the years, and seldom recorded.

SEPT RÉPONS DES TÉNÈBRES: MAY-OCTOBER 1961

Aside from an early May trip to Bordeaux to hear the premiere of Sauguet's cantata *Plus loin que la nuit et le jour,* Poulenc spent the month at Noizay with Richard Chanlaire, his friend since *Aubade* and *Concert champêtre.*

> I am working on my *Répons de la semaine* [FP 181] for Bernstein [he told Milhaud]. It is not going badly as I have renounced everything I did last autumn and started again. I thought it would be like Zurbarán, but it has turned out more like Mantegna.[34]

Poulenc seldom destroyed major portions of works in progress, but did so in this case. Just after having presented a conference on Milhaud's theatrical works at Aix-en-Provence on 24 July with Armand Lunel, Poulenc noted:

> Work is going miraculously well. Whether it is Rocamadour or St Anthony I don't know. All of a sudden this work enthralls me. I have restarted everything from the beginning. To be sure the choruses are *easy* because I am writing essentially for children. The solo is written from D to F sharp, which I believe is normal. The trick was to find the precise color. I believe that that's it.[35]

In early August he added:

> Work continues to go well. Yes, it was necessary to begin again at zero, to destroy pages which were *too* happy. In the end I am going back to the austerity and violence that I sought from the outset.[36]

The allure of the theater struck Poulenc in June when he witnessed two performances in a five-day period of Leonard Bernstein's musical *West Side Story* at the Théâtre de l'Alhambra-Maurice Cheva-

---

this interview Poulenc indicates that he had also thought of using Colette's *Chéri* for a libretto and that Duval had encouraged him to think of Anouilh's *La Folle de Chaillot* because she was interested in portraying a mad woman. See also the discussion in Buckland/Chimènes: l, p. 259, where Waleckx suggests that Poulenc was also considering Henri Million de Motherlant's *Le Cardinal d'Espagne.*
[34] Poulenc also intended to record Sauguet's *Trois mélodies* in early June, but no recording is known. 23 May [1961] letter to Milhaud in Poulenc 1994, 61-17 (Poulenc 1991, no. 331), and unpublished 23 May [19]61 letter to Rose Dercourt-Plaut in US-NH. He more than once referred to his music by analogy with the paintings of Andrea Mantegna (1431-1506) and Francisco de Zurbarán (1598-1644). Poulenc admired both their work, particularly that of Zurbarán.
[35] Fragment of Poulenc's "jeudi" [27 July 1961] letter to Bernac in Poulenc 1994, p. 981, note 1.
[36] Fragment of Poulenc's "lundi" [Aug. 1961] letter to Bernac in Poulenc 1994, p. 981, note 1.

lier.[37] He continued to compose throughout the summer with the goal of finishing by 2 October. Five of seven movements were copied, but two remained *very* partially incomplete.[38] From the Hotel Beau-Rivage Poulenc declared the work complete on 1 November, a month past his self-imposed deadline.[39] The orchestration occupied his time at the beginning of 1962, and five movements were finished by the second week of February.[40] On 26 March 1962 the work was complete.[41] He sent Bernac a moving letter placing it in perspective.

> The *Ténèbres* are finished. I think it is beautiful and don't regret having taken so much time because it is carefully wrought. I have, with the *Gloria* and *Stabat*, three good religious works. May they spare me several days of purgatory, if I manage avoiding going to hell.[42]

Poulenc did not live to witness the premiere.

MISCELLANEOUS EVENTS OF 1961

Poulenc's activities later in 1961 are difficult to trace. According to a report in *Musique et Radio,* he participated in a conference entitled "La Plastique musicale: Forme et Language" at the Centre français d'humanisme musical with Henry Barraud, Jacques Chailley, Edmond Costere, Maurice Jarre, Daniel-Lesur, and Sauguet.[43] He was in Noizay on 26 August when the present author visited with him and on 8 September he and Denise Duval performed *La Voix humaine* at the Théâtre d'Amboise to benefit restoration of the church at Noizay (Plate 23).[44] Then Poulenc was in Brussels at the Lambiottes in conjunction with a concert tour of Holland. He returned on 22 September and expected an evening visit from Rose Dercourt-Plaut. After his brief respite at Noizay he intended to leave on the 26th to visit his companion Louis Gautier in the south.[45] At the end of October he played his Concerto in D minor with Jacques Février

---

[37] 1 Nov. 1961 letter to Bernstein in Poulenc 1994, 61-26. Poulenc told Bernstein that the music fascinated him.

[38] "Samedi" [23 Sept. 1961] letter to Audel in Poulenc 1994, 61-22 (Poulenc 1991, no. 333).

[39] 1 Nov. 1961 letters to Bernstein and Gold and Fizdale in Poulenc 1994, 61-26, and 61-25 (Poulenc 1991, no. 334).

[40] [11 Feb. 1962] letter to Hell in Poulenc 1994, 62-2 (Poulenc 1991, no. 336).

[41] 26 Mar. 1962 letter to Bernac in Poulenc 1994, 62-4 (Poulenc 1991, no. 337). Curiously enough, Poulenc dated the piano-vocal score "Avril-Octobre 1961," the choral part "Avril 1961-mars. 1962," and the score "Bagnols-en-Forêt— avril 1962." Schmidt 1995, FP 181, p. 499.

[42] 26 Mar. 1962 letter in Poulenc 1994, 62-4 (Poulenc 1991, no. 337).

[43] 51 (July 1961), 253.

[44] See Boulet nos. 58 and 59 for an advertisement and program for this benefit performance. Both were illustrated by Marie-Thérèse Mabille.

[45] Unpublished [28 Aug. 1961] letter to Rose Dercourt-Plaut from Brussels in US-NH.

Plate 20: Francis Poulenc at Noizay (Noizay, 26 August 1961 by the author)

in Lausanne, and they also recorded Poulenc's "valse-musette" for two pianos entitled *L'Embarquement pour Cythère*.[46]

His letters to Robert Douglas Gibson yield scraps of information.[47] At the end of October, Poulenc gave a small 13 November London concert. As was his habit, he stayed at the Hotel Piccadilly and requested that £75 from his Chester account be left for him with the hotel cashier. A week before Christmas he wrote cards to various friends including one to Rosine Lambiotte-Donhauser in New York City (Plate 21). Three days before Christmas, he wrote again to Gibson registering his total opposition to a transcription of *Trois mouvements perpétuels* for wind quintet, and saying that he was studying the problem of orchestrating *Histoire de Babar*. We also know that sometime during 1961 Poulenc and Suzanne Peignot were involved in a serious automobile accident from which they escaped unscathed. According to Peignot Poulenc told her, "I would rather have died in that fashion, from a brutal death without warning."[48]

EARLY 1962

The last full year of Poulenc's life followed the now familiar pattern of a winter concert tour, composition at Brive, Noizay, and Bagnols-en-Forêt, quick trips to Italy, London, Menton, Aix-en-Provence, Milan, and Venice to attend or give concerts, as well as treks to summer spots such as Rocamadour and Le Tremblay. In January Poulenc participated in a radio forum ("Tribune de la musique vivante") on the R.T.F. in collaboration with Jeunesses Musicales de France and held in the auditorium of the Théâtre Récamier. The session, led by Olivier Alain and Claude Samuel, was attended by about two hundred listeners. Poulenc spoke out about the inadequacy of some of his own works (Sonatas for Violin and Piano, and Cello and Piano among others) and also discussed the situation of Schönberg today with Max Deutch.[49] Early in January he described for Denise Duval a joint Italian tour for 3-16 February imploring her to learn the notes quickly and reassuring her she would not be involved in endless concert tours.[50] He stressed the need to have two elegant gowns, one for evening concerts in Trieste and Turin and the other for afternoon concerts.[51] Knowing that Duval was uncomfortable as a recitalist, he carefully arranged the tour to leave breaks between con-

[46] [1 Nov. 1961] letter to Gold and Fizdale from the Hôtel Beau-Rivage in Ouchy-Lausanne in Poulenc 1994, 61-25 (Poulenc 1991, no. 334).
[47] Unpublished 30 Oct. [19]61 and 22 Dec. [19]61 letters in GB-Lchester.
[48] Peignot, p. 5.
[49] Lonchampt.
[50] "Jeudi" [early Jan. 1962] letter to Duval in Poulenc 1994, 62-1 (Poulenc 1991, no. 335).
[51] Duval had previuosly been robbed by Dior, who was now deceased. Poulenc told her that the talented Marc Bohan was keeping the firm on track.

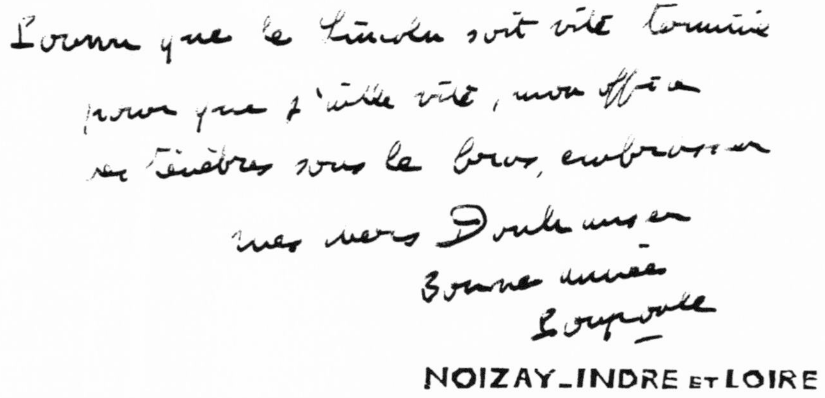
Pourvu que le Lincoln soit vite terminé
pour que j'aille vite, mon Office
des ténèbres sous le bras, embrasser
mes chers Donhauser
Bonne année
Poupoule
NOIZAY_INDRE ET LOIRE

Plate 21: Christmas card from Poulenc to Rosine Lambiotte-Donhauser postmarked Bagnols, 18 December 1961. "Le Lincoln" is a reference to* Sept. répons de ténèbre. *The text reads: "Pourvu que le Lincoln soit vite terminé / pour que j'aille vite, mon Office / des ténèbres sous le bras, embrasser / mes chers Donhauser / Bonne année / Poupoule /* NOIZAY-INDRE ET LOIRE.*" (Collection of Rosine Lambiotte-Donhauser and used with her kind permission.)

certs and suggested a single program. (The sequence of events is listed in Appendix 2.)

Poulenc suggested four Debussy *mélodies* (*Beau soir, L'Echelonnement des haies, La Chevelure,* and *Mandoline*), his own new cycle *La Courte Paille* plus a slightly cut version of *La Voix humaine,* and three Ravel *mélodies.* The repertoire was adjusted, however, because Duval disliked *La Courte Paille* and chose not to sing it. Apparently the tour went very well, and he reported to Henri Hell that Duval had triumphed in Florence.[52]

While in Bagnols Poulenc corrected *Trois mouvements perpétuels* for Robert Douglas Gibson at Chester.[53] This was not the first time he had revisited this youthful work, changing the spelling of a few accidentals or altering a detail. He also wrote Bernac about personal matters. Louis Gautier, his morale low due to lack of work (he did plumbing and odd jobs) and the loneliness of Bagnols, had decided to move to Cannes. Moreover, his relationship with Gautier had changed, as had his earlier relationship with Raymond Destouches, and he now thought of him as a child he adored. "Bagnols of the *Gloria* and *Les Ténèbres* thus joins Anost in my fond-

[52] [11 Feb. 1962] letter in Poulenc 1994, 62-2 (Poulenc 1991, no. 336).
[53] Unpublished 23 Feb. [19]62 letter in GB-Lchester. A copy of the 1939 edition inscribed "Corrigé mars 62" is also at GB-Lchester. Schmidt 1995, FP 14, p. 33.

est memories," Poulenc told Bernac.[54] In response, Bernac said that Poulenc should be delighted with such excellent choral works and might want to change genres the way Louis Gautier was changing residences.[55]

Just before Christmas 1961 Poulenc was asked by the publisher Hansen to orchestrate *Histoire de Babar, le petit éléphant*.[56] Not interested in undertaking the task himself, Poulenc suggested Jean Françaix, who was charmed by the piece. Françaix discussed orchestral details with Poulenc who broke the news of Françaix's acceptance of the commission to Gibson.[57] By the second week of June, the orchestration was complete, and Françaix played it for Poulenc, who called it a *chef d'œuvre*.[58] In this version, like Prokofiev's more famous *Peter and the Wolf*, the work is frequently played at children's concerts and has been commercially recorded.

Early in the year Poulenc spent time in Venice at the festival.[59] He continued to work on his Sonata for Clarinet and Piano, and much of May was spent with Richard Chanlaire at Noizay composing.[60] After *Sept répons*, Poulenc seemed to have temporarily lost his compositional way, as he confided to Yvonne de Casa Fuerte in early May.[61] A trip to Rocamadour and early July work on the wind sonatas on Marthe Bosredon's piano, however, steadied him. He interrupted his composing only to make a short hop to England in mid-May to see Duval in *Pelléas et Mélisande* on the 21st. By early June, he had reorchestrated and arranged *Les Mamelles de Tirésias* for a 1963 La Scala performance, composed several short numbers for the late summer Baalbeck performance of Cocteau's play *Renaud et Armide* (FP 183), and was practicing the piano for an upcoming Milhaud concert.[62] Shortly thereafter he recorded his incidental music for Cocteau's play, telling Bernac, "The recording of my music for *Renaud*

---

[54] 26 Mar. 1962 letter in Poulenc 1994, 62-4 (Poulenc 1991, no. 337).

[55] "Jeudi matin" [29 Mar. 1962] letter to Poulenc in Poulenc 1994, 62-5 (Poulenc 1991, no. 338).

[56] Fragment of Poulenc's 22 Dec. 1961 letter to Gibson in Schmidt 1995, FP 129, p. 364 and Poulenc 1994, p. 989, note 1.

[57] 2 Apr. 1962 letter to Françaix in Poulenc 1994, 62-7 and the fragment of his 2 Apr. [19]62 letter to Gibson in Poulenc 1994, p. 989, note 3. In an unpublished 24 Apr. [19]62 letter to Gibson Poulenc inquired if anything had yet become of the commission. GB-Lchester.

[58] Unpublished 12 June [19]62 letter to Gibson in GB-Lchester. Poulenc suggested that Françaix wanted a £300 fee.

[59] Unpublished 17 Apr. [19]62 letter to Rose Dercourt-Plaut in US-NH.

[60] Unpublished 24 Apr. [19]62 letter to Gibson in GB-Lchester.

[61] "Jeudi" [10 May 1962] letter in Poulenc 1994, 62-9.

[62] Unpublished 2 June [19]62 letter to Rose Dercourt-Plaut in US-NH. For *Mamelles*, among other things, he reduced the instrumentation.

is *splendid* and I think that these few notes will sound very well."[63] As spring ended, Poulenc made a second short trip, this time to Milan to hear Manuel de Falla's "cantata scènique" *Atlantide* on 18 June as finished by Falla's student, Ernesto Halffter.[64] Long a devotée of Falla's music, Poulenc was anxious to hear a work which had only once been performed in a concert version in Barcelona on 24 November 1961. He was not enthralled by what he heard as he lamented to Simone Girard.[65] Yet the trip to Milan was useful for Poulenc; he met with the conductor Thomas Schippers who had not only led *Atlantide,* but was scheduled to conduct the premiere of *Sept répons* in 1963. After four days in Bagnols Poulenc was in Paris from 26 June to 2 July before departing for his summer rounds. During the late spring he also saw a superb production of Richard Strauss' *Salomé* by Frankfurt Opera followed by Hans Werner Henze's *Der Prinz von Homburg,* which he disliked.[66]

SUMMER 1962

Poulenc's disorganized summer, as he referred to it, took on a now familiar shape. Early in July he was in Brive from where he made his customary pilgrimage to Rocamadour on the 3rd. That day he wrote Yvonne Gouverné saying he had prayed to the Holy Mother for a good recording of *Figure humaine,* a thought which had occupied his mind since early April.[67] While staying with Marthe Bosredon in Brive several works began to take shape on her piano. "I found the elements of a Sonata for Oboe.[68] The first movement will be elegiac, the second scherzando, and the last a sort of liturgical chant. I think that writing for winds is presently the correct solution for me," he told Bernac.[69] The *brouillon* of the first movement is dated "Brive juillet 62."[70] Poulenc considered his stay in Brive "exquisite," calling it his true vacation.[71] After a brief return to Bagnols, Poulenc went to Aix on July 22nd for three days. While

---

[63] Unpublished 3 July [19]62 letter in US-NH. Poulenc intended to go to Baalbeck for the production because his friend Louis Gautier, who never budged, wanted to come.
[64] Several telegrams to Valcarenghi concerning tickets to the performance are in I-Mr.
[65] 22 June [1962] letter from Bagnols in Poulenc 1994, 62 and his comments to Bernac in an unpublished 3 July [19]62 letter in US-NH and 6 Aug. 1962 letter in Poulenc 1994, 62-17 (Poulenc 1991, no. 344).
[66] Unpublished 3 July [19]62 letter to Bernac in US-NH.
[67] Fragments of Poulenc's 5 Apr. and 21 July 1962 letters to Michel Garcin, artistic director of Erato records, in Poulenc 1994, p. 995, note 1.
[68] Schmidt 1995, FP 185.
[69] 14 July 1962 letter in Poulenc 1994, 62-13 (Poulenc 1991, no. 340).
[70] Schmidt 1995, FP 185, p. 510.
[71] 14 July 1962 letter to Bernac in Poulenc 1994, 62-13 (Poulenc 1991, no. 340).

there he heard Mozart's *Die Entführung auf dem Serail* on the 22nd, a solo recital by Teresa Berganza on the 23rd, and Duval in Milhaud's *Les Malheurs d'Orphée* followed by Stravinsky's *Les Noces*.[72] Although he thought the décor of *Les Malheurs* ravishing, he found Duval in poor voice and felt she understood little about the music.[73] After Aix Poulenc departed for Menton on the 29th to perform on the 31st with baritone Bernard Kruysen, a young Bernac student from Holland, and flautist Christian Lardé.[74] The outdoor concert included eight Debussy *mélodies* and Poulenc's Sonata for Flute and Piano.[75] Although he enjoyed performing with Kruysen, his pleasure was mitigated by an extreme case of food poisoning.[76]

The month ended with both joy and sadness. Sauguet wrote on 23 July that Poulenc's *Gloria*, under Walter Susskind's baton, had triumphed at the summer music festival in Aspen, Colorado.[77] Poulenc also authorized Robert Douglas Gibson to use the *Sinfonietta* for a ballet at Covent Garden.[78] However, Poulenc also learned the tragic news that his London friends Vere and Honor Pilkington had been involved in an automobile accident in Portugal in which Honor was killed.[79]

Poulenc was at Noizay in early August before going to Milan on the 20th, but at the last minute he was unable to go to Baalbeck. Three hours before his flight, he suffered a severe angina. Assisted by a Hotel Continental porter and loaded with penicillin by a doctor, he flew back to Paris by plane. Once cleared medically, Poulenc went immediately to Le Tremblay.[80] Cocteau's *Renaud et Armide* went on without him between the 18th and the 20th.

---

[72] 14 July 1962 letter in Poulenc 1994, 62-13 (Poulenc 1991, no. 340). The performance of *Noces* made Poulenc so nostalgic he wrote Stravinsky on 5 Aug. 1962 from Noizay. Poulenc 1994, 62-16 (Poulenc 1991, no. 343).

[73] Fragment of Poulenc's 28 July 1992 letter to Bernac in Poulenc 1994, p. 998, note 4. Poulenc found Annelise Rothenberger and Luigi Alva excellent in *Die Entführung*.

[74] Unpublished 28 July [19]62 letter to Bernac in US-NH. Block, p. 218 indicates that Poulenc and Lardé recorded the sonata on 3 July 1962 and that it was broadcast on 26 Aug., but the recording was almost surely made on 31 July. Lardé was a member of the Quintette M.C. Jamet (Jamet hp., Lardé fl., J. Sanchez vn., C. Lequien vla., and P. Degenne vc.), which also performed on the Menton program. I am grateful to the Festival de musique de Menton for providing me with a copy of the program.

[75] See Appendix 3 for specifics about the Debussy pieces.

[76] Unpublished 20 Aug. [19]62 letter to Bernac in US-NH.

[77] 3 July 1962 letter to Poulenc in Poulenc 1994, 62-15 (Poulenc 1991, no. 342).

[78] Unpublished 28 July [19]62 letter in GB-Lchester.

[79] Unpublished "jeudi" [27 July 1962] letter in US-NH. A letter to Poulenc from Vere discusses the circumstances of Honor's death. (Francis Poulenc Collection).

[80] Unpublished 20 Aug. [19]62 letter to Bernac in US-NH.

FALL 1962

Rose Dercourt-Plaut visited him in September while he continued to work on the wind sonatas. The Sonata for Clarinet and Piano (FP 184), dedicated to Honegger's memory, was finished first and re-copied during the early fall.[81] The Sonata for Oboe and Piano (FP 185), dedicated to Prokofiev's memory, took longer to complete and was still unfinished in early November.[82] Poulenc also wrote a brief encomiastic "Hommage à Benjamin Britten" which appeared in *Trib-ute to Benjamin Britten on his 50th Birthday*.[83] In it he summarized the many pleasures he had enjoyed performing with Britten, listening to the Britten-Pears duo, and the Aldeburgh production of *Les Mamelles de Tirésias*. Shortly after 22 October Poulenc left for a multi-week stay in Cannes.[84]

While in the Midi Poulenc planned his April 1963 trip to the United States for the premieres of *Sept répons des ténèbres* by the New York Philharmonic and the two wind sonatas.[85] (See Appendix 2.) He planned to give a concert of his works for winds including Sextet, *Elégie*, Sonata for Flute and Piano, [intermission], Sonata for Oboe and Piano, and the Trio in Chicago.

Poulenc was still in Cannes on 12 November when he visited his dentist, had his cholesterol checked, and met someone named Stehelin, probably a doctor because Poulenc complained about a liver problem.[86] He planned to return to Paris on the 23rd and then de-part for Asolo, Italy on 3 December to serve on the Trieste Prize jury. The unusual location, in the foothills of the Apennines, was chosen because it was the home of Gian Francesco Malipiero, the jury presi-dent, who was in poor health. Poulenc remained in Asolo from the 3rd to the 6th; he then went to Venice where he stayed at the Gritti Palace Hotel for a few days before visiting Milan on the 11 and 12th to oversee planning for the 5 April 1963 Piccola Scala production of *Les Mamelles de Tirésias*.[87] The weather in Venice was unbelievably beautiful and the city was empty of tourists. Poulenc assured Bernac that he would then return for ten days to Bagnols, but would defi-nitely not take an apartment in Cannes. As usual, plans changed slightly. At the end of the year Poulenc spent Christmas in Bagnols and New Years with his family and the Destouches in Paris, where his apartment was now newly refurbished.

[81] References in Poulenc's letters published in Schmidt 1995, FP 185, p. 511.

[82] Unpublished 8 Nov. [19]62 letter to Bernac in US-NH.

[83] Poulenc 1963b, Poulenc 1994, 62-23 (Poulenc 1991, no. 348).

[84] Unpublished 22 Oct. [19]62 letter to Rose Dercourt-Plaut in US-NH. In a 1 Nov. 1962 letter he told Fournier that he would spend a month in the Midi. Poulenc 1994, 62-24. His Paris apartment was painted while he was away.

[85] Unpublished 8 Nov. [19]62 letters to Fred Plaut and Bernac in US-NH.

[86] Unpublished 8 Nov. [19]62 and 10 Nov. [19]62 letters to Bernac in US-NH.

[87] Malipiero confirms the dates in his homage to Poulenc in JournalMF 1963, 3.

POULENC'S LAST DAYS: JANUARY 1963

In January, while at Noizay for ten days with Richard Chanlaire, Poulenc worked at his last wind sonatas as well as *Sept répons*.[88] He also refined planning for his New York trip telling Rose Dercourt-Plaut that he wished to stay at his familiar Wyndham Hotel, and that Bernac and Suzanne Peignot would precede him on 30 March. Poulenc raised the possibility of a commission from Edward Benjamin on behalf of the Philadelphia Orchestra and asked Rose precisely how and what instrument Benjamin played. Benjamin was actually a wealthy patron who paid for commissions requested by the Orchestra.[89] At the end of 1962 Poulenc had learned that his American agent Franco Colombo intended to publish arrangements of several numbers from *Dialogues des Carmélites* including *Ave verum* and *Salve regina*. He expressly forbade Colombo from carrying out the plan, chastising him for having sent proofs before he had even received permission.[90]

Stéphane Audel was also at Noizay, and in April 1963 wrote an extensive preface to interviews with Poulenc which provides precious details about the composer's last weeks. According to Audel Poulenc devoted the first four of his last days at Noizay correcting proofs of *Sept répons*. To keep Audel productively occupied Poulenc lent him books about the Ballets Russes and Viennese twelve-tone composers. Their only time away from Noizay was an afternoon in neighboring Tours during which Poulenc purchased epicurean provisions. When the proofs were corrected, Audel quotes Poulenc as having said, "This will be my last religious work." During the next few days Poulenc complained that his own music bored him, that he would trade all of *Dialogues* for *La Voix humaine*, and that he didn't like the country, preferring Paris instead. Recounting their last Noizay evening together, Audel wrote:

> The evening before our return to Paris Francis lit a great wood-fire on the hearth, settled himself comfortably into his chair, and gave himself up to the pleasure of conversation. He was dazzling. Once again I admired the range of his culture. His knowledge of music, painting and literature was bewildering. Evoking the memories of his youth he brought to life again, with spirit, buffoonery and a fantastic sense of observation, the surrealists, the Princesse de Polignac, Diaghilev, Wanda Landowska, Anna de Noailles, not forgetting Satie, Georges

---

[88] Unpublished 8 Jan. [19]63 letter to Rose Dercourt-Plaut in US-NH.

[89] In the 1960s Benjamin paid for commissions to Eugene Zador, Virgil Thomson, Miklós Rózsa, Alberto Ginastera, Gottfried von Einem, Nicolas Nabokov, among others. I am grateful to the Philadelphia Orchestra archivist JoAnne Barry for this information.

[90] Copy of Poulenc's unpublished 3 Jan. [19]63 letter to Colombo in I-Mr. This copy was sent to Valcarenghi along with a brief explanation.

Auric, Cocteau, Éluard, and Marcel Proust, from whose *Sodome et Gomorrhe* he read a passage about Monsieur de Charlus.[91]

Poulenc left Noizay for frigid Paris on 14 January and mailed Robert Douglas Gibson the Sonata for Clarinet and Piano manuscript on the 18th saying that the Sonata for Oboe and Piano would follow in a week.[92] Poulenc and Audel dined together on two occasions before attending the theater. On the first evening they attended a Comédie française performance and on the second they went to the Théâtre de l'Ambigu, a venue which sent Poulenc into raptures because of its beautiful architecture, which he likened to an Honoré Daumier lithograph.

In the fourth week of January, Poulenc toured with Duval. They spent four days in Holland giving concerts and on the 26th gave one in Maastricht with the Limburgs Symphonie Orkest. André Rieu conducted a program that included Poulenc's Suite from *Les Biches, Concert champêtre, La Dame de Monte-Carlo,* and arias from *Les Mamelles de Tirésias.* The program also included Ravel's *Daphnis et Chloé* (2nd Suite).[93] After the concert Poulenc sent flowers to Duval's hotel room along with the message: "My Denise, it is to you I owe my last joy. Your poor Fr."[94] He returned to Paris on Monday, 28 January and the next day telephoned Duval to say he would like to lunch with her on Wednesday the 30th. However, on that same morning, suffering from a sore throat, he called to say he could not go out. A 6:30 pm recording session for an interview with Audel had also been scheduled for the 30th in the rue François 1er. They had planned to continue their interviews with four new broadcasts devoted to Diaghilev, Landowska, Schönberg/Berg/Webern, and Théâtre lyrique, but fate willed otherwise.[95] At one o'clock in the afternoon Poulenc died of a heart attack in his 5, rue de Médicis apartment. Many years later Auric spoke to François Mauriac about seeing Poulenc on his death bed: "Poulenc wasn't handsome, I said with-

[91] Poulenc 1963a, p. 20 (Poulenc 1978, pp. 21-2).

[92] Unpublished 18 Jan. [19]63 to Gibson in GB-Lchester. On 8 Jan. 1963 Poulenc had sent M Burdon a copy of the Sonata for Oboe and Piano with a request to film it and make two copies which he would pick up when he came to Paris. Schmidt 1995, FP 185, p. 512.

[93] Dijk, pp. 108-09 and Poulenc 1994, p. 1008 (Poulenc 1991, p. 298). For an advertisement of the program see *Die Nieuwe Limburger* (24 Jan. 1963); for reviews see T. F. in *Die Nieuwe Limburger* (26 Jan. 1963) and Jef Somers in *Limburgs Dagblad* (28 Jan. 1963); Berenguer, p. 68.

[94] Poulenc 1994, p. 1008 (Poulenc 1991, p. 298).

[95] "The Last Days at Noizay" in Poulenc 1963a, p. 9 (Poulenc 1978, p. 13).

out the slightest irony, he was no Apollo. But in death, his face took on a serenity, an admirable sweetness."[96]

FUNERAL AND MEMORIALS

Poulenc's funeral mass was celebrated on Saturday morning 2 February at St Sulpice, a most important church on the left bank of the Seine. Those attending the service, on a very cold morning, remarked that not a note of Poulenc's music was played.[97] Instead, Marcel Dupré, who had succeeded Charles Widor as organist at St Sulpice in 1934, performed music by Bach. The choir, famous for its plainsong, sang the traditional monophonic liturgy. Poulenc was placed in a tomb at Le Père Lachaise cemetery, the largest and most famous Parisian burial ground, which occupies more than one hundred acres. Named after Louis XIV's Jesuit confessor, this cemetery is the final resting place of numerous dignitaries, artists, and statesmen. Included among them are Guillaume Apollinaire, Christian Bérard, Colette, Claude Delvincourt, the Eluards (Nusch and Paul), Marie Laurencin, Ginette Neveu, Jean Nohain, and Raymond Radiguet.[98] When Brigitte Manceaux died several months after Poulenc, she was placed in the same tomb.

Poulenc's sudden death deeply shocked the music world and tributes filled not only the pages of French newspapers, but those of journals abroad. He had few detractors, for he seldom if ever involved himself in polemical debates about musical aesthetics. At the same time his music had touched countless individuals around the world. When news reached Poulenc's old friend Vittorio Rieti in New York, he penned a moving letter to Milhaud on 30 January which began, "I am deeply distressed by the news of Francis' death —I can hardly believe it, it seems impossible to me."[99] The *Journal musical français* included a lengthy "Hommage à Francis Poulenc" in its 6 March 1963 issue. Below a famous Lipnitzki portrait of *Les Six*, Cocteau wrote a moving tribute noting that with Poulenc's death a "lovely branch of our genealogical tree *[Les Six]* fell." Cocteau's "Hommage" preceded nineteen others written by Auric, Milhaud, Tailleferre, Bernac, Britten, Dumesnil, Duruflé, Février, Gavoty, Hell, Jolivet, Malipiero, and Rostand to name but a few. There were also numerous obituaries or memorial tributes by notables such as Lennox Berkeley,[100] Bernard Gavoty,[101] Roland Gelatt,[102] Michel

---

[96] Mauriac, p. 241.
[97] Schneider, p. 221.
[98] Langlade, passim.
[99] Ricci, p. 360.
[100] *The Musical Times* 104 (Mar. 1963), 205.
[101] "Hommage à Poulenc," *Le Figaro* (13 Dec. 1963), 6.
[102] "The 'Last' French Composer," *The Reporter* (28 Mar. 1963), 52-6.

Hayoz,[103] Henri Hell,[104] Allen Hughes,[105] Irving Kolodin,[106] François Mauriac,[107] Roy McMullen,[108] Ned Rorem,[109] Claude Rostand,[110] and Marcel Schneider[111] in the months following his passing.

Poulenc was memorialized in other ways. The 10 April concert at New York's Carnegie Hall, during which his Sonata for Clarinet and Piano was premiered, became a "Composers' Showcase Francis Poulenc Memorial Concert," and Leonard Bernstein accompanied Benny Goodman in Poulenc's place. This concert was the first of three organized by Doda Conrad.[112] *Sept répons* was premiered a day later at Philharmonic Hall by the Walter Baker Chorus, the boys of The Little Church Around the Corner and St Paul's Church Flatbush, Jeffrey Meyer, soprano, and the New York Philharmonic Orchestra conducted by Thomas Schippers.[113] The Sonata for Oboe and Piano, originally scheduled for performance by Poulenc on 27 April, was played instead by Pierre Pierlot and Jacques Février on 8 June at the Festival International in Strasbourg. Conrad's other two concerts took place at the Abbey of Royaumont during the summer season, and at the Salle Gaveau on 18 November.[114] There was also an homage to Poulenc at the Théâtre Graslin in Nantes on 21 October.[115]

Alice Esty, accompanied by David Stimer, sang a concert in homage to Poulenc at Carnegie Recital Hall on Monday evening 13 January 1964. For the occasion, at the suggestion of her longtime accompanist and coach, she commissioned twelve composers to write an "Hommage à Francis Poulenc." The contributors included Henk

---

103 "In Memoriam: Francis Poulenc et son temps," *Schweitzerische Musikzeitung* 103, no. 6 (1963), 352-5.
104 "Hommage à Francis Poulenc," *Musica* (Chaix), no. 109 (Apr. 1963), 36-42.
105 "Poulenc's Music Reflected Man: Works, Like Writer, 'Half Monk, Half Bounder'," *The New York Times* (2 Feb. 1963), 5 and "Francis Poulenc," *Musical America* 83 (Feb. 1963).
106 "The Merit of Poulenc," *Saturday Review* 46 (23 Feb. 1963), 49-50.
107 "Bloc-Notes," (9 Feb. 1963).
108 "Notes from Abroad: Paris," *High Fidelity* 13 (May 1963), 18.
109 "Poulenc - A Memoir," *Tempo*, no. 64 (spring 1963), 28-9.
110 "Francis Poulenc; hier et demain," *Le Figaro littéraire* (9 Feb. 1963), 17 and "Visages de Poulenc" *Feuilles musicale, Revue musicale de Suisse romande* 16 (30 Apr. 1963), 9-12.
111 "Si Poulenc m'était conté," *Les Nouvelles littéraires* (7 Feb. 1963), 10.
112 Other performers included Jennie Tourel, the Collegiate Chorale under Abraham Kaplan, and Gold and Fizdale. See Conrad 1997, pp. 411-12.
113 Reviews in Schmidt 1995, FP 181, p. 501. Peignot and Bernac both came to New York for this premier. See Peignot, p. 6.
114 Repertoire and performers in Conrad 1997, pp. 412-13.
115 See the advertising poster listed in Boulet, no. 61.

Badings, Lennox Berkeley, Henri Dutilleux, Frank Martin, Darius Milhaud, Vittorio Rieti, Ned Rorem, Manuel Rosenthal, Henri Sauguet, Germaine Tailleferre, Virgil Thomson, and Ben Weber.[116] The program began with Poulenc's *Dernier poème* and *La Courte Paille* and ended with "Dans l'herbe" (from *Fiançailles pour rire*) and *La Fraîcheur et le feu*. Shortly after Esty's concert, Gold and Fizdale presented New York premieres of Poulenc's *Elégie* and *Capriccio* as well as the Sonata for Two Pianos, and Gérard Souzay sang a group of Poulenc *mélodies*.[117] Benjamin Britten and Peter Pears were also involved in a tribute to Poulenc in Thorpeness on 15 June 1964.[118]

Poulenc has also been memorialized in less ephemeral ways. At Rocamadour a *Musée trésor Francis Poulenc* was inaugurated on 4 May 1969.[119] Earlier Poulenc had donated a silver chalice and a silver ciborium designed by Jean Puiforcat, which were incorporated into the Museum's collection. The former is inscribed with music from the "Ayez pitié de nous" section of *Litanies de la Vierge noire* signed "Francis Poulenc 1938." The latter, inscribed "Deo gratias Juin 1957 Francis Poulenc," commemorates completion of *Dialogues*.[120] In Amboise, near Poulenc's Noizay estate, a room in the city hall is named after him.

On the outside wall of his 5, rue de Médicis Paris apartment is affixed a plaque inscribed "DANS CETTE MAISON VÉCUT FRANCIS POULENC MUSICIEN FRANÇAIS DÉCEDÉ LE 30 JANVIER 1963," and the corner of the rue de Vaugirard and the rue de Tournon is now called "Square Francis Poulenc."[121] Likewise in Noizay, a plaque is affixed to the column supporting the front gate of Le Grand Coteau inscribed "Dans cette maison vécut Francis POULENC Musicien français." A number of French cities and towns have added streets or squares named after Poulenc, and festivals and competitions further honor his name.

Finally, a few poets and composers have written poems or music in Poulenc's memory. The British poet Thomas Tessier included a twelve-stanza poem entitled "Francis Poulenc" in his 1971 collec-

---

[116] I am grateful to Claire Brook for generously giving me a program of this recital. See also Buckland's note in Poulenc 1991, p. 304 and Rorem 1983, p. 231, who points out that Esty also commissioned the poetry of some of these songs. For a review see C. S. S., "Alice Esty," *Musical America* 84 (Feb. 1964), 34.

[117] Theodore Strongin, "Poulenc Tribute Given at Museum: Gold-Fizdale, Pianists, and Souzay, Baritone, Perform," *The New York Times* (27 Jan. 1964), 20.

[118] See Buckland's note in Poulenc 1991, p. 300.

[119] Lherm: the catalogue lists 116 items.

[120] Gouverné, photographs 10 & 11. Poulenc told Marthe Bosredon that he intended to make this gift ". . . as an act of thanks once *Les Carmélites* is finished." 27 Aug. [1955] letter in Poulenc 1994, 55-12 (Poulenc 1991, no. 266).

[121] Gouverné, photograph no. 12: "In this house lived Francis POULENC Musicien française (deceased the 30th of January 1963)."

tion *In Sight of Chaos*.[122] In 1982 Sándor Szokolay's *Déploration à la mémoire de Francis Poulenc pour piano solo, chœur mixte, orgue et orchestre de chambre* was published, and in 1995 Ernesto Halffter's *Hommages: petite suite pour trio (violon, violoncelle & piano)*, written earlier and containing movements honoring Poulenc, Stravinsky, and Adolfo Salazar, was published.[123]

LAST WILL AND TESTAMENT

Poulenc's original will, drawn up on 2 June 1954 and dated a day later, was quite simple.

Ceci est mon testament	This is my will Francis Poulenc
Francis Poulenc	
2 juin 54 - Paris - le 3 juin 1954	2 June 54 - Paris - 3 June 1954
<u>Seule,</u> je dis bien <u>seule</u>	<u>Alone,</u> state clearly <u>alone,</u>
Mademoiselle Brigitte Manceaux,	Mademoiselle Brigitte Manceaux,
mon héritiere testamentaire,	my heir by will,
aura le droit de s'occuper du	will have the right to deal with
destin posthume de mon oeuvre,	the posthumous destiny of my
<u>sous toutes ses formes.</u>	works, <u>in all their manifestations.</u>
Francis Poulenc	Francis Poulenc

A more detailed version of Poulenc's will probated after his death included gifts of property, royalties, and possessions not only to his niece Brigitte Manceaux, but also to his daughter Marie-Ange, to his faithful friend Raymond Destouches, and to another niece Mme Jean Seringe. Matters became complicated when Brigitte died within months of Poulenc. A different distribution of Poulenc's estate ensued and Mme Seringe inherited Le Grand Coteau at Noizay which she and her husband maintain to this day.[124] Bernac, Poulenc's long-standing concert partner and friend, was not included in his will.[125]

EPILOGUE

In death as in life, Poulenc remains a series of paradoxes. No one has captured this better than Allen Hughes, who wrote in 1963:

> He hired the solitude of a hotel and despised solitude, preferring to be surrounded by many people. He did not like the country very much, but maintained a home in the middle of it. He adored Paris and could not bear to stay there for more than a few weeks at a time.

---

[122] Tessier, pp. 10-11.
[123] See A. Leduc (A.L. 24.428) and M. Eschig (M.E. 8919) respectively.
[124] Copyright renewal information for Poulenc's works appears in Schmidt 1995, passim.
[125] Several of Poulenc's friends have suggested to me that this is owing to French law, which makes it difficult to designate gifts outside the immediate family.

He did not like to walk, but neither drove nor owned a car. He was enough of a gourmand to enjoy eating pastries before lunch but was given to restricting himself to the strictest of diets. He loved dogs, particularly those that attached themselves to only one person, but would not allow himself to have one in his later years. Known all his life for his exuberant wit and drollery, he was always subject to attacks of melancholy.[126]

There were also the paradoxes of Poulenc's sexuality, his financial situation, and his self confidence. In letters he occasionally shared aspects of his private life in a boastful manner while at the same time cautioning the recipient not to divulge the contents to faithful and trusted associates. Inherited family money assured his financially security despite two world wars, but he was not above pleading poverty to aristocratic friends or meticulously collecting royalties and fees wherever he could. Confidence in his own abilities, unflinching when it came to performing at the piano, was sometimes lacking in matters of composition as discussion of the Piano Concerto and *Dialogues des Carmélites* suggests.

Perhaps the peripatetic nature of his yearly routine, which saw frequent travel between Paris and Noizay, hotels in France and Switzerland where he set up multi-week residencies, and inexorable touring on various continents speaks to his need for constantly changing stimuli. He longed for positive reinforcement from friends and relatives, many of whom graciously lodged and entertained him, but his stays were brief and while at one place he was already looking ahead to the next and planning for the future. He counted on them and they were only too willing to accommodate "Poupoule," whom they adored and respected.

Paradoxes aside—and the list is far longer than that recounted here—Poulenc was and is genuinely admired by the vast majority of those who knew him personally and by countless thousands whose sole contact with him has been through his music. He was an enormously cultured man possessed of a wide knowledge of art and literature.[127] His musical repertory was also enormous, bridging all periods and ranging from the music hall to what he delighted in calling Darmstadt "dodécaca." Yet if his music is his portrait, then no composer could be more pleased with its continuing reception. With the one-hundredth anniversary of Poulenc's birth on 30

[126] Hughes 1963, p. 29.

[127] A fascinating glimpse into Poulenc's literary likes and dislikes is offered by his response to Raymond Queneau, a French writer who surveyed numerous "personalities" in 1950 in an attempt to establish an ideal library. Poulenc's response is published in *Pour une bibliothèque idéale* (Paris: Gallimard, 1956) and in Buckland/Chimènes: h. Poulenc lists 128 "books that I would like to own" and 11 "books I would detest owning."

January 1999 now history, interest in the man and his music not only remains strong but appears to be growing. In honor of the centenary EMI has reissued its extensive Poulenc catalogue on compact disks (including the large majority of his works), Charles Dutoit has recorded another comprehensive group of instrumental works, and Poulenc's music publishers have been busy issuing corrected copies of important compositions and anthologies.

More than twenty years ago Ned Rorem wrote:

> Certain composers when they die, like Hindemith, are placed in cold storage for a generation, sometimes forever. A far smaller group—Bartók, for instance—are no sooner cold than they suffer a resurgence. What Parisian in 1950 would have dreamed that Poulenc, not Milhaud or Honegger, would eventually be the composer to represent his generation.[128]

Much the same could be said today as all members of *Les Six* have celebrated their centenaries. Friends of Poulenc societies flourish in France and the United States and a small number of works discovered in the 1990s have even been added to Poulenc's canon. Among those who noted Poulenc's promise early in his career, several stand out. Cocteau's was a clarion voice from the beginning, and let us not forget those who ventured to publish music by a young man not yet twenty. Writers for the *Chesterian* such as Albert Roussel, Louis Durey, and André George helped bring Poulenc to public attention in the late teens or early twenties and in the late 1920s influential critics including Henry Prunières were singing his praises. By the early 1930s, Rollo Myers had already spotted Poulenc's major characteristics.

> Poulenc is always Poulenc; he never tries to be anybody else, although it would be idle to deny that his music shows traces of inevitable influences ranging from Gounod and Chabrier to Satie and Stravinsky. If asked to describe in a few words Poulenc's musical style I should say that it showed the influence of Stravinskian technique upon a melodic inspiration deriving from the classics. I should also say that his music seems to me chiefly remarkable for (*a*) its melody, (*b*) its spontaneity and youthful freshness, (*c*) its "charm" by which I mean a definitely pleasing character, (*d*) a certain quality that for want of a better term I would call "musicality."[129]

Poulenc was also greatly appreciated during his lifetime for excellence as a pianist. His finest work was undoubtedly with Bernac, but he also toured successfully with Fournier and Duval and col-

[128] Rorem 1977, p. 15.
[129] Concerning early articles in the *Chesterian* see Durey, George, and Roussel respectively. Myers, pp. 129-30.

laborated successfully with Février on his Concerto in D minor. Recordings, which he made with all but Fournier, remind us today of his excellence. His deep-seated need for interaction with others is manifested not only through his performances, but also through his extensive correspondence with numerous friends and business acquaintances. Among his friends may be numbered not only musicians and wealthy patrons, but also important artists and writers. As this writer can attest, however, he was never too busy to entertain a stranger from whom he could have little to gain.

In two telling statements Poulenc spoke candidly of how he wanted to be remembered: "If on my tomb could be inscribed: 'Here lies Francis Poulenc, the musician of Apollinaire and Eluard,' I would consider this my finest claim to glory,"[130] and "I would like that people think of me as 'the poet's musician'."[131] Poulenc also instructed his close friend Marie-Blanche de Polignac, "Think often of your Poupoule. Love his music, that is all I ask of you."[132] But Stravinsky, for whom Poulenc had the greatest reverence, said it best: "Very dear Poulenc, send me, I beg of you, a little of your music. You know what loyal and tender sentiments I have always had for your entrancing muse."[133] Stravinsky's sentiment was echoed by Nadia Boulanger who said, "We thank God for it, Francis, for your presence, your friendship, your work; these change one's life."[134] To this she added, "What a great musician you are, dear Francis, and a great heart."[135]

[130] Poulenc 1964, p. 69; Poulenc 1993, p. 39 (May 1945 entry).
[131] 15 Sept. [1948] letter to Thomson in Poulenc 1994, 48-6.
[132] [28 Aug.] 1939 letter to Marie-Blanche in Poulenc 1994, 39-9 (Poulenc 1991, no. 147).
[133] Stravinsky's 10 Jan. 1946 letter to Poulenc in Poulenc 1994, 46-1 (Poulenc 1991, no. 188).
[134] Boulanger's 31 Dec. 1936 letter to Poulenc in Poulenc 1994, 36-33.
[135] Boulanger's 6 Oct. 1939 letter to Poulenc in Poulenc 1994, 39-17.

APPENDIX I

Dramatis Personae

MEMBERS OF POULENC'S FAMILY:

Manceaux, André (1883-1967)—Poulenc's brother-in-law who married Jeanne Poulenc in 1913. He was a Parisian notary.

Manceaux, Brigitte (1914-63)—Poulenc's niece. She was a pianist who studied with Marguerite Long. Poulenc frequently relied on her advice, and she was particularly helpful when he wrote the Concerto in D minor. She inherited Poulenc's estate, but died four months after him following an operation.

Manceaux, Jeanne [née Poulenc] (1887-1974)—Poulenc's older sister who married the notary André Manceaux in 1913. She had three children: Brigitte Manceaux, Rosine [Manceaux] Seringe, and Denis Manceaux. She studied singing with Jeanne Raunay and Claire Croiza and is the dedicatee of "La Grâce exilée" from *Calligrammes*. Poulenc often visited her in Normandy at Le Tremblay (Tremblay Omonville), where she and her husband had purchased a château in 1927.

Marie-Ange (b. 1946)—daughter of Francis Poulenc and Frédérique (b. 1907). As a young girl she aspired to a career as a dancer.

Poulenc, Camille (1864-1942)—Poulenc's uncle and one of the founders of Etablissements Poulenc frères. He held the degree "Docteur ès sciences" and contributed to the chemical literature of the day.

Poulenc, Émile (1855-1917) — Poulenc's father and one of the founders of Etablissements Poulenc frères.

Poulenc, Mme Émile [née Jenny Royer] (1865-1915)—Poulenc's mother. An amateur pianist with a particular interest in the arts, she was nurturing in this respect to her young son,who was sixteen when she died.

Poulenc, Étienne (1823-78) — Poulenc's grandfather and father of Camille, Émile, and Gaston Poulenc.

Poulenc, Gaston Joseph (1852-1948)—Poulenc's uncle and one of the founders of Etablissements Poulenc Frères.

Poulenc, Gérard [Frère Jérôme] (1925-89)—son of Étienne Poulenc who took the Franciscan habit in 1945 and subsequently entered the priesthood. It is he who asked Poulenc to compose *Quatre petites prières de Saint François d'Assise*.

Royer, Marcel (1862-1945)—frequently referred to as "Uncle Papoum," Royer was the brother of Poulenc's mother. Poulenc noted that he could not pronounce the word "parrain" which became "Papoum." Royer was an amateur painter and devotée of the arts who delighted in overseeing Poulenc's development in this area. His connections to the artistic community fascinated Poulenc.

Seringe, Rosine [née Manceaux] (b. 1918)—daughter of Jeanne and André Manceaux, she is Poulenc's niece and goddaughter. When Brigitte Manceaux died only months after Poulenc, she inherited the major portion of his estate. She is the general secretary of Les Amis de Francis Poulenc and a generous friend to those involved with all aspects of her uncle.

POULENC'S FRIENDS AND ACQUAINTANCES:

Anouilh, Jean (1910-87)—author of numerous plays including *Léocadia* (1940), *Le Voyageur sans bagages* (1943-44), and *L'Invitation au château* (1947) for which Poulenc wrote music.

Ansermet, Ernest (1883-1969)—Swiss conductor who not only organized the Orchestre de la suisse romande in Geneva, but was also closely associated with Diaghilev's Ballets Russes.

Apollinaire, Guillaume (1880-1919)—poet, playwright, and art critic who had an enormous influence on arts and letters of early twentieth-century France. Poulenc greatly admired his poetry and set numerous poems as songs. He made an opera out of *Les Mamelles de Tirésias*.

Ardoin, Alice [née Linossier] (1893-1964)—sister of Raymonde Linossier and Suzanne Latarjet. She was a doctor with whom Poulenc remained friendly until the end of his life and was the recipient of the famous letter in which Poulenc asked her to intercede in securing Raymonde's hand in marriage.

Audel, Stéphane (d. 1984)—actor who also hosted a series of radio interviews with Poulenc which were broadcast on Radio Suisse-Romande in 1953, 1956, and 1962.

Auric, Georges (1899-1983)—member of *Les Six* who was a composer, pianist, critic, and arts administrator. He and Poulenc were the closest of friends who not only shared concerts, but also recorded together.

Auric, Nora [née Vilter] (1903-82)—painter allied to the surrealists who married Auric in 1930. She painted portraits of prominent figures in the arts, including Poulenc, Auric, Éluard, and Cocteau.

Balguerie, Suzanne (1888-1973)—soprano who premiered Satie's *Socrate* at Adrienne Monnier's La Maison des Amis du livre. Poulenc occasionally accompanied her.

Bartók, Béla (1881-1945)—Hungarian composer, pianist, and ethnomusicologist whom Poulenc met in 1922. Poulenc liked his music and said he wished he had written his six String Quartets.

Bathori, Jane (1877-1970)—mezzo-soprano who made her operatic debut in Nantes in 1900. She championed the vocal music of French composers such as Poulenc, Auric, Milhaud, Debussy, Ravel, and Satie.

Beach, Sylvia (1887-1962)—proprietress of Shakespeare and Company bookstore at 12, rue de l'Odéon across the street from Adrienne Monnier's bookstore.

Beaumont, Count Etienne de (1883-1956)—wealthy member of Parisian society who organized "Soirées de Paris" in 1924 and was the host of numerous lavish costume balls at his rue Duroc residence. Poulenc met him when he was eighteen.

Bérard, Christian [called Bébé] (1902-49)—noted painter and decorator who worked with Édouard Vuillard. He had a particularly important association with Jean Cocteau with whom he collaborated on a number of projects. Poulenc was very fond of Bérard and dedicated his *Stabat Mater* to Bérard's memory.

Bernac, Pierre ([Pierre Louis Bertin] 1899-1979)—eminent baritone and teacher who changed his name so as not to be confused with the actor Pierre Bertin. Bernac formed a duo with Poulenc in 1935; they performed and recorded for twenty-four years. Poulenc frequently sought his advice about prosody, range, and dramatic effect.

Bernanos, Georges (1888-1948)—Catholic writer of numerous novels whose screen play *Dialogues des Carmélites* Poulenc set as an opera.

Bernstein, Leonard (1918-90)—composer, pianist, and conductor whom Poulenc met on his first American tour in 1948. He helped commission *Sept répons des ténèbres* for the opening of Lincoln Center in New York.

Bertin, Pierre (1895-1984)—actor, singer, and playwright who performed at the Théâtre de l'Odéon, the Comédie-Française, and the Compagnie Renaud-Barrault. In the teens he was a co-director with Jane Bathori of concerts at the Théâtre du Vieux-Columbier, one of which featured Poulenc's *Rapsodie nègre*.

Blanche, Jacques-Emile (1861-1942)—painter, writer, and art critic well known for his portraits of important people including Poulenc when he was still in military service following World War I.

Bosredon, Marthe (?)—amateur pianist and friend. At her home in Brive Poulenc composed works such as *Histoire de Babar, le petit éléphant* and the Sonata for Cello and Piano. He dedicated "Hôtel" from *Banalités* and "C'est ainsi que tu es" from *Métamorphoses* to her.

Boulanger, Nadia (1887-1979)—renowned composition teacher who taught numerous Americans from Aaron Copland to Philip Glass. She taught at the Ecole normale de musique, the American Conservatory at Fontainebleau, and privately. Boulanger read proofs of Poulenc's compositions in the 1930s and conducted the private premiere of his Concerto in G minor.

Bourdet, Denise (1892-1967)—journalist who had known Poulenc since 1917. She occasionally wrote about Poulenc, and he dedicated "Je n'ai envie que de t'aimer" (from *Tel jour telle nuit*) and "Violon" (from *Fiançailles pour rire)* to her.

Bourdet, Edouard (1887-1945)—a playwright who wrote *La Reine Margot* for which both Poulenc and Auric contributed music. Denise Bourdet was his second wife.

Britten, Benjamin (1913-76)—English composer, conductor, and pianist who was the longtime partner of tenor Peter Pears. Poulenc met Britten in 1945, and the two performed Poulenc's Concerto in D minor. Later Britten invited Poulenc to perform at his Aldeburgh Festival.

Casa Fuerte, Yvonne de [née Yvonne Giraud] (1895-1984)—originally a violinist who studied at the Paris Conservatory with Milhaud, she was a founder of the Parisian concert society called La Sérénade. Poulenc valued her musical judgments, and she is the dedicatee of *Sécheresses*.

Casella, Alfredo (1883-1947)—Italian composer and pianist who studied at the Paris Conservatory with Gabriel Fauré and Louis Diémer. In Italy he founded various musical organizations including the Società Nazionale di Musica. Casella encouraged Poulenc to resurrect his *Trois pastorales* which became *Trois pièces pour piano*.

Chabrier, Emmanuel (1841-94)—composer who earlier took a degree in law and worked for the French government. Two great influences on his compositions were Richard Wagner and the music of Spain.

Chanel, Gabrielle [called Coco] (1883-1971)—couturière who amassed an immense fortune. Her first major costuming job was for Cocteau's *Antigone* in 1922, and she also designed the costumes for Diaghilev's Ballets Russes production of Milhaud's *Le Train bleu*.

Chanlaire, Richard (d. early 1970s)—painter who maintained shops both in Paris and Tourrettes-sur-Loup. He sold not only traditional paintings, but hand-painted scarves and screens. Poulenc met Chanlaire in the 1920s, and their relationship developed into a passionate affair by the end of the decade. They remained friendly until Poulenc's death.

Chanlaire, Suzette (?) — Richard Chanlaire's sister-in-law. Poulenc dedicated several pieces to her including his first Nocturne and "Sanglots" from *Banalités*.

Cocteau, Jean (1889-1963)—important contributor to numerous artistic and literary disciplines who was responsible for some of Poulenc's earliest compositional opportunities. Poulenc set several Cocteau texts early in his life and set *La Voix humaine* at the end of his life. The two first met when Satie composed *Parade* for Diaghilev.

Colette [Sidonie-Gabrielle] (1873-1954)—writer of numerous works including a series of books involving a character called *Chéri*. Poulenc set only one of her texts, *Le Portrait*, but the two were good friends, and she decorated Poulenc as a *Grand officier de la Légion d'Honneur*.

Collaer, Paul (1891-1989)—Belgian musicologist, pianist, and promoter of avant-garde music who began his career as a professor of chemistry and physics. He founded the Pro Arte Concerts and from 1937-53 was musical director of the Flemish service of Belgian Radio. He arranged performances of works by Poulenc and his contemporaries and wrote monographs on Milhaud, Stravinsky, and twentieth-century music.

Collet, Henri (1885-1951)—composer and music critic who was responsible for coining the term *Les Six*.

Conrad, Doda (1905-98)—Polish bass, son of the singer Marya Freund. A member of Boulanger's ensemble during the 1930s, he was a superb organizer of concerts, recordings, and publications. Poulenc wrote *Hymne* for Conrad when he visited the United States.

Coolidge, Elizabeth Sprague (1864-1953)—American patroness who established the Berkshire Festival of Chamber Music in 1918 and later sponsored the Elizabeth Sprague Coolidge Foundation at the Library of Congress. This foundation commissioned numerous composers including Poulenc.

Croiza, Claire [Claire Connolly] (1882-1946)—mezzo-soprano who sang at the Paris Opéra and throughout Europe. She was a renowned teacher at the Ecole normale de musique and after 1934 at the Paris Conservatory. Poulenc occasionally accompanied her recitals.

Dallapiccola, Luigi (1904-75)—Italian composer and teacher. Poulenc admired his music, and he and Bernac premiered Dallapiccola's *Rencesvals*. The two occasionally judged competitions together.

Danco, Suzanne (b. 1911)—Belgian soprano who won her first international prize in Venice in 1936. She sang both opera and lieder, and Poulenc wrote several soprano parts with her voice in mind.

Delmas-Marsalet, Dr. Maurice (b. 1929)—the son of Professor Paul Delmas-Marsalet, he was a neuropsychologist and poet. Poulenc found him a room in Paris when he was studying medicine.

Delmas-Marsalet, Prof. Paul (1899-1979)—professor of neuropsychology at Bordeaux. Poulenc met him on the steamship De Grasse in 1952 and the Professor helped him during his depression in 1954. In gratitude Poulenc gave him a manuscript of *Dialogues des Carmélites*.

Dercourt-Plaut, Rose (d. 1992)—soprano of Polish origin who studied in Paris with Marya Freund. She was married to Fred Plaut, a recording engineer for Columbia who was also a prolific photographer. Poulenc met her in New York during his first trip to the United States in 1948. She was his social secretary on subsequent American trips. He dedicated "Nuage" from *Deux mélodies* to her and they recorded one album for Turnabout in 1957.

Désormière, Roger (1898-1963)—conductor who studied at the Paris Conservatory and gained prominence with both the Ballets Suédois and the Ballets Russes during the 1920s. Poulenc greatly admired his intelligence as a conductor.

Destouches, Raymond (d. 1988)—a chauffeur by trade whom Poulenc met at Noizay. Their relationship, which spanned approximately thirty years, ran the gamut from passionate to fraternal. Destouches was devoted to Poulenc, and Poulenc dedicated *Mélancolie* to him. The Concerto for Piano is co-dedicated to Destouches and Denise Duval. Later in life Raymond married Céline, and "Le Hérisson" from *Petites voix* is dedicated to their son Jean.

Diaghilev, Serge (1872-1929)—Russian impresario who established the Ballets Russes in Paris. He commissioned various ballets from Stravinsky including *Le Sacre du Printemps* and *Les Noces*. He also commissioned ballets from members of *Les Six: Les Biches* from Poulenc, *Les Fâcheux* from Auric, and *Le Train bleu* from Milhaud.

Dugardin, Hervé (1910-69)—music editor and theater director. Poulenc became involved with him when he was director of Editions Ricordi in Paris in 1953. He was also director of the Opéra-Comique and the Théâtre des Champs-Élysées. Poulenc dedicated *La Voix humaine* to Hervé and his wife Daisy (a niece of Princess Edmond de Polignac).

Dullin, Charles (1885-1949)—actor and theater director, Dullin was part of the company established by Jacques Copeau at the Théâtre du Vieux-Colombier. He and Poulenc worked together on Charles Exbrayat's *La Fille du jardinier* in 1941.

Durey, Louis (1888-1979)—composer and member of *Les Six*. The oldest of them, he produced the least music. Durey resigned from the group early on, moved to St Tropez, and was active in the French Communist Party from 1936. Poulenc dedicated *Le Bestiaire* to him.

Duval, Denise (b. 1921)—French soprano whose career began at the Folies-Bergères. She and Poulenc were brought together by Max de Rieux. She sang at both the Paris Opéra and Opéra-Comique and was the featured singer in all Poulenc's operas. Poulenc toured Europe and the United States with Duval after Bernac's retirement. She is the co-dedicatee with Raymond Destouches of the Concerto for Piano, and Poulenc also dedicated his cycle *La Courte Paille* to her and her first husband Richard Schilling.

Eluard, Paul [Eugène-Emile-Paul Grindel] (1895-1952)—poet with whom Poulenc had a close friendship. Eluard was, along with Aragon, Breton, and Soupault, a founder of the Surrealist movement. Poulenc set many Eluard poems, and Eluard also supplied titles for several of Poulenc's song cycles.

Esty, Alice (1904-2000)—American soprano who studied with Pierre Bernac. She commissioned songs from a number of composers, including a group in Poulenc's memory which she performed in Carnegie Recital Hall in 1964. Poulenc dedicated *Le Travail du peintre* to her, and they premiered it together.

Falla, Manuel de (1876-1946)—Spanish composer who went to Paris in 1907, where he met Ravel, Debussy, and others. Among his most important works are *El Sombrero de tres picos,* his ballet remade for Diaghilev, and the puppet opera *El Retablo de Maese Pedro.* His Concerto for Harpsichord, requested by Landowska, was premiered several years before Poulenc's *Concert champêtre.* Poulenc's Trio for Oboe, Bassoon, and Piano is dedicated to Falla.

Février, Jacques (1900-79)—a student of Edouard Risler and Marguerite Long, he was trained at the Paris Conservatory. In 1932 he and Poulenc premiered the Concerto in D minor which they played frequently together and recorded.

Fizdale, Robert (1920-95)—American pianist who studied at the Juilliard School of Music. He made his duo-piano debut with Arthur Gold in 1944 and toured widely thereafter. Original works were written especially for the Gold/Fizdale duo by Poulenc, Barber, Milhaud, Auric, Virgil Thomson, Ned Rorem, and others.

Fournier, Pierre (1906-85)—cellist who studied with Paul Bazelaire and André Hekking at the Paris Conservatory and the Ecole normale de musique. Poulenc wrote his Sonata for Cello and Piano for Fournier and arranged his *Suite française* for their concert tours together in the early 1950s.

Françaix, Jean (1912-97)—composer who studied with Nadia Boulanger. Poulenc chose Françaix to orchestrate his *Histoire de Babar,* and Françaix also arranged Poulenc's Sonata for Flute and Piano as a concerto with orchestra.

Freund, Marya (1876-1966)—Polish soprano particularly noted for her association with the music of Mahler, Schönberg, and Stravinsky. She was Doda Conrad's mother. When she retired from the concert stage she taught singing in Paris.

Gaigneron, Jean de (1890-1976)—artist who painted a portrait of Poulenc.

Gautier, Louis (?)—Poulenc's lover who was part of his life from early 1957 until his death. In 1958 Louis began building a house in Bagnols-en-Forêt (called "La Garchette"), which accounts for Poulenc's frequent visits there. In March 1962 Louis, who could not find work in Bagnols, decided to move to Cannes.

Gavoty, Bernard [nom de plume "Clarendon"] (1908-81)—writer on music and organist. He studied at the Sorbonne and the Paris Conservatory and from 1945 was the music critic for *Le Figaro*.

Gibson, Robert Douglas (1894-1985)—music editor at Chester Editions in London. He began as an assistant to Otto Marius Kling in 1919 and succeeded Kling's son Harry as director in 1936.

Girard, Simone (1898-1985)—amateur pianist who founded the Société avignonnaise de concerts. Bernac and Poulenc gave their first of many concerts in this series in 1936. Poulenc dedicated "Quem vidistis pastores" from *Quatre motets pour un temps de Noël* to her.

Giraudoux, Jean (1882-1944)—writer with whom Poulenc collaborated in 1933, when he supplied incidental music for *Intermezzo* and in 1941, when he wrote music for the film *La Duchesse de Langeais*.

Gold, Arthur (1917-90)—Canadian pianist who studied at the Juilliard School of Music. Concerning his duo-piano career see Fizdale, Robert above.

Gouverné, Yvonne (1890-1983)—choral director of the French Radio Chorus from 1935. Poulenc frequently sought her artistic advice during visits to Uzerche in the 1930s. He dedicated two pieces to her: "Nous avons fait la nuit" from *Tel jour telle nuit* and one of his *Quatre motets pour un temps de pénitence*. A capable pianist, she accompanied Bernac in recitals before the Bernac/Poulenc duo formed.

Grey, Madeleine (1897-1979)—soprano who studied piano with Cortot. Later she was an important singer of the contemporary French repertoire who recorded *Chansons Madécasses* under Ravel's direction. Poulenc occasionally accompanied Grey, and they made a recording in 1938 which Poulenc advised her not to release.

Gross, Valentine (see Hugo, Valentine).

Hamnett, Nina (1890-1956)—English artist, the so-called "Queen of Bohemia." She was friendly with numerous French artists and knew Poulenc from the early 1920s.

Hell, Henri (1916-91)—music critic, writer, and accomplished pianist who met Poulenc during his tour of North Africa with Maria Modrakowska in the 1930s. Hell wrote for numerous journals, including *Fontaine* from 1940-47, and was Poulenc's first book-length biographer. The eleventh piano Improvisation is dedicated to Hell.

Hely-Hutchinson, Victor (1901-47)—composer, pianist, and arts administrator who was associated with the BBC for many years.

Hirsch, Georges (1895-1974)—Poulenc's long-time friend who was administrator of the Réunion des Théâtres lyriques nationaux.

Honegger, Arthur (1892-1955)—prolific Swiss composer. After study at the Paris Conservatory (violin and composition), he became a member of *Les Six*. Like Durey, he belonged to the French Communist Party. In 1926 he married the pianist-composer Andrée Vaurabourg. Poulenc's Sonata for Clarinet and Piano is dedicated to him.

Horowitz, Vladimir (1904-89)—Russian pianist who became a U.S. resident. He recorded Poulenc's "Pastourelle" from *L'Eventail de Jeanne* in 1932 and *Presto in B-flat* in 1951. Poulenc always sent Horowitz copies of his piano music with effusive dedications.

Hugo, Jean (1894-1984)—painter, illustrator, and designer of theatrical entertainments who was friendly with Cocteau, Radiguet, and members of *Les Six*. From 1919-29 he was married to the artist Valentine Gross; in 1921 he designed the costumes for *Les Mariés de la Tour Eiffel.*

Hugo, Valentine [née Gross] (1887-1968)—painter, illustrator, and designer of theatrical entertainments. She drew dancers such as Nijinsky as they rehearsed for the Ballets Russes, and created the décor for some of the early "Nouveaux Jeunes" entertainments. Poulenc dedicated several works to her including *Trois mouvements perpétuels.* She also drew many illustrations for Eluard's poetry collections.

Jacob, Max (1876-1944)—poet, painter, and novelist who converted to Catholicism and took refuge in the monastery of Saint-Benoît-sur-Loire. Jacob was very well connected with important French artists and writers including Picasso and Radiguet and met Poulenc in 1917. Poulenc wrote two sets of songs on Jacob texts in addition to *Le Bal masqué* and *Parisiana*. Jacob died in the Drancy prison camp.

James, Edward (1908-84)—eccentric English art collector and poet who commissioned Poulenc to write *Sécheresses* based on his poems. He was the godson of King Edward VII.

Jean-Aubry, Georges (1882-1949)—writer on music who lived in London after World War I. There he edited the *Chesterian* in which numerous advertisements and articles about Poulenc were published. In the 1930s he returned to France.

Jourdan-Morhange, Hélène (1892-1961)—violinist and critic who was responsible for Poulenc's earliest public performances.

Kiesgen, Charles (?)—Parisian artistic agent who represented the Bernac/Poulenc duo.

Kling, Otto Marius (1866-1924)—director of J. and W. Chester Editions in London from 1915-24. He was succeeded by his son Harry who was in turn succeeded by Robert Douglas Gibson in 1936. Kling was responsible for publishing Poulenc's first works.

Koechlin, Charles (1867-1950)—composer and teacher who gave Poulenc his only formal composition lessons in the early 1920s. Poulenc attributed to Koechlin his success as a writer of choral music.

Lagut, Irène (1893-?)—painter, illustrator, and theater decorator who was close to members of *Les Six*. She illustrated Raymond Radiguet's *Devoirs de vacances* and created the décor for *Les Mariés de la Tour Eiffel*. She was friendly with Picasso and Cocteau.

Lambiotte, Rose [sometimes referred to in correspondence as Mme Chapdelaine] (1891-1964)—married to Auguste Lambiotte, a wealthy Belgian industrialist and book collector. She, her husband, and daughters Claudine and Rosine became Poulenc's Belgian family in the mid-1940s. Poulenc frequently stayed at their rue Saint-Bernard mansion. He dedicated "Adelina à la promenade" from *Trois chansons de F. Garcia-Lorca* and his thirteenth Improvisation to her.

Landowska, Wanda (1879-1959)—Polish-born French harpsichordist, pianist, and early music expert. Poulenc first met her in 1923, and she commissioned his *Concert champêtre* as well as a concerto from Falla. Poulenc greatly admired her playing and counted her of great importance in his life.

Latarjet, André (1877-1947)—anatomy professor on the Faculty of Medicine at Lyons. He was artistically inclined and functioned as President of the "Chœurs de Lyon." He and his wife Suzanne, constant supporters of Poulenc, were at least in part responsible for some of his earlier choral commissions.

Latarjet, Suzanne [née Linossier] (1886-1962)—she was the sister of Alice Ardoin and Raymonde Linossier. As a child she was friendly with Jeanne Manceaux. It was to her that Poulenc dedicated his first composition, *Processional pour la crémation d'un mandarin*. With her husband André she organized musical events in Lyons.

Laurencin, Marie (1885-1956)—painter who had a tempestuous association with the poet Apollinaire, whose mistress she was for a time. She created the décor and costumes for *Les Biches* and *L'Eventail de Jeanne*. Poulenc unwittingly set some of her poetry and dedicated one *mélodie* to her, "L'Anguille" from *Quatre poèmes de Guillaume Apollinaire*.

Leguerney, Jacques (1906-97)—composer and pupil of Nadia Boulanger and Samuel-Rousseau who wrote many *mélodie*s.

Linossier, Raymonde (1897-1930)—sister of Alice Ardoin and Suzanne Latarjet, she was Poulenc's closest childhood friend and confident. For a brief period he entertained the idea of marrying her. She was a lawyer and student of orientalism who worked at the Musée Guimet at the time of her death. Poulenc dedicated a number of his most important works to her or to her memory including Sonata for Horn, Trumpet, and Trombone, *Les Animaux modèles*, *Épitaphe*, *Ce doux petit visage*, and "Voyage" from *Calligrammes*.

Lockspeiser, Edward (1905-73)—English musicologist who studied with Alexandre Tansman and Nadia Boulanger. For many years he worked for the BBC. He also translated Henri Hell's biography of Poulenc.

Long, Marguerite (1874-1966)—pianist and teacher particularly noted for her interpretation of the music of Fauré, Debussy, and Ravel. She was married to the writer Joseph de Marliave.

Lunel, Armand (1892-1977)—professor of philosophy and writer particularly associated with Darius Milhaud. At one time Poulenc consulted Lunel in hopes of collaborating on an opera.

Malipiero, Gian Francesco (1882-1973)—Italian composer and musicologist who edited the first collected editions of Monteverdi and Vivaldi. Malipiero was in Paris when World War I broke out and was one of the first Italian composers with whom Poulenc became friendly. In later years they served on juries together.

Manceaux, André (1883-1967)—*see* Poulenc's family.

Manceaux, Brigitte (1914-63)—*see* Poulenc's family.

Manceaux, Jeanne (1887-1974)—*see* Poulenc's family.

Marie-Ange (b. 1946)—*see* Poulenc's family.

Markevitch, Igor (1912-83)—composer and conductor who studied with Nadia Boulanger and was a Diaghilev protégé. Poulenc met him in the late 1920s.

Mauriac, Francois (1885-1970)—writer who knew Poulenc from his early years. Mauriac presented Poulenc with his decoration as *Chevalier de la Légion d'Honneur*. Poulenc was also acquainted with Mauriac's son Claude.

Messiaen, Olivier (1908-92)—composer, organist, and theorist admired by Poulenc, who spoke frequently about him in letters and interviews.

Meyer, Marcelle (1897-1958)—pianist who studied with Marguerite Long, Alfred Cortot, and Ricardo Viñes. An ardent champion of *Les Six* she also recorded music by Ravel and Chabrier. She frequently performed Stravinsky's works and played in the premiere of *Les Noces*. The actor Pierre Bertin was her husband.

Milhaud, Darius (1892-1974)—prolific composer and member of *Les Six* who, along with Auric, was close to Poulenc. Poulenc wrote *Les Mamelles de Tirésias* for Milhaud's return to France after World War II.

Milhaud, Madeleine (b. 1902)—actress and devoted wife of Darius Milhaud. She studied piano with Marguerite Long and dramatic arts with Charles Dullin. After a career as an actress and narrator she devoted her life to teaching and, after his death, to most generously assisting those who seek to research the life and music of her husband and his contemporaries.

Modrakowska, Maria (1896-1965)—Polish singer who studied with Henry Melcer, Hélène Kedroff, and Nadia Boulanger. She sang at the Paris Opéra and Opéra-Comique and was also a teacher, critic, and novelist. Poulenc toured to North Africa with her in 1935.

Monnier, Adrienne (1892-1955)—writer and owner of the famous Maison des Amis des Livres on the rue de l'Odéon in Paris. It was there that Poulenc heard some of the most important writers of the day (Apollinaire, Fargue, Valéry, Claudel, Gide) recite their works.

Munch, Charles (1891-1968)—conductor and violinist who succeeded Serge Koussevitzky as conductor of the Boston Symphony Orchestra. Munch conducted premieres of Concerto for Piano and *Gloria*.

Munch, Fritz (1890-1970)—choral conductor who spent his career in Strasbourg. Fritz, the brother of Charles Munch, conducted the premiere of *Stabat Mater*.

Noailles, Viscount Charles de (1891-1981)—nephew of the poet Anna de Noailles and husband of Marie-Laure de Noailles, he had a great interest in botany and excelled in landscape architecture. (See below.)

Noailles, Marie-Laure (Viscountess Charles de) (1902-70)—writer, painter, and wealthy patroness of artists in a variety of métiers. She was Poulenc's long-time friend who commissioned *Aubade* and *Le Bal masqué*, and who also financed films by Buñuel, Dali, and Cocteau. The Noailles maintained a *hôtel particulier* in Paris at 11, Place des États-Unis and an extraordinary modern home in Hyères (southern France) designed by Robert Mallet-Stevens.

Nohain, Jean [alias Jaboune] (1900-81)—son of Maurice Legrand [alias Franc-Nohain], he was a classmate of Poulenc's at the lycée Condorcet. Poulenc used his poetry in *Quatre chansons pour enfants*.

Parr, Audrey (1892-1940)—married to the diplomat Raymond C. Parr until she separated from him in 1930 and married Norman Colville in 1938. She was the designer for Milhaud's ballet *L'Homme et son Désir* and probably met Poulenc shortly after she returned to Paris from Brazil in 1918. Poulenc dedicated his Sonata for Clarinet and Bassoon and the *mélodie Hyde Park* to her.

Pecci-Blunt, Countess Anna Laetitia [called Mimi] (1885-1971)— she and her husband maintained two residences, one in Paris and one in Rome, which had a private theater. In 1933, with Vittorio Rieti and Mario Labroca, she founded a concert society called Concerti di Primavera which was allied with *La Sérénade* in Paris. Poulenc participated in her concerts and in her Sabati di Primavera lecture-concerts.

Peignot, Suzanne (1895-1993)—soprano who gave first performances of several Poulenc *mélodies* and was his life-long friend. They made recordings together between 1932 and 1952, and Poulenc found her without peer as a performer of his early *mélodies*.

Picasso, Pablo (1881-1973)—incomparable artist whom Poulenc met in connection with the ballet *Parade* in 1918. Picasso illustrated the covers of several Poulenc compositions and is the dedicatee of "Bonne journée," from *Le Travail du peintre*, and of the cantata *Figure humaine*.

Pincherle, Marc (1888-1974)—musicologist and critic who was also artistic director of the Société Pleyel from 1927-55. He was general secretary of the Aix-en-Provence Festival from 1950. Poulenc probably first met him because of his association with Wanda Landowska at Saint-Leu-la-Forêt.

Plaut, Fred (?)—sound engineer with Columbia Records in New York City and gifted photographer. Plaut took hundreds of photographs of Poulenc the negatives of which are preserved. He was the husband of Rose Dercourt-Plaut.

Polignac, Countess Charles de [née Jeanne de Montagnac, called Pata] (1882-1966)—reputed to have had a fine voice with a large range, she sang in various Parisian salons, notably that of Coco Madrazo. Her second husband was Count Charles de Polignac (brother of Jean de Polignac and nephew of Princess Edmond de Polignac). Poulenc gave her numerous signed copies of his music, and she was influential in the commission of his Concerto in D minor.

Polignac, Countess Jean de [née Marguerite di Pietro, called Marie-Blanche] (1898-1958)—daughter of Jeanne Lanvin, she was an accomplished singer who sang in Nadia Boulanger's vocal ensemble. She and her husband Jean de Polignac frequently entertained Poulenc at their rue Barbet-de-Jouy Parisian *hôtel particulier* and at Kerbastic, their summer residence in Brittany. Poulenc dedicated numerous pieces to her, and she sang the premiere of *Trois poèmes de Louise de Vilmorin* with him in 1938 at the Salle Gaveau. Poulenc also dedicated pieces to her husband Jean (1888-1943).

Polignac, Princess Edmond de [née Winnaretta Singer] (1865-1943) — heiress to the Singer Sewing Machine fortune, she had a passionate interest in music and maintained a superb salon at her Avenue Henri-Martin Paris *hôtel particulier*. She was associated with Diaghilev, and Nadia Boulanger was later her musical advisor. She commissioned both Poulenc's Concerto in D minor and his Concerto in G minor.

Poulenc, Camille (1964-1942)—*see* Poulenc's family.

Poulenc, Émile (1855-1917)—*see* Poulenc's family.

Poulenc, Étienne (1823-78)—*see* Poulenc's family.

Poulenc, Mme Émile (1865-1915)—*see* Poulenc's family.

Poulenc, Gaston Joseph (1852-1948)—*see* Poulenc's family.

Poulenc, Gérard [Frère Jérôme] (1925-89)—*see* Poulenc's family.

Prêtre, Georges (b. 1924)—conductor who has given many performances of Poulenc works including the premiere of *La Voix humaine*. He has also made many highly successful recordings.

Printemps, Yvonne (1894-1977)—singer/actress who was married to Sacha Guitry and then Pierre Fresnay. She recorded Poulenc's "Les Chemins de l'amour" from *Léocadia* and "A sa guitare" from *Margot*.

Prokofiev, Serge (1891-1953)—Russian composer and pianist who was closely linked with Diaghilev's Ballets Russes. Poulenc wrote an article about Prokofiev, dedicated his Sonata for Oboe and Piano to him, and during the 1920s rehearsed Prokofiev's piano concertos with him. The two also played bridge together.

Prunières, Henry (1886-1942)—musicologist who founded *La Revue musicale* in 1919 and was its chief editor until 1939. He also organized the *Concerts de La Revue musicale* at which music by *Les Six* was performed.

Radiguet, Raymond (1903-23)—precocious poet and novelist who was a protégé of Jean Cocteau and who died of typhus at the age of twenty.

Rampal, Jean-Pierre (1922-2000)—well-known flutist, conductor, and teacher who gave the world premiere of Poulenc's Sonata for Flute and Piano. He made numerous recordings and was decorated by the French government.

Rieti, Vittorio (1989-1994)—Italian composer (born in Egypt) who moved to America in 1940. Like Poulenc, whom he met in 1922, he wrote ballets for Diaghilev (*Barabau* and *Le Bal*). Rieti's early works were championed by Alfredo Casella, who also encouraged Poulenc.

Rosenberg, Léonce (1879-1947)—Parisian art dealer who, with his brother Paul, directed the Galerie Rosenberg. He also sponsored multimedia events at the Galerie L'Effort moderne at which works such as *Le Bestiaire* were performed.

Rostand, Claude (1912-70)—music critic and writer about music who produced important interviews for the radio with Milhaud, Poulenc, Markevitch, and others. Poulenc dedicated "Chanson d'Orkenise" from *Banalités* to Rostand.

Roubert, Lucien (1908-55)—traveling salesman from Toulon who was living in Marseilles when Poulenc met him in the spring of 1950. Poulenc had a complicated emotional relationship with him while writing *Dialogues des Carmélites*. Roubert, whose illness paralleled the opera's composition, died of cancer the day it was finished.

Rouché, Jacques (1862-1957)—important theater director who directed the Paris Opéra from 1915-45. Poulenc's work with Rouché included production of *Les Animaux modèles*, among others.

Roussel, Albert (1869-1937)—composer greatly admired by Poulenc as much for his music as for his advice. Poulenc enjoyed visiting the Roussels; after the composer's death Mme Roussel presented Poulenc with the manuscript of *L'Accueil des muses*. (Poulenc 1994, p. 1048).

Royer, Marcel ["Papoum"] (1862-1945)—*see* Poulenc's family.

Salacrou, Armand (1899-1989)—playwright for whose *Le Soldat et la Sorcière* Poulenc contributed music.

Salles, Georges (1889-1966)—initially a curator at the Louvre, he was later director of the Musées de France. Until he had his own apartment, Poulenc frequently stayed at Salles' 24, rue du Chevalier-de-la Barre home behind Sacré-Coeur.

Satie, Erik (1866-1925)—composer who influenced a generation of young French composers including Poulenc. The latter's relationship with Satie, nurturing and cordial at the outset, ended distastrously. In spite of this, Poulenc maintained a life-long respect for Satie.

Sauguet, Henri (1901-89)—composer from Bordeaux and member of the "École d'Arcueil" who came to Paris in 1922. Like Poulenc he studied with Charles Koechlin and was much influenced by Satie. Sauguet and Poulenc were close friends.

Schaeffner, André (1895-1980)—prolific musicologist and ethnomusicologist who was also involved with some of Paris' most important musical institutions. He had intended to write a book about Poulenc, but left only a significant article entitled "Francis Poulenc, musicien français."

Seringe, Rosine (b. 1918) — *see* Poulenc's family.

Sert, Misia [née Marie Sophie Olga Zenaïde Godebska] (1872-1950)—married successively to Thadée Natanson, Alfred Edwards, and José-Maria Sert; patroness of the arts in Paris who was closely associated with Serge Diaghilev and the Ballets Russes. She maintained an important salon at which Arthur Gold and Robert Fizdale (her future biographers) played.

Sienkiewicz, Geneviève (1878-1971)—friend of Poulenc's mother, Sienkiewicz was a fine amateur pianist and sightreader who often played with musicians such as Edouard Risler, Gabriel Fauré, and André Messager. She was particularly associated with the salon of Marguerite de Saint-Marceaux. Poulenc dedicated his *Thème varié* to her.

Souberbielle, Edouard (1899-1986)—organist and composer who taught organ at the Schola Cantorum. Poulenc first met him in 1916, and their correspondence about some of Poulenc's earliest compositions illuminates many details which would otherwise be forgotten. Poulenc dedicated to him his early Sonata for Two Clarinets, but in later years their friendship became more distant.

Stravinsky, Igor (1882-1971)—important Russian composer who lived in France, Switzerland, and the United States. From the first time Poulenc heard his music, his admiration for Stravinsky was unequivocal. They remained friendly and often exchanged letters and music. "Entrancing muse," part of the title of this documented biography, comes from a letter Stravinsky wrote to Poulenc requesting he send music after World War II.

Tacchino, Gabriel (b. 1934)—pianist who studied at the Paris Conservatory with Jacques Février and subsequently won celebrated European piano competitions. He has recorded virtually the entire corpus of Poulenc piano works, and the composer held his playing in high esteem. Poulenc met Tacchino in 1958.

Tailleferre, Germaine (1892-1983)—composer, pianist, and member of *Les Six*. Cocteau compared her compositional style to that of the painter Marie Laurencin.

Thomson, Virgil (1896-1989)—American composer and music critic who traveled to France for the first time with the Harvard Glee Club in 1921. This trip led to his study with Nadia Boulanger and a life long attachment to French arts and letters. He visited Poulenc in France and from his position as a revered New York critic was helpful when Poulenc visited the United States.

Valcarenghi, Guido (1893-?)—director of Editions Ricordi in Milan who was responsible for suggesting that Poulenc consider Bernanos' *Dialogues des Carmélites* as the libretto for an opera. Poulenc's extensive correspondence with Valcarenghi adds important information about *La Voix humaine* as well.

Vaurabourg, Andrée (1894-1980)—pianist who studied with Raoul Pugno and composition with Charles Widor. She married Arthur Honegger on 10 May 1926 and is well known for her performances of her husband's piano music.

Vilmorin, Louise de (1902-69)—French poetess and novelist admired by both Poulenc and Bernac.

Viñes, Ricardo (1875-1943)—Catalan pianist who lived in Paris from 1887. He studied piano, composition, and harmony at the Paris Conservatory. Viñes became one of the foremost champions of piano music by the younger French and Spanish composers including Debussy, Ravel, and Poulenc. He was Poulenc's most important piano teacher, who also gave first performances of various of his early piano works.

APPENDIX II

Summaries of Poulenc's Concerts, Tours, and Radio Broadcasts

A. Modrakowska/Poulenc North African Concert Tour: February 1935
B. Bernac/Poulenc Concerts in England and Ireland: February and March 1939
C. Bernac/Poulenc Paris Concerts: January-March 1941
D. Bernac/Poulenc Concerts in England: March 1945
E. Bernac/Poulenc Concerts in England: November-December 1945
F. Bernac/Poulenc Concerts in England: February-March 1947
G. Radio Broadcasts (1947-48): "A Bâtons Rompus"
H. Poulenc's first North American Tour: October-December 1948
I. Radio Broadcasts (1949): "A Bâtons Rompus"
J. Concerts in England: February 1949
K. Poulenc's second North American Tour: December 1949-March 1950
L. Poulenc's third American Tour: January-March 1952
M. Poulenc's fourth North American Tour: February-March 1960
N. Poulenc's last American Tour: January 1961
O. Duval/Poulenc Italian Tour: February 1962
P. Poulenc's anticipated April 1963 Tour to America

A. MODRAKOWSKA/POULENC NORTH AFRICAN CONCERT TOUR: FEBRUARY 1935

Date	Location	Theater	Total Fee
13	Oran, Algeria	Amis de Musique	Not given
14	Mostaganem, Algeria	Salle du Grand Hôtel	2,000 francs
18	Algiers	Post Radio-Alger	800 francs
19	Algiers	Salle des Beaux-Arts	4,000 francs
22	Tunis, Tunisia	Théâtre Municipal	4,000 francs

B. BERNAC/POULENC CONCERTS IN ENGLAND AND IRELAND: FEBRUARY AND MARCH 1939

Date	Location	Repertoire
February		
19+	London BBC regional, 9:05-9:35 pm	All Ravel
21++	Cardiff	?
22+	London BBC national, 6:35-7:00 pm	All Roussel
23+	London BBC regional, 6:35-7:00 pm	All Poulenc
24+	London BBC national, 5:30-6:00 pm	Ravel-Poulenc
25++	London, Queen's Hall	?
26++	Liverpool	?
March		
1++	London BBC	?
2++	Nottingham	?
4++	Haslemere (Surrey)	?
6++	Cambridge	?
7*	London Contemporary Music Center	Premiere of Sauguet's "Le Chat" [part of the cycle *Six mélodies sur des poèmes symbolistes*] plus Milhaud, Auric, Ibert, and Poulenc[1]

+Information from documents in GB-Rbbc (Francis Poulenc Artists file 1a [1937-1945]).
++Information from a financial ledger in the Ibbs and Tillett materials at GB-Rcm.
*Program

C. BERNAC/POULENC PARIS CONCERTS: JANUARY-MARCH 1941

Date	Location	Performers	Repertoire
January			
25	Théâtre de l'Atelier	Bernac and Poulenc	Poulenc *mélodies*
February			
4	Théâtre des Mathurins	Janine Micheau, Bernac, and Poulenc	*Ce doux petit visage* (first perf.),*Colloque* (first perf.), Chabrier, and Debussy
14	?	Bernac and Poulenc	Auric, *Trois poèmes de Léon-Paul Fargue, Trois poèmes de Louise de Vilmorin*

[1] Poulenc joyfully noted that he would return to Paris just in time to attend Sauguet's new opera *La Chartreuse de Parme* and asked Sauguet to arrange for a ticket. [Early Mar. 1939] letter in Poulenc 1994, 39-2 (Poulenc 1991, no. 142).

| 16 | Salle de l'Ancien Conservatoire | Poulenc | *Concert champêtre* |
| 28 | Salle Chopin | Poulenc and others | ? |

March

2	Ancien Conservatoire	Marcelle Meyer, Février, Poulenc, and Soulima Stravinsky	Stravinsky, *Les Noces*
15	Salle Gaveau	Bernac and Poulenc[2]	Duparc, Fauré, Debussy, Honegger, Poulenc
23	Salle Albert-legrand	Bernac and Poulenc	?
25	Ancien Conservatoire	Poulenc	*Aubade*

D. BERNAC/POULENC CONCERTS IN ENGLAND: MARCH 1945

Date	Location	Performers	Repertoire*
10+	Brighton	Poulenc	*Aubade?* (with orchestra)
11+	London BBC	Bernac	?
12	London BBC	Bernac and Poulenc	Fauré, *La Bonne Chanson*
12+	London	Bernac and Poulenc	?
12	Wigmore Hall	Neveu and Poulenc	Poulenc, Sonata for Violin and Piano** Debussy, Sonata for Violin and Piano
13+	Sheffield	Bernac and Poulenc	?
14+	Birmingham	Bernac and Poulenc	?
15+	Chelsea Town Hall	Bernac and Poulenc	Lully, Chausson, Chabrier, Fauré, Poulenc, Ravel (Fauré's *Mandoline* and Stravinsky's *Tilimbom* were added [GB-Lcm])
16+	Bletchley	Bernac and Poulenc	?
18+	Cambridge	Poulenc	*Aubade?* (with orchestra)

*Some concerts included other artists. Only Poulenc's participation is noted.
**First performance in England.
+Listed in Ibbs and Tillett ledgers.

---

[2] Entitled "Baudelaire, Verlaine, Apollinaire et cinq de leurs musiciens, Henri Duparc, Gabriel Fauré, Debussy, Honegger, Poulenc," this performance featured narration of the poems by Madeleine Renaud. In a "mercredi" [15 Jan. 1941] letter to M Gret Poulenc suggested a 3,000 franc fee for the Bernac/Poulenc duo and 1,500 (or better 2,000) franc fee for Renaud. Poulenc 1994, 41-2.

[19++	Leicester	Bernac and Poulenc	?]
20	Fyvie Hall	Bernac, Teyte, and Poulenc	Debussy, *Pelléas et Mélisande* (final scene)
22	National Gallery	Neveu, Bernac, and Poulenc	Debussy *mélodies* and Sonata for Violin and Piano, Poulenc *Tel jour telle nuit* and Sonata for Violin and Piano
22+	Cowdray Hall	Bernac and Poulenc	?
23+	BBC	Bernac and Poulenc	?
[24	BBC	BBC Chorus, Woodgate, conductor]	*Figure humaine* (premiere)
26	BBC	Bernac and Poulenc	?
26+	Manchester/ London?	Bernac and Poulenc	?
27+	Wigmore Hall	Bernac and Poulenc	Jaubert, *L'Eau vive: Chants du métiers de Haute-Provence***; Françaix, *L'Adolescence clémentine;*** Stravinsky, *Trois histoires pour enfants;* Poulenc, *Banalités,*** *Chansons villageoises***

**First public performance in England.
+Listed in Ibbs and Tillet ledgers.
++Listed in Ibbs and Tillet ledgers, but cancelled.

E. BERNAC/POULENC CONCERTS IN ENGLAND: NOVEMBER-DECEMBER 1945

Date	Location	Performers	Repertoire
November			
29+	Cambridge	Poulenc	(with orchestra)
December			
1+	Hereford	Bernac and Poulenc	?
2+	London	Bernac and Poulenc	Gounod, Milhaud, Poulenc
2	London	Bernac and Poulenc	Ravel, Poulenc, Fauré, Debussy

4+	Chelsea Town Hall	Bernac and Poulenc	Dowland, Duparc, Debussy, Hahn, Poulenc (program in GB-Lcm indicates that Poulenc played *Trois mouvments perpétuels* at the end)
5+	Harpenden	Bernac and Poulenc	?
8+	Oxford	Bernac and Poulenc	?
9+	Marlborough	Bernac and Poulenc	?

+Listed in Ibbs and Tillet ledgers.

F. BERNAC/POULENC CONCERTS IN ENGLAND: FEBRUARY AND MARCH 1947

Date	Location	Performers	Repertoire*
February			
9	London	Bernac and Poulenc	Grétry fragments from *Le Jugement de Midas,* Schumann's *Dichterliebe,* Berkeley's *Five Poems of Walter de la Mare,* Poulenc's *Chansons villageoises*
10+	London BBC	Bernac and Poulenc	?
13+	London BBC	Bernac and Poulenc	?
21+	Welwyn	Bernac and Poulenc	?
26+	London BBC	Bernac and Poulenc	?
[26++	Oldham	Bernac and Poulenc	?]
27+	London BBC	Bernac and Poulenc	?
28+	Chelsea Town Hall	Poulenc	Poulenc Sextet and *Aubade*
March			
4+	Wigmore Hall	Poulenc	Chamber music
5+	London BBC	Bernac and Poulenc	?
6+	London BBC	Poulenc	? Piano

*Some concerts include other artists. Only Poulenc's participation is noted.
++Listed in Ibbs and Tillett ledgers, but in pencil. Concert probably did not take place.
+Listed in Ibbs and Tillett ledgers.

G. RADIO BROADCASTS (1947-48): "A BÂTONS ROMPUS"[3]

Subject	Date Recorded (Broadcast)
Maurice Chevalier	[1947] (?)
Espagne I & II	[1947] (?)
Paris et la musique symphonique	[1947] (?)
Trois grandes chanteuses: Claire Croiza, Maggie Teyte, Ninon Vallin	[1947] (?)
Maurice Ravel	[1947] (28 Dec. 1947)
André Messager	29 Nov. 1947 (31 Jan. 1948)
Walton et Britten	? (?)
Serge Prokofiev	12 Feb. 1948 (13 Mar. 1948)
Musique sainte	? (?)
L'Exquise mauvaise musique*	? (?)
Le Folklore du XXe siècle I, II, & III	? (?)
Darius Milhaud	? (?)
Influence de la foire	? (?)
Igor Stravinsky et l'ascétisme	? (?)
Charles Gounod	29 Apr. 1948 (15 May 1948)
Carl Maria von Weber	29 Apr. 1948 (22 May 1948)
Francis Poulenc et ses mélodies	? (29 May 1948)

*Délicieuse mauvaise musique in Buckland/Chimènes: e, p. 385.

H. POULENC'S FIRST NORTH AMERICAN TOUR: OCTOBER-DECEMBER 1948

Date	City	Events [Poulenc 1994 and Poulenc 1991]
October		
22	Le Havre?	Departs France by ship[4]
23-7		Aboard ship
28	New York	Probably arrives
29	New York	Tells Thomson that he will see him [48-6]
30	Boston	Hears a performance of his Concerto in G minor
31	?	

[3] According to *Le Guide du concert et des théâtres lyriques* 29 (issues of Jan.-June 1948), passim., broadcasts in the series took place on 24 Jan., 14 Feb., 6 and 20 Mar., 10 and 24 Apr., and 15 and 22 May. Unfortunately the *Guide* does not indicate the content of the broadcasts.

[4] Photograph of the pair aboard ship returning from the U.S.A. in Poulenc 1963a, pp. 64/5 and Ivry, pp. 154-5.

November

1-2	?	
3	New York	St Moritz Hotel, leaving for Washington D.C. [48-8; no. 194]
4	Wash., D.C.	Stays with Reine Bénard [48-8; no. 194]; American debut at Dumbarton Oaks
5	?	
6	New York?	Going to a Toscanini concert [48-8; no. 194][5]
7	New York	First Town Hall concert
8	New York	Cocktail party chez Lily Pons [48-8; no. 194]
9	Boston	Jordan Hall concert with Bernac[6]
10	Boston	[48-9; no. 195]
11	New York	Concert with Mitropoulos [48-8; no. 194] (plays *Concert champêtre*)
12	New York	Concert with Mitropoulos [48-8; no. 194]
13	?	
14	New York	Concert with Mitropoulos [48-8; no. 194]
15	North Hampton, MA	Concert at Sage Hall (sponsored by Smith College Department of Music)[7]
16-18	?	
19	New York	St Moritz Hotel [unpublished letter to Gibson in GB-Lchester]
20	New York	Second Town Hall concert
21	New York	Leaving for Québec, Chicago, Los Angeles, Oakland [48-10; no. 196]
22-26	?	
27	Detroit?	
28	Chicago	Chicago Arts Club concert
29	Los Angeles?	[48-11 says he spent 5 days in Los Angeles]
30	Los Angeles?	

[5] While in New York Poulenc dined with Dior at a friend's house [48-9; no. 195].
[6] Program in US-Bp (Poulenc Clipping File).
[7] An article announcing this recital was published on the front page of *Scan (Smith College Associated News)*, 12 Nov. 1948. The 19 Nov. issue contained an unsigned review which begins "Pierre Bernac and Francis Poulenc lived up to their reputations as the finest combination in leider [sic] singing toda[y], as they performed Tuesday evening before a record audience." I am grateful to Nanci A. Young, Smith College Archivist, for her kindness in supplying this information.

December

1	Los Angeles	Biltmore Hotel, concert at the Wilshire Ebell theater [Craft, p. 145 and 23 Nov. 1948 letter to Stravinsky]
2	Los Angeles	Bernac/Poulenc lunch with the Stravinskys [Craft, p. 145]
3	?	
4	Salt Lake City	Hotel Utah [48-11]
5	Salt Lake City	Hotel Utah [48-11]
6-10[8]	?	
11	New York	Last concert under the auspices of the League of Composers honoring Poulenc at the Museum of Modern Art [48-10; no. 196]
12	Pittsburgh	Concert[9]
13	Philadelphia	Concert in Barclay Hotel Ballroom[10]
14	New York-Le Havre	Returns to France by ship [48-10; no. 196]

I. RADIO BROADCASTS (1949): "A BÂTONS ROMPUS"

Subject	Date Recorded (Broadcast)
Retour d'Amérique	7 Jan. 1949 (?)
Igor Stravinsky: portrait américain	7 Jan. 1949 (?)
Samuel Barber et Gian Carlo Menotti	19 Jan. 1949 (?)
Wanda Landowska	22 Jan. 1949 (?)
Francis Poulenc et sa musique instrumentale	29 Jan. 1949 (?)
Claude Debussy	12 Feb. 1949 (?)
Béla Bartók et Alban Berg	19 Feb. 1949 (?)
Henri Sauguet	19 Feb. 1949 (?)
Ravel orchestrateur	? (?)
La Mélodie italienne	? [but after Bartók & Berg] (?)
Erik Satie	17 Mar. 1949 (19 Mar. 1949)
Louis Ganne	27 Feb. 1949 (26 Mar. 1949)

[8] The duo had played Denver, but I have been unable to find the precise date.
[9] This is mentoned in Max de Schauensee's review of the Philadelphia concert in *The Evening Bulletin, Philadelphia* (14 Dec. 1948), 50.
[10] Landowski and note above.

J. CONCERTS IN ENGLAND: FEBRUARY 1949

Date	Location	Performers	Repertoire*
8	London	Bruce Belfrage and Poulenc	Poulenc, *Histoire de Babar, le petit éléphant***
10+	London BBC	Bernac and Poulenc	?
11+	Edinburgh	Bernac and Poulenc	?
13+	Amersham	Bernac and Poulenc	?
14+	London BBC	Bernac and Poulenc	Poulenc, *Calligrammes***; Debussy *mélodies*
16+	Doncaster	Bernac and Poulenc	?
17++	Cambridge	Bernac and Poulenc	?
17+++	London BBC	Bernac and Poulenc	?
18+	London BBC	Bernac and Poulenc	Ravel, Mallarmé settings; Poulenc, *Le Bal masqué*
20+	Tunbridge Wells	Bernac and Poulenc	?

*Some concerts included other artists. Only Poulenc's participation is noted.
**First public performance in England.
+Listed in Ibbs and Tillett ledgers.
++Listed in Ibbs and Tillett ledgers in pencil. Concert probably did not take place.
+++Listed in BBC contracts.

K. POULENC'S SECOND NORTH AMERICAN TOUR: DECEMBER 1949-MARCH 1950

Date	City	Events [Poulenc 1994 and Poulenc 1991; FA = Feuilles Américaines, F-Pn (Mus. Rés. Vmc MS 124)

December 1949

28	Paris-New York City	Departs Paris for New York by air [FA]
29	New York	
30	New York	Has been rereading *Don Quichotte* for three days [FA]
31	Boston	

January 1950

1-2	Boston	
3	Boston	First rehearsal of Concerto for Piano [50-1; no. 201; FA]
4	Boston	Second rehearsal of Concerto [FA]
5	Boston	Spends afternoon chez Prof. M. G...[FA]
6	Boston	Premiere of Concerto [FA]

7	Boston	Additional performance of Concerto; visits Museum of Fine Arts [FA]
8	Boston	Buys a recording of Debussy's *Jeux* for Prof. M. G... [FA]
9-11	?	
12	Washington, D.C.	Plays Concerto; Bernac has rejoined him [50-2]
13	?	
14	New York	Plays Concerto at Carnegie Hall with Boston Symphony Orchestra under Munch [50-2]
15	New York	Visits with Wanda Landowska [FA]
16	Philadelphia	Philadelphia recital with Bernac[11]
17	?	
18	Boston	Jordan Hall recital with Bernac[12]
19-20	?	
21	New York	Photograph of Poulenc and Landowska taken this date in Bloch, fig. 11
22	New York	Town Hall recital with Bernac; dinner with Jenny Tourel, Conrad, and friends [50-3]
23	New York	[FA]
24	Toronto	Recital with Bernac
25	Toronto	Royal York Hotel [50-3]
26	?	
27	Pittsfield, MA	[FA]
28-31	?	

February 1950

1	?	
2	Montreal	Plays Concerto (finale reprised) [50-4; no. 202; FA; see also the fragment of Poulenc's 1 Mar. 1950 letter to Collaer in 50-6, note 7]
3	?	
4	Pittsfield	Recital at Pittsfield High School[13]
5	New York	Horowitz picks him up — plays Barber's Sonata for Piano, Clementi sonatas, parts of Moussorgsky's *Pictures*, finale of Prokofiev's Sonata no. 7, transcription of a Souza march [FA]

[11] Max de Schauensee, "Bernac and Poulenc Heard in Recital," *The Evening Bulletin, Philadelphia* (17 Jan. 1950), 43. Schauensee acknowledged Mrs. Edith C. Corson "for giving Philadelphia the privilege of hearing the Messers Poulenc and Bernac."

[12] Program in US-Bp (Poulenc Clipping File).

[13] *The Berkshire County Eagle* (25 Jan. 1950), 13 and Jay Rosenfeld, "Frenchmen Score Hit in Concert," *The Berkshire Evening Eagle* (6 Feb. 1950), 13. Apparently the audience was quite small.

6	New York	
7	New York	Visits Metropolitan Museum. Speaks at length of paintings [FA]
8	New York	Day with Landowska [FA]
9-11	?	
12	New York	St Moritz Hotel [50-6; no. 204]
13-16	?	
17	Chicago	[50-6; no. 204]
18	Chicago	Visits a Van Gogh exhibition at the Chicago Museum [FA]
19	?	
20	Chicago	Hotel Ambassador, North State Street [50-9]
21-2	?	
23	Toledo	Hillorest Hotel [50-10]
24	Near Cleve-land[14]	[Letter to Munch in Honegger, p. 202]
25	?	
26	San Francisco	Mark Hopkins Hotel; recital with Bernac at St Francis Hotel Colonial Room [50-11; no. 205][15]
27	?	
28	Carmel	Staying 3 days following San Francisco; recital with Bernac [50-12; no. 206; 50-13]

March 1950

1	Carmel	[50-14]
2-5	?	
6	[Tucson?]	Hotel Santa Rita
7-8	?	
9	Colorado Springs	Antlers Hotel [50-16]; [F-Po Lettres autographes de Poulenc, no. 43 to Georges Hirsch]
10	Colorado	Antlers Hotel [50-17; no. 207]
11	Santa Barbara, CA	Lotte Lehmann comes to his recital [FA]
12-15		
16	Birmingham	Hotel Tutwiler [unpublished 16 Mar. letter to Mme Lambiotte]

[14] He also visited Cincinnati to gave a "Causerie au Conservatoire" [FA]. We are unable to establish the precise date of this visit.

[15] Alexander Fried, "Composer in Joint Recital," *San Francisco Examiner* (27 Feb. 1950).

[16] FA indicates that the recital was on the 10th.

17	Birmingham	Hotel Tutwiler in US-NYlambiotte-donhauser; recital with Bernac at Phillips High School Auditorium[17]
18	New York	Evening with Stravinsky [FA]
19	New York	[FA]
20	?	
21	New York	St Moritz (returns to NY this day) [50-17; no. 207]
22	New York	Attends Menotti's *The Consul* [FA]
23-4	?	
25	New York	Records with Bernac [50-17; no. 207]
26	?	
27	New York	Records with Bernac [50-17; no. 207]
28	New York	The Stravinskys and Poulenc share a box at Carnegie Hall to hear Thomson's Concerto for Cello
29	New York-Paris	Return flight to Paris [50-14]

L. POULENC'S THIRD AMERICAN TOUR: JANUARY-MARCH 1952

Date	City	Events [Poulenc 1994 and Poulenc 1991]
January		
18		Arrival date in New York undetermined
19-20	?	
21	Washington, D.C.	Dumbarton Oaks recital with Bernac[18]
22-3	?	
24	New York	Dines with Casa Fuerte [52-1; no. 223]
25	New York	[52-1; no. 223]
26	New York	Wyndham Hotel [52-2; no. 224]. Speaks of going to Venezuela for four concerts. Has already seen Strauss' *Salomé* at the Metropolitan Opera
27	New York	Performance of Bach's Mass in B minor with Robert Shaw [52-2; no. 224][19]
28-31	?	

[17] Donald Deagon, "French Duet Bring Popular Music Event," *The Birmingham Age-Herald* (18 Mar. 1950), 9.

[18] In a 4 Feb. 1952 letter to Marie-Blanche de Polignac, Bernac says they got excellent press in Canada early in the tour. Poulenc 1994, 52-4 (Poulenc 1991, no. 225).

[19] Poulenc's [27 Jan. 1952] letter to Girard in Poulenc 1994, 52-3 (Poulenc 1991, no. 222) says that the Concerto had a great success in Cincinnati. I have been unable to trace the date of this performance.

February

1	?	
2	Caracas	Recital with Bernac? [52-4; no. 225]
3	[Caracas]	[Probably performs *Concert champêtre* with Celibidache]
4	Caracas	Hotel Potomac [52-4; no. 225]; recital with Bernac
5	[Caracas]	
6	Caracas	Hotel Potomac; recital with Bernac [52-4; no. 225 and 52-5; no. 226]
7	Caracas-New York	Return to New York [52-2; no. 224]
8-9	?	
10	New York	Town Hall recital; dinner after with Elsa Maxwell [52-2; no. 224 and 52-4; no. 225]
11	New York	
12	Lakeville, CT	Visits Landowska [52-6]
13	Middlebury, VT	Concert
14	?	
15	New York	Records Barber's *Mélodies passagères*[20]
16	New York	Unpublished letter to Edith Borroff in US-Cn
17-20	?	
21	New York	St Moritz Hotel
22-9	?	

March 1952

1-4	?	
5	New York-Paris	[52-4; no. 225]

M. POULENC'S FOURTH NORTH AMERICAN TOUR: FEBRUARY-MARCH 1960

Date	City	Events [Poulenc 1994 and Poulenc 1991]

February

15	Paris	Initial unkept departure date
18	Paris-New York	Arrives at 7:00 pm Wyndham Hotel [60-2]
19-22	?	

---

[20] Ramey, p. 3.

23	New York	Performance of *Les Mamelles de Tirésias* and *La Voix humaine* at Carnegie Hall (Prêtre)
24	New York	Wyndham Hotel [unpublished 24 Feb. (1960) letter to Valcarenghi in I-Mr]
25	Philadelphia	Performance of *Les Mamelles de Tirésias* and *La Voix humaine* at the Academy of Music (Prêtre)
26	New York	Wyndham Hotel [60-3]
27	New York-Ithaca	Flies to Ithaca for a concert [60-3 and 60-6, note 1]
28	?	
29	Chicago	Rehearsal at 2:30 pm

March

1	Chicago	Rehearsal at 9:00 am and concert including *La Voix humaine* [60-4; no. 312]
2	Chicago	Ambassador Hotel [60-3; no. 312 misdated Feb.]
3	New York	Presented New York University Medal: Duval and Poulenc perform excerpts from *La Voix humaine* following the presentation
4-5	?	
6	Detroit	Concert at the Detroit Institute of Arts Auditorium[21]
7-9	?	
10	New York	Town Hall recital [60-6, note 1; see Poulenc 1991, p. 408]
11-12	?	
13	Washington, D.C.	[Unpublished letter to Bernac in F-Pn]
14-16	?	
17	New York	Records Sextet at Columbia Records Studio from 6-11 pm [12 Feb. 1997 private communication from Mason Jones]
18-19	?	
20	New York-Paris	[60-4; no. 312]

N. POULENC'S LAST AMERICAN TOUR: JANUARY 1961

Date	City	Events [Poulenc 1994 and Poulenc 1991]
13	Paris-New York	[Unpublished 26 Dec. (19)60] letter to Rose Dercourt-Plaut, Wyndham Hotel

[21] *The Detroit News* (28 Feb. 1960), 7G and (6 Mar. 1960), 7G.

14	New York	
15	New York-Boston	
16	Boston	Lunch chez Munch [61-3; no. 323]
17	Boston	Sheraton Plaza Hotel; rehearsal with the chorus and a substitute soloist for the *Gloria* followed by the first orchestral rehearsal [61-3; no. 323]
18	Boston	Rehearsal for *Gloria* and Concerto in D minor [61-4; no. 325]
19	Boston	Rose Dercourt-Plaut arriving that evening; takes her to hear Marlene Dietrich [61-4; no. 325]
20	Boston	Premiere of *Gloria* and performance of Concerto postponed due to snow
21	Boston	Actual premiere of program
22	Boston	Repeat of 21st program [61-6; no. 326]
23	Boston-NY	[61-7]
24	New York	While in New York, Poulenc meets Leontyne Price, sees Laurence Olivier in *Becket*, visits Horowitz, and sees Rosine Lambiotte-Donhauser and Rubinstein [61-6; no. 326]. This may be the night he had dinner with Allen Hughes at Mc-Ginnis' on Broadway and went shopping [Hughes 1963, p. 29]
25	New York	
26	New York	[Letter to Milan in I-Mr]
27	New York	[61-8]
28	New York	
29	New York-Paris	
30	Paris	

O. DUVAL/POULENC ITALIAN TOUR: FEBRUARY 1962

Date	City	Events [Poulenc 1994, 62-1 and Poulenc 1991, no. 335]
3	Paris-Trieste	Evening departure by train
4	Trieste	Arrive around 11 am; dinner in their honor chez Favello Bamfield
5	Trieste	Concert
6	Trieste-Milan	Stay in Milan for three nights
7	Milan-Turin	Concert (return to Milan by car)
8	Milan	Luncheon in honor of Duval; gala evening performance of Verdi's *Don Carlo* at La Scala[22]

[22] Poulenc wrote Philippe Heugel on this date from the Grand Hotel Continental concerning plans for the Feb. 1963 performance of *Les Mamelles de Tirésias* in Milan. Original in the Heugel family archives.

9	Milan-Florence	Take train; retire early
10	Florence	Concert
11	Florence-Perugia	[Take train?]; Concert (80 Km from Florence)
12	Perugia-Rome	Take train; stay with the Peccis
13	Rome	Rest
14	Rome-Naples	Take train; retire early
15	Naples	Concert
16	Naples-Paris	Return flight

P. POULENC'S ANTICIPATED APRIL 1963 TOUR TO AMERICA

Date	Location	Event
2	Paris	Leave at 7:00 pm on Air France[23]
3	New York	Arrive in New York and stay at Wyndham Hotel
5	New York	Dinner at Bobsy Goodspeed's
6	New York	Record for the radio
10	New York	Carnegie Hall: Showcase Concert featuring the premiere of Sonata for Clarinet and Piano[24]
16	New York	Party at the Plaut's in his honor
18	NY-Chicago	Arrive in Chicago during the morning
27	Chicago	Sonata for Clarinet and Piano

[Departure date to France undecided]

[23] 22 Jan. [1963] letter to Rose Dercourt-Plaut in Poulenc 1994, 63-1 (Poulenc 1991, no. 350).

[24] In the end, this concert was a memorial to Poulenc. Benny Goodman and Bernstein premiered the Sonata for Clarinet and Piano, and other performers included Gold and Fizdale, Jenny Tourel, Simon Sargon, Abraham Kaplan, and the Collegiate Chorale. Originally, Donald Gramm was to sing at this concert and Poulenc suggested he do *Priez pour paix*, *Le Bestiare*, and two numbers from *Chansons villageoises*. See also his 9 Dec. [19]62 letter to Rose Dercourt-Plaut in Poulenc 1994, 62-25 (Poulenc 1991, no. 349).

APPENDIX III

Recordings by Poulenc as Piano Soloist or Accompanist[1]

Key	B.A.M.	Boîte à Musique (France)
	BBC	British Broadcasting Corporation
	CD	Compact Disc
	FR	France
	H.M.V.	His Master's Voice (England)
	Phonothèque	Bibliothèque Nationale, Département de la Phonothèque Nationale et de l'audiovisuel
	U.S.	United States
	V.S.M.	Voix de son maître (France)

Date	Repertoire [artists]	Label
1928	*[Trois] mouvements perpétuels*	FR Columbia D 13053
1928	Trio (for pn., hb., bsn.) [Poulenc pn., Lamorlette hb., Dhérin bsn.]	FR Columbia D 14213/4
1928 (XI)	*Le Bestiaire;* Duparc: *L'Invitation au voyage* [Poulenc pn., Croiza Mez.]	FR Columbia D 15041
1928	*Les Biches* (1. Rondeau in F major; 2. Adagietto in B-flat major) [Poulenc pn.]	FR Columbia D 15094
1929	Debussy: *Ariettes oubliées* (2. "Il pleure dans mon cœur") [Poulenc pn.,Croiza Mez.]	FR Columbia D 13084

[1]Prepared in large part from Bloch (who cites rereleases through the early 1980s). A number of these recordings have been rereleased on CDs.

ca. 1929	Fauré: *Prison, Claire de lune* [Poulenc pn., Croiza Mez.]	FR Columbia D 13033
1930	*Aubade* (Poulenc pn., Straram cond.)	FR Columbia LF 33/5
1930	*Airs chantés* (Poulenc pn., Peignot S.)	FR Columbia LF 5
1932	*Deux novelettes* and *Caprice en ut majeur* arranged from *Le Bal masqué*	FR Columbia LFX 266
1934	Nocturnes 1, 2, 4	FR Columbia LF 142
1934	Improvisations 2, 5, 9, 10	FR Columbia LF 143
[1935	Ravel	See 1946: H.M.V. DA 1869]
ca. 1935	*Chansons gaillardes* (3. "Madrigal," 8. "Sérénade"), *Quatre poèmes de Guillaume Apollinaire* (1. "L'Anguille," 2. "Carte postale," 3. "Avant le cinéma") [Poulenc pn., Bernac Bar.]	Ultraphone BP 1531
1936 (VII)	Fauré: *Mirages* (3. "Le Jardin nocturne"); *Prison* [Poulenc pn., Bernac Bar.]	V.S.M. DA 4889
1936 (VII)[2]	Debussy: *Trois chansons de France* [Poulenc pn., Bernac Bar.]	V.S.M. DA 4890
1936 (VII)	Fauré: *Sur l'herbe, Sainte* [Poulenc pn., Bernac Bar.]	V.S.M. DA 4891
1936 (VII)[3]	Chabrier: *L'Ile heureuse, Ballade des gros dindons* [Poulenc pn., Bernac Bar.] [Poulenc 1994, 36-18]	V.S.M. DA 4892
1936 (VII)[4]	Auric: *Trois interludes pour chant & piano* (2. "Le Gloxinia"); Satie: *Trois mélodies* (1. "La Statue de bronze," 3. "Le Chapelier") [Poulenc pn., Bernac Bar.]	V.S.M. DA 4893
1936 (VII)[5]	Milhaud: *Quatre poèmes de Léo Latil* (4. "La Tourterelle"); Poulenc: *Chansons gaillardes* (4. "Invocation aux Parques," 7. "La Belle Jeunesse") [Poulenc pn., Bernac Bar.]	V.S.M. DA 4894

[2] The liner notes for "The Essential Pierre Bernac" (Testament SBT 3161) list July/ Nov. This set of three CDs was released in 1999 commemorating the one hundredth anniversary of Bernac's birth.

[3] The liner notes for "The Essential Pierre Bernac" (Testament SBT 3161) list July/ Nov. for "L'Ile heureuse."

[4] The liner notes for "The Essential Pierre Bernac" (Testament SBT 3161) list July/ Nov. for the two Satie pieces.

[5] The liner notes for "The Essential Pierre Bernac" (Testament SBT 3161) list July/ Nov.

1937	Satie: *Parade* (piano 4 hands), *Deux morceaux en forme de poire* [Poulenc & Auric pn.]	B.A.M. 16/7
1937 (I)	Fauré: *Le Secret* [Poulenc pn., Bernac Bar.]	V.S.M. DA 1884
1937 (I)	Fauré: *L'Automne* [Poulenc pn., Bernac Bar.]	V.S.M. DA 1885
1937 (I)	Fauré: *Aurore, Mandoline, Arpège, Les Présents* [Poulenc pn., Bernac Bar.]	V.S.M. (not released)
1938 (II)	Liszt: *Freudvoll und Leidvoll, Es muss ein Wunderbares sein, Nimm einen Strahl der Sonne* [Poulenc pn., Bernac Bar.]	V.S.M. DA 4914
1938 (IV/V)[6]	Roussel: *Cœur en péril, Le Jardin mouillé* [Poulenc pn., Bernac Bar.]	V.S.M. DA 4918
1938 (IV)	Gounod: *Ce que je suis sans toi, Prière* [Poulenc pn., Bernac Bar.]	V.S.M. DA 4915
1940 (XII)	Chausson: *Le Colibri;* Duparc, *Soupir* [Poulenc pn., Bernac Bar.]	V.S.M. DA 4928
1940 (XII)	Fauré: *Après un rêve, Lydia* [Poulenc pn., Bernac Bar.]	V.S.M. DA 4931
1942 (VI)[7]	Vellones: *A mon fils* [Poulenc pn., Bernac Bar.]	V.S.M. W 1516
1943	Debussy: *Ariettes oubliées* ("C'est l'extase," "Il pleure dans mon cœur," "L'Ombre des arbres"); *Aquarelles* (2."Spleen") [Poulenc pn.,Tragin S.]	FR Columbia LFX 650
1943	Debussy: *Ariettes oubliées* ("Paysages belges," 4. "Chevaux de bois," 5. *Aquarelle no.1* "Green;") *L'Echelonnement des haies;* "La Vierge Erigone" (excerpt from *Le Martyre de Saint-Sébastien*)[Poulenc pn., Tragin S.]	FR Columbia LFX 651
1945 (5 II)	Stravinsky: *Les Noces* [Poulenc, Geneviève Joy, Monique Haas, Pierre Sancan pn., Rosenthal cond.]	Phonothèque (private)
1945 (18 II)	*[Trois] mouvements perpétuels* [Poulenc pn.]	Phonothèque (private)

[6] The liner notes for "The Essential Pierre Bernac" (Testament SBT 3161) list Apr. for "Cœur en péril." Bloch gives Feb. for both.

[7] Date from the liner notes for "The Essential Pierre Bernac" (Testament SBT 3161). Bloch gives 23 June 1943.

1945 (18 II)	Sonata for Violin and Piano [André Asselin vn., Poulenc pn.]	Phonothèque (private)
1945 (18 II)	*Poèmes de Ronsard* (4. "Je, n'ai plus que les os," 1. "Attributs"); *Cinq poèmes de Max Jacob* [Poulenc pn., Suzanne Peignot S.]	Phonothèque (private)
1945 (III)	Fauré: *La Bonne Chanson* [Poulenc pn., Bernac Bar.]	H.M.V. DB 8931/3
1945 (XII)	Gounod: *Au rossignol, Sérénade* [Poulenc pn., Bernac Bar.]	H.M.V. DB 6250
1945 (XII)	*Métamorphoses, Deux poèmes de Louis Aragon* [Poulenc pn, Bernac Bar.]	H.M.V. DB 6267
1945 (XII)	*Le Bestiaire ou Le Cortège d'Orphée, Montparnasse* [Poulenc pn., Bernac Bar.]	H.M.V. DB 6299
1945 (XII)	Duparc: *Élégie sur la mort de Robert Emmet, L'Invitation au voyage* [Poulenc pn., Bernac Bar.]	H.M.V. DB 631
1946 (VI)[8]	Ravel: *Don Quichotte à Dulcinée* [Poulenc pn., Bernac Bar.]	H.M.V. DA 1869
1946 (VI & VII)	*Tel jour telle nuit;* "*Deux poèmes de Guillaume Apollinaire* (1. "Dans le jardin d'Anna") [Poulenc pn., Bernac Bar.]	H.M.V. DB 6383/4
1946 (VI & VII)[9]	Debussy: *Trois ballades de Villon, Fêtes galantes* ("Colloque sentimental") [Poulenc pn., Bernac Bar.]	H.M.V. DB 6385/6
1947 (20 X)	*Rapsodie nègre* [Poulenc pn., Jean Chefnay fl., André Vacellier cl., Poulet Quartet, voice]	Phonothèque (private)
1947 (XII)	Fauré: *Soir* [Poulenc pn., Bernac Bar.]	V.S.M. DA 1884
1947 (XII)	Fauré: *Soir, Les Berceaux* [Poulenc pn., Bernac Bar.]	H.M.V. DA 1907
1947 (XII)	Fauré: *Les Berceaux* [Poulenc pn., Bernac Bar.]	V.S.M. DA 1885
1947 (XII)	Fauré: *Le Secret, Aurore, Soir* [Poulenc pn., Bernac Bar.]	Testament SBT 3161

[8] Poulenc 1994, p. 408 says the first recording by FP/PB was in 1935.

[9] The liner notes for "The Essential Pierre Bernac" (Testament SBT 3161) list Mar. but this must be an error.

1950   *[Trois] mouvements perpétuels;* Nocturne 5;
(II)   *Suite française;* Satie: *Gymnopédie 1, Sara-*
        bande 2, Gnossienne 3, Descriptions auto-
        matique, Avant-dernières pensées, Croquis
        et agaceries d'un gros bonhomme en bois
        [Poulenc pn.]   U.S. Columbia ML 4399

1950   *Quatre poèmes de Guillaume Apollinaire, Mi-*
(II & *roirs brûlants* (1. "Tu vois le feu du soir"),
III)   *Main dominée par le cœur, Calligrammes;*
        Chabrier: *L'Ile heureuse, Villanelle des petits*
        canards; Debussy: *Beau soir, L'Echelonnement*
        des haies, Le Promenoir des deux amants; Satie:
        Trois mélodies [Poulenc pn., Bernac Bar.]   U.S. Columbia ML 4484

1950   *Banalités, Chansons villageoises;* Ravel:
(II & *Histoires naturelles, Trois chants hébraïques*[10]
III)   [Poulenc pn., Bernac Bar.]   U.S. Columbia MM 958

1950   Concerto for Piano [Poulenc pn.,
(24 VII) Charles Munch cond.]   Phonothèque (private)

1950   Sonata for Violin and Piano
(IX)   [Louis Kaufman vn., Poulenc pn.]   Phonothèque (private)

1952   Barber: *Mélodies passagères*
(15 II) [Poulenc pn., Bernac Bar.]   New World Records NW 229
                                          (Originally recorded in New York for
                                          Columbia XLP 9280, but never released)

1952   *Suite française* [Poulenc pn.]
(26 V)   Phonothèque (private)

1952   Duparc: *Élégie, Le Manoir de Rosemonde,*
(on or   *Soupir, L'Invitation au voyage;* Debussy:
before   *Trois ballades de Villon;* Ravel: *Don Quichotte*
26V)   *à Dulcinée;* Poulenc: *Tel jour telle nuit, Chan-*
          sons villageoises [Poulenc pn., Bernac Bar.] Phonothèque (private)
                                          (Festival de Bordeaux, 1952)

1952   *Paul et Virginie* [Poulenc pn., Peignot S.]
(6 VII)   Phonothèque (private)

1952   *Le Gendarme incompris* [Poulenc pn.,
(6 VII) Jacques Hilling, Bertin, etc.]   Phonothèque (private)

1953   *La Fraîcheur et le feu, Miroirs brûlants*
(15 IV) (1. "Tu vois le feu du soir") [Poulenc pn.,
        Bernac Bar.]   Phonothèque (private)

[10] This includes "Chanson hébraïque" from *Chants populaires* and *Deux mélodies hébraïques.*

1954   *L'Embarquement pour Cythè*re
(11 I)   [Poulenc & Février pn.]   MS 6450[11]

1954   *Fiançailles pour rire, Trois chansons de*
(VI)[12]   *F. Garcia-Lorca;* Debussy: *Ariettes oubliées*
           (1."C'est l'extase," 4."L'Ombre des arbres,"
           2."Il pleure dans mon cœur"); Roussel:
           Deux poèmes chinois, Cœur en péril
           [Poulenc pn., Touraine S.]   B.A.M. LD 012

1954   *Quatre poèmes de Guillaume Apollinaire,*
(23 VII) *Métamorphoses,* (2. "C'est ainsi que tu es"),
           Chansons villageoises, Le Bestiaire
           [Poulenc pn., Bernac Bar.]   Phonothèque (private)

1954   Trio (for hb., bsn., pn.) [André Lardrot
(29 VII) hb., Poulenc pn., Gérard Tantot bsn.]   Phonothèque (private)

1955   Satie: *Prélude de La Porte héroïque du ciel;*
(21 XI)   *Gymnopédie 1.Sarabande 2. Gnossienne 3;*
           Avant-dernières pensées, Descriptions auto-
           matiques; Croquis et agaceries d'un gros bon-
           homme en bois ("Tyrolienne turque," "Danse
           maigre"); *Prélude posthume* [Poulenc pn.]   B.A.M. LD 023

1955   Chabrier: *Trois valses romantiques*
           [Poulenc & Meyer pn.]   Discophiles français 151/2

1956   *Le Bal masqué* [Poulenc pn., Bernac Bar.,
           Louis Frémaux cond.]   Véga C 35 A 35

1957[13]   *Cinq poèmes de Paul Éluard; Huit chansons*
           polonaises; Le Travail du peintre; Airs chantés
           (1. "Air romantique"); *Deux mélodies*
           (2. "Nuage"); *La Grenouillère; Quatre poèmes*
           de Guillaume Apollinaire (3. "Avant le cinéma")
           [Poulenc pn., Rose Dercourt-Plaut S.]   Turnabout 4489

1957[14]   *Histoire de Babar, le petit éléphant* [Poulenc
           pn., Pierre Fresnay reciter]   Discophiles français DF425.105

ca.1957[15]*Histoire de Babar, le petit éléphant* [Poulenc
           pn., Noël Coward reciter]   Aurora ABA 253 (not released)

---

[11] "Bande magnétique d'origine radiophonique." See Bloch, p. 215.
[12] Month from Hughes 1963, p. 29. Hughes turned pages during the session.
[13] Poulenc did not finish "Nuage" until Sept. 1956.
[14] In his unpublished 6 June [1954] letter to R. Douglas Gibson Poulenc indicated
he originally intended to make this recording on 2 July 1954.
[15] In an unpublished Mar. [1957] letter o Gibson Poulenc expressed the hope that

1957   Debussy: *Beau soir, L'Echelonnement des*
(10 V) *haies, Le Promenoir des deux amants, Trois*
        ballades de Villon [Poulenc pn., Bernac
        Bar.]   Phonothèque (private)

1957   Sonata for Flute and Piano [Jean-Pierre
(18 VI) Rampal fl., Poulenc pn.]   Phonothèque (private)

1957   Gounod: *Ce que je suis sans toi, Au ros-*
(IX?)[16] *signol, Venise, Prière, Chanson de printemps,*
        L'Absent, Viens, les gazons sont verts, Envoi
        de fleurs, Mignon [Poulenc pn., Bernac Bar.]
                        The Friends of Pierre Bernac PB1 and
                                   Testament SBT 3161

1957   *Le Travail du peintre* [Poulenc pn.,
(IX?)[17] Bernac Bar.]   Testament SBT 3161

[1958?] *Deux poèmes de Guillaume Apollinaire, Le*
        Bestiare, "Le Pont,"*Montparnasse, Cinq*
        poèmes de Paul Eluard, La Fraîcheur et le
        feu [Poulenc pn., Bernac Bar.]   Véga C 35 A 33

[1958?] *Deux poèmes de Louis Aragon* (1. "C"), *Le*
        Disparu, Miroirs brûlants (1."Tu vois le feu
        du soir"), *Paul et Virginie, La Grenouillère,*
        Parisiana, Métamorphoses (2."C'est ainsi que
        tu es"), *Épitaphe, Chansons gaillardes, Priez*
        pour paix [Poulenc pn., Bernac Bar.]   Véga C 35 A 34

1958   Concerto in D minor [Poulenc & Février
        pn., Pierre Dervaux cond.]   FR Columbia 33 FCX 677

1958   Gounod: "La Romance de Baucis" (from
(16 V) Act 1 of *Philémon et Baucis*) "Viens les ga-
        zons sont verts;" Chabrier: "O petite étoile
        du destin" (from Act 1 of *L'Étoile),* "Hélas
        dans l'esclavage" (from *Le Roi malgré lui*);
        Debussy: *Les Proses lyriques;* Ravel: *Shéhéra-*
        zade (2."La Flûte enchantée," 3. "L'indifférent"),
        Noël des jouets; Poulenc: *Trois poèmes de Louise de*
        Vilmorin, Un poème, Main dominée par le cœur,
        from *Dialogues des Carmélites* (Act 1), from
        Les Mamelles de Tirésias (Scene 1), *Toréador*
        [Poulenc pn., Poulenc voice, Duval S.]   CLIO 001

Coward would record the work in April,. See the letter in GB-Lchester.
[16] This recording was made by the BBC Third Programme just after Bernac and
Poulenc gave two concerts at the Edinburgh Festival on 5 and 6 Sept. 1957. It
was broadcast on 9 Oct. 1957.
[17] See note 15.

1958 (20XI)	*Concert champêtre* [Poulenc pn., D. E. Inghelbrecht cond.]	Phonothèque (private)
1958 (28 XII)	*Concert champêtre* [Poulenc pn., Eugène Bigot cond.]	Phonothèque (private)
1959 (VI)	*Le Travail du peintre* [Poulenc pn., Bernac Bar.]	Phonothèque (private)
1959 (VI)	Trio (for pn., hb., bsn.) [Poulenc pn., Pierre Pierlot hb., Maurice Allard bsn.]	Véga C 35 A 181
ca. 1959	Debussy: *Trois ballades de Villon;* Duparc: *Élégie, Le Manoir de Rosemonde, Soupir,* *L'Invitation au voyage;* Poulenc: *Tel jour* *telle nuit;* Barber: *Mélodies passagères* [Poulenc pn., Bernac Bar.]	U.S. Columbia XLP 9280/81
1960	*Elégie* [Lucien Thévet hn., Poulenc pn.]	Véga C 30 S 244
1960 (VI)	*Banalités, Tel jour telle nuit, Calligrammes, Le* *Travail du peintre* [Poulenc pn., Bernac Bar.]	Véga C 30 A 293
1960 (21 VI)	Concerto in D minor [Poulenc & Février pn., Charles Bruck cond.]	Phonothèque (private)
1961	*Aubade* [Poulenc pn., Prêtre cond.]	Véga C 30 A 303
1961	Sextet [Poulenc pn., Robert Cole fl., John De Lancie hb., Anthony Gigliotti cl., Sol Schonbach bsn., Mason Jones hn.]	U.S. Columbia ML 5613
1961	*Suite française* [orch. version with Poulenc hps.]	Club français du disque 265
1961	Satie: *Trois morceaux en forme de poire* [Poulenc & Février pn.]	Club français du disque 272[18]
ca. 1962	Satie: *La Belle Excentrique, En habit de* *cheval* [Poulenc & Février pn.]	Club français du disque 273
1962	Concerto in D minor [Poulenc & Février pn., Prêtre cond.]	V.S.M. FALP 737
1962	Concerto in D minor [Poulenc & Février pn., Rosenthal cond.]	Phonotèque (private)
1962 (23 V)	*Air chantés,* excerpt from *Dialogues des Car-* *mélites* [Poulenc pn., Rosanna Carteri, S.]	Phonothèque (private)

---

[18] This recording won the *Grand Prix du Disque de l'Académie Charles Cros.*

?[19]   Satie: *Aperçus désagréables*
            [Poulenc & Février pn.][20]   Fidélio-Monestier 34002

?   Sonata for Flute and Piano [Poulenc
            pn., Edmond De Francesco fl.]   Phonothèque (private)
                                                    [from Radio Suisse-Romande]

?   *Histoire de Babar, le petit éléphant* [Poulenc
            pn., Bruce Belfrage reciter] [English]   BBC (private)

?   Five Debussy Songs [Poulenc pn.,
            Bernard Kruysen Bar.]   INA Mémoire vive 262010[21]

[19] Posthumous release in 1967.
[20] Also includes music found on Club français du disque 272 and 273.
[21] Cited in Ivry, p. 234. I am unaware of which Debussy songs are on this recording. Poulenc and Kruysen performed together at the Menton Festival on 31 July
1962. On that occasion they performed eight Debussy songs including: *Le Son du
cor s'afflige, L'Echelonnement des haies, Trois chansons de France,* and *Fêtes galantes*
("Les Ingénues," "Le Faune," and "Colloque sentimental").

APPENDIX IV

Portraits and Drawings of Francis Poulenc

A PRELIMINARY LIST

Artist	Date and Description	Location and Publication
Jacques-Emile Blanche (1861-1942)	18-7-1920; Poulenc in military uniform. Oil on canvas, 60 x 50 cm	Tours, France: Musée des Beaux-Arts (gift of Virginie Liénard). Poulenc 1994 cover; Machart, p. 240; Blanche, p. 187
Jacques-Emile Blanche	19-7-1920; Poulenc in profile. Oil on canvas, dedicated to Darius Milhaud	Private collection. Description only in Blanche, p. 186
Jacques-Emile Blanche	ca. 19-7-1920; Poulenc wearing a hat. Oil on canvas	Known only from a photograph of the artist's studio in 1920. See Blanche, p. 186
Jean Oberlé	1920; Jean Cocteau presenting Auric, Milhaud, and Poulenc to Satie.	Originally appeared in *Le Crapouillot* (1 Feb. 1921) Albrechtskirchinger, pl. 124; Machart, p. 31
Pedro Pruna	1920; Group portrait entitled "Les nouveaux dieux de l'Art: Max Jacob, Georges Auric, Igor Stravinsky, Jean Cocteau, Francis Poulenc, Darius Milhaud, Pablo Picasso quand Paris les découvraient"	Paris, Collection of Madeleine Milhaud. Albrechtskirchinger, pl. 100

Valentine Hugo (1887-1968)	Early 1920s?; Portrait. Pencil on tracing paper, 17.5 x 25 cm	Paris, Bibliothèque Nationale. Margerie, p. 50
Roger de La Fresnaye (1885-1925)	Feb. 1921; Portrait. Pencil on paper 27 x 21.6 cm signed "Grasse le 1 er Février 21 R de la Fresnaye"	Not located. Former collections of Claude Delvaincourt and Germain Seligman (New York); Seligman, no. 489
Roger de La Fresnaye	Feb. 1921; Portrait. Pencil on paper. Unsigned, but inscribed "Grasse - Portraits Photographie d'art"	Not located. Former collection of Georges Salles? Seligman, no. 490
Jean Cocteau (1889-1963)	1921; Caricature collage of the heads of *Les Six* signed "Jean Cocteau". Ink on paper, 28 x 22 cm	Formerly in private collection of Pierre and Marie Bertin. Albrechtskirchinger, pl. 119
Jean Cocteau	1922; Caricature of Poulenc playing the piano	Not located. Cocteau 1972, no. 9
Jacques-Emile Blanche	[ca. 1922] Poulenc pictured with Tailleferre, Milhaud, Honegger, Wiéner, Meyer, Cocteau, and Auric. Oil on canvas, 188 x 112 cm	Rouen, Musée des Beaux-Arts (Inv.924.1.29). Volta 1990, p. 9; Blanche, p. 189; Albrechtskirchinger, pl. 102, detail p. 86
Marie Laurencin (1885-1956)	1923; Portrait. Pencil on paper	Private collection of Francis Poulenc. Kochno 1924
Jean Cocteau	1924; Caricature of Poulenc signed "Jean Monte Carlo 1924"; the original is inscribed "à Francis Poulenc son ami Jean 1924 Monte Carlo"	Private collection of Francis Poulenc. Cocteau 1972, no. 10; Hell 1978, pl. 8
Nina Hamnett (1890-1956)	1925; Oil on canvas	Not located. Described in Hooker
Nina Hamnett	1925; Portrait. Pencil on paper?	Not located. Described and reproduced in Hooker, p. 168; it first appeared in *Apollo*
Christian Bérard (1902-49)	?; Poulenc seated at a piano under a picture of Mozart. Signed "à Francis Poulenc Ch. Bérard"	Private collection of Francis Poulenc. Machart, p. 119; Hell 1978, pl. 12; Roy 1994, p. 151

Louis Marcoussis (1878-1941)	Before 1941; Portrait. Pencil on paper, 45 x 32 cm	Paris, Musée National d'Art Moderne. Lafranchis, pp. 164-6. Reproduced on p. 164
Louis Marcoussis	Before 1941; Portrait. Pencil on paper, 29 x 33 cm	Paris, Musée National d'Art Moderne. Lafranchis, pp. 164-6
Jean de Gaigneron (1890-1976)	ca. 1944; Poulenc seated. Oil on canvas	Paris, Bibliothèque de l'Opéra
Scribner Ames	1950; Portrait. Pencil on paper, 9.5 x 8 inches	Not located. For an exhibition see Arts Club
Pablo Picasso (1881-1973)	13-3-1957; Poulenc seated. Pencil on paper, 54 x 37 cm	Paris, Musée Picasso. Albrechtskirchinger, pl. 105; Zervos, no. 317
Nora Auric (1903-82)	?; Portrait	Not located. Mentioned in Poulenc 1994, p. 1011
M Beur	?; Portrait. Pencil, 21.5 x 16.5 cm	Former collection of Raymond Destouches. Boulet, no. 60
M Tournade	?; Caricature in ink	Former collection of the artist

Bibliography of Works Cited and Poulenc's Published Writings

[Some periodical articles, particularly reviews, are cited only in footnotes.]

Adéma   Adéma, Pierre-Marcel, *"Les Mamelles de Tirésias: Essai bibliographique"* in *Guillaume Apollinaire, La Revue des lettres modernes*, nos. 123-6, ed. Michel Décaudin (1965), 55-63.

Albrecht   Albrecht, Carol Padgham, *"'Let's Do Lunch': Francis Poulenc Enters the Real Estate Market,"* in *Himmlischer Godt!: A Little Offering for Irving Godt on His Seventieth Birthday March 13, 1993*, ed. Theodore Albrecht (Kent, OH: Five-Minute Festschriften, Inc., 1993).

Albrechtskirchinger   Albrechtskirchinger, Geneviève, *Jean Cocteau et ses amis artistes* (Ludion: Musée d'Ixelles, 1991). [Exhibition Catalogue.]

Allorto   Allorto, Riccardo, "Intervista con Francis Poulenc: Nascità dei 'Dialoghi delle Carmelitane'," *Ricordiana* 2 (1957), 5-7. [Interview with Poulenc.]

Alsop   Alsop, Susan Mary, *To Marietta from Paris* (Garden City, NY: Doubleday & Company, Inc.,1975).

Ancelin   Ancelin, Pierre, "Le Musicien dans la société de son temps" in *Henri Sauguet: L'homme et l'œuvre. La Revue musicale* 361-3 (1983), 214-25.

Anderson   Anderson, Alexandra, and Carol Saltus, eds. *Jean Cocteau and the French Scene* (New York: Abbeville Press, 1984).

Archives Roland-
Manuel

*Archives Roland-Manuel et divers lettres auto-
graphes et manuscrits. Correspondances de Maurice
Ravel.* Drouot Richelieu - Salle 2, 24 Mar. 2000
(sale catalogue).

Arts Club

*Sixty Years on the Arts Club Stage: A Souvenir
Exhibition of Portraits* (17 November 1975-3
January 1976).

Aschengreen

Aschengreen, Erik, *Jean Cocteau and the Dance,*
trans. Patricia McAndrew and Per Avsum
(Copenhagen: Gyldendal, 1986).

Auric 1971

Auric, Georges, "A propos du 'Gendarme
incompris',"*Cahiers Jean Cocteau* 2 (1971), 39-42.

Auric 1979

— *Quand j'étais là* (Paris: Bernard Grasset, 1979).

Avant scène 1983, L'

L'Avant scène opéra, No. 52, May 1983. [Issue
devoted to *Dialogues des Carmélites.*]

Baedeker: NFrance

Baedeker, Karl, *Northern France From Belgium and
the English Channel to the Loire Excluding Paris and
Its Environs,* 5th ed. (Leipzig: Karl Baedeker;
London: T. F. Unwin; New York: Charles
Scribner's Sons, 1909).

Baedeker: Paris

— *Paris and Environs with Routes from London to
Paris,* 15th ed. (Leipzig: Karl Baedeker; London:
Dulau and Co.; New York: Charles Scribner's
Sons, 1904).

Baedeker: SFrance

— *Southern France Including Corsica,* 6th ed.
(Leipzig: Karl Baedeker; London: T. F. Unwin;
New York: Charles Scribner's Sons, 1914).

Barry

Barry, Richard, "Poulenc and the Twentieth-
Century: The Songs on Poetry of Paul Eluard,"
Ars Musica Denver 2 (1989), 1-11.

Baschet

Baschet, Roger, "L'Habitation d'un compositeur," *Images de France: Plaisir de France* 8 (Dec.
1941), 41-4.

Baxter

Baxter, John, *Buñuel* (London: Fourth Estate,
1994).

Beaumont

Beaumont, Cyril, *Complete Book of Ballets: A Guide
to the Principal Ballets of the Nineteenth and Twentieth Centuries* (London: Putnam, 1956).

Beevor and Cooper

Beevor, Antony and Artemis Cooper, *Paris After
the Liberation 1944-1949* (New York: Doubleday,
1994).

Béhar

Béhar, Henri, *Le Théâtre Dada et surréaliste* (New ed: [Paris]: Gallimard, 1979).

Bellas 1964

Bellas, Jacqueline, "Francis Poulenc ou le 'son de voix de Guillaume'," *La Revue des lettres modernes*, 3rd series, nos. 104-07 (1964), 130-48

Bellas 1965

— "*Les Mamelles de Tirésias* en habit d'Arlequin" in *Guillaume Apollinaire, La Revue des lettres modernes*, nos. 123-6, ed. M. Décaudin (1965), 30-54.

Bellas 1967

— "Apollinaire et Poulenc: peut-on mettre 'Alcools' en musique?" in *Apollinaire et la musique, Journées Apollinaire: Actes du Colloque (Stave-lot 27-29 août 1965)* (Stavelot: Les Amis de G. Apollinaire, 1967), 49-57.

Benedikt

Benedikt, Michael and George E. Wellwarth, *The Avant-Garde, Dada, and Surrealism* (New York: E. P. Dutton & Co., Inc., 1964).

Berenguer

Berenguer, Bruno, "Denise Duval - Francis Poulenc: Une amitié intime à la base d'une étroite collaboration artistique," *Poulenc et ses amis* in *Revue internationale de musique française* 31 (1994), 49-71.

Bernac 1965

Bernac, Pierre, "Poulenc's Songs," *Recorded Sound: The Journal of the British Institute of Recorded Sound* 18 (Apr. 1965), 315-21. A "Pierre Bernac Discography" by Erich Hughes and Patrick Saul, follows Bernac's article on pp. 322-27.

Bernac 1977a

— *Francis Poulenc: The Man and His Songs,* trans. Winifred Radford (New York: W. W. Norton, 1977).

Bernac 1977b

— "A Certain Grace," trans. Thomas Grubb, *Opera News* 41 (5 Feb. 1977), 28-32.

Bernac 1978

— *Francis Poulenc et ses mélodies* (Paris: Éditions Buchet/Chastel, 1978).

Bernier

Bernier, Olivier, *Fireworks at Dusk: Paris in the Thirties* (Boston: Little, Brown, 1993).

Blanche

Jacques-Emile Blanche, peintre (1861-1942) (Rouen: Musée des Beaux-Arts, 1997)

Bloch

Bloch, Francine, *Phonographies Francis Poulenc 1928-1982* (Paris: Bibliothèque Nationale, 1984).

Blum

Blum, Daniel, *Theatre World Season 1949-50* (New York, 1950).

Bothorel   Bothorel, Jean, *Louise ou la vie de Louise de
                                Vilmorin* (Paris: Bernard Grasset, 1993).

Boulet   Boulet, Louis-Dominique, *Exposition Georges
                                Bernanos-Francis Poulenc et les Dialogues des
                                Carmélites* (Tours: Musée des Beaux-Arts, 1970).
                                [Exhibition catalogue.]

Bourdet 1936   Bourdet, Dénise, *Margot* in *La petite Illustration*,
                                No. 755, Théâtre No. 382 (11 Jan. 1936).

Bourdet 1957   — "Images de Paris, Francis Poulenc," *La Revue
                                de Paris* (Mar. 1957).

Bourdet 1961   — "Francis Poulenc: 'Monte-Carlo c'est pour
                                moi Venise'," *Le Figaro littéraire* (2 Dec. 1961), 19.
                                [Interview with Poulenc.]

Breitrose   Breitrose, Henry, "Conversation with Milhaud,"
                                Music Educators Journal 56 (Mar. 1970), 55-6.

Brody 1977   Brody, Elaine,"New Light on Twentieth-Century
                                Performance Practice," *A Musical Offering:
                                Essays in Honor of Martin Bernstein*, Edward H.
                                Clinkscale and Claire Brook (eds.), pp. 45-62
                                (New York: Pendragon Press, 1977).

Brody 1987   — *Paris: The Musical Kaleidoscope 1870-1925* (New
                                York: George Braziller, 1987).

Brooks   Brooks, Jeanice, "Nadia Boulanger and the Salon
                                of the Princesse de Polignac," *Journal of the
                                American Musicological Society* 46 (1993), 415-68.

Bruyninckx   Bruyninckx, Walter, *Swing, 1920-1985: Swing-
                                dance Bands & Combos* (Mechelen, Belgium: Copy
                                Express, 1985).

Bruyr   Bruyr, José, "Bonjour Monsieur Poulenc ou les
                                rencontres,"*Musica: Revue d'informations et
                                d'actualités musicales* (Nov. 1954), 9-12.

Buckland/Chimènes: Buckland, Sidney and Chimènes, Miriam eds.,
                                Francis Poulenc: Music, Art and Literature (Lon
                                don: Ashgate, 1999). [Buckland translates nu-
                                merous passages from Poulenc's letters, supple-
                                menting those in Poulenc 1991.]

            a   Buckland, Sidney, "'The Coherence of Oppo-
                                sites:' Eluard, Poulenc and the Poems of *Tel jour
                                telle nuit*," pp. 145-77.

            b   Chimènes, Myriam, "Poulenc and His Patrons:
                                Social Convergences," pp. 210-51.

c   Daniel, Keith W., "Poulenc's Choral Works with
           Orchestra," pp. 48-86.

d   Gendre, Claude, *Dialogues des Carmélites:* The
           Historical Background, Literary Destiny and
           Genesis of the Opera," 274-319.

e   Kayas, Lucie, "Francis Poulenc — Disc Jockey,"
           pp. 363-88.

f   Orledge, Robert, "Poulenc and Koechlin: 58
           Lessons and a Friendship," pp. 9-47.

g   Poulenc, Francis, "All My Pleasure is in Making
           New Discoveries:' Francis Poulenc Visits Ameri-
           can Museums of Art. From *Feuilles américaines.*
           Extraits de journal," pp, 196-8.

h   — "'My Ideal Library'," pp. 140-4.

i   Reed, Philip, "Poulenc, Britten, Aldeburgh: A
           Chronicle," pp. 348-62.

j   Robert, Sophie, "Raymonde Linossier: 'Lovely
           Soul Who Was My Flame," pp. 87-139.

k   Schmidt, Carl B., "Distilling Essences: Poulenc
           and Matisse," pp. 199-209.

l   Waleckx, Denis, "In Search of a Libretto," pp.
           252-73.

m   — "'A Musical Confession:' Poulenc, Cocteau
           and *La Voix*," pp. 320-47.

n   Wharton, Marjorie Running, "Nogent Music:
           Poulenc and Dufy," pp. 178-95.

Buckle   Buckle, Richard, *Diaghilev* (New York: Ath-
           eneum, 1979).

Burrin   Burrin, Philippe, *France Under the Germans:*
           Collaboration and Compromise, trans. Janet Lloyd
           (New York: New Press, 1996).

Cadieu   Cadieu, Martine, "Duo avec Francis Poulenc,"
           Les Nouvelles littéraires (4 May 1961), 179. [Inter-
           view with Poulenc.]

Calvocoressi   Calvocoressi, Michel Dimitri, *Musicians Gallery:*
           Music and Ballet in Paris and London (London:
           Faber and Faber Limited, 1933).

Camfield   Camfield, William A., *Francis Picabia: His Art,*
           Life and Times (Princeton: Princeton Univ. Press,
           1979).

Carpenter   Carpenter, Humphrey, *Geniuses Together: American Writers in Paris in the 1920s* (Boston: Houghton Mifflin Co., 1988).

Casa Fuerte   Casa Fuerte, Illan de, *Le Dernier des Guermantes*, ed. Philippe Michel-Thiret (Paris: Editions Julliard, 1994).

CatM   *Catalogo delle manifestazioni: 1928-1997. Teatro Comunale di Firenze Maggio Musicale Fiorentino*, ed. Aloma Bardi and Maurio Conti, 2 vols. (Florence: Le Lettere, 1998).

Cayez   Cayez, Pierre, *Rhône-Poulenc 1895-1975: Contribution à l'étude d'un groupe industriel* (Paris: Armand Colin/Masson, 1988).

Chamfray   Chamfray, Claude, "Le Clavecin glorifié: Entretien avec F. Poulenc," *Beaux Arts* (November 1935), 6. [Interview with Poulenc.]

Charles-Roux   Charles-Roux, Edmonde, *Chanel*, trans. Nancy Amphoux (London: Harvill, 1989).

Chester   *The Complete Works of Francis Poulenc*, preface by Claude Rostand (London: Chester, 1946).

Chevaillier   Chevaillier, Lucien, "Un Entretien avec Francis Poulenc,"*Le Guide du concert et des théâtres lyrique* 30 (26 Apr. 1929), 855-7. [Interview with Poulenc.]

Christout   Christout, Marie-Françoise, *Théâtre du Vieux Colombier: 1913-1993* (Paris: Institute français d'architecture Norma, 1993).

Ciry   Ciry, Michel, *Le Temps des promesses: Journal 1942-1949* (Paris: Librairie Plon, 1979).

Ciupa   Ciupa, Karine, *Yvonne Printemps: L'heure bleue* (Paris: Robert Laffont, 1989).

Cocteau 1918   Cocteau, Jean, *Le Coq et l'Arlequin - Notes autour de la musique* (Paris: Éditions de la Sirène, 1918).

Cocteau 1921   — *Cock and Harlequin; Notes Concerning Music*, trans. Rollo Myers (London: The Egoist Press, 1921).

Cocteau 1946   — *Œuvres complètes.* (11 vols.; Geneva: Marguerat, 1946-51).

Cocteau 1965   — "Les Mariés de la Tour Eiffel," *L'Approdo musicale* 19-20 (1965), 145-8.

Cocteau 1969 — "Poémes inédits," *Cahiers Jean Cocteau* 1 (1969).

Cocteau 1971 — *"Le Gendarme incompris," Cahiers Jean Cocteau* 2 (1971), 43-69.

Cocteau 1972 — *Jean Cocteau Drawings: 129 Drawings from "Desseins,"* foreword by Edouard Dermitt (New York: Dover Publications, 1972).

Cocteau 1974 — *A Call to Order*, New York: Haskell House Ltd., 1974). [Includes *Cock and Harlequin, Professional Secrets,* and other critical essays.]

Cocteau 1983 — *Le Passé défini*, vol. 1, 1951-52 (Paris: Gallimard, 1983). English trans. in Cocteau 1987.

Cocteau 1985 — *Le Passé défini*, vol. 2, 1953 (Paris: Gallimard, 1985). English trans. in Cocteau 1988.

Cocteau 1987 — *Past Tense*, "Diaries," vol. 1, trans. Richard Howard (San Diego: Harcourt Brace Jovanovich, New York and London, 1987).

Cocteau 1988 — *Past Tense*, "Diaries," vol. 2, trans. Richard Howard (San Diego: Harcourt Brace Jovanovich, New York and London, 1988).

Cocteau 1989a — *Journal 1942-1945*, ed. Jean Touzot (Paris: Gallimard, 1989).

Cocteau 1989b — *Le Passé défini*, vol. 3, 1954 (Paris: Gallimard, 1989).

Cocteau 1992 — *Jean Cocteau-Darius Milhaud Correspondance*, ed. Pierre Caizergues and Josiane Mas (Montpellier: Centre d'études littéraires françaises du XXᵉ siècle Université Paul Valery, 1992).

Collaer 1965 Collaer, Paul, "I 'Sei': Studio dell'evoluzione della musica francese dal 1917 al 1924," *L'Approdo musicale* 19-20 (1965), 11-78.

Collaer 1974 — "La Musique française de 1917 à 1924: La fin des Six et de Satie," *La Revue générale: perspectives européenes des sciences humaines* 6-7 (June-July 1974), 1-25.

Collaer 1988 — *Darius Milhaud*, trans. Jane Hohfeld Galante (San Francisco: San Francisco Press, Inc., 1988).

Collaer 1996 — *Correspondance avec des amis musiciens*, ed. with annotations by Robert Wangermée (Sprimont, Belgium: Pierre Mardaga, 1996).

Complete Works	*The Complete Works of Francis Poulenc with a Foreword by Claude Rostand* (London, 1946).
Conrad 1983	Conrad, Doda, "Souvenirs," *Henri Sauguet: l'homme et l'œuvre,* ed. Pierre Ancelin, *La Revue musicale* 361-3 (1983), 67-82.
Conrad 1995	— *Grandeur et mystère d'un mythe: Souvenirs de quarante-quatre ans d'amitié avec Nadia Boulanger* (Paris: Éditions Buchet/Chastel, 1995).
Conrad 1997	— *Dodascalies: Ma chronique du XXe siècle* (Arles: Actes Sud, 1997).
Copeau	Copeau, Jacques and Martin du Gard, Roger, *Correspondance [de] Jacques Copeau [et] Roger Martin du Gard,* introd. by Jean Delay, ed. Claude Sicard, 2 vols. (Paris: Gallimard, 1972).
Copland 1984	Copland, Aaron and Perlis, Vivian, *Copland 1900 through 1942* (London/Boston: Faber and Faber, 1984).
Copland 1989	— *Copland Since 1943* (New York: St Martin's Press, 1989).
Cortot	Cortot, Alfred, *La Musique française de piano,* III (Paris: Presses universitaires de France, 1948).
Cossart	Cossart, Michael de, *The Food of Love: Princesse Edmond de Polignac (1865-1943) and Her Salon* (London: Hamish Hamilton, 1978).
Costumes	*Costumes and Curtains from the Diaghilev and De Basil Ballets,* Catalogues for the 17 July 1968 and 19 Dec. 1969, Sotheby and Co. auctions, intro. by Richard Buckle, preface by Léonide Massine (New York: The Viking Press, 1972).
Craft 1985	Craft, Robert, *Dearest Bubushkin: The Correspondence of Vera and Igor Stravinsky, 1921-1954, with Excerpts from Vera Stravinsky's Diaries 1922-1971,* trans. from the Russian by Lucia Davidova (New York: Thames and Hudson, 1985).
Craft 1992	— *Stravinsky: Glimpses of a Life* (New York: St. Martin's Press, 1992).
Crespin	Crespin, Régine, *La Vie et l'amour d'une femme* (Paris: Fayard, 1982).
Cronin	Cronin, Vincent, *Paris on the Eve: 1900-1914* (New York: St. Martin's Press, 1990).

Crosland

Crosland, Margaret, *Raymond Radiguet* (London: Peter Owen, 1976).

Cuneo-Laurent

Cuneo-Laurent, Linda, "The Performer as Catalyst: The Role of the Singer Jane Bathori in the Careers of Debussy, Ravel, 'Les Six' and Their Contemporaries in Paris, 1904-1926," Ph.D. thesis (New York Univ., 1982).

Daniel

Daniel, Keith W., *Francis Poulenc: His Artistic Development and Musical Style*, Studies in Music, No. 52 (Ann Arbor: UMI Research Press, 1982).

Décaudin 1965

Décaudin, Michel, ed., *Guillaume Apollinaire, La Revue des lettres modernes*, nos. 123-6, (1965).

Décaudin 1967

— *Apollinaire et la musique, Journées Apollinaire: Actes du Colloque (Stavelot 27-29 août 1965)* (Stavelot: Les Amis de G. Apollinaire, 1967).

De Nobel

De Nobel, Felix, "Memories of Francis Poulenc," *Sonorum Speculum* 15 (June 1963), 39-43.

Despart

Despart, Jehan, Francis Poulenc: *Musicien du cœur*. Conférence prononcée à l'occasion du centenaire de la naissance de Francis Poulenc, qui fut un familiar du salon de Winnaretta Singer, princesse de Polignac ([Paris]: Fondation Singer-Polignac, 1999).

Diaghilev

Diaghilev: Les Ballets russes (Paris: Bibliothèque Nationale, 1979). [Exhibition catalogue.]

Dijk

Dijk, Hans van, *LSO: Geschiedenis van het Maastrichts Stedelijk en het Limburgs Symphonie Orkest 1883-1983* (Maastricht: Stichting Historische Reeks Maastricht, 1988).

Drot

Drot, Jean-Marie, *Les Heures chaudes de Montparnasse* (Paris: Editions Hazan, 1995).

Dumesnil

Dumesnil, René, "Francis Poulenc," *Revue des deux mondes* (June 1963), 587-92.

Dunoyer

Dunoyer, Cecilia, *Marguerite Long: A Life in French Music, 1874-1966* (Bloomington & Indianapolis: Indiana Univ. Press, 1993).

Durey

Durey, Louis, "Francis Poulenc," *Chesterian* 25 (Sept. 1922), 1-4.

Duruflé

Duruflé, Maurice, "Poulenc's Organ Concerto," *Music* 8 (July 1974), 22.

Dutilleux   Dutilleux, Henri, "Au service de tous," in *Roger Désormière et son temps*, ed. Denise Meyer and Pierre Souvtchinsky (Monaco: Éditions du Rocher, 1966), 115-26.

Ehrler   Ehrler, Hanno, *Untersuchungen zur Klaviermusik von Francis Poulenc, Arthur Honegger und Darius Milhaud*, Mainzer Studien zur Musikwissenschaft 26 (Tutzing: Hans Schneider, 1990).

Eluard 1968   Eluard, Paul, *Œuvres complètes* (2 vols.; Paris, 1968). [Detailed information about the publication history of all of Eluard's poems set by Poulenc. In addition to the specific references contained in the catalogue, see vol. 2, pp. 1281-8.]

Eluard 1989   — *Letters to Gala*, trans. Jesse Browner (New York: Paragon, 1989). French ed.: *Lettres à Gala* (Paris: Gallimard, 1984).

Erté   Erté, Romain, *Erté: My Life/My Art* (New York: E. P. Dutton, 1989).

Faucigny-Lucinge   Faucigny-Lucinge, Jean-Louis de *Legendary Parties* (New York: Vendome Press, 1987). [See also *Fêtes mémorables bals costumés, 1922-1972* (Paris: Herscher, 1986).]

Faucigny-Lucinge   — *Un gentilhomme cosmopolite* (Paris: Perrin, 1990).

Feschotte   Feschotte, Jacques, *Histoire du Music-Hall* (Paris: Presses universitaires de France, 1965).

Fouché   Fouché, Pascal, *La Sirène*. Bibliothèque de litterature française contemporaine de l'Université Paris 7 (Paris, 1984).

Franck   Franck, Nino, *Candide* (28 Apr. 1932).

Gallois   Gallois, Jean, *Les Polignacs: Mécènes du XXᵉ siècle* (Monaco: Éditions du Rocher, 1995).

Garafola   Garafola, Lynn, *Diaghilev's Ballets Russes* (New York: Oxford Univ. Press, 1989).

Gateau   Gateau, Jean-Charles, *Paul Eluard ou Le frère voyant 1895-1952* (Paris: Éditions Robert Laffont, 1988).

Gavoty   Gavoty, Bernard, *Chroniques de Clarendon: Au bonheur des soirs (1945-1981)* (Paris: Éditions Albatros, 1990).

Gelatt — Gelatt, Roland, "A Vote for Francis Poulenc," *Saturday Review* 33 (28 Jan. 1950), 57-8.

George — George, André, "Francis Poulenc," *Chesterian* 6 (Mar.-Apr. 1925), 141-6.

Georgel — Georgel, Pierre, *Jean Cocteau et son temps 1889-1963* (Paris: Institut de France Musée Jacquemart-André, 1965). [Exhibition catalogue.]

Gimpel — Gimpel, René, *Diary of an Art Dealer* (London: Hamish Hamilton, 1986).

Glee Club — *Harvard Glee Club European Tour 1921* (Cambridge, MA, 1922).

Gold — Gold, Arthur and Fizdale, Robert, *Misia: The Life of Misia Sert* (New York: Alfred A. Knopf, 1980).

Goll-Wilson — Goll-Wilson, Kathleen, "Jean-Pierre Rampal on Making Music," *Flute Talk* 10 (May 1991), 9-13.

Gosling — Gosling, Nigel, *The Adventurous World of Paris 1900-1914* (New York: William Morrow, 1978).

Gouverné — Gouverné, Yvonne, "Poulenc et Rocamadour," *Zodiaque*, No. 99 (Jan. 1974), 1-52.

Griffin — Griffin, John Howard, *The John Howard Griffin Reader*, ed. Bradford Daniel (Boston: Houghton Mifflin Company, 1968.

Griffiths — Griffiths, Paul, "Leguerney, Jacques (Alfred Georges Emile)" in *The New Grove Dictionary of Music and Musicians*, ed. Stanley Sadie 10 (London: Macmillan, 1980), 619.

Gruen 1960 — Gruen, John, "Poulenc," *Musical America* 89 (April 1960), 6-7 & 26. [Interview with Poulenc and Duval.]

Gruen 1978 — *Menotti: A Biography* (New York: Macmillan, 1978).

Guth 1952 — Guth, Paul, "Des 'Mamelles de Tirésias' au 'Stabat Mater' Francis Poulenc a deux côtés...," *Le Figaro littéraire* (17 May 1952), 4. [Interview with Poulenc.]

Guth 1954 — *L'Académie imaginaire. Texte de Paul Guth, Portraits de Jean-Marie Marcel* (Paris: Éditions d'histoire et d'art, Librairie Plon, 1954).

Häger	Häger, Bengt, *Ballets Suédois (The Swedish Ballet)*, trans. Ruth Sharman (New York: Abrams, 1990).
Halbreich	Halbreich, Harry, *Arthur Honegger*, trans. Roger Nichols (Portland: Amadeus Press, 1999).
Hamnett 1932	Hamnett, Nina, *Laughing Torso* (London: Constable, 1932).
Hamnett 1955	— *Is She a Lady? A Problem in Autobiography* (London: Allan Wingate, 1955).
Harding 1972	Harding, James, *The Ox on the Roof: Scenes from Musical Life in Paris in the Twenties* (London: Macdonald, 1972).
Harding 1975	— *Erik Satie* (London: Secker and Warburg, 1975).
Hausser	Hausser, Elisabeth, *Paris au jour le jour: les événements vus par la presse. 1900-1919* (Paris: Les Éditions de Minuit, 1968).
Hell 1958	Hell, Henri, *Francis Poulenc musicien français* (Paris: Plon, 1958).
Hell 1959	— *Francis Poulenc*, trans. Edward Lockspeiser (New York: Grove Press, 1959).
Hell 1978	— *Francis Poulenc musicien français* (Paris: Fayard, 1978).
Hell n.d.	— "Francis Poulenc au travail: La musique de 'La voix humaine' sera mon œuvre la plus aiguë, la plus fouillée." [Contains quotations by Poulenc.] [Interview with Poulenc.]
Heyman	Heyman, Barbara, *Samuel Barber: The Composer and His Music* (New York: Oxford Univ. Press, 1994).
Hilmar	Hilmar, Ernst, ed., *Arnold Schönberg (13. Sept. 1874-13. Juli 1951): Gedenkausstellung 1974* (Vienna: Universal Editions, 1974).
Honegger 1966	Honegger, Arthur, *I Am a Composer*, trans. William O. Clough and Allan Arthur Willman (London: Faber and Faber Ltd., 1966).
Honegger 1992	Honegger, Geneviève, *Charles Munch: un chef d'orchestre dans le siècle* (Strasbourg: La Nuée bleue, 1992).
Hooker	Hooker, Denise, *Nina Hamnett, Queen of Bohemia* (London: Constable, 1986).

Houdin 1964a

Houdin, Maurice, "La Jeunesse nogentaise de Francis Poulenc," *Bulletin de la Société Historique et Archéologique de Nogent-sur-Marne (Seine) et du canton de Nogent* 15 (1964), 70-9.

Houdin 1964b

— "Le rendez-vous de Francis Poulenc," *La République du Centre* 26 (Feb. 1964).

Hughes 1963

Hughes, Allen, "Francis Poulenc: A Portrait," *Show: The Magazine of the Arts* (June 1963), 29-31.

Hughes 1998

Hughes, Angela, *Pierre Fournier: Cellist in a Landscape with Figures* (Aldershot/Brookfield USA/Singapore/Sidney: Ashgate, 1998).

Hugo 1975

Hugo, Jean, "Pages de journal 'Les Mariés de la Tour Eiffel',"*Cahiers Jean Cocteau* 5 (1975), 19-23.

Hugo 1976

— *Avant d'oublier: 1918-1931* (Paris: Fayard, 1976).

Hugo 1983

— *Le Regard de la mémoire* (Paris: Actes Sud, 1983).

Hunt

Hunt, Eileen, "E. Power Biggs: Legacy of the Performing Artist" (DMA thesis, Boston Univ., 1986).

Hurard-Viltard 1988

Hurard-Viltard, Eveline, *Le Groupe des Six ou Le Matin d'un jour de fête* (Paris: Méridiens Klinck-sieck, 1988).

Hurard-Viltard 1989

— "Jean Cocteau et la musique: à travers *Le Coq et l'Arlequin,* du manuscrit à l'œuvre publiée," *Revue de l'Université de Bruxelles* (1989), 85-100.

Ivry

Ivry, Benjamin, *Francis Poulenc* (London: Phaidon Press Ltd., 1996).

Jourdan-Morhange

Jourdan-Morhange, Hélène, *Mes amis musiciens* (Paris: Les Editeurs français réunis, 1955).

JournalMF1963

"Hommage à Francis Poulenc," *Le Journal musical français* 116 (6 Mar. 1963).

Kahnweiler 1946

Kahnweiler, Daniel-Henry, *Juan Gris sa vie, son œuvre, ses écrits* (Paris: Gallimard, 1946).

Kahnweiler 1947

— *Juan Gris His Life and Work,* trans. by Douglas Cooper (New York: Curt Valentin, 1947).

Keck

Keck, George R., *Francis Poulenc: A Bio-Bibliography.* Bio-Bibliographies in Music, No. 28 (New York: Greenwood Press, 1990).

Kessler

Kessler, Charles, ed. and trans. *The Diaries of a Cosmopolitan Count Harry Kessler (1918-1957)* (London: Weidenfeld and Nicolson, 1971).

Klüver

Klüver, Billy, *A Day with Picasso* (Cambridge, MA and London: The MIT Press, 1997).

Kochno 1924

Kochno, Boris, compiler, *Théâtre de Serge de Diaghilew: Les Biches* (2 vols., Paris, 1924).

Kochno 1970

— *Diaghilev and the Ballets Russes*, trans. Adrienne Foulke (New York: Harper & Row, 1970).

Kochno 1987

— *Christian Bérard* (Paris: Herscher, 1987). For an English trans. see Kochno 1988.

Kochno 1988

— *Christian Bérard*, trans. Philip Core (New York, 1988). For the French see Kochno 1987.

Koechlin

Koechlin, Charles, "Charles Koechlin 1867-1950: Correspondance," *La Revue musicale*, nos. 348-50 (1982).

Lacretelle

Lacretelle, Jacques de, *L'Écrivain public* (Paris: Gallimard, 1936).

Lafranchis

Lafranchis, Jean, *Marcoussis sa vie, son œuvre: catalogue complet des peintures, fixées sur verre, aquarelles, dessins, gravures* (Paris: Les éditeurs du temps, 1981).

Lake

Lake, Carlton, *Confessions of a Literary Archaeologist* (New York: New Directions Books, 1990).

Laloy

Laloy, Louis, *La Musique retrouvée* (Paris: Librairie Plon, 1928).

Landowski

Landowski, Marcel, "Francis Poulenc nous revient d'Amérique," *Opéra* (2 Feb. 1949). [Interview with Poulenc.]

Langlade

Langlade, Vincent de, *Le Père Lachaise: Plan du cimetière* (Paris: Éditions Vermet, n.d.).

Laurent

Laurent, Linda and Tainsy, Andrée, "Jane Bathori et le Théâtre du Vieux-Colombier, 1917-1919," *Revue de musicologie* 70 (1984), 229-57.

Lawson

Lawson Rex, "Stravinsky and the Pianola," in *Confronting Stravinsky: Man, Musician, and Modernist*, ed. Jann Pasler (Berkeley: Univ. of California Press, 1986), pp. 284-301.

Léger

Léger, Fernand, *Fernand Léger et le spectacle: 30 juin-2 octobre 1995*, Musée national Fernand

Léger, Biot, Alpes Maritimes (Paris: Réunion des musées nationaux, 1995).

Lherm — Lherm, Marcel, *Musée trésor Francis Poulenc: Catalogue* (Rocamadour: n. pub., n.d.).

Lhotse — Lhotse, Pierre, "M. Jean Giraudoux nous parle du cinéma pendant les prises de vues de *La duchesse de Langeais* où Edwige Feuillère, par suite de froid, doit mourir dix fois" in *Cahiers Jean Giraudoux* 19: enquêtes et interviews II (Paris: Société des amis de Jean Giraudoux, 1990), pp. 287-90. Originally published in *Paris-midi* (27 Jan. 1942).

Linossier 1918 — Linossier, Raymonde, *Bibi-la-bibiste* (Paris: Paul Birault, 1918).

Linossier 1991 — *Bibi-La-Bibiste* (Paris: La Violette noire, 1991). [New edition.]

Lonchampt — Lonchampt, Jacques, "A la radio: La Tribune libre de la musique vivante," *Le Monde* (18 Jan. 1962).

Lowe — Lowe, John, *Edward James: Poet-Patron-Eccentric, A Surrealist Life* (London: Collins, 1991).

Macdonald 1992 — Macdonald, Hugh, "*Roi d'Ys, Le*" in *The New Grove Dictionary of Opera*, ed. Stanley Sadie 4 (London: Macmillan Press Ltd., 1992), 6-7.

Macdonald 1975 — Macdonald, Nesta, *Diaghilev Observed by Critics in England and the United States 1911-1929* (New York & London: Dance Horizons and Dance Books Ltd., 1975).

Machart — Machart, Renaud, *Poulenc* (Paris: Éditions du Seuil, 1995).

Macnutt — *A Selection from Our Stock. . . .* Catalogue 115. [Richard Macnutt, Ltd. sale catalogue, 1991.]

Maré — Maré, Rolf de, *Les Ballets Suédois dans l'art contemporain* (Paris: Éditions du Trianon, 1931).

Margerie — Margerie, Anne de, *Valentine Hugo, 1887-1968* (Paris: J. Damase, 1983).

Maur — Maur, Karin von, "Music and Theatre in the Work of Juan Gris," trans. David Britt, in *Juan Gris*, ed. Christopher Green, (London: Whitechapel Art Gallery in association with Yale Univ. Press, 1992), pp. 267-82.

Mauriac
Mauriac, Claude, *Bergère, ô tour Eiffel* (Paris: Bernard Grasset, 1985).

Mayer
Mayer, Denise and Souvtchinsky, Pierre, *Roger Désormière et son temps: textes en hommage* (Monaco, 1966).

Medvedeva
Medvedeva, Irina Andreevna, *Fransis Pulenk* (Moscow: Sovetskii kompozitor, 1969).

Mellers
Mellers, Wilfrid, *Francis Poulenc* (Oxford, New York: Oxford Univ. Press, 1993).

Michel
Michel, François, "Passé-Présent: Les Souvenirs de François Michel (1)," *Symphonia: La Revue de la musique* (Dec. 1995), 26-9. [Interview with Jacques Drillon.]

Milhaud 1944
Milhaud, Darius, "Musique and Politics," *Modern Music* 22 (Nov.-Dec. 1944), 5-6.

Milhaud 1953
— *Notes Without Music*, trans. Donald Evans, ed. Rollo H. Myers (New York: Alfred A. Knopf, 1953). French edition: *Notes sans musiques* (Paris: René Julliard, 1949).

Milhaud 1970
— "Conversation with Milhaud," *Music Educators Journal* 56 (Mar. 1970), 55-6.

Milhaud 1987a
— *Ma Vie heureuse* (Paris: Pierre Belfond, 1987).

Milhaud 1987b
— *Notes sur la musique: Essais et chroniques,* ed. Jeremy Drake (Paris: Flammarion, 1987).

Miniature Essays
Miniature Essays: Francis Poulenc (London: Chester, 1922).

Monnier 1953
Monnier, Adrienne, *Les Gazettes d'Adrienne Monnier 1925-1945* (Paris: René Julliard, 1953).

Monnier 1976
— *The Very Rich Hours of Adrienne Monnier,* trans. with commentary by Richard McDougall (New York: Charles Scribner's Sons, 1976).

Morton
Morton, Brian N., *Americans in Paris* (New York: William Morrow, 1986).

Mussulman
Mussulman, Joseph A., *Dear People . . . Robert Shaw: A Biography* (Bloomington: Indiana Univ. Press, 1979).

Myers
Myers, Rollo H., "Francis Poulenc," *Monthly Musical Record* 61 (1 May 1931), 129-30.

Nichols 1988   Nichols, Roger, *Ravel Remembered* (New York: W. W. Norton, 1988).

Nichols 1996   — *Conversations with Madeleine Milhaud* (London: Faber and Faber, 1996).

Nohain 1952   Nohain, Jean, *J'ai cinquante ans* (Paris: René Julliard, 1952).

Nohain 1980   — *La Main chaude* (Paris: René Julliard, 1980).

O'Connor   O'Connor, Garry, *The Pursuit of Perfection: A Life of Maggie Teyte* (New York: Atheneum, 1979).

Orledge 1990   Orledge, Robert, *Satie the Composer* (Cambridge: Cambridge Univ. Press, 1990).

Orledge 1995   — ed., *Satie Remembered* (Portland, OR: Amadeus Press, 1995.

Oury   Oury, Marcelle, *Lettre à mon peintre: Raoul Dufy* (Paris: Librairie academique Perrin, 1965).

Owen   Owen, Barbara, *E. Power Biggs, Concert Organist* (Bloomington: Indiana Univ. Press, 1987).

Parrot   Parrot, Louis, *L'Intelligence en guerre: Panorama de la pensée française dans la clandestinité* (Paris: La Jeune Parque, 1945).

Parton   Parton, Anthony, *Mikhail Larionov and the Russian Avant-garde* (Princeton: Princeton Univ. Press, 1993).

Paxton   Paxton, Robert O., *Vichy France: Old Guard and New Order, 1940-1944* (New York: Knopf, 1972).

Peignot   Peignot, Suzanne, Typescript of an article on Poulenc written for Miron Grindea, editor of the review *Adam*. [Typescript dated "Paris -Février 1964 kindly supplied by Sidney Buckland, to whom it was presented by Mme Peignot in 1989.]

Penrose 1945   Penrose, Roland, *In the Service of the People* (London: William Heinemann Ltd., 1945).

Penrose 1981   — *Picasso His Life and Work,* 3rd ed. (Berkeley and Los Angeles: Univ. of California Press, 1981).

Perloff   Perloff, Nancy, *Art and the Everyday: Popular Entertainment and the Circle of Erik Satie* (Oxford: Clarendon Press, 1991). See my review in *Notes: The Quarterly Journal of the Music Library Association* 49 (1992), 126-8.

Perreux   Perreux, Gabriel, *La Vie quotidienne des civils en France pendant la grand guerre* (Paris: Hachette, 1966).

Pistone   Pistone, Danièle, "Suzanne Peignot et son époque," *Poulenc et ses amis* in *Revue internationale de musique française* 31 (1994), 9-48.

Plaskin   Plaskin, Glenn, *Horowitz: A Biography of Wladimir Horowitz* (New York: William Morrow, 1983).

Poiret   Poiret, Paul, *King of Fashion: The Autobiography of Paul Poiret*, trans. Stephen Haden Guest (Philadelphia & London: J.B. Lippincott,1931).

Polunin   Polunin, Vladimir, *The Continental Method of Scene Painting*, ed. Cyril W. Beaumont (London: C. W. Beaumont, 1927).

Poulenc 1920   Poulenc, Francis, "Accent populaire," *Le Coq* 4 (June 1920).

Poulenc 1921a   — "Catalogue des œuvres de Francis Poulenc[:] Paris juillet 1921."[Facsimile in Poulenc 1995, pp. xxi-xxiv.]

Poulenc 1921b   — "Paris Note — Music: Three String Quartets," *Fanfare, a Musical Causerie*, ed. Leigh Henry (Goodwin & Tabb, Ltd., London), I, no. 4 (15 Nov. 1921), 79-80. [Reviews Stravinsky's *Concertino*, Malipiero's *Rispetti e Strambotti*, and Bartók's String Quartet No. 2.]

Poulenc 1921c   — "Paris Notes: Music," *Fanfare, a Musical Causerie*, ed. Leigh Henry (Goodwin & Tabb, Ltd., London), I, no. 6 (15 Dec. 1921), 117-18. [Discusses compositions by Albert Roussel.]

Poulenc 1922   — "La Musique: A propos de 'Mavra'," *Les Feuilles libres* 27 (June-July 1922), 222-4.

Poulenc 1926   —"Festival d'œuvres posthumes d'Erik Satie," *Le Ménestral* 88 (4 June 1926), 253-5.

Poulenc 1928a   — *Arts phoniques*, no. 5 (June 1928), 17-19. [Review of six instrumental recordings.]

Poulenc 1928b   — *La Nouvelle Revue musicale* 1 (Nov. 1928), 14. [Review of Fauré's A Major Sonata played by Cortot and Thibaud.]

Poulenc 1928c — *Arts phoniques*, no. 10 (Nov.-Dec. 1928), 18-20. [Review of fifteen instrumental recordings.]

Poulenc 1929 — *Arts phoniques*, no. 11 (Jan. 1929), 22-3. [Review of twenty instrumental recordings.]

Poulenc 1931 — "A propos de la 'Symphonie de Psaumes' d'Igor Strawinsky," *Le Mois* (Feb.-Mar. 1931), 249-50. Excerpt in English trans. in Stravinsky/Craft, p. 297.

Poulenc 1934a — "A propos d'*Elektra* de Richard Strauss," *Le Figaro* (1 Sept. 1934), 4. [Reviews a performance at the Salzbourg *Festspielhaus*.]

Poulenc 1934b — "A propos d'*Oberon*," *Le Figaro* (4 Sept. 1934), 5. [Reviews a Bruno Walter performance at the Salzburg *Festspielhaus*.]

Poulenc 1935a — "Mes maîtres et mes amis," *Conferencia: Journal de l'Université des Annales* 29/2 (15 Oct. 1935), 521-9. [Transcript of a 7 Mar. 1935 talk by Poulenc, assisted by Modrakowska and the Société des instruments à vent.]

Poulenc 1935b — "Eloge de la banalité," *Présence* 3 (Oct. 1935), 24-5. For Ernest Kreneck's response to this article, see "Banalité," *Présence* 3 (Nov. 1935), 36.

Poulenc 1936 — Preface to Kerrieu, Marthe de, *Mélie, histoire d'une cocotte de 1900* (Tours: Chez Arrault et Cie maîtres imprimeurs, [1936]), pp. 9-12.

Poulenc 1941a — "Igor Stravinsky," *L'Information musicale* (3 Jan. 1941), 195.

Poulenc 1941b — "Le Cœur de Maurice Ravel," *Nouvelle revue française* 323 (Dec. 1940-June 1941), 237-40.

Poulenc 1941c — "Centenaire de Chabrier," *Nouvelle revue française* 329 (July-Dec. 1941), 110-14.

Poulenc 1942a — "La Leçon de Claude Debussy," *Claude Debussy, Chronologie de sa vie et de ses œuvres* compiled by Auguste Martin (Paris: Réunion des Théâtres lyriques nationaux, 1942). [Exposition from 2-17 May 1942 in the foyer of the Opéra-Comique]. Homages written by Henri Busser, Jean Cocteau, Léon-Paul Fargue, and Poulenc prefaced the printed volume. [Copy in F-Po C 10756.]

Poulenc 1942b   — "A propos d'un ballet," *Comœdia* (29 Aug. 1942).

Poulenc 1943a   — "L'Orchestration de Fauré," *Comœdia* (20 Mar. 1943), 3-4.

Poulenc 1943b   — "Sur deux premières auditions," *Comœdia* (19 June 1943).

Poulenc 1944   — "Hommage à Louis Laloy (1874-1944)," *L'Information musicale* 4 (31 Mar. 1944), 247. [One of a group of commemorative letters written by colleagues and friends of Laloy after his death.] Rpt. in Poulenc 1994, pp. 222-3, note 2.

Poulenc 1945   — "Le Musicien et le sorcier," *Lettres françaises* (5 May 1945), 5.

Poulenc 1946a   — "Une Enquête," *Contrepoints* 1 (Jan. 1946), 49. Rpt. *La Revue musicale*, 306-07 (1977), 33-4. [Response to a question posed to various composers.]

Poulenc 1946b   — "Œuvres récentes de Darius Milhaud," *Contrepoints* 1 (Jan. 1946), 59-61.

Poulenc 1946c   — "Un nouveau musicien: Anton Heiller," *Contrepoints* 4 (May-June 1946), 60.

Poulenc 1946d   — "Francis Poulenc on His Ballets," *Ballet* (Sept. 1946), 57-8.

Poulenc 1946e   — "A Letter from Poulenc," *Harper's Bazaar* (Nov. 1946), 229, 397-9.

Poulenc 1946f   — "Edwin Evans," *Adam*, no. 161 (Aug. 1946), 26.

Poulenc 1947a   — "Rêverie monégasque," *Opéra/Revue* (22 Jan. 1947).

Poulenc 1947b   — "A propos des Mamelles de Tirésias," *Opéra* (28 May 1947).

Poulenc 1947c   — "Mes mélodies et leurs poètes," *Conferencia: Journal de l'Université des Annales* 36 (15 Dec. 1947), 507-13. [Transcript of a talk by Poulenc, assisted by Bernac on 20 Mar. 1947.]

Poulenc 1949a   — "Contribution to Opéra Forum," *Music Today* (London 1949). [Brief reply to the question of tonality and atonality in modern operas.]

Poulenc 1949b   — "Tribute to Christian Bérard," *Ballet* (1949), 30-1.

Poulenc 1950a   — Spiral notebook in F-Pn (Rés. Vmc. Ms. 124) entitled: "Francis Poulenc | [rule] | Feuilles américaines | [rule] | Extraits de Journal | [rule]." Contains a daily account of Poulenc's American tour beginning with his departure from France on 28 Dec. 1949 through his viewing of a Menotti opera in New York on 22 Mar. 1950. [See Poulenc 1999.]

Poulenc 1950b   — "Encore BOLIVAR!," *Le Figaro* (6 June 1950), 6.

Poulenc 1950c   — "Feuilles américaines," *La Table ronde* 30 (June 1950), 66-75. (Extrait de journal.) See Poulenc 1950a.

Poulenc 1950d   — Program note concerning his Concerto for Piano and Orchestra, program for the 24 July 1950 Aix-en-Provence Festival. [Not seen: mentioned in Poulenc 1994, p. 687.]

Poulenc 1950e   — "Pour le clavecin. Wanda Landowska a terminé à New York 'la somme de sa vie'," *Le Figaro littéraire* (27 May 1950).

Poulenc 1952   — "La Musique de piano d'Erik Satie," *La Revue musicale* 214 (1952), 23-6. Dated "Noizay, avril 1952." Rpt. *La Revue musicale* 386-7 (n.d.), 102-05. English trans. in Orledge 1995, pp. 149-50.

Poulenc 1953a   —"'Souvenirs,' *Jean Giraudoux et 'Pour Lucrèce'.*" Cahiers de la compagnie Madeleine Renaud - Jean-Louis Barrault. Première année, deuxième cahier (Paris: René Julliard, 1953), pp. 29-32.

Poulenc 1953b   — "La Musique de piano de Prokofieff," *Musique russe*, vol. 2, ed. Pierre Souvtchinsky (Paris: Presses universitaires de France, 1953), 269-76.

Poulenc 1953c   — "Souvenirs sur Jean Giraudoux," *Samedi-Soir* (5 Nov. 1953).

Poulenc 1953d   — *Yvonne Printemps ou l'impromptu de Neuilly*, ed. Roland Laudenbach (Paris: Editions de la Table ronde, 1953), pp. 46-7. [Poulenc's voice is heard in a play lauding Printemps' singing ability.]

Poulenc 1954 — *Entretiens avec Claude Rostand* (Paris: René Julliard, 1954). See also several excerpts published in Jan Mul, "Gesprekken met Francis Poulenc," *Mens en melodie* 7 (1955), 205-07 and "De Componist Francis Poulenc" 10 (1955), 291-4.

Poulenc 1955 — "Hommage à Béla Bartok," *La Revue musicale* 29 (1955), 18-19. Eng. trans. in Malcolm Gillies, *Bartók Remembered* (New York: W. W. Norton, 1991), pp. 98-9.

Poulenc 1956a — "Lorsque je suis mélancolique. . .," *Mercure de France* (1 Jan. 1956), 72-3. [Remembrance of Adrienne Monnier.]

Poulenc 1956b — "Inventar der modernen französischen Musik," *Melos* 23 (Feb. 1956), 35. [Extract from *Entretiens*.]

Poulenc 1956c — Preface to *Albéniz, sa vie, son œuvre* by Gabriel Laplane (Paris: Éditions du Milieu du monde, 1956). [Preface dated "Paris, le 6 décembre 1952.]

Poulenc 1956d — [Obituary for Arthur Honegger] in *Melos* (Jan. 1956), 1-11.

Poulenc 1957 — "Comment j'ai composé les 'Dialogues des Carmélites'," *L'Opéra de Paris* 14 (1957), 15-17.

Poulenc 1961a — *Emmanuel Chabrier* (Paris-Geneva: La Palatine, 1961). English trans. in Poulenc 1981.

Poulenc 1961b — "Opera in the Cinema Era," [As told to Elliott Stein], *Opera* 12 (Jan. 1961), 11-12.

Poulenc 1961c — "Extrait du 'Journal de mes mélodies'," *Feuilles musicales* (May-June 1961), 64.

Poulenc 1962 — "A propos d'une lettre d'Arthur Honegger," *Schweizerische Musikzeitung* 102 (1962), 160-1.

Poulenc 1963a — *Moi et mes amis* (Paris: Éditions La Palatine, 1963). English trans. in Poulenc 1978. A Russian translation was issued in [Leningrad] in 1977.

Poulenc 1963b — "Hommage à Benjamin Britten,"*Tribute to Benjamin Britten on his Fiftieth Birthday.* (London: Faber and Faber, 1963), p. 13. Rpt. in Poulenc 1991, p. 296.

Poulenc 1963c

— "La Musique et les Ballets russes de Serge Diaghilev," *Encyclopédia de la Pléiade, Histoire de la musique,* vol. 2, ed. Roland-Manuel (Paris: Libraire Gallimard, 1963), 985-91.

Poulenc 1963-64

— "Appunti su Emmanuel Chabrier," "Appunti su Ravel," and "Appunti su Satie," *Enciclopedia della Musica Ricordi,* ed. Claudio Sartori (Milan: Ricordi, 1963-64), I, 454-5; III, 540-1; and IV, 119-20 respectively.

Poulenc 1964

— *Journal de mes mélodies.* (Paris: Bernard Grasset, 1964). English edition *Diary of My Songs [Journal de mes mélodies],* trans. by Winifred Radford (London: Victor Gollancz Ltd., 1985; rpt. 1989).

Poulenc 1965

— *Hommage à Marie-Blanche de Polignac* (Monaco: Jaspard, Polus et Cie, 1965). [Poulenc's contribution on pp. 90-2.]

Poulenc 1967

— *Correspondance 1915-1963,* compiled by Hélène de Wendel, preface by Darius Milhaud (Paris: Éditions du Seuil, 1967).

Poulenc 1978

— *My Friends and Myself.* Conversations assembled by Stéphane Audel, trans. James Harding (London: Dennis Dobson, 1978). For the French see Poulenc 1963a.

Poulenc 1979

— "Journal de vacances: extraits: Luchon, août 1911, Biarritz, avril 1912," *Francis Poulenc dans ses jeunes années,* ed. Jacques Soulé (Boulogne-sur-mer: Association des Amis de Francis Poulenc, 1979). [See also Poulenc 1999.]

Poulenc 1981

— *Emmanuel Chabrier,* trans. Cynthia Jolly (London: Dobson, 1981). For the French see Poulenc 1961a.

Poulenc 1989

— *Diary of My Songs [Journal de mes mélodies],* trans. by Winifred Radford (London: Victor Gollancz Ltd., 1985; rpt. 1989).

Poulenc 1991

— *Francis Poulenc "Echo and Source:"Selected Correspondence 1915-1963.* Ed. and trans. by Sidney Buckland (London: Victor Gollancz Ltd., 1991).

Poulenc 1993   — *Journal de mes mélodies.* Complete edition with notes by Renaud Machart (Paris: Cicero/Éditions Salabert, 1993). In this edition, square brackets indicate text omitted from the version found in Poulenc 1964.

Poulenc 1994   — *Francis Poulenc: Correspondance 1910-1963*, ed. with annotations by Myriam Chimènes (Paris: Fayard, 1994).

Poulenc 1999   *A bâtons rompus: écrits radiophoniques; précédé de Journal de vacances, et suivi de Feuilles américaines*, ed. Lucie Kayas (Arles: Actes Sud, 1999).

Poulenc n.d.   — "Paris Notes: Music," *Fanfare* 1 (Nos. 4 and 6).

Poulenc nw   "Poulenc of Les Six," *Newsweek* 32 (15 Nov. 1948), 84-5.

Pozharskaya   Pozharskaya, M. N., *The Russian Seasons in Paris: Sketches of the Scenery and Costumes, 1908-1929* (Moscow: Iskusstvo Art Publishers, 1988).

Prêtre   Prêtre, Georges, "Recherche du Francis Poulenc," *Music Journal* 23 (1965), 58 and 72.

Prunières   Prunières, Henry, "Francis Poulenc," *The Sackbut* 8 (1928), 189-93.

Radford   Radford, Winifred, "Pierre Bernac, the Man and the Artist," *Recorded Sound: The Journal of the British Institute of Recorded Sound* 70-1 (Apr.-July 1978), 772-6.

Ramey   Ramey, Phillip, Interview with Samuel Barber. Liner notes, "Songs of Samuel Barber and Ned Rorem," New World Records Recorded Anthology of American Music. NW 229, 1978.

Rampal   Rampal, Jean-Pierre, *Music, My Love: An Autobiography*, with Deborah Wise (New York: Random House, 1989).

Rasponi   Rasponi, Lanfranco, "The Voice of Poulenc: Lanfranco Rasponi Talks with Denise Duval," *Opera News* 41 (5 Feb. 1977), 17-19.

Reibel   Reibel, Emmanuel, *Les Concertos de Poulenc* (Bourg-la-Reine: A. Zurfluh, 1999).

Ricci   Ricci, Franco Carlo, *Vittorio Rieti* (Naples & Rome: Edizioni Scientifiche Italiane, 1987).

Richardson 1991 Richardson, John, *A Life of Picasso*, vol. 1: 1881-1906 (New York: Random House, 1991).

Richardson 1996 Richardson, John, *A Life of Picasso*, vol. 2: 1907-1917 (New York: Random House, 1996).

Ries   Ries, Frank W.D., *The Dance Theatre of Jean Cocteau*. Theater and Dramatic Studies Series, no. 33 (Ann Arbor: UMI Press, 1986).

Robert   Robert, Frédéric, *Louis Durey: L'âiné des "Six"* (Paris: Les Éditeurs Française Réunis, 1968).

Roland-Manuel Roland-Manuel (with Nadia Tagrine), *Plaisir de la musique* (Paris: Éditions du Seuil, 1947).

Ronze-Neveu 1952 Ronze-Neveu, M.-J., *Ginette Neveu* (Paris: Pierre Horay, 1952).

Ronze-Neveu 1957 — *Ginette Neveu*, trans. Joyce L. Kemp (London, 1957).

Rorem 1966   Rorem, Ned, *The Paris Diary of Ned Rorem* (New York: George Braziller Inc., 1966).

Rorem 1977   — "Monologues and Dialogues: A Composer/ Friend Recalls Francis Poulenc, the Man and His Music," *Opera News* 41 (5 Feb. 1977), 11-16.

Rorem 1983   — *Setting the Tone: Essays and a Diary* (New York: Coward, McCann & Geoghegan, 1983).

Rorem 1984   — "Cocteau and Music," in *Jean Cocteau and the French Scene* (New York: Abbeville Press, 1984), 153-83.

Rorem 1994   — *Knowing When to Stop: A Memoir* (New York: Simon & Schuster, 1994).

Rosenfeld   Rosenfeld, Paul, *Musical Chronicle (1917-1923)* (New York: Harcourt, Brace and Company, 1923; rpt. New York: B. Bloom, 1972).

Rosenstiel   Rosenstiel, Léonie, *Nadia Boulanger: A Life in Music* (New York: W.W. Norton, 1982).

Rosenthal   Rosenthal, Manuel, *Satie, Ravel, Poulenc* (Madras & New York: Hanuman Books, 1987).

Rostand 1957   Rostand, Claude, "Francis Poulenc parle des 'Mamelles de Tirésias' (Grand Prix du Disque 1954)," *Arts* (5 May 1957) (Reprinted from Poulenc 1954, pp. 144-52.) [Interview with Poulenc.]

Rostand 1963   — "Visages de Poulenc," *Feuilles musicale* 16 (30 Apr. 1963), 9-12.

Rostand 1970   — *Dictionnaire de la musique contemporaine* (Paris: Librairie Larousse, 1970).

Rothschild   Rothschild, Deborah Menaker, *Picasso's "Parade:" From Street to Stage* (London: Sotheby's Publications, 1991).

Roussel   Roussel, Albert, "Young French Composers," *Chesterian* 2 (Oct. 1919), 33-7.

Roy 1949   Roy, André Jean, *Le Chœur des anges* (Paris 1949).

Roy 1964   Roy, Jean, *Francis Poulenc: L'Homme et son œuvre* (Paris: Seghers, 1964).

Roy 1994   — *Le Groupe des six* (Paris: Éditions du Seuil, 1994).

Rubinstein 1973   Rubinstein, Arthur, *My Young Years* (New York: Alfred A. Knopf, 1973).

Rubinstein 1980   — *My Many Years* (New York: Alfred A. Knopf, 1980).

Sachs 1933   Sachs, Maurice, *The Decade of Illusion, Paris, 1918-1928*, trans. Gwladys Matthews Sachs (New York: Alfred A. Knopf, 1933).

Sachs 1987   — *Au temps du boeuf sur le toit* (Paris: Bernard Grasset, 1987).

Salabert   *Francis Poulenc: 1899-1963*. Catalogue des œuvres. Conception and realization by M. Ramezani and T. Vilbert (Paris: Éditions Salabert, 1993).

Sams 1988   Sams, Jeremy, "Poulenc," *Songs on Record* 2, ed. Alan Blyth (Cambridge: Cambridge Univ. Press, 1988), 118-27.

Sams 1992   — "*Mamelles de Tirésias, Les*," *The New Grove Dictionary of Opera*, ed. Stanley Sadie 3 (London: Macmillan Publishers Ltd., 1992), 173-4.

Satie — *The Writings of Erik Satie* , ed. and trans. by Nigel Wilkins (London: Eulenburg Books, 1980).

Saudinos — Saudinos, Dominique, *Manuel Rosenthal: Une vie* (Paris: Mercure de France, 1992).

Sauguet — Sauguet, Henri, *La Musique ma vie* ([Paris]: Librairie Séguier, 1990).

Schaeffner 1933 — Schaeffner, André, "Paris Season Under the Crisis," *Modern Music* 10 (Mar.-Apr. 1933), 167-70.

Schaeffner 1946 — — "Francis Poulenc: Musicien français," *Contrepoints* 1 (1946), 50-8.

Schmidt 1995 — Schmidt, Carl B., *The Music of Francis Poulenc (1899-1963): A Catalogue* (Oxford: Clarendon Press, 1995). [FP numbers are taken from this source.]

Schmidt 1996 — — "In Search of Francis Poulenc (1899-1963): Entrancing Muse," *Towson State University Lecture Series* 12 (Towson, MD: Towson State Univ., 1996), 31-44.

Schneider — Schneider, Marcel, *Le Palais des mirages*, Mémoires intimes, 3 (Paris: Bernard Grasset, 1992).

Seligman — Seligman, Germain, *Roger de la Fresnaye, with a Catalogue Raisonné* ([Greenwich, CN]: New York Graphic Society, 1968).

Serouya — Serouya, Henri, "Comme Lorca, Saint-Pol et Max Jacob, Robert Desnos," *Les Lettres françaises* (11 Aug. 1945), 1 and 3.

Sert — Sert, Misia, *Two of Three Muses: The Memoirs of Misia Sert*, trans. Moura Budberg (London: Museum Press Ltd., 1953).

Shattuck — Shattuck, Roger, *The Banquet Years: The Arts in France, 1885-1918* (New York: Harcourt, Brace and Company, 1961).

Shead — Shead, Richard, *Music in the 1920s* (New York: St Martin's Press, 1976).

Silver — Silver, Kenneth E., *Esprit de Corps: The Art of the Parisian Avant-Garde and the First World War, 1914-1925* (Princeton: Princeton Univ. Press, 1989).

Simon

Simon, Matila, *The Battle of the Louvre: The Struggle to Save French Art in World War II* (New York: Hawthorn Books, Inc., 1971).

Sokolova

Sokolova, Lydia, *Dancing for Diaghilev: The Memoirs of Lydia Sokolova,* ed. Richard Buckle (London: John Murry, 1960; pbk. ed. San Francisco: Mercury House Inc., 1989).

Sotheby 1991

Collection Boris Kochno. Catalogue of the 11-12 Oct. 1991 Sotheby's Monte Carlo sale.

Souhami

Souhami, Diana, *Mrs Keppel and Her Daughter* (New York: St Martin's Press, 1997).

Soulé

Soulé, Jacques, *Francis Poulenc dans ses jeunes années.* Published with *Francis Poulenc: Journal de vacances (1911-1912).* Privately printed for "Les Amis de Francis Poulenc," n.d.

Speaight

Speaight, Robert, *Georges Bernanos: A Study of the Man and the Writer* (New York: Liveright, 1974).

Spratt

Spratt, Geoffrey K., *The Music of Arthur Honegger* (Cork: Cork Univ., Press, 1987).

Sprigge

Sprigge, Elizabeth and Kihm, Jean-Jacques, *Jean Cocteau: The Man and the Mirror* (New York: Coward-McCann, 1968).

Spycket 1987

Spycket, Jérôme, *Nadia Boulanger* (Paris: Lattès and Payot: Lausanne, 1987).

Spycket 1992

— *Nadia Boulanger,* trans. M. M. Shriver (Stuyvesant, NY: Pendragon Press, 1992).

Steegmuller 1963

Steegmuller, Francis, *Apollinaire: Poet Among the Painters* (New York: Farrar, Straus, and Co., 1963).

Steegmuller 1970

— *Cocteau: A Biography* (Boston: Little, Brown and Co., 1970).

Steegmuller 1984

— "Jean Cocteau: 1889-1963, A Brief Biography" in Anderson, pp. 15-36.

Steuermann

Steuermann, Edward, *The Not Quite Innocent Bystander. Writings of Edward Steuermann* (Lincoln: Univ. of Nebraska Press, 1989).

Stravinsky 1982

Stravinsky, Igor and Robert Craft, *Stravinsky Selected Correspondence,* ed. and with commentary by

Robert Craft, vol. 1 (New York: Alfred A. Knopf, 1982).

Stravinsky 1984   — *Stravinsky Selected Correspondence,* ed. and with commentary by Robert Craft, vol. 2 (New York: Alfred A. Knopf, 1984).

Stravinsky 1985   — *Stravinsky Selected Correspondence,* ed. and with commentary by Robert Craft, vol. 3 (New York: Alfred A. Knopf, 1985).

Stravinsky/Craft   Stravinsky, Vera and Craft, Robert, *Stravinsky in Pictures and Documents* (New York: Simon and Schuster, 1978).

StravinskyV   Stravinsky, Vera, *Dearest Bubushkin: The Correspondence of Vera and Igor Stravinsky, 1921-1954, with Excerpts from Vera Stravinsky's Diaries, 1922-1971,* ed. Robert Craft (London: Thames and Hudson, 1985).

Stuckenschmidt   Stuckenschmidt, H[ans] H[einz], *Schoenberg: His Life, World and Work,* trans. Humphrey Searle (London: Calder, 1977).

Tailleferre   Tailleferre, Germaine, "Mémoires à l'emporte-pièce," ed. Frédéric Robert, *Revue internationale de musique française* 19 (1986), 7-82.

Taruskin   Taruskin, Richard, *Stravinsky and the Russian Traditions: A Biography of the Works Through Mavra,* 2 vols. (Berkeley and Los Angeles: Univ. of California Press, 1996).

Tessier   Tessier, Thomas, *In Sight of Chaos* (London: Turret Books, 1971).

Thomson 1966   Thomson, Virgil, *Virgil Thomson* (New York: Alfred A. Knopf, 1966; pbk. ed. New York: E.P. Dutton, 1985).

Timbrell   Timbrell, Charles, *French Pianism: A Historical Perspective,* 2nd ed. (Portland: Amadeus Press, 1999).

Tint   Tint, Herbert, *France Since 1918,* 2nd ed. (London: Batsford Academic and Educational Ltd., 1980).

Tual   Tual, Denise, *Le Temps dévoré* (Paris: Fayard, 1980).

Vidal

Vidal, Pierre with Dominique Villemot and Nicole Rose, *Francis Poulenc et les poètes* (Paris: Bibliothèque Nationale,1995) [Catalogue of the 14 June-22 July 1995 exhibition at the Bibliothèque Nationale de France, Galerie Colbert.]

Vilmorin 1962

Vilmorin, André de, *Essai sur Louise de Vilmorin*. Poètes d'aujourd'hui 91 ([Paris]: Éditions Pierre Seghers, 1962).

Volta 1989

Volta, Ornella, *Satie Seen Through His Letters*, trans. Michael Bullock, intro. John Cage (London: Marion Boyars, 1989).

Volta 1990

— ed. *Album des 6*. "Le Groupe des Six et ses amis 70e anniversaire"(Paris: Éditions du Placard. 1990). [Catalogue of an exhibition held 6 Mar.-9 Apr. 1990 at the Hôtel Arturo-Lopez, Neuilly-sur-Seine.] See my review in *Notes: The Quarterly Journal of the Music Library Association* 49 (1992), 126-8.

Volta 1992

— *Satie et la danse* (Paris: Plume, 1992).

Volta 1993

— *Satie/Cocteau: Les malentendus d'une entente* (Paris: Le Castor Astral, 1993).

Volta 1996

— *A Mammal's Notebook: Collected Writings of Erik Satie*, trans. Anthony Melville, Atlas Arkhive Five: Documents of the Avant-Garde (London: Atlas Press, 1996).

Volta 1997

— *Erik Satie*, trans. Simon Pleasance (Paris: Éditions Hazan, 1997).

Vreeland

Vreeland, Diana, *D.V.* (New York: Alfred A. Knopf, 1984).

Wallmann

Wallmann, Margarita, *Les Balcons du ciel* (Paris: Éditions Robert Laffont, 1976).

Watkins

Watkins, Glenn, *Pyramids at the Louvre: Music, Culture, and Collage from Stravinsky to the Postmodernists* (Cambridge, MA: Harvard Univ. Press, 1994).

Weber

Weber, Eugen, *France, fin de siècle* (Cambridge, MA and London: The Belknap Press of Harvard Univ. Press, 1986).

White White, Eric Walter, *Stravinsky: The Composer and His Works* (Berkeley and Los Angeles: Univ. of California Press, 1979).

Whiting Whiting, Steven Moore, *Satie the Bohemian: From Cabaret to Concert Hall* (Oxford: Oxford Univ. Press, 1999).

Wiéner 1966 Wiéner, Jean, *Roger Désormière et son temps* (Monaco: Editions du Rocher, 1966).

Wiéner 1978 — *Allegro appassionato* (Paris: Pierre Belfond, 1978).

Wood Wood, Vivian Lee Poates, *Poulenc's Songs: An Analysis of Style* (Jackson, MI: Univ. Press of Mississippi, 1979).

Zervos Zervos, Christian, *Pablo Picasso: Oeuvres de 1956 à 1957* (Paris: Éditions "cahiers d'art," 1957).

A Partial List of Unpublished Theses and Dissertations on Francis Poulenc

Allard, Maurice, "The Songs of Claude Debussy and Francis Poulenc" (DMA thesis., Univ. of Southern California, 1964).

Allen, Joy Ann, "Stylistic Analysis of *Banalités* by Francis Poulenc" (MM thesis, North Texas State Univ., 1968).

Allison, Ruth, "Analysis of a Poulenc Trio (for Bassoon, Oboe, and Piano)" (MM thesis, Univ. of Rochester, 1947).

Almond, Frank W., "Melody and Texture in the Choral Works of Francis Poulenc" (Ph.D. diss., Florida State Univ., 1970)

Amos, Shaun McClelland, "The Sacred Choral Works for Women's Voices of Francis Poulenc" (DMA thesis, Univ. of Alabama, 1994).

Anderson, Bert A., "The Harmonic Idiom of Francis Poulenc" (MS thesis, Boston Univ., 1963).

Anderson, Charlotte, "The Work of the Painters, the Poet, the Composer: An Examination of Francis Poulenc's *Le Travail du peintre*" (DMA thesis, The Peabody Institute of The Johns Hopkins Univ., 1993).

Barnard, Jack Richard, "Choral Problems in the Unaccompanied Music of Francis Poulenc" (MM thesis, North Texas State Univ., 1966).

Barrett, Kathryn Ann, "An Analysis of the Tonal Language of Poulenc's *Gloria*" (MA thesis, Univ. of Notre Dame, 1989).

Baserman, Paul William, "Tonal Structure and Aesthetics in Francis Poulenc's Musical Development Between the Wars 1919-1939 (Ph.D. diss., New York University, in preparation).

Becker, John Wellman, "The Sacred Choral Works of Francis Poulenc" (MA thesis, Union Theological Seminary, 1954).

Belland, Douglas Keith, "An Examination of the Persichetti, Poulenc, and Szymanowski 'Stabat Mater' Settings with Pertinent Information on the Text" (DMA thesis, Univ. of Cincinnati, 1993).

Berry, Richard Arnold, "Francis Poulenc's Settings of Poems of Paul Eluard for Solo Voice and Piano: A Reflection of French Artistic Moods from 1920 to 1960" (DMA thesis, Univ. of Missouri-Kansas City, 1985).

Bobbitt, Richard, "The Harmonic Idiom in the Works of 'Les Six'" (Ph.D. diss., Boston Univ., 1963).

Boyer, Douglas R., "A Description of the Choral Music of Marc-Antoine Charpentier, Maurice Duruflé, Ernest Bloch, Francis Poulenc" (MM thesis, Univ. of Texas at San Antonio, 1998).

Brandes, Jeffrey Harold, "The Organ as an Ensemble Instrument: Concerto Techniques in the Sinfonia of Cantata BWV 169 by Johann Sebastian Bach, Concerto for Organ and Chamber Orchestra, op. 46, no. 2 by Paul Hindemith, and Organ Concerto in G Minor by Francis Poulenc" (DMA thesis, Ohio State Univ., 1977).

Browning, John Curtis, "A Survey and Analysis of Stylistic Features and Formal Processes in the Motets of Francis Poulenc" (DMA thesis, Claremont Graduate School, 1995).

Card, P. Catherine, "A Comparison-study of Poulenc's *Deux poèmes de Guillaume Apollinaire* and *Deux poèmes de Louis Aragon*" (MM thesis, Bowling Green State Univ., 1986).

Carlson, Donna L., "A Study of Francis Poulenc's Sonata for Clarinet and Piano Incorporating Formal and Structural Analyses" (MM thesis, Bowling Green State Univ., 1982).

Co, Margaret Y., "An Analysis for Performance of Hindemith, Concerto for Organ and Chamber Orchestra and Poulenc, Concerto for Organ, String Orchestra and Tympani" (DM diss., Indiana Univ., 1982).

Corbett, Denise L., "An Analytical Study of the Songs of Francis Poulenc" (MM thesis, Ball State Univ., 1977).

Cox, Jeremy N., "Dadaist, Cubist and Surrealistic Influences in Settings by Francis Poulenc of Contemporary French Poetry "(Ph.D. diss., New, Oxford, 1986).

Crumpler, Nancy Elaine, "The Effect of French Impressionism on Traditional Harmony as Seen in Selected Songs of Debussy, Poulenc and Ravel" (AB thesis, Sweet Briar College, 1974).

Dawson, Terrence Evan, "Unifying Devices in Poulenc: A Study of the Cycles 'Banalités' and 'Tel jour telle nuit'" (DMA thesis, The Univ. of British Columbia, 1991).

Ebensberger, Gary Lee, "The Motets of Francis Poulenc" (DMA thesis, Univ. of Texas at Austin, 1970).

Edwards, Paula Turney, "A Survey of the Sacred Choral Music of Francis Poulenc" (MM thesis, Hardin-Simmons Univ., 1978).

Engebretson, Stanley, "Francis Poulenc, *Sept chansons*: A Performance Study and Analysis" (DMA thesis, Stanford Univ., 1978).

Feratty, Frédéric, "La Musique pour piano de F. Poulenc, ou le temps de l'ambivalence" (Thèse de Doctorat, Univ. de Toulouse, 1998).

Foley, Bridget Ann, "A Comparison and Contrast of Schoenberg's and Poulenc's One Woman Operas" (MM thesis, Bowling Green State Univ., 1997).

Fox, Larry Phillip, "A Comparative Analysis of Selected Dramatic Works and Their Twentieth Century Operatic Adaptions" (Ph.D. diss., Univ. of South Carolina, 1992). [Discusses *Dialogues des Carmélites*.]

Frick, Susan Elizabeth Salmon, "A Study of Poulenc's *Calligrammes:* An Accompanying Paper for a Creative Project" (Master's degree thesis, Southeast Missouri State Univ., 1987).

Fritschel, James Erwin, "The Study and Performance of Three Extended Choral Works: Mass in G, by Francis Poulenc, Missa Brevis, by Dietrich Buxtehude, Stabat Mater, by Antonio Caldara, and Introits and Graduals for Holy Week for Chorus and Wind Instruments" (Ph.D. diss., Iowa State Univ., 1960.

Gabrielse, Kenneth J., "A Conductor's Analysis of Gloria Settings from Five Masses and a Pedagogical Approach to Their Performance" (DMA thesis, New Orleans Baptist Theological Seminary, 1996). [Discusses the Gloria from Mass in G major.]

Garcia, Loretta Siasat, "Analysis of the Mass in G for Mixed a cappella Choir by Francis Poulenc" (MA thesis, Univ. of Rochester, 1961).

Glagla, Gisela, "Die Kammermusik Francis Poulencs" (Ph.D. diss., Frankfurt am Main, 1978).

Goode, Elizabeth Ann, "A Study to Determine the Classical Characteristics in the Flute Sonatas of Hindemith, Prokofiev, and Poulenc" (MM thesis, Univ. of Tennessee at Knoxville, 1985).

Granger, Milton Lewis, "The Piano Music of Paul Dukas; The Piano Music of Francis Poulenc; The Partitas of Bach" (D. Mus., Northwestern Univ., 1978).

Grant, Cheryl Kay, "Analysis of the *Banalités* by Francis Poulenc" (MA thesis, Texas Women's Univ., 1969).

Gregg, Noel Virginia, "The Piano Solo Works of Francis Poulenc" (MM thesis, Univ. of Texas at Austin, 1960).

Griffith, Bob, "Mass Settings by Three Twentieth-Century Composers: Poulenc, Stravinsky, and Bernstein" (MM thesis, Baylor Univ., 1981).

Grizzell, Anna Renée, "Poulenc and Roussel: A View of Early Twentieth-Century French Chamber Music for Flute" (MA thesis, California State Univ. at Long Beach, 1986).

Guelker-Cone, Leslie K., "Stylistic Considerations and Their Implications for the Modern Performer in Two Works from a Master's Choral Conducting Recital" (MA thesis, San Jose State Univ., 1985) [Considers Mass in G major.]

Guyard, Marie-Liesse, "*Les Biches:* décors, chorégraphie, musique" (Maîtrise, Paris IV, n.d.).

Hanson, John Robert, "Macroform in Selected Twentieth-Century Piano Concertos" (Ph.D. diss., Eastman School of Music, 1969).

Hardee, Elizabeth F., "The Solo Songs of Francis Poulenc" (MA thesis, Univ. of North Carolina at Chapel Hill, 1952).

Harden, Cheryl Vianne, "Compositional Characteristics of Music for Women's Chorus and Orchestra as Seen in the Selected Works of Three Twentieth-Century French Composers: Debussy, Honegger and Poulenc" (DM diss., Northwestern Univ., 1995). [Discusses *Litanies à la Vierge noire*.]

Hargrove, Guy A., "Francis Poulenc's Settings of Poems of Guillaume Apollinaire and Paul Eluard" (Ph.D. diss., Univ. of Iowa, 1971).

Harman, Nancy Kay, "Poulenc's Sonata for Flute and Piano: Some Observations on Melody, Harmony, and Form" (MA thesis, Univ. of Connecticut, 1984).

Harrison, Joel Miller, "Song Cycles and Sets of Francis Poulenc" (DM diss., Northwestern Univ., 1990).

Herrold, C. M., Francis Poulenc's *Dialogues des Carmélites:* An Historical, Literary, Textual, Musical Analysis" (MA thesis, Univ. of Rochester, 1975).

Howells, Mari R., "The Harmonic and Stylistic Development of Francis Poulenc with Emphasis on the Sonata for Two Clarinets (1918) and the Sonata for Clarinet and Piano (1962)" (MM thesis, Bowling Green State Univ., 1991).

Hugo, John William, "Relationships Between Text and Musical Setting in Selected Choral Works by Debussy, Ravel, Poulenc, and Bonheur" (DMA thesis, Arizona State Univ., 1987).

Jackerson, Gloria, "Selected Vocal Works of Francis Poulenc" (MA thesis, Brown Univ., 1971).

Jewett, Diana Skroch, "The Piano Works of Francis Poulenc" (MA thesis, Univ. of North Dakota, 1977).

Jones, Donald R., "An Analysis of Poulenc's *Concert champêtre*" (MA thesis, Univ. of Rochester, 1950).

Jones, Steven David, "A Study of *Chansons gaillardes* (1926) by Francis Poulenc" (MM thesis, Bowling Green State Univ., 1981).

Keltner, Karen, "A Conductor's Analysis for Performance of the Two A Cappella Cantatas of Poulenc, with a Survey of His Secular Choral Works" (DM diss., Indiana Univ., 1980).

Kipling, Diane, "Harmonic Organization in *Les Mamelles de Tirésias* by Francis Poulenc" (MA thesis, McGill Univ., 1995).

Kolar, Marilyn Davis, "The Relationship of Text and Music in Selected Choral Works by Francis Poulenc," (MA thesis, Ohio State Univ., 1975).

Landreth, Joe Alton, "The Unaccompanied Mass, Motets and Cantatas of Francis Poulenc" (MM thesis, Southern Methodist Univ., 1953).

Lawrence, Arthur Peter, "The Organ Concerto in G Minor of Francis Poulenc" (DMA thesis, Stanford Univ., 1968).

Lee, Carole Ann. "The Piano Toccata in the Twentieth Century: A Selective Investigation of the Keyboard Styles and Performance Techniques" (Ph.D. diss., Boston Univ., 1978) [Includes a discussion of Toccata from *Trois pièces*.]

Leonard, Edward, "A Study of Nine Songs of Francis Poulenc" (MM thesis, Univ. of Rochester, 1943).

Lewis, Charles Edward, "A Conductor's Analysis of Four Penitential Motets by Francis Poulenc and Requiem by Maurice Duruflé" (MCM thesis, Southwestern Baptist Theological Seminary, 1972).

Lincoln, Dorothy Ashbacher, "Musical Analysis and Stylistic Interpretation of Five French Choral Works by Francis Poulenc" (Ed.D. diss., Arizona State Univ., 1973). [Includes *Chanson à boire, Quatre petites prières, Petites voix, Huit chansons françaises,* and *Sept Chansons.*]

McKinney, David Conley, "The Influence of Parisian Popular Entertainment on the Piano Works of Erik Satie and Francis Poulenc" (DMA thesis, Univ. of North Carolina at Greensboro, 1994).

Magill, Kathryn L., "An Interpretive Guide to Francis Poulenc's *Airs chantés, Fiançailles pour rire* and *La Courte Paille*" (MM thesis, California State Univ. at Fullerton, 1977).

Margason, Roger Boyd, "A Conductor's Analysis of *Cantata from Job* by Darius Milhaud and *Sept répons des ténèbres* by Francis Poulenc" (MM thesis, Southwestern Baptist Theological Seminary, 1974).

Michel, Cheryl Ann, "*La Voix humaine* of Francis Poulenc as a Problem in Operatic Translation" (MA thesis, Univ. of Wyoming, 1974).

Mooney, Joan Mary, "The Songs of Francis Poulenc Set to Poems of Guillaume Apollinaire" (BM thesis, Univ. of Queensland, 1972).

Neely, James Kilford, "The Sacred Choral Music of Francis Poulenc" (MM thesis, Univ. of Texas at Austin, 1952).

Nelson, Philip Francis, "Francis Poulenc: An Examination of His Choral Technique" (MA thesis, Univ. of North Carolina at Chapel Hill, 1956).

Nelson, Jon Ray, "The Piano Music of Francis Poulenc" (Ph.D. diss., Univ. of Washington, 1978).

Neufeld, Charles W., "A Conductor's Analysis of Selected Works by Jan Pieterszoon Sweelinck, Andrea Gabrieli, Heinrich Schütz, Marc-Antoine Charpentier, Johann Sebastian Bach, César Franck, Anton Bruckner, Francis Poulenc, Richard Feliciano, and Edmund Rubbra" (MM thesis, Southwestern Baptist Theological Seminary, 1987).

Oates, Jennifer Lynn, "A Stylistic Analysis of the Concerted Sacred Choral Works of Francis Poulenc"(MM thesis, Univ. of Kansas, 1997).

Oey, Un Cho, "A Conductor's Analysis of Missa Brevis by Wolfgang Amadeus Mozart and *Gloria* by Francis Poulenc" (MM thesis, Southwestern Baptist Theological Seminary, 1994).

Pampell, Martha Ann, "Elements of Surrealism in *La Courte Paille* by Francis Poulenc" (MM thesis, North Texas State Univ., 1976).

Pariot, Christian, "Francis Poulenc, musicien polyphonique" (Maîtrise, Toulouse II, 1990).

Poulin, Pamela Lee, "Three Stylistic Traits in Poulenc's Chamber Works for Wind Instruments" (Ph.D. diss., Univ. of Rochester, 1983).

Prud'homme, Barbara, "Tonality in Four Sacred Choral Works by Francis Poulenc" (MM thesis, Southwestern Baptist Theological Seminary, 1989).

Ragsdale, Dana, "The Revival of the Harpsichord in the Twentieth Century with Particular Attention to the Harpsichord Concerti of Manuel de Falla and Francis Poulenc" (DMA thesis, Univ. of Cincinnati, 1989).

Rahm, Dana Marilyn, "Analysis of the Sonata for Two Pianos by Francis Poulenc" (MA thesis, Univ. of Rochester, 1962).

Riccinto, Leonard L., "An Analysis of the Glorias of Vivaldi, Poulenc, and Rutter" (DMA thesis, Michigan State Univ., 1985).

Romain, Edwin P., "A Study of Francis Poulenc's Fifteen Improvisations for Piano Solo" (DMA thesis, Univ. of Southern Mississippi, 1978).

Romza, Patricia-Andrea, "Female-Choir Music by French Composers: An Annotated Bibliography of Selected Works (Choral Music, Women's Choir, Francis Poulenc, Olivier Messiaen, Gabriel Fauré, Claude Debussy, Marie-Madeleine Duruflé-Chevalier)" (DMA thesis, Univ. of Georgia, 1997).

Rose, Donna, "Investigative Report: Francis Poulenc and the Sonata for Flute and Piano" (M. Mus. Ed. thesis, Northwestern State Univ. of Louisiana, 1971).

Rumery, Leonard, "A Survey of the Choral Music of Francis Poulenc" (DMA thesis, Stanford Univ., 1975).

Sanford, Elizabeth Pate, "Francis Poulenc: Musician of Apollinaire and Eluard: An Examination of His Settings of Selected Poetic Texts from *Calligrammes* and *Le Travail du peintre*" (MM thesis, California State Univ. at Fullerton, 1988).

Sass, Ronald D., "An Analysis of Francis Poulenc's "Quatre motets pour le temps de Noël" (MS thesis, Moorhead State Univ., 1986).

Scherler, Kathy Louise, "An Analysis of Performance Factors in *Airs chantés* by Francis Poulenc" (MM thesis, East Texas State Univ., 1982).

Sellers, Henry Alois, "The Place of Francis Poulenc as Seen in Some of His Choral Works" (MA thesis, Texas Christian Univ., 1975).

Shafer, Gloria, "The Childrens Song Cycle: A Study, Analysis, and Performance of Selected Childrens Songs from Song Cycles with an Original Cycle" (Ed.D. diss. Columbia Univ., 1978) [includes a discussion of *La Courte Paille*.]

Shearin, Arthur Lloyd, "Francis Poulenc's Use of the Chorus in His Operas *Les Mamelles de Tirésias* and *Dialogues des Carmélites*" (DMA thesis, Univ. of Colorado, 1977).

Sherer, John W. W., "The Organ Concerto of Francis Poulenc" (DMA thesis, The Juilliard School, 1999).

Shimensky, Roberta Nyberg, "An Analysis forRecital Performance of Selected Piano Works of Beethoven, Chopin, Brahms, and Poulenc [*Trois Mouvements perpétuels*]" (MA Thesis, Univ. of Portland, 1999).

Sitton, Michael Randy, "The 'Album des Six' and Pianism in the Works of *Les Six*, 1917-1925" (DMA thesis, Univ.of Illinois at Urbana-Champaign, 1991).

Sloan, Timothy Bruce, "A Study of the Piano Works of Francis Poulenc" (MM thesis, Univ. of Cincinnati, 1981).

Stirzaker, Thomas D., "A Comparative Study of Selected Clarinet Works by Arthur Honegger, Darius Milhaud and Francis Poulenc" (Ph.D. thesis, Texas Tech Univ., 1988).

Strange, John-Michael, "Recital/Thesis: Francis Poulenc and His *Trois chansons de F. Garcia-Lorca*" (MM thesis, Northwestern State Univ. of Louisiana, 1986).

Stringer, Mary Ann, "Diversity as Style in Poulenc's Chamber Works with Piano" (DMA thesis, Univ. of Oklahoma, 1986).

Stutzenberger, Linda Pruett, "The Published Solo Piano Works of Francis Poulenc (1899-1963): A Performance Tape with Commentary" (DMA thesis, Univ. of Maryland, 1979).

Swift, Daniel, "La Collaboration Jean Cocteau-Francis Poulenc dans les années vingt: étude comparative de la pensée musicale de Jean Cocteau et des œuvres produites en collaboration avec Francis Poulenc" (MA thesis, Univ. Laval, 1983).

Teal, Terri Denise, "Tempo Determination in the Choral Works of Francis Poulenc" (MM thesis, Univ. of North Texas, 1989).

Totten, Nancy Kinsey, "*Le Bal masqué*: A Compendium of Poulenc's Style" (MA thesis, Univ. of Houston, 1987).

Trickey, Samuel Miller, "Les Six" (Ph.D. diss., North Texas State College, 1955).

Valente, Harry Robert, "A Survey of French Choral Music of the Twentieth Century: With a Performance and Interpretive Analysis of Selected Works" (Ed.D. diss., Columbia Univ., 1968). [Includes the *Gloria*.]

Van Boskirk, Lee, "Style Elements in Four Concertos by Francis Poulenc" (DM diss., Indiana Univ., 1982).

Vantine, Bruce Lynn, "Four Twentieth-Century Masses: An Analytical Comparison of Style and Compositional Technique" (DMA thesis, Univ. of Illinois at Urbana-Champaign, 1982). [Includes Mass in G major.]

Waleckx, Denis, "La Musique dramatique de Francis Poulenc (les ballets et le théâtre lyrique)" (Doctoral thesis, Université Paris IV, 1996).

Weiser, Daniel Eric, "The Visual Stimulus: The Influence of the Visual Arts on the Musical Compositions of Emmanuel Chabrier, Erik Satie, and Francis Poulenc (DMA thesis, The Peabody Institute of The Johns Hopkins Univ., 1998).

Werner, Warren Kent, "The Harmonic Style of Francis Poulenc" (Ph.D. diss., Univ. of Iowa, 1966).

Wharton, Marjorie Running, "Visual Art and Poetry in the Songs of Francis Poulenc" (Ph.D. diss., Univ. of Iowa, 1998).

Wiley, John R., "The Sacred Choral Music of Francis Poulenc" (Senior Honors Project, Stanford Univ., 1963).

Will, Ethyl Lynn, "An Analysis of *La Voix humaine*: Opera by Poulenc and Cocteau" (MA thesis, Cornell Univ., 1976).

Wipfli, Steven P., "A Conductor's Guide to *Quatre motets pour le temps de Noël* by Francis Poulenc" (MM thesis, Bowling Green State Univ., 1986).

Wood, Marc, "The Influence of Igor Stravinsky on the Music and Thought of Francis Poulenc" (Ph.D. diss., Goldsmiths College, London, n.d.).

General Index

Dates for many persons appear in Poulenc 1994 and Schmidt 1995.
Appendices I-IV are not indexed.

Brunhoff, Michel de, 312, 313
Brussel, Robert, 84, 108, 109
Brussels: 54ff, *passim*
    Conservatoire, 197, 261
    Orchestre du Conservatoire
      royal de Bruxelles, 197
    Pro Arte Concerts, 106, 119, 142,
      149, 150, 151, 188, 197
    Queen Elizabeth Competition,
      440, 443
    Radio, 253
    Rue Saint-Bernard, 320
    St Bernard's Palace, 321
    Salle du Conservatoire, 105-06
    Théâtre de Bruxelles, 334
    Théâtre de la Monnaie, 168, 393
    Ysaye Concerts, 119
Brusset, Max, 219
Bruyninckx, Walter, 75
Bry sur Marne, 7
Buckland, Sidney:
    acknowledged, xii, 43, 202, 265,
      289, 388
    Buckland/Chiminès, *passim*
    commentary in Poulenc 1991,
      346, 387, 465
    Poulenc 1991, *passim*
Buckle, Richard, 35, 128, 131, 133, 134
Budapest, 107, 109, 135
Budry, Paul, 120
Buenos Aires: Teatro Colon, 382
Buet, les dames, 217
Buirette, Jean-Joseph, 339
Buñuel, Luis, 169, 172, 193
Burdon, M, 462
Bureau international Charles Kiesgen,
    212, 213
Burgin, Richard, 353
Burgundy, 243
Burkat, Leonard, 438, 443, 444
Burkhardt, Carl, 364
Burkhardt, Mrs. Carl, 364
Burrin, Philippe, 264, 265
Busoni, Ferruccio, 115

Cabrera, M, 177
Cabrol, Daisy de, 364
Caccini, Giulio, 279
Cadanal, Olga, 265
Cadieu, Martine, 451
Café-concert, 62, 80
Caffaret, Lucie, 170
Cahors, 267, 270
Cahuzac, M, 185

Cairo:
    Conservatoire, 392
    Société de Musique d'Egypte,
      392
Calais, 163
CALA (records), 333
Caldara, Antonio, 286
California, 369, 344
Callas, Maria, 414, 422, 443
Calvet, Joseph, 316
Calvet Quartet, 315-16
Calvocoressi, Michel Dimitri, 20
Cambridge (USA):
    Eda Kuhn Loeb Music Library,
      xiii
    Harvard University, 106, 320
    Harvard University Glee Club,
      xii, 90, 99, 100, 115, 118, 225
    Harvard University Libraries,
      xiii
    Harvard University Orchestra,
      353
Cameron, Basil, 304, 363
Camfield, William, 75, 77, 87
Campagnola, Léon, 14
Campra, André, 284, 372
Camus, Albert, 301
Candler, Miss, 330
Cannes: 116ff., *passim*
    Boulevard Carnot, 148
    Café de Paris, 146
    Casino, 146
    Film Festival, 400
    Hôtel des Négociants, 364
    Hôtel des Princes, 217
    Hôtel Majestic, 390, 398, 400, 403,
      407, 410, 412, 419, 423, 425
    Pavillon Henry IV, 146
Cantebury: Cantebury Cathedral, 254,
    261
Canteloube (de Calaret), (Marie)
    Joseph, 247
Canudo, Ricciotto, 135
Cap d'Ail, 93
Capdeville, M, 311
Capelle, Fernande, 55
Capelle Quartet, 55
Capet Quartet, 11
Caplet, André, 41, 108, 112, 257
Capuana, Franco, 423
Caracas, 369-70
Caratgé, F., 260
Carbuccia, M et Mme Horace de, 219
Carcassonne, 222

Carco, Francis, 191
Cardinal, Mme, 169
Carême, Maurice, 1, 441, 442
Carlisle (Cumberland), 399
Carmel (CA), 357
Carpenter, Humphrey, 90
Carqueiranne, 123
Carrell, Norman, 421
Carré, Marguerite, 34
Carrières-sous-Poissy, 338
Carteri, Rosanna, 429, 430, 434, 449
Carter, Nick, 79
Caryathis (née Elise Toulemon, later
    Mme Elise Jouhandeau), 64, 65
Casablanca: Rue de Madrid, 364
Casadesus, Henri, 132
Casadesus, Robert, 119, 379
Casa Fuerte, Yvonne, Marquise de (née
    Yvonne Giraud):
        and James, 244
        letters from Poulenc, 309, 311,
            315, 352, 357, 358-9, 362, 372,
            373, 374, 375, 446, 457
        as performer, 204
        photographed, 193
        Poulenc plays *La Voix humaine*
            for, 425
        Sérénade, La, 189
        social life, 340, 370, 371
Casati, La, 219
Casella, Alfredo, 23, 45, 47, 71, 80, 90,
    111, 125, 151, 168, 198
Casella, Georges, 95
Casella, Hélène, 275
Castelnuovo[-Tedesco], Mario, 71
Castries, Mme de, 183
Castrillo, Aurelio, 177
Castro, Dino, 329
Catania, 428, 430, 431
Causerie de M. René Chalupt, 44
Caussade, Georges, 23, 284
Cavalli, Francesco, 279
Cayez, Pierre, 4
Cazotte, Jacques, 238
CBS (records), 84
Celibidache, Sergiu, 366, 370
Cellier, Frédéric, xiii, 277
Cendrars, Blaise, 43, 55, 71, 75, 77, 122
Cernobbio: Villa d'Este, 427, 428, 442
Chabannes, Mme de, 207
Chabrier, Emmanuel:
    A la Musique, 11
    Bernac/Poulenc duo performs,
        215, 280, 292, 352, 357, 390, 404

Desaynard on, 210
Dix pièces pittoresques, 18
Duval/Poulenc team performs,
    426
Étoile, L', 18
Gwendoline, 199
Ile heureuse, L', 233
orchestration, 40
piano music, 17, 256
Poulenc on, 436, 440, 442, 443,
    450
Poulenc's affection for, 18, 21, 62,
    118, 213, 242, 271, 275, 435,
    436, 468
Roi malgré lui, Le, 199
Une education manquée, 126, 127,
    131, 132
Valses romantiques (waltzes), 150,
    163, 392, 420
Chadourne, Georgette, 178, 233, 311,
    404
Chadourne, Paul, 178, 268, 311, 393
Chagall, Marc, 401, 414, 428
Chailley, Jacques, 453
Chaîne nationale (radio), 313, 335, 346
Châlons-sur-Marne, 52
Chalupt, René, 23, 25, 44, 93, 149, 185,
    339
Chamberlain, Neville, 264
Chaminade, Cécile, 76, 402
Champaigne, Philippe de, 246
Champigny, 7, 164
Chanel, Gabrielle (called Coco), 64,
    130, 191
Chanlaire, Richard, 159, 160, 177, 180,
    402, 403, 423, 452, 457, 461
Chanlaire, Suzette, 180, 474
Chantavoine, Jean, 294
Chanvin, Charles, 26
Chapdelaine, Mme de, 419, 427, 436,
    441, 442
Chapelain-Midi, Roger, 314
Chaplin, Alvide (Mrs. Anthony
    Chaplin), 252, 304
Chaplin, Anthony, 252, 304, 379
Chaplin, Charlie, 378, 379
Chapman, Edmund, 202
Charenton-le-Pont: 375
    Rue de Gravelle, 9
Charleroi, 442, 450
Charles, M, 271
Charles-Roux, Edmonde, 64
Charrat, Jeanine, 358
Chartrette, 254

Domaine Musical, 390
Exposition Coloniale de Paris, 196
Exposition Internationale des Arts et Techniques, 223, 240
Exposition Picabia, 87
Festival Albert Roussel, 278
Festival Chausson, 348
Festival de Mélodies [Poulenc], 308, 309
Festival d'œuvres posthumes d'Erik Satie, 150
Festival du XXᵉ siècle, 361, 371, 373
Festival Erik Satie, 78
Festival Fauré, 279
Festival Maurice Ravel, 286
Gala de musique moderne, 204
Grande Saison d'art de la VIIIᵉ Olympiade, 132
Initiative musicale, 279
International Exposition 1937, 241
Jeunes musiciens polonaise, 176
Picasso Exhibition, 413
Recital de mélodies contempor- aines, 279
Saturday Soirées, 73, 74
Séance Francis Poulenc, 272
Séance Music-Hall, 33, 57, 58, 60, 64, 70
Sérénade, La, 189, 191, 193, 199, 200, 204, 217, 237, 240, 246, 250, 256
Société des Concerts du Con- servatoire, 294, 327
Société Lyre et Palette, 43, 55
Société Nationale de Musique, 348
Soirée de danses, 178
Soirée musicale, 176
Spectacle-Concert, 77, 78, 80
Spectacle de Théâtre bouffe, 86, 98
Triptyque, Le, 285, 286, 288
Triton Society, 199
Paris — institutions, landmarks, churches, streets, museums, and locales:
Archives de la Fondation Erik Satie, xii
Archives Sonores INA, 378
Arcueil, 28, 35, 147, 247
Au nain bleu, 136

Austerlitz station, 375
Avenue Daumesnil, 235
Avenue d'Iéna, 113, 162
Avenue Henri-Martin (Polignac Hôtel particulier), 191, 200
Avenue Latour-Maubourg, 68
Avenue Niel, 21
Avenue Victor Hugo, 114
Bastille, La, 125, 235, 356
Belle Jardinière, La, 10
Bibliothèque de l'Arsenal, 201
Bibliothèque de l'Opéra, 126
Bibliothèque Nationale [de France], La, xii, 124, 347
Bœuf sur le toit, Le, 74, 111, 423
Bois de Boulogne, 6, 11
Boulevard de Clichy, 122, 145
Boulevard de Grenelle, 252, 257
Boulevard de la Chapelle, 157
Boulevard du Montparnasse, 65
Boulevard Péreire, 41
Boulevard St-Germain, 4
Café de Paris, 190
Centre français d'humanisme musical, 453
Champs-Élysées, 4, 11, 286
Chapel des Dominicains, 251
Chinese pavilion, 12
Cirque Médrano, 73, 78, 79, 237
Club des Trois Centres, 436
Conservatoire Nationale de Musique, 6, 20, 23, 24, 33, 74, 84, 101, 127, 189, 283, 284, 302, 317, 324, 327, 347, 393, 399, 405, 407
Ecole normale de musique, 45, 178, 199, 205, 208, 286, 413
Eglise d'Arcueil, 147
Eglise de Saint-Roch, 373
Eiffel Tower, 95
Élysée Palace, 3
Etoile, L', 373
Fair of Montmartre, 73
Faubourg St Honoré, 29, 38, 64, 304
Gare d'Orsay, 12, 111
Gauclair's, 74
Gaya, La, 74, 75, 94
Grand Véfour, 328
Halles, Les, 369
Hôtel Continental, 113
Hôtel Crillon, 260
Hôtel de Ville, 99
Hôtel Drouot, 18, 199

Index of Compositions and Titles by Poulenc

"Videntes stellam" (*see Quatre motets pour un temps de Noël*, No. 3)

"Village abandonné, Le" (*see Sécheresses*, No. 2)

Villageoises (petites pièces enfantines pour piano) (FP 65), 189, 201, 211

"Villanelle" (FP 74: *see Pipeaux*)

"Vinea mea electa" (*see Quatre motets pour un temps de pénitence*, No. 2)

"Visions de beauté" (no FP number: not listed in Schmidt 1995), 74

Viva Nadia (FP 167), 418

Vocalise (FP 44), 161, 212, 214, 215

Voix humaine, La (FP 171), 31, 325, 417, 421-31, 434, 436, 437, 438, 439, 441, 450, 452, 453, 456, 461

"Violon" (*see Fiançailles pour rire*, No. 5)

"Vous n'écrivez plus?" (*see Parisiana*, No. 2)

"Voyage à Paris" (*see Banalités*, No. 4)

Voyage en Amérique, Le (FP 149), 219, 365

"Voyage" (*see Calligrammes*, No. 7)

Voyageur sans bagage, Le (FP 123), 219, 286, 295, 314

Wandlung des Tirésias, Die (*see Mamelles de Tirésias, Les*)

Zèbre (FP 4), 44, 45, 49, 58

Index of Compositions and Titles by Others